The Cabling Handbook

ISBN 0-13-080531-9

9 780130 805317

90000

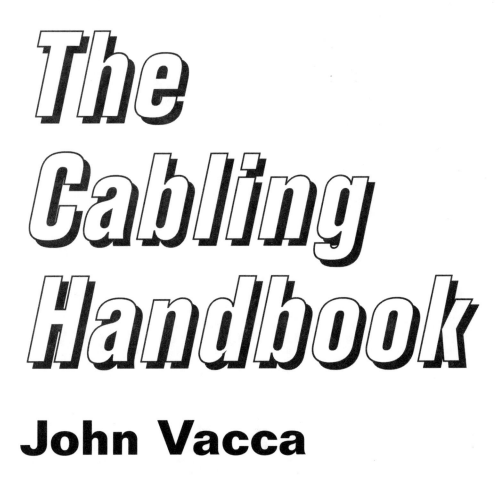

The Cabling Handbook

John Vacca

Prentice Hall PTR
Upper Saddle River, NJ   07458
http://www.phptr.com

Library of Congress Cataloging-in-Publication Date

Vacca, John
　　The cabling handbook / John Vacca.
　　　p.　cm.
　　Includes index.
　　ISBN 0-13-080531-9
　1. Telecommunication wiring--Handbooks, manuals, etc.
　2. Telecommunication cables--Handbooks, manuals, etc. 3. Computer
　　networks--Handbooks, manuals, etc. I. Title.
　TK5103.12.V33　　1998
　621.382--dc21　　　　　　　　　　　　　　　　98-22951
　　　　　　　　　　　　　　　　　　　　　　　　　　CIP

Editorial/Production Supervision: *Craig Little*
Acquisitions Editor: *Jeffrey Pepper*
Buyer: *Alexis R. Heydt*
Marketing Manager: *Dan Rush*
Cover Design: *Talar Agasyan*
Cover Design Direction: *Jerry Votta*
Art Director: *Gail Cocker-Bogusz*

Prentice Hall books are widely used by corporations and government agencies for training, marketing, and resale.

The publisher offers discounts on this book when ordered in bulk quantities.
For more information, contact the Corporate Sales Department, Phone: 800-382-3419;
Fax: 201–236-7141; email: corpsales@prenhall.com or write: Corporate Sales Department, Prentice Hall PTR, One Lake Street, Upper Saddle River, NJ 07458.

A number of entered words in which we have reason to believe trademark, service mark, or other proprietary rights may exist have been designated as such by initial capitalization. However, no attempt has been made to designate as trademarks or service marks all personal computer words or terms in which proprietary rights might exist. The inclusion, exclusion, or definition of a word or term is not intended to affect or to express any judgment on, the validity or legal status of any proprietary right that may be claimed in that word or term. All product names mentioned herein are the trademarks of their respective owners.

Some material in this book has been reproduced by Prentice Hall with the permission of Cisco Systems Inc., COPYRIGHT © 1998 Cisco Systems, Inc., ALL RIGHTS RESERVED.

Every effort has been made to make the contents of this book as accurate and understandable as possible. However, neither the author nor the publisher makes any warranty, and neither assumes any liability with regard to the uses to which its contents may be put.

Printed in the United States of America
10 9 8 7 6 5 4 3

ISBN 0-13-080531-9

Prentice-Hall International (UK) Limited, *London*
Prentice-Hall of Australia Pty. Limited, *Sydney*
Prentice-Hall Canada Inc., *Toronto*
Prentice-Hall Hispanoamericana, S.A., *Mexico*
Prentice-Hall of India Private Limited, *New Delhi*
Prentice-Hall of Japan, Inc., *Tokyo*
Simon & Schuster Asia Pte. Ltd., *Singapore*
Editora Prentice-Hall do Brasil, Ltda., *Rio de Janeiro*

DEDICATION

To David Lee for his invaluable support and friendship; and, for changing my life by introducing me to Bee.

–John R. Vacca

ACKNOWLEDGMENTS

There are many people whose efforts on this book have contributed to its successful completion. I owe each a debt of gratitude and want to take this opportunity to offer my sincere thanks.

A very special thanks to my editor Jeff Pepper, without whose initial interest and support would not have made this book possible. And editorial assistant Christy Schaack, who provided staunch support and encouragement when it was most needed. Special thanks to my technical editor, John LaBoube, who ensured the technical accuracy of the book and whose expertise in cabling and telecommunications system technology were indispensable. Thanks to my production editor, Craig Little, whose fine editorial work has been invaluable. Thanks also to my marketing manager, Kaylie Smith, whose efforts on this book have been greatly appreciated. Finally, thanks all the other people at Prentice Hall whose many talents and skills are essential to a finished book.

Thanks to my wife, Bee Vacca, for her love, her help, and her understanding of my long work hours.

I wish to thank the organizations and individuals who granted me permission to use the research material and information necessary for the completion of this book.

As always, thanks to my agent, Margot Malley, for guidance and encouragement over and above the business of being an agent.

CONTENTS

Part II: Designing Cabling Systems 163

Chapter 5: Network Design Issues 165

Chapter 6: Cost Justification and Consideration 191

Chapter 12: Data Compression 331

INTRODUCTION

The Cabling industry is becoming a full-service provider as it evolves its infrastructure into an all-digital superhighway. Both the telephone and computer industries are suggesting that their networking models—traditional point-to-point and extended distributed local area network (LAN) and wide area network (WAN) technology—become part of the cable industry solution. Cable is creating the multimedia networking model solution for the next millennium as a full-service provider through its migration to higher bandwidths.

Migrating to High-Bandwidth Cabling Solutions

Network cabling may not always be the first thing mentioned in the marketing literature for high-speed LAN technologies, but it certainly is the first thing considered by experts contemplating a migration to high-bandwidth solutions. That's why, according to recent cable industry research studies and cabling professionals, many large companies are turning to wiring such as Category 5 copper cable and multimode fiber. Furthermore, such cabling is becoming more prevalent for desktop connections.

The push to upgrade both backbone and desktop wiring is indicative of the fear IT managers have that older cabling will not be able to handle next-generation technologies such as ATM and fast Ethernet. This migration is calling into question the value of 25Mbps ATM and fast-Ethernet technology designed to run over Category 3 cable.

Category 5 is now the most dominant form of cabling for large installations, and multimode fiber is the most popular medium for vertical connections between floors and buildings in those organizations. Experts in the cabling industry say that massive Category 5 upgrades are indeed under way to prepare for future technologies. Most cabling experts agree that when faced with a choice between Category 3 and Category 5 copper, most people find Category 5 worth the extra cost, mostly because the cost of the cable itself is trivial in comparison with installation costs, so one might as well go to Cat 5. Cable industry experts have also found that many of the companies that are planning cable changes are also putting fiber in at the desktop level. A lot of people are installing Category 5 and fiber to prepare for the future.

The primary application driving the desire for greater bandwidth, cable industry analysts found, was desktop videoconferencing. Sixty-five percent of the large organizations surveyed said they planned to implement desktop videoconferencing. In the long run, videoconferencing is much cheaper than travel. Nevertheless, although big companies are bulking up on Category 5, technology vendors continue to tout the potential to run high-bandwidth applications over Category 5's older sibling, Category 3. Naturally, that's because of the huge installed base of Category 3.

Members of the ATM25 Alliance claim that 25 Mbps ATM can run over Category 3 cabling, but implementations of such technology are hard to find. Concerns such as these are driving IT managers to update their cable plants. But as long as copper remains the predominant cable source, testing problems will continue to occur. Because of the difficulty in testing Category 5 (caused mostly by the connections between cable segments), networks will still experience cable-related problems—although technology is minimizing cable-related problems. In other words, testing Category 5 is a real problem and there is virtually no way to certify a cable installation. Eventually we're all going to go to fiber optic or optical systems anyway. So, can widening the fiber highway or optical systems through wave division multiplexing deliver the bandwidth promise?

Widening the Optical Systems Highway

Recent advances in wave division multiplexing (WDM) technology have offered the potential for the deployment of cost-effective, highly reliable, high-capacity fiber optic network solutions. This is particularly important since the sustained growth of increasingly bandwidth-hungry applications requires an unprecedented rate of fiber optic network expansion, and places increasing demands on network design and planning. Development of time division multiplexing (TDM) transport systems has reached a plateau and operators can no longer wait for technology, such as managed Synchronous Transfer Mode-64 (STM-64) transmission, to mature. As a result, operators are increasingly pursuing WDM solutions to address evolving capacity issues. Cost-benefit analysis however, reveals that the deployment of currently available small-scale (four wavelength) stand-alone systems only makes sense in long-distance carrier networks—of the kind found in North America, for example. For European intra-operator networks, efficiencies only begin to be realized with 16 wavelength systems.

As a longer-term strategy, the creation of a high-capacity managed WDM network layer using optical add-drop multiplexers or wavelength routers is gaining acceptance in the formulation of future network architectures. The biggest challenge in implementing an all-optical fiber network will be in the delivery of an optical layer network management platform and the successful integration with existing synchronous digital hierarchy (SDH) network management systems. Most modern fiber optic networks today use time division multiplexing techniques to send data down the physical layer. But, experts say, most TDM equipment utilizes only about two percent of the intrinsic capacity of fiber. Dense wavelength division multiplexing is a technology that allows multiple data streams to be simultaneously transmitted over a single fiber at data rates as high as the fiber plant will allow—typically 3.5 Gbps. The WDM approach multiplies the simple 3.5 Gbps system by up to 16 times. So a 16-channel system (with ITU-recommended channel-spacing) will support 50 Gbps in each direction over a fiber pair. Also under development are 50-channel systems that will support 200 Gbps—the equivalent of over 20 STM-64 transmitters.

Current WDM technology utilizes a composite optical signal carrying four, eight, or 16 data streams, each transmitted on a distinct optical wavelength. Although WDM has been a known technology for years, its early application was restricted to providing two widely separated wavelengths. Only recently has the technology evolved to the point where parallel wavelengths can be densely packed and integrated into a transmission system with multiple, simultaneous, extremely high frequency signals in the 192 to 200 Terahertz (Thz) range. The 16-channel system in essence provides a virtual 16-fiber cable, with each frequency channel serving as a unique STM-16 carrier. The most common form of WDM uses a fiber pair—one for transmission and one for reception. The availability of precise demultiplexers and erbium-doped fiber amplifiers has allowed WDM with eight and 16 channel counts to be commercially delivered. Incoming optic streams are split into individual wavelengths using a newly developed technique of embedding a component (known as a fiber Bragg grating) so that the refractive index of the core is permanently modified to allow only a specific wavelength to pass through. A series of such gratings are used to split the carrier into a required composite wave. The fiber gating creates a highly selective, narrow bandwidth filter that functions somewhat like a mirror and provides significantly greater wavelength selectivity than any other optical technology.

So, would wireless technology be any better?

Wireless WANs and LANs

As school districts struggle with how to interconnect local area networks that they have in operation at various campuses to form a wide area network, one viable solution that is not well known is the use of wireless technology. Wireless network bridges to transmit data within or between buildings, using spread spectrum radio waves or infrared technologies or microwaves, can be used to connect LANs that are separated by as much as 30 miles. Many of the less powerful bridges, however, may be limited to a range of three to six miles. These wireless links can provide data transfer rates from less than 1 Mbps to more than 10 Mbps. As one might expect, the greater the link distance capability, and the higher the data transfer rate, the more expensive the equipment. For example, a pair of bridges operating at a radio frequency of 900 MHz may cost over $7000, provide a link distance of two to three miles, and transfer data at 1 Mbps. A 2.4 Ghz bridge might cost over $6000, provide a reliable link over a distance of four to seven miles, and transfer data at 2 Mbps. On the other hand, a microwave link at 31 Ghz may provide a connection over eight to 11 miles at 10 Mbps (full duplex) for an equipment cost of less than $40,000.

One really attractive feature of wireless connections, and their major advantage, is that there is a one-time cost for the equipment and installation. There are no recurring, on-going monthly costs! Thus, when compared to connection options that have continuing monthly fees associated, the wireless solution quickly pays for itself.

The potential drawbacks to a wireless solution include environmental factors. Terrain may eliminate wireless as an option; intervening hills and tall buildings or trees can block the radio frequency (RF) signals. Wireless RF technology is referred to as line-of-sight. This means that the antennas on the wireless bridge units must be able to see each other. There must be no obstacles in the way to block or reflect the transmitted signals. Severe weather, such as torrential rains, can adversely affect signal transmission and temporarily down the link. Similarly, the link might be susceptible to other radio frequency interference. Dense fog could possibly be a problem for microwave links.

The bottom line: wireless connectivity must be seriously considered if the terrain allows its use. Some reports indicate that microwave links can be more reliable than leased data lines. Furthermore, there are some major potential benefits to wireless solutions. For example, school district administrators could enter a conference room, turn on their laptop computers, and achieve high-speed connectivity to the district network. Teachers could sit down in the cafeteria with their notebooks and instantly update class schedules, grades, and attendance records in a centralized database. Students can take hand-held devices outside of the classroom, collect scientific data, and share their findings in real-time with peers via the Internet.

Sound like a vision for the 21st century? Actually, all of these scenarios are taking place today thanks to recent advances in mobile computing and wireless technology. Already, wireless local area networks (WLANs) have extended, or replaced, traditional LANs in hundreds of educational sites, and many more IT managers are carefully examining the benefits of wireless solutions. Actually, the bottom line to all of this is that although the initial investment for WLAN hardware might be higher, long-term cost savings can be realized because technicians never need to pull wire through walls or ceilings to expand the network.

Who This Book Is For

This book can be used by domestic and international system administrators, government computer security officials, network administrators, senior managers, engineers, sales engineers, marketing staff, WWW Developers, military senior top brass, network designers and technicians, cabling project managers, cable installers, LAN and PBX administrators, and other satellite communications personnel. In short, the book is targeted for all types of people and organizations around the globe who have responsibility for cabling decisions and/or project implementation, network cabling installation, cost justification and investments, and standards. Others who may find it useful are scientists, engineers, educators, top-level executives, information technology and department managers, technical staff, and the more than 600 million Internet, intranet, and extranet users around the world. Some previous experience with cabling installation is required.

What's So Special About This Book?

This book is unique in its comprehensive coverage of network cabling installation, cost justification and investments, and the latest standards. Key features include

- intermediate- to advanced-level instruction to help you install the latest copper, fiber, and wireless network cabling systems
- practical tips on cost-justifying your cabling investments
- tips on how to manage contractor/client relationships.
- extensive coverage of how to certify cabling system requirements performance to 100 Mbit/second and beyond
- discussion of the latest LAN design issues: optimal use in structured cabling systems; how to drive a project from design to certification; and how to ensure today's cable design supports emerging workgroup technologies
- a thorough discussion of all of the latest national and international cabling standards
- an installation section covering testing techniques, installation, certification of system performance.

The book is organized into seven parts and includes appendixes as well as a glossary of network cabling terms and acronyms at the back. It provides a step-by-step approach to everything you need to know about network cabling as well as information about many topics relevant to the planning, design, and implementation of high-performance network cabling systems. The book gives an in-depth overview of the latest structured cabling technology and emerging global standards. It discusses what background work needs to be done, such as developing a cabling technology plan, and shows how to develop network cabling plans for organizations and educational institutions. More importantly, this book shows how to install a network cabling system, along with the techniques used to test the system, as well as the certification of system performance. It covers many of the common pieces of network cabling equipment used in the maintenance of the system, as well as the ongoing maintenance issues. The book concludes with a discussion about future planning, standards development, and the cabling industry.

Part I: Overview of Cabling Technology

In this part of the book, the three cabling media (copper, fiber, and wireless) are discussed, followed by a discussion about the six major types of networks: Local Area Network (LAN), Wide Area Network (WAN), Virtual Area Network (VAN), intranet, extranet, and Internet. Some companies are fortunate to have all six types connecting their systems. Next, we'll examine how all three cabling media can be used with one or all six of the network types to allow your organization to soar beyond the traditional constraints of network cabling. You'll be shown how and when to expand, contract, or redeploy your network type(s) virtually anywhere, anytime, as quickly as today's accelerating pace of change demands. Finally, Part I reaches its climax with an in-depth presentation of the various cabling standards (TIA/EIA568A, ISO/IEC 11801, IEEE 802.x, FDDI, ISDN, LATM, etc.), and concludes by taking a close look at some third-party vendor cabling systems—AT&T (Lucent) Systimax and Powersum, IBM Cabling System, DECconnect, Northern Telecom IBDN, AMP Connect, KRONE, Mod-Tap, BCS, ITT, IBCS, etc.

Part II: Designing Cabling Systems

Part II begins by giving an overview of network design issues and how they can help you design and install a better cabling system. Next, it discusses the various Category 5 structured wiring components and how they all fit together. Part II also discusses the cost justification issues to consider during the design phase of your cabling system. It provides an overview of the various aspects of cabling system standards design issues and of cabling system architectural design considerations (structured cabling system, wiring closet design, cabling facilities, and user-to-outlet ratios). Additionally, Part II discusses copper design considerations (layout, components, connectors, and shielding and maintenance). Furthermore, it presents a brief overview of fiber optic design considerations (layout, system migration, loss budget calculations, and fiber-to-desk). It concludes with a discussion of wireless design considerations (spread spectrum, microwave, infrared, wireless WANs and LANs, etc.).

Part III: Planning for High-Speed Cabling Systems

Part III covers high-speed real-time data compression and how to plan for higher-speed cabling systems. It also describes the development of the high-speed cabling system implementation plan (scheduling, analyzing site surveys, connectivity requirements, equipment, security, and performance).

Part IV: Installing the Cabling System

This part begins by taking a look at the installation of the cabling system, starting with a presentation on testing techniques as part of pre-installation activities including the preparation of cable facilities, testing the cable and components, and code compliance and safety considerations. Next, it describes in detail the installation of the cabling system and covers specific areas such as core drilling considerations; conduit installation and fill guidelines; grounding, shielding and safety; pulling the cable without damage; splicing and patching; blown fiber; labeling schemes; and quality control and installation standards. Part IV concludes by taking a close look at the following post-installation activities: cable fault detection with OTDR; cabling system troubleshooting and testing; copper and fiber optic loss testing; documenting the cabling system; cabling system performance certification; and accuracy levels testing as defined in Telecommunications System Bulletin (TSB) 67.

Part V: Maintaining Cabling Systems

Opening up with a discussion on how to maintain your cabling system, this part examines the facilitation of ongoing cabling system maintenance by covering the building of the Cable Plant Management (CPM) database, vendor CPM products, and the EIA/TIA 606 standard.

Part VI: Future Directions

This part of the book examines the future standards in development (ATM, 300-600Mhz cable systems [Category 6], zone wiring, TIA/EIA-T568-B, EN50174, 100BaseT2, and 1000BaseT [Gigabit Ethernet]). Finally, the book concludes by taking a peak at the cabling industry as it continues on its way to becoming a full information service provider in the next millennium via the ever-changing cable specification process.

You'll find a glossary of network cabling-related terms at the end of the text.

Part VII: Appendixes

Nine appendixes provide direction to additional resources available for cabling. Appendix A is a discussion of TV-based high-speed cable Internet services, Appendix B is a list of top cable installation companies. Appendix C is a list of top fiber optic cable companies, and Appendix D is a Cabling Directory—an interactive buyer's guide for cabling products as well as for all cabling-related topics with direct links to each company's website. Appendix E is an EENET Interconnect Directory—a comprehensive listing of interconnect companies in different categories. Appendix F is a list of top cable labeling companies, Appendix G is a list of top SCSI companies, Appendix H is a list of wireless LAN products and sites, and Appendix I is a list of CCITT/ISO standards.

Conventions

This book has two conventions to help you find important facts.

- **Sidebars:** used to highlight related information, give an example, discuss an item in greater detail, or help you make sense of the swirl of terms, acronyms, and abbreviations so prevalent in this field. The sidebars are meant to supplement each chapter's topic. If you're in a hurry on a cover-to-cover read, skip the sidebars. If you're quickly flipping through the book looking for juicy information, read only the sidebars.

John R. Vacca
34679 TR 382
Pomeroy, Ohio 45769
jvacca@hti.net

Part I

Overview of Cabling Technology

Types of Cable
and Hardware

     As the demand for high-speed telecommunications increases across the globe, copper, fiber optic, and wireless systems are being deployed to fulfill the needs of telephone companies, cable TV companies, and businesses with high-speed LANs. The battle for supremacy between copper, fiber, and wireless systems in telecommunications and data communications continues to increase in complexity rather than becoming more clear. This has put serious pressure on the copper wire and cable industry, which has seen its market share decline steadily over the past decade as fiber and wireless systems take hold. A number of major copper cable suppliers have either pulled out of the copper cable business and embraced fiber optics or redesigned their organizations around adding value to traditional copper wire and cable products. This has provided market opportunities for some nimble market-oriented firms with lower manufacturing costs to enter niche markets.

     The copper-based network equipment manufacturers continue to fight back, using recent developments in digital signal processing technology to extend the bandwidth and usefulness of copper cabling, in order to preserve both the embedded base of copper cabling and to retain market share for present and future installations. In the telephone network, Asymmetric Digital Subscriber Line (ADSL), High-bit-rate Digital Subscriber Line (HDSL), and

Very-High-Data-Rate Digital Subscriber Line (VDSL) technologies are delivering megabit speeds over the local loop, allowing for the delivery of high-speed Internet access, telecommuting, and eventually video services. For premises networks,.100 Mbps (megabits per second) Ethernet equipment has quickly eclipsed Fiber Distributed Data Interface (FDDI) technology, and standards are underway for gigabit Ethernet and copper-based Asynchronous Transfer Mode (ATM) LANs.

This chapter provides detailed assessments of competing cable types and hardware technologies and discusses cabling solutions for telecommunications and data networks that set the stage for the rest of the book. It describes the global copper cable market and briefly analyzes the effect of sweeping regulatory reforms (standards. The chapter also provides major players in the fiber optics, copper cable, and wireless industry (copper wire manufacturers, copper wire companies seeking joint ventures or acquisitions, copper producers, telecommunications suppliers, telecommunications systems vendors, fiber optics manufacturers, networking equipment vendors, investors, consultants, long range planners, strategic planners, and presidents and CEOs) with a brief look at the range of strategies that can be pursued in order for them to remain competitive in this changing marketplace.

Copper, Fiber, or Wireless Media: Choose One

Perhaps your company thrives on copper cabling. Perhaps you're considering fiber optic alternatives. Or maybe you have problems that only a wireless LAN can solve.

Private network providers are often involved with providing systems to support future applications, while at the same time they're confronted with the seemingly contradictory objectives of lowering costs. Today, network providers are often faced with the question of whether to install an unshielded twisted pair (UTP) copper or multimode fiber cabling system or a wireless Local Area Network (LAN) when searching for an answer to these objectives. Unfortunately, this question does not have a clearly defined answer. In order to create the most cost-effective networks for voice, video, and data, most private networks require a mixture of all three media. UTP is unquestionably the right choice for traditional telephone and fax services. However, the answer is not as clear for data services. With rates from 100 to 155 Mbps, high performance Category 5 UTP provides the lowest initial cost for Local Area Networks (LANs). Nevertheless, recurring operational costs can be reduced by fiber-based networks. Furthermore, with wireless systems, you can bring 21st-century technology to older buildings without disturbing a single historic brick; go mobile for on-the-spot presentations, and even create instant extensions to an existing LAN anywhere in the building. These savings can, over time, far exceed the higher initial costs.

Cable by definition is the medium through which information usually moves from one network device to another. As previously mentioned, there are several types of cable media which are commonly used with LANs. In some cases, other networks will use a variety of cable media, while a network will utilize only one type of cable media. The type of cable media chosen for a network is related to the network's size, topology, and protocol. Therefore, what is necessary for the development of a successful network is an understanding of the characteristics of different types of cable media and how they relate to other aspects of a network.

The choice of media depends largely on the customer's present and future applications and business situations. A selection made without considering these fundamentals has little chance of providing the best solution. That is why it is important to understand not only the capabilities of each media, but also specific customer needs.

Overall, this chapter briefly examines the situation surrounding each of the cable media today; and when and how to use them. The following sections discuss the types of cable media and hardware used in networks and other related topics.

Copper Media

If cost concerns are more critical than high bandwidth, you should consider a copper media cabling solution. There are two main reasons for the broad acceptance and rapid growth of copper media: low initial cost and the ability to deliver high data rate LAN services.

Copper media encompasses basically two major types of cable: Unshielded Twisted Pair (UTP) and Shielded Twisted Pair (STP). There's actually a third type, Coaxial cabling, which will also be discussed.

Unshielded Twisted Pair (UTP)

Twisted pair cabling comes in two varieties: unshielded and shielded. Unshielded twisted pair (UTP) is the most popular and is generally the best option for school networks as shown in Figure 1–1 [1].

Figure 1–1: Unshielded twisted pair.

UTP quality may vary from extremely high-speed cable to telephone-grade wire. Four pairs of cable wires exist inside the jacket. In order to help eliminate interference from adjacent pairs and other electrical devices, each pair is twisted with a different number of twists per inch. The EIA/TIA (Electronic Industry Association/Telecommunication Industry Association) has established standards of UTP and rated five categories of wire as shown in Table 1–1. For further information on these UTP standards, see Chapter 3, "Standards."

Table 1–1: Categories of unshielded twisted pair.

Category	Use
1	Alarm systems, voice only (telephone wire), characteristics specified up to 0 (MHz) and other noncritical applications.
2	Voice, EIA-232, data to 4 Mbps (LocalTalk), characteristics specified up to 0 (MHz) and other low speed data.
3	10BaseT Ethernet, 4-Mbits/s token ring, 100BaseT4, 100VG-AnyLAN, basic rate ISDN, Data to 10 Mbps (Ethernet) and characteristics specified up to 16 (MHz). Generally the minimum standard for new installations.
4	16-Mbits/s token ring. Not widely used, data to 20 Mbps (16 Mbps token ring) and characteristics specified up to 20 (MHz).
5	TP-PMD, SONet, OC-3 (ATM), 100BaseTX. The most popular for new data installations, data to 100 Mbps (Fast Ethernet) and characteristics specified up to 100 (MHz).

The tightness of the twisting of the copper pairs is one difference among the different categories of UTP as shown in Table 1–1. The higher the supported transmission rate and greater cost per foot, the tighter the twisting. Buy the best cable you can afford. Most schools purchase Category 5 or Category 3. Category 5 cable comes highly recommended.

Remember, the Category 5 cable will provide more *room to grow* as transmission technologies increase—especially if you are designing a 10 Mbps Ethernet network and are considering the cost savings of buying Category 3 wire instead of Category 5. A maximum segment length of 100 meters exists in both Category 3 and Category 5 UTP. In most schools, Category 5 cable is required for retrofit grants. Also, the specifications for unshielded twisted pair cable (Category 3, 4, or 5) carrying Ethernet signals is referred as 10BaseT as shown in Table 1–2.

Unshielded Twisted Pair Connector

An RJ-45 connector is the standard connector for unshielded twisted pair cabling. This is a plastic connector that looks like a large telephone-style connector as shown in Figure 1–2 [2]. The placement of a slot allows the RJ-45 to be inserted only one way. RJ stands for Registered Jack. The implication here is that the connector follows a standard borrowed from the telephone industry. Thus, which wire goes with each pin inside the connector is designated by this borrowed standard.

Shielded Twisted Pair (STP)

Unfortunately, a disadvantage of UTP is that it may be susceptible to radio and electrical frequency interference. Shielded twisted pair (STP), on the other hand, is suitable for environments with electrical interference. However, the extra shielding can make the cables quite bulky. Shielded twisted pair is often used on networks using token ring topology, the industry standard (Project 802.5 of the IEEE) that specifies protocols for connection and transmission in local area networks. As a media access method, it operates at layers 1 and 2 in the OSI (Open System Interconnection) model. Token ring transmits at 4 or 16 Mb/s.

A Comparison: STP Versus UTP

This section continues the debate of UTP versus STP, presenting an in-depth comparison of the advantages and disadvantages of how and when to use cables and systems.

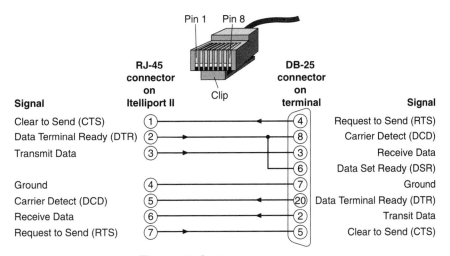

Figure 1–2: RJ-45 connector.

A debate has recently arisen on the advantages and disadvantages of unshielded twisted-pair (UTP) cable and shielded twisted-pair (STP) cable. Without adequately presenting both sides of the story, advocates of STP cable (a category that includes screened twisted-pair cable and foil twisted-pair cable) have attempted to claim that their product is superior to UTP cable. In order to provide reliable connectivity of electronic equipment, STP and UTP's purpose should still be the same, even though it is true that they are inherently different in design and manufacture. The true test comes when you look at the performance of each of these cable types within its respective end-to-end system, although, in theory, both types of cable should perform this task successfully.

In order to form a twisted pair, two copper wires, each encased in its own color-coded insulation, are twisted together. But, to form twisted-pair cable, multiple twisted pairs are packaged in an outer sheath, or jacket. The possibility of interference between pairs in the same cable sheath can be minimized by varying the length of the twists in nearby pairs.

Twisted-pair cable has been around for quite a while. In fact, early telephone signals were sent over a type of twisted-pair cable. Just about every building today still uses twisted-pair cable to carry telephone and other signals. Evolving from 1200 bps to over 100 Mbps, signals have become more complex over the years. Today, there are many more sources of interference that might disrupt those signals than there were at the turn of the century. Coaxial cable and fiber optic cable were developed to support emerging technologies and handle higher-bandwidth applications. Now, high-data-rate signals can be carried because of the evolution of twisted-pair cable.

To reduce the potential for electromagnetic interference (EMI), some twisted-pair cables contain a metal shield. Signals from other sources such as electric motors, power lines, high-power radio and radar signals cause EMI. If these signals are in the vicinity, they may cause disruptions or interference, called noise. Thus, shielded twisted-pair (STP) cable encases the signal-carrying wires in a conducting shield. At first glance, it may appear that because STP cable is physically encased in a shield, all outside interference is automatically blocked. However, this is not true.

The shield acts as an antenna (just like a wire) when it has been properly grounded, converting received noise into current flowing in the shield. In turn, this current induces an opposite and equal current flowing in the twisted pairs. The two currents cancel each other out and deliver no net noise to the receiver as long as they are symmetrical. However, the current in the twisted pairs is interpreted as noise if any discontinuity in the shield or other asymmetry in the current in the shield exists. As long as the entire end-to-end link is shielded and properly grounded, STP cable is effective at preventing radiation or blocking interference. Every component of a shielded cabling system must be just that—fully shielded—in order to work properly.

STP cable also has drawbacks. For instance, STP cable's attenuation may increase at high frequencies. Also, STP cable's balance (or longitudinal conversion loss) may decrease if the effects of the shield are not compensated for (which leads to crosstalk and signal noise). The shielding effectiveness depends on the material of the shield, its thickness, the type of EMI noise field, its frequency, the distance from the noise source to the shield, the grounding structure used, and any shield discontinuity. There's also no guarantee that the shield itself will contain no imperfections.

A thick braided shield is used by some STP cables. Harder to install than their UTP counterparts, these cables are heavier and thicker. A relatively thin overall outer foil shield is also used by some STP cables. Thinner and less expensive than braided STP cable, these cables are also known as screened twisted-pair (ScTP) cables or foil twisted-pair (FTP) cables. However, they are not any easier to install. When these cables are installed, the minimum bending radius and maximum pulling tension force must be rigidly observed; otherwise, the shield may experience a tear.

On the other hand, unshielded twisted-pair (UTP) cable does not rely on physical shielding to block interference. But UTP does rely on balancing and filtering techniques through media filters and/or baluns. Noise is induced equally on two conductors. The noise then cancels out at the receiver. This technique is easier to maintain than the shielding continuity and grounding of an STP cable if the UTP cable has been a properly designed and manufactured.

UTP cable has evolved over the years, with the result that there are different varieties of UTP cable available for different needs. Basic telephone cable (also known as direct-inside wire or DIW) is still available. Improvements over the years (such as variations in the twists or in individual wire sheaths or overall cable jackets), have led to the development of EIA/TIA-568 standard-compliant Category 5 (for specifications on signal bandwidth up to 100 MHz and greater) UTP cable, Category 4 (for specifications on signal bandwidth up to 20 MHz), and Category 3 (for specifications on signal bandwidth up to 16 MHz). Millions of nodes have been and continue to be wired with UTP cable (even for high-data-rate applications), because UTP cable is lightweight, thin, and flexible, as well as versatile, reliable, and inexpensive. UTP cable should be used as part of a well-engineered structured cabling system for best performance.

STP Cabling Systems Versus UTP Cabling Systems

Overall signal quality will be degraded if STP cable is combined with improperly shielded connectors (connecting hardware, or outlets, or if the foil shield itself is damaged). Also, degradation of emission and immunity performance can often result if the connectors are improperly shielded. Therefore, every component within the cabling system must be fully and seamlessly shielded, as well as properly installed and maintained for it to succeed totally in interference reduction.

An STP cabling system, likewise, requires good earthing and grounding practices. A primary source of emissions and interference can result if a system is improperly grounded The frequency of the application dictates whether this ground is at one end or both ends of the cable run. At a minimum (for high-frequency signals), an STP cabling system must be grounded at both ends of the cable run–and, it must be continuous. There is no effect against magnetic field interference if a shield is grounded at one end. A source of problems can also be the length of the ground conductor itself. It no longer acts as a ground if it is too long. Therefore, since it depends on the application, optimum grounding for an STP cabling system is not possible. This problem does not exist with UTP cabling systems.

A UTP cabling system inherently has fewer points for potential failure and is easier to install. Moreover, an STP cabling system is dependent on such factors as physical continuity of the cable shield itself or installation with adequately shielded and grounded components.

EMC and STP Versus UTP Cabling Systems

Another factor to consider when choosing a cabling system relates to the recent adoption of the electromagnetic compatibility (EMC) directive. This directive is in addition to requirements for precision design and manufacture, as well as end-to-end integrity. EMC refers to the ability of an electronic system to function properly in its environment. This would be an environment where several pieces of equipment are located in the same workspace, each radiating electromagnetic emissions. EMC becomes increasingly more important here (with the existence of an increased amount of electronic equipment in the average workspace) as excess radiation from one piece of equipment can adversely affect performance of another piece of equipment. This means that every electronic system (which includes either an STP or UTP cabling system) must meet this directive.

EMC regulations have existed for years in some countries, such as the U.S. and Germany. However, attention on EMC has refocused since the implementation of the European EMC Directive in 1989. The European EMC Directive 89/336/EEC states that all electronic equipment and apparatus must comply with the directive. These systems must pass the essential requirements of the directive before they can be sold anywhere in the European Economic Area (EEA). Some national regulations (such as Amtsblatt Verfugung 243/91 of Germany) currently exempt STP-based systems from immunity testing. However, as of January 1, 1996, these national regulations no longer apply, and all systems must be tested. Those that do not pass will not be able to be sold in the EEA.

How well do STP- and UTP-based systems stand up to rigorous EMC testing? Not all STP based systems can automatically pass EMC tests (contrary to some popular assumptions), while a well-designed UTP cabling system can. Further discussions on this topic will be addressed in Chapter 4, "Types Of Vendor And Third-Party Cabling Systems."

Coaxial Cable

Now let's briefly look at the third type of copper media, Coaxial cabling. This is the copper media type most frequently used in cable television systems, the transmission line for television and radio signals.

Coaxial cabling has a single copper conductor at its center. A plastic layer provides insulation between the center conductor and a braided metal shield as shown in Figure 1–3 [3]. The metal shield helps to block any outside interference from fluorescent lights, motors, and other computers.

Coaxial cabling is highly resistant to signal interference, despite the fact that it is difficult to install. Also, it can support greater cable lengths between network devices than twisted pair cable. The two types of coaxial cabling are thin coaxial and thick coaxial.

Thin coaxial cable is also referred to as thinnet. 10Base2 refers to the specifications for thin coaxial cable carrying Ethernet signals as shown in Table 1–2 [4]. The 2 refers to the approximate maximum segment length being 200 meters. In actual fact, the maximum segment length is 185 meters. Thin coaxial cable is popular in school networks, especially linear bus networks.

Table 1–2: Ethernet cable comparison summary.

Cable Type	10BaseF	10Base5	10Base2	10BaseT	Single Mode Fiber	Multi-Mode Fiber *	Standard AUI	Office AUI
Maximum Length	2000m	500m	185m	100m	5Km	1Km	50m	16.5m
Number of Taps	n/a	100	30	n/a	n/a	n/a	n/a	n/a
Tap Spacing	n/a	2.5m	5m	n/a	n/a	n/a	n/a	n/a
Propagation Delay	n/a	less than or = .00433	less than or = .00514	less than or =.0057	less than or = .005	less than or = .005	less than or = .00514	less than or = .0156
Maximum Segment Delay	n/a	2.165 micro-seconds	.95 micro-seconds	1.0 micro-seconds	25 micro-seconds	5.0 micro-seconds	.257 micro-seconds	.257 micro-seconds
Velocity of Propagation	n/a	greater than or = .77c	greater than or = .65c	greater than or = .585c	greater than or = .66c	greater than or = to .66c	greater than or = .65c	greater than or = .65c

Note: The IEEE 802.3 Fiber Optic Inter-Repeater Link (FOIRL) standard specifies 1 kilometer, while the 802.3j standard allows for 2 kilometers.

Figure 1–3: Coaxial cable.

Thick coaxial cable is also referred to as thicknet. 10Base5 refers to the specifications for thick coaxial cable carrying Ethernet signals as shown in Table 1–2. The 5 refers to the maximum segment length being 500 meters. Thick coaxial cable has an extra protective plastic cover that helps keep moisture away from the center conductor. This makes thick coaxial a great choice when running longer lengths in a linear bus network. One disadvantage of thick coaxial is that it is difficult to install and does not bend easily.

Coaxial Cable Connectors

The most common type of connector used with coaxial cables is the Bayone-Neill-Concelman (BNC) connector as shown in Figure 1–4 [5]. Different types of adapters are available for BNC connectors, including a T-connector, terminator, and barrel connector. The weakest points in any network are the connectors on the cable. Always use the BNC connectors that crimp, rather than screw onto the cable, to help avoid problems with your network.

Fiber Optic Media

Let's look at the next type of cabling media, fiber optic cable. This section presents light-speed technology through fiber optic systems, where 10BaseF (as shown in Table 1–2) refers to the specifications for fiber optic cable carrying Ethernet signals. It's one of the most sophisticated cabling media solutions available today, with a range of more than 70 miles (120 kilometers) and certified performance up to gigabit speeds.

Figure 1–4: BNC connector.

Fiber optic cabling consists of a center glass core surrounded by several layers of protective materials as shown in Figure 1–5 [6]. It transmits light rather than electronic signals. This eliminates the problem of electrical interference. Fiber optic is ideal for certain environments that are subject to a large amount of electrical interference. Its immunity to the effects of moisture and lighting has also made fiber optic cabling the standard for connecting networks between buildings. Some facts about fiber optic cables include:

- The outer insulating jacket is made of Teflon or PVC (Permanent Virtual Circuit).
- Kevlar fiber helps to strengthen the cable and prevent breakage.
- A plastic coating is used to cushion the fiber center.
- The center (core) is made of glass or plastic fibers.

Fiber optic cable has the ability to transmit signals over much greater distances than twisted pair and coaxial. It also has the capability to carry information at vastly greater speeds. This capacity broadens communication possibilities to include services such as interactive services and video conferencing. The cost of fiber optic cabling is comparable to copper cabling. Nevertheless, it is more difficult to install and modify. A comparison between the two media will be given later in the chapter.

So, how would you know which is the right fiber cable type for your network? The next section addresses this question. Let's take a look.

The Right Fiber Optic Cable

One of the design considerations is the type of fiber to use when deciding to install optical fiber in buildings or across a campus.. What should you install: singlemode (SMF), multimode (MMF) or both types of fiber? The choice is usually guided by a few key issues. For example, the primary considerations are the intended applications support, distance, data (baud) rate, and the difficulty and expense of retrofitting at a later time. Table 1–3 addresses the first three considerations for local area networks (LANs) and video applications.

Figure 1–5: Fiber optic cable.

Note:

Singlemode and/or multimode are fiber cable that use light pulses instead of electricity to carry data. In multimode cable, the light bounces off the cable's walls as it travels down, which causes the signal to weaken sooner and therefore data cannot travel as much distance as with single mode fiber. In SMF cables, the light travels straight down the cable. The size of the cable/cladding is 62.5/125 micron for MMF, and 8/125 micron for SMF.

Table 1–3: Standardized distances for LANs over singlemode and multimode.

Application	Data Rate	Fiber Distance (meters) and Type	
		Singlemode (9/125 micron)	**Multimode** (62.5/125 micron)
10BaseF (Ethernet)	20 Mbaud	non-standard	2,000
100BaseFX	125 Mbaud	non-standard	2,000
100VG-AnyLAN	120 Mbaud	non-standard	2,000
1000BaseX	1250 Mbaud	3,000	440 (draft)
ATM and SONET	155 Mbaud	40,000	2,000
	622 Mbaud	40,000	500
Baseband Video	6 MHz	65,000	10,000
Broadband Video	500 MHz	20,000	not applic.
FDDI	125 Mbaud	60,000	2,000
Fiber Channel	133 Mbaud	non-standard	1,500
	266 Mbaud	10,000	1,500
	531 Mbaud	10,000	350
	1062 Mbaud	10,000	300
Token Ring	32 Mbaud	2,000	non-standard

To date, all LAN standards specify 62.5/125 micron multimode fiber and some also specify singlemode fiber. Table 1–3 lists the standardized distances for LANs over both media. All LANs operating up to 266 megabaud have sufficient distance capability on multimode fiber to span most campuses. Above that rate, the distance capabilities of multimode fiber LANs are sufficient to cable most buildings using single point administration (centralized cabling) architecture. For longer distances, singlemode fiber provides the LAN solution at these higher rates. Multimode-to-singlemode converters are available to convert multimode signals to singlemode, even for those LANs where singlemode fiber is non-standard. Converters typically have 20- to 50-kilometer singlemode capability.

For video, multimode fiber is capable of delivering baseband (single channel) video over distances exceeding the span of most campuses. Multimode fiber is also capable of providing several channels of video (multichannel), but not capable of cost-effective broadband (20-80 channel) video delivery today. However, singlemode fiber is quite capable of providing broadband video services.

As Table 1–3 indicates, multimode fiber has the capability to meet both the distance and data rate demands of most LAN networks. Generally, multimode systems cost far less than singlemode systems since the optoelectronics that can be used with multimode fiber are much less costly than those used with singlemode fiber. This cost advantage explains the popularity of multimode fiber over singlemode fiber in premises networks.

Note:

Optoelectronics has a rapidly growing range of applications that includes optical communications, optical data storage and optical sensing. It is fundamentally concerned with the interaction of light and matter and with devices which interface between electronics and optics.

However, singlemode fiber is practically the only fiber used by telephone and cable television companies. These industries require the very long distance capability and high information carrying capacity of singlemode fiber. In these longer distance applications, singlemode systems are cost-effective because fewer optoelectronic devices are needed overall.

Today, most premises networks are being installed with multimode fiber in the building backbone and campus backbone segments. Some forward-looking companies are also installing singlemode fiber in backbones along with the multimode fiber.

Note:

Backbone is a fairly nebulous term for a part of the network that interconnects other parts of the network. For example, a campus might have an FDDI ring that interconnects a number of Ethernets. The FDDI ring could be called the network's backbone.

Multimode fiber is growing in the horizontal cabling scheme also, bringing the benefits of fiber all the way to the desktop. A few companies are even installing singlemode fiber to these work areas. Most of these companies are not using the singlemode fiber at this time, but are installing it in the event that they will need its higher information carrying capacity in the future. Also, because of its popularity with telephone and cable television companies, singlemode fiber is capable of extending telephony and cable services throughout a campus. For information regarding cost-related issues with installing both singlemode and multimode fiber at the same time, see Chapter 15, "Installation."

Note:

> Horizontal cabling extends from the telecommunications outlet/ connector to the horizontal cross-connect. All horizontal wiring must be placed in a physical star topology with the floor wiring closet (FWC) as the center. Physical topology is a star (each telecommunications outlet/connector has its own mechanical termination position at the horizontal cross-connect in the telecommunications closet)

The published building cabling standards, ANSI/TIA/EIA-568-A, ISO/IEC 11801, and EN-50173, recognize both multimode and singlemode fiber for building and campus backbones. However, these standards do not recognize singlemode fiber for horizontal segments to the work area or desktop. This position reflects the present view of fiber-based services within premises networks, taking into consideration practical issues of active equipment availability, relative cost, and the remote likelihood of needing at the desktop the type of information carrying capacity that singlemode fiber can provide. Looking into the future from a fiber distribution perspective, the most likely scenario (for data that may be delivered to a building or campus on singlemode fiber) is that the singlemode fiber will terminate at an electronic multiplexing device. This multiplexer then extracts lower speed signals for delivery to the desktop over multimode fiber.

Looking into the future from a technology perspective, several technologies exist for extending the capability of multimode fiber. For example, no LAN standards have yet to use multilevel coding on multimode fiber to increase transmission capacity using less bandwidth, a technique very popular in copper-based LANs. Nor have any LANs used wavelength division multiplexing (WDM), which provides additional channels over the same fiber by using different colors of light. However, some multichannel video links on multimode fiber and long distance telephony on singlemode fiber use WDM today. Also, new devices, such as short wavelength lasers and vertical cavity surface emitting lasers (VCSELs), are emerging as the transmitter technology capable of providing cost-effective gigabit-rate data links over multimode fiber.

Considering these largely untapped technologies, it appears that multimode fiber has the capability to provide desktop LAN services far into the future. In the backbone however, where speeds and distances are generally ten times greater than to the desk, the clear trend is toward singlemode solutions.

The remaining consideration is the cost of retrofitting a network with singlemode fiber at a later time. This issue depends on many variables that are customer specific and often complex. For example, items such as the cable placement method (directly buried, in conduits, or aerial), obstacles (streets, lakes, rivers, fire stops), right-of-way passage, and work disruption all affect this decision. For these reasons it is often prudent, particularly in campus backbones, to place both multimode and singlemode cables at the same time. Again, for information regarding cost-related issues with installing both single mode and multimode fiber at the same time, see Chapter 15, "Installation."

It is important to install enough fiber to support the present and future applications that will simultaneously share the cable segment. Take into account the type and number of fibers that each application requires and add in spare capacity for future proofing. Generally, LAN applications will each require two fibers, while video applications will require one or two fibers depending on whether they are unidirectional or bi-directional. Video links that use bi-directional communications include those that return video, audio, camera control, or data signals. Add in at least 50 percent spare capacity and round the fiber-count upward to the next standard cable size.

If you decide to place both multimode and singlemode fibers along the same route, the general recommendation is that you run separate cables for each type. Composite cable, with both multimode and singlemode fibers in one sheath, are specifically not recommended in outside plant (OSP) applications. Initially, these cable types may appear attractive. However, in practice, OSP composite cable can prove problematic because of increased difficulty in fiber-type identification. This can lead to inappropriate use of splice and connector hardware; and, unintended interconnection of multimode to singlemode fibers at splice points. Using separate OSP cables helps to identify and segregate the two fiber types, reducing confusion during installation, maintenance, and administration. Furthermore, composite cables have more limited availability and higher cost than non-composite cable. However, for applications inside buildings, the issues of fiber-type identification and resulting mix-ups at splice and termination points have been mitigated by the design of composite building cables. The tight-buffer construction of the composite building cable uses a color-coded plastic coating over each individual fiber within the cable. This buffer carries special markings that easily identify the singlemode fibers within the cable. Therefore, the general recommendation would be to use the composite cable (see Figures 1–6 and 1–7) in buildings where both singlemode and multimode fibers are required along the same route [7].

To improve the management of the fiber system for administration and record keeping, route the two fiber types to separate patch panels in closets or equipment rooms. The fiber type should be identified by distinctive labeling. Color coding the connectors and couplings (adapters) is recommended. The use of blue for singlemode and beige for multimode connections is consistent with ANSI/TIA/EIA-568-A, ISO/IEC 11801, and EN-50173.

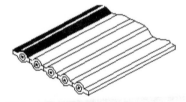

Figure 1–6: Composite cable.

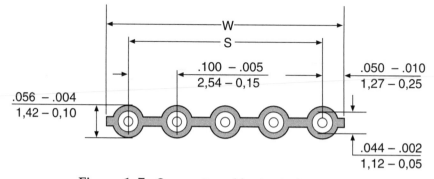

Figure 1–7: Composite cable circuit dimensions.

Fiber Optic Cable Connectors

The most common connector used with fiber optic cable is a Straight Tip (ST) connector. It is barrel shaped, similar to a BNC connector. A newer connector, the Subscriber Connector (SC) is becoming more popular. It has a squared face and is easier to connect in a confined space.

Copper Versus Fiber Cable

At this point in the chapter, it's quite appropriate to make a quick comparison of copper versus fiber media before going on to wireless media.

There are two main reasons for the broad acceptance and rapid growth of Category 5 UTP as a horizontal media: low initial cost and the ability to deliver high data rate LAN services. A standard media for LAN applications up to 155 Mbps is Category 5 UTP. However, copper-based LANs require more complex and expensive electronics as speeds increase. This trend, combined with continuing decreases in fiber media and optoelectronics prices, causes the initial price of the two solutions to converge as data rates increase. Today, for example, the price differential between copper and fiber (fiber being more expensive) for 155 Mbps ATM electronics is as small as 14 percent—with the 14 percent differential gap closing rapidly.

A third reason for the popularity of Category 5 UTP is that it allows customers to use only one media for both voice and data. In some instances though, customers select lower performance Category 3 UTP to support voice services, leaving the choice between Category 5 UTP and fiber for data services.

62.5/125 micron multimode fiber is already popular as a backbone media and its popularity is growing as a horizontal media. Although fiber is presently deployed in less than nine percent of horizontal cabling systems, analysts project it will triple or quadruple in some vertical markets over the next four years. The main reasons for this growth are the need for high-bandwidth services and the desire to never need to install cabling again over the life of the building. In addition, fiber eliminates potential problems of radio frequency interference, crosstalk, and lightning, thereby increasing the reliability of the network.

However, many customers may not realize one of fiber's greatest strengths. Fiber's longer distance capability permits cabling architectures that reduce recurring network operational costs. Fiber allows a centralized cabling design with a single point of administration. By collecting all hubs, switches, routers, and gateways into one location, the network requires less active equipment, maintenance, and administration effort. This generates substantial savings in initial and recurring operating costs. For example, the simplicity and flexibility of centralized electronics facilitates rapid rearrangements of distributed workgroup networks, and avoids expensive protocol conversions and switching that are often deployed between traditional horizontal and backbone cabling. In addition, centralization increases electronic equipment efficiencies, resulting in reduced equipment costs due to higher port usage. These savings multiply when supporting more than one LAN technology simultaneously, as is almost always the case when migrating to higher speed networks. All of these advantages can make fiber very cost-effective, even for lower-speed applications.

As mentioned earlier, it is critical to consider the customer's needs and business situation in order to make the best choice of horizontal media. Important issues include present and future data speed requirements, upgrade migration strategy, workgroup rearrangement frequency, building ownership and tenancy, remaining building occupancy, work area environment, horizontal distances, suitability of telecommunications closets, and long-term and short-term cost sensitivity. With these issues in mind, some conditions that indicate a centralized fiber architecture as the best choice for desktop connectivity include:

- A need to migrate efficiently to speeds above 155 Mbps at the desktop.
- A need to configure special workgroup networks quickly and easily.
- A need to support multiple LAN technologies efficiently.

- Long-term single-tenant occupancy.
- High security, high electromagnetic field, high lightning strike, or corrosive environments.
- Extreme intolerance to data errors or radiated emissions.
- Horizontal distances exceeding 100 meters (325 feet).
- Small, overcrowded, or insufficient numbers of telecommunications closets.
- A need to increase control over network operations.
- A need to reduce recurring operational costs.

If the customer's situation matches a number of these conditions, then fiber is probably the best choice. If the match is minimal, or if addressing the condition is not critical, then copper is probably the best choice. For some conditions, such as the need to exceed the standardized rates of UTP or support horizontal distances longer than 100 meters, fiber may be the only solution.

Wireless Media

Finally, let's take a look at the last cabling media type, wireless networks. This part of the chapter discusses how, through wireless media technology, you can create an instant stand-alone network—even linking the local area networks of several buildings—with a complete, integrated system of hardware and software that can extend wireless connectivity to an existing LAN.

Not all networks are connected with cabling; some networks are wireless. Wireless LANs use high frequency radio signals or infrared light beams to communicate between the workstations and the file server. Each workstation and file server on a wireless network has some sort of transceiver/antenna to send and receive the data. Information is relayed between transceivers as if they were physically connected. For longer distances, wireless communications can also take place through cellular telephone technology or by satellite as shown in Figure 1–8.

Wireless media is great for allowing laptop computers or remote computers to connect to the LAN. Wireless networks are also beneficial in older buildings where it may be difficult or impossible to install cables.

So What Really is a Wireless LAN?

Today many personal computers are interconnected with local area networks (LAN). Individuals are able to access and share data, applications, and services via the LAN. Most of these individuals use their computers in a fixed location where wired networking is possible as shown in Figure 1–9 [8].

Wireless Network

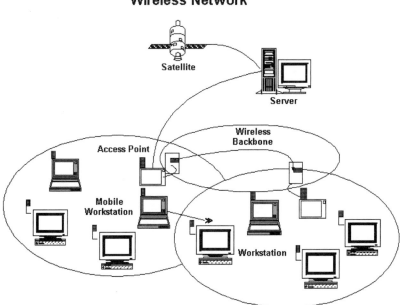

Figure 1–8: Wireless network.

Standard Wired Ethernet

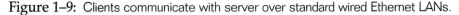

Figure 1–9: Clients communicate with server over standard wired Ethernet LANs.

However, a growing number of applications require mobility and simultaneous access to a network. Until recently, if an application required information from a central database, it had to be connected to a wired network using a docking station. A wireless LAN enables mobile computers to be in constant contact with servers and each other. Healthcare, warehousing, and education are examples of some of the industries which utilize wireless LANs as shown in Figure 1–8.

The computers in Figure 1–8 must all be in range of each other to maintain the wireless connection. However, most computers require greater range and flexibility since servers are often located on a wired Ethernet LAN somewhere else in the facility or at another site on an enterprise network. A *wireless access point* solves this problem by connecting wireless clients to Ethernet as shown in Figure 1–10 [AMP, 1–2].

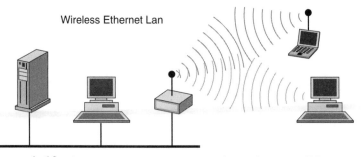

Figure 1–10: Access points connect wireless clients to Ethernet.

An access point will usually provide 50,000 to 250,000 square feet of coverage depending on your building structure. Numerous access points will allow wireless clients to roam and function in all the necessary areas. Roaming occurs seamlessly and transparently to the wireless client. Figure 1–11 shows roaming conceptualized [AMP, 2]. Implementing mobile or wireless applications in an existing environment consists of two simple steps:

- Step 1: Replace the PCMCIA (PC Card) wired network interface card (NIC) or the Industry-Standard Architecture Broadcast And Unknown Server (ISABUS) wired NIC with a wireless NIC.

- Step 2: Replace the Ethernet driver with a wireless Ethernet driver [AMP, 1]

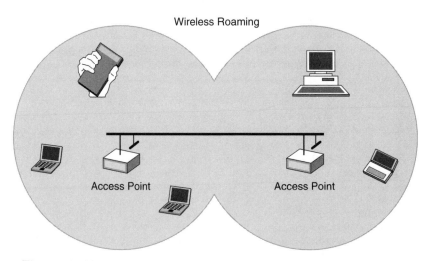

Figure 1–11: Wireless clients roam seamlessly throughout a facility.

Wireless drivers exist for all versions of Windows and DOS. ND&Is, ODI, and packet drivers are also offered. These drivers support a wide range of network operating systems, protocol stacks (Netware, Vines, TCP/IP, Lantastic, LAN server, etc.), and applications.

Nevertheless, wireless LANs also have some disadvantages. They are presently very expensive, provide poor security, and are susceptible to electrical interference from lights and radios. They are also slower than LANs using cabling. But they do have many advantages over traditional LANs. It's the way we're going to be doing business in the next millennium.

The next part of the chapter covers the questions that are most frequently asked when considering the functionality and performance of a wireless LAN.

Security

Because wireless technology has roots in military applications, security has long been a design criterion for wireless devices. Security provisions are typically built into wireless LANs, making them more secure than most wired LANs. It is extremely difficult for unintended receivers (eavesdroppers) to listen in on wireless LAN traffic. Complex encryption techniques make it impossible for all but the most sophisticated to gain unauthorized access to network traffic. Individual nodes must be security-enabled before they are allowed to participate in network traffic.

Coverage and Range

The distance over which Radio Frequency (RF) waves can communicate is dependent on the building or environment the wireless LAN is installed in. Interactions with typical building objects, including walls, metal, and even people, can affect how energy propagates and thus what range and coverage a particular system achieves. A wireless LAN system uses RF because radio waves can penetrate many indoor walls and surfaces. The range of a wireless LAN is up to 500 ft in normal office environments and up to 1000 ft in open space. Coverage can be extended, and true freedom of mobility via roaming is provided through microcells.

Safety

The output power of wireless LAN systems is very low, much less than that of a hand-held cellular phone. Since radio waves fade rapidly over distance, very little exposure to RF energy is provided to those in the area of a wireless LAN system. Wireless LANs must meet stringent government and industry regulations for safety. No adverse health affects have ever been attributed to wireless LANs.

Throughput

As with wired LAN systems, actual throughput in wireless LANs is dependent on your set-up. Factors that affect throughput include airwave congestion (number of users), propagation factors such as range and multipath, as well as the latency and bottlenecks on the wired portions of the wireless LAN. Typical data rates range from 1 to 10 Mbps.

Note:

The term "multipath" describes a situation in which a transmitted signal follows several propagation paths from a transmitter to a receiver. This may result from the signal reflecting off several objects to arrive at the receiver.

Users of traditional Ethernet LANs generally experience little difference in performance when using a wireless LAN and can expect similar latency behavior. Wireless LANs provide throughput sufficient for the most common LAN-based office applications, including electronic mail exchange, access to shared peripherals, and access to multiuser databases and applications.

Mobile and Flexible

Because it's wireless, this type of media or network can go where no other network has gone before. It can plug right into your existing network.

But what can a wireless network do for you? You might be surprised. Imagine the gains in productivity you'll achieve when everyone on the factory floor has instant access to your parts database, on the spot, without traveling to a distant terminal for information. Think about how much you'll save in labor costs with a network that requires virtually none of the planning, installation or reconfiguration traditional LANs require to keep pace with rapidly changing business conditions.

Now, imagine the improvements in both retail sales and customer service you'll achieve when point-of-sale terminals can be moved to areas of peak demand overnight, or even over a lunch break. Next, imagine six notebook computers hastily opened on a conference table and sharing data minutes later. Imagine being able to do the same thing an hour after that—in a client's office, on a factory floor, or at a trade show.

Finally, imagine linking the networks of two buildings a mile apart virtually overnight, without the expense of a leased telephone line. And, think about having an instant LAN set up and ready to cope—anywhere, anytime—when sudden business opportunities beckon or when a midnight phone call brings unthinkable news.

Connectivity

The pivotal role of LANs is more obvious every day. In just three years, the number of PCs sold that were linked to networks doubled and, by 1995, had reached a level of 50 percent.

Even that figure may seem laughably low. Odds are that far more than 50 percent of your company's computers are on a LAN. Well, the desktop computers, anyway. But what about all those new portables? Are they still mute and isolated, unable to tap the power of your network?

That situation won't last long. Recent surveys estimate that portables will comprise more than 60 percent of the computer market by 1999.

Chaining down all these portables with patch cords makes little sense. With a wireless network, you don't have to sacrifice mobility for connectivity. You can plug a small PCMCIA card into each portable—laptops, notebooks, pen-based computers—for an instant connection to the network. Depending on the configuration you choose, a wireless network can provide a seamless, continuous network link to each portable computer even while roaming.

Installation

Take an empty room, add half a dozen work stations and link them all in a fast, partially secure local area network—within a few minutes. Impossible? Well, the security part maybe.

Installing a wireless network actually can be just that simple. There's no wiring or conduit pathways to consider. All you need to create a fully functioning stand-alone network comes packed in a small box. Plug a card into each computer, install the software and your LAN is ready to go.

Could this unprecedented freedom help solve a few problems for you? Consider the possibilities. Cabling can be difficult or impossible to install in some situations. Asbestos makes older buildings problematic, hospitals can't accommodate new conduit pathways, warehouses can be simply too vast to rewire. But in each case a wireless network can be up and running virtually overnight.

Construction costs of recabling can overwhelm companies that change the workplace frequently. Retailers alter floor plans, manufacturers retool, banks redeploy branches. A wireless network effortlessly glides into place anywhere—and immediately becomes a versatile asset rather than a burdensome construction expense.

From Here

Today's businesses require constant communication and instant access to information—both in and away from the office. The three cabling media (copper, fiber, and wireless) discussed in this chapter provide you with the mobility and flexibility you need—but you also have to manage the network that provides your communication requirements.

The next chapter discusses the six major types of networks: Local Area Network (LAN), Wide Area Network (WAN), Virtual Area Network (VAN), intranet, extranet, and Internet. Some companies are fortunate to have all six types connecting their systems. This chapter will cover how all three cabling media can be used with one or all six of the network types to allow your organization to soar beyond the traditional constraints of network cabling. The chapter will show you how and when to expand, contract, or redeploy your network type(s) virtually anywhere, anytime, as quickly as today's accelerating pace of change demands.

End Notes

[1] "Local Area Network Cables," Remee Products Corp., P. O. Box 488, 186 North Main Street, Florida, NY 10921, USA, 1998, p. 1.

[2] "Connecting Terminals and PCs with DB-25 Connectors," Computone Corporation, 1100 Northmeadow Parkway, Suite 150 Roswell, GA 30076, 1995, p. 1.

[3] "CATV, CCTV & Communication Coaxial Cable," Remee Products Corp., P. O. Box 488, 186 North Main Street, Florida, NY 10921, USA1998, p. 2.

[4] "Ethernet Cable Comparison Chart," Cabletron Systems, 35 Industrial Way, Rochester, NH 03866 U.S.A., 1998, p. 1.

[5] Scientific Instrument Services, 1027 Old York Rd., Ringoes, NJ 08551, 1997, p. 1.

[6] "Fiber Optic Cabling Installations," Advanced Cable Connection Inc., 922A E. 124 Avenue, Tampa, FL 33612, 1997, p. 1.

[7] Molex Incorporated, 2222 Wellington Court, Lisle, Illinois 60532 U.S.A., 1998, p. 1.

[8] "What Is A Wireless LAN?," Reprinted with the permission of AMP Incorporated, Investor Relations, 176-42, PO Box 3608, Harrisburg, PA USA 17105-3608, 1997, p. 1.

2

TYPES OF NETWORKS

We are in the middle of another information revolution that is reaching out and touching every aspect of our professional and personal lives. This time, the revolution has less to do with creating new information and more to do with resistance to change—that tension between centrifugal and centripetal forces. In cabling, the tension lies between the effects of different types of networking technologies that pull computing power out to the fringes of the network, and the effects that tend to centralize it. Finding and maintaining the dynamic balance between these forces is what makes the job of information technology (IT) professionals so hard.

A network consists of two or more computers that are linked in order to share resources (such as printers and CD-ROMs), exchange files, or allow electronic communications. The computers on a network may be linked through cables, telephone lines, radio waves, satellites, or infrared light beams. This chapter discusses the six major types of networks, Local Area Network (LAN), Wide Area Network (WAN), Virtual Area Network (VAN), Internet, intranet, and extranet, that are available to organizations. The chapter also address ways in which the three cabling media (copper, fiber, and wireless) can be used with the various network types to allow your organization to be able to add and integrate new capabilities into their existing cabling infrastructure.

Local Area Network

Let's begin our journey by looking at the first of these major types of networks: Local Area Network (LAN).

A LAN or Local Area Network is a computer network (or data communications network) which is confined to a room, a building, or a group of adjacent buildings as shown in Figure 2–1 [1]. Rarely are LAN computers more than a mile apart.

A similar network on a larger scale is sometimes referred to as a WAN (Wide Area Network), or in some cases more specifically, a VAN (Virtual Area Network) or MAN (Metropolitan Area Network), if it is confined to a single metropolitan area. VANs are discussed later in the chapter.

The term LAN is most often used to refer to networks created using a certain class of networking equipment. This equipment is tailored to communication over a short distance and is in contrast to networks which happen to span long distances. These networks are constructed using *WAN* equipment (equipment capable of transmitting long distances). LAN-style networking equipment typically transmits data at a higher rate than WAN-style equipment. The equipment's design takes advantage of the short distance to supply a high transmission-rate at a relatively low cost.

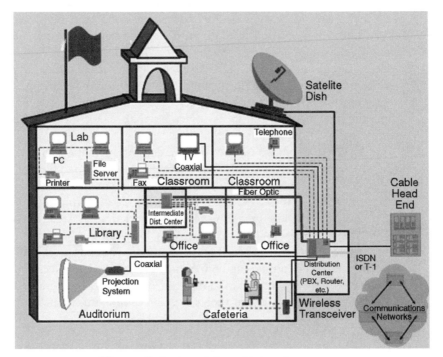

Figure 2–1: Local Area Network.

NOTE:

Both LAN and WAN equipment typically offers faster data transfer than even the fastest ordinary modem/phone-line access (LAN transfers being on the order of a million times faster).

If you are familiar with network access using a modem and an ordinary telephone line, the graphics that are loaded through a LAN network can be displayed significantly faster. In other words, there are things that are practical to do on a LAN that you would never do with a modem. For example, rather than setting up your computer to load your word processing application through your hard disk, you should load it from the LAN. In either case, the time you have to wait while it loads would be similar (a few seconds). In contrast, loading such an application through a modem would require minutes or hours.

A typical use of a LAN is to tie together personal computers in an office in such a way that they can all use a file server and a single printer. A file server is a computer set up so that other computers can access its hard disk as if it were their own.

LANs are also used to transmit e-mail between personal computers in an office. Additionally, they are also used to attach all the personal computers in the office to a WAN or to the Internet.

However, there is some variation in the way the term LAN is used. As previously stated, for example, it is used to refer to a file server and printer and often to the personal computers that are tied to them. People refer to saving their files on the PC LAN, or on the LAN. But the term LAN is also used more specifically to refer to the equipment and data communications wiring that ties the personal computers to the printer and file server.

In a typical LAN configuration, one computer is designated as the file server. It stores all of the software that can be shared by the computers attached to the network, as well as the software that controls the network. Thus, computers connected to the file server are called workstations. The workstations can be less powerful than the file server. They may even have additional software on their hard drives. Furthermore, cables are used to connect the network interface cards in each computer on most LANs.

Some other types of LANs (or in the jargon: other LAN technologies) are token ring, FDDI (Fiber Distributed Data Interface), and Fast Ethernet. Ethernet is the most common type in use today. It's an example of what is called LAN technology; or, in the more specific sense of the word LAN—one of several types of LANs.

Equipment of two different technologies cannot be plugged together without a special device (bridge or router) between that can translate from one technology to the other. In other words, equipment cannot be interconnected by a piece of wire if your file server has an Ethernet adapter and your PC has a token ring adapter. But if each adapter were attached to the same bridge—specifically, one that translates between Ethernet and token ring—then they could communicate (although it might cost a few thousand dollars).

Today, organizations are lured by the many benefits of distributed computing over LANs and WANs. They are faced with the daunting task of bringing workability to the diversity and complexity of today's data communications landscape. The need to interconnect dissimilar LANs and diverse equipment becomes even more urgent as enterprise networks continue to grow and expand to include telecommuters, small branch offices, and far-flung international locations. Among the key challenges facing network managers today is how to meld legacy systems and LANs, consolidate multiprotocol traffic over a single WAN backbone, and tie together incompatible LANs. Furthermore, without inflicting performance penalties on end users, all of this must be done at minimum cost.

Wide Area Network

With that in mind, let's continue with our journey and take a look at the next network type, the Wide Area Network.

Sometimes referred to as "long haul networks," Wide Area Networks (WANs) can cover large distances. Multiple buildings, cities, or even continents can be connected by WANs. Dedicated transoceanic cabling or satellite uplinks may be used to connect the type of network shown in Figure 2–2 [2].

Now (without having to pay enormous phone bills), schools in the United States can communicate with places like Tokyo in a matter of minutes using a WAN. A WAN is complicated. It uses multiplexers (a device that allows multiple logical signals to be transmitted simultaneously across a single physical channel) to connect local and metropolitan networks to global communications networks like the Internet. To users, however, a WAN will not appear to be much different from a LAN or a VAN. WANs operate at bandwidths ranging from 9.6 Kbps (thousand bits per second) up to and beyond 655 Mbps (million bits per second), as shown in Figure 2–3 [3]. Delays are usually large. They range from 10 milliseconds up to several hundred milliseconds across a satellite network.

NOTE:

Even though it is not shown in Figure 2–3, several of the Internet backbone providers are currently running or planning to run OC-24/OC-48 (1.2/2.4 Gbps) on their backbones.

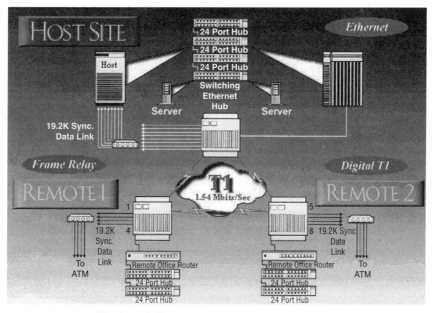

Figure 2–2: Wide Area Network.

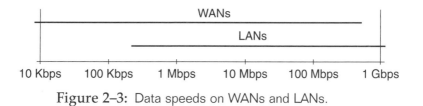

Figure 2–3: Data speeds on WANs and LANs.

Virtual Area Networks

Now, let's take a look at one of the most obvious and significant industries which will rise out of bandwidth abundance and our next type of network, Virtual Area Networks (VANs).

Virtual Area Networks (VANs) or metropolitan area networks (MANs)
have been around for several years. But the development of MANs has been
limited due to the lack of bandwidth.

Initially, MANs were designed to cover larger geographic areas, such as cities or school districts as shown in Figure 2–4 [4]. Information is easily disseminated throughout the network by interconnecting smaller networks within a large geographic area. A MAN is often used by local libraries and government agencies to connect citizens and private industries. The Fife and Tayside Metropolitan Area Network (FaTMAN) located at the University of Dundee in, Scotland, is one example of a MAN. The links (University of Dundee to University of Abertay Dundee: 1.5km; University of Dundee to University of St Andrews: 23km; and, University of St Andrews to University of Abertay Dundee: 23.3km) totaling 47.8km (28 miles), are very long for directly driven fiber optic connections and use special purpose drivers to cover these distances. A High Speed ATM Network is used to support teaching and research activities in Fife and Tayside.

In the near future, VANs will become the gathering place for communities, both geographical and special interest. VANs may return some sense of community which has been eroded by the automobile and urban sprawl. Additionally, VANs will create opportunities for special interest communities to form over widely dispersed geographical areas. They will empower telecommuting for company employees, individuals, government, and independent business.

The Telecommuting Factor

One of the goals of telecommuting is to allow a worker to accomplish from home the same things he or she would accomplish by traveling to the office. The virtual trip to the office can closely simulate the actual trip by utilizing interactive video and audio technology. You will be able to say hello to your secretary and co-workers once you are at your computer, and before you *sit down to work*. You will pass the coffee lounge (virtual or real) and notice who is there. You will see

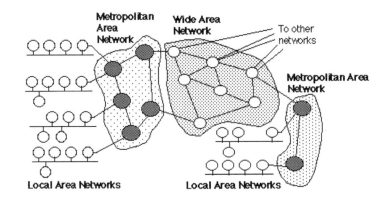

Figure 2–4: Virtual Area Network (VAN) or Metropolitan Area Network (MAN).

that Diane the secretary is already on the phone and that the boss's office door is closed. You can discuss a new idea with a visitor you run into in a casual room or in the hall. Also, when someone new arrives in the *area*, computer-generated sounds of footsteps will alert you. Thus, a new meaning will take on with the possibilities for telecommuting from your home or office.

Through the creation of a new social context for communities, the benefits of a virtual office will be offered to the public at large. The interactive technology which was developed for multiuser computer games will be incorporated by VANs. VANs serve a number of community and social functions, as well as businesses A virtual site will be created through chance encounters, social interaction, and multiple public sites that will closely resemble being together.

VAN Example

Residents in the town of Bozeman, Montana, have the opportunity to see each other on the University campus, meet for coffee, travel to each others' offices, and conduct business. A growing number of citizens work at home. The lack of social barriers is a distinguishing characteristic of Bozeman and the surrounding area. With a minimum amount of distraction or attracting attention, movie stars and business moguls are common in the shops and coffee houses and are free to interact in the community. This type of interaction will be possible in virtual communities anywhere in the world. People can limit their exposure to selected groups, interact anonymously and electronically, and still allow for chance encounters and random visits.

In a virtually connected community, citizens can address the school board or the city commission without leaving home. Customers can talk to their accountants and bankers. Home-bound students can talk to teachers. Merchants can market their products. And home office workers can look into connected coffee houses, see who is there, and decide whether or not to take a break.

VAN technology will be limited to perhaps 600 participants per system. Numerous VANs will develop in larger cities. A directory of VANs and access codes will also evolve. Each viewer will be able to display numerous participants on the computer screen at one time among the potential 600 participants of a VAN. Clicking on one participant will bring it to full screen view.

The legal and medical communities may initially receive the greatest benefits from VANs. Prisoners can be arraigned virtually, eliminating of expensive and dangerous transportation. They could receive routine health care virtually. Medical specialists can consult without leaving their offices and clinics. Lawyers can telecommute to the courthouse and their clients. Private rooms on the VAN will provide confidentiality for business in general, attorney-client privilege, and medical confidences. A quick return on investment for the VAN will result from savings in time and travel. Payback periods of less than one year may be realistic. Additional benefits will be less stress, reduced traffic, and increased efficiency. More professions, businesses and individuals will benefit directly from the virtual connection to their community as VAN develops.

The question of privacy must be addressed by this technology. Access to certain individuals or groups can be limited by participants. Members of a private group can go to a virtual private room where only other group members and their guests are granted access. Control of access and exposure on the VAN will be given to each participant. VANs may shift our cities back towards the communal nature of small towns (with their benefits and drawbacks). Standards for privacy can be agreed upon and implemented to fit individual values and the community.

Connectivity Factor

Hardware and software to implement VANs can be developed with existing technology. Bandwidth has been the limiting factor to date. Some major steps in bandwidth are listed in Table 2–1 [5].

Table 2–1: Major bandwidth steps.

home/small office use	year	faster than previous	improvement factor
0.3 Kbps modem	1990		
1.2 Kbps modem	1991	4.0	4
14.4 Kbps modem	1992	12.0	48
28.8 Kbps modem	1994	2.0	96
128 Kbps BRI-ISDN	1996	4.5	428
768 K—2.0 Mbps HDSL with PairGain	1997	6.0	2560
6 Mbps ADSL on AT&T GlobeSpan	1998	7.8	20,000
10 Mbps to 36 Mbps Cable Modem	1999	6.0	120,000
10 GbpsGbps wave multiplexed fiber	2001	1000.0	33,333,333
1,700 GbpsGbps wave multiplexed fiber	2006	170.0	5,666,666,610

Each step in Table 2–1 represents a dramatic improvement over the previous. Cable modems have already been deployed in northern California. And BRI-ISDN (Basic Rate Interface-Integrated Services Digital Network) has begun to spread in much of the country. PairGain Technologies has shipped 768 Kbps *Mega Modems* which now operate over copper lines. AT&T Paradyne claims their 6.0 Mbps GlobeSpan asymmetric digital subscriber line (ADSL) service is now available in most parts of the country. With the significant benefits of increased bandwidth, the question for anyone looking into VANs becomes which connectivity technology should be implemented? In most parts of the country, the highest step economically currently available is BRI-ISDN. But everything short of cable modems could soon be obsolete. Processing and storing data at this flow rate will push the limits of the fastest and most memory-endowed computers.

Among connected office computers, the high speed of local area networks (LAN) connections allows for high quality audio and video (10 Mbps for Ethernet, 4 or 16 Mbps for token ring). But quality and speed for inter-LAN multimedia connections is greatly limited by bandwidth of publicly switched telephone lines. High-bit-rate Digital Subscriber Line (HDSL) connection devices operating at 768 Kbps are available for connections over unconditioned *dry* copper pairs. The HDSL connection devices can be rented from the Local Exchange Carrier (LEC), usually a Bell Operating Company. This speed is adequate for high quality audio and video connection between remote LANs and over the Internet. AT&T Paradyne has unveiled an application of ADSL which is capable of providing 6 Mbps over copper wires. This is reportedly on the market now in most parts of the country. AT&T claims that rates are comparable to standard phone service.

Cable Modem Technology

Cable modem technology, which will spread in 1998, may make all the other connection schemes obsolete. Cable modem technology could provide access to VANs and the Internet at speeds in the 10 Mbps to 36 Mbps range downstream (network to computer). Computer connection will usually be based on Ethernet 10BaseT. Early cable modems will probably operate asymmetrically, with downstream bandwidths considerably wider that upstream bandwidths (computer to network). @Home, a venture of the Silicon Valley venture capital group of Kleiner, Perkins, Caufield and Beyer, reportedly has a cable modem Internet access trial currently underway in Fremont, California. Continental Cablevision is planning to use LANCity cable modems to provide high-bit-rate service in New England. Bozeman, Montana, the birth place of TCI Cable, is leveraging existing connections for a VAN in anticipation of cable modems.

Computer and interface limitations will lower these bandwidths in the early days of cable modems. Downstream bandwidths may be 3 to 10 Mbps and upstream bandwidths may be 200 Kbps to 2 Mbps. Cable modems do MOdulate and DEMolulate, but they are actually a combination modem, tuner, bridge, encrypter, router, Network Interface Card (NIC), Simple Network Management Protocol (SNMP), and hub.

NOTE:

Cable modem is a descriptive but inaccurate term.

Even cable operators with older one-way delivery systems will be able to provide bi-directional Internet access. The availability of bandwidth at this magnitude will lead to the next limiting factor of the digital age: the global telecommnunication backbone. The backbone will undergo radical upgrade in the next few years. Phone companies installed an estimated 10 million kilometers of fiber in the 1980s, and only a fraction of the potential bandwidth has been utilized. Wave division multiplexing is a method of sending different wavelengths or colors down the fiber and filtering them at the other end. Four colors increases the 2.4 Gbps capacity of a single fiber to 9.6 Gbps. This is the equivalent of sending 1000 novels per second. By the year 2000, that is expected to rise to 40 Gbps. This would send a small bookstore in less than a second. Theoretically, approximately 700 separate wavelength streams could be sent and filtered, resulting in a capacity of 1,700 Gbps over a single fiber.

In addition to being radically faster than other forms of digital connectivity, cable modems will offer much simpler installation. ISDN installation and connection is notoriously complicated, requiring the customer to act as his or her own systems integrator. Cable companies will be able to offer turnkey ready to operate systems.

Internet

Web pages today are mainly for disseminating information, not receiving it (beyond vital statistics). The proliferation of video conferencing equipment combined with increasing bandwidth will create more Internet users looking for virtual places to go. That brings us to the next type of network, the Internet.

The Internet, also known as the first wave of the World Wide Web (WWW) evolution, is the largest network in existence. It can be defined as the physical network that connects many different computer systems in a loosely associated network that spans the globe. The Internet carries most of the information shared on a worldwide scale. It currently connects 60 to 120 million machines located throughout ninety percent of the world, as shown in Figure 2–5, and is growing at an astounding rate [6].

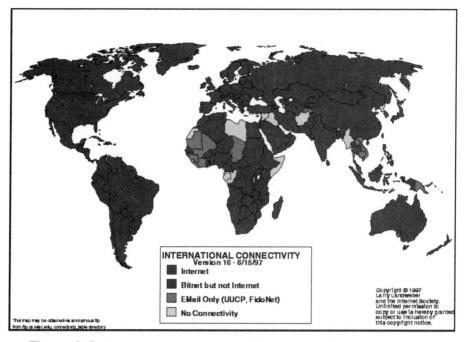

Figure 2–5: Internet connectivity to different parts of the world.

Current estimates indicate that there were 168 million Internet users at the end of 1997, up from 56 million Internet users in 1996, an annual growth of nearly 50%. Estimates by independent research organizations indicate that another 400 million users will join the Internet by 2001. With this many users, the Internet has grown far beyond the expectations of its designers when it was created 29 years ago.

Wave One: The Public Domain Internet

The Internet and WWW have provided unprecedented ways of linking people with information. With the web's ubiquitous software and technology, global access to data, text, documents, pictures, sound, animation, video, and other information from any web-enabled computer or workstation is now a reality. The recent awareness and popularity of this medium has been fueled primarily by the fundamental simplicity and adaptability of the Internet's open and standard protocols. More than simply a vehicle for information dissemination, the Internet is leading networking computing shifts away from fat clients, closed proprietary systems, and costly Network Operating System (NOS) environments.

Internet Use

With millions of interconnected systems and users, the Internet offers a way for organizations to compete globally. The low cost of entry and global reach associated with establishing a website level the playing field among organizations with respect to size or technology investment. However, the quality of that presence plays a much bigger role in terms of its technical and communicative function.

The World Wide Web is by far the most popular choice for a public presence on the Internet. It can provide a single platform for developing a corporate identity, advertising, and marketing products and services. In a recent study by an independent research organization, 68 percent of the companies surveyed felt that using Internet technology resulted in an improvement in their respective business environments [7]. An increasing number of organizations are using Internet technologies for useful business applications such as Federal Express's computerized cargo tracking system. But is Internet technology the right choice for you? Remember, the answer depends on the goals and objectives of your organization and how they match up against criteria such as the types of communications and the nature of transactions.

For example, the objective of The New York Times was to develop an interactive version of its daily newspaper. Internet technology was a good choice because the information in its publication is public and freely available. Security is not a major issue. The Internet also provides a convenient way to offer timely coverage of major news stories to readers at their desktops anywhere around the world.

Although the well-known Ben & Jerry's ice cream Internet site started out as a private business system for its employees and franchisers, the focus of the site was soon shifted to the consumer. To satisfy the universal desire for its product, the company developed an Internet website that offers information such as ice cream flavors and products, scoop shop locations, company-sponsored film and music festivals, factory tours, and Ben & Jerry's business philosophy.

In some cases, a public website on the Internet is needed to provide the easiest and most wide-ranging access, while still ensuring a high degree of security for sensitive transactions. The Chicago Board of Trade (CBOT) implemented its integrated website to allow the exchange to conduct secure electronic commerce and communications on a global basis. Visitors seeking recent quotes, educational material, or other information can get it all on-line 24 hours a day.

From just a brief look at these few business cases, it's clear that successful networking choices begin with well-defined goals and objectives based on an organization's needs and capabilities. Only then are the objectives matched to available network technologies. Specific networking strategies and tactics are negotiated from this match-up. For some objectives, intranets (which will be discussed next) are the clear choice, especially when internal communications must be kept secure or when the bandwidth and throughput must be optimized for multimedia and real-time communications.

For other objectives, the Internet offers an unprecedented opportunity to reach a global base of users in a manner that is convenient and has a low cost of entry and maintenance. Ultimately, the real question is not Internet versus intranet, but rather when and how each networking strategy should be used to serve the many and changing needs of an organization.

Intranets

Now let's take a look at intranets.

Intranets, also known as the second wave of the Internet evolution, are secured areas that utilize the Internet and WWW to conduct internal communication and collaboration activities. When the Internet and the World Wide Web architecture are brought inside of a company and used to distribute a company's private information, you have an intranet. Adopted by companies at an increasingly phenomenal rate, intranets have produced efficiencies for businesses that allow users to manage their organizations more efficiently and effectively *behind the firewall*. To date, three-fourths of Fortune 500 corporations and thousands of other companies have already established intranets, the majority of which are being used to manage tasks, information, and group work within individual organizations [8].

Whether network managers are considering Internet access or intranet implementation, they need to understand that both are important new approaches to networking technology. As such, they must be in every network manager's bag of tricks. More important, intranets are a technology, or more accurately a collection of technologies, that dramatically change how companies do business internally and with their customers and suppliers. As a telecommunications technology, intranet technology truly re-engineers communications. This is its real value.

Application and Services

The Internet and intranets comprise not only the physical connection of the systems, but also the wide range of software that allows the creation, organization, and distribution of information, including the World Wide Web. These technologies are revolutionizing the way information is produced, gathered, distributed, and used.

Most businesses agree that the availability of cheap, organized information is a benefit and a requirement to staying competitive. However, most businesses are unsure of exactly how to take advantage of the Internet/intranet information pipeline and how to integrate this pipeline into their existing mission-critical networks which were built as the result of a decade of expensive investments.

The problems of building and integrating a network infrastructure suitable to support mission-critical intranets are manifold. They include:

- The question of whether intranets are a practical investment.
- The consideration of today's LAN infrastructure, which may not be suitable for hosting a high-speed intranet.
- The requirements for hosting a mission-critical intranet [9].

A number of challenges have arisen because of the growing importance of intranets and the World Wide Web. Two of the most important are how to enable the wide spread exchange of information and how to deal with the type and structure of this new information. IT (Information Technology) and network managers are facing the challenge of enabling the exchange of information on a scale that is broader than the LAN. This requires implementing a technology gateway between an organization's existing infrastructure and the infrastructure improvements needed to support intranets.

So, how practical is it to build the client/server infrastructure necessary to support an intranet? The client/server concept and its associated issues are well understood; so are its benefits and pitfalls. Not only are there issues in building client/server applications, but there are also issues related to building the physical cabling infrastructure to support the wide-scale deployment of these applications.

Building the Physical Cabling Infrastructure

Fortunately, building a cabling infrastructure that can support an intranet is a logical step in moving a network toward the support of client/server applications. Today an intranet, with its client-side browser and its service-side servers, is the best low-cost, widely available implementation of a client/server architecture. In addition, an intranet can be built to incorporate and support many different computing platforms. Furthermore, most of the software needed to implement intranets is available at a relatively low cost.

Intranets, therefore, can benefit an organization by providing information on an organizational or worldwide scale, and also serve as a low-cost proving ground for the implementation of additional client/server applications. If a cabling infrastructure can support an intranet, it is well on the way toward supporting other client/server applications. Many CIOs now are asking: can my current cabling architecture support the new high-speed intranet software?

Supporting the Intranet

So, can your cabling architecture support an intranet? The answer to this question is most likely *no* if your network has the following characteristics:

- Congested network backbones with poor server-to-workstation or internetwork response time.
- Microsegmentation to control excess broadcast traffic.
- Lack of available bandwidth caused by a large number of end-stations trying to access a smaller number of servers (Gluck, 3).

When evaluating the potential return on investment of an intranet, cabling architects must decide on the type of technology that will be used to build the intranet backbone. Today's technologies offer ATM (Asynchronous Transfer Mode), FDDI (Fiber Distributed Data Interface), or fast Ethernet as solutions that will meet the bandwidth requirements of servers and backbones in the campus or metropolitan network. It is important to understand the differences among these technologies, especially where scalability is concerned.

When delivery of the right amount of bandwidth to where it is needed is important, ATM is a better solution than FDDI or fast Ethernet. One key difference between ATM and FDDI is that FDDI is a shared-media token-passing technology similar to token ring. ATM, on the other hand, is a switched-technology media.

Because an FDDI backbone is built as a token ring, the total available 100 Mbps is shared among all attached users. For example, connecting 16 users (or devices) to an FDDI ring means that these devices will be competing for a maximum available bandwidth of 100 Mbps, thereby giving each device an average bandwidth of only 6 Mbps. With this shared architecture, there is no way to allocate a specific amount of bandwidth to any one of the connections, and no way to scale available bandwidth.

Connectivity

Connect the same 16 devices to an ATM network, and each of the 16 devices can be allotted a dedicated 155 Mbps of bandwidth or, in fact, any amount of bandwidth from 25.6 Mbps to over 1 Gbps. This bandwidth is available because the architecture of ATM allows direct connections or circuits to be established between two end points over a meshed network where each of the circuits can be allocated a fixed amount of bandwidth.

Why is this an advantage? First, scalability allows each section of the network to be given bandwidth according to its particular needs. While desktop applications might find 25.6 Mbps more than adequate, workgroups or corporate servers might require 100 Mbps or 155 Mbps, and corporate backbones might need even more. With ATM networks, the cabling architect can scale the available bandwidth to provide exactly the amount needed using a single network topology from the desktop through the backbone.

Second, meshed networks allow scalability and can be built as a collapsed backbone either inside a chassis or over a wide area. This allows available scalable bandwidth to be allocated exactly where it is needed.

Finally, bandwidth within a meshed network is additive. This characteristic allows the construction of large multigigabit networks that can provide high throughput at the top of a bandwidth hierarchy.

Switching and Scalability

ATM and fast Ethernet are best when combined in a single solution that supports cost-efficient operation of the data center—each technology doing what it does best. Why? ATM and fast Ethernet are both switched and scalable technologies. As a bandwidth hierarchy is built, both Ethernet and ATM can scale to support the needs of users, LANs, and data centers. Fast Ethernet also is considered to be simpler in sites where Ethernet is the only topology. In pure Ethernet sites, there is no packet-to-cell conversion or heterogeneous bridging necessary to move data from one point to another. Fast Ethernet does not scale well over large geographical areas. It is limited to five miles, so problems may arise when installing backbones across a campus. Fast Ethernet cannot provide WAN solutions. ATM addresses this issue.

Fast Ethernet cannot support the connection of token ring networks if it is used as a backbone. It also cannot be meshed because of the requirement that spanning tree algorithms should be implemented to prevent loops in a network. However, ATM can be used to build meshed networks or backbones for redundancy and efficiency.

One other fact to consider: connecting servers directly to ATM is technologically feasible and rapidly dropping in price. It can be implemented today with almost no network changes other than the addition of an ATM network interface card (NIC) to the server. Based on these considerations, it is best to consider ATM as the technology for high-speed backbones and fast Ethernet as the technology for the LAN section of the network.

Many technologies cross our desks each year in the never-ending march to deliver information where it is needed. The second and first Internet technology wave, intranets, and the World Wide Web have already proven themselves as highly useful paradigms that can improve information availability in the business and even the home environment. Always keep in mind that the benefits that intranets can bring may be lost in an overwhelming avalanche of network over-load and uncompleted projects if not implemented correctly. Learn, plan, start slowly, and factor in growth from the beginning. Intranets can then deliver all that they promise.

Extranet

Now that you know all about intranets, the next logical step in your thought processes might involve an extranet—the third wave of the Internet evolution, and the last of the network types. Let's look at how organizations are intelligently joining their intranets to create *extranets.*

The *extranet* represents the bridge between the public Internet and the private corporate Intranet. It connects multiple and diverse organizations on-line behind virtual firewalls, where those who share in trusted circles can network in order to achieve commerce-oriented objectives. The extranet defines and supports this extended business enterprise including partners, suppliers, distributors, con-tractors and others that operate outside the physical walls of an organization but are nonetheless critical to the success of business operations. With the Internet providing for public outreach or communication, and the Intranet serving inter-nal business interests, the extranet serves the business-critical domain between these extremes where the majority of business activity occurs.

Nailing It Down

The exact definition of an extranet still is shaking out, but the most uni-versally accepted one defines an extranet as a network that links business part-ners to one another over the Internet by tying together their corporate intranets. Put simply, an extranet means expanding your intranet to include perhaps customers, clients, suppliers, and almost anyone else who has contact with your business on a daily basis. You actually give people outside your company (who somehow relate to your business) access to your intranet using Internet technology. Extranets can help businesses improve customer service, increase revenue and save time, money and resources.

The unification of robust enabling technologies and ubiquitous access through the web is resulting in unique and interesting market dynamics that are changing the way many companies are doing business. Interactive communities are beginning to emerge that exist solely in cyberspace, where information trav-els faster, more cost effectively, and with greater accuracy when compared to other forms of communication and information exchange. These interactive communities are the driving and sustaining force behind the extranet concept, and their insatiable collective need to access content when, where, and how they want to see it will continue to push the limits of what is technologically possible.

Extranet solutions built to engage and support these interactive communities are designed to emphasize and foster the customer relationship. As successful businesses know, the cost of obtaining a new customer far outweighs the cost of maintaining a current one. With commerce-enabled extranets, companies are now able to establish and maintain one-to-one relationships with each of their customers, members, staff or others at very low cost through the web, offering a customized and individualized experience that can be dynamically generated or modified based upon a user's privileges, preferences, or usage patterns. Information entered by the user (registration form, on-line surveys, etc.) can be compiled with statistics and other information that is captured automatically by the system (searches performed, products purchased, time spent in each site area, etc.) to provide the company a complete picture for each and every visitor to the system. This comprehensive user profile offers unprecedented opportunity to present relevant information, advertising, product and service offerings, and other content to a qualified, targeted interactive user community on a one-to-one basis.

A company that supplies tools to other companies, for example, might allow its customers to browse its catalog and place orders online, eliminating the need for customer service representatives. Or a hospital could link up with health maintenance organizations (HMOs) and others in the healthcare field. Other user profiles for an extranet includenewsgroups to share experiences and ideas among colleagues, suppliers, clients, etc.; collaboration to develop a new application all interested parties could use; and providing training programs or other educational material.

Obstacles

Building an extranet is hard work—even harder than building an Intranet! Many issues—compatibility, access, and culture—must be worked out ahead of time. An extranet will require more planning than an intranet. And it will cost a lot more, too. Funding needs to be built in for training, security, additional firewalls, and ID/password controls.

While the benefits of an extranet greatly outweigh the drawbacks in the long run, various obstacles must be overcome. They include

- A system that runs over the Internet is not fully secure and could be vulnerable to attack. Certain data (for instance, financial) is sensitive.
- When something on your extranet isn't working, who is responsible? Is it broken on your end or theirs? Support for applications, etc.— especially when developed jointly—may fall through the cracks.

- Your site is only as fast as its slowest link and many applications that would be used on an extranet (for instance, videoconferencing) are still very slow.
- Having an extranet may require that employees become familiar with new technologies they current know nothing about. This can lead to frustration among staff.

Running through the right planning process can help alleviate or eliminate many of these problems. Those companies developing an extranet can learn from those companies who have been there. Good planning processes include

- Meeting with key employees to determine your goals.
- Meeting with key customers, suppliers, etc. (those who will be using your extranet) to determine what kind of information they expect to be able to find.
- Developing processes to keep your information up to date.
- Building in time and money for training. In addition to your employees, clients, suppliers, etc. will need to use your site. Training is an integral part of keeping everyone on the same page.

System Maintenance

To make the system maintenance process more cohesive, some organizations have instituted extranet web committees or councils to promote and facilitate the use of the extranet as a knowledge and information dissemination vehicle. In addition to designating cross-organizational standards such as a document and style guides and providing user training and support, the cross-organizational and cross-functional collaborative nature of the council fosters and promotes best practices while avoiding structural or bureaucratic hurdles.

Industry Standards

Proprietary elements that exist within an extranet's architecture can severely hamper the flexibility to interface with new applications, the portability for the system to be moved to a larger HTTP or database server, and the scalability to incorporate new objects, users, or features. Organizations within an extranet cannot afford to be *held hostage* by any single vendor due to lock-in strategies instituted by software companies. Extranets are best built upon industry cabling standards (such as TIA/EIA established UTP standards) to allow for maximum flexibility in system growth and sustainability—the subject of Chapter 3,"Standards."

Communication among all interested parties is the key to a successful extranet. Take your time and develop your site at a pace everyone can handle.

From Here

This chapter discussed the six major types of networks: Local Area Network (LAN), Wide Area Network (WAN), Virtual Area Network (VAN), Internet, intranet, and extranet. The next chapter presents an in depth overview of the various cabling standards (TIA/EIA568A, ISO/IEC 11801, IEEE 802.x, FDDI, ISDN, LATM, etc.) that are associated with the cabling technologies discussed in Chapter 1. Further discussions of cabling standards are presented in Chapter 7, "Standards Planning And Design Issues;" and, Chapter 20, "Standards Development."

End Notes

[1] "Networking In The School," AT&T, 32 Avenue of the Americas, New York, NY 10013-2412 1997, p. 1.

[2] "LAN/WAN Services," PM Systems Corporation, 115 Clark Street, Chapin, S.C., 1998, p. 1.

[3] Bradley H. Lamont, "A Guide to Networking a K-12 School District," University of Illinois at Urbana-Champaign, Urbana, Illinois, 1996, p. 18.

[4] Godred Fairhurst, "Metropolitan Area Networks (MANs)," Electronics Research Group, Department of Engineering at the University of Aberdeen, Fraser Noble Building, King's College, Old Aberdeen, Abereden, United Kingdom, AB24 3UE UK, 1998, p. 1.

[5] Claud E. Matney, P.E., "Virtual Area Networks (VANs)," Digital Horizon, Telephony Newsletter, Broadband Guide, PennWell Media Online L.L.C., 2875 South Congress Avenue, Delray Beach, Florida, 33445, 1997, p. 5.

[6] Internet Society, Post: 12020, Sunrise Valley Drive, Reston, VA 20191-3429, USA, 1997.

[7] Paul David Henry and Gene De Libero, "Intranet or Internet," Telecommunications® Online, Horizon House Publications, Inc., 685 Canton Street, Norwood, MA 02062, (January, 1997), p. 8.

[8] "The Extranet Solution: The Business Software Application for the 21st Century," OneSoft Corporation, 7010 Little River Turnpike, Suite 410, Annandale, VA 22003-3241, 1997, p. 2.

[9] Fredric B. Gluck, "The Basics of Building Intranet Infrastructure," Telecommunications® Online, Horizon House Publications, Inc., 685 Canton Street, Norwood, MA 02062, (January, 1997), p. 1.

3

STANDARDS

Remember the good old days when network cabling requirements consisted of telephone connections and precious little else? If you were moving into a new building, you had one telephone number to remember—that of the Bell Telephone Co. Computer cabling was proprietary and complicated. Eventually coaxial and shielded cabling systems became the norm. Then, with the advent of LANs and the breakup of the Bell system, our world changed. By the late 1980s, proprietary network cabling systems were being phased out. Even then, knowledgeable observers were predicting the future—increasing dependency on network cabling.

Those predictions were accurate. Manufacturers have developed cabling systems that accommodate both voice and data transmission. Open systems have become universal, and proprietary systems are hard to find. Standard media and connecting components such as jacks and patch panels are UTP (Unshielded Twisted Pair) or STP (Shielded Twisted Pair). In the United States, UTP cabling systems have become dominant. Shielded cabling systems are more common in Europe.

As we move toward higher data rates—100 Mbps (megabits per second) and beyond—we are once again on the precipice of a major change. That shift is reflected in the new cabling standards being developed by the major network cabling standards institutes around the world.

Cabling Standards Organizations

Cabling standards are documented agreements containing technical specifications or other precise criteria to be used consistently as rules, guidelines, or definitions of characteristics to ensure that cabling materials, products, processes, and services are fit for their purpose. Standards thus contribute to making life simpler and to increasing the reliability and effectiveness of the goods and services we use. Before delving into an in-depth discussion of cabling standards, it's appropriate to briefly identify the major international, regional, and national standards institutes found on the WWW since they will be mentioned periodically from time to time in later chapters. All of these organizations are involved in one form or another in the development of network cabling standards around the world.

International

The growth of the international cabling industry has been well-documented over the last 11 years. The major reason for this growth has been due to the following major international standards organizations that have been instrumental in developing new cabling standards:

International Organization for Standardization

The International Organization for Standardization (ISO) is a worldwide federation of national standards bodies from some 100 countries, one from each country. ISO is a non-governmental organization established in 1947. The mission of ISO is to promote the development of standardization and related activities in the world with a view to facilitating the international exchange of goods and services, and to developing cooperation in the spheres of intellectual, scientific, technological, and economic activity. ISO's work results in international agreements which are published as International Standards. For a list of some ISO/CCITT (International Organization for Standardization/Consultative Committee for International Telegraph and Telephone) standards see Appendix I, "List Of CCITT/ISO Standards."

International Electrotechnical Commission

The object of the International Electrotechnical Commission (IEC) is to promote international cooperation on all questions of standardization and related matters in the fields of electrical and electronic engineering and thus to promote international understanding. The IEC is composed of National Committees, of which there are 50 at present, representing all the industrial countries in the world.

Video Electronics Standards Association

VESA (Video Electronics Standards Association) is the international organization that sets and supports industry-wide interface standards for the PC, workstation, and other computing environments. VESA promotes and develops timely, relevant, and open standards for the electronics industry, ensuring interoperability and encouraging innovation and market growth.

International Telecommunication Union

The ITU (International Telecommunication Union) is an intergovernmental organization within which the public and private sectors cooperate for the development of telecommunications. The ITU adopts international regulations and treaties governing all terrestrial and space uses of the frequency spectrum as well as the use of the geostationary-satellite orbit within which countries adopt their national legislation. It also develops standards to facilitate the interconnection of telecommunication systems on a worldwide scale regardless of the type of technology used.

The Internet Engineering Task Force

The Internet Engineering Task Force (IETF) is the protocol engineering and development arm of the Internet. The IETF is a large open international community of network designers, operators, vendors, and researchers concerned with the evolution of the Internet architecture and the smooth operation of the Internet. It is open to any interested individual. The actual technical work of the IETF is done in its working groups, which are organized by topic into several areas (routing, network management, security, etc.). Much of the work is handled via mailing lists, however, the IETF also holds meetings three times per year. Chairs and presenters might find it helpful to read the instructions for sessions and plenaries. First-time attendees might find it helpful to read *The Tao of IETF*.

United National Educational, Scientific and Cultural Organization

The main objective of UNESCO (United National Educational, Scientific and Cultural Organization) is to contribute to peace and security in the world by promoting collaboration among nations through education, science, culture, and communication in order to further universal respect for justice, for the rule of law, and for the human rights and fundamental freedoms which are affirmed for the peoples of the world, without distinction of race, sex, language or religion, by the Charter of the United Nations. Its constitution was adopted by the

ference in November 1945, and entered into effect on 4 November
20 states had deposited instruments of acceptance. It currently has
nber States.

The Internet Society

The Internet Society is a non-governmental international organization for
global cooperation and coordination for the Internet and its internetworking
technologies and applications. The Society's individual and organizational
members are bound by a common stake in maintaining the viability and global
scaling of the Internet. The Society comprises the companies, government
agencies, and foundations that have created the Internet and its technologies
as well as innovative new entrepreneurial organizations contributing to maintain the dynamic global scaling of the Internet. The Society is governed by its
Board of Trustees elected by its membership around the world.

The World Wide Web Consortium

The World Wide Web Consortium exists to realize the full potential of the
web. W3C (World Wide Web Consortium) is an industry consortium which
develops common standards for the evolution of the web by producing specifications and reference software. Although W3C is funded by industrial members, its products are freely available to all. The Consortium is run in the United
States by MIT Laboratory for Computer Science and in Europe by INRIA
(National Institute for Research in Computer Science and Control), in collaboration with CERN (acronym translates to: European Laboratory for Particle
Physics), where the web originated.

The Institute of Electrical and Electronics Engineers

The Institute of Electrical and Electronics Engineers (IEEE) is the world's
largest technical professional society. Founded in 1884 by a handful of practi-
tioners of the new electrical engineering discipline, today's Institute comprises
more than 430,000 members who conduct and participate in its activities in 158
countries. The men and women of the IEEE are the technical and scientific professionals making the revolutionary engineering advances which are reshap-
ing our world today. The technical objectives of the IEEE focus on advancing
the theory and practice of electrical, electronics, and computer engineering and
computer science. To realize these objectives, the IEEE sponsors technical conferences, symposia, and local meetings worldwide and publishes nearly 36% of
the world's technical papers in electrical, electronics, and computer engineering. It provides educational programs to keep its members' knowledge and
expertise state-of-the-art. The purpose of all these activities is two fold: (1) to
enhance the quality of life for all peoples through improved public awareness

of the influences and applications of its technologies; and (2) to advance standing of the engineering profession and its members.

Regional

The regional network cabling standards organizations consist of the Comite Europeen de Normalisation, the European Telecommunications Standards Institute, and the European Workshop on Open Systems. The following major cabling and cable standards organizations are a significant force to deal with for everyone working with cabling:

Comite Europeen de Normalisation

The European Committee for Standardization is responsible for European standardization in all fields except electrotechnical (CENELEC) and telecommunications (ETSI). A related project of the CEN (Comite Europeen de Normalisation) on the web is the standardization of the European character set in the fields of identification, coding, and more.

The European Telecommunications Standards Institute

The European Telecommunications Standards Institute was set up in 1988 to set standards for Europe in telecommunications and in the related fields of broadcasting and office information technology with cooperation of the EBU (European Broadcasting Union) and CEN. This organization includes technical committees such as for signaling, protocols, switching, network aspects, transmission, multiplexing, and other fields related to telecommunications, but also special committees that are assembled from time to time to inspect specific and well-defined tasks.

The European Workshop on Open Systems

The European Workshop on Open Systems is the open European forum for one-stop development of technical guidance and pre-standards in the information and communications technologies (ICT) field. This standards organization works for the benefit of vendors, planners, procurers, implementers and users.

National

Finally, the national network cabling standards organizations are and have been instrumental in creating cost-effective, efficient cabling systems that would support the widest possible range of applications and equipment. However, significant differences do exist between the various organizations in their development of cabling standards specifications.

the

ds Association of Australia (SAA)

ards Association of Australia is the Australian representative on the
international standardizing bodies: the International Organization
dardization (ISO) and the International Electrotechnical Commission
Standards Australia was founded in 1922. Its original name was the Aus-
n Commonwealth Engineering Standards Association. The organization
sion is to excel in meeting the needs of Australia's technical infrastructure
r contemporary, internationally aligned standards and related services which
enhance the nation's economic efficiency and international competitiveness
and fulfill the community desire for a safe and sustainable environment.

Standards Council of Canada (SCC)

The Standards Council coordinates the contribution of Canadians to the
two most prominent international standards-writing forums—the International Organization for Standardization (ISO) and the International Electrotechnical Commission (IEC). The SCC's activities are carried out within the
context of the National Standards System, a federation of organizations providing standardization services to the Canadian public. The SCC is manager of
the System.

Deutsches Institute für Normung (DIN)

DIN, the German Institute for Standardization, is a registered association
with its head office in Berlin. It is not a government agency. The work of standardization as undertaken by DIN is a service in the field of science and technology that is provided for the entire community. The results of standardization
benefit the whole of the national economy.

National Standards Authority of Ireland (NSAI)

NSAI operates under Forf's, the Irish National Policy Advisory and Coordination Agency for Industrial Development, in respect of the Industrial Research
and Standards Act, 1961, and the Industrial Development Act, 1993, and, on
behalf of the Minister for Enterprise and Employment, for the development and
publication of Irish Standards including harmonized European Standards of
CEN, CENELEC, ETSI (European Telecommunications Standards Institute) and
the international standards of ISO and IEC. NSAI also provides a comprehensive
product and management system certification service. NSAI activities are focused
in two distinct areas: Standards Development and Standards Application, which
in turn comprises Certification Services and the Irish Agriment Board.

Ente Nazionale Italiano di Unificazione (UNI)

UNI—Italian National Standards Body—established in 1921, is a legally recognized association whose function is to prepare, publish, and disseminate standards in all sectors except for the electrotechnical and electronic one, which falls under the responsibility of CEI (not on the web). The EEC directive 83/189 of March 28, 1983—enacted in Italy as law no. 317 of June 21, 1986— recognizes UNI as the only national body entrusted with the adoption of technical standards in all fields except the electrical one.

Standards and Industrial Research of Malaysia (SIRIM)

The Standards and Industrial Research Institute of Malaysia (SIRIM) is a national multidisciplinary research and development agency under the Ministry of Science, Technology and the Environment. Established in 1975 under the SIRIM (incorporation) Act 157, SIRIM was set up to assist companies in solving technical problems through the use of technology and help their business growth.

Standards and Metrology Institute (SMIS)

SMIS prepares, adopts, and issues Slovenian standards, while also coordinating the tasks according to the rules of international standardization. Slovenian standards are therefore either international or European standards adopted according to the rules of the ISO IEC Guide 21. SMIS establishes technical committees, coordinates their work, links, and integrates them through corresponding regional and international technical committees.

American National Standards Institute

The American National Standards Institute (ANSI) is the United States private sector voluntary standardization system for 80 years. Founded in 1918 by five engineering societies and three government agencies, the Institute remains a private, nonprofit membership organization supported by a diverse constituency of private and public sector organizations. ANSI was a founding member of ISO and plays an active role in its governance. ANSI is one of five permanent members to the governing ISO Council and one of four permanent members of ISO. U.S. participation, through the U.S. National Committee (USNC), is equally strong in the IEC. The USNC is one of 12 members on the IEC. Through ANSI, the United States has immediate access to the ISO and IEC standards development processes. ANSI participates in almost the entire technical program of both the ISO (79% of all ISO technical committees) and the IEC (92% of all IEC technical committees) and administers many key committees and subgroups (17% in the ISO; 18% in the IEC). As part of its responsibilities as the U.S. member body to ISO and IEC, ANSI accredits U.S. Technical Advisory Groups (U.S. TAGs) or USNC Technical Advisors (TAs). The U.S. TAG purpose is to develop and transmit, via ANSI, U.S. positions on activities and ballots of the international technical committee.

National Institute of Standards and Technology

The National Institute of Standards and Technology (NIST) was established by Congress to assist industry in the development of technology needed to improve product quality, to modernize manufacturing processes, to ensure product reliability, and to facilitate rapid commercialization of products based on new scientific discoveries. As an agency of the U.S Department of Commerce's Technology Administration, NIST's primary mission is to promote U.S. economic growth by working with industry to develop and apply technology, measurements, and standards.

Accredited Standards Committee X3

The Accredited Standards Committee X3 was established in 1961, and is accredited by ANSI to develop voluntary standards. X3 sets standards in dynamic areas of commerce, technology and society. It contains Technical Committees such as X3T10 which is responsible for Lower-Level Interfaces, X3T11 (Fiber Channel, HIPPI (High Performance Parallel Interface), and IPI (Intelligent Peripheral Interface)), and X3T13 (ATA (AT Attachment) and ATAPI (AT Attachment Packet Interface)).

National Information Standards Organization—USA

The National Information Standards Organization (NISO) is a nonprofit association accredited as a standards developer by the American National Standards Institute—the national clearinghouse for voluntary standards development in the U.S. NISO's voting members and other supporters include a broad base of information producers and users including libraries, publishers, government agencies, and companies that provide information services. NISO is a leader in shaping international standards.

ASTM

ASTM (American Society of Testing Materials) has developed and published 10,000 technical standards, which are used by industries worldwide. ASTM members develop the standards within the ASTM consensus process.

Technical publications, training courses, and statistical quality assurance programs are other ASTM products.

This concludes the presentation of the major international, regional, and national standards organizations. The stage is now set to delve into the various cabling standards (ANSI TIA/EIA-T568-A, ISO/IEC 11801, IEEE 802.x, FDDI, ISDN, 100BaseTX, etc.) that are associated with the major network cabling standards organizations just discussed.

Network Cabling Standards

Network cabling standards are the lifeline for the entire information technology network. They are the foundation on which all other network activities depend. A properly designed, installed, and administered standards-based cabling system reduces costs through each phase of its life cycle—installation; moves, adds, and changes; maintenance; and administration. The importance of network cabling standards should be neither overlooked nor underestimated.

Inferior cabling systems are the cause of up to 75% of network downtime. With costs that range between $2,000 and $60,000 per hour it is easy to see how important it is to control downtime. By installing a standards-based compliant network cabling system much of this downtime can be effectively eliminated.

Although a cabling system will outlive most other networking components, it represents only 6% of the total network investment. A standards-based network cabling system represents a sound investment in the productivity of your organization.

Cabling is the longest life cycle component of the entire network, outlived only by the building shell. A standards-compliant cabling system can *future-proof* your network and guarantee future application support, ensuring that your investment will continue to serve you for the full extent of its life cycle.

With that in mind, let's look at the latest major network cabling standards (ANSI TIA/EIA-T568-A, ISO/IEC 11801, IEEE 802.x, FDDI, ISDN, 100BaseTX, etc.) that are available today for building telecommunications cabling systems worldwide. This part of the chapter will begin the discussion of these standards with an in-depth look at the ANSI TIA/EIA-T568-A cabling standard.

ANSI TIA/EIA-T568-A

Prior to 1991, telecommunications cabling was controlled by the manufacturers of computer equipment. End-users were confused by manufacturers' conflicting claims concerning transmission performance and were forced to pay high installation and administration costs for proprietary systems.

The telecommunications industry recognized the need to define a cost-effective, efficient cabling system that would support the widest possible range of applications and equipment. The Electronic Industries Association (EIA), Telecommunications Industry Association (TIA), and a large consortium of leading telecommunications companies worked cooperatively to create the ANSI/EIA/TIA-568-1991 Commercial Building Telecommunications Cabling Standard. Additional standards documents covering pathways and spaces, administration, cables and connecting hardware were released subsequently. ANSI/EIA/TIA-568-1991 was revised in 1995, and is now referred to as ANSI/TIA/EIA-T568-A.

This part of the chapter covers the key aspects of the TIA/EIA-T568-A Commercial Building Telecommunications Cabling Standard (Canadian equivalent: CSA T529). TIA/EIA-T568-A incorporates the technical content of TSB-36 (Technical Systems Bulletin-36), TSB40-A, and draft TSB53. As published, the new cabling standard (TIA/EIA-T568-A) takes precedence over these technical bulletins. New specifications for 62.5/125 μm optical fiber and singlemode optical fiber cables, connectors, and cabling practices have been added. Guidelines are provided on UTP and optical fiber link performance.

The purpose of the TIA/EIA-T568-A standard is to first specify a generic voice and data telecommunications cabling system that will support a multiproduct, multivendor environment. Second, provide direction for the design of telecommunications equipment and cabling products intended to serve commercial enterprises. Third, enable the planning and installation of a structured cabling system for commercial buildings that is capable of supporting the diverse telecommunications needs of building occupants. Finally, establish performance and technical criteria for various types of cable and connecting hardware and for cabling system design and installation.

TIA/EIA-T568-A specifications are intended for telecommunications installations that are *office-oriented*. Requirements are for a structured cabling system with a usable life in excess of 10 years. Specifications address:

- Minimum requirements for telecommunications cabling within an office environment.
- Recommended topology and distances.
- Media parameters which determine performance.
- Connector and pin assignments to ensure interconnectability.
- The useful life of telecommunications cabling systems as being in excess of ten years [1].

The goal of standard TIA/EIA-T568-A is to define *structured cabling*—a telecommunications cabling system that can support virtually any voice, imaging, or data application that an end-user chooses. This part of the chapter highlights the key points or cabling elements of the TIA/EIA-T568-A Standard by looking at the structured cabling system design considerations.

Design Considerations

The structured cabling system design considerations for the TIA/EIA-T568-A Standard are concerned with six subsystems as shown in Figure 3–1 (Anixter and TIA/EIA, 1).

1. Building Entrance.
2. Equipment Room.
3. Backbone Cabling.
4. Telecommunications Closet.
5. Horizontal Cabling.
6. Work Area.

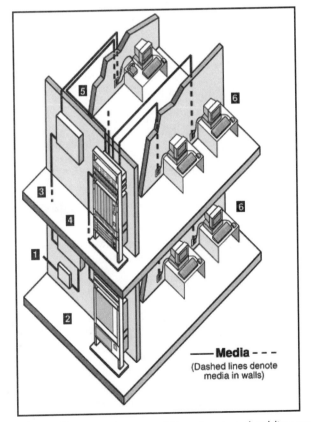

Figure 3–1: The six subtypes of the structured cabling system.

Building Entrance

Building entrance facilities provide the point at which outside cabling interfaces with the intrabuilding backbone cabling. The physical requirements of the network interface are defined in the EIA/TIA-569 Standard (TIA/EIA-T568-A).

Equipment Room

The design aspects of the equipment room are specified in the EIA/TIA 569 Standard. Equipment rooms usually house equipment of higher complexity than telecommunication closets. Any or all of the functions of a telecommunications closet may be provided by an equipment room.

Backbone Cabling

The backbone cabling for the TIA/EIA-T568-A Standard provides interconnection between telecommunication closets, equipment rooms, and entrance facilities as shown in Figure 3–2 (Anixter and TIA/EIA, 2). It consists of the backbone cables, intermediate and main cross-connects, mechanical terminations, and patch cords or jumpers used for backbone-to-backbone cross-connection. The backbone also extends between buildings in a campus environment.

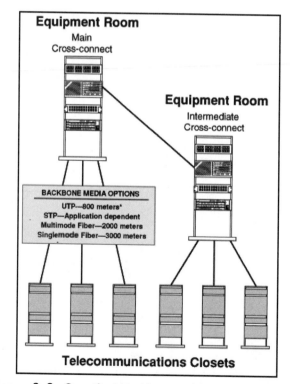

Figure 3–2: Specified backbone cabling topology: Star.

This includes:

- Vertical connection between floors (risers).
- Cables between an equipment room and building cable entrance facilities.
- Cables between buildings (interbuilding).

Backbone distances are application-dependent as shown in Table 3–1 (Anixter and TIA/EIA, 2). The maximum distances specified in Table 3–1 are based on voice transmission for UTP and data transmission for STP and fiber. The 90-meter distance for STP applies to applications with a spectral bandwidth of 20 MHz (Megahertz) to 300 MHz. A 90-meter distance also applies to UTP at spectral bandwidths of 5 MHz—to 16 MHz for Category 3, 10 MHz to 20 MHz for Category 4, and 20 MHz to 100 MHz for Category 5.

Table 3–1: Backbone cabling types and distances.

Cabling Types Recognized	Backbone Distances Maximum
100 ohm UTP (24 or 22 AWG (American Wire Gauge))	800 meters (2625 ft) Voice
150 ohm STP	90 meters (295 ft) Data
Multimode 62.5/125 µm optical fiber	2,000 meters (6560 ft)
Singlemode 8.3/125 µm optical fiber	3,000 meters (9840 ft)

Lower speed data systems such as IBM 3270, IBM System 36, IBM System 38, AS 400, and asynchronous (RS232, 422, 423, etc.) can operate over UTP (or STP) for considerably longer distances, typically from several hundred feet to over 1,000 feet. The actual distances depend on the type of system, data speed, and the manufacturer's specifications for the system electronics and the associated components used (baluns, adapters, line drivers, etc.). Current state-of-the-art distribution facilities usually include a combination of both copper and fiber optic cables in the backbone. See the sidebar, "Other Design Requirements," for specific information on the backbone cabling subsystem.

Other Design Requirements

Some points specified for the backbone cabling subsystem include:

- Equipment connections to backbone cabling should be made with cable lengths of 30m (98 ft.) or less.
- The backbone cabling should be configured in a star topology as shown in Figure 3–2. Each horizontal cross-connect is connected directly to a main cross-connect or to an intermediate cross-connect, then to a main cross-connect.

- The backbone is limited to no more than two hierarchical levels of cross-connects (main and intermediate). No more than one cross-connect may exist between a main and a horizontal cross-connect and no more than three cross-connects may exist between any two horizontal cross-connects.

- Cross-connects for different cable types must be located in the same facilities.

- A total maximum backbone distance of 90 m (295 ft.) is specified for certain applications. This distance is for uninterrupted backbone runs. (No intermediate cross-connect).

- The proximity of backbone cabling to sources of electromagnetic interference (EMI) should be taken into account. (Specific distances are provided in ANSI/EIA/TIA-569.)

- The distance between the terminations in the entrance facility and the main cross-connect should be documented and should be made available to the service provider.

- Recognized media may be used individually or in combination, as required by the installation. Quantity of pairs and fibers needed in individual backbone runs depends on the area served. Recognized backbone cables are shown in Figure 3–3 [2].

- Multipair cable is allowed, provided that it satisfies the power sum crosstalk requirements.

- Bridged taps are not allowed.

- Main and intermediate cross-connect jumper or patch cord lengths should not exceed 20 meters (66 feet).

- Avoid installing in areas where sources of high levels of EMI/RFI (Electromagnetic Interference/Radio Frequency Investigation) may exist.

- Grounding should meet the requirements as defined in the EIA/TIA 607 standard (Siemon, 1).

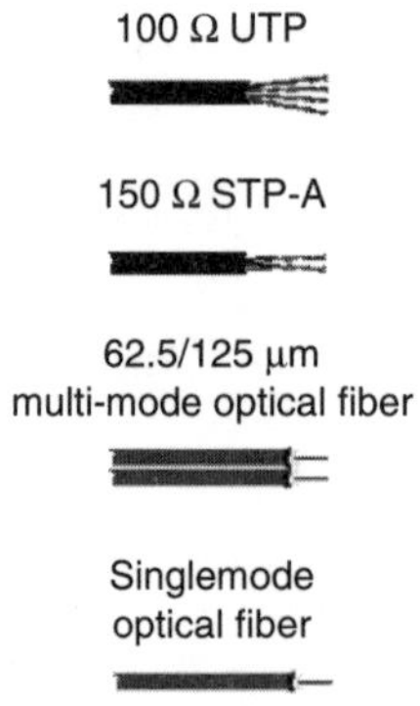

100 Ω UTP

150 Ω STP-A

62.5/125 μm
multi-mode optical fiber

Singlemode
optical fiber

Figure 3–3: Recognized backbone cables.

NOTES:

In ISO/IEC 11801 (which is discussed later in this chapter), the equivalent cabling elements to the main cross-connect (MC) and intermediate cross-connect (IC) are called the campus distributor (CD) and building distributor, respectively. In addition to those listed, two alternate backbone cabling types allowed by ISO/IEC are 120 ohm twisted-pair and 50/125 μm multimode optical fiber. 50 ohm coaxial cabling is recognized by 568-A, but is not recommended for new installations. It is recommended that the user consult with equipment manufacturers, application standards, and system providers for additional information when planning shared sheath applications on UTP backbone cables.

Telecommunications Closet

A telecommunications closet is the area within a building that houses the telecommunications cabling system equipment as shown in Figure 3–2. This includes the mechanical terminations and/or cross-connect for the horizontal and backbone cabling system. Please refer to EIA/TIA-569 for the design specifications of the telecommunications closet as discussed in the sidebar, "Other Telecommunications Closet Design Specifications."

Other Telecommunications Closet Design Specifications

Some specifications related to telecommunications closets are:

• Closets should be designed and equipped in accordance with ANSI/EIA/TIA-569-A.

• Cable stress from tight bends, cable ties, and tension should be avoided by well-designed cable management.

• Cables and cords used for active equipment connections are outside the scope of the standard (10 m (33 ft.) total allowed for patch cords and equipment cables on both ends of each link).

• Only standards-compliant connecting hardware should be used.

• Equipment connections at a cross-connect may be made by way of *interconnections* or *cross-connections* as shown in Figure 3–4 (Siemon, 1). Cross-connections are used for connections between cabling subsystems and for connections to equipment with multiport connectors. Interconnections are used for connections to equipment with single-port connectors.

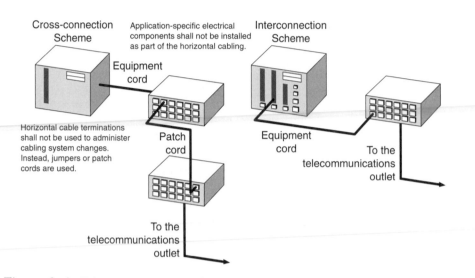

Figure 3–4: Telecommunications closet interconnections or cross-connections.

Horizontal Cabling

The horizontal cabling system for the TIA/EIA-T568-A Standard extends from the telecommunications outlet in the work area (or workstation) to the horizontal cross-connect in the telecommunications closet as shown in Figure 3–5 (Anixter and TIA/EIA, 4). It includes the telecommunications outlet (see Figure 3–6), an optional consolidation point or transition point connector, horizontal cable, and the mechanical terminations and patch cords (or jumpers) that comprise the horizontal cross-connect.

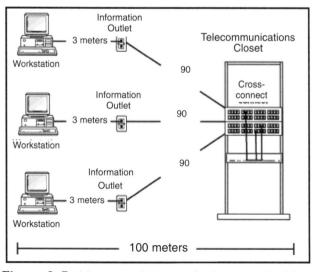

Figure 3–5: Maximum distances for horizontal cabling.

Three media types are recognized as options for horizontal cabling, each extending a maximum distance of 90 meters as shown in Figure 3–6 (Anixter and TIA/EIA, 5):

- 4-pair 100 ohm UTP cable (24 AWG solid conductors).
- 2-pair 150 ohm STP cables.
- 2 fiber 62.5/125 μm optical fiber cable.

NOTE:

In addition, two alternative horizontal cabling types allowed by ISO/IEC 11801 are 120 Ohm twisted pair and 50/125 μm multimode optical fiber.

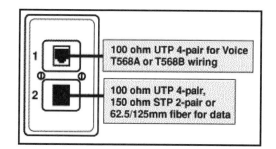

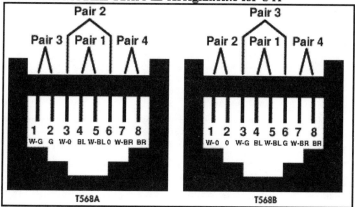

Figure 3–6: Telecommunications outlet.

At this time, 50 ohm coaxial cable is a recognized media type. It is not, however, recommended for new cabling installations and is expected to be removed from the next revision of the ANSI/EIA/TIA-569-A standard. See the sidebar, "Other Horizontal Cabling System Structure Design Specifications," for further information on the ANSI/EIA/TIA-569-A and 568-A standards.

Other Horizontal Cabling System Structure Design Specifications

Some points specified for the horizontal cabling subsystem include:

- The proximity of horizontal cabling to sources of electromagnetic interference (EMI) should be taken into account. Specific guidelines are provided in ANSI/EIA/TIA-569-A.

- One transition point (TP) is allowed between different forms of the same cable type (where undercarpet cable connects to round cable). NOTE: The definition provided for a *transition point* in ISO/IEC 11801 is broader than 568-A. It includes transitions to undercarpet cabling as well as consolidation point connections.

- A minimum of two telecommunications outlets are required for each individual work area. The first outlet: 100 ohm UTP; and, the second outlet: 100 ohm UTP,150 ohm STP-A or 62.5/125 µm multimode fiber.

- Grounding must conform to applicable building codes, as well as ANSI/TIA/EIA-607.

- Additional outlets may be provided. These outlets are in addition to and may not replace the minimum requirements of the standard.

- Bridged taps and splices are not allowed for copper-based horizontal cabling. Splices are allowed for fiber.

- Multiunit cables are allowed, provided that they meet hybrid crosstalk requirements.

- The horizontal cabling should be configured in a star topology; each work area outlet is connected to a horizontal cross-connect (HC) in a telecommunications closet (TC).

In addition to the 90 meters of horizontal cable (see Figure 3–5), a total of 10 meters is allowed for work area and telecommunications closet patch and jumper cables. Each work area should have a minimum of TWO information outlet ports, one for voice and one for data. The cabling choices are indicated in Figure 3–6.

NOTE:

Application-specific components should not be installed as part of the horizontal cabling. When needed, they must be placed external to the telecommunications outlet (or horizontal cross-connect).

Work Area

The work area components extend from the telecommunications (information) outlet to the station equipment. Work area wiring is designed to be relatively simple to interconnect so that moves, adds, and changes are easily managed. Work area components consist of:

- Station Equipment: computers, data terminals, telephones, etc.
- Patch Cables: modular cords, PC adapter cables, fiber jumpers, etc.
- Adapters: baluns, etc.—must be external to telecommunications outlet.

The goal of the ANSI TIA/EIA-T568-A standard is also to define the media and connecting hardware performance specifications. This part of the chapter continues looking at the key points or cabling elements of the TIA/EIA-T568-A Standard by discussing the performance of networking equipment or hardware.

Media and Connecting Hardware Performance Specifications

Today, as more and more end users move to open systems, active media and connecting hardware is being developed based upon the assumption that the cabling portion of the physical layer is standards compliant (reliable and capable of specific transmission performance). The risks of non-compliant cabling are numerous: substandard network performance; higher costs for moves, adds, and changes; and the inability to support emerging technologies. As the acceptance of standards-compliant structured cabling has grown, the price of installed networking media and connecting hardware has dropped and performance has exponentially increased. The physical layer has evolved into an affordable bandwidth-rich business resource. This part of the chapter will take a close look at the physical layer of the ANSI/TIA/EIA-T568-A standard by focusing on the following cabling elements:

- UTP Cabling
- Optical Fiber Cabling
- STP-A Cabling
- Hybrid and Undercarpet Cables
- Modular Wiring Reference
- TSB-67
- TSB-72

Unshielded Twisted Pair (UTP) Cabling

As transmission rates have increased, higher performance UTP cabling has become a necessity. The 568-A specifications on 100 ohm unshielded twisted-pair cabling supersede TSB-36 and TSB40-A. In addition, some means of classifying horizontal UTP cables and connecting hardware by performance capability had to be established. These capabilities have been broken down to a series of categories as follows:

- *Category 3:* Cables/connecting hardware with transmission parameters characterized up to 16 MHz.
- *Category 4:* Cables/connecting hardware with transmission parameters characterized up to 20 MHz.
- *Category 5:* Cables/connecting hardware with transmission parameters characterized up to 100 MHz

UTP Categories 1 and 2 are not specified. Characteristic impedance of *horizontal* categorized cables equal 100 ohms ± 15 percent from 1 MHz to the highest referenced frequency (16, 20, or 100 MHz) of a particular category as shown in Table 3–2 (Anixter and TIA/EIA, 1). Components and installation practices are subject to all applicable building and safety codes.

Table 3–2: Horizontal UTP cable attenuation/NEXT (Near-End-Crosstalk) loss (worst pair).

Frequency (MHz)	Category 3 Decibel (dB) Attn/NEXT	Category 4 Decibel (dB) Attn/NEXT	Category 5 Decibel (dB) Attn/NEXT
0.064	0.9 / -	0.8 / -	0.8 /
0.150	- / 53	- / 68	- / 74
0.256	1.3 / -	1.1 / -	1.1 / -
0.512	1.8 / -	1.5 / -	1.5 / -
0.772	2.2 / 43	1.9 / 58	1.8 / 64
1.0	2.6 / 41	2.2 / 56	2.0 / 62
4.0	5.6 / 32	4.3 / 47	4.1 / 53
8.0	8.5 / 27	6.2 / 42	5.8 / 48
10.0	9.7 / 26	6.9 / 41	6.5 / 47
16.0	13.1 / 23	8.9 / 38	8.2 / 44
20.0	- / -	10.0 / 36	9.3 / 42
25.0	- / -	- / -	10.4 / 41
31.25	- / -	- / -	11.7 / 39
62.5	- / -	- / -	17.0 / 35
100.0	- / -	- / -	22.0 / 32

NOTE:

Attenuation: per 100 meters (328 feet) @ 20 degrees C. NEXT: 100 meters (328 feet)

NOTE:

Category 3 requirements are consistent with the UTP specifications for horizontal cable and connecting hardware in the original edition of 568.

Characteristic Impedance of *backbone* cabling equals 100 ohms ± 15 percent from 1 MHz to the highest referenced frequency of a particular category (16, 20, or 100 MHz). Performance markings should be provided to show the applicable performance category. These markings do not replace safety markings.

Services with incompatible signal levels should be partitioned into separate binder groups. Transmission requirements are equivalent to horizontal cables except that NEXT loss performance shown in Table 3–3 is based on power-sum rather than worst-pair characterization to allow for multiple disturbing signals in the same sheath (Anixter and TIA/EIA, 2).

Table 3–3: Backbone UTP cable attenuation/power sum NEXT (Near-End-Crosstalk).

Frequency (MHz)	Category 3 (dB) Attn/NEXT	Category 4 (dB) Attn/NEXT	Category 5 (dB) Attn/NEXT
0.064	0.9 / -	0.8 / -	0.8 / -
0.150	- / 53	- / 68	- / 74
0.256	1.3 / -	1.1 / -	1.1 / -
0.512	1.8 / -	1.5 / -	1.5 / -
0.772	2.2 / 43	1.9 / 58	1.8 / 64
1.0	2.6 / 41	2.2 / 56	2.0 / 62
4.0	5.6 / 32	4.3 / 47	4.1 / 53
8.0	8.5 / 27	6.2 / 42	5.8 / 48
10.0	9.7 / 26	6.9 / 41	6.5 / 47
16.0	13.1 / 23	8.9 / 38	8.2 / 44
20.0	- / -	10.0 / 36	9.3 / 42
25.0	- / -	- / -	10.4 / 41
31.25	- / -	- / -	11.7 / 39
62.5	- / -	- / -	17.0 / 35
100.0	- / -	- / -	22.0 / 32

NOTE:

Attenuation: per 100 meters (328 feet) @ 20 degrees C. NEXT: 100 meters (328 feet).

NOTE:

Tip conductors have colored insulation that corresponds to that of the binder group. Ring conductors have colored insulation that corresponds to that of the pair.

Backbone UTP cables consist of solid 0.5 mm (24 AWG) cables that contain more than four pairs (typically multiples of 25 pairs are used). An overall shield is optional.

To ensure that installed *UTP connecting hardware* (telecommunications outlets, patch cords and panels, connectors, cross-connect blocks, etc.) *and cords* will have minimal effect on overall cabling system performance, the characteristics and performance parameters presented in this section are based on specifications that cover all types of connectors used in the cabling system including the telecommunications outlet/connector.

UTP connecting hardware and cords do not cover work area adapters, baluns, protection, MAUs, filters, or other application-specific devices. Temperature can range from 10°C (14°F) to 60°C (140°F).

Outlets should be securely mounted. Outlet boxes with unterminated cables must be covered and marked.

Transmission requirements are much more severe than cable of a corresponding category as shown in Table 3–4 (Anixter and TIA/EIA, 3). Performance markings should be provided to show the applicable transmission category and should be visible during installation (for example, CAT 5) in addition to safety markings. Installed connectors should be protected from physical damage and moisture.

Table 3–4: UTP connecting hardware attenuation NEXT (Near-End-Crosstalk) loss.

Frequency (MHz)	Category 3 (dB)	Category 4 (dB)	Category 5 (dB)
1.0	0.4 / 58	0.1 / 65	0.1 / 65
4.0	0.4 / 46	0.1 / 58	0.1 / 65
8.0	0.4 / 40	0.1 / 52	0.1 / 62
10.0	0.4 / 38	0.1 / 50	0.1 / 60
16.0	0.4 / 34	0.2 / 46	0.2 / 56
20.0	- / -	0.1 / 44	0.2 / 54
25.0	- / -	- / -	0.2 / 52
31.25	- / -	- / -	0.2 / 50
62.5	- / -	- / -	0.3 / 44
100.0	- / -	- / -	0.4 / 40

NOTE:

The preferred termination method for all UTP connecting hardware utilizes the insulation displacement contact (IDC).

Patch cords must use stranded cable for adequate flex-life. The following requirements apply only to wire and cable used for patch cords and cross-connect jumpers (see Table 3–5 (Anixter and TIA/EIA, 3)). For example, jumper/patch cord maximum length limitations:

- 20 meters (66 feet) in main cross-connect.
- 20 meters (66 feet) in intermediate cross-connect.
- 6 meters (20 feet) in telecommunications closet.
- 3 meters (10 feet) in the work area.

Table 3–5: Maximum attenuation of cable used in patch cords.

Frequency (MHz)	Category 3 (dB)	Category 4 (dB)	Category 5 (dB)
1.0	3.1	2.6	2.4
4.0	6.7	5.2	4.9
8.0	10.2	7.4	6.9
10.0	11.7	8.3	7.8
16.0	15.7	10.7	9.9
20.0	-	12.0	11.1
25.0	-	-	12.5
31.25	-	-	14.1
62.5	-	-	20.4
100.0	-	-	26.4

NOTE:

Attenuation: per 100 meters (328 feet) @ 20 degrees C = Horizontal UTP cable attenuation +20 percent (due to stranded conductors).

To ensure overall system integrity, horizontal cables need to be terminated with connecting hardware of the same category or higher. Also, cables used for patch cords and cross-connect jumpers need to be of the same performance category or higher as the horizontal cables they connect to. Lastly, UTP cabling systems are not Category 3, 4, or 5 compliant unless all components of the system satisfy their respective category requirements.

Optical Fiber Cabling

The new specifications on *optical fiber cabling media* for the TIA/EIA-568A Standard consist of one recognized cable type for horizontal subsystems and two cable types for backbone subsystems:

- Horizontal—62.5/125 µm multimode optical fiber (minimum of two fibers) as shown in Table 3–6 (Anixter and TIA/EIA, 5).
- Backbone—62.5/125 µm multimode and singlemode (10/125 µm) optical fiber as shown in Table 3–7 (Anixter and TIA/EIA, 5).

All optical fiber components and installation practices should meet applicable building and safety codes.

Table 3–6: Cable transmission performance parameters multimode (horizontal and backbone).

Wavelength nanometers (nm)	Maximum Attenuation (dB/km)	Minimum Bandwidth megahertz over one kilometer (MHz-km)
850	3.75	160
1300	1.5	500

Table 3–7: Cable transmission performance parameters singlemode (backbone).

Wavelength nanometers (nm)	Maximum Attenuation (dB/km)
1310	0.5
1550	0.5

With regard to optical fiber connectors, the recommended adapter (coupler) and connector is designated as 568SC (duplex SC or specified connector) as shown in Figure 3–7 (Siemon, 2). ST connectors are allowed where an installed base exists. In cross-connects, a simplex or duplex connector is allowed.

For the work area side of the telecommunications outlet, the 568SC duplex SC connector is specified. 568SC patch cords are required for two-fiber applications. Outlets should be securely mounted at planned locations.

The two positions in a duplex connector are referred to as position A and position B. 568SC connectors are rated for a minimum of 500 mating cycles. The 568SC adapter performs a cross-over between position A and position B of two mated connectors as shown in Figure 3–7.

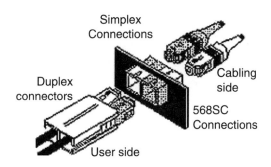

Simplex
Connections

Duplex
connectors

Cabling
side

568SC
Connections

User side

Figure 3–7: Optical fiber cabling system.

NOTES:

(a) Color identification of fiber types should have a beige 62.5/125 μm multimode connector/coupling and a blue 8.3/125 μm singlemode connector/coupling. (b) Applications with an installed base of ST-type fiber connectors are *grandfathered* for continued use in both current and future updates of existing optical fiber networks. (c) A key reason the standard now specifies the 568SC-type fiber connector is to harmonize with the IEC specified interface currently in use in Europe.

On the other hand, the optical fiber telecommunications outlet , should have the capability to store unterminated fibers within its outlet box. Other required features of the outlet include:

- Capability to terminate minimum of two fibers into 568SC couplings.
- Means of securing optical fiber and maintaining minimum bend radius of 30 mm (1.18 in.).
- Ability to store a minimum of 1 meter (3.28 ft.) of 2-optical fiber cable.
- A surface-mount box that attaches directly over standard 4" x 4" electrical box.

Shielded Twisted Pair (STP-A) Cabling

The recognized shielded twisted pair (STP) cables for the TIA/EIA-T568-A Standard are IBM type 1A for backbone and horizontal distribution and IBM type 6A for patch cables. Cable and connector specifications are extended to 300 MHz. Prior specifications are no longer supported. All STP-A components and installation practices should meet applicable building and safety codes.

The same mechanical and transmission requirements apply to backbone and horizontal STP-A cables as shown in Table 3–8 (Anixter and TIA/EIA, 4). Additional requirements are provided for outdoor cables.

Table 3–8: Horizontal and backbone STP-A cable balanced mode attenuation/ NEXT loss (worst pair).

Frequency (MHz)	Attn/NEXT (dB)
4.0	2.2 / 58.0
8.0	3.1 / 54.9
10.0	3.6 / 53.5
16.0	4.4 / 50.4
20.0	4.9 / 49.0
25.0	6.2 / 47.5
31.25	6.9 / 46.1
62.5	9.8 / 41.5
100.0	12.3 / 38.5
300.0	21.4 / 31.3

NOTE:

Attenuation: 100 meters (328 feet) @ 25 degrees C

Standard outlet interface and pair assignments are the same as the ISO 8802-5 TokenRing Connector (IEC 807-8) except that performance requirements are much more severe. 150 ohm data connectors should be marked shielded twisted pair (STP-A) in addition to any safety markings required by local or national codes as shown in Table 3–9 (Anixter and TIA/EIA, 4).

Table 3–9: 150 ohm STP-A data connector attenuation/NEXT loss.

Frequency (MHz)	Insert Loss/NEXT (dB)
4.0	.05 / 65
8.0	.10 / 65
10.0	.10 / 65
16.0	.15 / 62.4
20.0	.15 / 60.5
25.0	.15 / 58.5
31.25	.15 / 56.6
62.5	.20 / 50.6
100.0	.25 / 46.5
300.0	.45 / 36.9

Specifications for 150 ohm STP-A patch cables call for 0.4 mm (2-pair, 26 AWG) stranded conductors. They allow for an overall shield (as opposed to individually shielded pairs).

Characteristic impedance equals 150 ohms ± 10% (3 MHz—300 MHz). Balanced mode attenuation of 150 ohm STP-A patch cable is about 1.5 times that of horizontal or backbone STP-A cable (4 MHz to 300 MHz). NEXT performance of 150 ohm STP-A patch cable measures approximately 6 dB less than horizontal or backbone STP-A cable (5 MHz to 300 MHz).

Hybrid and Undercarpet Cables

Hybrid cables that contain multiple units of recognized copper cables for the TIA/EIA-T568-A Standard are subject to additional NEXT loss requirements between cable units. These requirements assure a minimum of 6 dB additional crosstalk isolation between applications that may operate on adjacent cables within the Sheath. All detailed specifications for the individual cable units used in the hybrid assembly still apply.

Undercarpet cables should not be used in wet locations. They should be separated from power cables by at least 152 mm (6 in.), except at crossings. The use of carpet squares is recommended for accessibility.

Modular Jack Styles

There are four basic modular jack styles for the TIA/EIA-T568-A Standard as shown in Figure 3–8 (Siemon, 1). The 8-position and 8-position keyed modular jacks are commonly and incorrectly referred to as RJ45 and keyed RJ45, respectively. The 6-position modular jack is commonly referred to as RJ11. Using these terms can sometimes lead to confusion since the RJ designations actually refer to very specific wiring configurations called Universal Service Ordering Codes (USOC).

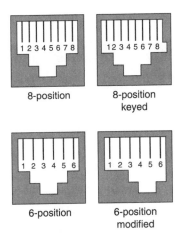

Figure 3–8: Basic modular jack styles.

The designation *RJ* means Registered Jack. Each of these three basic jack styles can be wired for different RJ configurations. For example, the 6-position jack can be wired as an RJ11C (1-pair), RJ14C (2-pair), or RJ25C (3-pair) configuration. An 8-position jack can be wired for configurations such as RJ61C (4-pair) and RJ48C. The keyed 8-position jack can be wired for RJ45S, RJ46S, and RJ47S.

The fourth modular jack style is a modified version of the 6-position jack (modified modular jack or MMJ). It was designed by Digital Equipment Corporation® (DEC) along with the modified modular plug (MMP) to eliminate the possibility of connecting DEC data equipment to voice lines and vice versa.

Two wiring schemes have been adopted by the 568-A standard with regard to common outlet configurations. They are nearly identical except that pairs two and three are reversed. T568A is the preferred scheme because it is compatible with 1- or 2-pair USOC systems as shown in Figure 3–9 (Siemon, 1). Either configuration can be used for Integrated Services Digital Network (ISDN) and high-speed data applications.

USOC wiring is available for 1-, 2-, 3-, or 4-pair systems as shown in Figure 3–10 (Siemon, 1). Pair 1 occupies the center conductors, pair 2 occupies the next two contacts out, etc. One advantage to this scheme is that a 6-position plug configured with 1 or 2 pairs can be inserted into an 8-position jack and maintain pair continuity. A note of warning though, pins 1 and 8 on the jack may become damaged from this practice. A disadvantage is the poor transmission performance associated with this type of pair sequence.

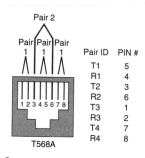

Figure 3–9: 568-A standard wiring schemes.

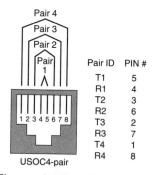

Figure 3–10: USOC wiring.

10BaseT wiring specifies an 8-position jack but uses only two pairs as shown in Figure 3–11 (Siemon, 2). These are pairs two and three of T568B and T568A schemes.

Token ring wiring uses either an 8-position or 6-position jack as shown in Figure 3–12 (Siemon, 2). The 8-position format is compatible with T568A, T568B, and USOC wiring schemes. The 6-position is compatible with 1- or 2-pair USOC wiring.

The MMJ is a unique wiring scheme for DEC® equipment as shown in Figure 3–13 (Siemon, 2). Furthermore, ANSI X3T9.5 TP-PMD uses the two outer pairs of an 8-position jack as shown in Figure 3–14 (Siemon, 2). These positions are designated as pair 3 and pair 4 of the T568A wiring scheme.

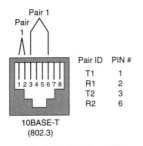

Figure 3–11: 10BaseT wiring.

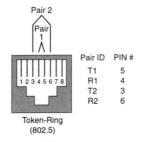

Figure 3–12: Token ring wiring.

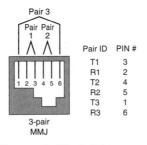

Figure 3–13: MMJ wiring.

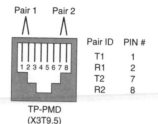

Figure 3–14: ANSI X3T9.5 TP-PMD wiring.

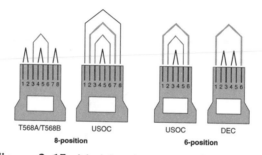

Figure 3–15: Modular plug pair configurations.

It is important when dealing with modular plug pair configurations that the pairing of wires in the modular plug match the pairs in the modular jack as well as the horizontal and backbone wiring. If they do not, the data being transmitted may be paired with incompatible signals. Furthermore, Figure 3–15 shows that modular cords wired to the T568A 8 pin position scheme on both ends are compatible with T568B systems and vice versa (Siemon, 3).

Modular cords are used for two basic applications. One application uses them for patching between modular patch panels. When used in this manner modular cords should always be wired straight-through (pin 1 to pin 1, pin 2 to pin 2, pin 3 to pin 3, etc.). The second major application uses modular cords to connect the workstation equipment (PC, phone, FAX, etc.) to the modular outlet. These modular cords may either be wired *straight-through or reversed* (pin 1 to pin 6, pin 2 to pin 5, pin 3 to pin 4, etc.) depending on the system manufacturer's specifications. This *reversed* wiring is typically used for voice systems. The following is a brief guide to determine what type of modular cord you have. Also, see the sidebar, "Recommended Cabling Practices," for some tips on the *Dos* and *Don'ts* of modular wiring.

So, how do you read a modular cord? You should first align the plugs side-by-side with the contacts facing you and compare for example, the 8 pin positions (pin 1 to pin 8, pin 2 to pin 7, pin 3 to pin 6, pin 4 to pin 5; or, pin 1 to pin 2, pin 3 to pin 6, pin 4 to pin 5, pin 7 to pin 8, etc.) from left to right. If the pin positions appear in the same order on both plugs, the cord is wired *straight-through* as shown in Figure 3–16 (Siemon, 3). If the pin positions appear reversed on the second plug (from right to left), the cord is wired *reversed*.

Recommended Cabling Practices

The following are some recommended cabling practices to follow when you're doing *modular wiring*, let's look at the *Dos* first:

Dos:

- Use connecting hardware that is compatible with the installed cable.
- Terminate each horizontal cable on a dedicated telecommunications outlet.
- Locate the main cross-connect near the center of the building to limit cable distances.
- Maintain the twist of horizontal and backbone cable pairs up to the point of termination.
- Tie and dress cables neatly, not exceeding the minimum bend radius.
- Place cabling at a sufficient distance from equipment that may generate high levels of electromagnetic interface.

Don'ts:

- Do not use connecting hardware that is of a lower category than the cable being used.
- Do not create multiple appearances of the same cable at several distribution points (called bridged taps).
- Do not locate cross-connects where cable distances will exceed the maximum.
- Do not leave any wire pairs untwisted.
- Do not over-tighten cable ties or make sharp bends with cables.

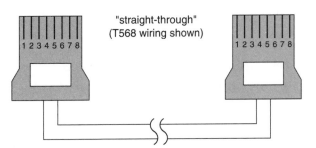

"straight-through"
(T568 wiring shown)

1 2 3 4 5 6 7 8   1 2 3 4 5 6 7 8

Figure 3–16: Reading a modular cord: straight-through.

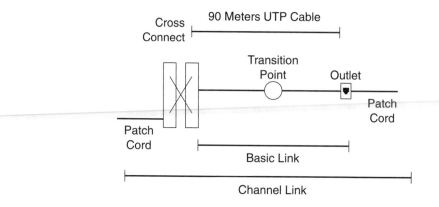

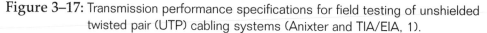

Figure 3–17: Transmission performance specifications for field testing of unshielded twisted pair (UTP) cabling systems (Anixter and TIA/EIA, 1).

TSB-67

TSB-67 (Telecommunications Systems Bulletin-67 standard) provides users with the opportunity to use comprehensive field test methods to validate the transmission performance specifications or characteristics of installed UTP cabling systems. The categories of UTP cabling systems in this bulletin also correspond with the UTP cabling categories of ANSI/TIA/EIA-T568-A.

For the purposes of testing UTP cabling systems, the horizontal link is assumed to contain a telecommunications outlet/connector, a transition point, 90 meters of UTP (Category 3–5), a cross-connect consisting of two blocks or panels and a total of 10 meters of patch cords. Figures 3–17, 3–18, and 3–19 show the relationship of these components (Siemon, 1). See the sidebar, "Specific Points for TSB-67," for some additional tips on transmission field testing for UTP cabling systems.

The two link configurations in Figure 3–17 are defined for testing purposes. The basic link (See Figure 3–20) includes the distribution cable, telecommunications outlet/connector or transition point and one horizontal cross-connect component. This is assumed to be the permanent part of a link. The channel link is comprised of the basic link plus installed equipment, user, and cross-connect jumper cable.

TSB-67 defines the allowable worst case attenuation and NEXT for an installed link as shown in Figure 3–20 (Siemon, 2). Tables 3–10 and 3–11 show the limitations for attenuation and NEXT respectively for both the basic and channel links (Anixter and TIA/EIA, 2).

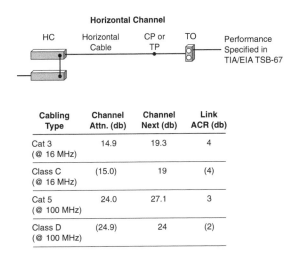

Cabling Type	Channel Attn. (db)	Channel Next (db)	Link ACR (db)
Cat 3 (@ 16 MHz)	14.9	19.3	4
Class C (@ 16 MHz)	(15.0)	19	(4)
Cat 5 (@ 100 MHz)	24.0	27.1	3
Class D (@ 100 MHz)	(24.9)	24	(2)

Figure 3–18: Transmission performance comparison for Cat. 3/Class C and Cat. 5/Class D channels. Numbers in parenthesis are calculated based on using 5 meters of additional flexible cables that meet the ISO/IEC 11801.

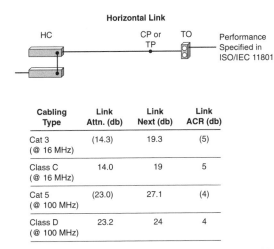

Cabling Type	Link Attn. (db)	Link Next (db)	Link ACR (db)
Cat 3 (@ 16 MHz)	(14.3)	19.3	(5)
Class C (@ 16 MHz)	14.0	19	5
Cat 5 (@ 100 MHz)	(23.0)	27.1	(4)
Class D (@ 100 MHz)	23.2	24	4

Figure 3–19: Transmission performance comparison for Cat. 3/Class C and Cat. 5/Class D Links. Numbers in parenthesis are calculated based on using 6 meters of patch cable that meets TIA/EIA-T568-A. Transition point/ consolidation point included.

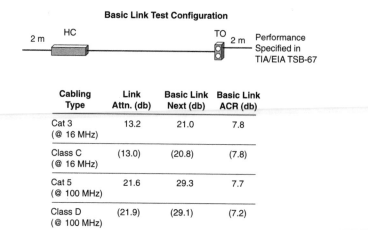

Cabling Type	Link Attn. (db)	Basic Link Next (db)	Basic Link ACR (db)
Cat 3 (@ 16 MHz)	13.2	21.0	7.8
Class C (@ 16 MHz)	(13.0)	(20.8)	(7.8)
Cat 5 (@ 100 MHz)	21.6	29.3	7.7
Class D (@ 100 MHz)	(21.9)	(29.1)	(7.2)

Figure 3–20: Transmission performance comparison for Cat 3/Class C and Cat 5/Class D basic links. Class C and D attenuation values are calculated based on 90 meters horizontal cable plus 4 meters of flexible cable and two connectors that meet ISO/IEC 11801. Class C and D NEXT values are based on voltage summations of the near-end connector and horizontal cable.

Table 3–10: Basic/channel link attenuation.

Frequency (MHz)	Category 3 (dB)	Category 4 (dB)	Category 5 (dB)
1.0	3.2/4.2	2.2/2.6	2.1/2.5
4.0	6.1/7.3	4.3/4.8	4/4.5
8.0	8.8/10.2	6/6.7	5.7/6.3
10.0	10/11.5	6.8/7.5	6.3/7
16.0	13.2/14.9	8.8/9.9	8.2/9.2
20.0	-	9.9/11	9.2/10.3
25.0	-	-	10.3/11.4
31.25	-	-	11.5/12.8
62.5	-	-	16.7/18.5
100.0	-	-	21.6/24

Table 3–11: Basic/channel link NEXT loss (pair-to-pair).

Frequency (MHz)	Category 3 (dB)	Category 4 (dB)	Category 5 (dB)
1.0	40.1/39.1	54.7/53.3	60/60
4.0	30.7/29.3	45.1/43.3	51.8/50.6
8.0	25.9/24.3	40.2/38.2	47.1/45.6
10.0	24.3/22.7	38.6/36.6	4.5/44
16.0	21/19.3	35.3/33.1	42.3/40.6
20.0	-	33.7/31.4	40.7/39
25.0	-	-	39.1/37.4
31.25	-	-	37.6/35.7
62.5	-	-	32.7/30.6
100.0	-	-	29.3/27.1

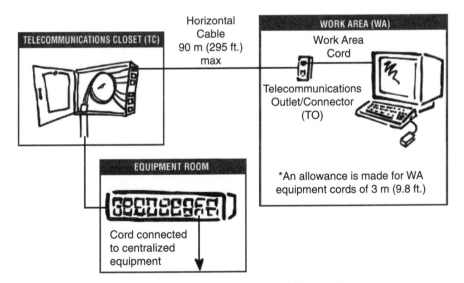

Figure 3–21: Typical schematic for centralized optical fiber cabling using an interconnection.

Specific Points for TSB-67

Some points specified for TSB-67 transmission field testing for UTP cabling systems include:

- UTP cabling systems comprise cables and connecting hardware specified in TIA/EIA-T568-A.

- Required test parameters include wiremap, length, attenuation, and crosstalk.

- Two levels of pass or fail are indicated, depending on measured margin compared to minimum specifications. Testing of NEXT is required in both directions.

- Level II equipment meets the most stringent requirements for measurement accuracy.

- Requirements are intended for performance validation and are provided in addition to '568-A requirements on components and installation practices.

TSB-72

Telecommunications Systems Bulletin-72 (TSB-72) provides the user with the flexibility of designing an optical fiber cabling system for either centralized or distributed electronics in conjunction with the ANSI/TIA/EIA-T568-A standard. It contains information and guidelines for centralized optical fiber cabling as shown in Figure 3–21 (Siemon, 1). See the sidebar, "Specific Points For TSB-72," for some additional tips on centralized optical fiber cabling systems.

Specific Points for TSB-72

Some points specified in TSB-72 for a centralized optical fiber cabling system include:

- Intended for single-tenant users who desire centralized vs. distributed electronics.

- Allows cables to be spliced or interconnected at the telecommunications closet such that cables can be routed to a centralized distributor for total cable lengths of 300m (984 ft.) or less.

- Allows for migration from an interconnection or splice to a cross-connection scheme that can also support distributed electronics.

- Allows for pull-through implementations when total length between the telecommunications outlet/connector and centralized cross-connect is 90 meters (295 ft.) or less.

- Connecting hardware required to:
    —Join fibers by re-mateable connectors or splices.
    —Connectors shall be 568SC interface.
    —Provide for simplex or duplex connection of optical fibers.
    —Provide means of circuit identification.
    —Allow for addition and removal of optical fibers.

ISO/IEC 11801

Now, let's briefly look at the next major network cabling standard: ISO/IEC 11801. This cabling standard is currently being developed by ISO (International Organization For Standardization).

ISO is currently developing a cabling standard on an international basis under the title Generic Cabling for Customer Premises Cabling ISO/IEC 11801. Heavily based on EIA 568, this standard extends the UTP bias of the American standards into 100 ohm STP cabling and 120 ohm cabling for the French market. The principal difference between EIA 568 and ISO 11801 is that, in the latter, four Application Classes (A, B, C, D) are specified for increasing data rates.

The ISO 11801E 1995 standard is being generally followed in Europe. This standard (like EIA 568) includes a Link performance level of NEXT (Near End Crosstalk) and has also introduced the concept of measuring ACR (Attenuation/ Cross Talk Ratio) for LAN cables.

Local Area Network (LAN) Cables

LAN cables are supposed to provide you with conformance to AS/NZS 3080:1996, ISO/IEC 11801, and EIA/TIA-T568-A. The cables should be verified and listed by Underwriters Laboratories—a U.S. firm. With regard to standard ISO/IEC 11801, the following categories and classes of cables will be covered:

- Balanced Twisted Pair Cable (Category 7 Cable).
- UTP Structured Cable (Enhanced Category 6 Cable).
- Horizontal Reticulation Cable (Category 6 Cable).
- Horizontal Reticulation in a Structured Cabling System (Category 5 Cable).
- Halogen-free Cable.
- Horizontal link in a Structured Cabling System (Category 3 Cable).

Balanced Twisted-Pair Cable

Balanced twisted-pair cable has been designed to meet the recently announced ISO/IEC Category 7 specifications for individually screened 4-pair horizontal distribution cable in a structured cabling system. This type of cable will support any protocol that requires a bandwidth up to 600MHz. The services expected to require this bandwidth include Ethernet 1000 BaseT, Asynchronous Transfer Mode (ATM) 2.4 Gbps and higher. This cable can also be used to extend well beyond the 90m horizontal link length for lower bandwidth services.

This type of cable can be described as a 4-pair individually foil-screened 23AWG twisted-pair STP LAN cable with overall braid and verified by 3P Test Laboratories to C6STP (proposed ISO/IEC Category 7 link specifications). The balanced twisted-pair cable complies with "AS/NZS 3080:1996, ISO/IEC 11801," and "TIA/EIA-T568-A Cable Construction PVC (Permanent Virtual Circuit) Outer Sheath Braid Screen Foil Screen Rip Cord Twisted Pair."

UTP Structured Cable

The UTP structured cable transmission performance far exceeds proposed Category 6 requirements as part of the ISO/IEC 11801 revision. This 4-pair cable is used in the horizontal reticulation of a structured cabling system, interfacing communications equipment in the floor distributor to the telecommunications outlet in the work area.

The UTP structured cable is a flexible cable when used as either a work area cable or an equipment cable in a structured cabling environment. 24-pair UTP is used in riser applications where high-speed data or large bandwidth is required. Consideration should be given to the shared sheath compatibility of difference services being transmitted in the same sheath.

This multipair 24 AWG UTP LAN cable exceeds proposed ISO/IEC Category 6 link specifications. Pair twist lengths and cable geometry, via central filler, are designed to maximize NEXT performance and product stability during installation. Complies with AS/NZS 3080:1996, ISO/IEC 11801, ACA/AUSTEL TS-008, and TIA/EIA-T568-A. The range is UL listed/verified.

Designed to operate beyond 400MHz, UTP structured cable takes cabling well beyond gigabit and ATM applications. Also, attenuation to crosstalk ratio (ACR or headroom) exceeds 30dB@100MHz.

AS/NZS 3080:1996 allows Category 5 links to extend beyond 90 meters (clause 4 and 7.1.2). UTP structured cable will allow you to run 10BaseT over a 300m link, and ATM 155 over a 130m link. Furthermore, a high degree of balance (LCL, LCTL), superior NEXT, and ACR provide a physical link that will enable a total system to comply with the EMC regime.

Horizontal Reticulation Cable

The horizontal reticulation cable is designed to meet the proposed Category 6 requirements as part of ISO/IEC 11801 revision. This category supports services requiring a bandwidth up to 200MHz. The horizontal reticulation cable range is tested to 350MHz to ensure performance capability.

This cable is used for horizontal reticulation between the floor distributor and the telecommunications outlet in a structured cabling system. The 24-pair horizontal reticulation cable is recommended for use in backbone applications where consideration has been given to shared sheath compatibility of different protocols transmitted in the same sheath.

The horizontal reticulation cable is a multipair 24 AWG UTP/FTP LAN cable that meets proposed ISO/IEC Category 6 link specifications. Pair twist lengths are designed to optimize NEXT performance. This cable complies to AS/NZS 3080:1996, ISO/IEC 11801, ACA/AUSTEL TS-008, and TIA/EIA-T568-A standards. The cable's range is UL listed/verified.

The horizontal reticulation cable is designed to operate to 350MHz. Attenuation to crosstalk ratio (ACR or headroom) exceeds 23dB@100MHz.

Horizontal Reticulation in a Structured Cabling System (Category 5 Cable)

Here, horizontal reticulation in a structured cabling system is a 4-pair Category 5 UTP cable suitable for high-speed LAN applications including Ethernet 10 BaseT, Ethernet 100 BaseT, Video Conferencing, 100VG-AnyLAN, and ATM155. The 4-pair Category 5 cable is individually screened and used where EMI (Electromagnetic Interference) is an issue, beyond the capabilities of UTP.

The 4-pair cable is used for patching equipment to patch panels or to interface the horizontal cable to the terminal equipment in the work area. The cable can be described as multipair 24 AWG UTP/FTP LAN cable meeting Category 5 specifications. It complies with AS/NZS 3080:1996, ISO/IEC 11801, ACA/AUSTEL TS-008, and TIA/EIA-T568-A. The range is UL listed/verified.

Halogen-Free Cable

The halogen-free cable's range is suitable (the range is suitable) in public areas where public safety is at stake in the case of fire breaking out. These cables are constructed of materials that do not emit halogens and reduce the speed of fire; little or no smoke is emitted. Halogen-free cables are ideal in confined spaces such as tunnels, vehicles, ships and aircraft.

Halogen-free cable is a multipair 24 AWG UTP/FTP zero halogen and low fire hazard LAN cable meeting Category 5 specifications. It complies with AS/NZS 3080:1996, ISO/IEC 11801, ACA/AUSTEL TS-008, and TIA/EIA-T568-A. Fire safety standards complied with include AS1660.5.3(Zero Halogen), AS 1660.5.2 (Low Smoke Density), AS 1660.5.1(Bunch Vertical Burn), AS 1660.5.6 (Single Vertical Burn). The cable's range is UL listed (CMR/CM)/verified.

In a fire, time is paramount. Halogen-free cables have been designed to minimize smoke and toxic fumes,thus maximizing the time available for evacuation and minimizing harm to building occupants in the event of a fire.

The chlorine used within PVC cables is an environmental hazard. Halogen-free cables are manufactured from environmentally friendly materials that do not contain PVC or fluoropolymer.

The smoke from cables sheathed in PVC, when brought into contact with moisture (say from sprinklers), will form corrosive acids that may damage equipment. Halogen-free cables are designed to protect equipment and do not contain halogens to produce acids.

Horizontal Link in a Structured Cabling System (Category 3 Cable)

Here, the cable range complies with the Category 3 cable requirements of AS/NZS3080 1996. This cable range is also suitable for applications requiring a bandwidth up to 16MHz (Category 3) such as Voice, ISDN, Ethernet 10 BaseT, and token ring 4 Mbps.

A horizontal link in a structured cabling system is a 4-pair UTP Category 3 cable. It is a flexible 4-pair UTP patch cable used as a work area cable or an equipment cable.

The cable is also a 100 pr UTP suitable for voice or 10 BaseT transmission in a backbone application. In other words, it's a multipair 24 AWG UTP/FTP LAN cable meeting Category 3 specifications. It complies with AS/NZS 3080:1996, ISO/IEC 11801, ACA/AUSTEL TS-008, and TIA/EIA 568A. The cable's range is UL listed/verified.

IEEE 802.x

Next, let's take a quick look at another major set of network cabling standards: IEEE 802.x. This set of cabling standards is currently being developed by the IEEE (Institute of Electrical and Electronics Engineers). There are many standards in the 802.x series. To discuss them all is beyond the scope of this book; therefore, only a few of the major ones are covered. They include:

- IEEE 802.1: Standards related to network management.
- IEEE 802.2: General standard for the data link layer in the OSI (Open System Interconnection) Reference Model. The IEEE divides this layer into two sublayers—the data link control (DLC) layer and the media access control (MAC) layer. The MAC layer varies for different network types and is defined by standards IEEE 802.3 through IEEE 802.5.
- IEEE 802.3: Defines the MAC layer for bus networks that use CSMA/CD (Carrier Sense Multiple Access Collision Detection). This is the basis of the Ethernet standard (10BaseT, 10BaseF, 10Base5, 10Base2, 10Broad36, Fast Ethernet).
- IEEE 802.3 (Fast Ethernet): Any of a number of 100 Mbps Ethernet specifications. Fast Ethernet offers a speed increase ten times that of the 10BaseT Ethernet specification while preserving such qualities as frame format, MAC mechanisms, and MTU. Such similarities allow the use of existing 10BaseT applications and network management tools on Fast Ethernet networks. This is the basis of the Fast Ethernet standard (100BaseFX, 100BaseT4, 100BaseTX).

- IEEE 802.4: Defines the MAC layer for bus networks that use a token-passing mechanism (token bus networks).
- IEEE 802.5: Defines the MAC layer for token ring networks.
- IEEE 802.6: Standard for Metropolitan Area Networks (MANs).
- IEEE 802.11: Standard protocols for wireless networks.
- IEEE 802.12: 100VG-AnyLAN. 100 Mbps Fast Ethernet and token ring media technology using four pairs of Category 3, 4, or 5 UTP cabling. This high-speed transport technology, developed by Hewlett-Packard, can be made to operate on existing 10BaseT Ethernet networks.

IEEE 802.1

The IEEE 802.1 standard refers to the broad subject of managing computer networks. There exists a wide variety of software and hardware products that help network system administrators manage a network. Network management covers a wide area, including:

- Security: Ensuring that the network is protected from unauthorized users.
- Performance: Eliminating bottlenecks in the network.
- Reliability: Making sure the network is available to users and responding to hardware and software malfunctions.

The IEEE 802.1 is also the specification that describes an algorithm that prevents bridging loops by creating a spanning tree. The algorithm was invented by Digital Equipment Corporation. The Digital algorithm and the IEEE 802.1 algorithm are not exactly the same, nor are they compatible.

IEEE 802.2

As previously stated, IEEE 802.2 is the general standard for the data link layer in the OSI (Open System Interconnection) Reference Model. ISO has defined a 7-layer model to clarify various tasks in communications systems as shown in Table 3–12. The main idea is to have independent standards for the different layers so that a change in a layer would not cause changes in other layers. In the layered approach it is possible to use different network hardware without changing the existing application programs, as shown in Figure 3–22 [3].

```
+---------------+                              +---------------+
| application  |<---------------------------->| application  |
+---------------+                              +---------------+
| presentation |<---------------------------->| presentation |
+---------------+                              +---------------+
|   session    |<---------------------------->|   session    |
+---------------+                              +---------------+
| transport    |<---------------------------->| transport    |
+---------------+         +----------+         +---------------+
|   network    |<----->| network  |<----->|   network    |
+---------------+         +----------+         +---------------+
| data link    |<----->|data link|<----->| data link    |
+---------------+         +----------+         +---------------+
| physical     |<----->|physical |<----->| physical     |
+---------------+         +----------+         +---------------+
```

Figure 3–22: ISO/OSI network architecture reference model.

Table 3–12: OSI Model.

Layer	Name	Function
7	Application	Provides for program-to-program communication.
6	Presentation	Manages data representation conversions. For example, the Presentation Layer would be responsible for converting from EBCDIC to ASCII.
5	Session	Establishes and maintains communications channels. In practice, this layer is often combined with the Transport Layer.
4	Transport	Controls end-to-end integrity of data transmission.
3	Network	Routes data from one node to another.
2	Data Link	Physically passes data from one node to another.
1	Physical	Manages putting data onto the network media and taking the data off.

Each layer in the OSI reference model communicates with its peer using services which the layer below provides. As can be seen from Figure 3–22, the transport layer and layers above it are end-to-end layers and they do not know anything about the network below them.

Here, the IEEE 802.2 data link layer defines how the network layer packets are transmitted as bits. Examples of data link layer protocols are PPP (Point-to-Point Protocol) and Ethernet framing protocol. Bridges work at the data link layer only.

The IEEE 802.2 LAN protocol also specifies an implementation of the LLC sublayer of the data link layer. IEEE 802.2 handles errors, framing, flow control, and the network layer (Layer 3) service interface. It's also used in IEEE 802.3 and IEEE 802.5 LANs.

Data Link Control

Data Link Control (DLC) is the second lowest layer in the OSI Reference Model of the IEEE 802.2 general standard. Every network interface card (NIC) has a DLC address or DLC identifier (DLCI) that uniquely identifies the node on the network. Some network protocols, such as Ethernet and token ring use the DLC addresses exclusively. Other protocols, such as TCP/IP, use a logical address at the network layer to identify nodes. Ultimately, however, all network addresses must be translated to DLC addresses. In TCP/IP networks, this translation is performed with the Address Resolution Protocol (ARP). For networks that conform to the IEEE 802 standards (Ethernet), the DLC address is usually called the Media Access Control (MAC) address.

IEEE 802.3

IEEE 802.3 is the IEEE LAN protocol that specifies an implementation of the physical layer and the MAC sublayer of the data link layer. IEEE 802.3 uses CSMA/CD access at a variety of speeds over a variety of physical media. Extensions to the IEEE 802.3 standard specify implementations for Fast Ethernet. Physical variations of the original IEEE 802.3 specification include 10Base2, 10Base5, 10BaseF, 10BaseT, and 10Broad36. Physical variations for Fast Ethernet include 100BaseT, 100BaseT4, and 100BaseX.

10Base2

10Base2 is a 10 Mbps baseband Ethernet specification using 50 ohm thin coaxial cable. 10Base2, which is part of the IEEE 802.3 specification, has a distance limit of 185 meters per segment.

10Base5

10Base5 is a 10 Mbps baseband Ethernet specification using standard (thick) 50 ohm baseband coaxial cable. 10Base5, which is part of the IEEE 802.3 baseband physical layer specification, has a distance limit of 500 meters per segment.

10BaseF

10BaseF is a 10 Mbps baseband Ethernet specification that refers to the 10BaseFB, 10BaseFL, and 10BaseFP standards for Ethernet over fiber optic cabling.

10BaseT

10BaseT is a 10 Mbps baseband Ethernet specification using two pairs of twisted-pair cabling (Category 3, 4, or 5): one pair for transmitting data and the other for receiving data. 10BaseT, which is part of the IEEE 802.3 specification, has a distance limit of approximately 100 meters per segment.

10Broad36

10Broad36 is a 10 Mbps broadband Ethernet specification using broadband coaxial cable. 10Broad36, which is part of the IEEE 802.3 specification, has a distance limit of 3600 meters per segment.

IEEE 802.3 (Fast Ethernet)

This part of the chapter describes the 802.3 100BaseT Fast Ethernet segments which are part of the Ethernet system. However, you should know that there are two LAN standards that can carry Ethernet frames at 100 Mbps.

When the IEEE standardization committee met to begin work on a faster Ethernet system, two approaches were presented. One approach was to speed up the original Ethernet system to 100 Mbps, keeping the original CSMA/CD medium access control mechanism. This approach is called 100BaseT Fast Ethernet.

Another approach presented to the committee was to create an entirely new medium access control mechanism, one based on hubs that controlled access to the medium using a demand priority mechanism. This new access control system transports standard Ethernet frames, but it does it with a new medium access control mechanism. This system was further extended to allow it to transport token ring frames as well. As a result, this approach is now called 100VG-AnyLAN.

The IEEE decided to create standards for both approaches. The 100BaseT Fast Ethernet standard described here is part of the original 802.3 standard. The 100VG-AnyLAN system is standardized under a new number, IEEE 802.12, which is discussed later in this section.

In any event, compared to the 10 Mbps specifications, the 100 Mbps system (100BaseT Fast Ethernet) results in a factor of ten reduction in the bit-time, which is the amount of time it takes to transmit a bit on the Ethernet channel. This produces a tenfold increase in the speed of the packets over the media system. However, the other important aspects of the Ethernet system, including the frame format, the amount of data a frame may carry, and the media access control mechanism, are all unchanged.

The Fast Ethernet specifications include mechanisms for auto-negotiation of the media speed. This makes it possible for vendors to provide dual-speed Ethernet interfaces that can be installed and run at either 10 Mbps or 100 Mbps automatically. There are three media varieties that have been specified for transmitting 100 Mbps Ethernet signals as shown in Figure 3–23 [4].

The three media types are shown in Figure 3–23 with their IEEE shorthand identifiers. The IEEE identifiers include three pieces of information. The first item, 100, stands for the media speed of 100 Mbps. The Base stands for baseband, which is a type of signaling. Baseband signaling simply means that Ethernet signals are the only signals carried over the media system.

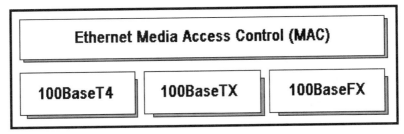

Figure 3–23: The three 100 Mbps Ethernet media varieties.

The third part of the identifier provides an indication of the segment type. The T4 segment type is a twisted-pair segment that uses four pairs of telephone-grade twisted-pair wire. The TX segment type is a twisted-pair segment that uses two pairs of wires and is based on the data grade twisted-pair physical medium standard developed by ANSI. The FX segment type is a fiber optic link segment based on the fiber optic physical medium standard developed by ANSI and that uses two strands of fiber cable. The TX and FX medium standards are collectively known as 100BaseX.

100BaseTX and 100BaseFX

The 100BaseTX and 100BaseFX media standards used in Fast Ethernet are both adopted from physical media standards first developed by ANSI, the American National Standards Institute. The ANSI physical media standards were originally developed for the Fiber Distributed Data Interface (FDDI) LAN standard (ANSI standard X3T9.5) and are widely used in FDDI LANs.

The 100BaseTX (100 Mbps baseband Fast Ethernet) specification uses two pairs of either UTP or STP wiring. The first pair of wires is used to receive data; the second is used to transmit. To guarantee proper signal timing, a 100BaseTX segment cannot exceed 100 meters in length.

The 100BaseFX (100 Mbps baseband Fast Ethernet) specification uses two strands of multimode fiber optic cable per link. To guarantee proper signal timing, a 100BaseFX link cannot exceed 400 meters in length.

100BaseT4

Rather than re-inventing the wheel when it came to signaling at 100 Mbps, the Fast Ethernet standard adapted the 100BaseTX and 100BaseFX ANSI media standards for use in the new Fast Ethernet medium specifications. The T4 standard was also provided to make it possible to use lower-quality twisted-pair wire for 100 Mbps Ethernet signals.

The 100BaseT4 (100 Mbps baseband Fast Ethernet) specification uses four pairs of Category 3, 4, or 5 UTP wiring. To guarantee proper signal timing, a 100BaseT4 segment cannot exceed 100 meters in length.

IEEE 802.4

IEEE 802.4 is the IEEE LAN protocol that specifies an implementation of the physical layer and the MAC sublayer of the data link layer.

Token Bus

The token bus is a LAN architecture using token-passing access over a bus topology. This LAN architecture is the basis for the IEEE 802.4 LAN specification.

In other words, the token bus is a type of local area network (LAN) that has a bus topology and uses a token-passing mechanism to regulate traffic on the bus. A token bus network is very similar to a token ring network, the main difference being that the endpoints of the bus do not meet to form a physical ring. Token bus networks are defined by the IEEE 802.4 standard.

IEEE 802.5

The IEEE 802.5 standard states that the token ring is intended for use in commercial and light industrial environments. Use in home or heavy-industrial environments, although not precluded, is not considered within the scope of the standard. These environments are identical to those specified for IEEE 802.3. IBM made the standard possible by marketing the first 4 Mbits/sec token ring network in the mid-1980s. While the network physically appears as a star configuration, internally signals travel around the network from one station to the next as shown in Figure 3–24. Therefore, cabling configurations and the addition or removal of equipment must ensure that the logical ring is maintained. Workstations connect to central hubs called multistation access units (MAUs). Multiple hubs are connected together to create large multistation networks. The hub itself contains a collapsed ring. If a workstation fails, the MAU immediately bypasses the station to maintain the ring of the network. Because the cable contains multiple wire pairs, a cut in the cable causes the ring to revert back on itself. Signals simply reroute in the opposite direction, creating a loop-back configuration.

IEEE 802.5 Medium-Access Control (MAC)

The token ring technique is based on the use of a small frame, called a token, that circulates when all stations are idle. A station wanting to transmit must wait to detect the next available token as it passes by. It takes the token by changing 1 bit in the token. This transforms the token into a start-of-frame sequence for a data frame. The station then transmits the remainder of the data fields necessary to complete a data frame. When a station seizes a token and begins to transmit a data frame, there is no token on the ring, so other stations wishing to transmit must wait. The frame on the ring will make a round trip and be absorbed by the transmitting station. The transmitting station will insert a new token on the ring when both of the following conditions are met.

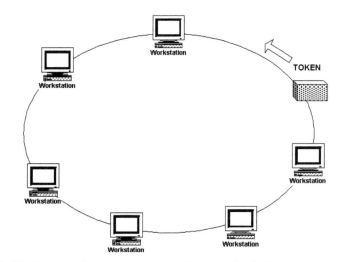

Figure 3–24: A type of computer network in which all the computers are arranged (schematically) in a circle. A token, which is a special bit pattern, travels around the circle. To send a message, a computer catches the token, attaches a message to it, and then lets it continue to travel around the network.

The station has completed transmission of its frame. The leading edge of the transmitted frame has returned to the station. Once the new token has been inserted on the ring, the next station downstream with data to send will be able to seize the token and transmit. Under lightly loaded conditions, there is some inefficiency with token ring, since a station must wait for the token to come around before transmitting. Under heavy loads, the ring functions in an efficient and fair round-robin fashion.

A field exists in the token in which the workstations can indicate the type of priority required for their transmission. The priority setting is basically a request to other stations for future use of the token. The other stations compare the workstation's priority with their own priority levels. If the workstations priority is higher than theirs, they grant the workstation access to the token for an extended period. Other workstations can override the priorities, if necessary. Workstations attached to the ring transfer packets to their downstream neighbors. Thus, each workstation acts as a repeater. When a new station is attached to the network, it goes through an initialization sequence to become part of the ring. This sequence checks for duplicate addresses and informs downstream neighbors of its existence. The role of an active monitor is assigned to one of the workstations on the network, usually the first workstation recognized when the LAN comes up. The active monitor watches over the network and looks for problems, such as errors in the delivery of frames, or the need to bypass a workstation at the MAU because it has failed. The active monitor basically makes sure the network runs efficiently and without errors. If the active monitor should fail, other workstations are available to take its place and basically bid for the job by transmitting claim tokens.

IEEE 802.6

IEEE 802.6 is a IEEE MAN specification based on DQDB technology. IEEE 802.6 supports data rates of 1.5 to 155 Mbps.

MAN

A metropolitan-area network is a network that spans a metropolitan area. Generally, a MAN spans a larger geographic area than a LAN, but a smaller geographic area than a WAN. A MAN is a relatively new class of network. There are three important features which discriminate MANs from LANs or WANs:

First of all, the network size falls between LANs and WANs. A MAN typically covers an area of between 5 and 50 km in diameter. Many MANs cover an area the size of a city, although in some cases MANs may be as small as a group of buildings or as large as the North of Scotland.

Second, a MAN (like a WAN) is not generally owned by a single organization. The MAN, its communications links, and equipment are generally owned by either a consortium of users or by a single network provider who sells the service to the users. The level of service provided to each user must therefore be negotiated with the MAN operator, and some performance guarantees are normally specified.

Third, a MAN often acts as a high speed network to allow sharing of regional resources (similar to a large LAN). It is also frequently used to provide a shared connection to other networks using a link to a WAN. A typical use of MANs to provide shared access to WAN is shown in Figure 3–25 [5].

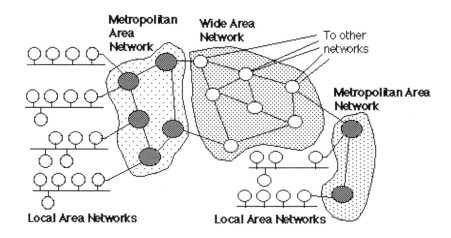

Figure 3–25: Use of MANs to provide regional networks which share the cost of access to a WAN.

DQDB

The Distributed Queue Dual Bus (DQDB) is a data link layer communication protocol, specified in the IEEE 802.6 standard, and designed for use in MANs. DQDB, which permits multiple systems to interconnect using two unidirectional logical buses, is an open standard that is designed for compatibility with carrier transmission standards and is aligned with emerging standards for BISDN (Broadband Integrated Services Data Network). SIP (SMDS Interface Protocol) is based on DQDB.

EEE 802.11

802.11 uses a contention mechanism to allow stations to share a wireless channel based on carrier sense multiple access (CSMA), like 802.3. 802.11 cannot use all of 802.3 because it is not possible in the wireless environment for a station to listen and transmit on the same channel, as would be required for the collision detection (CD) used in 802.3. Because of this, a station on a wireless LAN will not be able to determine that a collision has occurred until the end of the packet transmission—making collisions more expensive in 802.11 than in 802.3. The 802.11 MAC uses a collision avoidance mechanism to reduce the probability of collisions. The 802.11 MAC is designed to operate over multiple physical layers, and does not specify various media-dependent parameters.

IEEE 802.12

A 100VG-AnyLAN network consists of a central hub or repeater, referred to as a level 1 (or root) hub, with a link connecting each node, creating a star topology. The hub is an intelligent central controller that manages the network access by continually performing a rapid round-robin scan of its network port requests, checking for service requests from the attached nodes. The hub receives the incoming data packet and directs it to only the ports with a matching destination address, providing inherent network data security.

Each hub may be configurable to support either 802.3 Ethernet or 802.5 token ring frame formats. All hubs located in the same network segment must be configured for the same frame format. A bridge may be used to connect a 100VG-AnyLAN network using an 802.3 frame type to an Ethernet network, or a 100VG-AnyLAN network using an 802.5 frame type to a token ring network. A router may be used to connect a 100VG-AnyLAN network to FDDI and ATM networks or to WAN connections.

Each hub includes one uplink port and *n* number of downlink ports. The uplink port functions as a node port but is reserved for connecting the hub (as a node) to an upper level hub. The *n* downlink ports are used to connect to 100VG-AnyLAN nodes.

Each hub port may be configured to operate in either a normal mode or a monitor mode. Ports configured to operate in normal mode are forwarded

only those packets intended (addressed) for the attached node. Ports configured to operate in a monitor mode are forwarded all packets that the hub
receives. The normal and monitor mode configuration may be automatically
learned for cascaded ports (an uplink or downlink to another hub) or manually configured for a port connected to network monitoring equipment.

A Node may be a client or server computer, workstation, or other 100VG-
AnyLAN network device such as a bridge, router, switch, or hub. Hubs connected
as nodes are referred to as "lower level," such as level 2 or level 3 hub devices. Up
to three levels of cascading may be used on a 100VG-AnyLAN network.

A node issues requests to the hub to initiate link training and to send a
packet onto the network. The 100VG-AnyLAN node also responds to incoming message commands from the hub.

The Link connecting the hub and the node may be 4-pair UTP cable (Category 3, 4, or 5), 2-pair UTP cable (Category 5), 2-pair STP cable, or fiber optic cable.
The maximum length of the cable from the hub to each node is 100 meters for Category 3 and 4 UTP 150 meters for Category 5 UTP and STP, and 2000 meters for
fiber optic cable. The UTP and STP cable must be wired straight through (pin 1
connects to pin 1, pin 2 connects to pin 2, etc.) for all node connections.

Now, let's take a look at the next major set network cabling standards
from ANSI (American National Standards Institute): FDDI, MMF, SMF and TP-
PMD. MMF, SMF and TP-PMD standards are presented here as extensions of
the FDDI standard. This set of cabling standards are continuously being developed and updated by ANSI.

FDDI

The Fiber Distributed Data Interface (FDDI) standard was produced by the
ANSI X3T9.5 standards committee in the mid-1980s. During this period, high-
speed engineering workstations were beginning to tax the capabilities of existing
LANs (primarily Ethernet and token ring). A new LAN was needed that could
easily support these workstations and their new distributed applications. At the
same time, network reliability was becoming an increasingly important issue as
system managers began to migrate mission-critical applications from large computers to networks. FDDI was developed to fill these needs.

After completing the FDDI specification, ANSI submitted FDDI to ISO,
which has created an international version of FDDI that is completely compatible with the ANSI standard version.

Today, although FDDI implementations are not as common as Ethernet or
token ring, FDDI has gained a substantial following that continues to increase
as the cost of FDDI interfaces diminishes. FDDI is frequently used as a backbone
technology as well as a means to connect high-speed computers in a local area.

Fundamentals

FDDI specifies a 100 Mbps, token-passing, dual-ring LAN using a fiber optic transmission medium. It defines the physical layer and media access portion of the link layer, and so is roughly analogous to IEEE 802.3 and IEEE 802.5 in its relationship to the Open System Interconnection (OSI) Reference Model.

Although it operates at faster speeds, FDDI is similar in many ways to token ring. The two networks share many features, including topology (ring), media access technique (token passing), reliability features (redundant rings, for example), and others.

One of the most important characteristics of FDDI is its use of optical fiber as a transmission medium. Optical fiber offers several advantages over traditional copper wiring, including security (fiber does not emit electrical signals that can be tapped); reliability (fiber is immune to electrical interference); and, speed (optical fiber has much higher throughput potential than copper cable).

SMF and MMF

FDDI defines use of two types of fiber: singlemode (sometimes called monomode) and multimode. Modes can be thought of as bundles of light rays entering the fiber at a particular angle. Singlemode fiber (SMF) allows only one mode of light to propagate through the fiber, while multimode fiber (MMF) allows multiple modes of light to propagate through the fiber. Because multiple modes of light propagating through the fiber may travel different distances (depending on the entry angles)—causing them to arrive at the destination at different times (a phenomenon called modal dispersion)—SMF is capable of higher bandwidth and greater cable run distances than MMF. Because of these characteristics, SMF is often used for interbuilding connectivity, while MMF is often used for intrabuilding connectivity. MMF uses light-emitting diodes (LEDs) as the light-generating devices, while SMF generally uses lasers.

Specifications

FDDI has four key components: the media access control (MAC) layer, the physical (PHY) layer, the physical media dependent (PMD) layer, and the station management (SMT) layer as shown in Figure 3–26 [6]:

- Media Access Control (MAC)—Defines addressing, scheduling, and routing data. It also communicates with higher-layer protocols, such as TCP/IP, SNA, IPX, DECnet, DEC LAT, and Appletalk. The FDDI MAC layer accepts Protocol Data Units (PDUs) of up to 9,000 symbols from the upper-layer protocols, adds the MAC header, and then passes packets of up to 4,500 bytes to the PHY layer.
- Physical Layer Protocol (PHY)—Handles the encoding and decoding of packet data into symbol streams for the wire. It also handles clock synchronization on the FDDI ring.

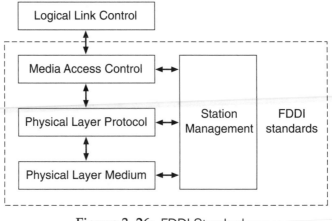

Figure 3–26: FDDI Standards.

- Physical Layer Medium (PMD)—Handles the analog baseband transmission between nodes on the physical media. PMD standards
  include TP-PMD for twisted-pair copper wires and Fiber-PMD for
  fiber optic cable.
- Station Management (SMT)—Handles the management of the FDDI
  ring. Functions handled by SMT include neighbor identification, fault
  detection and reconfiguration, insertion and de-insertion from the
  ring, and traffic statistics monitoring.

Twisted Pair Physical Layer Medium (TP-PMD)

In June 1990, ANSI established a subgroup called the Twisted Pair-Physical
Medium Dependent (TP-PMD) working group to develop a specification for
implementing FDDI protocols over twisted-pair wire. TP-PMD replaces the proprietary (or prestandard) approaches previously used for running FDDI traffic
over copper wires. The TP-PMD standard is based on an MLT-3 encoding
scheme; prestandard implementations used the less reliable NRZ encoding
scheme. TP-PMD interfaces are compliant with U.S. and international emission
standards and provide reliable transmission over distances up to 100 meters.
With TP-PMD in place, network managers now have a standard means to implement FDDI over inexpensive UTP cable, cutting cabling costs by about a third
compared with fiber optic cabling.

ANSI approved the TP-PMD standard in February 1994. Approval of the standard is pending in Europe.

Configuration

FDDI is a link layer protocol, which means that higher-layer protocols operate independently of the FDDI protocol. Applications pass packet-level data using higher-layer protocols down to the logical link control layer in the same way that they would over Ethernet or token ring. But because FDDI uses a different physical layer protocol than Ethernet and token ring, traffic must be bridged or routed on and off an FDDI ring. FDDI also allows for larger packet sizes than lower-speed LANs; for this reason, connections between FDDI and Ethernet or token ring LANs require the fragmentation and reassembly of frames.

FDDI can be implemented in two basic ways: as a dual-attached ring and as a concentrator-based ring. In the dual-attached scenario, stations are connected directly one to another. FDDI's dual counter-rotating ring design provides a fail-safe in case a node goes down. If any node fails, the ring wraps around the failed node. However, one limitation of the dual counter-rotating ring design is that if two nodes fail, the ring is broken in two places, effectively creating two separate rings. Nodes on one ring are then isolated from nodes on the other ring. External optical bypass devices can solve this problem, but their use is limited because of FDDI optical power requirements.

In other words, FDDI specifies the use of dual rings. Traffic on these rings travels in opposite directions. Physically, the rings consist of two or more point-to-point connections between adjacent stations. One of the two FDDI rings is called the primary ring; the other is called the secondary ring. The primary ring is used for data transmission, while the secondary ring is generally used as a backup.

There are 4 types of stations (DTEs or concentrators):

1. Dual Attached Station (DAS), which is connected to both rings.
2. Single Attached Station (SAS), which is attached only to the primary ring.
3. Dual Attached Concentrator (DAC), which is connected to both rings and provides connection for additional stations and concentrators. It is actually the root of a tree.
4. Single Attached Concentrator (SAC), which is connected only to the primary ring (through a tree).

Class B or single-attachment stations (SAS) attach to one ring; Class A or dual-attachment stations (DAS) attach to both rings. SASs are attached to the primary ring through a concentrator, which provides connections for multiple SASs. The concentrator ensures that failure or power down of any given SAS does not interrupt the ring. This is particularly useful when PCs, or similar devices that frequently power on and off, connect to the ring.

Another way around this problem is to use concentrators to build networks similar to a typical FDDI configuration (with both DASs and SASs), shown in Figure 3–27 [7]. Concentrators are devices with multiple ports into which FDDI nodes connect. FDDI concentrators function like Ethernet hubs or token ring multiple access units (MAUs). Nodes are single-attached to the concentrator, which isolates failures occurring at those end-stations. With a concentrator, nodes can be powered on and off without disrupting ring integrity. Concentrators make FDDI networks more reliable and also provide SNMP management functions. For this reason, most FDDI networks are now built with concentrators.

Each FDDI DAS has two ports, designated A and B. These ports connect the station to the dual FDDI ring. Therefore, each port provides a connection for both the primary and the secondary ring, as shown in Figure 3–28 (Cisco, 3).

In practice, most user stations are attached to the ring via wiring concentrators, since then only a single pair of fibers is needed and the connection cost is lower. The basic fiber is dual core with polarized duplex connectors at each end. This means that each end of the cable has a different physical key so that it can only be connected into a matching socket (to prevent faulty interchanging of wires, which can cause a total breakdown of the network). Special coupling units (either active or passive fiber devices) are used to isolate (bypass) a station when its power is lost. Stations detecting a cable break will go into wrap mode, using the secondary ring as backup so both rings are connected to form a single ring.

Physical Interface

As opposed to a basic token ring network, where at any instant there is a single active ring monitor which supplies the master clock for the ring, in FDDI this approach is not suitable because of the high data rates. Instead, each ring interface has its own local clock, and outgoing data is transmitted using this clock.

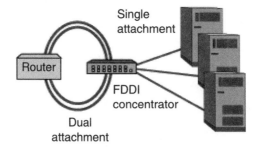

Figure 3–27: FDDI concentrators function like token ring MAUs or Ethernet hubs. Concentrators make FDDI networks more reliable by isolating failures that occur at end-stations and by providing SNMP management functions.

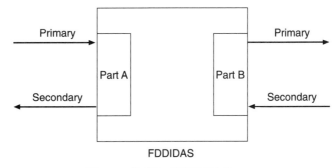

FDDIDAS

Figure 3–28: FDDI DAS ports.

All data to be transmitted is encoded prior to transmission using a 4-of-5 group code This means that for each 4 bits of data a corresponding 5-bit code word or symbol is generated by the encoder. Some of these symbols are used for link control functions, such as indicating the start and end of each transmitted frame or token. In general, the meaning and use of FDDI frame (or token) fields is the same as with the basic token ring. But, because of the use of symbols rather than bits, there are some differences in the structure of each field.

Traffic

FDDI supports real-time allocation of network bandwidth, making it ideal for a variety of different application types. FDDI provides this support by defining two types of traffic: synchronous and asynchronous. Synchronous traffic can consume a portion of the 100 Mbps total bandwidth of an FDDI network, while asynchronous traffic can consume the rest. Synchronous bandwidth is allocated to those stations requiring continuous transmission capability. Such capability is useful for transmitting voice and video information, for example. Other stations use the remaining bandwidth asynchronously. The FDDI SMT specification defines a distributed bidding scheme to allocate FDDI bandwidth.

Asynchronous bandwidth is allocated using an eight-level priority scheme. Each station is assigned an asynchronous priority level. FDDI also permits extended dialogues, where stations may temporarily use all asynchronous bandwidth. The FDDI priority mechanism can essentially lock out stations that cannot use synchronous bandwidth and have too low an asynchronous priority.

Fault-Tolerant

FDDI provides a number of fault-tolerant features. The primary fault-tolerant feature is the dual ring. If a station on the dual ring fails or is powered down or if the cable is damaged, the dual ring is automatically wrapped (doubled back onto itself) into a single ring, as shown in Figure 3–29 (Cisco, 4). In this figure, when Station 3 fails, the dual ring is automatically wrapped in Stations 2 and 4, forming a single ring. Although Station 3 is no longer on the ring, network operation continues for the remaining stations.

Figure 3–30 shows how FDDI compensates for a wiring failure (Cisco, 5). Stations 3 and 4 wrap the ring within themselves when wiring between them fails.

As FDDI networks grow, the possibility of multiple ring failures grows. When two ring failures occur, the ring will be wrapped in both cases, effectively segmenting the ring into two separate rings that cannot communicate with each other. Subsequent failures cause additional ring segmentation.

Optical bypass switches can be used to prevent ring segmentation by eliminating failed stations from the ring. This is shown in Figure 3–31 (Cisco, 5).

Critical devices such as routers or mainframe hosts can use another fault-tolerant technique called "dual homing" to provide additional redundancy and help guarantee operation. In dual-homing situations, the critical device is attached to two concentrators as shown in Figure 3–32 (Data Communications, 2).

One pair of concentrator links is declared the active link; the other pair is declared passive. The passive link stays in backup mode until the primary link (or the concentrator to which it is attached) is determined to have failed. When this occurs, the passive link is automatically activated.

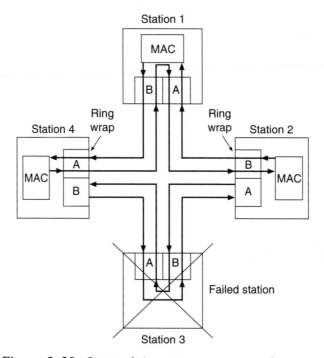

Figure 3–29: Station failure, ring recovery configuration.

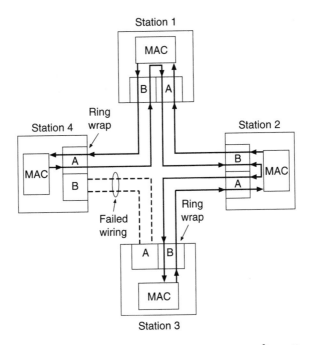

Figure 3–30: Failed wiring, ring recovery configuration.

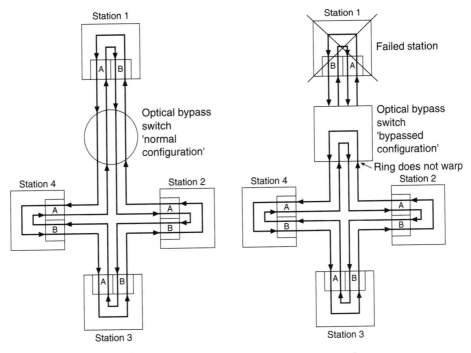

Figure 3–31: Use of optical bypass switch.

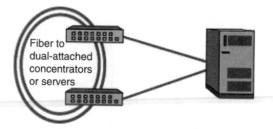

Figure 3–32: In dual-homed applications, mission-critical servers are connected to redundant concentrators, which in turn are connected to a dual-attached ring for maximum redundancy.

Frame

FDDI frame formats (shown in Figure 3–33) are similar to those of token ring (Cisco, 6). See the sidebar, "FDDI Frame Fields," for more information.

FDDI Frame Fields

The fields of an FDDI frame are as follows:

- Preamble—Prepares each station for the upcoming frame.
- Start delimiter—Indicates the beginning of the frame. It consists of signaling patterns that differentiate it from the rest of the frame.
- Frame control—Indicates the size of the address fields, whether the frame contains asynchronous or synchronous data, and other control information.
- Destination address—Contains a unicast (singular), multicast (group), or broadcast (every station) address. As with Ethernet and token ring, FDDI destination addresses are 6 bytes.
- Source address—Identifies the single station that sent the frame. As with Ethernet and token ring, FDDI source addresses are 6bytes.
- Data—Contains either information destined for an upper-layer protocol or control information.
- Frame check sequence (FCS)—Filled by the source station with a calculated cyclic redundancy check (CRC) value dependent on the frame contents (as with token ring and Ethernet). The destination station recalculates the value to determine whether the frame may have been damaged in transit. If so, the frame is discarded.
- End delimiter—Contains nondata symbols that indicate the end of the frame.
- Frame status—Allows the source station to determine if an error occurred and if the frame was recognized and copied by a receiving station.

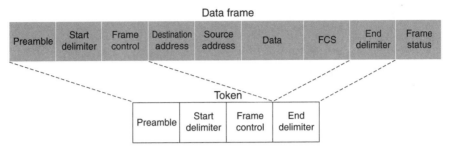

Figure 3–33: FDDI frame format.

CDDI

The high cost of fiber optic cable has been a major impediment to the widespread deployment of FDDI to desktop computers. At the same time, shielded twisted-pair (STP) and unshielded twisted-pair (UTP) copper wire is relatively inexpensive and has been widely deployed. The implementation of FDDI over copper wire is known as Copper Distributed Data Interface (CDDI).

Before FDDI could be implemented over copper wire, a problem had to be solved. When signals strong enough to be reliably interpreted as data are transmitted over twisted-pair wire, the wire radiates electromagnetic interference (EMI). Any attempt to implement FDDI over twisted-pair wire had to ensure that the resulting energy radiation did not exceed the specifications set in the United States by the Federal Communications Commission (FCC) and in Europe by the European Economic Council (EEC). The following three technologies reduce energy radiation: scrambling, encoding and equalization.

Scrambling

When no data is being sent, FDDI transmits an idle pattern that consists of a string of binary ones. When this signal is sent over twisted-pair wire, the EMI is concentrated at the fundamental frequency spectrum of the idle pattern, resulting in a peak in the frequency spectrum of the radiated interference. By scrambling FDDI data with a pseudo-random sequence prior to transmission, repetitive patterns are eliminated. The elimination of repetitive patterns results in a spectral peak that is distributed more evenly over the spectrum of the transmitted signal.

Encoding

When using an encoding scheme, signal strength is stronger, and EMI is lower when transmission occurs over twisted-pair wire at lower frequencies.

MLT3 is an encoding scheme that reduces the frequency of the transmitted signal. MLT3 switches between three output voltage levels so that peak power is shifted to less than 20 MHz.

Equalization

Equalization boosts the higher frequency signals for transmission over UTP. Equalization can be done on the transmitter (predistortion), or at the receiver (postcompensation), or both. One advantage of equalization at the receiver is the ability to adjust compensation as a function of cable length.

NOTE:

Of the many categories and types of twisted-pair wire, the ANSI standard only recognizes Category 5 UTP and Type 1 STP.

ISDN

Finally, let's take a brief look at the major network cabling standard from the ITU (International Telecommunications Union): ISDN. Standards for ISDN are continuously being defined and updated by ITU.

The public telephone and telecommunications networks are rapidly evolving to the exclusive use of digital technology. The move toward digital technology has been pushed by the competitive desire to lower cost and improve quality of voice transmission and network services. As the use of distributed processing and data communication has grown, this evolution of an all-digital network has been pulled by the need to provide a framework for ISDN (Integrated Services Digital Network).

Concept

Standards for ISDN are being defined by ITU-T. This part of the chapter will look at the following ISDN concept:

- Principles of ISDN.
- The user interface.
- Objectives.
- Benefits.
- Services.

Principles

The main feature of the ISDN concept is the support of a wide range of voice and non-voice applications in the same network. A key element of the service integration for an ISDN is the provision of a range of services using a limited set of connection types and multipurpose user-network interface arrangements.

ISDN supports a variety of applications, including both switched and non-switched connections. Switched connections in ISDN include both circuit-switched and packet-switched connections.

New services introduced into an ISDN should be arranged to be compatible with 64 Kbps switched digital connections. Also, an ISDN will contain intelligence for the purpose of providing service features, maintenance, and network management functions.

A layered protocol structure should be used for the specifications of the access to an ISDN. Access from a user to ISDN resources may vary depending upon the service required and upon the status of implementation of national ISDNs. Additionally, it is recognized that ISDNs may be implemented in various configurations according to specific national situations.

User Interface

The user has access to the ISDN by means of a local interface to a digital pipe of a certain bit rate. Pipes of various sizes will be available to satisfy differing needs. At any given point in time, the pipe to user's premises has a fixed capacity, but the traffic on the pipe may be a variable mix up to the capacity limit. Thus a user may access circuit-switched and packet-switched services, as well as other services, in a dynamic mix of signal types and bit rates. To provide these services, the ISDN will require rather complex control signals to instruct it how to sort out the time-multiplexed data and provide the required services. These control signals will also be multiplexed onto the same digital pipe.

Objectives

It is essential that a single set of ISDN standards be provided to permit universal access and to permit the development of cost-effective equipment. Transparency permits users to develop applications and protocols with the confidence that they will not be affected by the underlying ISDN.

The ISDN should provide dedicated point-to-point services as well as switched services. This will allow users to optimize their implementation of switching and routing techniques.

Benefits

The integration of voice and a variety of data on a single transport system means that the user does not have to buy multiple services to meet multiple needs. The requirements of various users can differ greatly in a number of ways; information volume, traffic pattern, response time, and interface types.

Services

The ISDN provides a variety of services. It supports existing voice and data applications as well as facsimile, teletex, and videotex.

Channels

The digital pipe between the central office and the ISDN user will be used to carry a number of communication channels. The capacity of the pipe may vary from user to user. The transmission structure of any access link is constructed from the following types of channels:

- B-channel: 64 Kbps.
- D-channel: 16 or 64 Kbps.
- H-channel: 384, 1536, and 1920 Kbps.
- The basic channel structure

B-channel

The B-channel is the basic user channel. It can be used to carry digital data, PCM-encoded digital voice, or a mixture of lower-rate traffic, including digital data and digitized voice encoded at a fraction of 64 Kbps. In the case of mixed traffic, all traffic must be destined for the same endpoint.

D-channel

The D-channel serves two purposes: First, it carries signaling information to control circuit-switched calls on associated B-channels at the user interface. In addition, the D-channel may be used for packet-switching or low-speed telemetry at times when no signaling information is waiting.

H-channel

H-Channels provide for user information at higher bit rates. The user may use such a channel as a high-speed trunk or subdivide the channel according to the user's own TDM (Time Division Multiplexing) scheme. Examples of applications include fast facsimile, video, high-speed data, high-quality audio, and multiple information streams at lower data rates.

Basic Channel Structure

The basic channel structure consists of two full-duplex 64 Kbps B-channels and a full-duplex 16 Kbps D-channel. Each frame of 48 bits includes 16 bits from each of the B-channels and 4 bits from the D-channel. See the sidebar, "ISDN Standards," for more information on these channels.

ISDN Standards

The ITU (International Telecommunications Union) has the following recommendations for ISDN:

H Series

The ITU makes the following recommendations for video conferencing and ISDN:

- H.221—The frame structures for 64 to 1920 Kbps channels when used with audiovisual teleservices.

- H.320—Narrow-band equipment recommendations for visual telephone systems and terminal equipment.

I Series

In 1988 the CCITT (currently the ITU) defined ISDN standards and published them as I series recommendations in a document called the *Blue Book* (not to be confused with the U.S. Air Force's *Project Blue Book* which ended in 1967). The following is a list of the applicable standards:

- I.100—General Concepts. Explains the ideas behind ISDN.

- I.200—Service Capabilities. Defines the extended services available to ISDN.

- I.300—Network Aspects. Defines the way the network for ISDN works.

- I.400—User-Network Interfaces. Explains the physical configuration for user network interfaces to ISDN.

- I.500—Internetwork Interfaces. Explains how to internetwork ISDN with other services.

- I.600—Maintenance Principals. Defines how to test networks and service levels.

Q Series

The Q Series Standards are the most commonly quoted ISDN standards. These standards have been devised by the ITU (International Telecommunications Union) and cover the standards of ISDN. The major Q standards are as follows:

- Q.920—Covers the network interface Data Link layer. Covers layer two of the OSI data model and controls the data flowing between two points in the network.

- Q.921—Defines the Data Link layer to an even higher degree.

• Q.930—Describes the Network layer of ISDN as it relates to the OSI data model. This standard defines how to find the pathway to complete the circuit that the connection makes.

• Q.931—Covers the basic call control of an ISDN call on the Network layer. Defines the envelope that information on an ISDN call is encapsulated in.

• Q.932—Defines the supplementary services that ISDN is capable of.

T.120 Series Video Conferencing

The ITU has also defined the use of ISDN with video conferencing in the T series of recommendations. They are as follows:

• T.122—Defines the multipoint communication for setting up multi-user tele-conference calls.

• T.123—Defines the protocol stacks for teleconferencing.

• T.124—Provides standards for Generic Conference Control (GFC) and how each user device will maintain communication.

• T.126—Defines the transfer of still images and the means to annotate them during conferences.

• T.127—Explains multipoint file transfers.

• T.128—Defines the use of real-time audio and video.

V Series Rate Adaption

When the device that is attached to an ISDN device cannot output data as fast as the ISDN service needs (such as a 28.8 Kbps being put on a 64k B channel), bits must be added to the stream to adapt the rate to what is being output. This is defined in the standards V.110 and V.120:

• V.110—Defines how to rate adapt 2.4 to 19.2 Kbps asynchronous rates into synchronous 56 or 64 Kbps rates. This standard is widely used in Europe, but does not have widespread adoption in North America. This protocol does not support any type of error correction.

• V.120—This standard is becoming widely accepted in North America. It is based on LAP-D (Link access procedure for the D channel), which is also the main protocol for all ISDN communications. This standard allows for bonding (combining) of B channels, into rates higher than 64 Kbps. The common speeds that are used with a Basic Rate Interface (BRI 2B+D) are as follows:

1 D Channel = 16 Kbps
1 B Channel = 64 Kbps
2 B Channels = 128 Kbps

X Series

• X.3—Defines the PAD (Packet Assembly/ Disassembly) for use in public data networks.

• X.25—Defines the interface between Data Terminal Equipment (DTE) and Data Communication (also called Circuit Terminating) Equipment (DCE) in packet networks.

- X.28—Defines start and stop mode for the X.25 interface for data terminal equipment (DTE) in a packet mode when both end points are in the same country.
- X.29—Defines the exchange of control information between two connections in a packet network.

From Here

This chapter presented an overview of the various cabling standards (TIA/EIA568A, ISO/IEC 11801, IEEE 802.x, FDDI, ISDN, 100—BaseTX, etc.) that are associated with the cabling technologies discussed in Chapter 1. Further discussions of cabling standards are presented in Chapter 7, "Standards Planning And Design Issues," and, Chapter 20, "Standards Development." The next Chapter will take a close look at some of the third party vendor cabling systems—AT&T (Lucent) Systimax and Powersum; IBM Cabling System; DECconnect; Northern Telecom IBDN, AMP Connect, KRONE; Mod-Tap, BCS, ITT, IBCS; etc.

End Notes

[1] "Guide to the TIA/EIA-T568-A Standard," Anixter Inc., 4711 Golf Road, Skokie, IL, 60076; and, TIA/EIA (Reproduced under written permission of the copyright holder (Telecommunications Industry Association)), 2500 Wilson Blvd., Suite 300, Arlington, Virginia 22011, 1997, p. 1.

[2] "Backbone Cabling System Structure," © The Siemon Company, Siemon Business Park, 76 Westbury Park Road, Watertown, CT 06795-0400 USA, 1997, p. 1.

[3] "OSI Reference Model," AMITCP/IP Group, Network Solutions Development Inc., P.O.Box 32, FIN-02151 ESPOO, Helsinki, FINLAND, EUROPE, 1994, p. 1.

[4] Charles Spurgeon, "100-Mbps Media Systems," Network Engineer, Computation Center Networking Services, The University of Texas, Austin, TX 78712, 1997, p. 1.

[5] Godred Fairhurst, "Metropolitan Area Networks (MANs)," Electronics Research Group, Department of Engineering at the University of Aberdeen, Fraser Noble Building, King's College, Old Aberdeen, Abereden, United Kingdom, AB24 3UE UK, 1998, p. 1.

[6] "FDDI," (some of the material in this book has been reproduced by Prentice Hall with the permission of Cisco Systems Inc.), Copyright © 1998 by Cisco Systems, Inc., All Rights Reserved, 170 West Tasman Drive, San Jose, CA, 95134-1706, USA, 1997, p. 2.

[7] "FDDI," Data Communications on the Web, 1221 Avenue of the Americas, New York, NY 10020-1095, 1997, p. 2 (Reprinted from *Data Communications* magazine December 1994; copyright The McGraw-Hill Companies, Inc., 1998, all rights reserved).

4

Types of Vendor and Third-Party Cabling Systems

Cost-effective cabling systems and the necessary infrastructure to support them are critical to the ongoing success of your business. Whether you are linking PCs within your office or connecting them to a host system across the country, you need a structured networking cabling system. And, because the cabling infrastructure is a substantial portion of total construction costs, flexibility and planning are essential, but the challenges are substantial.

The open office environment (partition based—no walls) presents a challenge to those installing vendor and third-party cabling systems. These challenges fall into three general categories; mechanics, scheduling, and churn. Each category is discussed in turn.

Mechanics

Open office partitions have no standard size, thickness, or base dimension. When open offices are networked, openings within the panel must contain communication cabling as well as the power wiring. Present telecommunications industry practice requires uninterrupted, 4-pair cable runs to each workstation receptacle.

The cabling industry is presently recommending four 4-pair receptacles be installed in each work station. This means four individual wires (16 pair) must be run to each work station. Large cable bundles are required. It is difficult and in many cases impossible to get these cables through the open office partition. In many cases, the two-inch power line to communication cable separation and routing required by Underwriters Laboratories (UL-1286 10.9) cannot be maintained.

Scheduling

Buildings utilizing open office partitions are seldom wired in one step. The open office furniture is not available at the time the building needs to be wired. Multiple callbacks become necessary. Time and costs increase dramatically.

For further information on scheduling, see Chapter 13, "Implementation Plan Development." This chapter discusses the development of the cabling system implementation plan with extensive and thorough coverage of all factors that impact schedules and tips on how to keep projects on schedule.

Churn

The major advantage of open office cabling systems is flexibility. Open office panels are frequently taken apart and reconfigured. The open office environment is in line with the adaptable, less hierarchical business paradigm today. This accounts in a large part for its popularity. Much of this flexibility is lost however, when the panels must be field-wired for LAN connections.

A vendor or third-party cabling system can be easily installed by a premise cabling company. It also can be installed by the same people installing the office furniture. In both cases, installation must be coordinated with the person or company with system responsibility. The final connection is made by plugging the cabling system in or in some cases punching it down to the building system. On the other hand, installing telephone and LAN wiring is a more agreeable task than having a premise cable company try to lay conventional cable in the panel.

Open office power wiring has used pre-manufactured and modular wire harnesses for many years. No one would even consider using standard field wiring practices to power an open office today.

Standard Vendor or Third-Party Cabling System Installation

In buildings using open office divider partitions, most vendor or third-party cabling systems start at the communications closet (TC) as described in TIA/EIA-T568 A/B or at a Multiuser Telecommunications Outlet (MTO) as defined in TIA/EIA TSB75. The end of this wiring is the user-accessible plug located in the individual work station. This final wiring step is commonly called horizontal cabling.

For pre-manufactured and plug-together systems, none can comply with all physical aspects of TIA/EIA-T568 A/B. The standard that applies here is Pre-Manufactured, Modular Telecommunications Cabling Standard, 1997, which is maintained by Dekko Engineering of Kendallville, Indiana.

Most standard vendor or third-party cabling system modules consist of multipair unshielded twisted pair (UTP) Category 5 performance-compliant cable segments. Fifty position Telco connectors are usually provided at opportune points. The head end connection is male in order to mate with a standard patch panel, hub or MTO. The user (work station) access is usually a female RJ-45 receptacle. Three to twelve users share a given cabling system run. User breakouts are positioned near the point of use. The breakout usually has a RJ-45 receptacle to accept the smaller cable leading to the user access face plate. The pin-out of the initial plug and face plate is specific to the LAN platform being served. This type of standard cabling system is usually available in twelve formats corresponding to common LAN and/or telephone arrangements. For more information on Category 5 and the new Category 6 cable standard, see Chapter 7, "Standards Design Issues" and Chapter 18, "Standards Development." Both LAN and telephone requirements are addressed here. Again, most standard cabling systems can provide both the LAN and telephone in a single run. Or, if the application dictates, platforms are usually available that bring either LAN or telephone. When both LAN and telephone exist in the same cabling system run, a profile cable with different sections for telephone and LAN is used.

Pre-manufactured cable designed for a specific LAN provides operational advantages not available with field wiring. Techniques can be applied to significantly reduce cross talk and interference susceptibility. In many cases, the performance of pre-manufactured cable is superior to that of field-wired cabling.

A step-up feature can significantly ease installation and reconfiguration. Most cabling system breakouts are usually the same. Each breakout brings out the next set of wire pairs in turn. It is not necessary for installers to concern themselves with which pair is brought out at a given breakout. The step-up feature is further described in the Chapter 15, "Installation."

Figure 4–1 is a typical application [1]. The run starts at the communication closet where it is attached to the LAN patch panel (large patch panel in the center of the communication closet) and the telephone punch down block (right side in Figure 4–1). The equipment shown on the left in the communication closet is the hub with its outside connection which in most cases is fiber. The cabling system proceeds to the open office area where the first breakout is located. The communication needs of the first work station are brought out here. One cable comes from the breakout to the office face plate. The cabling system then proceeds with the second breakout where the communication needs of the second work station are met.

NOTE:

> Except for length, all the breakouts are the same. They can be exchanged and placed in any order. In all cases, the LAN and telephone needs of the next work station are brought out in order.

The next part of the chapter will take a close look at some specific vendor and third party cabling systems—AT&T (Lucent) SYSTIMAX and Power Sum; IBM Cabling System; DECconnect; Nortel IBDN, AMP Connect, KRONE; Mod-Tap, BCS, and ITT, etc. Cabling system warranty and certification are also covered.

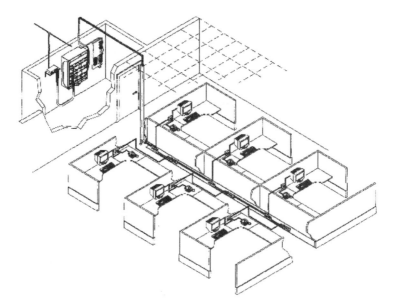

Figure 4–1: Typical application.

AT&T (Lucent) SYSTIMAX and Power Sum

Since many customers today are installing both copper and fiber cabling systems, many vendors are introducing products that accommodate both media at the same time. These products allow customers to migrate from one media to the other as conditions change.

For example, Lucent Technologies offers three different sets of products that provide both fiber and copper management. The first is a complete line of multimedia outlets for both surface-mount and flush-mount applications at the work area. The second product is the Multimax panel with new accessories for fiber management. Designed for smaller cross-connects, the Multimax panel accommodates up to 24 duplex fiber or 4-pair copper connections per panel. The third is the PatchMax family of patch panel products. In addition to the modular patching arrangement for high performance UTP, fiber modules are included as well. Both the panels and the outlets allow the installation of fiber and copper within the same housing.

The panels and the outlets also allow a smooth migration from one media to the other while preserving the investment in the hardware. For example, customers may migrate from copper to fiber by replacing the copper connectors (jacks) with fiber adapters (couplings) without replacing the outlet or panel.

The next part of the chapter presents a brief overview of Lucent Technologies' cabling system: SYSTIMAX®. It offers an end-to-end cabling solution that enables high-speed transmission rates at 622 Mbps. For more information on higher speed transmission rates and how to plan for higher-speed cabling systems as a result of changes in standards, see Chapter 12, "Data Compression."

SYSTIMAX Structured Connectivity Solutions (SCS) Cabling System

As previously stated, Lucent Technologies also has a cabling system: SYSTIMAX. It is composed of a number of Structured Connectivity Solutions (SCS). But, before taking a look at the SYSTIMAX SCS, a quick definition of a premises distribution system and a structured cabling system is in order.

Premises Distribution System

A premises distribution system is the transmission network inside a building or campus of buildings. It connects voice and data communications, video and building automation devices, switching equipment ,and other information management systems to one another as well as to outside communications networks. It includes all the cabling and associated distribution components between the point where the building wiring connects to the outside network or telephone company lines and the voice, data, and video terminals at work locations. The system can also serve a building or group of buildings on a campus-like premises. A distribution system consists of various families of components, including transmission media, circuit administration hardware, connectors, jacks, plugs, adapters, transmission electronics, electrical protection devices, and support hardware. These components are used to build elements, each having a specific purpose, that allow easy implementation and smooth transition to enhance distribution technology as the communications requirements change. A well-designed distribution system is independent of the equipment it serves and is capable of interconnecting many different devices, including data terminals, analog and digital telephones, personal computers, and host computers, as well as system common equipment.

Structured Cabling System

A structured cabling system is a set of cabling and connectivity products deployed according to specific engineering design rules. It enhances a premises distribution system and consists of the following:

- Open architecture.
- Standardized media and layout.
- Standard connection interfaces.
- Adherence to national and international standards.
- Total system design and installation.

SYSTIMAX SCS

SYSTIMAX SCS is the structured cabling system which was developed by Bell Laboratories, the research and development arm of Lucent Technologies. SYSTIMAX SCS is an integrated unshielded twisted-pair copper, fiber optic, and wireless networking solution that supports multiple applications, including voice, data, video, and building controls, seamlessly and simultaneously. Lucent Technologies provides all the components used in SYSTIMAX. This is a very important factor as the standards bodies continue research on high speed LANs and multimedia protocols. At some point, it will be necessary to migrate from copper to fiber. There is a comfort level knowing that you will be dealing with only one company, not two or even three as is the case now, when that time comes.

SYSTIMAX SCS is modular. It uses star topology—the same physical topology used by the telephone industry and adopted by EIA/TIA-T568-A Commercial Building Standard. Expansion is simple in a star topology because stations are added outward from a central point. Each link is independent of the others, so changes and rearrangements affect only those links actually being changed. Such a topology makes troubleshooting and maintenance easy, since problems can be localized while the reports of those problems can be centralized. The star configuration is versatile, because it can be reconfigured easily to other topologies, such as ring or bus, needed by other applications. While keeping your equipment and wiring in a star arrangement, you can integrate additional topologies simply by adjusting the circuits at administration points.

The star topology makes possible a subsystem approach to SYSTIMAX SCS. With SYSTIMAX SCS, you can design a distribution system that is, in effect, built of the following elements:

- Horizontal Cabling.
- Backbone Cabling.
- Work Area.
- Telecommunications Closet.
- Equipment Room.
- Entrance Facilities.
- Administration [2].

Like each link in the star topology, an element is a discrete unit; changes to one element need not affect others. An example would be a copper backbone element which is changed to add fiber for greater bandwidth. It can still be viable to use the copper horizontal cabling, equipment room, and telecommunications closet elements to work with the fiber.

Open Architecture

SYSTIMAX SCS solutions are implemented on an open architecture platform for maximum connectivity for existing products. At the same time, this cabling system provides a foundation for evolution to emerging technologies, such as multimedia, ATM (Asynchronous Transfer Mode), and Gigabit Ethernet.

Standardized Media and Layout

The SYSTIMAX SCS cabling system has a standard media, both copper and fiber, for each of the elements. For copper media, the choice is unshielded twisted pairs (UTP). There are three grades of UTP—Category 3 for voice and some low bandwidth LANs up to 16 MHz, Enhanced Category 5 tested for Power Sum for high bandwidth LANs up to 100 MHz, and GigaSPEED cable developed to support emerging bandwidth-intensive applications such as Gigabit Ethernet and featuring high bandwidth channel capability up to 200 MHz.

For fiber media, the fiber of choice is multimode 62.5 micron core for all elements. Singlemode 8.3 micron core fiber cable is allowed in backbone elements for high bandwidth applications. For more information on standardized media and layout with regard to how Category 6 fits into this scheme, see Chapter 18, "Standards Development."

Standard Connection Interfaces

SYSTIMAX SCS has standard connection interfaces, both copper and fiber, for each of the elements. For copper, interconnect and jack panels are deployed according to the category rating of the media: Category 3 for bandwidths up to 16 MHz, Enhanced Category 5 to 100 MHz, and GigaSPEED connection interfaces to support bandwidths up to 200 MHz. The same applies to the information outlets in the work area. For fiber, patch panels and fiber connector types are deployed based upon location, fiber type, and quantity.

Total System Design and Installation

SYSTIMAX SCS has instituted training courses for design and engineering as well as installation and maintenance which are requirements for working on certified projects. It provides application guides for designers which address all the major LANs and many of the building management control offerings. This ensures that the system design adheres to the LAN standards and product specifications. Additionally, the cabling system's installation guidelines are provided for installation and maintenance personnel to ensure that the system is installed properly and the system functions as designed. A 15-year extended product warranty and applications assurance program is provided to all certified projects. The cabling system's applications assurance covers all applications currently contained in the SYSTIMAX SCS performance specification as well as any applications introduced in the future by recognized standards bodies or user forums such as ATM, IEEE, etc. that require EIA/TIA-T568-A or ISO/IEC IS 11801 for component and link/channel specifications.

New Developments

The current standard for commercial buildings is based upon minimum requirements at a component level. The standard does not take into consideration connectivity between components. The result is a standard which lists minimum performance specifications for individual components. The SYSTIMAX SCS cabling system, on the other hand, takes a systems approach and works to try and improve margins for attenuation, cross-talk, structural return loss and impedance matching on a link/channel basis.

The same is true for Power Sum. SYSTIMAX SCS introduced the Power Sum Solution with the following features:

- Certified 622 Mbps performance to the Desk.
- Superior Power Sum Near End Crosstalk performance.
- Support up to 550 MHz (77 Channels) broadband video.
- SYSTIMAX SCS Expansion Option [Paradine, 5].

Bell Laboratories proved with the 622 Mbps Demonstration Unit that by using more than one pair of UTP conductors for transmission in the same direction, called Parallel Transmission Schemes (PTS), LAN speeds could improve dramatically. Thus, the SYSTIMAX SCS cabling system offers two UTP cabling systems: the Power Sum Solution and the GigaSPEED Cabling System, a fiber system with all the components required for both multimode and singlemode fiber and the WaveLAN wireless system for those nodes that exceed standard cabling distances.

Certified 622 Mbps to the Desk

The SYSTIMAX SCS's 622 Mbps to the desk capability is based on power sum technology and enables customers to send and receive information at higher speeds across multiple pairs. The technology supports various applications including asynchronous transfer mode (ATM) for simultaneous voice, data, and video.

Power sum technology refers to the more stringent industry requirements placed on cabling systems with applications that use multiple pairs of wires in the same cable. Power sum is an electrical performance testing method that takes into account crosstalk, or interference, from every pair of wires in a cable.

This kind of transmission speed has an impact on the way the business world communicates. For example, a healthcare network utilizing 622 Mbps technology could pull up a patient's x-ray and simultaneously videoconference with a team of physicians across the country to formulate a real-time prognosis—all on the same terminal.

The 622 Mbps capability is accomplished by transmitting 155 Mbps over each of four twisted pairs in what is known as parallel transmission. Parallel transmission uses four pairs that transmit signals simultaneously, providing four times the capacity of Category 5.

Power Sum Near End Crosstalk (NEXT) Performance

The SYSTIMAX SCS cabling system has engineered a solution that diminishes the harmful effects of NEXT. Power sum is an advanced method of measuring NEXT which identifies cable with performance margins. Applying power sum technology to 4-pair cabling results in a product with superior performance characteristics that is ideally suited to the demands of emerging and future high-speed applications.

Although standards committees have just begun studying the issue of sheath sharing, Bell Laboratories tested and qualified the fastest available LANs for compatibility. The 16 Mbps token ring, 100 Mbps Twisted Pair-Physical Media Dependent (TP-PMD), and 155 Mbps ATM are all compatible and warranted under the cabling system's guidelines. Furthermore, 25-pair cabling was qualified as an option for horizontal zone cabling.

NOTE

> that the following products meet the Power Sum specification: 4-pair 1061+ and 2061+ High Performance LAN Cables, 25-pair 1061 and 2061 High Performance LAN Cables, 110 Patch Panel System, PATCHMAX® Distribution Hardware, 1100CAT5PS Modular Jack Panels, MPS-100 Information Communication Outlet, and 1074 Impedance Matched Cordage [Paradine, 5].

550 MHz Broadband Video

The SYSTIMAX SCS cabling system includes a 384A Video Adapter for broadband applications. It has passed tests for radiated emissions in compliance with FCC Part 76 regulations. This cabling system provides applications assurance for up to 77 channels of broadband video (Channel 2 to Channel 78; frequency range 55 to 550 MHz).

Expansion Option

This cabling system option is in support of move and change activity. Lucent Technologies guarantees the sharing of qualified high-speed data systems over a single 4-pair or 25-pair cable link/channel using the enhanced (power sum) qualified products. The cabling system's guidelines specify options to meet EIA/TIA and ISO standards while providing another option for cabling customers. This option allows for expansion of supported applications using breakout assemblies until additional cabling can be installed.

In continuing with the SYSTIMAX Structured Connectivity Solutions (SCS) cabling system, let's look next at how Bell Laboratories demonstrates achievement of NEXT channel performance requirements for the GigaSPEED cabling system.

Achieving NEXT Channel Performance Requirements for the GigaSPEED Cabling System

The SYSTIMAX Structured Connectivity Solutions (SCS) Department of Bell Laboratories has designed and built a research experiment to demonstrate that the SYSTIMAX SCS GigaSPEED cabling system has achieved near end crosstalk (NEXT) channel performance requirements set at the inception of the project. The system demonstrated comprises 1071 GigaSPEED 4-pair UTP cable, MGS100 GigaSPEED Telecommunications Outlet, and GigaSPEED 110 Wiring Blocks and 110GS Patch Cords. The GigaSPEED cabling system has been introduced to support emerging bandwidth-intensive applications such as gigabit data transmission, multimedia, shifting LAN traffic patterns, and the use of network computers.

The GigaSPEED Cabling System

Currently the IEEE Gigabit Ethernet Alliance is developing a gigabit standard titled 1000BaseSX and LX for fiber and 1000BaseT for UTP. IEEE has set a completion schedule for the fiber standard for UTP. Additionally, the ATM (Asynchronous Transfer Mode) Forum is working on a fiber specification for 1.2 Gbps ATM and is evaluating a research project for UTP.

Bell Laboratories has developed design requirements for the GigaSPEED cabling system and has introduced and is selling the GigaSPEED 1071/2071/ 3071 Cable. Lucent Technologies introduced the remaining SYSTIMAX GigaSPEED apparatus. As Ethernet evolves from 100 Mbps to 1000 Mbps and becomes a standard, the SYSTIMAX SCS GigaSPEED cabling system will provide the capability to support it and future technologies and provide a 20-year extended product warranty and application assurance program.

While it is understood that the emerging gigabit standard for Ethernet will be based upon generic Category 5 cabling, research has shown that Category 5 performance is inadequate for robust 100-meter solutions using inexpensive electronic hub technology. The standard committee evaluated two proposals: (1) to support horizontal distances of 50 to 60 meters with inexpensive electronic hubs or (2) to support full 100 meter when coupled with very expensive and complex electronic hubs. The Gigabit Ethernet Standard has subsequently decided to support proposal (2). The GigaSPEED cabling system offers a cost-effective approach by providing a more robust system which can use less expensive hub electronics at the full 100 meter distances. Lucent Technologies Microelectronics Division is currently developing the integrated circuit chips that will be used in these hubs. The GigaSPEED cabling system has incorporated the following criteria:

- All components designed as a total system with backwards compatibility.
- A system designed for current and future applications that customers can use.
- A system that exhibits acceptable EMC performance for all intended applications [Paradine, 2].

GigaSPEED Cable

Incorporating all the principles previously outlined, the GigaSPEED cable has been designed for electrical performance specified out to 550 MHz and for channel performance supporting gigabit transmission to the desk at 100 meter distances. Employing optimized balance design, the cable exhibits lower emissions, stable electrical performance to higher frequencies, and greater noise immunity. On a worst case basis (or achievable for 100% of the cables installed), GigaSPEED cable guarantees the following electrical performance across the frequency spectrum relative to the Category 5 specification:

- 10 dB of Margin for Pair-to-Pair Near End Crosstalk.
- 8 dB of Margin for Power Sum Near End Crosstalk.
- Greater than 4% Margin for Attenuation.
- 10+ dB of Margin for Attenuation to Crosstalk Ratio.
- 3 dB of Margin for Structural Return Loss [Paradine, 2].

NOTE:

Typical values are based on an average of several cables tested and will show even better margins. They are, however, not guaranteed. When making comparisons between cables, it is most important to compare guaranteed-to-guaranteed or typical-to-typical values.

GigaSPEED Connectivity Components

GigaSPEED components have been designed with drastically improved crosstalk performance and balance. Additionally, major improvement in return loss and further reduction in attenuation have been achieved. The components have been designed and tested to 200 MHz and provide substantially more bandwidth when compared to the existing Category 5 standard. The GigaSPEED components have been designed to be fully compatible with existing hardware and plugs. Termination requires no new tools nor special installation procedures. The components include:

- MGS100 Telecommunications Outlet which fits all existing M series openings.
- DM2151 PatchMax Module with the same footprint as current product.
- D8GS Modular Cord with new 1074+ GigaSPEED Cordage and new plug.
- 110GS Patch Cords with new 1074+ GigaSPEED Cordage.
- 110 Wiring Block [Paradine, 3].

GigaSPEED Channel Performance

Figure 4–2 compares projected GigaSPEED channel performance values to those of Category 3 and 5 [Paradine, 4]. Specified out to 200 MHz, the GigaSPEED channel dramatically increases available bandwidth. The values shown for the GigaSPEED channel are part of the system's development requirements but are considered projected since some development work is ongoing and the values could improve.

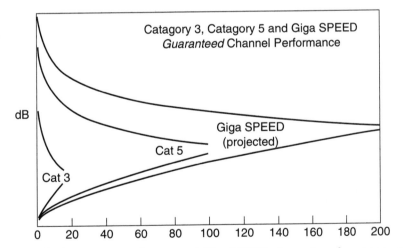

Figure 4–2: Comparison of projected GigaSPEED channel performance values to those of Category 3 and 5.

Demonstration of GigaSPEED NEXT Channel Performance

The GigaSPEED demonstration was designed and built by the SYSTI-MAX SCS Department of Bell Laboratories, Middletown, New Jersey. The demonstration was designed to show that the GigaSPEED cabling system provides dramatically improved NEXT channel performance when compared to the Category 5 standard. A 4-pair termination module for common and differential mode testing and a software program using new algorithms were developed by Bell Laboratories for ongoing research and this demonstration.

The demonstration provided a swept frequency test of NEXT specified to 200 MHz. The results for the NEXT of each pair-combination of the GigaSPEED channel were overlaid onto a grid on the PC monitor which displayed the Category 5 channel requirements. The following test sets and equipment were used:

- Custom 4-pair Test and Termination Module.
- Hewlett-Packard 35677A S-Parameter Test Set.
- Hewlett-Packard 3577A Network Analyzer.
- Hewlett-Packard Attenuator/Switch Drive.
- PC with 21" Monitor.
- GigaSPEED Cabling System Display [Paradine, 5].

The results demonstrated that the GigaSPEED channel not only met the initial objectives but exceeds them.

The IBM Cabling System

Now, let's take a very brief look at the next type of vendor and third-party cabling system: The IBM Cabling System. The IBM cabling system has the option of using five different types of cable as shown in Figures 4–3 to 4–7 [3]. The sidebar, "Types of Cable," discusses the physical characteristics of IBM's Cabling System.

NOTE:

IBM recommends Category 5 UTP for all token ring environments.
IEEE 802.5q discusses Category 3 cable in an active configuration only.

Figure 4–3: Type 1.

Figure 4–4: Type 3.

Types of Cable

The IBM cabling system has the option of using six different types of cable with the following physical characteristics.

Type 1:

- Two pairs twisted together, then overall shield applied.
- 22 AWG gauge, tested to 16Mbps.
- Impedance is 150 ohms, plus or minus 10 percent, at 3-20Mhz.
- Attenuation is 22dB per kilometer.
- Crosstalk must be less than -58dB between pairs.
- LAN use: between MAUs and from MAU to wallplate.

Type 2:

- Two pairs twisted and shielded, then shielded together, and an additional four pairs that can be used for voice (unshielded twisted pair Category 3 Cable).
- 22 AWG gauge, tested to 16 Mbps.
- Impedance is 150 ohms, plus or minus 10 percent, at 3-20Mhz.
- Attenuation is 22dB per kilometer.
- Crosstalk must be less than -58dB between pairs.
- LAN use: through the walls to the station wallplate typically carrying voice, token ring, and possibly 10BaseT Ethernet.

Type 3:

- Unshielded twisted pair.
- 22 AWG gauge or 24 AWG gauge wire.
- Minimum 2 twists per foot.
- Impedance is 100 ohms at 256Khz to 2.3Mhz.
- LAN use: throughout the network for token ring over unshielded twisted pair.

Type 5:

- Two 62.5/125 micron multimode fiber optic cable. 50/125 and 100/140 micron have also been used.
  - 62.5/125 micron is the defacto standard for FDDI:
    — Attenuation: 3.75 dB/km using 850 nm source.
    — Attenuation: 1.5 dB/km using 1300 nm source.
  - 8.3/125 for singlemode cable.
  - Connector types: SMA, ST, and SC.

Type 6:

- Two pairs twisted together, then shielded.
- 26 AWG stranded cable.
- Impedance: 150 ohms, plus or minus 10 percent, at 3–20Mhz.
- LAN use: typically connecting from the wall plate to the station adapter; patch cables only, to a 30 meter maximum.

Type 9:

- Two pairs twisted together, then shielded.
- 26 AWG solid or stranded cable.
- Impedance is 150 ohms, plus or minus 10 percent, at 3-20Mhz.
- Accepts RJ45 termination (smaller diameter).
- LAN use: typically used connecting from the wall plate to the station adapter [Cabletron, 1–2].

Figure 4–5: Type 5.

Figure 4–6: Type 6.

Figure 4–7: Type 9.

Next, let's look at how S/3X and the AS/400 are using the IBM cabling system (ICS).

S/3X and AS/400

System/3X and AS/400 connectivity can be accomplished using either unshielded twisted pair (UTP) or twinax cable. A UTP star-wired cabling system offers the ability to make changes to the system by simply moving a patch cord on a patch panel, while a twinax cabled system provides a high degree of immunity to electrical noise. The cabling scheme shown in Figure 4–8, however, offers the best of both twinax and UTP wired systems [4]. In addition, see the sidebar, "Twinax and UTP Wired Cabling Systems Product List," for a numbered list of products that correspond to the numbers shown in Figure 4–8.

Twinax and UTP Wired Cabling Systems Product List

The following is a numbered list of products that correspond to the numbers shown in Figure 4–8.

1. Part No. 501724 Type 1 Surface Mount Box.

2. Part No. 10148 Type 1 Faceplate.

3. Part No. 501405 Patch Cable.

4. Part No. 501174 MCL Metal Panel.

5. Part No. 30607 Distribution Panel.

6. Part No. 32873 84" Distribution Rack.

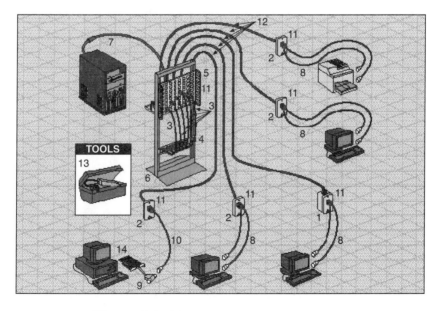

Figure 4–8: Twinax and UTP wired cabling systems.

7. Part No. 10143 Twinax Impedance Matching Device.
8. Part No. 501289 Twinax Y Assembly.
9. Part No. 502187 Twinax Green Terminator, 150 ohm.
10. Part No. 501399 Twinax Direct Cable.
11. Part No. 10087 Data Connector.
12. Part No. 10063 or 10061 PVC or Plenum Type 1 Cable.
13. Part No. 10138 Cable Test Kit.
14. Part No. 32330 Twinax Adapter Card.

Based on the IBM cabling system, the scheme shown in Figure 4–8 uses shielded twisted pair cabling. Since the cabling is star-wired to a distribution panel, moves, changes and additions can be made by simply moving a patch cord on the distribution panel. There is also a high degree of immunity to electrical noise, because the cable is shielded. This cabling system (shown in Figure 4–8) is able to support both token ring and 5250 type devices, so there is a great amount of flexibility when connecting the AS/400 to a token ring network. By simply changing the attachment cables and devices at the equipment rack and the workstation, the existing cabling can be adapted to a variety of systems and interfaces such as 16 Mbps token ring, 10BaseT Ethernet, RS-232 and RS-422. The benefits of this cabling scheme are:

* Combines the benefits of Twinax and UTP Cabling.
* Allows easy moves, changes, and additions.
* Highly reliable in electrically noisy environments.
* Able to support both token ring and 5250 type devices.
* Compatible with other networking schemes [South Hills Datacomm, 1].

Nortel IBDN

Next, let's take a look at the next type of vendor and third-party cabling system: Nortel IBDN. The Integrated Building Distribution Network (IBDN) is a universal wiring system designed to meet communications needs as they expand.

IBDN is a global in-building cabling system communications infrastructure that addresses distribution needs from the building entrance to the workstation with a single wiring system. Nortel's Category 5 IBDN structured wiring system is a UTP copper technology that provides 100 Mbps data rates and connectivity up to 100 meters. This comprehensive line of fully integrated products covers all of the needs for networking current and future computers, voice, and video communications equipment.

IBDN also covers end-to-end certified UTP gigabit cabling system solutions. The IBDN System 1200 and System 2400 UTP gigabit cabling system solutions go beyond Category 5 standards by providing additional margin to support emerging gigabit data rate applications.

Gigabit Cabling System Solutions

The availability of two enhanced IBDN structured cabling systems—IBDN gigabit cabling system solutions, System 1200 and System 2400—allows gigabit networking environments to be optimized over unshielded twisted-pair cabling. With the growing demand for Internet commerce, intranet deployment, and video conferencing, gigabit networks will become increasingly prevalent.

Evolved from the field-proven Category 5 IBDN structured cabling system, the IBDN gigabit cabling system solutions go well beyond existing Category 5 standards to meet increasing high-speed applications and network user demands. With the rapid increase in computer processing power, higher-performance networks will be required to support gigabit data rate applications.

The IBDN gigabit cabling system solutions allow end users the choice of two performance options to meet the varying needs of different enterprises. For example, IBDN System 1200 is built using IBDN PS5 enhanced connectivity and 1200 series UTP cable. It delivers a higher signal-to-noise margin than conventional Category 5 systems. It also provides a system bandwidth of 160MHz and an information bit-rate capability of 1.2 Gbps. The System 1200 is a very cost-effective solution to install and operate, thus making it a preferred cabling solution for gigabit ethernet.

The IBDN System 2400 comprises PS5 enhanced connectivity and 2400 series UTP cable and delivers 200 MHz of system bandwidth. It is capable of delivering an information bit-rate of 2.4 Gbps. Medical and financial institutions and other industries that constantly move large amounts of data benefit from the added speed, reliability, and assurance provided by the System 2400.

Developing a complete end-to-end enhanced system with matched components was the key engineering design criteria for the IBDN gigabit cabling system solutions. IBDN cable and connectivity work together to provide superior network performance. As such, these solutions are designed to exceed critical performance parameters such as power sum NEXT, FEXT (Far End Crosstalk), attenuation, and return loss.

To complement the new system offering, Nortel has extended its product warranty from 15 years to 25 years. In addition, IBDN gigabit cabling system solutions can be certified for application assurance over the life of the structured cabling system. End users will also benefit from Nortel's performance guarantee supplied in the form of a bandwidth and data-rate certification.

MOD-TAP

Let's now take a look at the next type of vendor and third-party cabling system: MOD-TAP's structured cabling system (SCS), which is composed of the residential cabling system (RCS) and the commercial structured cabling system (CSCS). The company provides structured cabling solutions to customers worldwide.

MOD-TAP is a manufacturer of structured cabling systems for information transport. The company designs and manufactures electronic, electrical and fiber optic components, flat cable, switches, and application tooling.

The MOD-TAP Structured Cabling System

The MOD-TAP Structured Cabling System (SCS) is an infrastructure for information transport within the office, building, or campus environment. It consists of a series of subsystems that support the analog and digital transmission of communication and building control signals. The SCS includes:

- Horizontal Cabling.
- Backbone or Vertical Cabling.
- Main Distribution Frame.

The MOD-TAP SCS is protocol-independent and is capable of supporting the following protocol technologies:

- ISDN.
- Voice.
- FDDI TP-PMD.
- ATM.
- 100BaseT.
- 10BaseT.
- Token ring.
- IBM Systems 3X/AS400.
- IBM 3270.
- RS232.
- AppleTalk Networks [5].

As previously stated, MOD-TAP's structured cabling system (SCS) is composed of the residential cabling system (RCS) and the commercial structured cabling system (CSCS). Let's look at the RCS first.

Residential Cabling System

Residential communication systems usually comprise a telephone line and a TV antenna. MOD-TAP RCS takes the home of today into the 21st century, providing access to, and distribution of the huge range of services available to the consumer including Internet, video services, home automation, LAN, and home theater as shown in Figure 4–9 [MOD-TAP, 1].

The MOD-TAP Residential Cabling System (RCS) is a structured solution to low voltage cabling in a new or existing home. RCS provides a plug-and-play modular approach to residential cabling for telephones, faxes, answering machines, video, computer equipment, and their devices such as security systems and control devices. RCS has adopted a four-part approach to residential cabling consisting of drops, feeds, system equipment, and an interconnect panel (central termination point).

Drops

Drops are equipment connection points located throughout the house for telephones, computers, video connections, and other devices. Each drop consists of one or more cables run to the panel.

Feeds

Feeds are gateways into the RCS telephone and cable TV services, an air antenna, a satellite dish, etc. Spare feeds can be installed for future use. A feed consists of one or more cables run to panel.

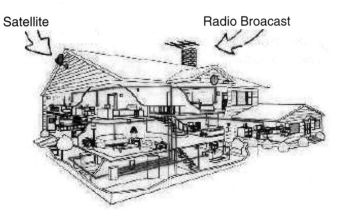

Figure 4–9: Residential Cabling System.

System Equipment

System equipment can include telephone key systems, door intercoms, video distribution panels, and computer LANs as well as lighting, security, and other control systems. Additionally, system equipment is cabled to the panel.

Interconnect Panel

InfoPanel™, the heart of the RCS, is a central terminating point for all residential twisted pair, coaxial, and/or fiber optic cabling. This is where all interconnections between drops, feeds, and systems are made.

Commercial Structured Cabling System

The commercial structured cabling system (CSCS) plays a critical role in all telecommunication systems, providing the physical link between sources and destinations of all information. Data, voice, video, and control signals are transmitted over this infrastructure linking devices across the room, and throughout a building as shown in Figure 4–10 [MOD-TAP, 1].

The CSCS may be quite small and simple, linking just a few nodes, or it may be massive, linking several buildings with tens of thousands of nodes, or a system somewhere in between. Essentially the CSCS is a simple physical link between active equipment, and is comprised of unshielded twisted-pair (UTP) cable or optical fiber cable or combinations of both.

Figure 4–10: Commercial structured cabling system.

However, to facilitate the day-to-day operations of a normal office environment, the link must enable the user to make adds, moves, and changes wherever and whenever necessary. Furthermore, the CSCS must also be universal in its ability to carry a wide variety of applications from voice and low-speed data to high-speed LAN applications.

MOD-TAP divides the entire system into subsystems (horizontal, backbone, and system) and addresses each individually, which collectively forms a system that meets all of the above criteria and more. CSCS is standards-based and complies with all relevant local and international telecommunications cabling standards.

Communication technology is developing at an astounding pace and it is essential for the survival of any business to utilize one of several possible technologies as shown in Figure 4–11 [MOD-TAP, 1]. No longer is the statement *Knowledge is Power* true. It is replaced by *Access to Knowledge is Power*. Business today needs an infrastructure to enable access to the vast knowledge base and to share this information.

Business Communication Systems (BCS)

Now, let's look at another type of vendor and third-party cabling system, the Lucent Technologies Business Communications Systems (BCS), a structured cabling system. World-class telecommunications is a vital element in any

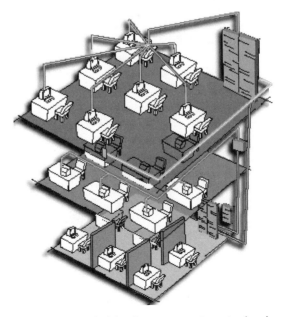

Figure 4–11: Communications technology.

business's plan to gain an edge over its competition. BCS is a developer, manufacturer, and supplier of multimedia communications services and products. These are services and products that combine the voice, data, and visual communications technologies that are currently available.

The BCS vision is to introduce its customers to the world of comprehensive, scalable multimedia communications. Through a manufacturing partnership with Honeywell, BCS in Australia manufactures its PABX, the DEFINITY Enterprise Communications Server (ECS), and exports it throughout the South Pacific. Particular emphasis is given to the following cabling system solutions:

Customer Sales and Service

Providing customers with twenty-four by seven access is becoming increasingly important to forward-thinking companies. The DEFINITY call center enables companies to handle the high volume of calls based on the individual caller's needs and expectations.

Conferencing and Collaboration

A personal computer is undoubtedly the most powerful tool available to modern businesses. Adding to that power is the Lucent Technologies Multipoint Control Unit (MCU). The MCU enhances productivity through video conferencing, applications sharing and data collaboration.

Distributed and Mobile Work Force

In today's workforce of increasing decentralization and mobility, there is a constant requirement for powerful support tools. The Lucent Technologies Forum Personal Communications Manager is a second-generation wireless communications system; it offers mobility, features, convenience, and, importantly, security.

Multimedia Messaging and Response

Effective and, above all, efficient, messaging and voice response solutions bring major benefits in a business's communications with its employees, customers, prospects, and partners. Lucent Technologies offers a range of solutions to assist businesses in messaging and response capabilities, and streamlining both the internal and external communications and workflow.

Networking

In today's business environment, there's the need to be faster, work better, and do more with less. The efficient dissemination of information is crucial to this need. Thus, many of the Lucent Technologies cabling system products offer the ability to link multiple locations into a unified private network with feature and functional transparency.

In creating solutions to meet the cabling system needs of Australian businesses, BCS works closely with Bell Labs. BCS also houses the South Pacific Regional Support Center (RSC). The Center provides technical expertise to its distributors and customers. Within the Center are specialist technical designers, test engineers, process specialists; custom software and hardware development staff, professional services consultants, application and business operations consultants; and, customer trainers.

ITT Cabling Systems

Next, let's take a quick look at a couple of vendor and third-party cabling systems: ITT Structured Cabling System (ISCS) and the ITT Structured Networking System (ISNS). This part of the chapter presents an on-going strategy aimed at the testing and development of both the ITT Structured Cabling System (ISCS) and the ITT Structured Networking System (ISNS). This strategy demonstrates a commitment that ITT has invested in—ensuring that the products and services delivered are designed for today's and tomorrow's standards and legislative frameworks.

Power Sum Cables, Connectors, and Systems

As previously discussed, the notion of power sum cables is not a new one; it is well-documented within both ISO/IEC 11801 and ANSI/TIA/EIA-T568A, where their performance requirements and limitations are described in some detail. In short, power sum cables are designed with improved NEXT parameters that allow standard Category 5 NEXT levels to be achieved on all pairs even when signals are generated on all other adjacent pairs within the sheath. Therefore the more pairs there are within the sheath the higher the crosstalk specification has to be to ensure a minimum standard for Category 5 performance is still attained even with active signals on all other pairs.

As there are many cables on the market capable of supporting power sum on 25 pairs, it puts into perspective just how easy it is to attain this level of performance for a 4-pair solution. Using the formula below, the improvement in

NEXT required to achieve power sum NEXT on a 4-pair cable is approximately 3 dBs at 100Mhz. This is an increase from the Category 5 standard of 32 dBs to 35 dBs.

$$\text{PSXTALK PR1} = \text{Square Root of } (pr2\text{-}1)^2 + (pr3\text{-}1)^2 + (pr4\text{-}1)^2$$

NOTE:

> A quality Category 5 cable such as ISCS20000DSC has a worst case acceptance criteria of 42 dBs at 100 Mhz and therefore far exceeds the requirement of power sum crosstalk.

Under section 7.5.1 of ISO/IEC 11801, power summation is described as cables whose NEXT loss performance values contained within the existing Category 5 specification can be met using power summation to determine total crosstalk energy. Power summation cables are not intended to support services with different signaling schemes (different protocols).

NOTE:

> Power sum crosstalk is based upon crosstalk between signals from the same type of application, and in particular those using the same spectral energy.

If one wishes to support multiple protocols within a single sheath without considerable limitations, power sum crosstalk performance is not adequate. Cables required to perform this task require an even more rigorous crosstalk performance criteria. NEXT loss between any cable unit (in the case of sheath sharing, a quad) supporting different kinds of applications simultaneously shall have an improvement in NEXT above Category 5 to the level specified in section 7.5.2 of ISO/IEC 11801 and is defined by the following equation:

NEXT = 6 dB + 10 log (n + 1) dB
where n = the number of adjacent units within the cable

Therefore, the installation of power sum cables does not give the end user carte blanche with respect to multiple protocol support. Power sum is a method of marketing systems in excess of Category 5 performance and differentiating them from standard Category 5 links and channels that can only support a single service of a single protocol rather than two services of the same or similar protocol.

This is not a major achievement; the majority of quality balanced cables exceed standard Category 5 by the power sum requirement. This is also the case with connector technology. The ITT Cannon 808 connector, for example, exhibits a performance criteria of between 48 and 58 dBs at 100 Mhz compared to the TSB40A requirement of 40 dBs. However, it is the performance of the system, post installation, that is the critical issue. It is for this reason that ITT Cannon has been using power sum crosstalk limits for the pass/fail criteria. These criteria are applied across the entire installation to ensure that optimum performance of the structured cabling system is guaranteed.

Table 4–1 depicts the TSB 67 link pass/fail NEXT and ACR (power sum) limits for the ITT Structured Cabling System (ISCS) and the requirements contained within standards-based test equipment [6]. ITT Cannon also insists on every installed link passing a full network test for all current and proposed MAC (Medium Access Control) level protocols.

Table 4–1: The TSB 67 link pass/fail NEXT and ACR (power sum) limits for the ITT Structured Cabling System.

Frequency (Mhz)	ATT	NEXT (TSB67)	*NEXT Power Sum*	ACR (IS 11801)	*ACR Power Sum*
1.00	2.1	60.0	61.8	n/a	59.7
4.00	4.0	51.8	52.7	40.0	48.7
10.00	6.3	45.5	46.8	35.0	40.3
16.00	8.2	42.3	43.7	30.0	35.5
20.00	9.2	40.7	41.7	28.0	32.5
31.25	11.5	37.6	39.6	23.0	28.1
62.50	16.7	32.7	34.5	13.0	17.8
100.00	21.6	29.3	31.4	4.0	9.8

While providing improved NEXT performance and increased ACRs (Attenuation/Cross Talk Ratio), protocol performance will still be affected by external RF and EMI. It is for this reason that to guarantee zero error operation, the enhanced bandwidth must be protected, as in the case of ISCS, with an effective foil screen.

622 Mbps OC-12 ATM Support for Copper

The sidebar, "ATM Physical Layer Standards," shows the current physical layer standards provided by the ATM Forum for the support of ATM services.

With respect to twisted-pair physical layer specifications, it is apparent that at present, no standard exists for the provision of 622 Mbps ATM services over twisted pair.

ATM Physical Layer Standards

The following are the current physical layer standards provided by the ATM Forum for the support of ATM services:

- ATM Physical Medium Dependent Interface Specification for 155 Mbps over Twisted-Pair Cable, af-phy-0015.000.
- DS1 Physical Layer Specification, af-phy-0016.000.
- Utopia Level 1 v2.01, af-phy-0017.000.
- Mid-range Physical Layer Specification for Category 3 UTP, af-phy-0018.000.
- 6,312 Kbps UNI Specification, af-phy-0029.000.
- E3 UNI, af-phy-0034.000.
- Utopia Level 2 v1.0, af-phy-0039.000.
- Physical Interface Specification for 25.6 Mb/s over Twisted Pair, af-phy-0040.000.
- A Cell-based Transmission Convergence Sublayer for Clear Channel Interfaces, af-phy-0043.000.
- 622.08 Mbps Physical Layer, af-phy-0046.000 (fiber only).
- 155.52 Mbps Physical Layer Specification for Category 3 UTP (See also UNI 3.1, af-uni-0010.002), af-phy-0047.000.
- 120 Ohm Addendum to ATM PMD Interface Spec for 155 Mbps over TP, af-phy-0053.000.
- DS3 Physical Layer Interface Spec, af-phy-0054.000.
- 155 Mbps over MMF Short Wave Length Lasers, Addendum to UNI 3.1, af-phy-0062.000.
- WIRE (PMD to TC layers), af-phy-0063.000.
- E-1, af-phy-0064.000 [ITT, 3-4].

Currently OC-12 622 Mbps ATM utilizes NRZ (Non-Return to Zero) encoding operating at a peak carrier frequency of 311.04 Mhz. This frequency range is far beyond the reach of any 100-ohm 4-pair structured cabling system available. Therefore support for 622 Mbps ATM over copper will obviously mean developing new encoding schemes that will be uneconomic to manufacture in the quantities anyone at present can perceive.

An alternative option is to put the ATM signal across all four pairs and use a methodology similar to that used under IEEE 802.12, 100VG-AnyLAN. In essence, this process demodulates the 622 Mbps signal and spreads it across all four pairs. Again, although undoubtedly possible, it would mean using proprietary, uneconomic technology.

Finally, as the ATM Forum has no plans to develop a standard copper interface for 622 Mbps ATM, no sensible switch vendor is going to put R&D dollars into developing a technology to support a dubious requirement with zero demand. The reluctance of switch and NIC (Network Interface Card) vendors to push for a OC-12c (Optical Carrier) copper interface will be further heightened by the IEEE 802.3z Gigabit Ethernet committee. This standard will contain a specification for delivering 1.0 Gbps over twisted pair at 100 meters. The ease of migration from existing Ethernet and Fast Ethernet environments along with the anticipated low cost may result in Gigabit Ethernet overtaking ATM as the most popular choice for tomorrow's backbone technology. The claims of 622 Mbps support over copper are at best marketing hype, an attempt for differentiation in a standards-based environment, or at worst a feeble effort to mislead the customer.

Radio Frequency (RF) Support via Structured Cabling Systems

Recent press releases featuring the capability to support 550 Mhz RF signals across twisted pair have certainly raised many questions both within the installer and end user community. This is not a new technology. Lucent Technologies, among others, has been producing RF baluns for over two years and has spent significant amounts of money in R&D on the subject. At first glance, the idea of delivering RF TV signals over structured cabling appears to offer end users increased flexibility. However, what are its limitations? And, what are the drawbacks of providing RF signals over twisted pair to the desk?

The main problem with RF TV distribution is that it was conceived for broadcasting from one single point to many points over free space in large geographical areas, and not to be used over premises cabling infrastructures in restricted environments such as an office building. Because higher frequencies suffer from more propagation attenuation than comparatively lower frequencies, it follows that the higher the frequency used to cover a given distance range, the higher the level of emitted signal required. This level is regulated by the ITU (International Telecommunications Union), which is the body of the United Nations that produces the international telecommunications regulations, and is enforced in each country by a national governmental department such as the FCC in the U.S. or the DTI (Department of Trade and Industry) in the U.K.

It is for these reasons that under FCC/DTI guidelines a TV-modulated RF bandwidth of 550 Mhz RF can be delivered over distances of only 196 feet of structured cabling. The number of channels assigned by the ITU for broadcasting over the 550 Mhz frequency band is very limited. The number of simultaneously usable channels is much smaller than that theoretical number due to the problem of frequency re-assignment, guard bands between channels, and inter-channel interference.

Traditional RF installations utilize double-shielded, double-braided coax cables and *F* connectors to ensure any leakage of RF signals into the environment and interference from the environment into the signals on those installations are kept to a minimum. It is very likely that serious interference from RF signals distributed over unshibuted twisted pair will appear on services operating over adjacent data cables. Any RF signals must be kept completely separated from voice and data signals in nearby cables and equipment as the effect of RF can be catastrophic.

The use of balanced transport lines will obviously reduce (not eliminate) the amount of RFI emanation, but it does not solve the problem of RF interference with voice and data services. The differences in wave form and consequently energy between networked data and RF carriers modulated with TV signals make it evident that such signals should not be put in the vicinity of each other.

Since the important thing in a trading floor or office environment is the data on the network and not the TV signals, it is obvious that alternative technologies must be used for business TV distribution. In short, customers do not want RF in their buildings. The only sensible way to achieve this scenario is to take RF from external sources and convert the signal into baseband. Once the signal is in this format, it can be safely transported around the building over twisted pair with relatively few restrictions on the number of channels available and transmission distance. This service is currently provided by systems such as Paragon's NEWS Link and Amulets TACSI.

International Cabling Systems

Now, let's take a look at some of the international vendor and third-party cabling systems. Even though some of the vendors just discussed were international in origin, this part of the chapter will take close at EMC Fribourg, a Swiss testing facility that conducted comparative EMC (Electro-Magnetic Compatibility) tests on four STP cabling systems and one UTP cabling system. Using personal computers (PCs) with IBM token ring Adapter Cards, all cabling systems were configured to support the IBM 16 Mbps token ring local area network (LAN) application according to ISO 8802.5 standards.

For the UTP cabling system, SYSTIMAX SCS 1061 Category 5 24-AWG High-Performance 4-Pair UTP cable was chosen, with an M1000 Multimax Panel and M100-type information outlets (IOs) used as the connecting hardware and a 370C1 Adapter (media filter) used to link the IBM card to the SYSTIMAX SCS UTP system.

Test Results

In radiated emissions testing for a frequency range of 30 MHz to 1 GHz in an anaechoic chamber and in an open area test site (OATS), the SYSTIMAX SCS UTP system met CISPR 22/EN5022 Class B requirements with a more than adequate margin. Class B requirements are for residential use and are more stringent than the Class A requirements for commercial use.

In conducting emissions on signal port testing at lower frequencies (150 kHz 30 MHz) with a current probe, the SYSTIMAX SCS UTP system met the proposed CISPR 22/EN55022 class B requirements. In IEC 801.4 electrical fast transient (EFT) noise-burst testing, the SYSTIMAX SCS UTP system did not fail even when subjected to the most strenuous test at 4,000 V. None of the STP cabling systems survived to that level.

In IEC 801.3 radiated immunity testing, which tests the ability of a system to withstand electromagnetic interference at defined severity levels (26 MHz to 1 GHz), the SYSTIMAX SCS UTP system experienced no errors. The one STP cabling system tested experienced errors when the media filter was used instead of the shielded work area cable at the PC. EMC Fribourg concluded that UTP cabling systems, and, more specifically, SYSTIMAX SCS UTP systems, can meet the above EMC requirements.

High-Speed Data Transmission and UTP Cabling Systems

Tests conducted in well-known testing facilities show that UTP cabling systems and, specifically, SYSTIMAX SCS using UTP cable, can meet standards specifications for transmitting high-speed data within acceptable levels and can pass all required tests. EMC tests were conducted on an ISO 8802.3 10 Mbps 10BaseT system that used SYSTIMAX SCS 1061 Category 5 24-AWG High-Performance 4-Pair UTP cable, with Category 5 patch panels, Category 5 M100-type IOs, and Category 5 patch cords, along with 486-type PCs and electronics from several major vendors. The tests were done at the Lucent Technologies Bell Laboratories Global Product Compliance Laboratory in Holmdel, New Jersey, and were sent to a German notified and competent body, Bundesamt fur Zulassungen in der Telekommunikation (BZT) for certification. The

SYSTIMAX SCS UTP system passed every test, in some cases even exceeding the current requirements under the EMC Directive. The tests were as follows:

- Radiated Emissions; specifications EN 55022, 1987, Class B Limit.
- Conducted Emissions (AC Mains); specifications EN 55022, 1987, Class B Limit.
- Conducted Emissions (Signal Ports); specifications EN 50081-1, 1992, Informative Annex A, CISPR 22 Amendment, CISPR/G (Sec 65), 1993, Class B Limit.
- Electrostatic Discharge (ESD) Immunity; specifications IEC 801.2, 1991, IEC CISPR 24, Part 2, prEN 55024, Part 2, Contact Discharge at 4,000 V (Level 2), Air Discharge at 8,000 V (Level 3).
- Radiated Field Immunity; specifications IEC 801.3, 1992, IEC CISPR 24, Part 3, prEN 55024, Part 3, 3 V/m (Level 2), 10 V/m (Level 3).
- EFT/Burst Immunity; IEC 801.4, 1988, IEC CISPR 24, Part 4, prEN 55024, Part 4, AC Mains at 1.0 kV (Level 2), Signal/Control Lines at 0.5 kV (Level 2) and 1.75 kV (Level 3) [7].

EMC tests were also conducted on an ISO 9314 (ANSI X3T9.5) 100 Mbps TP-PMD LAN that used SYSTIMAX SCS 1061 Category 5 24-AWG High-Performance 4-Pair UTP cable, with Category 5 patch panels, Category 5 M100-type IOs, and Category 5 patch cords, along with 486-type PCs and electronics from several major vendors. The tests were done at the Lucent Technologies Bell Laboratories Global Product Compliance Laboratory in Holmdel, New Jersey, and were sent to BZT in Germany for certification. The SYSTIMAX SCS UTP system again passed every test, in some cases even exceeding the current requirements under the EMC Directive. The tests were as follows:

- Radiated Emissions; specifications EN 55022, 1987, Class B Limit.
- Conducted Emissions (AC Mains); specifications EN 55022, 1987, Class B Limit.
- Conducted Emissions (Signal Ports); specifications EN 50081-1, 1992, Informative Annex A, CISPR 22 Amendment, CISPR/G (Sec 65), 1993, Class B Limit.
- ESD Immunity; specifications IEC 801.2, 1991, IEC CISPR 24, Part 2, prEN 55024, Part 2, Contact Discharge at 4,000 V (Level 2), Air Discharge at 8,000 V (Level 3).
- Radiated Field Immunity; specifications IEC 801.3, 1992, IEC CISPR 24, Part 3, prEN 55024, Part 3, 3 V/m (Level 2).
- EFT/Burst Immunity; IEC 801.4, 1988, IEC CISPR 24, Part 4, prEN 55024, Part 4, AC Mains at 1.0 kV (Level 2), Signal/Control Lines at 0.5 kV (Level 2) [Lucent, 7].

Furthermore, research conducted by the SYSTIMAX SCS Department of Lucent Technologies Bell Laboratories, together with the Advanced Multimedia Communications Department of Lucent Technologies Bell Laboratories, has demonstrated that SYSTIMAX SCS UTP systems, using 328 ft (100 m) of 1061 Category 5 24-AWG High-Performance 4-Pair UTP cable, with M1000 MULTIMAX Panels and M100-type IOs for connecting hardware along with Category 5 D8AU patch cords, can successfully transmit up to 622 Mbps, the equivalent of 23,000 pages of text per second. The test used off-the-shelf high-quality red/green/blue (RGB) video equipment to provide the data stream. A studio-quality RGB video camera was used to capture a full-motion high-resolution image. Using a codec, the analog video signal from the camera was converted to an industry-standard D1 protocol digital video data stream and, at the transmitter, encoded into a 64-point Carrierless Amplitude and Phase (64 CAP) signal. The 64 CAP encoding method was used to partition the data stream into four 155 Mbps channels at the transmitter, which were each then sent over one pair of the 4-pair cable, and then decoded and recombined into a single 622 Mbps data stream at the receiver end of the link. A codec at this end converted the signal back into an analog RGB video signal that was displayed on the monitor.

The Advantages of Using UTP Cabling Systems

STP cabling systems are more expensive and harder to install and maintain than UTP cabling systems, but are not necessarily better. As demonstrated in EMC and other test results, UTP cabling systems succeeded—even excelled—in rigorous testing. Furthermore, because it was chosen as the representative UTP cabling system, SYSTIMAX SCS demonstrated the benefits of Lucent Technologies' testing and manufacturing under rigid ISO 9000 quality control conditions. This underscores the importance of using a structured cabling system made up of products designed and manufactured to work together that meet or exceed international standards.

AMP Connect

This part of the chapter will not cover any vendor and third-party cabling systems, but instead will take a close look at a service that provides electrical and electronics industries with a fast, easy way to find information on over 90,000 cabling system products. This service is called AMP Connect, and the search engine is called Step Search (http://connect.ampincorporated.com/).

The database is searchable by viewing pictures of cabling system products, by reviewing an alphabetical listing of products and industry names for them, or by requesting information on a specific part number.

The database presents information on cabling system products in any of the languages you select (Chinese, English, French, German, Italian, Japanese, Korean and Spanish) as shown in Figure 4–12 [8]. The membership registration process allows you to customize your profile by selecting a language and a country of delivery.

The search engine is called Step Search. It was co-developed with Saqqara Systems, Inc. to provide customers with a way to select the products AMP offers quickly from the thousands of parts available worldwide. Other examples of the Step Search engine can be seen at the Saqqara website (http://www.saqqara.com/). These provide you with some idea of how Step Search functions and are particularly useful if you are not interested in the electrical/electronics industry.

Information available from this site includes product information currently available from Saqqara Systems, Inc. catalogs, and from the AMP Fax fax-back system. 3D CAD models in IGES (Initial Graphics Exchange Specification) format are also available for approximately 6,000 of the part numbers.

What's on AMP Connect?

Well, for one thing, there's over 90,000 part numbers on-line. Additional features are the direct result of customer input and AMP's move toward serving customers on a global basis. Customer requests have resulted in the following system enhancements:

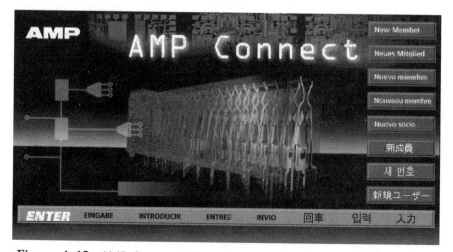

Figure 4–12: AMP Connect's Step Search search engine database menu.

- 3D Models On-Line.
- Comparison Table.
- Additional Languages.
- Smaller Graphics.

3D Models

3D models of over 6,000 AMP connectors are on-line and available for downloading. AMP has been providing IGES versions of 3D model files for use in many popular CAD systems through the Electronic Assistance Design System (EADS) since 1991. Previously, these models were available only via CD-ROM. The addition of these files to the AMP Connect website means that customers can obtain these same IGES files over the Internet for immediate use in their CAD systems. Customer interviews have indicated that the availability of 3D models can save up to 2 days of design work for each model available. Models will continue to be available on CD-ROM. A *Model On Demand* request system is being prepared for future release to enable customers to request 3D model files for AMP part numbers which do not currently have CAD files available. 3D model availability was the most requested addition to the AMP Connect website from on-line customer feedback.

Comparison Table

To facilitate selection of parts a comparison table feature has been incorporated into the Step Search portion of AMP Connect. When the *Compare Parts* button appears on the Detail View screen, you will be able to compare up to five part numbers on one screen to see the actual differences between the products. Hyperlinks to each part number's Detail View screen speed access to detailed part number information and documentation. Side-by-side comparison of several parts was also a feature requested by customers using the AMP Connect website.

Additional Languages

Another feature is the addition of translations for much of the website information into Japanese, Mandarin Chinese, and Korean languages. Users with browser software capable of viewing these Kanji character-based languages will be able to use Step Search to select cabling system products using their native language. These translated versions of AMP Connect will appear as gibberish to browsers not able to handle the Kanji character sets.

Graphics

In further response to customer feedback, the graphics for the welcome screen and the main menu page are being improved. The file sizes are also being reduced for faster download time.

AMP Connect currently has information on over 90,000 part numbers. The Step Search software allows members (currently over 46,000 worldwide) to search for interconnect devices via photographs, alphabetic lists of product names, or part numbers. Documentation is available for every part number, including customer drawings, product and application specifications, and instruction sheets. AMP plans to offer information on all standard connector part numbers through AMP Connect with over 400,000 available by the year 2000.

Certification and Warranty

Last, but not least, it's now time to take a look at certification and warranty for these vendor and third-party cabling systems. There are a number of reliable cabling system certification and warranty services available.

Design and installation of cabling systems is in accordance with TIA/EIA-T568A/569/606/607. Cabling system certification in accordance with TSB-67. This part of the chapter will review some of the most reliable cabling system certification and warranty services currently available:

- KRONE.
- LRS.
- Millennium Technologies of New Boston.
- 3P.
- PerfectSite.
- SYSTIMAX SCS.

KRONE

Networking information systems are becoming more and more crucial to the survival and success of companies struggling to compete in increasingly complex global markets. These networked information systems are dependent on the reliability of a behind-the-scenes physical foundation consisting of a conglomeration of copper wiring and optical fiber. Frequently this conglomeration has evolved in a haphazard, ad hoc fashion. Because of this, many of these wiring systems are unable to support some of the high-speed LAN technologies that are becoming increasingly necessary for companies attempting to stay abreast of rapidly changing technology and keep ahead of their competition.

The best way to ensure that your company's investment in a cabling system is capable of supporting high-speed networks is to install a structured cabling system. All components of a structured cabling system must meet rigorous standards. The cable and the connectors must all comply with strict requirements. A structured cabling systems provides many benefits to the customer including:

- Eliminates network segmentation.
- Provides logical data paths.
- Ensures that the physical requirements for communications and cabling are met.
- Simplifies adds, moves, and changes.
- Simplifies troubleshooting and fault isolation.
- Provides facilities management and tracking of the system [9].

Insist on Quality

By using the highest quality components to build a system, and only experienced, well-trained installers who can test and certify the system's performance, you can be confident that you have invested in a foundation that is capable of supporting the inevitable advances in LAN technology. As the performance potential of copper wiring continues to climb, industry analysts have had to reevaluate the long term role of copper wiring. According to some industry experts, data rates as high 622 Mbps are well within the potential of 4-pair copper cable. This means that copper wiring is capable of supporting data at rates four times greater than the fastest rates being used today (ATM at 155 Mbps). As the data speed continues to climb, the importance of having a well-engineered, performance certified structured cabling system becomes more and more critical.

KRONE Recommends Full Category 5 Compliance

When installing a new cabling system or upgrading an existing site, it only makes sense to comply with the current industry standards for structured cabling. Most of the cable will be hidden in walls or run above ceilings or under floors. It will be difficult to upgrade in the future. Money saved by using Category 3 cabling for voice or a low-speed LAN currently in use will be lost if the system needs to be retrofitted. In the same vein, if all circuits are Category 5 compliant, then all ports can be used for voice or data, providing much more versatility for moves, adds, or changes, and making installation much easier in areas where a large concentration of data devices is essential.

There has been some confusion by what actually is meant by a *Category 5 compliant system*. With industry experts arguing about the importance of good installation practices, the confusion is increasing daily. However, by setting a performance standard that exceeds Category 5 levels and backing this with a 15-year warranty for link performance, KRONE is showing that high performance cabling systems can be installed and certified by well-trained installers with the latest test equipment and the highest quality cable and components.

The Channel is the Key

At the core of any cabling system is the horizontal channel. Figures 4–13 and 4-14 respectively show the horizontal channel models for both the U.S. standard, TIA/EIA-T568-A, and the European or International Standard, ISO/IEC 11801 [KRONE, 2-3]. The major difference between the two standards is the recommended lengths between areas within the channel, but the differences are minor, and both standards are the same in the recommended distance from the station field to the telecom outlet of 90 meters maximum.

Because the link is so important, KRONE bases its system solution and its system warranty around the link. KRONE's cabling system certifier program guarantees the performance of the installed link for 15 years.

In partnership with KRONE-approved cable companies, KRONE is able to provide an installed end-to-end solution with these benefits:

- Field verifiable to exceed current standards.
- Link bandwidth characterized up to 350 MHz.
- 15-year product warranty.
- 15-year performance warranty.
- Application independent [KRONE, 3-4].

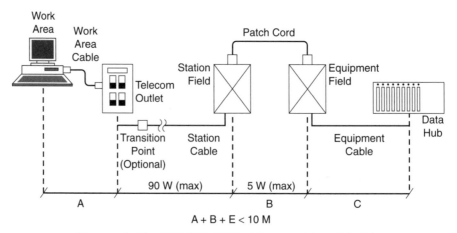

Figure 4–13: ISO/IEC 11801 Horizontal Link Model.

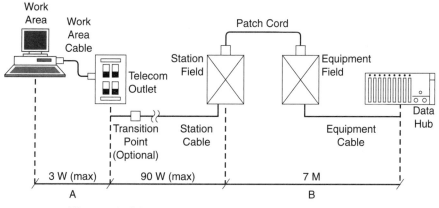

Figure 4–14: TIA/EIA-T568-A Horizontal Link Model.

KRONE can be the Backbone of any LAN Standard

Because of this strict conformance with standards, the basic KRONE system is suitable for any of the current LAN standards such as 10BaseT, 100BaseT, token ring 16, AnyLan, 100BaseVG, 3270, AS400, System 36, AppleTalk, and ISDN.

Interconnection Versus Cross-Connection

Two basic wiring schemes for the telecommunications closet are addressed in the TIA/EIA-T568-A standard, interconnection and cross-connection. Both the backbone and the horizontal cabling are terminated on connecting hardware that meets the requirements of the TIA/EIA-T568-A standard.

However, the standard prohibits the use of these terminations for moves, adds, and changes. Any connection between the backbone and horizontal cabling must be accomplished through the use of a horizontal cross-connect between the common equipment and the connecting hardware to which the horizontal cabling is terminated as shown in Figure 4–15 [KRONE, 4]. This connection may be made using an Interconnection or a cross connection cabling scheme, which provides for a direct connection between two cables with the use of patch cords or jumper wires.

A cross-connection is a cabling scheme between cabling runs, subsystems, and equipment using patch cords or jumper wires that attach to connection hardware on each end as shown in Figure 4–16 [KRONE, 5]. Common equipment which uses cables that extend an individual port may be permanently terminated or interconnected to the connecting hardware for the horizontal cabling. Direct interconnections such as this reduce the number of connections in a link, but may also reduce the flexibility.

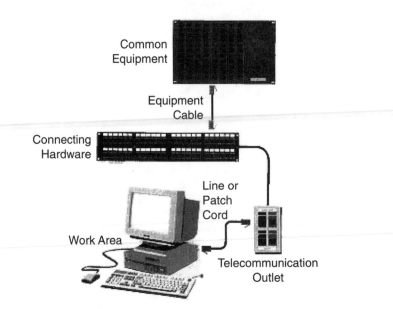

Figure 4–15: A horizontal cross-connect between the common equipment and the connecting hardware.

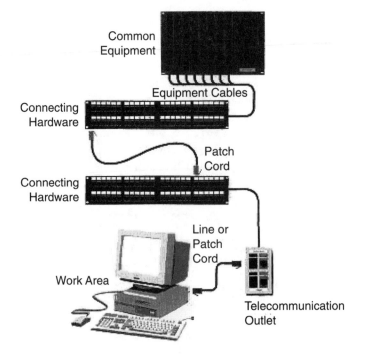

Figure 4–16: A cross-connection.

Common equipment which uses cables that consolidate several ports on a single connector (such as a 50-pin connector) must first be terminated to connecting hardware to break out the individual ports. The connecting hardware fields for the common equipment and the horizontal cabling may then be cross-connected using patch cords or jumper wires.

The DOs and DON'Ts of Common Installation Practices

A successful, high-performance premises wiring system requires more than simply purchasing the proper standards-compliant cables and hardware. Care must be taken to ensure that the components are installed properly according to industry-recognized practices. Performance specifications called out in the TIA/EIA-T568-A standard are based on the assumption that proper installation techniques and management practices have been followed. If recommended cabling precautions and installation methods are not observed, specified transmission capabilities of cabling components may not be achieved as discussed in the sidebar, "Common Installation Practices DOs and DON'Ts." Installation should be performed by trained, certified installers, such as the authorized Belden/KRONE cabling system certifiers who can provide a product and performance warranty for 15 years.

Common Installation Practices DOs and DON'Ts

If the recommended cabling precautions and installation methods are not observed, specified transmission capabilities of cabling components may not be achieved.

Do:

- Pull cables to minimize the distance of the run and eliminate large loops.
- Bundle cables in a neat, orderly fashion.
- Follow recommendations for cable bend radius. In spaces with UTP terminations, cable bend radius should not be less than four times the cable diameter for horizontal cable, and should not be less than ten times the cable diameter for multipair cable.
- Make sure that pair twists are maintained within 1/2 inch (12mm) of the termination point.

Don't:

- Exceed 110 newtons (25lb/f) of pulling forces when running cables.
- Cinch cable bundles too tightly.
- Ever bend or kink cable too sharply.
- Untwist pairs when terminating [KRONE, 5-6].

NOTE:

The information presented in the sidebar will receive expanded coverage in Chapter 18, "Standards Development." The chapter goes into great depth to discuss the TIA/EIA standard with regard to the use of cable ladders, how much cables can be bent, etc.

Structured Cabling Services

High speed networks require sophisticated cabling systems to support the increasing demands for speed and reliability. The LRS (Levi,Ray & Shoup, Inc.) network consulting practice assists organizations with their cabling system needs including:

- Hardware and Software Selection.
- Facilities Review.
- Diagnostics and Troubleshooting.
- Cabling Design and Testing.
- Professional Infrastructure Documentation [10].

Structured cabling systems support a wide variety of connections and systems. Today, many technologies, including telephony, networks, multimedia, and much more, are now carried over a single wiring system. Proper design and compliance with industry standards are two of the many issues that must be considered when initiating or rehabilitating a structured cabling system.

LRS cabling specialists provide assistance with all phases of your wiring project. Obviously, the best time to install cable is during the planning stage of a new building. addition, or remodeling project. However, LRS can assist in all projects during any phase, including renovations, remodels, and upgrades to existing equipment.

Cabling is a game of standards. Each platform required has a different set of requirements and equipment which must be in compliance. LRS consultants are trained to comply with all EIA/TIA/NEC specifications and certification criteria.

With the multitude of cable types now available, it is difficult to find a vendor well-versed in all of them. There are many types, including phone, shielded twisted pair (STP), unshielded twisted pair (UTP), coax, and optical fiber. LRS can help you select the appropriate media type for the environment required.

What can you do when your cabling system is already in place? Oftentimes you are faced with a decision to enhance, upgrade, or replace the entire system. LRS has the latest testing and certification tools required to determine the current status of your cabling infrastructure.

Cabling systems are complex vehicles for the information super highway and, as with any technology based product, problems can and do arise. Many instances of cabling failure can be resolved with minimal trouble. However, there are some cases which require sophisticated tools and techniques to fully isolate the problem. This service is just a small part of the many other diagnostic services the LRS network consulting practice offers.

Millennium Technologies of New Boston

The building industry has been all too slow to recognize the importance of modern communications cabling systems. In planning, architects have always provided for adequate electrical, plumbing, and HVAC (heating, ventilation, and air conditioning) systems. Apart from small closets designed for the telephone company, space for other cabling systems and components has all but been ignored in new construction. New construction requires forethought and planning for the inevitable computer that sits next to the telephone.

Cable Infrastructure

Building owners, architects and contractors take no responsibility for the lack of proper communications support within a new structure. After all, intent of use is not their problem. Yet today, it is almost inconceivable that any tenants would be without computer networks or computers. Intelligent buildings use cabling systems for energy management. Security-conscious owners and tenants require cabled security systems and cameras. The list of cabled devices is endless. Installation of these systems is an afterthought.

New cable installations begin just before or shortly after people move in. Over time people move out, new ones move in, and the cabling mess starts all over. If walls are torn down, contractors cut the old wiring flush with the ceiling. The other 90% of it remains in a ceiling above the hallways. If a network problem occurs and technicians can't resolve the problem, they quickly install a new cable eliminating that as the potential culprit.

The end result of continuous cabling is generally a series of unmarked outlets. In the hallways outside the offices, the suspended ceilings have a series of broken ceiling tiles damaged by careless cable installers. Above the tiles, invisible to the building occupants, a cable installer has broken through a fire wall to pull in some new cable. The careless installer failed to refill the opening with fire retardant foam. A week later, fire and smoke race through the compromised fire wall and several people die needlessly. Paradoxically, it was another well-engineered cable system that sent a signal to close a fire door not more than three feet below the compromised fire wall. It functioned as planned but could not help the hapless victims.

Of far less concern, old cable is generally abandoned in place. After all, when is the last time you heard of cable being removed from the ceiling when somebody moves? Nobody knows where the old cable goes and what it was used for. There are no records available. It's a mystery and it's far easier to install new cable. The old cable becomes a permanent fixture and part of the building architecture. Eventually, the area above the drop ceiling becomes congested. It is impossible to efficiently install any new infrastructure including electrical cable, plumbing, and HVAC.

Cable installations vary in quality and resultant performance. Unfortunately, lack of compliance to standards has caused a great deal of concern for those who have the responsibility for maintaining building infrastructure. This task normally falls on the building engineers and facility managers. The rush to get wired has created a gold rush for cable installers. The quality of low-voltage cable installations is all over the map.

The BICSI logo on the home page (http://www.bicsi.org/corpmemb.htm) identifies Millennium Technologies of New Boston as a corporate member of BICSI. The company supports BICSI and their RCDD (Registered Communications Distribution Designer) certification program. RCDD designation provides assurance that a cable installation will meet the qualifications required for technical craftsmanship, performance, safety, and many other standards. The company encourages anyone who wants to seek a career in low-voltage cable installation to obtain a coveted certification.

Companies intent on saving money sometimes exacerbate poor installation practices by selecting low bidder to an RFP (Request for Proposal). The lowest bid may not be the most qualified bid and may invite trouble. Millennium Technologies of New Boston urges buyers of cable systems to check installers' qualifications carefully. In the RFP, find out how many certified installers the cable company proposes to use on your job. Make sure that number appears in the contract along with the names of those on the job. Your project consultant should check for certifications. Certification within an installation company can run from all installers to only supervisors or a project manager. If work is closely supervised and inspected, perhaps certification at the supervisory level is adequate. In a typical two-person installation team, one person should be certified. Millennium Technologies of New Boston feels it is impossible for a project manager who holds RCDD certification to guarantee the quality of a large installation. A large installation could use several two-person teams installing cable in a large building or campus environment over a period of days, weeks, or months. A certified project manager cannot be with every installer all the time, particularly on larger projects.

In the days before divestiture, telephone company installers worked with pretty much the same type of installations daily. Installers of telephones used plain old telephone wire. There are installations still working today that are older than most of the readers of this book. The information age, the digital age, or just plain evolution of technology changed all that. It seems everything is wired. There is even a magazine called *Wired*! Cable-connected devices all have an interface specification that dictates the type of connection required for that wired device.

Typically, a television will use a coaxial cabling system. A telephone can use a Category 3 copper cable for connection to a network but a computer may require a high performance Category 5 cable. An MRI (magnetic resonance imaging) system may specify multimode fiber optic cabling. The options and configurations are almost endless depending on intended use and the environment.

If you prefer to manage a major installation internally, do so with a dedicated staff to make the project a success! A retrofit or new project of several hundred distribution points or more will require from one to three staff members. Selecting a cable installation company should be accomplished through the RFI (Request for Information) and RFP processes. Use the same due diligence you would use in selecting a software application vendor. The RFP process is an important tool to use in the selection process.

3P: Third Party Link Testing and Certification of Existing Cable for Data Applications

Link testing is still the superior way for the end user to prove the quality of his or her installation. National and international requirements have been agreed to through the standards ISO/IEC 11801 and EN 50173, which fortunately are identical with respect to link specifications.

The benefits for end users are evident. They can let the link requirements in the above standards form the contractual conditions for accepting the final installation. Using standards for acceptance testing does not depend on supplier warranties to secure transmission performance. In addition, users can have a larger extent of supplier and installer independence. And they will get the highest possible quality just by requiring an installation acceptance test. What supplier or installer would risk a re-cabling by failing a final installation testing?

Today's problem is not link requirements, which are generally clear (except maybe for the different definitions of links, basic links, horizontal links, and channels). The main obstacle has been and still is how to make a fast and reliable verification of a Class D installation (going to 100 MHz). Two different methods may be applied: measurements with laboratory equipment (network analyzers, etc.) and measurements with hand-held field testers.

Measurements with Laboratory Equipment

Link measurements with laboratory equipment may be performed accurately by the very experienced operator, but it is a slow, difficult, and impractical way to demonstrate performance. A few very tricky pitfalls exist if you are not experienced in measuring short lengths of cable, for instance with respect to impedance measurements. However, it is outside the scope of this chapter to discuss details of link testing with laboratory equipment. 3P recommends that laboratory equipment be used only to verify performance in case of disputes, to demonstrate performance on a limited statistical basis, and to verify precision of hand-held testers.

Measurements with Hand-Held Field Testers

Link measurements with hand-held testers can be performed fast by a trained operator allowing a 100% verification of all links of an installation. Testers for Class D installations have been available for approximately four years, but the quality of some early testers has been questionable, both with respect to precision and extent of testing performed. Most testers can perform verification of only some of the specified requirements. Low-quality testers may both accept bad installations and reject good installations. The first point normally makes everyone happy (maybe only until traffic on the network is later stressed or transmission rate is increased), while the second point may create a million dollar panic without reason.

Quality of testers has been continuously improved by the manufacturers and parallel work in development of a specification for hand-held testers has been completed. The resulting document, TIA telecommunications Service Bulletin TSB 67, has been agreed to and specifies two different quality levels of testers (Accuracy Level I and Accuracy Level II testers). Performance of Level II testers is the best, and some early model testers would probably have difficulties even in passing the Level I requirements.

Accurate and complete link testing with hand-held testers is a key issue for modern cabling. Therefore, 3P will evaluate the quality of commercial testers and continue to publish summarized performance data sheets on their website (http://www.3ptest.dk/). Recommendations on how to perform an installation test with a specific type of hand-held tester is found in the performance data sheet of the tester in question.

PerfectSite

PerfectSite[SM] helps define requirements that match your organization's connectivity needs. It specifies structured cabling systems that give performance and value over the structured cabling system life cycle.

Problems typically arise in an open office environment when cubicles are torn down and reconstructed. Unexpected re-cabling costs occur because of a poor up-front needs analysis of the company churn rate. By providing strategically located consolidation points and multiuser outlets, the future costs of moves, adds, and changes to your structured cabling system will be reduced over its life cycle.

Bid Creation and Evaluation

It's easy to get confused by vendors' differing terminology. That applies to contractor performance and service as well as hardware components.

When providing bid specifications, it has become a de facto standard to say, "Yes, Yes, Yes," when bidding on a poorly written Request for Proposal (RFP). Then, upon execution of the contract say, "No, No, No," on as many items as possible (and being legally right), thus increasing the value of the contract many times over the original award price.

Manufacturer Product Evaluation

There are many different manufacturers of structured cabling systems. The components are independently tested for transmission performance as required by TIA/EIA-T568-A, ISO/IEC 11801, and other standards.

In addition to the testing that already exists, PerfectSite^SM tests the functionality of the mechanical design of the components. Is the vertical management that came with your rack adequate for high-density patching? This might seem like a harmless question until you start installing a lot of patch cords and end up with a rat's nest. Or is the multiuser outlet designed for easy access, but, when installed on a surface, activates a defective hinge, making it difficult to open and causing possible future breakage?

An end user typically finds out about these problems when it is too late—after an installation. In addition to PerfectSite's testing, feedback on products is gathered from 600+ contractors who have worked with them all over the world.

System Warranty Evaluation

For peace of mind and protection of your investment, the system warranty is an excellent option. However, every manufacturer's warranty can be different and unclear. How do you know what you are getting? If a problem arises down the road, where do you go to get it corrected? Who is responsible, the certified contractor or the manufacturers?

You installed a Category 5, UTP structured cabling system last year and have recently migrated to 100BaseT, but are experiencing intermittent problems with transmission. First, you call in your firm's data consultant. After exhaustive testing (all billable), the consultant blames it on the cabling system. Second, you contact the certified cabling contractor who performed the installation. After more testing, the contractor finds out that it is a delay skew problem with the 2x2 construction of the Category 5 UTP plenum cable. Third, the certified contractor notifies the manufacturer, but finds that it is not covered under the 15-year warranty because it met the TIA/EIA-T568-A standard at the time of installation. The final result—all of the Category 5, UTP cabling must be replaced at your expense.

Service companies like PerfectSite can sift through the legalese and paperwork to try and ensure that you get the full benefits of the warranty that you paid for. The service company is a member of U.S. and international standards committees and can respond to potential problems that are presently being addressed in the standards but may take years to resolve and incorporate into existing or new standards. This insight can save clients thousands of dollars in the life cycle of their structured cabling system and provide a more comprehensive system warranty, with fewer contractual loop holes.

SYSTIMAX SCS

For UTP cabling systems such as the Lucent Technologies SYSTIMAX Structured Cabling Systems (SCS), all of the individual products certified for use are manufactured by Lucent Technologies and individually tested, as well as tested in conjunction with other products in the SYSTIMAX SCS offering. All cables, for example, are tested on the reel at the point of manufacture and are also tested as a complete cabling system within the individual applications for which they are certified. All products certified for use in SYSTIMAX SCS also carry a 15-year warranty.

SYSTIMAX SCS utilizes Lucent Technologies Bell Laboratories-developed design rules for all certified end-to-end applications. Such design rules, which are fully documented in Lucent Technologies application guidelines, cite which products may be used (for example, only Category 5 products for some higher-speed applications), how cable must be terminated and administered, and maximum distances for cable runs. All applications are also tested in Lucent Technologies Bell Laboratories test labs and are certified for a period of 15 years. Consequently, both products and systems are fully tested and warranted.

622 Mbps Warranty Guarantee

This final part of the chapter is written to provide supplemental information concerning the inclusion of 622 Mbps coverage in the SYSTIMAX SCS extended product warranty and application assurance program. Lucent Technologies will guarantee that each SYSTIMAX SCS channel comprised of end-to-end power sum products is capable of delivering 622 Mbps to the workstation. In the short term, this can be accomplished with an implementation that transmits 155 Mbps over each of the four pairs in a parallel transmission scheme using 64-point Carrierless Amplitude and Phase (64 CAP) encoding technology.

64 CAP is a bandwidth-efficient transmission scheme that sends multiple symbols simultaneously. Utilizing a two dimensional modulation constellation, 64 CAP uses a set of 8 points in each dimension, for a total of 8 x 8 or 64 points. Specialized symbol waveshaping and orthogonal modulation mean that they do not interfere with each other and can be recognized and distinguished at the receiver. The transmission rate is 25.92 M_Symbols per second. Two orthogonal symbols each carry 3 bits of information. With this, each pair supports 155 Mbps. To achieve 622 Mbps, all four pairs are used. The data stream is partitioned into four 155 Mbps channels at the transmitter. The four channels are recombined into a single data stream at the receiver.

Lucent Technologies and Bell Laboratories (formerly the research and development arm of AT&T) have been demonstrating the feasibility of delivering a 622 Mbps data stream using parallel transmission schemes over a 100-meter channel. Their evaluation, testing, and understanding of this concept, coupled with improved electrical performance, now allows Lucent to move from a laboratory experiment to a SYSTIMAX guarantee.

As future networking standards are developed and issued, other methods of delivering 622 Mbps will become available. Future LAN equipment will be tested and evaluated by Bell Laboratories for coverage under the SYSTIMAX SCS Applications Assurance Program.

Summary

This chapter covered different types of vendor and third party cabling systems (AT&T (Lucent) Systimax and Powersum; IBM Cabling System; Nortel IBDN, AMP Connect, KRONE; Mod-Tap, BCS, ITT, etc.) as well as a number of cabling system certification and warranty service companies.

End Notes

[1] Dekko Engineering , P.O. Box 2,000, Kendallville, IN 46755, 1998, p. 3.

[2] R.J. Paradine Jr., RCDD, "An Overview of SYSTIMAX® Structured Connectivity Solutions (SCS)," 200 Laurel Avenue, Middletown, NJ 07748, Lucent Technologies Inc., 600 Mountain Avenue, Murray Hill NJ 07974, U.S.A., (Copyright © 1997), p. 2.

[3] "The IBM Cabling System, " Cabletron Systems, 35 Industrial Way, Rochester, NH 03866 U.S.A, 1998, pp. 1–2.

[4] South Hills Datacomm, 760 Beechnut Drive, Pittsburgh, PA 15205, 1998, p. 1.

[5] "Residential Cabling System," MOD-TAP USA, Box 706, 285 Ayer Road, Harvard, MA 01451-0706, 1998, p. 1.

[6] "An investigation into the ability of Power Sum cables to support Radio Frequency (RF) and OC-12c ATM," ITT Cannon, Systems & Services, Jays Close, Viables Estate, Basingstoke, Hampshire, England, RG22 4BW, 1996, p. 3.

[7] "UTP vs STP: A Comparison of Cables, Systems, and Performance Carrying High-Data-Rate Signals," Lucent Technologies Inc., 600 Mountain Avenue, Murray Hill NJ 07974, U.S.A., (Copyright © 1996), pp. 6–7.

[8] Reprinted with the permission of AMP Incorporated, REGIONAL CENTER, Harrisburg, PA, USA, 1996, p. 1.

[9] "Standards-Based Structured Wiring," KRONE Asia Pacific, KRONE (Australia) Technique Pty Ltd, 2 Hereford Street, Berkeley Vale, N.S.W. 2261, Australia, 1996, p. 2.

[10] "Structured Cabling Services," Levi, Ray, & Shoup, Inc., 2401 West Monroe Street, Springfield, IL 62704, 1998, p. 1.

Part II

Designing
Cabling Systems

5

NETWORK DESIGN ISSUES

Traditionally, most computer system and network designers have developed their products with the idea in mind that they will operate on a specific type of cable using a specific type of connector. Each manufacturer has its own cable and connector standard, which is another way of saying, *There are no general or independent standards that everyone must follow*! Here are some examples:

- DEC: 3-pair UTP & Modified Modular Connectors.
- FDDI: 62.5 Micron Fiber & MIC Connector.
- IBM S/3x and AS/400: 100 Ohm Twinax & Twinax Connectors.
- IBM 3270: 93 Ohm Coax & BNC Connectors.
- IBM token ring: 150 Ohm Shielded Twisted Pair & IBM Data Connector.
- Hewlett Packard 3000: RS-232 Cable & DB Connectors.
- Ethernet: 50 Ohm Coaxial Cable & BNC or N Connectors.
- Wang: Dual 75 Ohm Coax & BNC-TNC Connectors [1].

It's easy to see from the list above that migrating from one type of computer system or network to another is very difficult in a traditionally wired cabling system. In most cases, the entire cabling system, and the investment it represents, must be abandoned. A new cabling system must be installed. The new cabling system can cost more than the networking hardware itself.

Another expense related to any traditionally wired cabling system is the cost of making moves, changes, or adds after the original installation is completed. The topology, or physical layout, of the cabling system has a lot to do with how easy it is to make changes. For example, the daisy chain or bus topology, which is used for both Thinwire Ethernet and IBM's System/3X and AS/400, does not lend itself well to change because cables either have to be moved, extended, or added whenever a new person is hired or an existing employee is moved. In a large network, this can become a full-time job in and of itself! The most common network topologies are shown later in the chapter.

The problems just previously described are common with these non-structured wiring systems. The two foremost characteristics of this type of cabling system are that it is difficult or impossible to migrate from one computer system to another without replacing the entire cabling system and, to make moves, changes, or additions, the cabling system has to be changed. In this sense, the cabling system has no real structure since it is constantly changing as user requirements change, hence the term *non-structured*.

To overcome these problems, many companies are installing structured wiring systems similar to the one shown in Figure 5–1 in which the cabling, once installed, rarely needs to be changed [Kayworth, 2]. Of the three topologies illustrated later in the chapter, the star is the most flexible, since all cable runs are brought to one central location. By pre-wiring all possible locations in a new or existing building in a star topology, all future moves, changes, and additions can be made quickly and easily by simply moving patch cables in a centralized wiring closet. Also, by simply changing the attachment cables and devices at the equipment rack and the workstation outlet, a structured cabling system can be adapted to a variety of systems and interfaces.

Components

As defined earlier, a structured cabling system is one in which the main components of the system, once installed, do not change. In its most basic form, a structured cabling system consists of horizontal wiring and appropriate connecting hardware. Before proceeding farther, let's define some of the terms used in structured cabling design as well as some of the network design issues.

Category

The EIA/TIA-T568-A standard specifies certain performance and speed characteristics for structured cabling systems. These specifications follow a *Category* system, where each category specifies a certain level of performance.

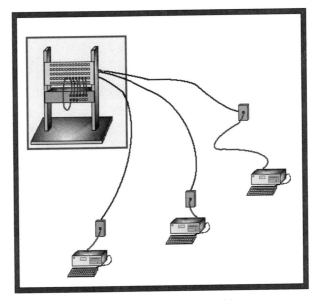

Figure 5–1: Typical structured cabling system.

The EIA/TIA-T568-A standard starts with Category 3, and goes to Category 5. Categories 1 and 2 are not officially recognized, but are generally used in the cabling industry as being useful at frequencies of 1 MHz and 4 MHz, respectively. Category 3 specifies a cable rated for frequencies up to 10 MHz, Category 4 cables are rated at up to 20 MHz, and Category 5 is rated up to 100 MHz. Nowadays, Category 3 cable is widely regarded as being a voice grade cable, and most new data installations use Category 5.

Topology

The topology is the physical layout of network components (cable, stations, systems equipment, etc.). A universal topology is where unshielded twisted-pair (UTP) cabling is used as the horizontal connection between wall plates and a distribution frame. A distribution frame serves as a concentration point and provides cross-connections between network components. When necessary, a backbone connects multiple distribution frames with file servers and other systems equipment. The backbone may be coax, optical fiber, UTP trunks, or a combination of these media. Communications systems can also be cabled to a distribution frame for cross connection.

Specific benefits are derived from this design. For example:

- A system can be easily reconfigured by simply changing cross connects at the distribution frames.

- LANs and other new applications can be added easily by bolting the equipment into the frame and connecting to the appropriate horizontal/ truck channels.
- Workstations can be moved by simply changing cross connections.
- Workstations can be added by installing patching into the expansion space provided.
- Phone lines can be cross-connected to computer LAN cabling to provide quick and easy fax/modem connections.

10BaseT Cabling Specification

The IEEE 802.3 10BaseT specification is the standard for Ethernet communications over unshielded twisted-pair (UTP) cabling. Application of this technology offers substantial advantages:

- It employs the most widely accepted standard for computer LAN connection providing the widest range of product options and future stability.
- Star topology provides clean attractive cable installations between distribution frames and wall plates. Systems can easily be relocated without termination concerns or modification of cabling.
- It eliminates daisy-chained terminals and their related problems such as cable-driven system failures.
- It has the potential for use of existing building data and voice cabling for implementation of a LAN.
- It provides the ability to integrate Ethernet into a UTP structured cabling system, including the capability to run token ring and Ethernet over the same cabling plan.
- It replaces RS232 UTP channels with Ethernet LAN service.

There are two major components in a 10BaseT communications link: a concentrator and a transceiver. The concentrator (or hub) is a multichannel device connecting multiple transceivers. It is usually located in a distribution frame in a wiring closet or other central location where it is patched to the building wiring. The concentrator interface will typically be a group of WE8W RJ45 modular jacks or a 50-position telco connector. The transceiver may be an independent device or a card in a personal computer which connects the workstation to the building wiring. Therefore, a concentrator supports multiple transceivers, each individually star-wired.

Horizontal Cabling

Horizontal cabling begins at a centrally located point called a distribution frame and ends where the user plugs a terminal in. A separate horizontal cable is run from a distribution frame to each wall plate where a computer or device might be connected to the network. Distribution frames should be located so horizontal cable length is limited to 300 feet to provide compatibility with high-speed LAN operation. When horizontal cabling is properly designed, each office interface is accessible from an appropriate distribution frame.

In other words, this is the wiring that runs from the telecommunications wiring closet to the workstation outlet. For each workstation outlet, there will be one or more cable runs back to the wiring closet, depending on how many jacks are needed at the workstation outlet.

Distribution Frames

The distribution frame is a central management point for horizontal cable runs. At this point, each cable run is punched down to a patching field. The patching field enables specific wall ports to be connected to a concentrator. Concentrators and other systems equipment in the distribution frame are connected via the backbone. Each distribution frame should be located so that the horizontal cabling length is limited to 300 feet to ensure compatibility with high-speed LAN operation. The cable run should be free of bridges, taps, and splices from the wall plate or other office interface to the cross connect product. The main distribution frame should be located in the same wiring closet or central location as the communications equipment. This enables easy cross-connection from phone lines to computer systems, as well as simplified and safe management of building wiring. Multiple distribution frames may be connected via the backbone.

Backbone Cabling

Backbone, or trunk cabling, provides the main feeder cable in a building. Backbone cabling can be either *campus style,* where it connects several buildings, or it can be run vertically between floors to connect several subdistribution frames to the main distribution frame. Each backbone segment must not exceed a cable length of 1000 feet.

In other words, this is the cabling that provides the interconnection between wiring closets and equipment rooms, whether in the same or different buildings. It includes the backbone cabling itself, as well as cross-connects, mechanical terminations, and patch cables used to provide backbone-to-backbone cross-connection.

Connecting Hardware

Connecting hardware (systems connections) is used to terminate the horizontal wiring in the wiring closet or at the workstation outlet. It exists between system equipment such as file servers, concentrators, patch bays, other devices installed in the distribution frame, and backbone cabling or trunk channels. Patch panels, used in the wiring closet, and wall plates, used at the desktop, fall into this category. The EIA/TIA-T-568A standard specifies RJ45 jacks to be used in these types of products. Patch panels provide multiple RJ45 jacks, often in multiples of twelve, and are designed to fit into standard racks or cabinets with 19-inch mounting rails. Wall plates come in a variety of types ranging from single outlet, flush mount styles to multioutlet, multimedia surface mount versions. Most connecting hardware will also accommodate other types of connectors, such as RJ11, BNC, and fiber optic, for use in telephone or non-EIA/TIA applications.

Category 5 (or 100 MHz capable) connecting hardware is routinely constructed using a circuit board design with RJ45 jacks mounted on the front and AT&T 110-type contacts mounted on the rear. The 110 contact uses insulation displacement technology to terminate the horizontal wiring to the RJ45 jack. Although the AT&T 110 contact is the most popular method of terminating the horizontal wiring to the jack, other types, such as the KRONE and 66 contact, are also used by some manufacturers.

Patch Cables

Patch cables are used to make the physical connection between the connecting hardware and the network or telecommunications equipment. At the wiring closet, patch cables are used to facilitate fast and easy moves, changes, or additions to the network. At the desktop, they make the connection to user equipment such as network interface cards.

It is debatable whether patch cables can be considered a part of the structured wiring system. By definition, they are not, because their use changes as the needs of the network users change, but they are so well-defined by the ANSI/TIA/EIA-T568-A standard that it is an easy intellectual jump to include them in any discussion of structured wiring.

Installation Planning and Practices

It has been said that a chain is only as strong as its weakest link. Similarly, a structured wiring system is only as fast as its slowest component. When planning and installing your wiring system, pay particular attention to the components you choose. It does no good, for example, to install the highest quality Category 5 cabling and connecting hardware and then use Category 3 patch cables. At best, your structured wiring system will provide you with Category 3 performance. Installing higher performance products may cost a bit more up front, but not so much as replacing components later. Pinching pennies makes short-term sense, but the long-term flexibility of your wiring system will be limited, and you could spend more upgrading to a Category 5 cabling system than you would have installing it in the first place.

Figure 5–2 illustrates the way in which the various components mentioned previously are connected together to create a structured wiring system [Kayworth, 4]. Keeping in mind that every connection you make is a point of weakness, plan your installation with as few connections as possible between the wallplate and patch panel. With the right products and careful planning, your structured wiring installation will be a great success.

Topology

There are two types of topology, physical and logical. The physical topology of a network refers to the configuration of cables, computers, and other peripherals. Logical topology is the method used to pass the information between workstations. Issues involving logical topologies are beyond the scope of this chapter.

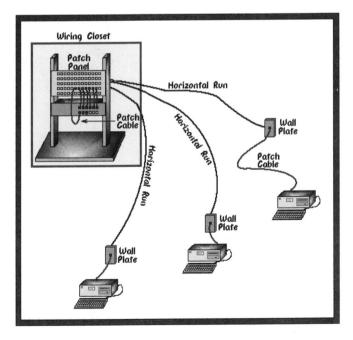

Figure 5–2: Structured cabling system.

Main Types of Physical Topologies

This part of the chapter discusses the physical topologies used in network design and other related topics or issues:

- Linear Bus.
- Star.
- Star-Wired Ring.
- Tree.

Linear Bus

The linear (shared multi-drop bus) topology is the traditional topology that most people think of when a computer bus is mentioned. VME, Ethernet and 1553 are all popular examples of this topology. Because a linear bus is inherently fault intolerant (any node can take the bus down and prevent communication by other nodes), military mission-critical computers using this topology usually implement it in a redundant format.

Basically, a linear bus topology consists of a main run of cable with a terminator at each end as shown in Figure 5–3. All nodes (file server, workstations, and peripherals) are connected to the linear cable. Ethernet and LocalTalk networks use a linear-hierarchical bus topology as shown in Table 5–1.

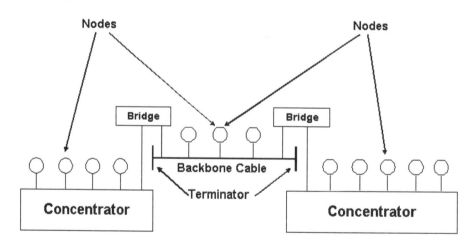

Figure 5–3: Linear Bus/Hierarchical topology.

Table 5–1: Comparison Chart.

Topology	Type Of Cable	Type Of Protocol
Linear Hierarchical Bus	Coaxial	Ethernet
	Twisted Pair	Fast Ethernet
	Fiber Optic	LocalTalk
Star	Twisted Pair	Ethernet
	Fiber Optic	Fast Ethernet
		LocalTalk
Star-Wired Ring	Twisted Pair	token ring
Tree	Coaxial	Ethernet
	Twisted Pair	Fast Ethernet
	Fiber Optic	

Advantages and Disadvantages of Linear Bus Topology

Some of the advantages of linear bus topology are that it's easy to connect a computer or peripheral to a linear bus and it requires less cable length than a star topology. The sidebar, "Choosing A Topology," expands further on the benefits. Nevertheless, the disadvantages of linear bus topology are that the entire network shuts down if there is a break in the main cable, terminators are required at both ends of the backbone cable, it is difficult to identify the problem if the entire network shuts down, and they are not meant to be used as a stand-alone solution in a large building.

Another disadvantage of this topology is that the physical constraints of the shared medium limit the number of nodes that can be attached. Futurebus+ and PI-bus, for example, have each a maximum limit of 32 nodes. To connect additional nodes, it is necessary to build a hierarchical topology, as illustrated in the Figure 5–3. Here a bridge node connects one physical linear bus to another, allowing nodes on one bus to communicate with nodes on another bus. More complex tree topologies can be created by adding bridges and buses as needed.

Choosing a Topology

The following are some of the considerations in choosing a topolgy:

Expenses:
 • The least expensive way to install a network is via a linear bus network. Concentrators do not have to be purchased.

Required Cable Length:

- Shorter cable lengths are used by the linear bus network.

Future growth potential:

- Expanding a network is easily done by adding another concentrator when using a star topology.

Type of cable:

- Unshielded twisted pair (UTP) is the most common cable in schools. It is most often used with star topologies.

Star

A star topology is designed with each node (file server, workstations, and peripherals) connected directly to a central network hub or concentrator as shown in Figure 5–4. Data on a star network passes through the hub or concentrator before continuing to its destination. The hub or concentrator manages and controls all functions of the network. It also acts as a repeater for the data flow. This configuration is common with twisted pair cable; however, it can also be used with coaxial cable or fiber optic cable as shown in Table 5–1.

The protocols used with star configurations are usually Ethernet or LocalTalk. Token ring uses a similar topology, called the star-wired ring.

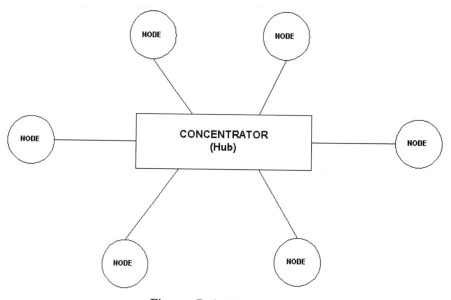

Figure 5–4: Star topology.

Advantages and Disadvantages of Star Topology

The advantages of star topology are that it is easy to install and wire, there are no disruptions to the network when connecting or removing devices, and it is easy to detect faults and to remove parts. The disadvantages of a star topology are that it requires more cable length than a linear topology, that attached nodes are disabled if the hub or concentrator fails, and it is more expensive than linear bus topologies because of the cost of the concentrators.

Star-Wired Ring

A star-wired ring topology may appear (externally) to be the same as a star topology. Internally, the MAU (multistation access unit) of a star-wired ring contains wiring that allows information to pass from one device to another in a circle or ring as shown in Figure 5–5. The token ring protocol uses a star-wired ring topology as shown in Table 5–1.

Tree

A tree topology combines characteristics of linear bus and star topologies. It consists of groups of star-configured workstations connected to a linear bus back-bone cable as shown in Figure 5–6. Tree topologies allow for the expansion of an existing network, and enable users to configure a network to meet their needs.

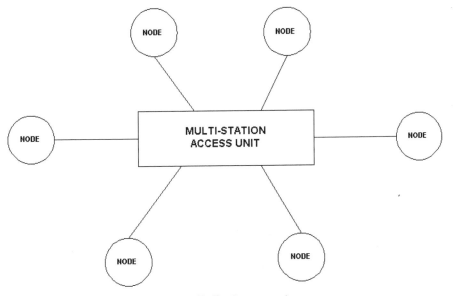

Figure 5–5: Star-wired ring.

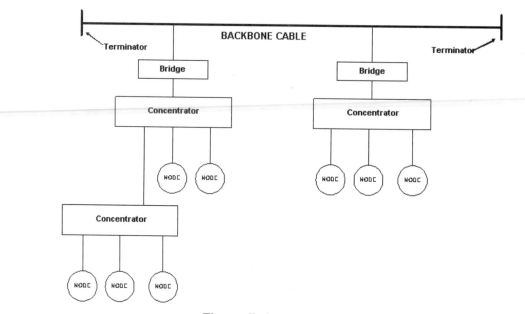

Figure 5–6: Tree topology.

Advantages and Disadvantages of Tree Topology

The advantages of tree topology are that they allow point-to-point wiring for individual segments and they are supported by several hardware and software venders. The disadvantages are that the overall length of each segment is limited by the type of cabling used, the entire segment goes down if the backbone line breaks and it is more difficult to configure and wire than other topologies.

5-4-3 Rule

A consideration in setting up a tree topology using Ethernet protocol is the 5-4-3 rule. One aspect of the Ethernet protocol requires that a signal sent out on the network cable reach every part of the network within a specified length of time. Each concentrator or repeater that a signal goes through adds a small amount of time. This leads to the rule that between any two nodes on the network there can only be a maximum of 5 segments, connected through 4 repeaters/concentrators. In addition, only 3 of the segments may be populated (trunk) segments if they are made of coaxial cable. A populated segment is one which has one or more nodes attached to it . In Figure 5–6, the 5-4-3 rule is adhered to. The furthest two nodes on the network have 4 segments and 3 repeaters/concentrators between them. This rule does not apply to other network protocols or Ethernet networks where all fiber optic cabling is used.

10BaseT Cabling Specification

Ethernet was originally designed to operate over a heavy coaxial cable and was later updated to also support a thinner, lighter, coaxial cable type. Both systems provided a network with excellent performance, but they used a bus topology which made changing the network a difficult proposition, and also left much to be desired in regard to reliability. Also, many buildings were already wired with twisted-pair wire which could support high-speed networks. Installing a coaxial-based Ethernet into these buildings would mean they would have to be rewired. Therefore, a new network type known as 10BaseT was introduced to increase reliability and allow the use of existing twisted-pair cable.

Topology and Cabling

10BaseT utilizes Category 3 (or higher) unshielded twisted-pair (UTP) cable in a star topology. Each node on the network has its own cable run back to a common hub, and each of these cable runs may be up to 100 meters (330 feet) in length. Figure 5–7 shows a simple 10BaseT network [2].

10BaseT can also be wired in a tree topology, where one main hub is connected to other hubs, which are in turn connected to workstations. It is also possible to combine 10BaseT with any combination of the other 10 Mbps Ethernet technologies in an infinite number of ways to meet nearly any requirement. Figure 5–8 shows a combination of 10BaseT and 10Base2 [Mazza, 2].

NOTE:

The depth of a 10BaseT tree network is limited to one layer below the main hub.

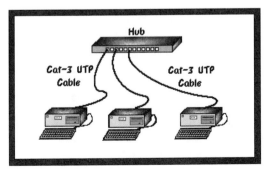

Figure 5–7: 10BaseT network.

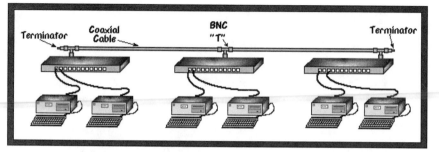

Figure 5–8: 10BaseT and thin Ethernet combination.

Advantages and Disadvantages

10BaseT has various advantages and disadvantages which make it suitable for some applications and less suitable for others. Some of them are listed below.

Advantages

Since each node on a 10BaseT network has its own cable connecting it to a central hub, it is far less likely that any node can cause the entire network to fail. The hub also has a partitioning function built into it which allows it to detect a problem on any of its ports. If a problem is found, the node is disconnected from the rest of the network. This isolates the problem until the node can be troubleshot and repaired.

Because of the partitioning function built in to the hubs and the star-wired topology, it is generally easy to troubleshoot a 10BaseT network. In a worst-case scenario, one can be troubleshot by simply disconnecting nodes from the hub one at a time until the network recovers. Usually, the hub will give an indication as to which node is causing a problem, allowing the technician to troubleshoot that node as opposed to spending many hours finding where the problem is.

Disconnecting a node from the network has no effect whatsoever on the rest of the network. Therefore, moving an attached device is simply a matter of unplugging it from the hub and reconnecting it somewhere else.

Many buildings are already wired with UTP cable which can support a 10BaseT network. Even in the event a building is not wired with UTP already, it is still preferable to install UTP than any other type of cable, as UTP will support other applications later, whereas other cable types will generally be specific to one network type. This allows leveraging the UTP cable investment for other applications many years later.

Disadvantages

10BaseT only allows distances from the hub to the node of 100 meters (330 feet). In some installations, this can be a major problem if nodes need to be located farther away.

Sensitive to Noise

The nature of UTP cable makes it considerably more sensitive to electrical noise than coaxial cable. Generally, this rules 10BaseT out as an option for installations in factory floor environments or other locations with a high ambient noise level.

Cabling Considerations

10BaseT uses two pairs of wires: one pair for transmission and the second pair to receive. The physical connector used is an 8-position modular plug, commonly referred to as an RJ45. All cables must be rated at a minimum of Category 3, and must be wired such that pins 1 and 2 are on one twisted pair and pins 3 and 6 are on a second pair. Common wiring standards which meet this requirement are EIA/TIA T568-A and T568-B.

There are two pinouts used: MDI for DTE devices (such as computers, printers, etc.) and MDI-X (hubs). Connecting an MDI port to an MDI-X port requires a straight through cable, and connecting either MDI to MDI or MDI-X to MDI-X requires a crossover cable. Pinouts of the MDI and MDI-X interfaces are shown in Table 5–2 [Mazza, 3].

Table 5–2: 10BaseT Pinouts.

MDI PINOUT	
Pin	**Signal**
1	T+
2	T-
3	R+
6	R-

MDI-X PINOUT	
Pin	**Signal**
1	R+
2	R-
3	T+
6	T-

There are several applications for crossover cables in 10BaseT networks. The most common reason is to cascade hubs together in a tree topology. If both hubs have only MDI-X ports then a crossover cable is needed. Another application for a crossover cable is to connect two DTE devices together without a hub. A standard 10BaseT crossover cable wiring diagram is shown in Table 5–3.

Table 5–3: Crossover Cable Pinout.

	10BaseT Crossover Cable	
SIDE 1	**WIRE COLOR**	**SIDE 2**
1	White/Orange	3
2	Orange/White	6
3	White/Blue	1
6	Blue/White	2

Horizontal Cabling

The cable used for horizontal wiring is constructed of four unshielded twisted pairs under one jacket and comes in two types, PVC and plenum. Both types of cable perform the same electrically; however, local and national building codes require the use of plenum cable when the cable is being run above certain types of dropped ceilings. If you are in doubt as to the type of cable you should install, check with your installer or local electrical inspector before pulling any cable. Pulling the wrong kind of cable can cost you dearly in time and materials.

When planning your installation, it's important to know where each workstation will be located in relation to the wiring closet. You must plan your installation so that the length of each run of horizontal wiring does not exceed 90 meters (295 feet). Keep in mind that we're talking about actual cable length, not the physical distance between the wiring closet and the workstation outlet. If any single horizontal wiring run is greater than the 90-meter limitation, there are products available that will allow you to exceed that distance; however, if you find that a large number of workstations will be located beyond the 90-meter limit, you should plan for more than one wiring closet. The two wiring closets can be connected together with either a copper or fiber backbone cable.

Often, it's not possible for horizontal cable runs behind walls to reach all the way to workstation outlets without crossing open floors. This is particularly true in open office settings using modular furniture clusters. To accommodate such situations, it is permissible for a horizontal cabling run to include one transition point where the round UTP cable connects to flat undercarpet cable. Category 5 undercarpet cable typically consists of four unshielded twisted pairs in a flat PVC jacket. When using it, you should use carpet squares rather than regular carpet in that area to allow access to the cabling later.

While you're still in the planning stage, consider your requirements for telephones or additional data jacks. It's more cost effective to install all of your cabling at one time rather incrementally. It is also a lot less disruptive if you're doing an installation in a working office.

When it comes time to actually install your cabling, here are some guidelines to follow that will help you avoid problems:

First of all, many networks that run on UTP cable use only two of the four pairs of wires available in the cable. It can be tempting to try to save a little money by pulling only one 4-pair cable and using the first two pairs for data and the second two pairs for telephone or additional data. While this may work in some instances, there exists a strong potential for problems caused by crosstalk between the two types of systems. To avoid problems of this kind, you should never run more than one type of data (token ring and 10BaseT) or data and telephone in the same cable. The rule of thumb is: if the pairs are under the same jacket, use them for only one system or type of data. If you're really trying to save money and want to pull only one cable, you can use a *Siamese* four-pair cable which consists of two two-pair cables in separate jackets physically fused together in a fashion similar to a lamp cord. Each two-pair cable meets the Category 5 electrical specification. Since each of the two-pair cables is under its own jacket, it is permissible to use one side for data and the other side for telephone or an additional data circuit, without the fear of crosstalk between the systems. The only caveat is that with just two pairs to work with, you will only be able to wire your data jack partially. This will limit you to wiring your system for specific applications, such as token ring or 10BaseT, but not both, thus defeating the universal nature of a structured cabling system. In addition, some network standards, such as 100VG-AnyLAN and 100BaseT4, require the use of all four pairs, which would not be available for use.

Second, UTP cabling is relatively immune to outside sources of interference that can corrupt data, but it's always good practice when routing your cables through walls and ceilings to keep them as far away as possible from sources of electromagnetic interference (EMI) and radio frequency interference (RFI). Likely sources of EMI/RFI include fluorescent lights, electric panels, and light dimmers. Electric motors, such as those found in air handlers and elevator rooms can also generate high levels of interference. Also, never run your data cables in the same conduit as electrical wiring. Not only is this a dangerous practice, but it's nearly guaranteed to result in high levels of EMI/RFI and lost data. When using undercarpet cabling, try to keep the undercarpet cable at least 6" away from any undercarpet electrical power circuits.

Third, pulling a cable with too much force (over 25 pounds) or bending it too sharply can change the electrical characteristics of the cable and degrade its performance, so care must be taken during the installation process to prevent any undue stress on the cable. The cable should move freely at all times and be protected from sharp edges while it is being pulled. When pulling around tight or multiple corners, you should generally pull the cable at the first bend, then the second, and so on until reaching the far end of the run. Do not attempt to install cable around multiple tight bends in one pull.

Finally, you will do yourself a big favor if you take a few extra minutes to mark both ends of each cable run with a wire marker of some kind. Taking a little time now will save you lots of time later when you don't have to hunt for which cable goes where.

Backbone Cabling

As previously discussed, the 90-meter limitation on horizontal cabling runs often necessitates the use of multiple wiring closets to serve users spread out over large facilities. A means for interconnecting wiring closets and equipment rooms, backbone cabling should use a tree topology, with each horizontal cross-connect in a wiring closet cabled back to one main cross-connect in a central equipment room, as illustrated in Figure 5–9 [Kayworth, 6]. If needed, there can be one intermediate cross-connect between horizontal cross-connects and the main cross-connect, but under no circumstances should there be more than three levels of cross-connects (main, intermediate and horizontal).

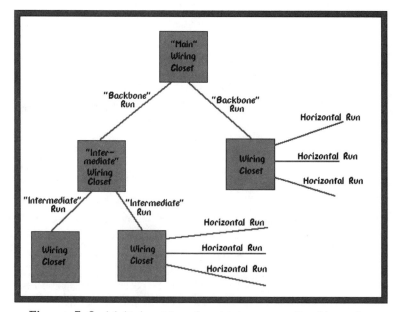

Figure 5–9: Multiple wiring closet interconnection hierarchy.

Multiple Wiring Closets with Backbone Connection

The backbone cabling media itself can be 100 ohm UTP, 150 ohm STP-A, 62.5/125 micron fiber optic cable, singlemode fiber optic cable, or any combination thereof. The cross-connect devices located in the wiring closets may be patch panels or 110-type connecting blocks. Patch panels are discussed in more detail below.

Connecting Hardware

The connecting hardware you choose will depend on the size of your network, the flexibility you will need, and the way in which you want to organize and manage your structured cabling installation. Connecting hardware components generally fall into two categories, either fixed or modular in design. Fixed components have a set number of RJ45 ports and cannot be reconfigured for other applications (telephone). Modular components can be configured and reconfigured for a variety of applications and can often be color-coded to help identify multiple systems running over the same structured cabling system.

For small, single system installations with few moves, additions, or changes, fixed type components are usually adequate. If, however, the structured cabling system is intended to support multiple networks plus telephones, a more flexible approach should be considered. In today's corporate computing environment, it's not uncommon to see token ring, 10BaseT, and IBM midrange being used under one roof. Having one wiring system that supports all of these, plus being able to color-code patch panel and wall plate jacks by system, is an advantage when moving or adding people, and for troubleshooting, it's invaluable!

Connecting hardware components that use the modular approach lets you create virtually any type of wall plate or patch panel. You don't have to settle for stock configurations anymore.

At the same time you are deciding what type of patch panels to purchase, consider how you are going to mount them. If ease of access is important, open distribution racks are a good choice. If, however, your concern is for security, a locking cabinet maybe preferable. Cabinets with clear plexiglass front doors allow you to view indicator lights that may be present on network concentrators or other equipment while still maintaining system security. For heat dissipation, cooling fans can be installed in most cabinets.

Smaller installations or ones with limited floor space can benefit from using wall mount distribution racks. These types of racks provide easy access for cabling to the back of the patch panels and take up no floor space.

Before purchasing any connecting hardware, it's vitally important to decide which wiring standard you are going to follow. The wiring standard designates which color wire from the horizontal wiring connects to which pin on the RJ45 modular jack. The preferred EIA/TIA wiring standard is known as T568-A. An alternate wiring standard, known as T568-B, conforms to the old AT&T 258A wiring standard and is the more commonly used standard in the U.S. Availability of products for both standards is good but will be somewhat better for T568-B. The proper wiring for each standard shown in Figure 5–10 and Table 5–4 illustrate T568-A; and, Figure 5–11 and Table 5–5 illustrate T568-B [Kayworth, 8-10].

NOTE:

The only difference between these standards is that the position of pairs 2 and 3 (pins) on the RJ45 jack is reversed.

Table 5–4: EIA/TIA-T568-A color code.

EIA/TIA-T568-A Standard	
Pin	Color
1	White/Green
2	Green/White
3	White/Orange
4	Blue/White
5	White/Blue
6	Orange/White
7	White/Brown
8	Brown/White

Table 5–5: EIA/TIA-T568-A color code.

EIA/TIA-T568-B Standard	
Pin	Color
1	White/Orange
2	Orange/White
3	White/Green
4	Blue/White
5	White/Blue
6	Green/White
7	White/Brown
8	Brown/White

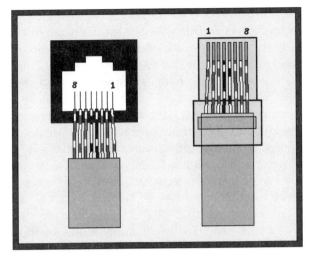

Figure 5–10: EIA/TIA-T568-A Wiring Standard.

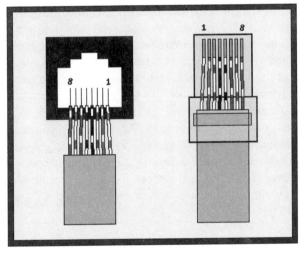

Figure 5–11: EIA/TIA-T568-B Wiring Standard.

Care must be taken when terminating the horizontal wiring at the connecting hardware so as to maintain the highest level of performance possible. The first step you can take to accomplish this is to use the proper terminating tool.

As mentioned earlier, the AT&T 110 contact is most commonly used to connect the wires from the horizontal cable to the connecting hardware. These contacts pierce the insulation to make contact with the wire underneath. Never try to use screwdrivers, pliers or cutters to push the wires into the 110 contact. This might work in an emergency but won't result in good, long-term connections. To get consistently reliable terminations, you must use what is called a 110 punch down tool. It is recommended that you use a tool that terminates only one wire at a time. There are tools that will terminate four pairs of wire simultaneously, but the termination quality is questionable, and they tend to put undue strain on connecting hardware that is based on a circuit board design.

The 110 contacts are normally color-coded, making it easy to connect the right color wire to the right spot on the modular jack. The color code on the jack will correspond to either T568-A or T568-B, depending on the wiring standard you have chosen. To terminate the wire, you simply lay it in the appropriate color coded slot and use the 110 tool to punch the wire down. Be sure to trim off any excess wire that is left after you have punched down the wire. Better quality punch-down tools will automatically do this for you. If yours does not, you will have to do it manually.

A typical 4-pair cable is shown in Figures 5–10 and 5–11. One important point to notice is that each pair is twisted. This twisting is very important to maintaining the electrical and performance specifications of the cable. To ensure peak performance, you *must* maintain the pair twisting to within one half inch or less of the point of termination on the connecting hardware. Any untwisting of the pairs greater than this length will adversely affect the performance of the cable and can reduce its ability to transmit data at a Category 5 level.

This one point may seem trivial but can cause major problems if not considered. You should use the same wiring standard, either T568-A or T568-B, throughout your structured wiring system. For example, if you use T568-B wall plates, you should also use T568-B patch panels and patch cables everywhere. Not doing this can cost you a lot of wasted time trying to troubleshoot non-existent cabling problems, when in fact the only problem that exists is a wiring standard mismatch between various components of your wiring system.

Patch Cables

The quality and performance of the patch cables you use for connecting to your patch panels and wall plates should not be minimized. They are as important as any other component in your structured cabling system.

By their very nature, patch cables are intended to be moved and flexed. For this reason, patch cables should be made from cable with stranded conductors, which offer a much greater flex life and are better suited for this application than solid conductors.

It was mentioned earlier that some patch panels and wall plates can be color-coded to help differentiate between various systems running on the same cabling system. Colored patch cables are available and can be used to color coordinate with color-coded patch panels and wall plates to make identification of various systems extremely fast and easy. For example, you might want to use blue patch cables for token ring and red patch cables for 10BaseT.

When planning your installation, you must take into account the length of the patch cables. As stated earlier, the maximum horizontal cable run cannot exceed 90 meters (285 feet). In addition, the EIA/TIA-T568 standard allows for a maximum patch cable length of 6 meters (20 feet) in the wiring closet and 3 meters (10 feet) at the workstation outlet. If either of these lengths is exceeded, the main horizontal cable run must be reduced by the excess amount, so as not to exceed an overall length of 100 meters, including both horizontal cabling and patch cables. Another decision you will need to make concerning patch cables is whether to purchase them pre-assembled or to build them yourself. On the surface, building your own may seem like a way to save money, but of all the components in a structured wiring system, patch cables are probably the most difficult and time-consuming to assemble.

To assemble your own patch cables you will need three things: the proper cable, the proper connectors and the proper crimp tool. The cable you choose must meet all of the mechanical, electrical, and performance specifications of Category 5 cable. In addition, you should choose the cable type and color based on the previous discussion.

Modular plugs are available for both solid and stranded conductors. It is recommended that you use plugs made for solid wire regardless of what type of cable you are using. It has been determined that, long term, this type of connector makes a more reliable contact with the wire.

The crimp tool you use should be a ratchet type tool or some other type that gives a repeatable crimp performance. Inexpensive tools that rely on the user's physical strength to determine the amount of crimp pressure applied to the RJ45 plug do not give consistent crimping results. With these types of tools, the quality of the crimp will vary from person to person and even from crimp to crimp. Ratchet type tools, on the other hand, will not release until the minimum acceptable crimp pressure has been applied. The only strength criteria a person needs to meet is that he or she can apply enough force to put the tool through the full crimp cycle.

You must also verify that the tool will crimp the connectors you are using. Even though all connectors are compatible once terminated on the cable, the way the tool terminates them may be different. Problems can arise when you use one manufacturer's tool to crimp another manufacturer's connector.

Although this is not always a problem, it is a safer bet to stay with one manufacturer for both the connectors and the tool.

When terminating the connector, you must maintain the pair twisting to within on half inch or less of the terminating point, just as you did when connecting your horizontal cable runs to the patch panels and wallplates. Ignoring this rule will degrade your overall system performance.

In contrast to building your own, purchasing pre-assembled patch cables takes one less worry out of your installation process. Most pre-assembled cables are crimped with air or electric presses, so the crimps are extremely consistent, resulting in a highly reliable termination. In addition, most manufacturers of pre-assembled patch cables have implemented quality assurance programs which ensure you top quality and top performance.

Application Testing and Network Certification Design Issues

Once you've completed your installation, you should spend some time testing each of your cable runs to ensure that they meet or exceed the electrical performance specifications for the intended application. The EIA/TIA provides guidelines for field testing of installed UTP channels for Category 5 compliance in TSB 67. For testing purposes, a UTP channel is defined as one entire cable run. This includes the workstation outlet—a transition point from under-carpet cable to round cable if applicable, the horizontal cable run of up to 90 meters, the horizontal cross-connect consisting of two patch panels or connecting blocks, and up to 10 meters of patch cables.

Hand-held field testers, or *cable scanners* as they are often called, are capable of measuring channel parameters such as attenuation and near-end crosstalk (NEXT). A cable scanner may also include a built-in time domain reflectometer, or TDR, that can determine the total channel length or pinpoint where on the channel a problem, such as a cable short or open, is located. Most testers can also provide a hard copy record of the measurements taken for each channel. When used properly, a cable scanner can be a valuable troubleshooting and diagnostic tool. It can also be used for documentation and acceptance of a cabling system for a specific network application.

If you are considering purchasing such a cable tester, be sure to choose a model that meets the guidelines for testing provided in TIA/EIA TSB 67. And always remember, your best guarantee of ending up with a compliant cabling system is to be certain that all components in the channel are Category 5 compliant and are installed according to ANSI/TIA/EIA-T568-A standards.

If you don't want to invest in test equipment of your own, there are independent companies that specialize in testing and certifying structured wiring systems for specific network applications. Also, firms that specialize in the installation of structured wiring systems usually have the equipment and know-how to properly test your cabling system. If you do hire an outside company to perform your testing, be sure to get hard copies of the test results for each channel and save them for future reference. Original test results can be a valuable point of reference when troubleshooting a network problem. With test results in hand, you can show that a particular UTP channel was good on a given date. You can then look at what changes have occurred since then to try to narrow down where a problem might exist.

For further information on testing and design issues, see Chapter 15, "Testing Techniques." This chapter includes practical tips on how to get the test done, how to interpret results, how to maintain documentation on test results, when to retest, and how to include requirements for test in contracts.

Network Design Documentation Issues

One of the worst things you can do is install an exemplary structured cabling system and then not label and identify where each wall plate and patch panel jack goes. That would almost be like returning a book to the wrong section of the library. It's as good as lost!

Each wall plate jack should be marked with a unique identifier that corresponds to a jack on a patch panel in the wiring closet. Once this is done, it's a simple matter to make moves, changes, or additions, since finding various locations throughout the building is as easy as comparing the identifiers on the wall plate and patch panel. Troubleshooting is also made easier when you know where to look. For more information concerning standards for documentation, you should refer to ANSI/EIA/TIA-606.

For more information about managing documentation beyond ANSI/EIA/TIA-606, see Chapter 18, "Standards Development." This chapter describes how to store drawings, where to store them, how to index them, how to update them, etc.

Network Design Standards and Technology Issues

In the time since the Category 5 standard was defined, many companies have introduced cabling products purported to be tested at speeds far exceeding the 100 MHz limit specified for Category 5. The benefits of using this type of cable in lieu of standard Category 5 cable may be hard to determine. There is no standard yet written or approved that addresses testing of cabling products at these higher speeds. The only claim that can really be made is that these types of cables exceed the electrical performance specifications of standard Category 5 cable by some variable factor. Does this mean that all the claims made for these enhanced Category 5 cables are nothing more than hype? Not necessarily.

Although it's not something we all like to think about, the reality is that not all installation jobs are perfect, so, if for no other benefit, these types of cables can provide a fudge factor to help overcome any marginal UTP channels. More to the point, however, is the fact that, while 100 Mbps networks are becoming commonplace, networks running at even higher speeds are anticipated. In order to be able to keep pace with changing technologies, installing the best cabling available can be economically prudent when compared to replacing a cabling system in the future. For information on Category 6 network design standards and technology issues, see Chapter 18.

From Here

This chapter was written with the goal of giving an overview of network design issues and how they can help you design and install a better cabling system. In addition, there was a discussion about various Category 5 structured wiring components and how they all fit together. Additional information regarding installations with multiple wiring closets, fiber optics, shielded twisted pair (STP) cable, plus much more can be found later in the book in Chapter 16, "Installation." Refer to the Appendices of this book for information on obtaining your own copies of these standards. The next chapter discusses the cost justification issues to consider during the design phase of your cabling system.

End Notes

[1] Stephen Kayworth, "Structured Cabling Systems," South Hills Datacomm, 760 Beechnut Drive, Pittsburgh, PA 15205, 1998, p. 1.
[2] John Mazza, "10BaseT," South Hills Datacomm, 760 Beechnut Drive, Pittsburgh, PA 15205, 1998, p. 1.

6

Cost Justification and Consideration

How do you justify buying a globe when the world still looks flat? What are the financial considerations?

When it comes to designing a high-speed network, there are many lower-cost alternatives; thus, when you present budget figures for the cabling system equipment to your managers, they will scream at the price. And when the noise ends, you will have some convincing to do.

Frankly, there isn't much hope that can be offered to most of you. The benefit that really sets most cabling systems apart—dedicated bandwidth—simply isn't there yet, thanks to a lack of applications support.

Dedicated bandwidth, which guarantees applications a predetermined slice of bandwidth and hence consistency of service, isn't available in shared-bandwidth infrastructures. Cabling systems using an ATM (Asynchronous Transfer Mode) connection can do it; however, it requires the widespread development and use of applications that have been designed to take advantage of it. Also, universal deployment, which offers the potential of an end-to-end solution from desktop to local segment to backbone to WAN, isn't feasible. Locally, too much money and upheaval is required.

Still, for those who can technologically justify it now, a few hints are offered here on how to get money set aside for cabling system expenditures. In fact, there are two approaches that may help you get your cabling system budget approved: the Foundation of the Near Future angle and the Derivative Benefit approach. But first, let's do a reality check.

Do Not Abandon Hope

Before you can convince anyone you need a cabling system, be certain of it yourself. Take a hard look at your network. Do you really need those benefits that only a cabling system can deliver? As previously mentioned, speed alone can be delivered in many different ways.

However, if you have a network that must run several critical processes simultaneously, a cabling system may be the only way to run these successfully over the same infrastructure. If slow, wide-area transmission is strangling your network, a well-designed cabling system's potential for providing heretofore unheard of bandwidth may eventually save your corporate life. Furthermore, if you spend an inordinate amount of time eliminating finger pointing and coordinating a host of different technologies and their vendors to keep your WAN afloat, the promise of end-to-end cabling system is very inviting, even in the misty distance.

If you are certain that the cabling system is truly relevant to your network, the preceding images are the ones you must share with your budget-approval authorities. Everyone who has so much as glanced at a business or networking publication in the past six years has heard of copper, fiber, and wireless cabling systems. This means your budget authorities are probably somewhat familiar with cabling systems. To persuade them to let you buy this technology right now, you'll have to adopt evangelical enthusiasm—and, to some extent, hyperbole. Make sure they also know that whatever type of cabling system technology they end up choosing, that it is sound technology in both theory and implementation, even if the latter is slow in coming. Also, make sure it offers things like dedicated bandwidth that shared technologies simply can't. Therefore, when justifying your budget proposal, you should design your cabling system in such a way as to get a jump on the technology that will be the premiere network infrastructure within three years.

It's important to stress that your network will require the latest type of cabling system in less than three years. The shortest depreciation schedule for cabling equipment is three years. Therefore, let's suppose you need to replace the switch in intermediate distribution frame A (IDFA) this year. If you know that before 2001 this switch in IDFA will need to be ATM, you should purchase an ATM switch this year. That's because if you purchase, say, a 100BaseT switch this year and it becomes obsolete and must be replaced before 2001, your company will take a capital loss. Therefore, you may be able to convince budget-approval authorities that purchasing any other high-speed switch for IDFA this year would soon result in a capital loss.

When selling your cabling system-expenditure proposals, don't forget to emphasize the *future-proofing* aspects of this technology. Most types of cabling systems (whether they be copper, fiber, or wireless) are very scalable, and for companies that have been replacing Category 3 cable with Category 5 cable while migrating from 10 Mbps technology to 20 Mbps and 100 Mbps speeds, this could be music to their ears.

Furthermore, don't forget to mention to your budget authority that you can *go a little bit here and there with the cabling system*. Part of the scalability of a well-designed cabling system (now that several vendors have LAN Emulation (LANE) working reasonably well) is that it can be integrated in phases.

Deriving Benefits

The Derivative Benefit approach was made popular by NASA when defending the space program. It states that new technology in your network will bring a host of derivative benefits on which you can now only speculate. What you can do is give your budget committee starting points from which to dream.

For example, draw the following scenario for your controller. Suppose the chairman has told the controller to pull a snapshot financial statement for the company immediately. Unfortunately, it's 8 p.m. and the end-of-day backup has begun, so the network is running like molasses. With ordinary shared protocols, it could take hours to prepare the report—with many time-outs and lost connections. The controller could be there until dawn.

Not with a well-designed cabling system's dedicated-bandwidth feature, however. With the appropriate applications support, the controller would have guaranteed service for accessing and transferring data over the network. The controller would be home in time for (a late) dinner.

It is guaranteed that this will get any beleaguered financial person's attention. Furthermore, this is just the beginning of what a well-designed cabling system's dedicated bandwidth may be capable of delivering to your company. When you present scenarios like this for each of the cabling system's benefits, managers start responding favorably.

You can find more fuel for high-tech speculation in the wide-area aspects of a cabling system. Although some types of cabling systems over the wide area aren't commonly available, it wouldn't hurt to take a look at your WAN bills. Determine how many different technologies and their respective vendors your company employs to maintain its WAN. Calculate totals of what you spend on each; don't forget to include a figure for the time you and your staff spend integrating and coordinating these different technologies and services. Then make an informed estimate of how many costs could be eliminated by having a single protocol end-to-end. Universal cabling system deployment may not be feasible now, but any manager who has played referee between the

IS and telecommunications departments will appreciate the potential harmony that a common frame of reference could provide.

Of course, you must be completely truthful with your budget authority about how far in the future these wide-area benefits may be. However, when taken in combination with the other benefits of a well-designed cabling system, future benefits make the expenditure all the more palatable.

You may need some help in getting your budget approvers to visualize what a cabling system can do for them. In this case, it never hurts to do a little show and tell. Enlist a vendor or group of vendors to put together demonstrations of the cabling system's technology. A lot of it will probably be simulated (you must be very honest about that) but it doesn't really matter. What you're trying to do is give nontechnical people some concept of how revolutionary your cabling system is and what it can mean to them before the end of its depreciation schedule.

Now, let's look at how to centralize network administration in order to justify LAN operating costs of your cabling system.

Justification of LAN Operating Costs

In an effort to reduce rapidly escalating operating costs, many corporations and institutions have installed all-fiber networks with centralized electronics—routers, bridges, hubs, and switches. These companies report increased efficiency in equipment utilization, along with greater flexibility, fewer outages, and simplified network management. Estimated annual savings in network operating costs range to $175 per user compared to typical systems with decentralized electronics.

Longer Passive Fiber Links

Fiber cables permit longer passive links between the electronics and the user workstation, which makes centralized network administration possible. Category 5 UTP copper systems, for example, have a 100-meter length limit on cable runs between the electronics and the workstation. This often necessitates distributing electronics in multiple communications closets near the workstations.

On the other hand, 62.5-fm optical fiber cable can support up to 2.5 Gbps over cable lengths ranging to 300 meters. So the electronics for an optical fiber system can usually be centralized in one communications room within a building. Centralization greatly simplifies moves orchanges or rearrangements of users on the network.

Centralized fiber networks best suit single-tenant buildings—preferably owned or under a long-term lease by the building occupant. The decision to deploy centralized electronics is much more convincing for the single-tenant owner. However, entrepreneur building owners or third-party network companies who provide both cabling and networking solutions may also find centralized fiber networks highly economical.

The building with a centralized network architecture should still contain telecommunications closets within 90 meters of each user; however, now they are passive, housing only splices and interconnects. Following installation, the closets are primarily useful for adding fiber cables to accommodate expansions.

Analyzing Network Costs

How do the various costs of LANs break down? Industry reports indicate that the initial cost of a LAN is only about five perfect cabling and 12 percent hardware or electronics. As for annual operating costs, Forrester Research states that the average corporation spends $280 per user for physical LAN support and $110 per user for bridge/router support. Losses for network outages run about $160 per user annually. This equates to an annual operating cost of $550 per user as shown in Figure 6–1, which will exceed the initial network cost based on Ethernet pricing [1]. Operating and life-time network costs far outweigh the initial costs of installation, and offer the greatest potential for savings.

To estimate the savings possible, assume that 25 percent efficiency can be gained in LAN support through a centralized fiber network administration. Also assume that 15 percent of the network problems relate to copper cable and that fiber solves 80 percent of them. Applying to the figures previously cited and shown in Figure 6–1, centralized fiber networks would have a total

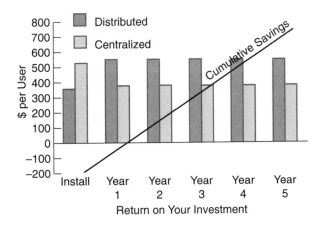

Figure 6–1: Network costs analysis.

annual operating cost of $375 per user, versus today's $550. This translates to an annual savings of $175 per user or a typical payback of the associated premium (cabling and electronics) by the end of the first year.

Equipment Utilization

If all LAN electronics reside in one central equipment room, the user can effectively reduce the number of ports and chassis throughout his or her network. The actual savings from equipment utilization depend greatly on the number of users per closet, number of closets, and the port size of the electronics. To illustrate these savings, assume a building with six telecommunications closets having 72 users per closet for distributed electronics. Also assume a 24-port hub, such as an Ethernet stackable hub. Strictly based on a mathematical probabilities, the distributed electronics would provide a mean probability of 70% utilization.

Alternatively, suppose the same building has 432 users served by a centralized room for network electronics. The centralized architecture provides a mean probability of 90% utilization. The 20% difference in equipment utilization equates to savings of $30 per user, based on system costs of $150 per user.

Centralized fiber networks provide even greater port and hub efficiencies to corporations and institutions having multiple data network technologies, such as Ethernet, token ring, FDDI, and ATM. This is true even if they have a relatively high concentration of users per closet. So all organizations should consider their future migration to higher-speed technologies, in which they may operate multiple types of networks.

With centralized network administration, a user experiences all these benefits plus the inherent benefits of optical fiber cabling. Because fiber is immune to EMI and RFI emissions, has no cross-talk, and has an extremely large operating margin both in attenuation and bandwidth, fiber is a near error-free transmission system.

Advantages

A key benefit of centralized network administration revolves around the simplicity, flexibility, and cost effectiveness of establishing special workgroup networks at a moment's notice. Today many corporations often form small workgroups among individuals scattered throughout a building. For one reason or another they need a dedicated network to perform their task.

If the users' horizontal cables terminate in one centralized communications room, it's easy to bring in the required electronics and provide connectivity to this workgroup. Such networks are often impossible or extremely difficult to configure with a distributed network architecture.

Open Plan Offices

Centralized optical fiber cabling can also be implemented in zone network architectures, such as those for open plan offices using modular furniture. In this case the horizontal distribution cable will typically have a 12- to 24-fiber count versus the normal 2- or 4-fiber count cable for single-user cabling.

Using a splice or interconnect option, the backbone cable remains the same and the installer simply splices the multiuser cable to the feeder or backbone cable. For ease of administration, the connecting or splice hardware in the local telecommunications closet and that in the centralized closet should stress organization and administration of the fibers in the multiuser cable.

Related Standards

The Fiber Optic Task Group of TR 41.8.1, the working subcommittee responsible for TIA/EIA-T568-A Commercial Building Telecommunications Cabling Standard, has recently gotten approval from the Centralized Optical Fiber Cabling Guidelines to publish a TSB. This document, referred to as PN-3523, provides recommendations for the proper implementation of this modified cabling topology in support of optical fiber cabling and fiber-to-the-desk within buildings. The draft results from nine months of discussions within the task group. This group, chaired by AMP, represents manufacturers, consultants, and contractors.

Financial Considerations and Acquisitions

Next, we will cover the financial considerations derived from the cost justification of planning and creating a well-designed cabling system. It will also cover the financial considerations during the acquisition of a cabling system.Careful planning can result in creating a network that has met and will continue to meet all of your client's expectations and, at the same time, has proved to be very cost-effective. Each planned enhancement to the network should be reevaluated at the appropriate time and any selections made should be based on component functionality and contribution to overall network efficiency. With those criteria as the driver for each decision, there will usually be no instance where the objective is compromised. The same criteria can also apply to the acquisition of a cabling system. Let the buyer beware!

Financial Considerations during the Acquisition of a Cabling System

In any acquisition, the buying organization must understand what it is acquiring. Although the buyer will have a general understanding of the seller's business and perhaps financial condition, the buyer may not know specific problems or considerations that may affect the structure, timing, and price of an acquisition. For this reason, a careful buyer—together with its counsel, and, as appropriate, its investment banker, accountant, and other professional advisers—will investigate the seller's assets and operations, its books and records, and the various documents that are important to the seller's business. The process will involve both an inspection of physical assets and a review of documents.

Discussions with the seller's managers and other important employees also will be necessary to carry out a complete due diligence investigation. Since a planned acquisition may be kept confidential, a buyer may need to conduct due diligence in a very low-key fashion. Although some interviews may be deferred, a buyer still may need to enlist the confidence of top-level officials in order to secure complete and reliable information.

A business and legal due diligence review has become a fairly typical early part of the acquisition process, and is essential if the buyer is to understand and assess the risks of its planned acquisition. As a result of due diligence, the buyer and its counsel should have enough information to prepare an appropriate acquisition agreement; for example, the buyer will know whether it needs to include any special representations, covenants, conditions, or indemnities, and whether to address legal, regulatory, or business risks identified through due diligence.

The due diligence process will require a careful balancing of costs and benefits. If the seller is a large company with assets throughout the country or the world (as might be true for a cable Mixed Signal Oscilloscope), the costs of time and travel to visit the seller's various offices and inspect its assets must be balanced against the potential benefits of such undertakings. Alternatively, a fast and superficial investigation could lead the unwitting buyer into a transaction with significant unexpected risks and problems. Among the important matters for a buyer to investigate in considering the acquisition of a cable system are the following:

Examination of Physical Assets

A buyer will want to inspect headend sites, local and central business offices, system plant, equipment in inventory, the repair and customer service fleet, and similar critical assets to ensure that they are in good working condition, comply with technical and legal standards and requirements, and are capable of supporting the level of operations desired by the buyer. The buyer also will want to ensure that these assets are properly owned or leased by the seller.

Franchise Agreements

FCC Licenses are probably the most critical assets of a cable system. A buyer cannot possibly consider a cable system acquisition unless it knows the franchise terms and conditions under which it must operate. The franchise agreement also is likely to specify any requirements for seeking the local government's consent to the planned acquisition, and may set forth the procedures for obtaining it. Such requirements and procedures also may be contained in state laws and rules, or in local ordinances and regulations. The buyer also must confirm that all regulated radio frequency transmission and reception devices have been properly licensed by the FCC, and that all FCC licenses are valid. In some cases, such as where a telephone company is involved, additional FCC approvals and state certifications also may be relevant.

Corporate Documents

A buyer should examine the organizational documents of an entity, its stock transfer (or similar equity ownership) records, and its corporate minutes book (for both owner and director meetings and actions). This inquiry should ensure the following:

- That the entity was validly formed.
- That its outstanding stock (or other equity) was legally issued and is fully paid.
- That the entity has observed legal formalities of electing officers and directors.
- That it obtained appropriate owner or director approval for past actions.
- That the approval requirements or impediments to closing exist as a result of articles of incorporation, by-laws, partnership agreements, or other similar constituent documents [2].

If the seller is a corporation, a buyer also will want to know about any agreements among stockholders (including any voting trust agreements), which may not be referenced in the corporate records or in the organizational documents. The buyer also should ensure that the seller has obtained all necessary licenses to operate in states other than its state of incorporation or organization.

Debt Agreements

If the seller has bank loans or other debt, a buyer will want to review the loan documents. Among the issues of concern are whether the planned transaction is permitted by the lender (and whether the lender's consent is required), the material terms of the loans, and the existence and extent of any security or pledge agreements to collateralize repayment.

Other Material Contracts

For similar reasons, a buyer will want to review a cable system's major contracts, particularly programming agreements, equipment and real property leases, pole attachment or conduit use contracts, and other similar important agreements. A careful buyer also will ask to review any agreements that pertain to any past or pending purchase or sale of assets by the seller (other than ordinary and routine purchases). Finally, union contracts and other collective bargaining agreements will be important. If senior managers will remain with the business, their employment contracts also should be reviewed.

Legal and Regulatory Compliance

In addition to examining FCC licenses and all franchise agreements, the buyer will want to assess whether the seller is operating in accordance with applicable federal, state, and local laws and rules. This would include those applicable to programming, access channel operations, rates,customer service and privacy, zoning, environmental hazards, taxes (including a complete review of past tax returns), copyright filings (for the compulsory cable license), and FCC rules regarding equal employment opportunities and maintenance of a public file. Any evidence of past violations, fines, or other government actions should be requested.

Pending and Threatened Litigation

The buyer should ask for all court papers relating to pending lawsuits or agency investigations, and also should request demand letters or other similar documents that may indicate a threat of litigation. Court and agency dockets and records should be reviewed to ensure that the buyer has a full understanding of any active, important litigation or other proceedings.

Insurance Coverage, Pension and Other Benefit Documents

All existing policies should be reviewed to ensure their adequacy and effectiveness. Also, the terms, conditions, and funding levels of defined and non-statutory plans should be reviewed.

Although not necessarily comprehensive, the foregoing provided a basic overview of the scope of an appropriate due diligence investigation. The participation of knowledgeable professionals is critical, to ensure that technical matters are properly evaluated.

Letters of Intent

If the buyer and seller believe that there is a deal to be done, they may seek to memorialize its basic terms and conditions in a letter of intent. This can be a relatively simple statement of basic principles for the deal or it can be a lengthy, detailed document—almost a first iteration of the ultimate transaction agreement. At the very least, a letter of intent will set out the purchase price, the form of the transaction, the assets or stock to be acquired, and the desired time for completion. Some or many other matters may be included, in great detail or in only summary fashion. If a publicly held company is involved in a transaction, execution of a letter of intent may trigger a requirement to disclose the proposed transaction to the public.

Not every transaction makes use of a letter or intent, and some lawyers advise against them. Legally, a letter of intent is an *agreement to agree*; under common contract law principles, it generally is not legally enforceable. A lawyer frequently will require that a letter state that it is not legally binding on either party; a buyer or seller would not want to find itself unwittingly committed to a transaction defined only in summary fashion under a letter of intent. In some cases, courts find that a letter of intent is meant to be binding; since this is hard to predict, it may be wise to state that a letter is not binding.

Although a letter of intent usually is not binding, it may serve various purposes. For example, it may be required by a lender before beginning the process of considering or seeking acquisition financing. A well-prepared, carefully planned letter of intent, which reflects the results of thoughtful negotiations, also may memorialize an agreement's critical terms. This will save the parties from uncertainty about what they originally agreed to do when— weeks or months later—the acquisition is being finalized. The letter also may be a helpful guide to the preparation of the final documents.

The letter of intent also may put in place certain legally enforceable arrangements intended to govern the process of negotiating a transaction. These might include an allocation of due diligence expenses between buyer and seller, an agreement regarding the confidentiality of information made available by the seller during the due diligence process, an agreement regarding the payment of fees to the buyer by the seller if the seller decides not to proceed with the transaction, or similar matters. Although the terms of the actual transaction in a letter will not be legally enforceable, these other pre-transaction matters are likely to be, unless the letter of intent is poorly drafted or conceived.

Confidentiality

As part of a letter of intent or as a separate agreement, the seller is likely to require the buyer to maintain the confidentiality of information about the seller acquired by the buyer during the due diligence process. The confidentiality agreement might contain the terms and conditions discussed in the sidebar, "Confidentiality Agreement Terms And Conditions." In the absence of such an agreement, the buyer may have an unrestricted ability to disclose confidential information about the seller and its business. This could be disastrous for the seller if the transaction with the buyer is not completed. The disclosure of non-public information about the seller could harm or embarrass the seller (and be helpful to the seller's competitors).

Confidentiality Agreement Terms And Conditions

A standard confidentiality agreement will include the following terms and conditions:

1. It will identify generally the information made available to the buyer, which is to be treated as confidential and proprietary. Some means of distinguishing between confidential and non-confidential information is advisable. The seller also may seek to include oral information communicated to the buyer, and any notes, charts, memos, or other derivative information created from or based upon the seller's confidential information.

2. It will state that the confidential information may not be disclosed to third parties, and may be used by the buyer only to evaluate its interest in the proposed transaction.

3. If the buyer is an entity, the agreement should permit the buyer to share this information with any officers, directors, employees, or professional advisors involved in evaluating the transaction who need to know the information. The agreement, however, should require the buyer to inform these individuals that the information is covered by a confidentiality agreement and should make the buyer responsible for ensuring their compliance with the agreement.

4. The agreement should exclude any disclosure made by the buyer that is required by law or court or government order. The agreement also usually will exclude information that is public or becomes public (except, of course, as a result of an impermissible disclosure by the buyer) that was known to the buyer before receiving the information from the seller (a condition that may be difficult to prove or disprove), and any information that the buyer receives from a third party (as long as the third party is not also bound by a confidentiality agreement or obligation).

5. The agreement should require the buyer to return all confidential written information upon request, and to destroy all notes, charts, memos, and other records created from, or containing, any confidential information. [Director, 5-6].

The seller probably will want this non-disclosure obligation to remain in effect permanently. The parties may agree upon a limited duration, particularly if the information is likely to go stale after a period of time.

Because damage caused by the disclosure of confidential information can be remedied (if at all) only if the disclosure is halted, a confidentiality agreement should allow the seller to obtain an injunction if the buyer (or its representative) breaches the restrictions. The agreement also should specify that the seller will be free to recover any and all other damages available to it.

In some circumstances, the seller will want the buyer to agree not only to refrain from disclosing confidential information, but also from using the information internally to compete with the seller, if the transaction is not completed. Any restriction on competition is likely to be a subject of difficult negotiation; it also can be hard to draft properly and accurately. The problem is that once a buyer has access to confidential information, it is likely to retain at least some of that information (in the memories of corporate officials), even if all original and derivative documents are returned and destroyed.

Because of these concerns, a seller may require the buyer to agree not to compete with it for a specified period of time if the acquisition is not completed. If the buyer agrees to this type of restriction, an important issue will be the scope of the restriction. Should it cover only cable service? What about wireless cable? Other forms of distribution? Should it apply only to the seller's current geographic market(s), or should it also include surrounding markets and perhaps markets into which the seller is planning to expand?

State courts vary widely on the scope and duration of an enforceable non-competition agreement. Because the law prefers competition as a means of achieving a variety of desirable ends, courts tend to refrain from restricting competition.

From Here

This chapter described how to centralize network administration in order to justify LAN operating costs of your cabling system. It also covered the financial considerations derived from the cost justification of planning and creating a well-designed cabling system; as well as the financial considerations during the acquisition of a cabling system. The next chapter provides an overview of the various aspects of cabling system standards design issues.

End Notes

[1] Tony Beam, "Centralizing Network Administration to Control LAN Operating Costs," Reprinted with the permission of AMP Incorporated, REGIONAL CENTER, Harrisburg, PA, USA, 1998, p. 2.

[2] Mark D. Director, "Cable System Sales: A Transactional Guideline," © Communications Media Center New York Law School, 57 Worth Street, New York, NY 10013, 1996, pp. 2–3.

7

STANDARDS DESIGN ISSUES

Do vendors have too much influence on the way cabling industry standards are designed, written and ratified? The answer is yes and no. Vendors will always have the dominant influence on the way cabling industry standards are designed and written. In a system which is driven in an effective self-correcting course by competition, the cabling industry has done a great job of updating and maintaining standards which have a primary focus on the consumer's interest.

Only recently has a new political animal raised its head and told the world that it can do the thinking for customers and users. When a vendor developed a cabling standard or a spec, you knew who was driving; and, if it did not work, you knew who to send your lawyer after. Now, there's a whole new set of players in the standards game—the unbiased and *totally independent* standards body which will do your thinking for you:

- ANSI—American National Standards Institute.
- TIA—Telecommunications Industry Association.
- EIA—Electronics Industry Association.
- BICSI—Building Industry Consulting Services International.
- NEMA—National Electrical Manufacturers Association.
- NECA—National Electrical Contractors Association.
- Underwriters Laboratories and many more [1].

What do they have in common? They are fine corporations and organizations which may not necessarily represent the end user's interest.

The behind-the-scenes power struggle to control the unbiased cabling standards is better than any espionage novel. If the power brokers can dictate the standards design through these associations, they can also insulate themselves from liability. Competitive pressures and liability issues tend to deliver a fairly good checks-and-balances system to the marketplace. Remove these drivers from the formula, and there is the risk of reduced accountability for the performance and safety in the products customers buy.

In addition to diminished accountability for the products, this process can create a "good old boy" system which almost certainly restrains the smaller independent companies from introducing new technologies. Competition is good. Do not support any system that inhibits or eliminates competition, or you will find out about the proverbial golden rule—those who have the gold, make the rules.

One of the great benefits of a vendor program for cabling standards design is quality, driven by competition. Vendors are darn careful about what they put their name on because of reputation and liability issues. However, if a small group of powerhouse vendors can get customers to buy into some third-party standards design system that they control (and they can hide from liability or criticism), customers may lose most of the benefits of free enterprise.

As an example of how the third-party system operates, let's look at BICSI and their standards deign committee. In September 1995—at a BICSI Standards meeting in Tucson, Arizona—a member at the meeting suggested the committee send a letter to the top end user communications organizations inviting them to send a representative to sit on the committee. The discussions were all positive and the vote was unanimous to extend the invitation and get the consumer organizations to add their perspective to the standards. The contact names and addresses for these groups (ICA—International Communications Assn; CMA—Communication Managers Assn; NASTD—National Association of State Telecommunications Directors; SETA—SouthEastern Telecommunications Assn; and TCA—Telecommunications Assn.) were handed over to the committee chairman.

In January 1997, at the BICSI annual conference at Disney World, a follow-up inquiry was made by members again to see if any action had been taken since the 1995 meeting to involve the end user organizations. The appropriate BICSI staffers told the members that they knew about the matter and the letter would go out as soon as they could develop the proper wording for the two-paragraph epistle. Who is in charge?

An industry observer might get the impression that the meetings and the standards process is being maneuvered so that only big boys and insiders with the deep pockets can play the standards design game. To make the big point about standards design, let's consider the plenum story. For a brief period, FEP (Front-End Processor) insulating material was in short supply and the situation was aggravated by hoarding of EIA/TIA Category 5 4-pair UTP plenum cable. During that period most cable companies developed alternative hybrid constructions for plenum Category 5 cable using polyolefin for one or two pairs. These constructions were difficult to manufacture in compliance with the electrical performance standards of EIA/TIA and the fire safety codes for plenum verified by UL.

Virtually all the manufacturers have returned to an all-FEP construction for insulation, for a host of sound reasons. Recently, Berk-Tek, the cable manufacturer who owns the patent for the 2x2 hybrid cable construction, came out with a very strong fire performance message recommending a return to the 100% FEP insulation for Category 5 plenum cable constructions.

Berk-Tek has created quite a ripple effect in the cabling industry. It even extends to the Internet. After this announcement, a lot of the cabling websites and chat groups on WWW were buzzing about the fire safety of communications cabling. Combine this with a special meeting held by UL (Underwriters Laboratories Inc.) to address fire safety concerns, and fire safety has finally reached shock wave status. To say that the big end users that have been discussed in this chapter are interested in these matters would be a gross understatement. They are eager to get their hands on the latest information so they can make better, more informed cabling decisions. When the subject turns to life safety and property protection, everyone listens.

From what has been gleaned from the cabling industry, a lot of research into fire safety performance has turned up the following three problem areas: First of all, some hybrid constructions (2x2's and 3x1's) may have variable fire performance properties. Sometimes they pass code requirements, sometimes they don't. This is where Berk-Tek's call for headroom makes sense and UL is investigating. Second, if certain hybrid constructions do pass, then there's still the question of long-term stability. Remember that the new insulation materials used as a substitute for FEP are compounds with a lot of different ingredients. Finally, there is more code work to be done to more precisely define what is permitted in plenum installations, based on fuel load and the NFPA (National Fire Protection Agency) requirement for Limited Combustibles.

It's ironic that new problems can be avoided with old solutions. Users have consistently recommended 100% FEP insulation when electrical performance and fire safety are top concerns. What can possibly be gained by saving a few pennies with something less than the best?

As is quite evident from what has just been discussed, for some time most cable manufacturers have been aware of a serious fire hazard safety problem.

However, from a standards design point of view, you have to ask yourself, who is really driving the process? Ask who will be responsible if the cable is retested after installation and no longer qualifies as CMP listed. Everyone may be charged with accountability as the attorneys go on a witch hunt.

Recently, the EIA/TIA was asked about end user involvement on the standards committee for Category 5 cabling. As of this writing, people are still waiting for an answer. There is a great deal of political in-fighting as each mega-manufacturer maneuvers to position their product in the standard design and eliminate their competition. Sometimes, it seems like a field and track event with everyone wearing concrete boots. Unfortunately, these standards groups may be anything but independent. It's up to you to figure out who is really in charge.

The Good without the Bad and the Ugly

Not all of the news is bad however. There is some good news about the Anixter Levels '97 Program. This program redefines cabling performance characteristics and, most importantly, gives users guidance in high-performance areas where EIA/TIA cannot seem to agree on a standard design.

Anixter, Inc., a global distributor of integrated communications systems and services, launched Anixter Levels '97, the most recent update of its cable performance specification program. Anixter Levels '97 defines the performance characteristics of unshielded twisted-pair (UTP) cabling beyond 100 MHz, a parameter necessary for advanced applications such as intranet technology, three-dimensional imaging, multimedia programs, video to the desktop, computer-aided design, and broadband video.

The revised program builds on the ANSI/TIA/EIA-T568-A Commercial Building Telecommunications Cabling Standard, which defines the expectations and limitations of cable and provides structure and direction for technological advances. It takes many years to ratify a standard and portions of ANSI/TIA/EIA-T568-A have become obsolete. Therefore, implementing advanced applications could cause cable that adheres to today's standards design to fail in the future. It's doubtful that many users in the network-infrastructure industry, including Anixter, could have predicted that applications requiring increased bandwidth would be developed so quickly that a lot of standard Category 5 cable would become electrically insufficient. Although Anixter has always stayed one step ahead of the industry in defining and evaluating performance requirements, the standards design organizations have been hard pressed to keep up with the developers of applications and access methods.

Anixter Levels '97 divides cable into three performance levels: Cable specified as Level 5 must meet the more stringent requirements for Category 5 cables as spelled out in the international standard ISO 11801, which allows cables meeting its requirements to be used globally. Level 6 increases cable performance to what some in the industry have called high-end Category 5 or Category 5+ cables. Finally, a new generation of recently launched products that meet at least twice the Category 5 bandwidth requirement constitute Level 7.

To be considered a specific Anixter level, cable must pass specification tests at the Anixter Structured Cabling Lab in Mount Prospect, Illinois. All Anixter levels cable must meet a stringent 4-pair crosstalk measurement called power sum testing.

Obviously, not all cable manufacturers distribute their products primarily through Anixter and not all of the manufacturers feel comfortable with the Anixter Levels Program. Just because a cable is not rated by Anixter doesn't mean that it doesn't meet or exceed Anixter's criteria.

Even Better News: Designing Distributed Cabling System Standards

The news is getting even better for the standards design issue. The standards design presented in this part of the chapter describes the functional, electrical, topological, and management standards for the intra-building telecommunications media at the University of Texas, Austin [2]. This media, its associated passive termination equipment, and dedicated floor space, constitutes the building distribution system (BDS). The BDS defined by these standards will permit transmission of voice, video, and computer communications.

These standards are intended to provide faculty and staff with general planning guidelines for BDS design, installation, and extension. However, with the variety of building architectures, telecommunication applications, and user requirements found in the UT (University Texas) Austin community, faculty, and staff should assume that each building's BDS will require custom planning.

Function

The BDS originates in offices, laboratories, conference rooms, and other general areas within a building. The BDS presence in each room or area takes the form of one or more faceplates typically mounted in the room's walls. These faceplates, similar in appearance to the faceplates that mount receptacles for electric power, are configured with two system information outlets (SIO).

Again, this arrangement is similar to the two receptacles found in a common duplex electric power outlet. The number of faceplates required to serve a particular room or area is determined by such factors as the number of people that use the room, their functions, and the extent to which their functions employ the University's information resources.

Each of the two SIOs per faceplate is capable of being independently configured for a particular type of connector, or connectors, as appropriate for the type of information that it will carry (bayonet network connector (BNC) for video or IBM 3270 type terminals; RJ11 modular jack for telephony applications; and RJ45/48 modular jack for LAN applications). Configuration of an individual SIO is accomplished by installing it as a unit in the faceplate housing. An SIO is therefore selected that provides the type of connector necessary for the specific information application and is installed in the faceplate housing that is intended to serve that application. This capability permits the SIOs that serve a particular room or location to be reconfigured to meet new information requirements as they evolve.

Each faceplate housing serves to terminate two independent cables, or sheaths, of wire. Each sheath contains eight wires, arranged as four pairs. Each sheath also provides information, via the faceplate housing, to one of the SIOs mounted in the housing.

The other end of each wire sheath either terminates directly in a common patch panel (CPP) configured with female modular jack receptacles or in a common cross-connection panel (CXP), implemented via a 110-type terminal block. Functionally, a CXP is differentiated from a CPP in that the CXP permits any of the eight wires within a sheath to be accessed and used in conjunction with any of the other wires in the sheath for a particular purpose. In contrast, a CPP establishes a permanent connection and configuration of all eight wires between the panel and the faceplate.

Both CPPs and CXPs may be employed in the same building and both are housed in common space within the building referred to as wiring closets (WC). A given wiring closet may contain CPPs or CXPs that terminate sheaths that originate in areas on the same floor as the WC, or if distance and cabling paths permit, multiple floors of the building can be served from the same WC. Thus, the WC serves to aggregate at a common location sheaths of wire serving rooms and other building areas that are proximate to it. The location and number of WCs within a building is almost exclusively a function of the size of the building and the availability of media routing paths within the building.

Each building contains one WC that performs the special function of housing the media and terminating equipment that is necessary to connect the building to external sources of information, (the telephone system, computer network backbone, and video network). This WC is called the gateway room

(GW) and it serves as the demarcation point between the BDS and external information distribution systems.

At this point, recall that the BDS consists of passive components (components such as wire, connectors, and mounting equipment) that do not produce information. The WCs may also contain active equipment (local area network hubs, terminal controllers, video modulators/demodulators) that connects to the BDS and uses it to distribute information. This active equipment and the information applications that it supports will determine how connections are implemented between the various WCs within a building. For example, high-speed computer information moving between hubs located in different WCs may require optical fiber interconnection, while a telephone connection between the GW and WC is carried on wire.

Electrical

The largest media element of the BDS is the cabling between the building's various faceplates and its WCs. This cabling is standardized to be eight conductor, carried as four unshielded twisted pair (UTP), copper wire conforming to the Category 5 performance level defined in EIA/TIA TSB 36. Further, this media is to be installed and terminated with procedures and connecting hardware that meets ANSI/EIA/TIA-T568-A Commercial Building Telecommunications Wiring Standard.

Properly installed and terminated, an analog bandwidth of 100 Mhz is specified for a Category 5 BDS. Digital information capacities corresponding to the synchronous transport signal-3 (STS-3) of 155.52 Mbps can also be supported with a Category 5 BDS.

Topology

A BDS is implemented in a star configuration having the WC at the center of the star and uninterrupted 4-pair sheaths as rays to each of the faceplate housings. In this configuration, the path distance (the distance measured along the actual path that the sheath will follow from the faceplate housing to the CPP or CXP) must not exceed 90 meters. Subject to this constraint, and the space available for connection hardware, a particular WC can serve as many rooms, areas, and floors of a building as desired. In particular, it may be possible to serve an entire building with a single WC that also serves as a GW.

The choice of CPP, CXP, or a combination of CPP and CXP termination of media in a WC is at the discretion of the department installing the BDS. In buildings that require multiple WCs, the method and routing of the interconnection of the WCs with each other and with the building's GW is determined by the specific information services that are distributed within the building. As these requirements change, this portion of the BDS is incremented appropriately.

Management

UT Austin maintains a central database containing information for each BDS installed at the University. In particular, this database contains the location of each WC, including the GW, and the locations of faceplates served by the respective WC. The database also contains the type of SIO installed in each faceplate. A common scheme for identifying each sheath and its originating and terminating points is employed throughout the database. This database is updated upon installation or modification of any BDS.

Once installed, a BDS can be managed on a day-to-day basis either by a central University utility (CUU) or jointly by the using department and a CUU. In the former case, the using department contracts with a CUU to perform all moves, changes, and reconfigurations of the BDS. In the latter case, the using department performs these functions and reports the changes to a CUU so that the University BDS database can be updated to reflect the new configuration.

New Standards Design Issues

Now, let's move on to some new standards design issues, Category 6, Category 7, and the new CENELEC standards. This final part of the chapter will answer such burning questions as are Category 6 or Category 7 products currently available on the market?

The direction taken by ISO/IEC is to standardize on the highest plateau of performance that unshielded, screened, and fully-shielded balanced cabling systems are able to support. Many manufacturers have issued claims about their high-performance systems with the intent of leading end users to believe that they already comply with a standard that, as of early 1998, does not yet exist. Although not much is known about any system solutions that offer end-to-end component or channel performance, it is only a matter of time before new product releases are announced.

Category 6 or Category 7

The Siemon Company is currently addressing the need for Category 6 and Category 7 system solutions [3]. The Category 6 standard has already been approved. At the time of this writing, Category 7 was still awaiting approval.

Now that ISO/IEC has released two performance categories, most copper experts agree that the proposed Category 6 NEXT values are about as good as twisted-pair cabling can get without individually shielded pairs, based upon a theoretical limit related to the effects of increasing twist rate. Category 6 is by no means a stepping stone to Category 7. For example, the system and component values for Category 6 are more stringent than the highest published commercial specifications for UTP and Screened Twisted-Pair (ScTP), including so-called gigabit offerings. Unshielded and screened twisted-pair systems have such a significant following and are so much more cost-effective than fully-shielded solutions that there is a low probability that they will be completely replaced. This point is especially compelling, considering that fully-shielded cabling provides less bandwidth than multimode fiber for about the same cost.

In addition, if a high-end UTP cable is endorsed and the connecting hardware is tweaked, Category 6 is achievable. This is probable, provided that a cable is found that meets the Category 6 requirements.

So, what type of connector interface will be required in order to achieve Category 7 performance? The standard 8-position plug/outlet connection is not expected to satisfy the proposed Category 7 transmission requirements for 4-pair systems. Consequently, it is likely that a new interface will be required to support 4-pair transmission to 600 MHz. There have been submittals to WG3 (the ISO/IEC's Working Group) on new connectors that claim to meet these requirements, but commercial availability of these products remains in question.

ISO/IEC and TIA

In view of earlier comments with regard to the credibility of ISO/IEC and TIA, will ISO/IEC objectives be accepted by TIA? It is likely that TIA will also select 200 MHz as the minimum frequency at which the difference between attenuation and multi-disturber NEXT is positive for Category 6 cabling channels. There is also strong evidence that supports a trend towards standards harmonization between the TIA and ISO groups. Two recent examples include the pending issuance of an ISO/IEC ballot with new Class D channel requirements that are well-aligned with the Category 5 channel values specified in TIA/EIA TSB 67 and ISO/IEC input to TIA on the pending return loss requirements for Category 5 channels and links.

Standardized Testing

There are many standardized testing issues for these new categories. So, is standardized testing good enough to use hand-held certification devices that test only to 100 MHz? Not at the time of this writing or in the immediate future. The reason being that the specifications for these new categories and classes will not be complete until a full system specification is available that is supported by procedures for laboratory and field testing. At this point, it is questionable whether even the most advanced field testers available today are able to test accurately up to 200 MHz, not to mention 600 MHz. Even if existing 100 MHz testers are used, their ability to make measurements at these new, higher performance levels up to 100 MHz with acceptable scatter (accuracy and repeatability) remains unknown. In addition, it is likely that there will be a need for additional test capabilities for parameters such as return loss, far-end crosstalk, skew, and perhaps others, that existing testers do not offer. If new applications standardize on a cabling category with requirements beyond 100 MHz, it would follow that accurate field testing to the new limits and extended frequencies will be needed.

Gigabit Ethernet

Categories 6 and 7 are also expected to handle gigabit Ethernet (1000BaseT). The objective is for new categories to be backward compatible. Applications that run on lower classes and categories must be supported by all higher classes. The existing IEEE 1000BaseT project (802.3ab) is clearly targeted for operation over Category 5 cabling. If IEEE is able to achieve this goal, the new categories will only be needed for LAN applications that operate with transmission rates in excess of 1 Gbps. If four pairs are required at each work area outlet, it is likely that Categories 5, 6, and 7 will support gigabit Ethernet.

Performance Requirements

Draft performance requirements for Category 6 are already available, but not for Category 7. Although the ISO/IEC committee has not released an expected project completion date for Category 7, they have agreed to provide updates to, and solicit input from, application and component committees. It is not the intention of ISO/IEC to develop a closet standard without input and guidance from industry working and developmental groups. Nevertheless, what ISO/IEC intends to do, and what they actually do remains to be seen. The question remains: Who's in charge?

ACR Values

Finally, what are the positive ACR (attenuation to crosstalk ratio) values at the maximum frequencies for these two new categories? At least as good as current Class D at 100 MHz (> 3dB) for channels, including equipment cords and work area cables, based on worst case pair-to pair performance, and greater than 0 dB based on worst case power sum performance.

Now, let's look at the new Comite Europeen de Normalisation Electrotechnical (CENELEC) standards design issues.

CENELEC Standards

The EU Commission in Brussels has recently prepared a new, complete family of cabling system standards, identified as Mandate 212. Work to prepare all documents in question was extremely intense in the involved committees and working groups. Some cable specifications and basic test documents are completely new (as for instance the 600 MHz cable standard) while other existing standards are revised and aligned with the overall standard family concept.

Mandate 212 CENELEC Standard Family

The Mandate 212 CENELEC standard family is intended as a complete, self-supporting set of standards containing:

- Basic reference standards specifying test methods, definitions, materials, guide to use, and environmental issues. These standards are identified with the title *EN BASIC* and referenced by the generic and sectional cabling system standards.
- Generic cable specifications for symmetrical and multi conductor cables, coaxial cables and optical fiber cables.
- Sectional cable specifications for symmetrical and multiconductor cables, and coaxial cables [4].

For people involved in generic cabling, the most interesting information will probably be the nature of the cable specifications. So far, the CENELEC cable standards EN 50167, EN 50168, and EN 50169 for screened horizontal, patch, and backbone cables, respectively, have been the only sectional CENELEC specifications available. These specifications have therefore been the only cable standards referenced by CENELEC EN 50173. They are now being revised.

Furthermore, new standards for UTP cables and screened 600 MHz cables are being prepared. The family of twisted-pair cable standards will then become complete. The present identifications of the cable standard proposals are:

- prEN 5046C-2-1—Screened horizontal and backbone cables to 100 MHz, corresponding to EN 50167 and EN 50169.

- prEN 5046C-2-2—Screened patch cables to 100 MHz, corresponding to EN 50168.

- prEN 5046C-3-1—Unscreened horizontal and backbone cables to 100 MHz.

- prEN 5046C-3-2—Unscreened patch cables to 100 MHz.

- prEN 5046C-4-1—Screened horizontal and backbone cables to 600 MHz.

- prEN 5046C-4-2—Screened patch cables to 600 MHz [3P, 3].

Cabling System Requirements

The coming symmetrical cable standard proposals have a number of new technical requirements which will be significant for everyone involved in cabling. These issues concern both specified cable types, electrical performance, EMC, and safety. See the sidebar "Significant New Cable Requirements" for more information on these issues.

Significant New Cable Requirements

The following points have the most significant market impact:

1. UTP cables will now get their own specifications. Earlier, only screened cable specifications existed due to uncertainty and disputes about true EMC performance of UTP cables. This problem has now been resolved (see point 2).

2. EMC performance of all cable types is now being specified by coupling attenuation measurements, which will again be specified in EN BASIC 5-4-6D. The earlier disputes about EMC performance will now be solved by this new measurement type which is applicable for both screened and unscreened cables. The different cable types can be specified and measured for EMC performance. The requirements apply from 30 MHz to 1 GHz for all cable types since it is an EMC and not a transmission performance parameter. Typical values between 30 MHz and 100 MHz are min. 40 dB, min. 55 dB and min. 80 dB for UTP, 100 MHz screened, and 600 MHz screened cables, respectively.

3. Electrical requirements are specified to 600 MHz for screened cables. For the sake of order it should be noted that cables are not identified as Category 6, even though those cables will undoubtedly form the cable requirements to any future Category 6 Class E specifications.

4. Safety of cables is modified to clearly specify IEC 332-1 flame retardancy only. Cables will all be of a Low Smoke Zero Halogen (LS0H) grade. In other words, the links between wiring closets are typically provided using multimode fiber optic cable, terminated using ST connectors on a patching field at each wiring closet. Low Smoke Zero Halogen (LS0H) interior/exterior grade cable is utilized, meeting both the requirements for fire resistance and for moisture protection without the need for intermediate termination points at building entry/exit. Each wiring closet comprises one or more standard 19 inch racks containing the fiber optic and UTP patch fields and the active equipment.

5. PVC cables will no longer be allowed, not even for UTP cables. However, flame retardancy requirements will not be more strict than for the presently common PVC cables [3P, 3].

Finally, most of the cabling standards have now been published. Stay tuned for future updates!

From Here

This chapter discussed the latest cabling system standards design issues. See Chapter 18, "Standards Development" for more information on these developing standards issues as well as the international issues in Europe, Japan, and South America. The next chapter presents an overview of cabling system architectural design considerations (structured cabling system, wiring closet design, cabling facilities, and user-to-outlet ratios, etc.).

End Notes

[1] "The Standards Game," Wireville, ACP (The Association of Cabling Professionals, Jacksonville, FL), 1998, p. 1.
[2] W.C. Bard, "Building Distribution System Standards," University of Texas at Austin, Austin, Texas 78712, p. 1.
[3] © The Siemon Company, Siemon Business Park, 76 Westbury Park Road, Watertown, CT 06795-0400, USA, p. 1.
[4] "New CENELEC Standards," *3P Newsletter No. 4*, 3P Third Party Testing, Agern Allé 3, DK-2970 Hoersholm, Denmark, 1997, p. 2.

8

ARCHITECTURAL DESIGN CONSIDERATIONS

The information technology age office is not just a place equipped differently from offices of the past, it's a place that will be designed in an entirely different way.

The best and most productive offices will be designed from the inside out, not the outside in. Foremost will be concern for the way the office environment supports people at work. Therefore, the design process must begin with an understanding of the work process.

Architects and interior designers need to understand power and data/communications delivery systems. Facility planners need to know what kinds of work will go in their buildings and how the facility must support the work process. The role of the facility manager as the integrator of varied disciplines and planning processes will be more and more important.

In short, things are getting more complicated. The purpose of this chapter is to provide an overview of the architectural design considerations with regard to power and data/communications distribution for architects, designers, facility managers, and others interested in designing and managing office environments. The complexity imposed by information technology means that each of these professions must learn the others' languages.

Complexity of Information Technology

The business of business, for most office workers, is the processing of information. The revolutionary change brought about by the information technology age is that now, at every level of the organization from clerical to executive, information is being processed with the help of electronic tools.

What changes will be required in the way organizations manage cabling? Plenty. Some of the immediately foreseeable ones:

- Each workstation must support a personal computer and often other electronic devices, in addition to providing power for lighting.
- Offices must be designed in such a way as to be open to a variety of cabling options.
- Electrical loads of 500 to 1000 watts or more per workstation will likely be the average [1].

Furniture systems can extend the building's power distribution and communications cable capacity. But cable paths may affect the reconfigurability of components, and facility planning must take this into account.

Building services for distribution of power and data/communications capabilities will be designed differently, for more horizontal cable capacity and to preserve adaptability to changes in technology. Furthermore, much more space will be required, particularly in high-rise office buildings, for cables delivering power and data/communications resources vertically through the building to each floor.

Realizing the link between productivity and adequate facilities, organizations will spend more money getting services right. Also, most observers agree that multiple wire and cable systems, such as coaxial cable for data next to twisted pair for phones, will be common for at least the next four years. Furthermore, coaxial cable may currently be installed in facilities for data, but is almost universally being replaced by Category 5.

All of the significant manufacturer strategies for office automation define separate physical networks for voice and data applications despite the fact that the technology exists that allows data and voice signals to be sent over the same physical wire. For the most part, coaxial and twisted-pair cables will continue to provide most of the physical linkages. Optical fibers will be used on a limited basis for point-to-point links between computer systems within buildings and on a more frequent basis for inter-building communication channels [Sullivan, 2].

In the near term, the typical workstation will not have applications which require the bandwidth capacity of fiber optics. Use of fiber optics is also limited due to lack of connecting capability in and between workstations.

The costs of not planning adequate capacity for power wiring and data/communications cabling will be tremendous. Some organizations report having to budget as much as $200 a foot for relocating cable every time a change is needed. One such organization, a large bank highly dependent on automated services, estimates spending $12 million per year moving wires and cables around. In other instances, companies have been unable to move into brand-new facilities because the services provided were insufficient to meet the demands of the equipment. Clearly, organizations without cabling management plans and design put themselves at a competitive disadvantage.

Electrical Design and Data/Communication Cabling Systems Distribution Considerations

Information technology exists to make people more productive. Making the technology work as effectively as possible requires well planned and designed power and data/communications cabling distribution systems.

Both electrical and data/communications cabling systems resources must travel through the building to get to where they can be used. Resources enter the building from the power company, phone company, or other sources. They must be distributed vertically to each floor, horizontally throughout each floor, and then out to each point of use: computer terminal, telephone, light, etc. The design of these various cabling distribution systems depends on the criteria imposed by the equipment in use and projected for future use.

Typically, designing cabling distribution systems requires the talents of architects and design professionals working with communications specialists, electrical engineers, and equipment specialists. A key role of the professional facility manager is one of integrating the contributions of each of these disciplines.

Distribution and Electrical Needs

Electricity can be a mixed blessing; it makes our organizations and culture work by running our machines, but it can be dangerous when misapplied, or hazardous to electronic equipment and stored information when voltage sags and spikes contaminate power supplies.

An electrical circuit requires three things,: a power source, conductors, and a load—a device like a lamp or terminal that uses the electricity. The conductors have to make a complete circle from power source to the load and back, no matter how many access points are available on the circuit. Electricity passes easily through conducting material like copper wire. The parts of the equipment where there is resistance to electrical flow is where the work gets done: where the light bulb lights, etc.

What does that mean in the office environment? Power distribution systems must provide not only sufficient capacity for present needs and flexibility for the future, as well as plenty of points of access, they must also accommodate new, specialized needs.

Often, equipment will dictate the need for additional, dedicated circuits and special accommodations for protecting power from outside interference. Designing circuits is the business of qualified electrical engineers and electricians. But facility managers, architects, and interior designers must understand the potentials and constraints imposed by power distribution systems on building structures and furnishing plans.

Single and Three-Phase Electrical Circuits

Utility companies deliver two kinds of power to commercial buildings: single-phase (120 volts to ground) and three-phase (208 Y/120). Three-phase systems are becoming standard, but you may encounter some cases of single-phase power. It's important to know if a building is supplied with single-phase power because it will affect later decisions about distributing power to workstations through furniture systems or flat wire.

Three-phase circuits have three hot wires (those which take the electricity along the first part of the circle, from source to load) from the electric utility source to a main distribution panel in the building service core. Hot and neutral wires are run through conduit to separate secondary distribution panels, usually located on each floor. These panels will have a bus bar, or a metal bar, for each wire or *phase leg* (one of the three phases of the three-phase system). From this panel, an electrician will run a hot wire with its own neutral wire to floor monuments or other termination points.

In a high-rise building, for instance, utilities can bring in very high voltage power (13,000 KV) through the core of the building, with transformers on each floor. This allows use of smaller cable for vertical distribution, saving space in backbone (riser) shafts.

Generation and distribution of alternating current (AC) is usually done with three-phase circuits for a variety of reasons. Three-phase circuits are more efficient than single-phase; they can use lighter, smaller conductors than single-phase circuits of the same power rating. Three-phase motors are also generally smaller, lighter, and more efficient than single-phase motors of the same horsepower. The large utility companies are geared to three-phase distribution lines and typically use three-phase generators.

Single-phase circuits have either one or two hot conductors and one neutral conductor running through conduit to secondary panels. From these, each incoming hot conductor connects to a separate bus bar with its own circuit breaker.

Designing Electrical Loads

Just how much electrical capacity must be provided within a specific office depends on the type of organization involved and the work processes that go on there. It is more important than ever that facility planners have accurate information, best gained from surveys, about each worker's equipment and about the organization's best estimates for future growth or automation.

Not all organizations have introduced technology to the same level, so the professional architect, designer, or facility manager will probably encounter widely varying levels of need. It is usually advisable to allow for different circuits for lighting, electrical devices, and electronic equipment. Some offices will need separate dedicated circuits, such as for a large computer. A very large installation may need several circuits.

When planning all the utility systems (HVAC (heating, ventilation, and air conditioning), electrical, data/communications), it's best to plan for the maximum feasible loads, based on the organization's long-range plans. Your building system might look perfectly adequate for today's needs. But will it be adequate for additional power wiring, communications cable, and HVAC loads that can be reasonably predicted five, eight, or ten years out? The slight cost for adding extra capacity during construction or redesign must be weighed against the high cost of correcting a deficient space.

Electrical Circuits

To understand circuit loads, you'll need to understand the rudiments of how electrical circuits work. The classic way to illustrate this is to think of an electrical system as being similar to a water circuit. In this analogy, voltage compares to water pressure: it is the pushing force. Amperage is comparable to the gallons per minute that travel through the pipe: it is the rate at which electrons pass along the wire, or the amount of current flowing.

Most people are used to thinking in watts—a 60-watt light bulb, etc. Wattage is the measure of power that can be supplied through a given circuit, calculated by multiplying voltage time amperage. If, for example, you have 120 volts with 5 amps of current moving through a wire, you have 600 watts. If you have ten amps of power moving through the wire, you have 1200 watts.

Just as the water-carrying capacity of a pipe is limited by its size and the material it's made of, electrical wire is limited by its size and material as to the number of electrons it can carry. Over-burdened wire will heat up and become dangerous if the electrical overload is not stopped; that's why protection devices like circuit-breakers and fuses exist. Wire size and circuit capacity relationships are listed in the National Electrical Code; state and local building codes often list more stringent limitations. Wire size and type determines the number of amps allowable per circuit. Total amperage needs are determined by how many circuits are required in the facility. The total must not exceed the total number of amps available at the secondary distribution panel for the floor.

In planning electrical circuits within the office environment, you'll need to know what equipment will be used on various electrical circuits to plan capacity. Particularly in the case of electronic equipment, circuit overloads causing power interruptions can be catastrophic not only for the work in process but also for the hardware itself. And even if the needs of today are accommodated, inadequately planned circuits can hobble future expansion.

Workstation Electrical Loads

When most office workstations had only typewriters and lights and maybe an occasional calculator, planning electrical circuits was a relatively simple job. The sudden influx of electronic equipment at every level of the organization has permanently changed the game.

An electronic load is any device that uses electricity: a lamp, a terminal, or any of the other conveniences and necessities of office life that depend on electricity to function. In the office, electrical loads can be divided into three categories: lighting, office machines and appliances, and electronic office equipment.

Computer terminals, printers, and similar equipment use considerable amounts of electrical power. Planning for power and lighting in an office installation requires: identifying the users need, estimating total load requirements, and calculating circuits.

It isn't the number of receptacles on a branch circuit that causes overload; it's what's plugged into those receptacles. This is why, in planning power distribution and access for offices where electric equipment is used, knowing what will be used at each workstation is extremely important.

Planning branch circuits must involve a qualified electrician or electrical engineer familiar with the National Electrical Code and with the code requirements of the state, city, or locality involved. But the facility planners or managers are the ones who must provide the information to guide the activity of these professionals, and planners can be more effective knowing their language.

Branch circuits

Now, let's look at an example of a process for calculating the number of outlets allowed on a general purpose branch circuit. The capacity of a circuit, remember, is calculated by multiplying amperage and voltage. A 15-amp circuit being supplied with 120-volt current has a total capacity of 1,800 watts. A 20-amp 120-volt branch circuit has a capacity of 2,400 watts.

The number of receptacles which may be placed on a circuit is limited by its capacity (15- or 20-amp), the load that will be connected to it, and by standards of the National Electrical Code. Where the connected load is not known, a 20-amp circuit may have a maximum of 13 receptacles and a 15-amp circuit may have a maximum of 10. The actual number of receptacles allowed on a circuit is subject to local or municipal codes which may be different from the NEC. Check with local authorities for specific constraints.

Branch circuits on which maximum or near maximum loads will be in use for three hours or more, such as circuits used for CRTs or for lighting, are defined as being in *continuous operation*. These circuits must be de-rated for the purpose of calculating electrical loads. For a de-rated circuit, the total load may not exceed 80% of the rating of the circuit. For example: A 20-amp circuit for office lighting would be de-rated to 16 amps (.80 x 20 = 16).

Specialized Types of Circuits

Electronic equipment may dictate the need for specialized types of circuits. Let's briefly discuss some of the most common:

Branch Electrical Circuit

Branch electrical circuits are circuit conductors between the final overcurrent device (fuse or circuit breaker) and a receptacle intended for use with an electrical load. The conductors in the circuit are not shared with any other branch circuit; this is also referred to as an isolated branch circuit.

Dedicated Branch Circuit

A *dedicated branch circuit* has one load or one piece of equipment connected to it, such as a copy machine or a paper shredder. This is a complete circuit consisting of hot, neutral, and ground wires, all connected to just one machine and not shared with any other equipment. This is usually done because the equipment uses the entire legal capacity of the circuit.

Designated Circuit

A *designated circuit* is a branch circuit used for a specific, designated kind of load, such as lighting only or personal computers only, or other equipment with compatible operating characteristics. Unlike a dedicated circuit, the designated circuit may share its neutral and ground wires with other circuits.

Isolated Ground Circuit

An *isolated ground circuit* has a separately wired ground from other circuits within the building. This helps avoid the problem of electrical noise being introduced to the internal circuitry of sensitive equipment.

The isolated ground is not a separate grounding system, but an isolated ground path back to the power system grounding point. Also, the isolated ground wiring does not connect to the conduit system at any other point. It is connected to the power system grounding point either directly or through an isolated ground bar in a distribution panel.

Clean Power

Users of electronic equipment sometimes report mysterious glitches, frozen screens, locked key-boards, and other computer malfunctions that seem to come from nowhere. Many such problems may be the result of irregularities in the power feeding the computer. Computers code and store information on the basis of very small changes in voltage; any deviation from standard voltage could cause them to malfunction.

Clean power can be defined as any power that is within a range of five percent above or ten percent below the standard 120 volts, and free from electrical noise generated by other machines using the circuit. A typical wall socket may supply electrical power more than ten percent below 120 V, and momentary deviations occur regularly due to outages, spikes, and electrical noise.

Power Problems

Computer makers have built in devices to protect equipment from some power problems, but four basic power problems still exist. The first problem has to do with power outages occurring when power is suddenly cut off. Most often due to power line damage by ice, lightning, etc. Large computers are usually protected by backup power sources, such as uninterruptible power supplies (UPS), but small PCs most often aren't. An outage can erase a computer's RAM (random access memory).

The second problem is voltage fluctuations, which are deviations either up or down in voltage. A *sag* occurs during a brown-out, when utilities deliberately reduce voltage to conserve power during peak loads. A surge can result during low demand periods, such as at night when other loads in the area shut down. Voltage fluctuations can last a few seconds or several hours. They can cause computer equipment to overheat or shut off, cause extensive data alterations (mysterious glitches), or damage circuitry. Voltage regulators or stabilizers can be installed to keep the voltage close to a stable 120 V.

Voltage spikes (the third problem) are instantaneous and very high surges. They can be caused by lightning striking a power line or the switching of large loads in the area (such as an elevator, copy machine, or other motor coming on or off). Spikes can wipe out stored data, alter data, or damage circuitry. Voltage spike suppressers are available to dissipate the excess voltage.

Electrical noise is an unwanted signal on a power line. It is caused by a series of voltage spikes of low magnitude. Fluorescent lights, business machines, elevators, HVAC equipment, and other sources can cause electrical noise, which in turn can cause the computer to process information erroneously. Noise isolation transformers and line conditioners will filter out noise.

Protection Systems

In the past, mainframe computers were protected from all these problems with discrete electrical systems, temperature- and humidity-controlled rooms, and other safeguards. But protecting personal computers spread all through an organization can be a special problem.

To determine whether to install protective devices, and if so which ones, compare the cost of the solution to the answers to a number of questions. For example, look at the type of information a personal computer is storing or processing. Does it contain critical financial information? Does it contain simple back files of correspondence? What would be the cost of losing that information if the computer malfunctions in one of the ways previously described? What would happen if the computer provided inaccurate information due to a glitch caused by one of the four basic problems described earlier?

Look at the function of the computer. What would be the cost of downtime? Consider the value of the user's time. What would it cost for that person not to work for an hour? Who else and what work processes would be affected?

Finally, look at the equipment. What would it cost to replace damaged circuitry or equipment?

Providing power to electronic equipment in the information technology age office is part of the story. Providing cabling systems to transmit data and telecommunications signals to each device is part two.

Cable Design Considerations

Facility planners need to understand the basics of cable management because, to design effective installations, they need to know how much cable management capacity is needed for the specific equipment to be used, how much bending the cables can tolerate, how much cable storage space they'll need, where the equipment will be located, and how the cables can be routed throughout the floor and the building.

As previously stated in Chapter 1, many types and sizes of data/communications cables exist, but they fall into a few categories based on their construction and transmission characteristics. The basic categories are twisted pair, coaxial, and fiber optic.

Twisted-pair cable is exactly what its name implies—two insulated wires wound together and covered by a protective coating, usually in combinations such as 3-pair or 4-pair. Ordinary telephone lines are twisted pair; 25-pair cable is the cable that the phone companies have used for years, though it is rarely used today in new installations.

Twisted pair wiring can be used for voice or data transmission. Though it is adequate for most office applications, twisted pair cable transmits data at slower speeds than newer technologies, and signals lose power when they move along this type of wire. If data is to be transmitted over some distance via twisted-pair wiring, the signal may have to go through one or more repeaters that amplify and retransmit it.

For example, IBM's cabling system offers two classes of cable in several types. One class is for data and one is for both voice and data. Both are twisted pair, but the data pairs are larger than normal, specially shielded, and precision-manufactured. These cables have bending restrictions that may affect how they can be routed through an installation. They are also much larger than most equivalent twisted pair.

NOTE:

IBM Type 5 Cable fiber and Type 6 Cable-STP Stranded for data is very flexible.

AT&T's system uses primarily 4-pair twisted cable. This consists of two cables per workstation: one for voice and one for data. Twisted-pair cable is discussed further in Chapter 9, "Copper Design Considerations."

Coaxial cable is made of a core conductor surrounded by a layer of insulation, then a metal sheath which acts as both a second conductor and a shield, then an insulated outer coating. Each layer shares the same geometric axis—hence the name coaxial.

Coaxial cables have greater data capacity than twisted-pair wiring. But coaxial cable can be expensive and more difficult to install because of its bending restrictions. It is also bulkier.

Twinaxial cable is similar to coaxial, except that there are two conductors in the core. Triaxial cable has a core conductor and two concentric conductive shields. Twinaxial cable is discussed further in Chapter 9, "Copper Design Considerations."

Fiber optic cables are the most sophisticated and newest cables on the scene. The special glass or plastic core of a fiber optic cable (the optical fiber itself) transmits light instead of electrical impulses. It is surrounded by a cladding which reflects the light. Signals in the form of light travel a zigzag path through the core by bouncing off the cladding. Cables containing from one to hundreds of fibers are protected with a coating much like that used for metal conductor cables.

Fiber optic cable offers a number of advantages—greater potential capacity; potentially lower cost; immunity to power surges, electrical noise, and grounding problems; very high rates of speed in transmitting data; small size; and flexibility. But most experts believe fiber optic technology will not be a major factor within most office buildings for several years because of a number of problems—too few installers experienced with the technicalities of coupling the cables, lack of standardization in the industry, fine cracks which develop over time in cables that are bent too tightly, and lack of need for the extra capacity fiber optics offer. Nevertheless, installation of fiber optic cable is easier then ever to learn and use, due to the configuration of the connection equipment, as well as the many pre-made connectors and adapters. Fiber optic cable is discussed further in Chapter 10, "Fiber Optic Design Considerations."

Backbone cable is the wiring used to route power or communications resources vertically to the floors of a building, or for major horizontal runs in large low-rise buildings. Telephone backbone cable, in particular, is very large and bulky (as much as three inches in diameter) and difficult to bend. Backbone cable is not a separate type of cable, but an application of one of the basic cable types previously described, with special fire-rating characteristics.

The type and brand of cable used for any specific application will be dictated by the kind of equipment in use and how that equipment must be connected. That's another reason why the facility planner must have information on the equipment planned for each workstation that is as accurate as possible. Cable manufacturers provide data on the bend radius restrictions and other important features of their products.

Local area networks

Some experts call the local area network (LAN) the major advance in office technology of the '80s. Networks extend the use of peripherals (printers, etc.) and databases to many users; they allow microcomputers or other digital-based equipment to communicate and share data.

Other major improvements in technology in the past two decades have resulted in the removal of functions to special centers—the information technology center, the word processing center, etc. LANs, in contrast, allow the decentralization of data and resources, preserving the independence of each workstation.

LANs are defined in different ways by different experts, but most definitions describe them as systems for moving and sharing information that include computers and peripherals, the transmission media connecting them, and sometimes additional components that amplify or interpret data signals to make them usable by another device.

LAN technology offers tremendous advantages to an organization. But making a LAN work requires interweaving skills and knowledge between communications systems designers and facility managers. LANs have implications for several aspects of facility planning:

- Wire and cable management, including the possible need for dedicated power circuits, cable paths and storage of service loops, etc.
- Savings in equipment and space; sharing resources is more efficient.
- Location of people on the network. It's easier to design the network for maximum flexibility at the outset than to move people.
- Relocatability of furnishings; some loss of flexibility may be the price to be paid.
- Extra equipment space in backbones or small equipment rooms on each floor may be needed [Sullivan, 10].

Cabling Topologies

Three physical layouts, in varying degrees of complexity, are most common for local area networks. As previously discussed in earlier chapters, these cabling topologies, or configurations, are also used for other applications.

Multiple personal computers within a department might be connected, for instance, by a ring topology and yet not constitute a true LAN.

Bus (or tree) networks use a single spine of cable throughout the location. A branch cable connects to each device. It is the simplest topology, but is has constraints such as limits to the length of the spine cable and the need for complex devices at each branch point to tap into the network. Any damage to the network may affect the whole system; one malfunctioning device can bring the entire network down.

Star networks connect each device through a length of cable to a central connection point. This in turn is connected by a separate cable to another device such as a mainframe computer. A typical telephone system has a star topology.

Ring (or loop) networks must be continuous throughout the location. Each device connected to the network has one cable for information entering the terminal and another for information exiting. A non-functioning device on the network can be bypassed.

Hierarchical networks are multiple networks, linking groups of connected devices at many levels. This kind of network can be very complex because each concentration point can only provide services to a few devices.

The type of LAN used in an office will depend on the type of equipment to be used and the interaction required, and will be determined by equipment specialists. This choice will determine the type of cable used to implement the LAN, which in turn affects facility decisions. Implementing a LAN requires close cooperation among information technology (IT), facility managers, and interior planners.

Building or Structured Cabling Considerations

So far, this chapter has dealt with power and data/communications cabling system design delivery issues separately because they are two different issues. They come together in discussion of distribution of these resources through the architectural (or structured cabling) systems, through the building itself.

Both power and data/communications cabling system resources must enter the building, be distributed vertically to each floor, and be available for access at points of use dictated by the needs of the people working there.

Adding to the confusion is the fact that multiple vendors are involved. The local phone company is one vendor, the long-distance company another, the cable television company yet another. Multiple computer and office equipment vendors are the rule, not the exception.

In designing cabling distribution systems, flexibility to accommodate future change is as important, if not more so, than accommodating present needs. Inadequate access to power and data/communications cabling system resources could prevent an organization from moving forward into a new technology and growth. Here too, structured cabling must be responsive to new functions imposed by the information technology age. See the sidebar, "Obstacles to Infrastructure Modernization Cabling," for further information on the responsiveness of new cabling technology to space, speed and future growth.

Obstacles to Infrastructure Modernization Cabling

Older construction, historic or otherwise, presents serious obstacles to infrastructure modernization. Creative solutions with cabling and wiring technologies ensure successful upgrades.

When do vintage 1980s buildings undergo historical renovations? When their wiring and cabling don't meet current needs.

That's what professionals at Briggs Corp. in Des Moines, IA, found when they investigated a new headquarters facility. The voice and data cabling was inadequate, inflexible, and prone to failure. If the phone or computer goes down, they would be out of business because that's the only way they sell.

The building was gutted, and core-drilled holes through the existing floors received poke-through devices—a flexible yet unobtrusive solution. Cabling was routed through center-spline cable trays in plenum space below, with data cables on one side of the tray and voice lines on the other to facilitate future moves. The cable tray saved a lot on labor. It's lightweight and easy to handle, and because it uses a single hanger instead of a trapeze, Wolin Electrical, a design/build firm in Des Moines, found they could put it up much faster than a conventional tray.

An in-floor cellular raceway was used for a training facility on the ground floor by cutting channels in the floor slab and refinishing over the raceway. It was easy to reconfigure the space just by opening the activation cover and plugging in.

In other instances, a gut renovation may be impossible, and even greater creativity is needed. For example, at Perry's Egyptian Theater, county and city owners wanted to save historical detail while bringing the 1924 facility up to date.

Part of a business and entertainment complex in Ogden, UT, the theater project was complicated by a historic design—and a fast-track schedule—that made pipe-and-wire cabling impossible. The 1924 theater has an unusual poured concrete structure, plastered masonry tile, and a rich art-deco facade with carved stone statues.

Pipe and wire could have been installed in 3-foot sections, but they never would have met the nine-month deadline. Instead, a metal-clad (type MC) cable was fished between the outer walls and the red interior tiles to serve convenience power and lighting throughout the theater.

A special, color-coded cable for fire alarm and control devices enhances the installed fire protection systems. A red stripe facilitates inspection, simplifies future rewiring, and helps prevent accidental disabling of the fire-security system.

Overall, the flexible type MC cabling is ideal for threading electrical circuits into existing walls, plenums, and anywhere that mechanical protection is required for safety. No alternative to flexible, pre-wired, metal-clad cable would have enabled them to meet that schedule in that type of environment.

Historic buildings present unique obstacles to telecommunications upgrades as well—especially in modernizing a turn-of-the-century facility. For example, a brick building with wooden beams and planks was modernized with contemporary offices and a decidedly futuristic cabling design.

Designed by US West and Plymouth, MN-based U.S. Premise Networking Services, the new system encompasses a total of seven telecommunications closets and three computer rooms serving some 2,000 workstations in modular furniture and hardwall offices.

The data networking environment offers Internet access and the capacity to install an asynchronous transfer mode (ATM) network for future increased bandwidth demands. US West's existing high-speed Ethernet networks are served by a fiber backbone and horizontal cable is supported by a single platform that goes beyond current needs for voice and data applications.

Certainly, this is the key for telecommunications and data cabling, say experts. Demand grows almost as rapidly as technologies evolve, so it's critical to allow space—and speed—for future growth [Sullivan, 1–3].

So, what is structured cabling? What does it mean to you? Let's take another look even though the U.S. version of structured cabling has been covered in earlier chapters to some extent. This discussion of structured cabling which follows is based on practices generally in use within the U.K. and in Europe.

Structured Cabling

In the past, buildings could have several different cabling systems for different communications systems, for example, block wiring for voice, coaxial for Ethernet, multipair for RS232, etc. Structured cabling replaces all the different cabling with a single cabling system which covers the whole building for all voice and data (including CCTV and video) requirements.

A structured cabling system consists of outlets which provide the user with an RJ45 presentation as shown in Figure 8–1 [2]. User outlets are usually supplied as either one or two RJ45 connectors mounted in a standard single gang face plate, or as single snap-in modules which can be fitted into floor boxes, single gang face plates (up to two modules), or dual gang face plates (up to four modules).

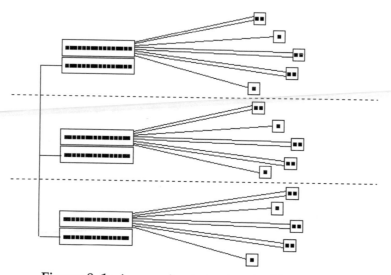

Figure 8–1: A generalized structured cabling system.

Each user outlet is cabled back to a hub using an individual cable containing four twisted pairs, this cabling is known as the *horizontal cabling*. In most cases, cable which meets the Category 5 specification is used for the horizontal cabling. The cable can be either unshielded, known as UTP (Unshielded Twisted Pair) or shielded, known as STP (Shielded Twisted Pair) or FTP (Foiled Twisted Pair).

The cable is connected to the back of the user outlet by means of an IDC (Insulation Displacement Connection) connector. The maximum length of cable between the hub and any outlet must be 90 meters to comply with EIA/TIA and ISO requirements. This is for Class D applications on Category 5 cable. The standards allow a further 10 meters for connecting leads and patch leads, making a total drive distance of 100 meters.

NOTE:

Some suppliers will warrant systems with longer drive distances, depending on the protocol being used.

In a true structured cabling system, the horizontal cabling and user outlets are the same for all services, so that any outlet can be configured for voice, Ethernet, RS232, video, or other service. As user requirements change, the service provided on the outlets can be changed simply by changing the patching configuration in the equipment room. If necessary, an adapter is used in the outlet to convert it to the service being provided (for example, a video balun will provide the standard RGB or composite video outputs required for CCTV).

When a structured cabling system is installed, the floors are usually *flood wired* with outlets being installed on a grid layout to a specified density, rather than to individual user positions. This allows for more flexibility, without having to re-cable, when changes are made to the layout of the building in the future.

At the hub, the individual 4-pair cables from the user outlets are terminated on patch panels. These patch panels usually have IDC (Insulation Displacement Connection) connectors on the rear for terminating the 4-pair cables, and provide an RJ45 presentation on the front for patching. Patch panels are usually mounted in standard 19-inch racks, either wall mounted or free standing. RJ45 patch panels usually come in multiples of 16 connectors; panels containing 16, 32, and 48 RJ45 connectors are common.

The hubs are connected together and to the main computer or equipment room using *riser* or *backbone* cables; these can either be copper or optical. In most systems, optical cables are used for the data backbone cables and multi-pair copper cables are used for the voice backbone cables.

NOTE:

> Voice backbone cables are almost always the 25-pair telco cables— where the interface to the Private Branch Exchange (PBX) is 66E Blocks at one end and to the patch panels in the Intermediate Distribution Frame (IDF) at the opposite end.

The equipment cabinets usually also contain equipment for the data network. Depending on the equipment used, the data channels may be presented in one of two different ways. Each data channel on the equipment may be fitted with an RJ45 connector, so that channels can be patched directly to the patch panels terminating the horizontal cables as shown in Figure 8–2 [Egerton, 2].

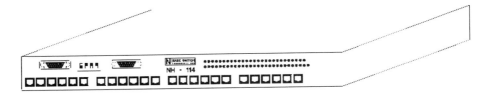

Figure 8–2: Data channels.

Alternatively, the equipment may be fitted with *telco* connectors. These are 25-pair connectors, each of which carries several (usually 12) data channels as shown in Figure 8–3 [Egerton, 3]. If the equipment is fitted with telco connectors, then these must be connected to *equipment side* patch panels using mass termination cables (25-pair cables fitted with a telco connector at one end, and no connectors at the other end, so that they can be punched down onto IDC connectors) to provide an RJ45 connector for each data channel.

If an optical fiber backbone is used, the hubs must also contain equipment to enable the optical cable to interface with the copper cables. Backbone cables are terminated on patch panels at the hub. Copper cables are terminated on RJ45 patch panels, the same as those used for the horizontal cabling. Optical cables are terminated in patch panels which usually provide the user with a 10Base-FL (STII) fiber optic or Stream Protocol Version 2 (STII) presentation. Fiber optic cables can be terminated by either fusion-splicing pigtails with factory-fitted connectors onto each fiber in the cable or by directly fitting *field mountable* connectors to each of the fibers. Factory fitted connectors are also available for interfacing copper to fiber.

Patch leads are used to connect the horizontal cables to either the data equipment or to the voice backbone cable, depending on which service is required at the user outlet as shown in Figure 8–4 [Egerton, 3]. Cable tidies are

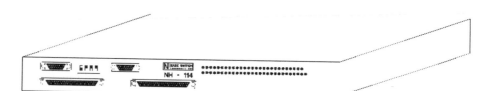

Figure 8–3: Telco connectors.

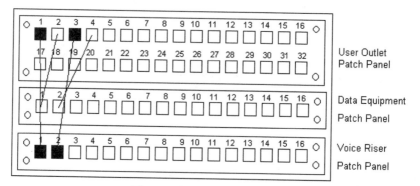

Figure 8–4: Patch leads.

used in the hub cabinets to enable patch leads to be routed neatly, these are 1U high 19-inch panels fitted with jumper rings. A 1U cable tidy is usually used below every 3U of patch panels.

The data backbone can be in either a star or ring configuration, depending on the equipment used as shown in Figure 8–5 [Egerton, 4]. In a star configuration, data backbone cables are usually taken to patch panels in the main computer (or equipment) room. Voice backbone cables are nearly always in a star configuration, and are taken to an MDF (Main Distribution Frame) or BDF (Building Distribution Frame). The MDF or BDF is usually a *KRONE* type frame utilizing 10-pair IDC connection strips. Furthermore, in large facilities, there are usually IDFs where voice and data are patched prior to being routed to the MDF.

A star and a ring backbone can be combined to provide resilience. In the event of the failure of any one cable in the backbone, the signal can be re-routed via another available route. This can be carried out automatically by the equipment, or by manually re-patching the backbone.

Equipment Rooms or Wiring Closets

Incoming communications cables interface with the building distribution systems in most office buildings and in main terminal rooms. Depending on the size of the building and the need, this interface can be anywhere from a relatively small wiring closet to a large temperature- and humidity-controlled room.

A rule of thumb cited by one manufacturer of electronic equipment is to provide a room a minimum of eight feet wide, with one square foot of floor space for each 2,000 square feet of usable floor space in the building. Satellite wire closets or equipment areas may be necessary, depending on the size and configuration of the building.

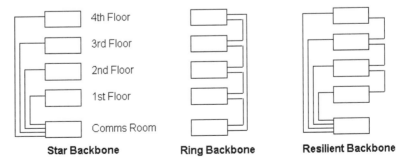

Figure 8–5: Data backbone.

For large office buildings, more than one equipment room may be necessary. A big high-rise might require a main equipment vault and satellite equipment rooms in other places throughout the building.

The main equipment room should be a separate, lockable room (this is advisable for satellite equipment rooms, too). It must be adequately ventilated and temperature-controlled (a 65- to 80-degree range is average, though some equipment makers may allow broader or narrower ranges for temperature and/or humidity). The humidity should generally be kept between 30 to 55 percent, and the room must be secure from flooding or seepage.

It's important to the functioning of the switching equipment that equipment rooms not become catchall storage areas. Switching equipment can be affected by copying machines and has to be housed separately; it has to be kept in a room free of chemicals or combustible gases such as ammonia, petroleum vapors, etc. It also should be kept as dust-free as possible.

Floor-loading requirements (the load-bearing capacity of the floor of the equipment room) will differ depending on the type of equipment. Usually, 125 to 175 pounds per square foot are typical recommended limits.

Special consideration should also be given to the availability of power wiring and AC outlets for communications equipment. Most manufacturers and building codes warn against joint use of equipment rooms for power system interface and communications system purposes.

NOTE:

A phone in each closet. No protocol data units (PDUs).

Nevertheless, most buildings will have two types of rooms to provide for the termination, protection, and management of various kinds of media and electronics that comprise the telecommunications network: entrance wiring closets and floor wiring closets. Let's take a specific look at the two different types of wiring closets.

Entrance Wiring Closets

The first type of room, the *entrance wiring closet* (EWC), will be located in the basement of the building it serves. In the absence of a basement, it will be on the ground floor.

All cables entering the building will be terminated in this room and the appropriate methods for high voltage protection will be applied. Electronic equipment associated with video and data interconnectivity will also be situated in this room. The EWC will be the focal point of all communications facilities and resources in the building. It is imperative that the EWC be an enclosed area secure from flooding and accidental damage, as well as sabotage.

In other words, the EWC is a room for the exclusive placement of electronics and terminations of cable of many types which supply the building with telecommunications. Security is required and the room cannot be shared with other functions in the building. Considerations for the facility are floor weight load factors, water avoidance, lighting, electrical access, room size, electrical grounding, HVAC, and location near the building entrance facility.

General

The room designated to be a EWC must be dedicated exclusively to that purpose. Access to the room should be direct without passing through other secure areas that would require additional keys for access. Conversely, access to the EWC should not be required in order to access another area. It cannot be shared with any other use such as storage, janitorial equipment or other electrical or mechanical installations. There should not be any plumbing fixtures in the room and pipes should not pass through the room that could cause flooding or require repair or replacement. There should not be any fire sprinklers in the room, if local fire codes will permit. Although, there should be some sort of smoke or fire monitoring.

Floor

The floor must be free of dust and static electricity. The floor should be tiled instead of carpeted. If the floor is left uncovered, it must be sealed and painted. The floor must be high enough to avoid any threat of flooding and have a minimum floor loading specification of at least 100 pounds per square foot.

Ceiling

The ceiling should be a minimum of 8 feet, 6 inches high. There should also not be a false ceiling.

Walls

The walls should be lined with _-inch, 4-foot by 8-foot plywood attached to the wall framing members or mechanically attached to the masonry walls. All surfaces are to be painted with fire resistant paint.

Doors

Doorways should be a minimum of 36 inches wide by 6 feet 8 inches high. Doors should be hinged outward and solid to provide security and resistance to fire. The door locks will be cored so that they will allow access to network personnel only.

Lighting

Lighting should be provided to a minimum level of 540 lx (50 foot candles) measured 3 feet above the floor. Light fixtures should be mounted a minimum of 8 feet, 6 inches above the floor.

Electrical

A 20 amp, 110 volt AC separately fused electrical circuit should be provided for electronic equipment. This circuit shall be extended to a power strip mounted on equipment racks in the center of the room. Additional outlets for tools, test instruments and work lights shall be placed at least at 6-foot intervals around the room.

Grounding

A minimum of a 6 AWG ground conductor from the main building grounding electrode and the power neutral shall be provided. It shall also be terminated on a copper ground bar properly installed in the room.

HVAC

HVAC provisioning shall be sufficient to provide a minimum of six air changes per hour. The temperature should be maintained at 55 F to 80 F 24 hours a day, 365 days a year. Care must be taken to not include the room in a zone that could have heating, air conditioning, or air exchange reduced during night or idle times, as the equipment will generate the same amount of heat at all times.

Location

A building should have only one EWC regardless of the building size. It should be located as close as possible to the point where telecommunications facilities enter the building while being centrally located to reduce the lengths of backbone cables.

Size

The minimum size for an EWC is 6 feet by 9 feet, but that size room will satisfy the needs of a building of up to 200,000 square feet of gross floor space. Figure 8–6 illustrates how that space would be utilized [3]. Table 8–1 specifies room sizes required for buildings of more square feet or gross floor space [VCCS, 2].

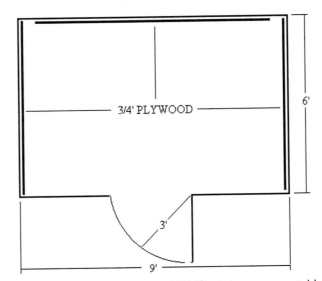

Figure 8–6: EWC space utilization and FWC minimum acceptable room size.

Table 8–1: Room Sizes.

Ground Floor Space Square Feet	Room Dimensions Feet
Up to 200,000	9 X 6
200,001 to 400,000	9 X 10
400,001 to 500,000	9 X 13
500,001 to 600,000	10 X 13.5
600,001 to 800,000	11 X 16
800,001 to 1,000,000	11 X 21

Floor Wiring Closets

The *floor wiring closet* (FWC) is the second type of room required. Backbone cables from the EWC are terminated here as are station cables. Pairs in these cables are connected in this room to establish continuous electrical paths from rooms/desktops to other rooms/desktops, and to communication devices. Electronic devices associated with the exchange of data and/or video information will also be situated in these FWCs.

In other words, the FWC has an exclusive location on each floor to facilitate the electronics and cabling distribution for the floor. If the floor is large enough, with long cable runs, more than one room may be required on each floor. Security requires that the room not be shared with other building functions. Considerations for the facility are floor loading factors, water avoidance, ceilings and walls, fire door, lighting, electrical access, room size, electrical grounding, HVAC, floor location, and cable run maximum lengths.

General

A room designated to be an FWC must be dedicated exclusively to that purpose. Access to the room should be direct without passing through other secure areas that would require additional keys for access. Conversely, access to the FWC should not be required in order to access another area. It cannot be shared with any other use such as storage, janitorial equipment or other electrical or mechanical installation. There should not be any plumbing fixtures in the room and pipes should not pass through the room that could cause flooding or require repair or replacement. There should not be any fire sprinklers in the room, if fire codes will permit However, the FWC should have a working phone in it.

Floor

The floor must be free of dust and static electricity. The floor should be tiled instead of carpeted. If the floor is left uncovered, it must be sealed and painted. The floor must be high enough to avoid any threat of flooding and have a minimum floor loading specification of 50 pounds per square foot.

Ceiling

The ceiling should be a minimum of 8 feet, 6 inches high. In addition, there should also not be a false ceiling.

Walls

The walls should be lined with 3/4-inch, 4-foot by 8–foot plywood attached to the wall framing members or mechanically attached to the masonry walls. All surfaces are to be painted with fire resistant paint.

Doors

Doorways should be a minimum of 36 inches wide by 6 feet, 8 inches high. Doors should be hinged outward and solid to provide security and resistance to fire. The door locks will be cored so that they will allow access to network personnel only.

Lighting

Lighting should be provided to a minimum level of 540 lx (50 foot candles) measured 3 feet above the floor. Light fixtures should be mounted a minimum of 8 feet 6 inches, above the floor.

Electrical

A 20 amp, 110 volt AC separately fused electrical circuit shall be provided for power strips to be installed with the steel equipment racks. Additional outlets for tools, test instruments and work lights shall be placed at least at 6-foot intervals around the room at a height of 6 inches above the floor.

Grounding

A minimum of a 6 AWG ground conductor from the main building grounding electrode and the power neutral shall be provided. It shall also be terminated on a copper ground bar properly installed in the room.

HVAC

HVAC provisioning shall be sufficient to provide a minimum of four (4) air changes per hour. The temperature should be maintained at 55 F to 80 F 24 hours a day, 365 days a year. Care must be taken to not include the room in a zone that could have heating, air conditioning or air exchange reduced during night or idle times as the equipment will generate the same quantity of heat at all times.

Location

Each floor must have at least one FWC. Additional FWCs may be required to meet maximum limits for station cable lengths defined below. FWCs should be located in the center of the area to be served. In multi-floored buildings, FWCs should be located directly above each other to minimize the lengths of backbone cables, thus reducing the lengths of circuits between floors in the building.

The FWC should be located in such a way that the average station cable length is 150 feet, and no individual station cable exceeds 295 feet in length. One FWC can effectively serve 20,000 square feet of usable floor space.

Size

The requirements to terminate fiber optic cables both to the individual room jack and in the building backbone system coupled with the video media terminations required in each FWC cause the minimum acceptable room size to be 6 feet by 9 feet as shown in Figure 8–6. This 54 square foot minimum requirement can effectively serve 15,000 square feet of usable floor space. As the usable floor space increases, so should the size of the FWC at the rate of 9 square feet per 5,000 square feet of usable floor space. A maximum 20,000 square feet of usable space would require a minimum FWC size of 6 feet by 12 feet.

Vertical Distribution

Power and data/communications cabling system resources are distributed vertically through tall buildings via backbone cables in one or more building shafts to the floors where they will be used. How this system is designed will vary greatly depending on the design of the building.

Increased use of information technology usually brings the need for more building core capacity to accommodate the additional cable used. Many high-rise buildings have created headaches for their owners because the backbone shaft is crammed full of cable and can't handle the demand for more. Where codes allow, even the elevator shafts are pressed into service in many high-rises as a way (though not a good one) of getting more data/communications capacity into the building. Nevertheless, there continue to be numerous instances of intermittent problems with high speed circuits that are routed over cables in elevator shafts.

Backbone shafts are either open or closed. Closed backbone shafts are vertically aligned closets on each floor connected by pipe sleeves or conduit through the floors. They have different fire code requirement than open-shaft systems, but they may be more versatile.

Backbone Raceways

Backbone raceways are a series of accesses that connect EWCs to FWCs. These paths permit cable to be placed between the floors. They may be slots, sleeves, conduits, or trays and racks in which cables may be routed for support and protection. Considerations are the size, quantity, and seals. If conduits or sleeves are used, the 4-inch size is preferred. Table 8–2 shows the number of paths needed, based upon building size [VCCS, 1].

NOTE:

The term backbone has replaced riser and house in cable terminology.

General

Backbone raceways may be slots or sleeves between floors. Or, they may consist of conduits or trays and racks in which cables may be routed for support and protection.

Design

When wiring closets are located above each other, sleeves or slots may be used. When they are so situated, conduits should be utilized to provide security and physical protection to the cables.

Size

The size of sleeves or conduits can be stated as one since sleeves will probably be made of pieces of conduit placed through the floor. A minimum of 4-inch conduits should be used. If space limitations prevent the use of 4-inch conduits then the number of 3-inch ducts provided should be doubled or if 2-inch ducts are used the number should be increased four fold. Slots should be a minimum of 4-inches inside dimension square. Slot sizes and/or numbers of slots can be determined by the number of 4-inch conduits or sleeves required under Table 8–2 [VCCS, 1].

Table 8–2: Slot sizes.

Ground Floor Space Square Feet	Numbers of Sleeves or Ducts
Up to 40,000	1
40,001 to 80,000	2
80,001 to 160,000	3
160,001 to 180,000	4
180,001 to 200,000	5

NOTE:

Table 8–2 does not include two spare ducts or sleeves.

Quantity

A minimum of one 4-inch conduit or sleeve should be provided per FWC plus two spares. If higher floors FWCs are supplied from lower floor FWCs (as with sleeves or slots) only one conduit for every two rooms need to be added to the backbone as shown in Figure 8–7 [VCCS, 1].

Seals

All conduits should be provided with seals until used to prevent the entrance of gases. Sleeves and slots should be sealed with firestop material to prevent the spread of fire.

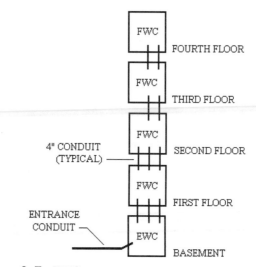

Figure 8–7: FWC minimum acceptable conduit or sleeve.

Horizontal Distribution

On each floor, power and data/communications cabling system resources are distributed horizontally through either the ceiling or the floor. Ceiling systems use metal conduit, raceways, and/or flexible conduit cable assemblies to distribute power and data/communications wiring in the plenum, or the space between a finished dropped or hung ceiling and the floor above. If the ceiling is an air-plenum ceiling, cable must be routed through conduit or must be fire-rated.

Wires and cables are brought down to each point of use through power poles, which typically interface with building electrical wiring through junction boxes at the top. Data/communications cables run through the power pole in separate raceways isolated from the electrical wiring by metal barriers (required by the National Electrical Code).

Features of ceiling systems include low initial cost, low labor costs (poles are prewired), unlimited choice of installation locations, and compatibility with just about any structural system or furniture choice. Constraints include the *forest* effect (a clutter of poles interrupting open office environments), small capacity, and limited reuse of ceiling tiles, which have to be cut.

Typical Floor Distribution Cabling Systems

Tubular duct systems use steel ducts to carry wiring. Access to these systems is through above-floor monuments or *tombstones*. Because the ducts have separate channels for power wires and data/communications cables, access to each usually requires a separate above-floor monument.

Features include ease of installation during construction and experienced builders, who have worked with such systems for years. Constraints include high first cost, potentially limited capacity (by raceway size), ease of damaging the ducts during other phases of construction, and necessity of a thicker concrete slab to meet fireproofing requirements.

Cellular floors are among the most popular architectural options. They are both structural floors and data/communications wiring. Trench headers, specially manufactured metal troughs, bring power wiring and data/communications cables through the floor from the wiring closets.

Trench duct is normally covered with removable flat steel cover plates for its entire length. Although access to the cellular floor can be through other feeder ducts, trench headers provide maximum flexibility to the system. The size and placement of the trench header will determine the accessibility of wiring and cabling.

Cellular floors can conceal power and communications outlets below the floor, or they can be used with above-floor monuments. Preset inserts are usually used with freestanding furniture because the density of the cells enables the inserts to be placed almost anywhere the furniture plan requires.

Features of cellular floors are that they can provide a great deal of capacity for numerous access points (depending on their design), are cost-effective in use of materials, and don't have the stability problems some users notice with raised floors. Constraints are that they can be slow or difficult to install because the concrete must be poured carefully around the presets, alignment during construction can be difficult, an electrician must be present during construction, adding wire can be difficult, fireproofing is required on the bottom plate, and access to the trench header must be maintained. Designing the cell spacing of a cellular floor system is critical to its later usefulness.

Raised floor (or raised-access floor) systems are mounted on steel pedestals and have removable floor panel sections to allow access beneath the floor, where power and data/communications wiring are distributed. Access can be through above-floor monuments or through access ports with a junction box mounted below a cutout on the floor panel.

Raised floors were used primarily in computer rooms before the invasion of the personal computer into most offices. Today they are widely used because of their capacity to handle volumes of cable. Features in addition to capacity include flexibility for additions or relocations of wiring, capacity to accommodate other services (HVAC, plumbing, etc.), no need for conduit to protect wires, cables where the floor plenum does not contain air return, and ease of construction.

Constraints include raising floor height; higher initial material cost, floor-height changes around stairwells and core areas, leveling problems, noise from footsteps, and potential code problems. Raised floor provides no additional shielding of cables. Its capacity, one of its greatest advantages, can also become a constraint by leading to lax wire management. It is seductively simple just to add more cable for a short-term solution instead of planning properly for the long term. See the sidebar, "Installing Communications Cabling Below a Raised Floor," for additional information.

Installing Communications Cabling Below a Raised Floor

When you are installing communications cabling below a raised floor in a room that doesn't meet the requirements of an Information Technology Processing Room (as defined in Article 645 [NFPA-70] of the National Electrical Code [NEC]), does the cable have to be type CMP or MPP, and does it have to be enclosed in conduit as outlined in Section 300-22(b)? The confusion stems from Section 800-53(a), which states: "*Cable installed in ducts, plenums, and other spaces used for environmental air shall be type CMP.*" However, the exception lists several types of cables allowed in plenums that must be installed in compliance with Section 300-22, and type CMP is listed as one of those types of cables. Also, Figure 800-2 depicts type MPP and CMP cable in a plenum, but not in conduit. Is type CMP cable in a plenum required to be installed in accordance with Section 300-22?

No, NFPA-70 does not require that CMP cable be installed in conduit in a plenum space, but it does not prohibit installation of CMP cable in conduit in a plenum space either. That is why CMP appears in both the requirement and the exception. The following citations should clear up any confusion:

• Section 800-50 of the NEC, "Listing, Marking, and Installation of Communications Wires and Cables," states: "Communications wires and cables installed as wiring within buildings shall be listed as being suitable for the purpose."

• Section 800-53(a), "Applications of Listed Communications Wires and Cables, (a) Plenum," states: "Cables installed in ducts, plenums, and other spaces used for environmental air shall be Type CMP. Exception: Types CMP, CMR, CMG, CM, and CMX and communications wire installed in compliance with Section 300-22."

• Section 300-22(c), "Other Space Used for Environmental Air," states: "Other type cables and conductors shall be installed in electrical metallic tubing, flexible metallic tubing, intermediate metal conduit, rigid metal conduit, flexible metal conduit, or, where accessible, surface metal raceway or metal wireway with metal covers or solid bottom metal cable tray with solid metal covers."

NOTE:

The listing of type CMP in the exception to 800-53(a) is not a typographical error. There are parts of the country that require all telecommunications cable to be installed in conduit. This wording allows for those folks to use CMP or MPP cable in those conduits [4].

Poke-through systems use the plenum of the floor below for access to wires and cables. A hole is drilled through the floor and wires or cables are literally poked through. A fire-rated monument must be installed in the floor to protect the floor fire rating. Fire codes and structural considerations usually limit the number of poke-through fittings that can be used in a space.

Features of poke-through systems include low initial cost. Constraints includes high cost of changing or maintaining the building once holes have been made, limited outlets (holes weaken the structure), relocation expense and difficulty, limited capacity, conduit or fire-rated plenum cable required for telephone and data wiring, risk (drilling could result in damage to hidden conduits), and mess and disruption when it's time to change.

Floor-surface raceways attach directly to the floor and enclose electrical and data/communications wiring in separate covered raceways. They're used with low profile junction boxes and fittings that are mounted directly on the floor, and they are usually used when the least expensive solution is desired. Surface-wall raceways are similar and attach directly to walls or columns.

Features of floor-surface raceways include low initial cost and ease of access. Constraints include aesthetic concerns and potential tripping hazards.

Flat conductor cable is one of the newest options. Flat cables can carry phone, electrical, and data transmission wiring in thin copper strips covered with insulation, lying flat beneath carpet squares where traditional round wires would be objectionable. Specially designed monuments allow access to the wiring. Outlets can be moved or new outlets can be added with a minimum of disruption.

Though only approved a few years ago, flat cable has become very popular for use with open-plan furniture systems because it can deliver services nearly anywhere in an installation, preserving the furniture system's relocatability and aesthetic advantages. Flat conductor must be used with carpet squares because of electrical codes, but this is desirable anyway because it makes access to the wire much easier.

The newest flat conductor products include optical fiber versions that can carry voice, data, and video signals, yet are immune to interference and electrical noise. Other developments include low-profile coaxial data cable, including some suitable for use with LANs.

Other features of flat conductor cable include moderate installed system cost depending on locality, suitability for renovation, compatibility with other systems such as cellular floors or tubular ducts, ease of relocation by backbone (in-house) workers, and distribution of wires and cables without altering floor height. Constraints include limited applications (not approved for hospitals, schools, or residential applications), limited capacity, relatively high cost of change because cable is not always reusable, distance limitations of data and voice cable, and trade problems (phone workers cannot move carpeting because of union rules).

Each of these building distribution systems has advantages and disadvantages, and often the right solution is a combination of approaches. But it is important for the facility planner to realize that higher initial costs for maximum power and data/communications capacity will very likely be justified by future needs. And the cost of retrofitting an inadequate installation will be much, much higher than planning for the maximum at the beginning of a project.

Open-plan furniture systems can be a valuable extension of building power and data/communications delivery systems. To accomplish this, the furniture system must provide an interface with the building distribution systems, means of distribution of wires and cables through the space, and points of access to resources.

Power poles and base power-in assemblies provide the interface between the building systems and equipment for both electricity and data/communications cables. Wires and cables travel from ceiling systems through separate channels in power poles to panels, where they are distributed horizontally. Whatever the method of distribution through the floor, the base power-in connects to the building electrical system and electricity is then distributed through electrically wired powerways. Cables can be routed through raceways at panel bases or tops.

Vertical distribution of cables is accomplished through cable management poles available for different geometries of panel connections. Storage of excess cable takes place in the raceways themselves or in special cable reels and troughs mounted under work surfaces.

Access is provided in a variety of ways. Electrical outlets can be placed at panel bases in simplex, duplex, or triplex receptacles. Outlets can be at work surface height as separate outlets or as part of worksurface powerways.

Cables can be brought through channels at worksurface height. Or, they can be brought through at the tops and bottoms of panels through a variety of options.

Planning and designing for adequate access can be trickier than it may seem. Plenty of outlets may be available in the panels, but when free-standing furniture such as desks or files is moved in, these access points can be blocked. For this reason, as well as for circuit capacity planning, the facility planner needs to know what equipment will be used in a space and where it will be located.

A wire management plan and design, continuously and accurately updated, provides the database required for managing power and data/communications wiring. As with everything else in facility management, what is designed and installed will only work as long as it is properly maintained.

The wire management plan should include a set of drawings that identifies each point of access to power or data/communications cabling system resources on each floor, as well as the overall view of the building. It should indicate what has been activated and what has not, what kind of cable is located where, and what each cable is connected to.

It's easier than it may seem. This information can easily be logged on a personal computer or simply kept in notebook form and updated any time changes are made. Software for managing power wiring and data/communications cabling is becoming increasingly sophisticated; several versions are already on the market, with more to come.

Make sure, too, that every vendor contract affecting power or data/communications cabling system delivery includes a provision stating that the vendor must adhere to the wire management plan and design. The key is having a plan and design, and then making sure everyone sticks to both.

From Here

This chapter presented an overview of cabling system architectural design considerations (structured cabling system, wiring closet design, cabling facilities, and user-to-outlet ratios, etc.). The next chapter discusses copper design considerations (layout, components, connectors, shielding and maintenance, etc.).

End Notes

[1] C. C. Sullivan, "Prehistoric Cabling," *Buildings OnLine*, Stamats Communications, Inc., 427 6th Avenue S.E., PO Box 1888, Cedar Rapids, IA 52406, 1997, pp. 1–3.

[2] "Structured Cabling," Egerton Communications Systems Ltd, Sound Lane, Nantwich, Cheshire, CW5 8BE, United Kingdom, 1997, p. 1.

[3] "Telecommunications Cabling and Electronics Specifications: Specific Guidelines," Virginia Community College System (VCCS), 101 North 14th Street 15th Floor, Richmond, Virginia 23219, 1998, p. 3.

[4] Jesse Tolliver, "Cabling Below a Raised Floor," ASAF Air Intelligence Agency/QA, Kelly afb, San Antonio, TX, *Cabling Installation & Maintenance*, (August, 1997), p. 44.

9

Copper Design Considerations

In any discussion about computers and communication, copper wiring design considerations are right at the top of any workarea layout decisions. These design decisions must fit into every layer that provides physical connections between the various devices like printers, dumb terminals, and computers. For example, let's imagine an analogy between the computer-based networks and an overnight carrier (FedEx, UPS, AIRBORNE Express, DHL, etc.). Here the computers would represent people on either side of the communication where the communication would take place in the form of packets of information (letters and boxes in the overnight carrier analogy). The network would be the mechanism responsible for carrying the packets of information from a computer to a computer or another device like a printer. In the analogy, this mechanism would be the overnight carrier system, where letters and boxes are carried from person to person. The overnight carrier system consists of counter employees, carriers, trucks, highways,. etc. Wiring in the analogy would be the roadways/highways over which the information is carried.

As discussed in earlier chapters, the International Standards Organization (ISO) has put forth a standard for communication between computer equipment and networks. This standard is referred to as Open System Interconnection (OSI) model and shows how the communication maps into 7 protocol layers as shown in the sidebar, "Open System Interconnect Model."

Open System Interconnect Model

This model explains what each layer does in the communication framework. The model is often used to explain any particular set of protocols (not just OSI) to the point where many people seem to believe that true data-communications requires these 7 layers. When talking about wiring we're mainly concerned with the first two layers, the physical layer and the data-link layer.

Top Layer 7. Applications:

This top layer identifies where the user applications software lies. Such issues as file access and transfer, virtual terminal emulation, interprocess communication, and the like are handled here. An example of this would be IBM's System Application Architecture (SAA).

6. Presentation:

This layer deals with differences in data representation. For example, UNIX-style line endings (CR only) might be converted to MS-DOS style (CRLF), EBCIDIC to ASCII character sets, blinking characters, reverse video and screen graphics.

5. Session:

This layer controls communications between applications across a network. Testing for out-of-sequence packets, two-way communication, security, name recognition, and logging are handled here.

4. Transport:

This layer makes sure the lower three layers (3, 2 and 1) are doing their job correctly, and provides a transparent, logical data stream between the end user and the network service being used. It also makes sure that the data received is in the right format and order. This is the lower layer that provides local user services.

3. Network:

This layer makes certain that a packet sent from one device to another actually gets there in a reasonable period of time. Routing and flow control are performed here. This is the lowest layer of the OSI model that can remain ignorant of the physical network.

2. Data Link:

This layer deals with getting data packets on and off the wire, error detection and correction, and retransmission. This layer is generally broken into two sub-layers: The LLC (Logical Link Control) on the upper half, which does the error checking, and the MAC (Media Access Control) on the lower half, which deals with getting the data on and off the wire. Also, some of the protocols the data-link layer uses are High Level Data Link Control (HDLC) and bisynchronous (bisync) communications.

Bottom Layer 1. Physical:

This bottom layer defines the nuts and bolts. Here is where the cable, connector and signaling specifications are defined [1].

Different Media for Physical Layer

Physical media for Ethernet can be one of several types including thin and thick coaxial cable, twisted-pair cable, and fiber optic cable. Coaxial cable (coax) is a metallic electrical cable used for RF (radio frequency) and certain data communications transmission. The cable is constructed with a single solid or stranded center conductor that is surrounded by the dielectric layer, an insulating material of constant thickness and high resistance. A conducting layer of aluminum foil, metallic braid or a combination of the two encompass the dielectric and act as both a shield against interference (to or from the center conductor) and as the return ground for the cable. Finally, an overall insulating layer forms the outer jacket of the cable. Coaxial cable is generally superior in high-frequency applications such as networking. However, for shorter distances (up to 100 meters), UTP or STP cable is generally just as reliable when using differential modulation techniques (such as with 10BaseT). Some well-known kinds are various cable TV cables, cables used by IBM 327x terminals, and cables used by Ethernet and IEEE 802.3.

Diagrams for STP and UTP

Twisted pair (TP) is the type of wire used by the phone company to wire telephones over shorter distances (like between your house and the central office). It has two conductors which are twisted. The twists are important: they give it electrical characteristics which allow some kinds of communications otherwise not possible.

UTP

UTP is what's typically installed by phone companies (though this is often not of high enough quality for high-speed network use) and is usually what 10BaseT Ethernet runs over. UTP is graded according to its data-carrying ability (Category 3, Category 4, Category 5). 10BaseT Ethernet requires at least Category 3 cable. Many sites now install only Category5 UTP, even though Category 4 is more than sufficient for 10BaseT, because of the greater likelihood that emerging high-speed standards will require cable with better bandwidth capabilities.

Unshielded Twisted Pair (UTP) Cable Vertical Cabling Design

When using Unshielded Twisted Pair (UTP) cable vertical (trunk) cabling, it is recommended that 100-pair cable maximum be used for ease of installation and to minimize data crosstalk. Where more than 100 pairs are required, as in a trunking application, it is recommended that multiple cables of 25- or 100-pair each be specified.

A block system uses 100 pairs per block, so using 100 pair cables enhances cable management and identification. Likewise, when using modular (RJ) patch panels, it is recommended that 2-pair channels that yield 100 pairs per 2U (2 rack position) patch panel (48 channels) be implemented.

Cabling crosstalk occurs when one channel within a multiconductor cable generates Electro-Magnetic Interference (EMI) which another channel receives. This is the most detrimental EMI for a data communications system. Limiting the maximum per-cable pair count to 100 pair minimizes potential cross-talk problems.

Installation Considerations

Historically, voice cables were constructed in 25-pair groupings and terminated in 100-pair sets. This caused cable manufacturers to research and develop cables with performance optimized within these configurations. Manufacturers of cross-connection products also configure products to handle the cables in 25- or 100-pair groups.

In the case of most block based systems, each block provides termination for 100 pairs. System layout on some products (66 blocks, for example) may define a termination implementation that reduces this to 50 pairs; but, this still supports a 25-pair grouping. Figure 9–1 shows a panel consisting of two 100 pair blocks [2].

High density modular (RJ) patch panels are generally 24 channels per rack position (1U) with a recommended frame layout of two patching positions between each ring run as shown in Figure 9–2 [MOD-TAP, 1]. It is recommended that vertical (trunk) UTP cabling in 2-pair channels be configured. This yields a single 100-pair cable per 2U (48 channels) patch field. Optionally, this is specifying 4-pair vertical channels that would yield a single row of channels per 100-pair cable (24 channels).

In either case, using a 25- or 100-pair cable offers substantial advantages in the area of cable design and management. Each section of the cross-connection field corresponds to a specific cable, which eases troubleshooting and maintenance. Likewise, during the installation, the cable must be routed and tied down. Using a larger cable (400-pair) requires removing the jacket for much more length and routing sections of the cable across a much larger area.

Figure 9–1: A panel consisting of two 100 pair blocks.

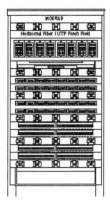

Figure 9–2: High density modular (RJ) patch panels.

Cable Channel Noise: Cause and Effects

Noise within the cable can come from many sources. But it is generally segmented into noise from outside the cable (external) and noise generated within the cable itself (internal).

External cable noise comes from the general environment. Common sources are TV and radio stations, nearby power cables, motors (often HVAC systems), and high voltage lighting. Properly designed cables minimize impact from broadcast sources such as TV and radio. Proper installation insuring a minimum distance from motors and high voltage devices minimizes problems from these sources.

Internal noise is generated either from other channels (signals) within the cable or from reflections caused by connections within the channel. Again, proper installation minimizes the number of connections and ensures the highest possible quality of the connections required. This eliminates problems caused by reflection. It also leaves crosstalk as the primary noise issue in your information cabling system.

Crosstalk is a type of Electro-Magnetic Interference (EMI) in which interference is generated by one channel and received by another. This can be especially detrimental to system operation where the two channels are common to the same system. The receiving channel will get data of the correct speed, timing, and protocol and therefore does not reject it as simple noise. The system instead may attempt to process or otherwise operate on this data.

Figure 9–3 is a graph of the signal effects as the transmission distance increases in an environment with no EMI [MOD-TAP, 2]. Starting at -0dB, the signal is attenuated (signal level reduced) as the distance increases. At some point, labeled *-dB,* the signal has attenuated to the point where the receiver can no longer accept the signal. This point is determined by the operating characteristics of the equipment interfaces. At this signal level the communications interface can no longer capture the signal and the channel fails. This distance, labeled *D1* on the horizontal axis, is the maximum distance attainable for this system on that media. When most manufacturers rate their products they use this distance, reduced by a percentage for a safety margin.

Figure 9–4 places this UTP channel in an environment where EMI is present [MOD-TAP, 2]. As the length of a cable increases, so does its ability to act as an antenna, generating a second line labeled *N* for noise. The intersection of these two lines defines a distance, labeled *D2*, which is the failure point of the channel within this specific EMI environment. At this point, the noise becomes high enough to overpower the signal and the communications interface fails.

NOTE:

Distance D2 is substantially less than the clear channel distance D1. Different EMI environments generate different noise curves and yield different failure (intersection) points.

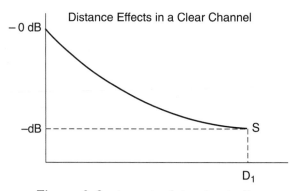

Figure 9–3: A graph of the signal effects.

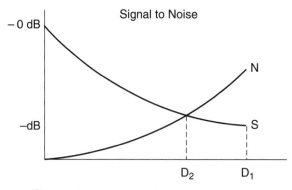

Figure 9–4: Placement of the UTP channel.

In Figure 9–5, the signal-to-noise graph (See Figure 9–4) and the clear channel failure graph (See Figure 9–3) are combined [MOD-TAP, 2]. This would be the case where the noise is really another channel carrying data of the same system and there is no current data on the receiving channel. In this case, the system accepts the noise as a signal, attempting to acknowledge and process it. This yields problems at distance *D3,* an even shorter distance than either D1 or D2. Therefore, the potential problems caused by crosstalk exceed the problems caused by other EMI.

Minimizing Crosstalk

The usual answer to EMI problems is to use shielded cable, an expensive proposition not only because of the higher cost of the media but also because of a more expensive installation due to shield termination and cable size. Shields must be correctly terminated. Shields which *float* (are unterminated) or which create ground loops (terminated at both ends) will make the EMI problem worse instead of better. This necessitates the purchase of grounding products and allocating additional labor to this process. Shielding also increases both the size and bend radius of the cable, requiring larger and more costly conduit or cable trays and making the installation more difficult. Furthermore, it's also very important that the plugs or connectors are shielded.

A properly installed cable with an overall shield (a shield around the entire cable) will minimize the effects of EMI from the outside of the cable. However, in the case of trunk cables, there will be many pairs of cable within the shield and, therefore, many channels of data. Each channel is not only a potential receiver but is also broadcasting EMI. An overall shield does not protect a cable from this crosstalk, only from the external EMI. Therefore, to shield against crosstalk in multichannel cabling (in addition to an overall shield), each channel must be shielded within the cable from all others. This requires individual shields for each pair of cable to provide maximum protection. Again, this increases media cost, installation cost, bend radius, and cable outside diameter (OD).

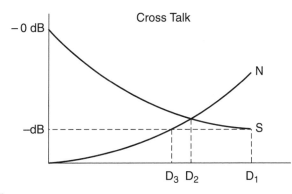

Figure 9–5: Combining the signal-to-noise graph and the clear channel failure graph.

An alternative to shielding is to minimize the coupling effect between the pairs by twisting each pair at a different rate from the others. This *variable lay-up* will not totally eliminate crosstalk but generally will reduce it to an acceptable level. Better cable manufacturers use a variable lay-up for all their cable and the higher the quality of the cable (Category 5 vs. Category 3) the higher the twist rate will be. In addition, the way the 25-pair groups are combined into a cable is critical to the crosstalk and other noise induced.

Use of High Pair Count Cabling

It is easy to implement a variable lay-up when manufacturing 25-pair cabling, but when using higher pair count cable (100-, 200-, 400-pair or higher) problems can occur. While the lay-up within a 25-pair group varies, there will be a repeat of twist rates group to group.

When combining the 25-pair groups into a larger cable it is possible to maintain low crosstalk capabilities up to 100-pair. In larger pair counts the groups are tightly bound together and the spatial relationships between the groups become very stable. Varying the spatial relationships minimizes the crosstalk potential by breaking the coupling between the pairs, thereby reducing the mutual antenna effects.

The potential crosstalk paths in 25-pair cable is 300, as shown by the matrix in Figure 9–6 [MOD-TAP, 3]. This shows a 25-by-25 matrix, eliminating the instances where a pair crosstalks to itself (not possible) and the duplication of paths (1 to 2 is the same path as 2 to 1). This yields an equation of:

$1/2 (X$ squared $-X)$ where X is the pair count of the cable.

Table 9–1 consists of potential crosstalk paths for different pair count cable by pair and channel for 2-, 3-, and 4-pair channels [MOD-TAP, 4].

25 Pair Cable Cross-Talk Matrix

	1	2	3	4	5	6	7	• • • 25
1	X							
2		X						
3			X					
4				X				
5					X			
6						X		
7							X	
•								
•								
•								
25								

Figure 9–6: Potential crosstalk paths.

Table 9–1: Number of Cross Talk Paths

Cable Pair Count	1-Pair Crosstalk Paths	2-Pair Crosstalk Paths	3-Pair Crosstalk Paths	4-Pair Crosstalk Paths
25	300	66	28	15
50	1,225	276	120	66
100	4,950	1,128	496	276
200	19,900	4,560	2016	1,128
400	79,800	18,336	8,128	4,560
600	179,700	41,328	18,336	10,296
1200	719,400	165,600	73,536	41,328

STP

Shielded twisted pair (STP) is a type of twisted-pair cable with a metallic shield around the twisted conductors. The shield reduces the noise from the cable and reduces the effects of noise on the communications in the cable, but changes the electrical characteristics of the cable so some equipment optimized to non-shielded cable runs worse on shielded cable. STP is typically used for token ring networks, where it is commonly referred to IBM Type 1 (or 2, 3, 6, 8, etc). However, there are several manufacturers of Ethernet equipment and interfaces that support Ethernet over STP. Nevertheless, Ethernet over STP is not officially defined in any standards.

Shielded Versus Unshielded Cables

Telephone wire in wide use today is typically between 19 AWG and 26 AWG, with the inside more likely to be 24 to 26 AWG. This wire is typically twisted, on average, with two twists per foot, and combined with other color-coded twisted pairs.

The twisting of a pair of wires resulted from the observation that when twisted, the radiated energy from current flowing in any one wire is almost completely canceled out by radiated energy from the same current flowing back in the return wire of that pair. This radiated energy is often referred to as electromagnetic radiation (EMR).

This twisting therefore, effectively and inexpensively minimizes crosstalk into adjacent pairs in a multipair cable. It also allows the pairs to be less susceptible to external noise, since they would be coupled equally into each wire in a pair, as well as being canceled out if properly terminated.

At voice frequencies, each pair appears to be balanced. The word *balanced* in this context is the approximate definition of a transmission pair that is balanced if equal energy is coupled from each wire within the pair to any point in space.

The wavelength of a signal (its propagation velocity divided by its frequency—where the speed of light at 186,000 miles per second is divided by 186,000 hz yielding a wavelength of one mile) at voice frequencies is much longer than the physical dimensions of a pair and its twist length. Therefore, it can be considered a balanced media.

However, at higher frequencies (at 10 mhz the wavelength would be less than 100 feet), the pair no longer agrees with the balanced theory and both crosstalk and noise susceptibility increase exponentially. Therefore, it is the desire to transmit at higher frequencies that has generated research and interest into shielded cables.

Shielding

The shield improves a wire pair's emission of and susceptibility to EMI, depending of course on the shield's construction materials and application. Shielding comes in many varieties and performance characteristics.

The general consensus among wire and cable providers is that transfer impedance is the most useful measurement of a shield's effectiveness. Transfer impedance is the ratio of the potential difference applied at a pair of terminals in a network to the resulting current at a second pair of terminals. The following information is a comparison of the transfer impedance of various shields at different frequencies.

When to Shield

The safe answer is to always install shielded cable, because although today's applications might get by on unshielded wire, clearly high digital rates of the future will work better over shielded cable. The difficulty is its higher cost over unshielded copper pair (2-3 pair unshielded costs less than .05 per foot, whereas shielded 2-3 pair can cost .30 per foot or more). In other words, shielded cable costs about 500% more than unshielded. For example, if you are installing conduits everywhere and applications don't need the services of shielding initially, then it might be appropriate to install unshielded today and install shielded only on an as-needed basis.

In the end, the commercial building standards make use of all types (UTP and STP) of cabling depending on the requirements. Nowadays, the most common type of wire to run distributions from the phone closet to the workstation is data-grade unshielded twisted pair (2-pair minimum, 4-pair recommended). Backbone runs phone closet to phone closet. Thin wire or thick wire is usable with multimode fiber being the better choice. As with all cases of wiring, the best possible thing to do is leave usable pathways for future expansion.

Data Link Layer Standard

The data link layer is directly above the physical layer. This the first layer in the logical communications layer. The most widely used standard here is Ethernet (it overlaps both in the physical layer and data link layer in the OSI model). It is a type of network cabling and signaling specifications originally developed by Xerox in the late 1970s. In 1980, Digital Equipment Corp. (DEC), Intel, and Xerox (the origin of the term DIX, as in DEC/Intel/Xerox) began joint promotion of this baseband (carrier sense multiple access with collision detection (CSMA/CD) computer communications network over coaxial cabling) and published the *Blue Book Standard* for Ethernet Version 1. This standard was later enhanced, and in 1985 Ethernet II was released.

The IEEE's (Institute of Electrical and Electronics Engineers') Project 802 used Ethernet Version 2 as the basis for the 802.3 CSMA/CD network standard. The IEEE 802.3 standard is generally interchangeable with Ethernet II— with the greatest difference being the construction of the network packet header.

A complete description of all Ethernet specifications is available in the IEEE 802.3 documents and in the ISO 8802-3 documents, as well. Ethernet/802.3 can now be run on two types of coaxial cable as well as multimode fiber and unshielded twisted pair.

NOTE:

Raw rate of data transmission is 10 Mbps.

10Base5, 10BaseT, 10Base2, 10Broad36 are the IEEE names for the different physical types of Ethernet. The *10* stands for signaling speed: 10MHz. *Base* means Baseband. *Broad* means broadband. Initially, the last section is intended to indicate the maximum length of an unrepeated cable segment in hundreds of meters. This convention was modified with the introduction of 10BaseT, where the *T* means twisted pair; and, 10BaseF, where the *F* means fiber. This actually comes from the IEEE committee number for that media as shown in the sidebar, "Different Physical Types Of Ethernet."

Different Physical Types of Ethernet

In actual practice:

10Base2   Is 10MHz Ethernet running over thin, 50 ohm baseband coaxial cable. 10Base2 is also commonly referred to as thin-Ethernet or Cheapernet.

10Base5   Is 10MHz Ethernet running over standard (thick) 50 ohm baseband coaxial cabling.

10BaseFL   Is 10MHz Ethernet running over fiber optic cabling.

10BaseT   Is 10MHz Ethernet running over unshielded, twisted-pair cabling.

10Broad36   Is 10MHz Ethernet running through a broadband cable [Velamparampil, 3-4].

FDDI (Fiber Distributed Data Interface) is another LAN data-link protocol designed to run on multimode fiber. The FDDI standard defines two physical rings that simultaneously send data in different directions. The raw rate of data transmission is 100 Mbps. The FDDI standard was developed by the American National Standards Institute. CDDI (Proprietary technology developed by Crecendo Corp) is FDDI-like technology adapted to unshielded twisted pair(UTP) as discussed in the sidebar, "CDDI Cabling," and shown in Figures 9–7 to 9–11 [3].

CDDI Cabling

The following contains pinout information for CDDI A/B ports, CDDI adapter ports, concentrator master ports, and the optical bypass switch connector:

CDDI/MLT-3 Installation:

MLT-3 is the new American National Standards Institute (ANSI) draft specification developed by Cisco Systems for compression of FDDI signals over UTP copper wire. Cisco Systems products that are upgraded to MLT-3 will interoperate with other vendors' equipment that complies with the draft standard.

Note: MLT-3 equipment can only be connected to other MLT-3 equipment.

Workgroup CDDI/MLT-3 installations require Category 5 equipment throughout. Two types of Category 5 modular cables (cross-connect and straight-through) are used to connect concentrators and adapters to the network as shown in Figures 9–7 and 9–8 respectively. Figures 9–7, 9–8, and 9–9, illustrate the EIA/TIA-T568-B wiring standard and CDDI transmit and receive pairs. Figure 9–10 shows the location of straight-through and cross-connect cabling for CDDI installations.

Note: The cross-connect cabling is used between the concentrator and the patch panel.

Bypass Connector Pinouts:

Figure 9–11 shows the optical bypass switch connector pinouts [Cisco, 1-3].

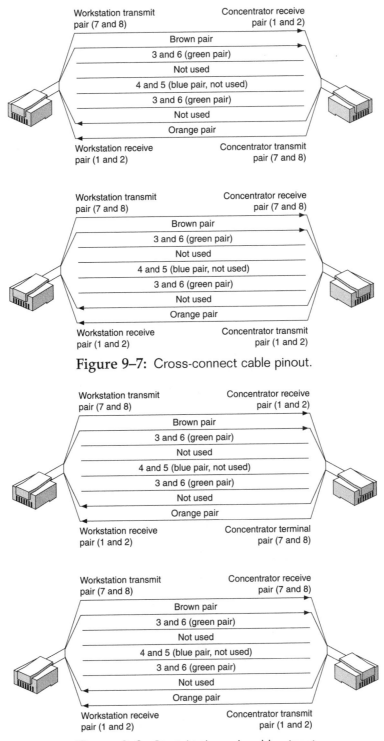

Figure 9–7: Cross-connect cable pinout.

Figure 9–8: Straight-through cable pinout.

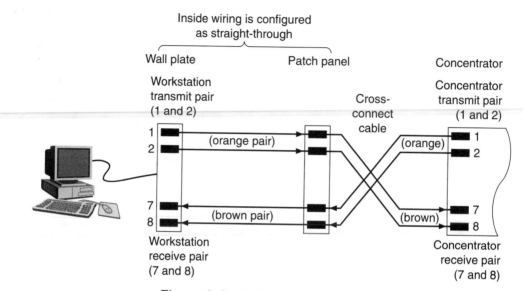

Figure 9–9: Patch panel connections.

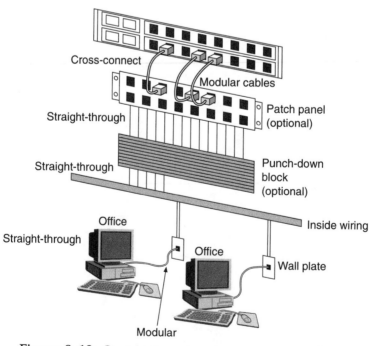

Figure 9–10: Straight-through and cross-connect cabling.

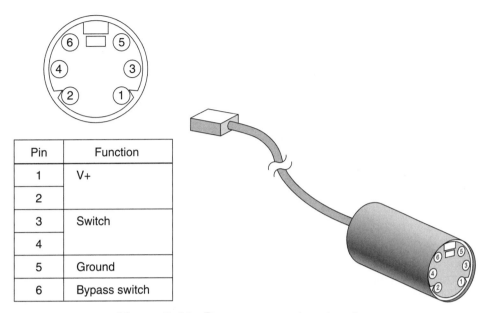

Pin	Function
1	V+
2	
3	Switch
4	
5	Ground
6	Bypass switch

Figure 9–11: Bypass connector pinouts.

Efforts to standardize CDDI have yielded TP-PMD (FDDI *Twisted Pair Physical Layer Media*), an ANSI specification for FDDI-like service over UTP. Limitations on how Ethernet is cabled vary according to the media used as shown in the sidebar, "Ethernet Cabling Distance Limitations."

Ethernet Cabling Distance Limitations

10Base2   Limited to 185 meters (607 ft) per unrepeated cable segment.

10Base5   Limited to 500 meters (1,640 ft) per unrepeated cable segment.

10BaseF   Depends on the signaling technology and media used but can go up to 2 km.

10BaseT   Generally accepted to have a maximum run of 100-150 meters, but is really based on signal loss in Dbs (11.5db maximum loss, source to destination).

10Broad36   Limited to 3,600 meters (almost 2.25 miles) [Velamparampil, 4].

Fundamentally, there are also limitations on the number of repeaters and cable segments allowed between any two stations on the network. There exists two different ways of looking at the same rules, the Ethernet way and the IEEE way.

The Ethernet Way

A remote repeater pair (with an intermediate point-to-point link) is counted as a single repeater (IEEE calls it two repeaters). You cannot put any stations on the point-to-point link, and there can be two repeaters in the path between any pair of stations.

The IEEE Way

There may be no more than five (5) repeated segments, and no more than four (4) repeaters between any two Ethernet stations. Of the five cable segments, only three (3) may be populated. This is referred to as the 5-4-3 rule (5 segments, 4 repeaters, 3 populated segments). A segment here is a piece of network wire bounded by bridges, routers, repeaters or terminators.

It can really get messy when you start cascading through 10BaseT hubs, which are repeaters unto themselves. Just try to remember that any possible path between two network devices on an unbridged/unrouted network cannot pass through more than 4 repeaters or hubs, and no more than 3 populated cable segments.

Finally, 10Base2 is limited to a maximum of 30 network devices per unrepeated network segment with a minimum distance of 0.5 meters (1.5 ft) between T-connectors. 10Base5 is limited to a maximum of 100 network devices per unrepeated segment, with a minimum distance of 2.5 meters (8.2ft) between taps or T-connectors (usually indicated by a marker stamped on the cable itself every 2.5 meters). 10BaseT and 10BaseF are star-wired, so there is no minimum distance requirement between devices, since devices cannot be connected serially. You can install up to the Ethernet maximum of 1024 stations per network with both 10BaseT and 10BaseF. In addition, the maximum number of stations on a thick Ethernet network is also 1024.

Building Wiring Standard

The Electronics Industries Association has defined a standard for commercial and industrial building wiring. The EIA/TIA-T568-A *Commercial Building Telecommunications Wiring Standard* defines a generic wiring system which will support a multiproduct, multivendor environment whose useful life span is in excess of 10 years.

The EIA/TIA standard is based on a star topology in which each workstation is connected to a central location (a telecommunications closet) situated within 90 meters of the workstation. Backbone wiring between telecommunications closets and the main cross-connect is also organized in a star topology. Direct connections between closets are allowed to accommodate bus and ring configurations. Distances between closets and the main cross-connect are dependent on cable types and applications (See Table 9–2) [Velamparampil, 5].

Table 9–2: Twisted Pair Cable Classifications

References	Applications
EIA/TIA Category 1	Analog, Digital Voice
EIA/TIA Category 2	ISDN (Data) 1.44 Mbps T1 (1.544 Mbps) Digital Voice
EIA/TIA Category 3	10BaseT ISDN Voice
EIA/TIA Category 4	10BaseT 16 Mbps token ring
EIA/TIA Category 5	10BaseT 16 Mbps token ring 100 Mbps DDI (proposed)

Each workstation is to be provided with a minimum of two communications outlets (can be on the same faceplate). One outlet is supported by a 4-pair, 100 ohm UTP cable. The other may be supported by an additional 4-pair UTP cable. For the backbone, four cable types are recognized for wiring: 100 ohm UTP multipair cable, 150 ohm STP cable, 50 ohm coaxial cable, and 62.5/125 micron fiber optic cable.

Looking back, nearly everyone thought wire was cable! Isn't Category 5 as shown in Table 9–2 enough? Aren't all Category 5 cables designed and created equal? Isn't this a standard? All of these questions are answered next.

Category 5 UTP Design Considerations

Is the reliable performance of your network infrastructure important to your organization's bottom line? According to industry analysts, failures at the physical layer (structured cabling) account for an average loss of $360,000 per year per 100 users. Losses are measured in user productivity, network manager effort, and business downtime. Couple this with the fact that the physical layer represents only about 11 percent of the overall network installation costs, when including the computers, software, structured cabling, and support costs, and you can see a big reason to be concerned. Fortunately for the people responsible for cable infrastructure, a system of acceptable standards exists that defines the expectations and limitations of cable, and provides structure and direction for technological advances.

Wire Is Wire

There seems to be indiscernible differences in communications cabling design considerations and construction. After all, isn't all wire created equal?

Today, words like *reflection, terminator,* and *vampire tap* have quickly faded from memory in the wake of robust and reliable 10 and 100BaseT LANs and *categorized* unshielded twisted-pair cabling systems. And *no,* all cables are *not* created equal. EIA/TIA has published cabling standards that set the baseline for interoperability in structured cabling and has provided a consistent platform for networking devices to be built to.

When you look at the original *categories,* someone entering the industry today wouldn't know (or care) about Category 1 telephone voice-grade copper cable or *POTS* (Plain Old Telephone Service) cable, as it was called. Category 2 handled IBM mainframe and minicomputer terminal transmission, as well as some early slow-speed (12 Mbps) LAN technologies like Arcnet. Category 3 was designated as the minimum quality twisted-pair cable that would handle 10 Mbps Ethernet and 4-16 Mbps active token ring without errors at the desktop.

Since these original categories were defined several years ago, we've all seen America being rewired, information transmission technologies advancing, and standards ratified. In 1992, a group of manufacturers marketed a copper version (CDDI) of an FDDI (Fiber Distributed Data Interface) transport system using thin coax and IBM Type 1 cabling products.

In 1993, ANSI ratified TP-PMD (twisted pair-physical media dependent) for FDDI over Category 5 UTP. Shortly after that, EIA/TIA signed the *568* standard document, followed immediately by TSB36.

It wasn't until the birth and availability of affordable 100BaseT in 1996 that institutions and organizations saw a reason to enable 100 Mbps desktops, and then largely because it was an inexpensive and well understood insurance policy. For a little extra money, whether turned on or left dormant, dual 10/100 Mbps Ethernet network interface cards became a no-brainer for network managers. Fiber optics and FDDI remained in the campus backbone, and became the server superhighways and intercloset infrastructures. In several short years (since Category 5 was introduced) the physical layer transport of the most future-thinking planners has been maxed out in terms of the high-speed networking options of the near future!

Category 5

Few of us can conceive of the need for anything beyond 100 Mbps. For example, 155 Mbps ATM (Asynchronous Transfer Mode) is seen by many to be a technology in search of an application, but we should remember how much things can change in a five-year period.

Today in the age of Pentiums, the chicken-and-egg routine continues. Processing power ultimately drives innovation in user applications, specifically media-rich and collaborative functions. These business and learning-enabled applications ultimately drive the need for more bandwidth when it's needed. Transport technologies like switching and ATM will likely catch on as the economic and sociological benefits of multimedia, distance learning, and media conferencing are realized. When thinking about where applications will be in five years, think about the size of hard drives and modem speeds in 1991. Hundred fold increases in performance and plummeting costs make these technology innovations solid drivers in today's corporate America, as well as in education and healthcare.

If you consider that several years ago the high-end wiring choice was Category 5 cabling in the LAN and multimode fiber optic systems in the backbone, then when LAN speeds became 10, 16, and 100 Mbps, the *headroom* or additional capacity that was built into the systems seemed more than adequate for the future. Recently though, the ATM Forum put its seal of approval on 155 Mbps ATM to run on existing Category 5 systems, and the first interface products have just recently started to appear on the market. One may ask what applications will require more than 100 or 155 Mbps at the desktop? But, the more visionary question is, will my Category *X* cabling system have enough additional *headroom* or *true* electrical bandwidth to provide error-free transmission when extra throughput is needed?

A few issues need to be explored to answer this question satisfactorily. All high-speed LAN standards require compliance with generic cabling specifications plus many additional parameters that are defined only in the specifications and standards for the network interface products. These extra requirements define the actual electrical and digital signaling, and usually assume a well-behaved and consistent cable and connectivity system. Figure 9–12 shows the

Generic Cabling Standards

All high-speed networking standards require compliance with generic cabling standards plus some additional parameters.

Examples:

SUPPLEMENTAL REQUIREMENT	NETWORK STANDARDS
Signal-to-noise ratio requirements	All
Maximum noise thresholds	All
Self NEXT noise (included above 100 MHz)	ATM
Pair skew	100BASE-T, 100VG
Total propagation delay of a cable link	100BASE-T, 100VG

To assure the opperation of networks over installed cabling, both must be tested.

Supplemental Network-Specific Requirements

Figure 9–12: Structured cabling standards versus network-specific standards.

relationship between cabling standards (center ellipse) and networking standards (outer ellipse), and demonstrates, unfortunately, that cabling requirements are just a subset of the overall requirements for a smooth-running network [4].

All high-speed standards need to conform to SNR (Signal-to-Noise Ratios) and maximum noise thresholds. But pair skew and propagation delay characteristics are important supplemental requirements for 100BaseT, 100BaseVG and for ATM above 100 MHz. Pair skew applies to technologies using multiple pairs for signaling. In essence, signals are divided between pairs and must be reassembled at the receiving end. If they arrive at different times, skewing of the signal occurs, resulting in transmission errors. Propagation delay, the time it takes for the signal to travel to the receiver, is a factor of the efficiency of the cable in moving the signal relative to the theoretical speed of electricity (light). Also known as the velocity of propagation, it is expressed as the percent of the speed of light represented by the cable's speed.

Network electronics manufacturers deal with electrical loss across cable distances by incorporating equalizers into their receivers. These equalizers attempt to amplify the received signal based on what they assume happened through attenuation or the electrical loss during transmission through the channel. This same received signal must also be identified within the noise picked up during its transmission and receipt, and in most cases a little bit of the noise is also reamplified. If this results in an incorrect representation of the original signal it is called a *bit error*. Bit errors often lead to garbled information and/or retransmissions of the data.

As in the case of 155-Mbps ATM running on Category 5 cable, anomalies can occur above the Category 5 maximum signal frequency (in excess of 100 MHz and as far out as 200 MHz) that when seen by the equalizer are amplified as if they were part of the signal. This results in higher than acceptable bit errors and therefore corruption of the information. No additional headroom will help in this case. If the attenuation performance of the cable is not smooth, then the ATM signal will probably not be interpreted correctly even though the cable installation passes Category 5 requirements below 100 MHz!

Category 5 Cables Are Created Equal

Standards by definition are derived by consensus and often are open to interpretation. *Delay Skew* is an addendum to the ANSI/EIA/TIA-T568-A specification that requires that another test be performed on the cable before it leaves the manufacturer. The TIA task group has rejected suggested names for the addendum (Category 5.1 or Category 6), and has elected not to have the cables that would comply with the new standard marked differently from the other eight billion feet of 4-pair cable already manufactured and currently installed in North America. The only way to know for sure if your cable meets this new requirement will be to get a copy of the actual product specification the manufacturer used to make the exact cable you purchased at that time. When was the last time you consulted the cable manufacturer's spec sheet? So, enhancements to cable can only be determined by looking at exactly what parameters the manufacturer has tested and guaranteed.

Performance is directly related to the chemical compounds used in the manufacture of cable. There are more than 105 different electrical designs of plenum cables, including 15 high-end Category 5 plenum designs and 33 standard and high-end non-plenum designs all with varying electrical performance characteristics, yet still Category 5-compliant.

In addition, a high-speed system must display Category 5 characteristics from input to output; in other words, across all connectors, cross-connects, patch panels, and outlets. So, assuming the Category 5 cable tests out at 155 Mbps, users must still contend with the quality of the components and the installation. Some of the various plenum flavors that used different numbers of Polyolefin pairs mixed in with the FEP pairs to reduce the amount of FEP consumed were very installer-friendly; others were not. This mixing of different materials can cause the propagation delay skew to exceed the 45 ns specified in the revised TIA-568 standard and has resulted in a recent addendum. See the sidebar, "Category 5 Plenum Cabling With FEP Insulation," for more information on FEP.

Category 5 Plenum Cabling with FEP Insulation

The University of Pennsylvania (Philadelphia, PA) has been specifying their Category 5 plenum cable by manufacturer and product number for some time now and it was always all-FEP (fluorinated ethylene propylene). But without any notification, the manufacturer changed the composition of the product to a 3+1 cable. Do any manufacturers still make plenum-rated Category 5 cabling with FEP insulation on all 4 pairs of conductors? How does the cost of this product compare with the 2+2 and 3+1 cables?

Even though the 4+0 construction may not be specified in their catalogs, most manufacturers make the 4+0 cable. With regard to cost, the University of Texas at Austin (UTA) has been buying low-bid and installing the 4+0 cable all along. Cabling manufacturers that have not made the 3+1 or 2+2 cables are very competitive bidders.

The Telecommunications Industry Association (TIA) UTP cable task group has been very active and expects to issue a delay-skew specification. For those readers not familiar with recent developments in the TR41.8.1 working group, in a recent press release, the TIA stated that all Category 5 cables may not support all 100 Mbps data applications. The reason is excessive delay skew, which is not a specified test parameter for UTP cable in the TIA-568A standard.

Delay skew is the difference of nominal velocity of propagation (NVP) between individual pairs in a link. Velocity of propagation is the speed at which a signal can be transmitted over a media. UTA is most familiar with velocity of propagation stated as a percentage of the speed of light (NVP = 72.5%); however, it can also be stated as time-to-distance, for example: 500 nanoseconds per 100 meters (500 ns/100 m).

The continuing shortage of FEP and a 40% to 50% annual growth in the demand for Category 5 plenum cable present a challenge for cable manufacturers. Traditionally, FEP has been used to insulate paired conductors in Category 5 plenum cable because it was perceived that only FEP would comply with the electrical performance requirements specified in the ANSI/EIA/TIA-T568A standard and the plenum requirements for communications cable in the National Electrical Code. With only two FEP suppliers— Daikin America (Orangeburg, NY) and Dupont (Wilmington, DE)—the supply-and-demand problem continues, causing manufacturers and distributors to scramble for the product.

Ingenuity produced several solutions. One solution is to use FEP for three of the four pairs of conductor in 4-pair cable and polyolefin for the fourth pair. This solution would save the manufacturer 25% of its FEP allocation. Polyolefin was not used to insulate all of the pairs because that construction would not pass the Underwriters' Laboratory (UL) flame test. Another solution is to use FEP for two of the four pairs of conductors in 4-pair cable and modified polyolefin for the other two. While these solutions result in a product that can pass the UL flame test and meet existing Category 5 requirements, some will not support high-speed data applications [5].

It's ironic that the original EIA/TIA-568-A was signed in the summer of 1991 and only covered what essentially was 10BaseT electricals, or the then current Category 3. Immediately after the standard was issued, the committee came out with TSB36 (Technical Systems Bulletin) for *Additional Cable Specifications for Twisted Pair Cables*, which defined the new Category 3, 4 and 5 electrical performance requirements based on work done at NEMA (National Electrical Manufacturers Association) and ISO.

A TSB is not a standard but a preliminary look at what a standard might be as generated by the TIA working group. That is, if they publish such a standard it might look like the TSB after the voting is done. So, a new standard can be approved then immediately made obsolete by the same working group. A rewrite of the 568 standard was signed into existence in October of 1995 as ANSI/EIA/TIA-T568-A; and, ANSI formed a working group to explore the issue of delay skew, resulting in another change or addendum. Many standards are obsolete the day they are signed because they cover existing, implemented, and proven technologies that, by design, must be available from a number of different sources.

Standards have become so prevalent that brand awareness has become less of an issue. Because of this, many manufacturers tend to minimally meet specifications, which in turn fosters a market environment where the products become commodities or articles of commerce. As a result, the advent of standards has impeded manufacturers from developing products that exceed the qualifications of standards.

What's Next?

Organizations may see the promise (or opportunity) of deploying even higher-speed technologies in the next five years as applications and processors address new creative and competitive business needs and continue to consume more and more of the available bandwidth. The Gigabit Ethernet Alliance has concluded that this technology will have a significant impact on cabling, pushing the limits. Regardless of product and installation quality, there will be no slack if implemented on the current Category 5 cabling.

So while it seemed that Category 5 would be all that would ever be needed in the horizontal cable infrastructure, it appears that headroom and *structural return* (performance specification reading returns) concerns will open the books again for organizations. This timely performance or quality assurance program is based on a stringent purchasing specification (based on performance specification readings) that requires the organization's suppliers to qualify their high-performance unshielded twisted pair products.

This stringent purchasing specification sets guidelines for electrical bandwidth in excess of 100 Mhz by reaching for a performance mark that has over twice the actual usable electrical bandwidth of the current Category 5. It also extends the data bandwidth to the 1.2 Gbps performance mark, making it useful in developing Gigabit Ethernet systems, while incorporating less sophisticated encoding schemes than those required for conventional Category 5 cabling.

The original Category 5 specification from 1992 was modified to cover the performance requirements for existing Category 5 cables. The more stringent requirements for what has been called High-End Category 5 or Category 5+ cables are referred to as Category 6 in the updated categories program. And a new generation of recently launched products that meet the twice Category 5 bandwidth requirement constitute Category 7. The chart in Figure 9–13 gives the basic requirements for these new performance categories [Serenbetz and Lockhart, 8].

NOTE:

Category 5+ is different from the standard Category 5 in that it now must meet the more stringent requirements included in the international standard ISO 11801. This standard allows cables meeting these requirements to be used globally. This new definition for cable performance creates a superset of the original Category 5 requirements.

100 ohm UTP					
Performance Level	Highest Test Frequency (MHz)	ACR ≥ 10 dB (MHz) Powersum	ATTM ≤ 33 dB (MHz)	ACR ≥ 0 dB (MHz) Powersum	Other Required Measurements
5	200	80	200	130	ISO IMP-SRL <45 ns SKEW LCL
6	350	100	200	165	ISO IMP-SRL <25 ns SKEW LCL
7	400	160	230	250	ISO IMP-SRL <25 ns SKEW LCL

Figure 9–13: Categories of acceptance cable performance.

Copper cabling technology has certainly come a long way in less than a decade! Beyond this, it looks like fiber optics is mandatory. Even today fiber is the clear future protection of choice.

As is usually the case, the implementation of a cabling infrastructure should fit the need. Corporations, financial institutions, healthcare providers, and colleges and universities are poised in many ways to take full advantage of the technology wave to enhance their competitive advantage. Is your organization ready to deploy tomorrow's technological advances? Is your physical layer infrastructure up to the task? Thankfully, there are cost-effective, future-proofing solutions in high-end copper still in the works. And as users move into the world of lightwave communications over optical fiber, the same guiding principles of price, performance, and ease of installation and maintenance are at work in the engineering and standards committees of the industry.

Nevertheless, in Europe, organizations are ready to deploy tomorrow's technological advances by the installation or implementation of a copper cabling design technology called Digital Subscriber Line (xDSL). But, if xDSL technology is the answer to the current bandwidth dilemma, why aren't vendors and service providers beating down the developers' doors? The final part of this chapter answers that burning question.

Digital Subscriber Line

In the operator and service provider world, it is now an accepted, inescapable conclusion that xDSL technologies will one day be installed on a global basis, in vast quantities. Despite other technology developments (not excluding recent announcements about the commercial viability of sending data down power lines), it is still the only viable technology capable of substantially increasing bandwidth on the local access loops without a substantial overhaul. These copper loops are ubiquitous over every home in Europe and it is unlikely that any mass scale upgrade to fiber will happen within the next 15 years.

The primary driver for xDSL is high-speed Internet service deployment to residential customers. So far, there have been two small commercial deployments and no less than 55 trials around the world, trying to prove that asynchronous DSL (ADSL) can provide a downstream connection of up to 8 Mbps and upstream connection of up to 1 Mbps over the existing telephony copper pair. See the sidebar, "Asymmetric Digital Subscriber Line Technology (ADSL)," for further Information ADSL.

Asymmetric Digital Subscriber Line Technology (ADSL)

ADSL (Asymmetric Digital Subscriber Line) technology is making a resurgence as telecommunication companies look for alternatives to costly network infrastructure upgrades such as HFC and fiber to the curb. ADSL takes the existing copper telephone line and turns it into a digital pathway capable of carrying up to 8 Mbps downstream and 1 Mbps upstream, making it ideal for high-speed Internet access services, telecommuting, remote LAN access, and other emerging residential broadband applications.

ADSL technology can also be used in business environments as a high-speed link between corporate intranets, or as a low-cost alternative to T-1 and Fractional T-1 lines. Questions remain as to ADSL's long-term viability in the marketplace, particularly in terms of equipment and operations costs, and its potential for integration with ATM transport and fiber-based network topologies [6].

Both IP and ATM network architectures are currently on trial. ATM is considered the probable choice in the future. Initial trials have used standalone ADSL modems with discrete IP interfaces for reasons of time-to-market and availability; these are evolving to highly integrated digital subscriber loop access multiplexers (DSLAM) solutions.

The complete network typically consists of a core which is based around SDH (Synchronous Digital Hierarchy), wrapped with broadband ATM switches, ATM access switches and DSLAMs. The DSLAMs provide the individual xDSL lines out to the customer premises and integrate with the existing POTS network connections. But even after having been in trial for more than 18 months, few operators seem close to commercial rollouts. What is taking them so long?

Some of the main barriers to large-scale adoption include the continuing standards battle and the lack of interoperability. The existence of two de facto standards, namely DMT (discrete multitone technology) and CAP (carrierless amplitude modulation/phase modulation), provides network operators with a dilemma; deciding which to adopt before a leader is clearly identifiable in case the choice ends up as the Betamax of the standards. There are two standard camps, one apparently led by Israel's Amati, which has developed modems using DMT for the line coding. Motorola and Alcatel are among the major manufacturers who have developed DMT modems. The second camp has adopted a technology developed by the former AT&T Paradyne, which championed CAP for the line coding. Westell, the company that made the ADSL modems being used in a Bell Atlantic's trial in Virginia, uses CAP. With no clear stance being taken, a general wait and see attitude is developing.

Lack of interoperability is also becoming a matter of concern. The current xDSL units on the market, from a variety of vendors, supporting different standards, do not interoperate. Interoperability between vendors' equipment is key to mass rollout and provisioning. The ultimate goal is for the end customer to be able to purchase their own ADSL termination units, much the same way that people buy off-the-shelf analog modems today. For this to happen, the ADSL termination unit technology needs to mature to the point were it is as simple as a modem to install and operate.

Operators are still deciding on suitable end-to-end architectures. Once these infrastructures have been agreed upon, the business and technology in place, services can then be rolled out in volume. These new architectures need to address the integration of network, service, and business management of these new broadband services. Without these seamless, end-to-end management systems in place, it is difficult to see how operators will be able to make any profit on broadband services.

Management Capabilities

The new broadband services being deployed by network operators and service providers are typically delivered over very complex network environments which include legacy equipment with primitive management capabilities and newer systems incorporating sophisticated element management based on the telecommunications management network (TMN). New network management infrastructures are required to mold these disparate information sources into a cohesive view of the end-to-end services being delivered. This can be complicated by the large scale of such services—typically involving hundreds of thousands or millions of network elements. The major requirements can be summarized as follows:

- Cost-effective, performance scaleability—a system with the ability to manage small pilot networks and expand as the network grows without performance degradation.
- Multiple protocol support—standards-based and proprietary management protocols must be supported in a manner transparent to the network applications.
- Powerful event management—as the network grows, the number of events grows exponentially. The ability to manage this volume of events in a way that helps the operator make sense of the status of the network is mandatory.
- Seamless application interworking—operators will use a number of different applications to manage aspects of the network, but they require the ability to move easily between applications, for example, to investigate problems or configure service for a particular customer.
- User access management—the information within the management system must be protected, but it must also be feasible to partition the data, and the access to it, in a way that supports operational processes [7].

Network Architecture

Some of the key management challenges when installing xDSL networks include potential element volumes. xDSL network elements are extremely complex devices that require real time management. As element volumes increase exponentially, operators are faced with the challenges of implementing end-to-end systems that can manage millions of highly complex access elements.

As an example, the 1994 BT video-on-demand (VOD) trial (conducted by telecommunications companies TCI, AT&T and US West in Colorado)supported 2,000 ADSL lines, equating to 4,000 access elements. Although this was classified as a small marketing trial, it is still the largest single xDSL installation in the world. This network generated a tremendous amount of management traffic, primarily with SNMP and performance monitoring information, all of which had to be processed in real time by the central management workstation.

Additionally, xDSL equipment, by virtue of its inherent built-in intelligence, generates a tremendous amount of management traffic. This information, be it alarms, performance monitoring information, configuration data, diagnostic commands, or inventory data, has to be processed, stored, prioritized, formatted, and displayed by the central management console. A single element management workstation cannot scale to support any major network growth.

Element and network complexity is also an issue that operators need to prepare for. xDSL equipment is becoming more complex with each generation.

The latest generation uses rate-adaptive transmission which causes a myriad of possible upstream and downstream speed permutations. Remote equipment now incorporates xDSL transmission hardware, IP routing equipment and IP or ATM CPE interfaces into a single unit. In addition, it has to be seamlessly integrated with the existing POTS network, leading to a wealth of configuration permutations, performance monitoring information, alarm and event reports, diagnostic functions, and inventory data being available to the network operator.

A typical end-to-end network capable of delivering high speed Internet, on-demand services, and data and voice from multiple service providers is extremely complex. Many issues can only be resolved with the use of integrated management applications and systems. This often results in a number of non-compatible element management systems being installed to manage different parts of the network, then integrated together to provide an overall end-to-end service management system. The eventual goal is to provide a *zero touch* system to allow the end customer to control and manage a large part of their own service offering in real time.

xDSL equipment is normally installed over existing telephony circuits but the devices at each end of the connection contain POTS splitters that allow both the telephony circuit and the xDSL circuit to use a single copper pair. This requires the integration of a new xDSL management system with existing POTS systems.

A range of issues also cloud the choice of the most efficient interface for the equipment on the customer premises. The two protocols in question are IP and ATM. Network operators are installing complex networking equipment in residential environments for the first time. This can lead to a multiplicity of new problems. These problems range from units being tampered with and cables being disconnected to PCs being reconfigured. This could result in a huge increase in the number of service-related calls and queries directed at the network operator. The operator has to be able to diagnose, isolate, and analyze problems from the central management system. Only when this type of network, system management, and control is achieved will broadband services become commercially viable.

Viability

The density of the technology must increase dramatically to enable operators to fit all the required ADSL termination units into their existing exchange real estate. xDSL technologies are still costly, and this is holding back general acceptance due to the costs of equipment investment and the ongoing line rental charge. Prices in the range of $260 to $310 would start to approach an acceptable level for the benefits of this new broadband technology.

But in most European countries, high capacity broadband ATM backbone networks have yet to be deployed. Without this backbone infrastructure, there is little benefit to be gained from introducing an upgraded access network. In the infrastructure context, the questions of how some major European operators will play off ADSL against their substantial ISDN services will be an interesting debate. As it now stands, current versions of ADSL cannot coexist with ISDN BRI lines. New versions of ADSL are being developed that will coexist with ISDN but as yet are only available in small trial volumes from one or two vendors.

Telecommunication companies s such as Deutsche Telekom, which bet its future on ISDN, are now involved in desperately trying to increase ISDN usage before ADSL establishes itself. The situation it faces (in common with many other operators in Europe) is that too much emphasis and keenly-priced ISDN will undermine ADSL; but, at the same time, not investing an adequate amount of resource on ADSL now might undermine its future as a broadband services provider.

Future

From the point of view of a commercial (profitable for both provider and user) service provision, xDSL can be considered an immature technology. xDSL has been proven an effective, reliable solution in many international trials. However, it is continually developing and progressing—which adds to the xDSL management complexities requiring the facilities for operators to download new algorithms on a regular basis.

xDSL standards are relatively new and are therefore prone to change on a regular basis. This involves regular, programmable equipment upgrades, such as software download of new versions of xDSL transmission and application code from a central management station.

As with all new technologies, technical and cost issues do get resolved in subsequent generations. xDSL is no different. The market demand for high-speed, broadband communications will drive the development of the technology and will produce an economic, reliable solution for end users. For network operators, xDSL is the most cost effective way of upgrading the copper infrastructure and competing against fiber and cable competitors. Another factor in determining market direction is the move for European PTTs (Post, Telegraph, and Telephones) from monopoly to deregulation and free competition. This will force network operators to unbundle their loops in a way similar to what has happened in the UK and US. These new competitors will aggressively target end customers with offers of high-speed broadband data communications, tempting them from the traditional service providers who may not be moving as quickly towards new service provision.

So, using the existing copper networks, xDSL will be made available which will motivate PTTs to respond, leading to a critical mass and explosion in xDSL deployments. While network operators, service providers, and vendors debate the standards, technology, and cost issues of deploying xDSL networks, customer demand is growing for cost-effective, high speed, broadband networks that unleash new services and new business potential for them. Looking at the rapid development of Internet and intranet business and services over the last few years, one can expect resolutions to the main issues and mass xDSL deployment within the next 3 to 5 years.

From Here

This chapter discussed copper design considerations (layout, components, connectors, shielding, maintenance, etc.). The next chapter presents a brief overview of fiber optic design considerations (layout, system migration, loss budget calculations, fiber-to-desk, etc.).

End Notes

[1] George Velamparampil, "Wiring," Computer Science Department, 1304 West Springfield, Office of Public Affairs and Computing and Communications Services Office, University of Illinois at Urbana-Champaign 61801, 1997, pp. 1–2.

[2] "UTP Trunk Cabling Design," MOD-TAP, a subsidiary of Molex Inc., 285 Ayer Road, P.O. Box 706, Harvard, MA 01451, 1997, p. 1.

[3] "Cabling and Pinout Information," (Some material in this book has been reproduced by Prentice Hall with the permission of Cisco Systems Inc.), COPYRIGHT © 1998 Cisco Systems, Inc., ALL RIGHTS RESERVED, 170 West Tasman Drive, San Jose, CA 95134-1706, USA, 1996, p.p. 1–3.

[4] Jim Serenbetz and Pete Lockhart, "Category 5: How Did We Get Here and Where Do We Go Next?" Anixter Inc, 4711 Golf Road, Skokie, IL 60076, 1997, p. 4.

[5] Donna Ballast, "Cabling Installation and Maintenance," (Copyright 1996 by Cabling Installation and Maintenance, PennWell, Nashua, NH, 03062. USA. Reprinted with permission), PO Drawer 7580, University of Texas, Austin, TX 78713, 1996, p. 1.

[6] "ADSL: Turning Copper into Gold," Textor Webmasters Ltd., The Barley Mow Centre, 10 Barley Mow Passage, London W4 4PH, 1996, p. 1.

[7] Bhawani Shanher, "The Copper Loop: From Barbed Wire to Broadband," *Telecommunications*, 685 Canton Street, Norwood, MA 02062, (November, 1997), p. 1.

10

Fiber Optic Design Considerations

Before fiber optic networks can be constructed, they must be properly designed and, once constructed, they must be managed. Efficiencies in these processes translate into lower cost layout and construction, more productive system migration and field operations, lower optical loss budget, and greater business profitability by bringing fiber to the desk.

The fiber optic network layout design plays an important role in error-free system reliability. Choice of the proper type of network layout depends on the type of process controlled, the possible need for expansion, and the degree of failure immunity desired—all of which must be balanced with cost considerations.

Basic Layout Network Designs

As is the case with electrical control system networks, four basic optical networks prevail: bus, star, ring, and collapsed backbone. For each type, the purpose of the network is to provide communication between the devices, or nodes, in the system. "Node" is a general term that refers to a programmable logic controller (PLC), remote input/output (I/O) drop, distributed control system (DCS) controller, or any communication device.

Network Layout Types

Each of the four network types has advantages and disadvantages, depending on the application. Historically, bus layouts have been preferred by PLC suppliers and star layouts by DCS suppliers—both on equipment OEM-configured for fiber optic signal transmission. Recently, both PLC and DCS suppliers have begun to offer more ring and collapsed backbone layouts than in the past.

Bus Network

In a bus network, all the nodes are attached in a line. This layout lends itself especially well to automobile assembly lines, lumber and paper mills, and other operations that begin with raw materials at one end, and end at the other end of a production line with a finished unit. The control devices are laid out in a linear array alongside the process machinery. Because the process machinery requires adequate clearances and right-of-way, it is usually easy to set up the cableways along the same right-of-way.

In an electrical bus signal transmission system, devices are connected to the nodes in parallel by direct attachment or attenuating taps. Attenuating taps allow higher speeds and greater bandwidth, but do not provide for easy network expansion.

In a fiber optic system, fibers cannot simply be *paralleled* as can copper conductors. Present fiber optic technology does not provide for effecting the equivalent of an electrical tap. In a fiber optic system, taps are effected through modems. All intermediate modems in the string (with the exception of the two at the extreme ends of the bus) are repeaters that interface with their respective nodes and send the optical signal on to all other modems on the bus.

Fiber optic systems are normally used in star wiring patterns or to connect wiring centers. Modems convert digital signals to analog signals and vice versa. They are normally used on analog circuits.

Star Network

The star network consists of a star (central) node device with arms extending out to other nodes. The star is used predominantly in facilities where different processes are physically separated, but must be centrally controlled, such as in petroleum refineries, chemical and pharmaceutical plants, and power-generating stations.

Outlying nodes handle individual complex tasks, or have many alternative paths, and must therefore function somewhat independently. For example, one node might be connected to thermocouples with slow temperature changes in a 4- to 20-ma control loop; a second node might be a high-speed remote computer on a 10 Mbps RS-485 link; and a third node might be a controller operating a motorized process control valve [1].

Because the controlled functions might have no well-defined path of their own, or the path might not readily lead back to the central devices, locating the cable ways and securing right-of-way can be more complex than with linear layouts. Also, in a star network, the central device is always a repeater, capable of transferring communications from one separate node to another. Sometimes the central node has overall control over the separated nodes. Each separated node is connected to the central device by a point-to-point link. Because each node receives and sends messages solely with the central device, only these two devices must understand the message. Thus, the different nodes can communicate at different speeds and use different protocols or languages. If the star node has enough power and intelligence, it handles many different speeds and protocols. This feature makes it easier to use devices utilizing various technologies from different manufacturers.

Furthermore, the central node is usually a hub or a multiplexer that utilizes repeaters to forward data. Some repeaters can interconnect cable segments using different physical media such as coaxial cables and fiber optic cables.

In a star network, however, each separated node requires two modems—one attaching to the star and other to the node for a point-to-point link. As a result, a star requires twice as many modems as a bus layout, and thus costs more.

NOTE:

> Fiber optics termination does not utilize modems. Cables are terminated in fiber optics patch panels, medium attachment units (MAU), fiber optic hubs, etc.

Ring Network

Devices in a ring layout are connected in a circular fashion. Each node is a repeater, and all nodes operate at the same speed under the same protocol. In theory, a simple ring handles complex processes but, in practice, relatively few processes lend themselves to a ring layout. A ring network can, however, be advantageous in high-reliability applications, because it can be installed in a modified *self-healing* configuration.

NOTE:

> With regard to FDDI, fiber optics is normally used to connect two wiring systems or in a star wiring plan.

Collapsed Backbone Network

Today, networks are composed of broadband, baseband, and fiber cables. Broadband is the same type of cabling used by Cable TV companies, the cable carrying multiple channels. Baseband is the typical ethernet cable used to connect machines, usually known as thicknet or thinnet. Fiber, of course, is cable composed of glass fibers and the signals are transmitted as light. This composition of multiple media makes the network environment hard to manage and the transition to future technologies difficult.

Within network environments today, there exists what has come to be known as the *collapsed backbone*. The idea behind collapsing the backbone is to bring all the inter-building connections into one location. This makes management easier and a chance of a cable plant problem affecting multiple buildings less likely. All the interconnect equipment usually resides in building with a controlled environment and backup power.

The daily management of the network will be greatly enhanced when the backbone is collapsed. Things that should be simple, like tracking down a bogus or bad host, are difficult in the environment today. Once the backbone is collapsed, network problems will be isolated to just one building or area. The TCP/IP topology of network environments today is only about 20% routed and the rest bridged. In the future, collapsed environment of the TCP/IP topology will be 100% routed. This will greatly increase network performance for users.

Layout Expansion Design Considerations

To expand a bus network, one adds to either end. Expansion is easy if growth is linear, but difficult if links must be added between the ends or on a branch.

The star is expanded by adding more arms with separated nodes, and their connecting cables. As long as cableways are available and the central device has enough capacity, expansion is straightforward. Moreover, it is possible for units to be added while the network is up and running.

In a ring layout, expansion is difficult. Because any addition requires disrupting the ring, it cannot be done quickly or while the network is running.

Achieving High Reliability

Studies show that in fiber optic telephone systems, 80% of interrupted service is due to cable damage. Much the same might be true in industrial environments, where cable is exposed to potential damage from sources such as forklift trucks, dropped tools and equipment, and cutting and welding torches.

In a bus or ring, the entire network usually goes down if a cable is damaged, because the network devices usually have neither the power nor the intelligence to operate as isolated entities. And in the rare event that a modem or repeater fails, communication is also disrupted throughout the network.

The *self-healing ring network* can be installed in a modified, ultrahigh-reliability configuration. The ring is made to send signals clockwise and counter-clockwise by duplicating the cable and installing two optical transmitters/ receivers at each node. Importantly, the two cables can be strung alongside each other in the same cableway, because operations are not disrupted if either or both cables are damaged. If one or both cables between any two devices is damaged, communication is disrupted at that point. However, the nodes adjacent to the break continue to receive communications from either the clockwise or the counter-clockwise signal stream. Likewise, if one node fails, communication continues among the other nodes.

A modular fiber optic design can bring down the cost of a self-healing ring layout. That is, rather than duplicating the entire modem, one need add only a transmitter/receiver module and a self-healing ring module to each modem. If regular modems are already in place in a bus layout, the network can become self-healing by connecting the two ends and inserting the additional modules. The ability to insert additional modules, rather than replace modems, also reduces installation time.

In practice, different parts of a network require varying levels of reliability. The most critical processes can be arranged in a self-healing ring, and less critical processes in a bus, star, collapsed backbone, or other hybrid configuration.

NOTE:

> Fiber optics are normally installed in a star configuration and/or used to connect two wiring systems—other than the FDDI hub topology.

Many hybrid variations on the basic network types are possible, incorporating the star in one form or another. If a cable is damaged in a star, communication stops only with the node served by the damaged cable; the other nodes continue to operate. It must be borne in mind, however, that if the star (center) node itself fails, all control is lost.

Bus-star layout is commonly used in PLC networks with distributed I/O modules. In a paper mill, for example, PLCs and I/O modules controlling various processes are typically laid out in a linear bus. However, the I/O drops that control chemical kitchens in the pulp preparation area have control points that radiate out in star configurations. If the bus cable is damaged, the star nodes can continue to control local pulp operations. And if a bus node fails, the other star-connected nodes can continue to communicate among themselves.

Star-bus hybrid configuration is often used in spread-out operations such as oil production fields or far-spread petrochemical processing operations. For example, each device, such as an individual oil well, local storage tank, or pump and valve controller, is regulated by nodes on a local bus. The many buses are linked back to a central control room in a star layout. If a local bus cable fails, other local buses in the layout continue to control their respective processes.

Ring-bus and *ring-star* configurations show how a ring network can be combined with either a bus or a star network. One node on the ring can be one of several nodes on a local bus, or it can be the central node for a local star. The ring is connected in a self-healing configuration for the most critical elements of the network, with less critical nodes connected in bus or star.

Quadruple-hybrid combinations combine all four basic networks into a ring-bus-star collapsed backbone configuration. The most critical items are connected in a self-healing ring; other items are connected in either bus or star or collapsed backbone as best satisfies their location and application.

Redundant Systems

While a hybrid layout can improve performance and enhance reliability, ultimate failure resistance often requires a redundant system—that is, a second or duplicate system that takes over in the event the first stops functioning. Depending on the layout and hazards involved, many system designers opt to duplicate the cable only. The redundant systems, however, need not be identical. The primary system might be fiber optic, with the backup system electrical, and wired with copper conductors. For maximum reliability in bus and star layouts, cables of the redundant systems should be placed in separate cableways some distance from the primary systems. Setting up a second cableway can be enormously expensive.

Duplicating only the cable poses a significant disadvantage in systems with long distances between modems. In order to send the signal down the duplicate cables, each modem needs an optical splitter and combiner. Each splitter introduces a signal loss of 3 to 6 dB, which can create distortion unless the distance between modems is limited.

In a star layout, if the central node is especially at risk of destruction, one option is to duplicate only the star node. It is usually not necessary to duplicate the outlying nodes, because other portions of the system can continue to operate if one node fails. Even duplicating only the star node can be expensive. This is because the central node is very powerful or complex. As with duplicate cables, the duplicate central node should be located some distance from the first, which also increases costs. Thus, for most industrial applications where operations must be preserved in the face of anticipated cable damage, a ring network cabled in a self-healing configuration usually provides the reliability needed at the most moderate cost.

The next part of chapter provides guidelines for fiber optic design considerations with regard to system migration. It covers the following areas: 10BaseF connection to FDDI, token ring connection to FDDI, and FDDI connection to ATM.

System Migration: Moving to Future Networks

The size of your networks and the distance between connections on your networks will depend on the type of signal, the signal speed, and the transmission media (the type of cable used to transmit the signals). For example, the most commonly used fiber optic medium type is the link segment. There are two fiber optic link segments in use, the original Fiber Optic Inter-Repeater Link (FOIRL) segment, and the newer 10BaseFL segment.

The original FOIRL specification from the Ethernet standard of the early 1980s provided a link segment of up to 1000 meters between two repeaters only. As the cost of repeaters dropped and more and more multiport repeater hubs were used, it became cost-effective to link individual computers to a fiber optic port on a repeater hub. Vendors created outboard FOIRL MAUs to allow this, although a repeater-to-DTE (Data Terminal Equipment) fiber connection was not specifically described in the FOIRL standard.

The distance and rate limits in these descriptions are the IEEE-recommended maximum speeds and distances for signaling. For instance, the recommended maximum rate for V.35 is 2 Mbps, but it is commonly used at 4 Mbps without any problems.

NOTE:

Even though you can usually get good results at speeds and distances far greater than those listed in this part of the chapter, exceeding the maximum distances is not recommended or supported. If you understand the electrical problems that might arise and can compensate for them, you can get good results with rates and distances greater than those shown in this chapter; however, do so at your own risk.

10BaseF Connection to FDDI

To deal with connections to FDDI and other aspects of fiber optic Ethernet, a set of fiber optic media standards, called 10BaseF, was developed. This set of fiber standards includes revised specifications for a fiber optic link segment that allow direct attachments to computers. The full set of 10BaseF specifications includes three segment types:

10BaseFL

The 10BaseFL standard replaces the older FOIRL specifications and is designed to interoperate with existing FOIRL-based equipment. 10BaseFL provides a fiber optic link segment that may be up to 2000 meters long, providing that only 10BaseFL equipment is used in the segment. If 10BaseFL equipment is mixed with FOIRL equipment, then the maximum segment length may be 1000 meters.

A 10BaseFL segment may be attached between two computers, or two repeaters, or between a computer and a repeater port. Because of the widespread use of fiber links, 10BaseFL is the most widely used portion of the 10BaseF fiber optic specifications, and equipment is available from a large number of vendors.

10BaseFB

The 10BaseFB specifications describe a synchronous signaling backbone segment that allows the limit on the number of repeaters that may be used in a given 10 Mbps Ethernet system to be exceeded. In other words, the 10BaseFB specification is *a synchronous Ethernet* link between repeaters that extends the limit for repeaters and segments in a single unbridged network.

10BaseFB links typically attach to repeater hubs, and are used to link special 10BaseFB synchronous signaling repeater hubs together in a repeated backbone system that can span long distances. Individual 10BaseFB links may be up to 2000 meters in length. This system has a limited market and equipment is available from only a few vendors.

10BaseFP

The Fiber Passive system provides a set of specifications for a fiber optic mixing segment that links multiple computers on a fiber optic media system without using repeaters. In other words, the 10BaseFP specification is a passive star configuration for fiber optics. The signal is shared with other fiber arms using a optical distribution system.

10BaseFP segments may be up to 500 meters long, and a single 10BaseFP fiber optic passive star coupler may link up to 33 computers. This system has not been widely adopted and equipment does not appear to be generally available.

FDDI Connections

The distance limitations for singlemode and multimode Fiber Distributed Data Interface (FDDI) stations are listed in Table 10–1 [2].Table 10–2 summarizes the characteristics of IEEE 802.3 Ethernet and Ethernet 10BaseFL [Cisco, 10]. The distance limitations for 10 Mbps transmission over multimode optical fiber cables are shown in Table 10–3. Table 10–4 lists multimode optical fiber parameters required for 10BaseFL.

Table 10–1: FDDI maximum transmission distances.

Transceiver Type	Maximum Distance Between Stations
Singlemode	6.2 miles (10 km)[1]
	Up to 9.3 miles (up to 15 km)[2]
Multimode	Up to 1.2 miles (2 km)[2]

[1] *For AGS+(modular router with slots for nine cards) applications of FDDI.*
[2] *For the VIP (Versatile Interface Processor) singlemode FDDI port adapter using SC-type optical fiber.*

Table 10–2: IEEE 802.3 Ethernet and Ethernet 10BaseFL physical characteristics.

Parameter	IEEE 802.3 Ethernet	10BaseFL Ethernet
Data rate	10 Mbps	10 Mbps
Signaling method	Baseband	Baseband
Media	50 ohm coax (thick)	Multimode optical fiber
Topology	Bus	Star

Table 10–3: 10 Mbps 10BaseFL transmission cable distance limitations

Parameter	ST Connections
Maximum segment lengths	1,322 ft (407 m) for any repeater-to-DTE fiber segment. 1,650 ft (508 m) with five repeaters and six segments. 3,290 ft (1012 m) for any inter-repeater fiber segment. 6,571 ft (2022 m) without a repeater.
Cable specification	Multimode fiber optic cable[1]

[1] *Commercially available cables.*

Table 10–4: 10BaseFL multimode optical fiber parameters.

Parameter	Multimode
Attenuation	< 3.85 dB/km, at 860 nanometers (nm)
Bandwidth	> 170 MHzkm, at 860 nm
Insertion loss	< 13.5 dB, at 860 nm
Propagation delay	< 6 microseconds/km
Size	62.5/125 micrometer (nominal diameter) optical fiber[1]

[1] *IEC Publication 793-2 specification.*

NOTE:

The singlemode and multimode optical fiber connections conform to the following optical power parameters: output power: –20 to –15 dBm; input power: –32 to –15 dBm; and input sensitivity: –32 dBm @ 2.6x11-11 BER @ 126 Mbps.

Token Ring Connection to FDDI

Another way to deal with connections to FDDI is through the fiber optic token ring. For example, an FTB (FDDI to token ring Translation Bridge) connects a token ring departmental LAN to an FDDI backbone as shown in Figures 10–1 and 10–2 [3]. The FTB plugs into the backplane of a *modular token ring hub* and connects to the FDDI interface from its front panel.

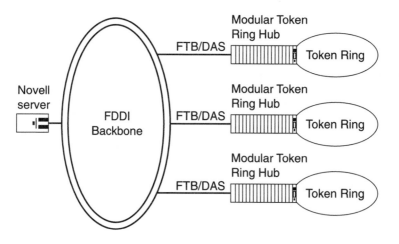

Figure 10–1: FDDI to token ring translation bridge.

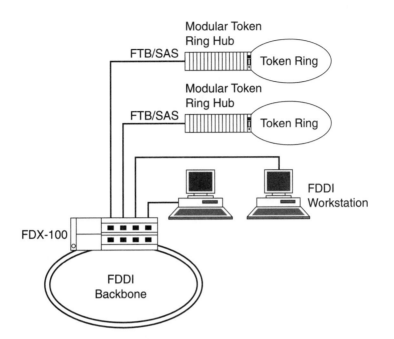

Figure 10–2: FDDI to token ring translation bridge where the FTB can be configured as a dual-attached or single-attached FDDI station.

The FTB can segment the network for improved performance and response times on each departmental LAN as well as between LANs. Servers can connect directly to the FDDI backbone and can communicate with token ring clients, providing a cost-effective, high-performance solution to client servers. In addition, FDDI's dual-ring capability, together with the FTB's singlemode and multimode FDDI interfaces, promotes a high-performance fault-tolerant backbone that operates over extended physical distances, ideal for campus networks.

The FTB performs positive filtering on the FDDI side and negative filtering on the token ring port side. All addresses on the token ring side are automatically learned by the bridge. An aging process causes inactive stations to be deleted from the bridge tables.

Any number of FTBs can be connected to the FDDI backbone. Additional bridges (transparent and source routing) can be connected on the token ring LANs, supporting up to 256 stations on the token ring side.

The FTB can be configured as a dual-attached or single-attached FDDI station as shown in Figure 10.2. It supports backup (dual homing) connection on the tree, using for example, port *B* as the main connection and port *A* as the redundant connection. For greater reliability, ports *A* and *B* can be connected to two different concentrators.

The FTB can be configured and fully diagnosed via a management port. Masks by protocol or by MAC (Media Access Control) address can be entered via the port, as well as by software downloading.

The FTB performs extensive testing and diagnostics. Whenever a problem is detected, a combination of LEDs (light emitting diodes) indicate the nature of the fault. If an FDDI Bypass Switch is installed, the FTB is bypassed.

Configuration and monitoring of the FTB can also be performed via the in-band Simple Network Management Protocol (SNMP) agent. This enables management by a SNMP Network Management System for LAN/WAN networks or any other SNMP management station. Alternatively, configuration and diagnostics can be performed from a terminal connected to a module management port.

The RISC processor architecture ensures a forwarding rate of 15,000 frames per second. The FDDI and token ring frames are filtered by hardware filters which support the maximum frame rates on both FDDI and token ring.

FDDI Connection to ATM

In reverse, a way to deal with connections *from* instead of *to* FDDI is through the fiber optic ATM. Here, the market gurus are not perfectly synchronized concerning the migration to ATM. Some of them advocate skipping the current high-speed LAN standard (FDDI) and moving directly to ATM. Some view such a strategy as risky for most corporate users because it could run into severe interoperability problems.

The ATM principles are to establish a completely transparent LAN/WAN network where a single technology could handle different speeds as well as match the needs (and the budgets) of corporate workgroups. The ideal picture of ATM implementation is a real end-to-end connection based on the same model as the telephone system.

However, most pictures of ATM deployment assume that it will be incorporated into the corporate LAN as a collapsed backbone. Standard LAN segments will be attached to this backbone via routers or special adapter interfaces on the ATM backbone switch. However, the needed interface standards between ATM and other subsystems is not stable. And even when they are finalized, first implementations may not be too efficient or may require extreme care to be tuned properly.

For example, Fibronics On-Demand Bandwidth Hierarchy (ODBH) is based on a transparent, then secure, four-layer evolution to ATM for the installed base of LAN protocols and equipment as shown in Figure 10–3 [4]. ODBH includes a series of high-speed interfaces together with the open GigaHUB architecture. In terms of costs, On-Demand Bandwidth Hierarchy provides a very attractive investment scheme that provides the most cost-effective solution to single user work group, and enterprise bandwidth problems.

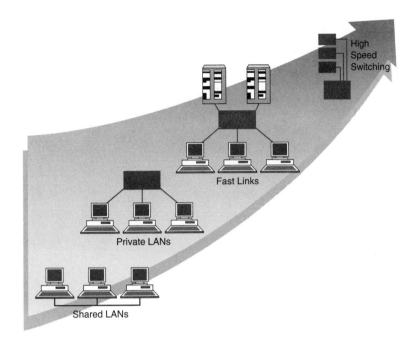

Figure 10–3: On-Demand Bandwidth Hierarchy (ODBH).

Layer 1

Shared LANs is the first layer as shown in Figure 10–3. It is the most popular networking implementation for office automation, data entry, client/server, etc.

Layer 2

Ethernet switching significantly increases network performance for workgroups or single users. Private LANs consist of two switching methods to match the customer's environment as shown in Figure 10–3. Switching simply provides multiples of 10 Mbps, allowing low speed data stream applications to gain performance at low cost.

Layer 3

FDDI is the best-suited technology for client/server applications. FDDI provide extensive reliability, 100 Mbps throughput, and copper or fiber support. In addition, FDDI collision-less technology enables the Ethernet LAN to operate with efficiency. Furthermore, FDDI and Ethernet are completely interoperable with all existing FDDI and Ethernet equipment including adapter cards, concentrators, bridges, routers and standard FDDI interfaces.

This level meets the users bandwidth requirements (fast links) at the desktop and at the server level as shown in Figure 10–3. Combining switched Ethernet and 100 Mbps will ensure a smooth network capacity upgrade for the more powerful computing devices.

Layer 4

Migrating to ATM can then be introduced at no risk of a network architecture change nor performance degradation at the server level or at the LAN level. With FDDI becoming more of a front-end LAN, new backbone implementation can be achieved through ATM. The lack of full ATM management today is not a major issue in this configuration. FDDI provides the pipe for local client/server applications while ATM will provide high-speed LAN interconnection (high speed switching), until the technology reaches a price level compatible with the desktop environment as shown in Figure 10–3.

During the process of deciding which optical fiber design to use and which system to migrate to, it is very important to keep your costs down. Next, we'll look at how you can maintain a lower optical loss budget.

Optical Loss Budget

The faster design and drafting can be completed, the lower the design costs will be. The more consistent and accurate the calculations and drafting are, the more efficient field construction and operations become.

For example, the typical fiber optic cable used for a fiber link segment is a multimode fiber cable (MMF) with a 62.5 micron fiber optic core and 125 micron outer cladding (62.5/125). Each link segment requires two strands of fiber, one to transmit data, and one to receive data. There are many kinds of fiber optic cables available, ranging from simple two-strand jumper cables with a PVC (Permanent Virtual Circuit) outer jacket material on up to large inter-building cables carrying many fibers in a bundle.

The fiber connectors used on link segments are generally known as *ST* connectors. The formal name of this connector in the ISO/IEC international standards is *BFOC/2.5*. The ST connector is a spring-loaded bayonet connector whose outer ring locks onto the connection, much like the BNC (Bayone-Neill-Concelman) connector used on 10Base2 segments. The ST connector has a key on an inner sleeve and also an outer bayonet ring. To make a connection, you line up the key on the inner sleeve of the ST plug with a corresponding slot on the ST receptacle, then push the connector in and lock it in place by twisting the outer bayonet ring. This provides a tight connection with precise alignment between the two pieces of fiber optic cable being joined.

NOTE:

> There are two other dominant types of optical connectors besides ST, SMA and SC. The SC connector is new, but is or has become the standard.

The wavelength of light used on a fiber link segment is 850 nanometers (850 nm). The optical loss budget for a fiber link segment must be no greater than 12.5 dB. The loss budget refers to the amount of optical power lost through the attenuation of the fiber optic cable, and the inevitable small losses that occur at each fiber connector.

The more connectors you have and the longer your fiber link cable is, the higher the optical loss will be. Optical loss is measured with fiber optic test instruments that can tell you exactly how much optical loss there may be on a given segment at a given wavelength of light. A standard grade fiber optic cable operating at 850 nm will have something in the neighborhood of 4 dB to 5 dB loss per 1000 meters. You can also expect something in the neighborhood of 0.5 to around 2.0 dB loss per connection point, depending on how well the connection has been made. If your connectors or fiber splices are poorly made, or if there is finger oil or dust on the connector ends, then you can have higher optical loss on the segment.

The older FOIRL segment typically used the same type of fiber optic cable and connectors and had the same optical loss budget. The 10BaseFL specifications were designed to allow backward compatibility with existing FOIRL segments. The major difference is that the 10BaseFL segment may be up to 2,000 meters in length if only 10BaseFL equipment is used on the segment.

Fiber on the backbone, copper to the desktop. For years, that's been the book on premises wiring management. That book has now been rewritten due to the dramatic cut in cost of installing fiber to the desktop. The continued price reductions for fiber cabling and components have brought the overall cost of fiber installation close to that of Category 5 unshielded twisted pair (UTP) copper wiring. This has resulted in greater business profitability by bringing fiber to the desk—the final topic of discussion for this chapter.

Fiber-to-the-Desk

The time for considering optical fiber as the main cabling medium for building cabling has finally arrived. No longer should fiber optics be considered an alternative to copper used only for applications with special requirements. Fiber optic technology is clearly superior in performance and is now competitive in price with the high-end twisted-pair cable required for today's high-speed networks.

Twisted-pair cable is the most prevalent type of cable used in wiring new buildings. These cables come in several grades based on performance: Category 3 for applications to 16 MHz, Category 4 for applications to 20 MHz, and Category 5 for applications to 100 MHz. Each supports cable runs of up to 100 meters. A standard fiber optic cable for building use can handle applications of several hundred megahertz at distances in excess of 2000 meters. As will be discussed in this chapter, Category 5 cable, the cable required for emerging high-speed applications like asynchronous transfer mode (ATM) and 100 Mbps Ethernet, present some challenges in installation and operation.

The bottom line in the fiber-versus-copper debate is this: fiber optic cable has a performance edge. Copper, on the other hand, is a more widely understood and accepted technology. More important, the costs of fiber components are competitive with their copper counterparts. And, if you add life cycle costs, including the costs of downtime and possible obsolescence, fiber is the better value.

The Seven Advantages of Fiber

Fiber optics would not even be considered if it did not offer distinct advantages over traditional copper media. These advantages translate into the following:

- Information-carrying capacity.
- Low loss.
- Electromagnetic immunity.
- Light weight.
- Smaller size.
- Safety.
- Security.

Information-Carrying Capacity

Fiber optic cable offers bandwidth well in excess of that required for today's network applications. The 62.5/125-micrometer fiber recommended for building use has a minimum bandwidth of 160 MHz-km (at a wavelength of 850 nm) or 500 MHz-km (at 1300 nm). Because bandwidth is a product of frequency and distance, the bandwidth at 100 meters is over 1 GHz. In comparison, Category 5 cable is specified only to 100 MHz over the same 100 meters.

With the high-performance singlemode cable used by the telephone industry for long distance telecommunications, the bandwidth is essentially infinite. That is, the information-carrying capacity of the fiber optic cable far exceeds the ability of today's electronics to exploit it as shown in Figure 10–4 [5].

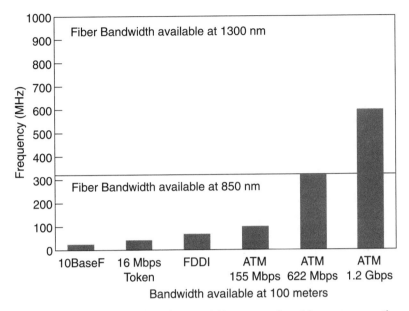

Figure 10–4: The bandwidth of optical fibers comfortably surpasses the needs of today's applications and gives room for growth.

Low Loss

A fiber optic cable offers low power loss. Low loss permits longer transmission distances. Again, the comparison with copper is important—in a network, the longest recommended copper distance is 100 meters; with fiber optic, it is 2000 meters as shown in Table 10–5 [AMP, 3].

Table 10–5: Copper Versus Fiber.

| | Copper | Fiber | |
		Multimode	Singlemode
Bandwidth (100 meters)	100 MHz	1 GHz	> 100 GHz
Transmission distance	100 meters	2000 meters	40,000 meters
FCC EMI concerns	Yes	No	
EMI susceptibility	Yes	No	
Crosstalk	Yes	No	
Ground loop potential	Yes	No	
Weight	Heavier	Lighter	
Size	Larger	Smaller	

A principal drawback of copper cable is that loss increases with the signal frequency. This means high data rates tend to increase power loss and decrease practical transmission distances. With fiber, loss does not change with the signal frequency.

Electromagnetic Immunity

By some estimates, 60% of all copper-based network outages are caused by cabling and cabling-related products. Crosstalk, impedance mismatches, and EMI susceptibility are major factors in noise and errors in copper systems. What's more, such problems can increase with incorrectly installed Category 5 cable, which is more sensitive to poor installation than other twisted-pair cable.

Because a fiber optic cable is a dielectric, it is immune to electromagnetic interference. It does not cause crosstalk, which is a critical limiting factor for twisted-pair cable. What's more, it can be run in electrically noisy environments, such as a factory floor, without concern because electrical noise will not affect fiber. There's no concern with proximity to noise sources like power lines or fluorescent lights. In short, fiber is inherently more reliable than copper.

Light Weight

Fiber optic cable weighs less than comparable copper cable. A dual-fiber cable is 20% to 50% lighter than a comparable 4-pair Category 5 cable. Lighter weight makes fiber easier to install.

Smaller Size

Fiber optic cable has a smaller cross section than the copper cables it replaces. Again, relative to Category 5 twisted-pair cable, a duplex optical fiber takes up about 15% less space.

Safety

Since the fiber is a dielectric, it does not present a spark hazard. What's more, cables are available with the same flammability ratings as copper counterparts to meet code requirements in buildings.

Security

Fiber optic cable is quite difficult to tap. Since it does not radiate electromagnetic energy, emissions cannot be intercepted. And physically tapping the fiber takes great skill to do undetected. Thus, the fiber is the most secure medium available for carrying sensitive data.

Basically, fiber optic cable offers high bandwidth over greater distances with no danger of electrical interference. Its small size and lighter weight give it an installation edge for pulling and installing, especially in tight spaces. And it's safe and secure. The clear advantages of fiber optics are too often obscured by concerns that may have been valid during the pioneering days of fiber, but that have since been answered by technical advances.

The Four Myths about Fiber Optics

A great deal of discussion has focused on the capabilities and shortcomings of high performance copper and fiber optic cables for the horizontal wiring system. Many misconceptions have clouded the facts surrounding the capabilities, survivability, and craft-friendliness of fiber. Technology improvements (coupled with more cost-effective solutions) have made fiber a viable and valuable option for high-performance wiring to the workstation. This part of the chapter dispels four myths which have surfaced about the feasibility of fiber as a complete communications system solution—from backbone links all the way to the desk.

Myth #1: Fiber Optic Cable is Fragile

An optical fiber has greater tensile strength than copper or steel fibers of the same diameter. It is flexible as shown in Figure 10–5 [AMP, 3], bends easily, , and resists most corrosive elements that attack copper cable. Optical cables can withstand pulling forces of more than 150 pounds—about six times that recommended for Category 5 cable. Fact is, Category 5 cable may be more fragile than optical cables: tight cable ties, excessive untwisting at the connector, and sharp bends can degrade the cable's performance until it no longer meets Category 5 performance requirements.

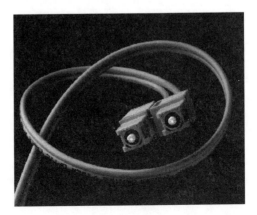

Figure 10–5: Fiber optic cable is flexible, sturdy and easy to work with.

Myth #2: Fiber Optic Cable Is Hard to Work With

Myth 2 derives from the early days of fiber optic connectors. Early connectors were difficult to apply; they came with many small parts that could tax even the nimble fingered. They needed epoxy, curing, cleaving, and polishing. On top of that, the technologies of epoxy, curing, cleaving, and polishing were still evolving. Today, connectors have fewer parts, the procedures for termination are well-understood, and the craftsperson is aided by polishing machines and curing ovens to make the job faster and easier.

Even better, epoxyless connectors eliminate the need for the messy and time-consuming application of epoxy. Polishing is an increasingly simple, straightforward process. Pre-terminated cable assemblies also speed installation and reduce a once (but no longer) labor-intensive process. Also, pre-engineered parts, cables, connectors, etc. make using fiber optics much easier.

Myth #3: Fiber Is Expensive

Fiber optic cable and related components are comparably priced to Category 5 copper counterparts. As fiber optic cable becomes increasingly easier to work with, it means that installation costs are becoming less expensive. Pulling costs are the same. Termination time is about equal (Category 5 cable takes more care, and time, than other UTP).

Is fiber more expensive than copper? On the installed cost side, fiber optic cable and Category 5 components are comparably priced. On the life cycle costs, fiber may be cheaper in the long run. Many users have found fiber optic cable installations easier to maintain and more reliable. The cost of network downtime and glitches can be enormous: the cable plant that minimizes these costs justifies the small premium in components/installation costs.

What's more, costs are changing every day and for every installation. Don't assume, any longer, that fiber optics cost more.

Myth #4: Fiber Has No Place to the Desktop

How much bandwidth is needed at the desktop? How much is too much? Underestimating a user's requirements has long been a mistake in the computer and networking industry. Critics of fiber optics argue that users don't need high bandwidth to the desktop, so that using fiber is wasted potential. Data rates of 25 Mbps and 51 Mbps are among those touted for desktop connectivity.

Yet, 4 Mbps token ring seemed fast at first, only to be replaced by the four-times-faster 16 Mbps version. Traditional Ethernet is being replaced by 100 Mbps flavors. Video, video teleconferencing, multimedia, and other bandwidth-hungry applications are vying for bandwidth. While the network backbone can certainly benefit from the high-speed, long-distance transmission achieved with fiber optics, don't count the desktop out. Demands at the desktop will invariably grow as new applications like ATM require more bandwidth.

Technology presents an important issue here. Category 5 cable may have been pushed to its limits in achieving 100 MHz performance. While advances in data encoding schemes may provide higher data rates within this frequency framework, the question remains whether Category 5 performance can be extended. Will we need Category 6 UTP? At the same time, fiber optic technology has room to spare. For the 100-meter distances recommended for links to the desktop, Category 5 cable has a bandwidth of 100 MHz, while the fiber optic bandwidth is over 1 GHz.

Today, networks can be the lifeblood of businesses, universities, and medical centers, so it is essential that the cable system perform reliably to the specifications required. Downtime can be costly. In the final analysis, fiber for workstation applications offers long-term performance, security and reliability advantages, and should be considered as part of the network solution into the 21st century.

From Here

This chapter presented an overview of fiber optic design considerations (layout, system migration, loss budget calculations, and fiber to disk, etc.). The next chapter discusses wireless design considerations (spread spectrum, microwave, infrared, wireless WANs and LANs, etc.).

End Notes

[1] John C. Huber, Ph.D., PE, "Understanding Fiber Optics: Selecting the Optical Network," Fiber Optics Laboratory Manager, 3M Telecom Systems Group, Austin, TX, 9May 8, 1995), p. 1.

[2] "Site Preparation," (Some material in this book has been reproduced by Prentice Hall with the permission of Cisco Systems Inc.), COPYRIGHT © 1998 Cisco Systems, Inc., ALL RIGHTS RESERVED, 170 West Tasman Drive, San Jose, CA 95134-1706, USA, 1997, pp. 9–10.

[3] "RADring Module: FTB-FDDI to Token Ring Translation Bridge," RAD Data Communications, 900 Corporate Drive, Mahwah, NJ 07430, and Corporation UNI, Russia, 1998, p. 4.

[4] "Product Strategy," NBASE Communications, Fibronics International, 16 Esquire Road, North Billerica, MA 01862, 1996, p. 1.

[5] "Why Fiber? Why Now," Reprinted with the permission of AMP Incorporated, Investor Relations, 176-42, PO Box 3608, Harrisburg, PA USA 17105-3608, 1997, p. 2.

11

Wireless Design Considerations

Today's wireless communication systems are designed as logically separate networks (separate from the normal fixed network). They are primarily designed to provide cost-efficient wide area coverage for a rather limited number of users with moderate bandwidth demands (voice + low rate data). The consumers of telecommunication services of tomorrow will expect to receive the same services in a wireless fashion as they receive today from a fixed network. These services require high bandwidths instantaneously. It is not expected that future users will be willing to sacrifice functionality for the added value of mobility—mainly because they will hardly be using any other stationary telecommunication devices. A wireless system should therefore be transparent to the user and thus be highly integrated with the fixed network. Personal wireless devices should by nature be small and consume a minimum of power.

Wireless systems design should also take into consideration practical design solutions for engineers and engineering managers working at the wireless systems level. Solutions should explore the design, simulation, and testing of wireless systems and subsystems, especially focusing on the interaction of a design's RF circuitry with its analog, baseband, DC, and digital sections.

This chapter discusses the design and implementation of wireless systems to support multimedia communications, with emphasis on a broadband downlink capable of supporting digital video. In particular, the development of integrated analog RF front-end and baseband digital interface circuitry, as well as the system simulations driving the design, are examined. In addition, the chapter also covers practical applications of the latest wireless technologies to help guide wireless design engineers and engineering managers in designing wireless infrastructures. Let's begin the discussion by first taking a look at the fundamental limitations of those wireless infrastructures.

Fundamental Limitations

Device technology is expected to make even more progress. This is why size reduction and functionality of personal devices is expected not to constitute a fundamental problem, per se. The fundamental factors limiting the design of high-capacity ubiquitous wireless systems are expected to be:

- Spectrum shortage.
- Device power consumption.
- Infrastructural investments.
- Distributed network complexity.

Spectrum shortage is mainly due to regulation and coordination with existing services. Device power supply technology, which is not expected to make substantial progress (1-2 orders of magnitude) in the next decade, is why power consumption has to be limited. Infrastructural investments could include both devices and fixed networks. Can all these limiting factors be set aside with no fundamental restriction on the capacity in numbers of wireless users and the user bandwidth provided? By limiting, for instance, the infrastructural investments (for example, the number of wireless access points to the fixed network), spectrum efficiency will be degraded and device power consumption will have to be increased due to higher transmitter power and increased signal processing burden due to adverse propagation conditions. The sheer numbers of radio ports and mobile devices in future high-density wireless systems will require efficient and reliable distributed network functions in order to avoid centralized system vulnerability and excess signaling data volume. Therefore, contrary to traditional network design, let's assume that the following factors are limiting:

- Fixed infrastructure communication capacity.
- Fixed infrastructure processing (switching).

Main Problem Areas

The design of efficient wireless infrastructures is a truly an interdisciplinary activity—spanning services and user behavior, infrastructural economics, telecommunication analysis down to implementation issues, and device technology. The main problem areas that can be identified are discussed in the sidebar, "Major Issues."

Major Issues

The following are the major problem areas (in the form of questions that need to be asked) in the design of wireless infrastructures:

User Behavior:

What is the traffic structure emanating from the use of personal wireless communication services? Will there be an imbalance (data received/transmitted) that could be exploited in efficient wireless systems design? Can source coding be employed? Can applications adapt to time-varying connection performance? What are the quality requirements.?

Economics:

How should infrastructures evolve to provide coverage and capacity with respect to operator revenues? How should investments be shared between users (personal devices) and operators ?

Device Technology:

What devices will be available (semiconductors, antennas, batteries, etc.)? What is the impact of multiple access techniques—Code Division Multiple Access (CDMA), Multicarrier techniques, Time Division Multiple Access (TDMA), and Frequency Division Multiple Access (FDMA)—on device technology and electronic system design? What will be their functionality, performance and power consumption? What user interface technology should be used?

Wireless Systems Security:

Which schemes can be devised to prevent wireless systems eavesdropping, jamming, terminal spoofing, illegal use of roaming information, etc.?

Network Architecture and Mobility Management:

What overall network architecture should be employed (packet-routing/(virtual) circuit switching)? How should efficient mobility management and/or signaling strategies be implemented? What are capacity requirements and the performance implications of these schemes? How should mixed architectures (satellite/ short range) be handled?

Radio Infrastructure Design and Performance:

What tools should be used to meet capacity demands and the restriction on spectrum, power, and cost? Which dynamic spectrum allocation architectures should be used to achieve adequate performance/spectrum utilization? How should multimedia traffic spectrum management be handled? How should radio infrastructures (radio port locations) be planned? What is the impact of layered (multi-range) cell structures?

Air Interface Design:

What multiaccess techniques, diversity, detection schemes, and antenna devices should be used? What is a suitable distribution of signal processing load (coding, detection, compression, equalization, etc.) between the fixed infrastructure and portable devices to maintain functionality but to conserve power?

Distributed Systems Implementation Technology:

How can we ensure reliability in large complex systems? How should systems be integrated and protocols designed?

In this next part of the chapter, the overall wireless system design, analog RF circuitry, and digital baseband circuitry are discussed—particularly emphasizing a single chip, the silicon Complementary Metal Oxide Semiconductor (CMOS) solution, for the mobile receiver. The discussion will focus primarily on the broadband downlink—given the high data rates, the need for low power consumption, and size in the portable unit.

Wireless System Design and Services

Over the past several years, wireless communications have seen dramatic advances in two distinct areas. On one hand, the demand for portable voiceband services has resulted in intense research efforts to improve performance and increase capacity through digital transmission. Such systems focus on wide-area narrowband communications, providing low-bandwidth network services to individual users in a portable fashion. On the other hand, the need for more flexible computer networks has led to the advent of wireless LAN's such as the ones discussed in the sidebar, "Wireless LANs" and Table 11–1 [1]. Such systems focus on local-area wideband communications, providing networking services to individual computers but usually not easily portable.

Wireless LANs

This sidebar discusses what a wireless LAN is and what products are out there to implement a wireless LAN. See Appendix I, "List Of Wireless LAN Products And Sites," for a list of many other sites where you can go to find more information on wireless LANs.

What Is a Wireless LAN?

In the last few years, a new type of local area network has appeared. This new type of LAN, the wireless LAN, provides an alternative to the traditional LANs based on twisted pair, coaxial cable, and optical fiber. The wireless LAN serves the same purpose as that of a wired or optical LAN—to convey information among the devices attached to the LAN. But with the lack of physical cabling to tie down the location of a node on a network, the network can be much more flexible—moving a wireless node is easy, as opposed to the large amount of labor required to add or move the cabling in any other type of network. Also, going wireless may be a better choice where the physical makeup of the building makes it difficult or impossible to run wire in the building.

Wireless networks are ideal for portable computers. Using wireless connections allows portable computers to still be portable without sacrificing the advantages of being connected to a network. These machines can be setup virtually anywhere within the building.

Wireless networks can be used in combination with cabled LANs, in that all the machines that will require relative mobility are connected wirelessly, while the stations that are for the most part permanent can be connected through cable. Wireless LANs use one of three transmission techniques: spread spectrum, narrowband microwave, and infrared.

Spread Spectrum

Spread spectrum is currently the most widely used transmission technique for wireless LANs as shown in Table 11–1. It was initially developed by the military to avoid jamming and eavesdropping of the signals (like radio-controlled torpedoes). This is done by spreading the signal over a range of frequencies that consist of the industrial, scientific, and medical (ISM) bands of the electromagnetic spectrum. The ISM bands include the frequency ranges at 902 MHz to 928 MHZ, at 2.4 GHz to 2.484 GHz, and at 5.8 GHz to 5.9 GHz, which do not require an FCC license.

The first type of spread spectrum developed is known as *frequency-hopping spread spectrum.* This technique broadcasts the signal over a seemingly random series of radio frequencies. A receiver, hopping between frequencies in synchronization with the transmitter, receives the message. The message can only be fully received if the series of frequencies is known. Because only the intended receiver knows the transmitter's hopping sequence, only that receiver can successfully receive all of the data. Most vendors develop their own hopping-sequence algorithms, which all but guarantee that two transmitters will not hop to the same frequency at the same time.

The FCC has made some rules for frequency-hopping spread spectrum technologies. The FCC dictates that the transmitters must not spend more than 0.4 seconds on any one channel every 20 seconds in the 902 MHz band and every 30 seconds in the 2.4 GHz band. Also, the transmitters must hop through at least 50 channels in the 902-MHz band and 75 channels in the 2.4-GHz band—a channel consists of a frequency width which is determined by the FCC. The IEEE 802.11 committee has drafted a standard that limits frequency-hopping spread spectrum transmitters to the 2.4 GHz band.

The other type of spread spectrum communication (used in cellular, Personal Communications Services (PCS), wireless LANs, and Global Positioning Satellite (GPS) systems) is called direct-sequence spread spectrum or pseudonoise. This method seems to be the one that most wireless spread-spectrum LANs use. The direct-sequence transmitter spreads its transmissions by adding redundant data bits called *chips* to them. Direct-sequence spread spectrum adds at least ten chips to each data bit. Like a frequency-hopping receiver, a direct sequence receiver must know a transmitter's spreading code to decipher data. This spreading code is what allows multiple direct-sequence transmitters to operate in the same area without interference. Once the receiver has all of the data signal, it uses a correlator to remove the chips and collapse the signal to its original length.

As with frequency-hopping spread spectrum, the FCC has also set rules for direct-sequence transmitters. Each signal must have ten or more chips. This rule limits the practical raw data throughput of direct sequence transmitters to 2 Mbps in the 902 MHz band and 8 Mbps in the 2.4 GHz band. Unfortunately, the number of chips is directly related to a signal's immunity to interference. In an area with lots of radio interference, you'll have to give up throughput to avoid interference. The IEEE 802.11 committee has drafted a standard of 11 chips for direct-sequence spread spectrum.

Frequency-hopping radios currently use less power than direct-sequence radios and generally cost less. Direct-sequence radios have a practical raw data rate of 8 Mbps; frequency hopping radios have a practical limit of 2 Mbps. So, if high performance is key and interference is not a problem, go with direct sequencing. But if a small, inexpensive portable wireless adapter for a notebook or Personal Digital assistant (PDA) is needed, a the frequency-hopping method should be good enough.

Furthermore, another frequency-hopping technique is when each terminal has it's own unique 10-bit code which is applied to the channel. That code allows the terminal and the base to recognize or not to recognize data intended for it. With either method of spread spectrum, the end result is a system that is extremely difficult to detect, does not interfere with other services, and still carries a large bandwidth of data.

Narrowband Microwave

Microwave technology is not really a LAN technology. Its main use is to interconnect LANs between buildings. This requires microwave dishes on both ends of the link. The dishes must be in line-of-sight to transmit and collect the microwave signals. Microwave is used to bypass the telephone company when connecting LANs between buildings.

One major drawback to the use of microwave technology is that the frequency band used requires licensing by the FCC. Once a license is granted for a particular location, that frequency band cannot be licensed to anyone else, for any purpose, within a 17.5 mile radius (4-6 GHz: 20-30 miles (analog), 10-12 GHz: 10-15 miles (digital), 18-23 GHz: 5-7 miles (digital).

Infrared

Infrared LANs use infrared signals to transmit data. This is the same technology used in products like remote controls for televisions and VCRs. These LANs can be set up using either a point-to-point configuration or a sun-and-moon configuration where the signals are diffused by reflecting them off of some type of surface. The major advantage of infrared is its ability to carry a high bandwidth, but its major disadvantage is that they can easily be obstructed, since light cannot pass through solid objects [Wood, 1-3].

Table 11–1: Wireless LAN transmission techniques.

	Spread Spectrum	**Narrowband Microwave**	**Infrared**
Frequency	902MHz to 928 MHz; 2.4 GHz to 2.4385GHz; 5.725 GHz to 5.825 GHz	18.825 GHz to 19.205 GHz	3×10^{14} Hz
Maximum coverage	105 to 800 feet, or up to 50,000 square feet	40 to 130 feet, or up to 5000 square feet	30 to 80 feet
Line of sight required	No	No	Yes
Transmit power	Less than 1 W	25 mW	N/A
License required	No	Yes	No
Interbuilding use	Possible with antenna	No	Possible
Rated speed (% of 10 Mbps wire)	20% to 50%	33%	50% to 100%

The distinction between these two wireless systems is rapidly blurring. As laptop computers place mobile computing resources in the hands of individuals, wireless technologies capable of providing wide-area, wideband services will clearly be needed. With this merging of computation and communications, individual users will have instantaneous and portable access to fixed information networks via a lightweight mobile unit. Furthermore, users will be capable of transferring data to other users and accessing fixed computing resources without any constraints on where or when such access takes place. As shown in Figure 11–1, the mobile unit will support a myriad of services, including full-motion digital video and high-quality audio, and combines the functionality of today's analog mobile telephones, radio pagers, and laptop personal computers [2].

Since portability places severe constraints on the physical weight of the terminal, the available battery power is quite limited. Thus, power minimization is crucial; power reduction in both the digital and analog hardware must be achieved. To this end, the terminal should only carry the bare minimum of computing resources necessary to support its functionality. User computation should be mainly performed by large, non-portable computing facilities, with the high-speed wireless link serving as the terminal's means of accessing the fixed computation servers and data networks. Direct point-to-point wireless communication is not allowed; the link only provides the final interface into the wired data network, much like a conventional telephone handset serves as the link into the telephony system. Whereas the capability of moving massive amounts of digital data within networks already exists, the problem of easily getting data in and out of those networks is now addressed.

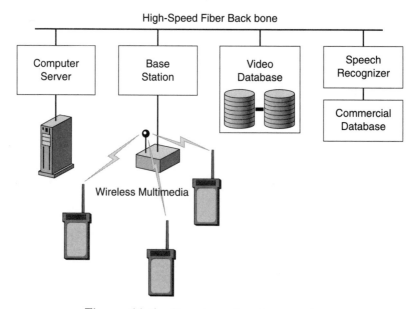

Figure 11–1: Overview of system services.

Although placing all computation services back in the wired network has immediate benefits in terms of reducing power consumption, it provides another advantage: data that is highly sensitive to corruption will not be transmitted over the wireless network. Existing distributed computation environments are crucially dependent on the fact that data transmitted over the network has high integrity (bit-error rates on wired Ethernet are typically on the order of 1 per 1012 bits and further protection is gained by packet retransmit in the case of an error). However, on wireless networks this is not true; even after extensive error-correction coding, it is still difficult to attain error rates even remotely as low as this. User computation data, such as spreadsheets or simulation results or bank transfers, simply cannot be allowed to sustain any corruption. For wireless systems, this translates into an inordinate amount of transmission overhead in terms of coding and data retransmission to compensate. On the other hand, user multimedia information, such as voice and image data, is relatively tolerant of bit errors. An error in a single video frame or an audio sample will not significantly change the meaning or usefulness of the data. Thus, the portable unit described above is truly a terminal dedicated to multimedia personal communications, and not simply a notebook computer with a wireless LAN/modem attached to it.

With the shift in emphasis from computation inside the mobile unit over to communications outside, it is evident that development of a wideband link capable of supporting the required user bandwidth becomes paramount. The uplink is used only for low-rate speech and control data. Although the system is still full-duplex, this asymmetry must be accounted for in the design, as the bandwidth requirements for maintaining the uplink are thus considerably less than those for the downlink.

NOTE:

The wideband video data is only supported in the downlink to the mobile.

Broadband Spread-Spectrum Communications

Even with a reliable, guaranteed latency backbone network, the issues of user capacity and overall system bandwidth consumption still remain. With the best compression schemes developed to date, data rates in excess of 1 Mbps per user would be needed to support full-motion video. However, this data rate is not needed on a continuous basis. When regular computational tasks are being performed on compute servers back on the network (such as using a word processor or a spreadsheet), the screen changes only slightly on a frame-by-frame basis; and, over only a small region—usually on the order of a single character or a few pixels. Hence, the peak data rate required by a user may easily be much larger than the overall time-average data rate. Thus, minimizing the overall system bandwidth consumption while supporting a large number of users accessing data simultaneously is of paramount importance.

The advantages in improved spectral efficiency afforded by cellular systems have long been known. They have already been employed to a limited extent by existing analog mobile telephony systems, with cell size on the order of square kilometers. Due to the tremendous bandwidth requirements of such a portable terminal, it is inevitable that future wideband systems will exploit picocellular networks with cell sizes on the order of meters to employ as much frequency reuse as possible.

NOTE:

Macrocell—large area; Microcell—smaller area; and Picocell—very small area.

The primary interference mechanism in such a cellular transmission environment is that of multipath fading, in which the transmitted signal interferes at the receiver due to reflections off of objects. From statistical measurements [Sheng, 3], the short-range indoor channel that's been considered has typical delay spreads ranging from 20 nsec to 60 nsec with Rician-distributed fading characteristics. This is far different from the typical outdoor large-cell transmission environment that has much more severe Rayleigh fading characteristics. Likewise, the indoor transmission environment changes far more slowly than the outdoor, given that the mobile unit will likely be stationary during use.

With this in mind, direct-sequence spread spectrum, or code-division multiple access becomes attractive for use in the downlink. It is naturally immune to multipath, since it can (with sufficient spreading) resolve the interfering multipath arrivals and combine them via a Rake Receiver (receiver having a number of individual digital channels, or tines, which can combine these channels to form a stronger received signal) as an intrinsic form of diversity. Also, CDMA can easily accommodate a wide range of user data rates by varying the transmit power for each user as a function of the required data rate. This concept of power modulation has already been exploited to improve the effective system capacity of next-generation digital cellular systems [Sheng, 3]. It is important to realize that traditional impairments of CDMA systems such as near-far interference and unsynchronized codes do not exist for the downlink, since all downlink transmissions originate from a single point—the base station. The broadcast nature of the signal, combined with the ability to resolve multipath arrivals and support variable data rates, makes CDMA extremely attractive for use in the high-performance wireless downlink in the system.

With these factors in mind, the system itself is a wideband extension of the U.S. IS-95 digital cellular CDMA standard [Sheng, 3], which utilizes a transmitted synchronization tone for timing recovery and Walsh orthogonal codes to multiplex users. A basic raw user data rate of 2 Mbps is assumed to allow a margin for channel error correction as well as the ability to explore various compression algorithms. The raw data is then modulated into a 1 Mbaud differential quadrature phase shift keying (DQPSK) symbol stream. In determining the cell size of 5 meters, a typical office environment consisting of soft-partition cubicles is assumed, with each cell typically containing 12 to 16 active users. Of those 16 users, it is assumed that approximately half are demanding the full 1 Mbaud data rate for video use, while the remainder are utilizing 128 Kbaud (256 Kbps) each for lower data rate applications such as voice or text and graphics. With a seven-cell reuse pattern at maximum capacity, a chipping rate of 64 Mchip/sec is sufficient to support this. Furthermore, given an average delay spread of 40 nsec, the resolvable number of paths is given by:

$$N = (Tdelayspread/Tchip) + 1$$

which translates to 2-3 resolvable paths by the receiver and dictates the size and complexity of the Rake receiver in the digital baseband hardware.

With a chipping rate of 64 Mchip/sec, a transmit bandwidth of 80 to 100 MHz will be required. Although this is a considerable amount of spectrum, this is amortized over large numbers of people using this spectrum simultaneously within multiple buildings. Considering that this bandwidth is designed to support full motion video and other multimedia network services for all users, this allocation of spectrum is not unreasonable given the level of service provided by the system, especially when compared to the spectrum allocated for existing systems by the National Television System Committee (NTSC) television standard.

For development and system verification for example, a baseband equivalent model for the transceiver system has been developed in the U.C. Berkeley Ptolemy simulation environment [Sheng, 4]. The schematic of the system utilizes a delay-locked loop keyed to the timing pilot tone to achieve synchronization/lock, and furthermore uses the pilot tone to provide an estimate of the channel impulse response. To simulate multipath effects, a baseband equivalent channel model has been developed from measured statistics [Sheng, 4]. This allows users to optimize the system for transmit power levels, number of parallel receivers, quantization levels in the receiver, etc.

As an example, the bit-error rate (BER) as a function of the number of users is shown in Figure 11–2, simulated under various conditions [Sheng, 5]. By Monte-Carlo methods, a worst-case (extreme fade) channel and a best-case channel were determined from the model, and then both channels were simulated with and without maximum-ratio Rake combining [Sheng, 4]. The benefits of the three-tap Rake receiver are apparent; under the worst-case fade condition, the Rake combiner provided a factor of up to 1000 improvement in BER over the uncompensated case. As the number of users increases, however, this not only degrades the base signal-to-noise ratio, but also degrades the accuracy of the channel estimate, reducing the effectiveness of the Rake combiner.

With high data rates and variable throughput requirements, developing the downlink has been of greatest importance, with CDMA providing an attractive means of both channel compensation and multiple access. The uplink, consisting of speech and pen input data, will require significantly lower data rates per user data rates (on the order of 32 Kbps), and due to near-far effects and the unsynchronized nature of the uplink signals, CDMA is not nearly as attractive. Instead, more conventional time-division multiple access (TDMA), frequency-hopped, or orthogonal frequency-division multiple access techniques are being explored for use in the uplink.

Monolithic RF Circuitry

Ostensibly, the linchpin of the wireless link lies in the development of the necessary radio-frequency components. In addition to the requirement of low

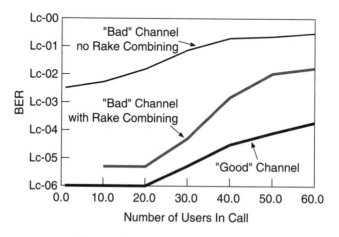

Figure 11–2: BER vs. number of users.

power consumption, the analog RF circuitry is complicated by the need to operate at frequencies above 1 GHz. Due to spectral congestion and competition from existing services, it will be impossible to accommodate such a wideband system at any lower frequencies. Such circuitry has been traditionally dominated by designs using discrete gallium arsenide semiconductors (GaAs) or silicon bipolar transistors and stripline filters, which consume significant amounts of area on a circuit board and excessive amounts of power, especially when matching to standard impedance levels (typically, 50 Ω).

First, the greatest power consumer in existing analog cellular is the transmitter. Since the transmit power must be scaled down as the cell radius is reduced, power consumed in the portable to drive the antenna drops correspondingly. Whereas existing cellular systems utilize 1 watt transmit power for RF links in 5 mile cells, a picocellular system with 5 meter cells only requires 0.1 to 1 milliwatt to maintain the link. The impact of this is tremendous; the traditional RF power amplifier is not needed, and transmit power becomes a small fraction of the overall system power consumption in a microcell or picocell environment.

Hence, power minimization of the remaining RF components becomes critical. Shown in Figure 11–3 is the block diagram of a conventional superheterodyne

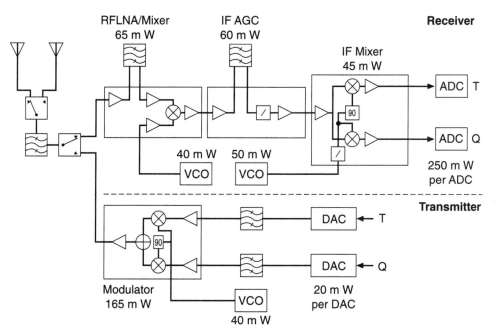

Figure 11–3: Superheterodyne transceiver architecture.

RF transceiver designed for picocell operation in the 902-928 MHz radio band [Sheng, 6]. Implemented using commercially available components, the power consumption for each active element in the transceiver is indicated. Even without the transmit power amplifier, the total consumption is impressive—1W overall, with 750 mW being consumed in the receiver. Furthermore, the component count is astronomical; over 200 passive and active devices are needed to implement the design, after taking into account external bypass, filter, and bias elements. Minimizing both the power and component count dictates the development of highly integrated analog technologies. From Figure 11–3, it is also apparent that the greatest gains are to be had from optimizing the receiver circuitry, given the complex chain of amplifiers, mixers, filters, oscillators, and Analog-to-Digital (A/D) converters required to implement it.

This part of the chapter will focus on the design and implementation of a single-chip, highly integrated receiver capable of operating in the 1 GHz frequency band and supporting a 64 Mchip/sec direct-sequence spread spectrum signal. To facilitate high integration levels, silicon CMOS is employed exclusively in the design.

Silicon CMOS for Microwave Applications

Digital technologies have seen a breakthrough in both performance and size through the use of device scaling, especially in the arena of silicon. However, the same benefits derived from Metal Oxide Semiconductor (MOS) scaling for digital circuits are reflected in analog applications as well. The figure of merit used to measure analog device performance is ft, which is the maximum operating frequency at which gain can still be derived. As a reference point, effective operation in the 1 GHz band requires a minimum device ft of around 7 GHz, with 10 GHz being a more conservative estimate. Currently available 1.2 micron processes can achieve peak fts in excess of 8 GHz; and, with an experimental 0.35 micron process, fts in excess of 25 GHz can be achieved. This argues very strongly that a 1 to 5 GHz analog RF transceiver can be built employing the same technologies traditionally used for digital, thus opening the possibility of a single-chip CMOS radio implementation.

As a demonstration, the RF amplifier design shown in Figure 11–4 has been fabricated and tested in a 1.2 micron technology (Sheng, 7]. The design is a two-stage transconductance-transresistance cascade, with the transresistance stage consisting of the tightly-coupled feedback loop formed by NMOS M2-M3. The presence of this feedback loop ensures that the circuit has no high-impedance nodes, thus achieving its broadband performance. Since the transconductance stage has gain gm1, the overall gain of the circuit is thus gm1/gm3, which can be shown to be process- and temperature-independent. The output buffers shown are needed to drive an off-chip filter stage, and are designed to be matched to 50W.

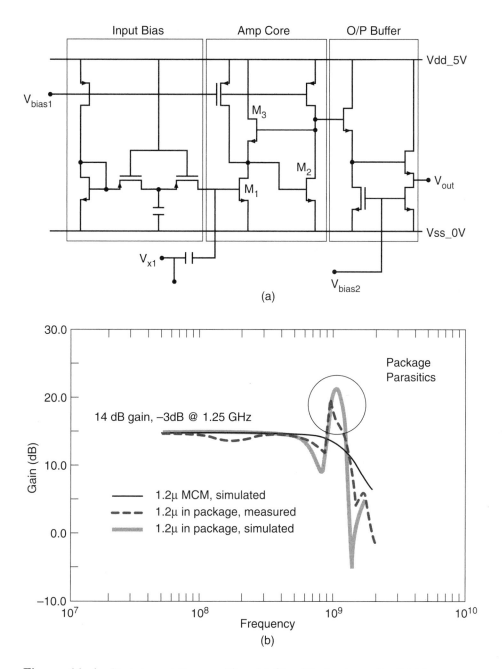

Figure 11–4: Prototype 1.2m amplifier. (a) Simplified schematic; (b) Measure performance from die photo.

The measured performance characteristics of the amplifier are shown in Figure 11–4, including the frequency response of the circuit. The circuit was originally designed for use in a low-parasitic multichip module; however, for testing it became necessary to package the device in a 44-pin leadless chip carrier. The sharp peaking near the rolloff corner is due to the extra parasitics introduced by the package. The Transistor Level Circuit Simulator or Simulation Program with Integrated Circuit Emphasis (SPICE) simulation for the amplifier with the package can be seen to fit quite well to measured values, and the SPICE simulation of the device in a multichip module is also shown. A version of this amplifier correcting for the package parasitics has been designed, and is fabricated as part of the integrated receiver circuit.

Sampling Demodulators

When sampling demodulators, a homodyne conversion method should be used that takes advantage of the fact that the underlying transmitted signal is inherently discrete-time [Sheng, 7]. If the incoming modulated RF signal at a carrier wc is subsampled at a frequency ws, where wc is assumed to be an integer multiple of ws, then the aliasing phenomenon intrinsic to the sampling operation will yield the required frequency conversion. This is akin to the passband sampling concept employed for many years by digital sampling oscilloscopes. Subsampling a passband signal is tantamount to a mixing operation. What was a complex series of active mixers and oscillators has been reduced to a single sampling operation, sampled at the Nyquist rate of the baseband signal. The hardware and power costs are now minimal: an accurate switch, implementable using standard MOS technologies, and a fixed-frequency crystal oscillator. A prototype demodulator has been fabricated to explore this concept. The modulated signal is a 20 kHz square wave riding on top of a 100 MHz carrier tone. The sampling rate is set to 1 MHz (100x subsampling ratio). Clearly, the sampled output is the recovered baseband envelope. The *return to zero* effect is a result of the sampling capacitors resetting during each cycle. Also, the slight curvature exhibited in the recovered baseband signal is due to the fact that wc is not a perfect integer multiple of ws. The frequency offset between the carrier frequency and the sampling rate is slight; in this case, it was measured to be 1.4 kHz.

In any case, the system design must take this phenomenon into account, since it is impossible to achieve zero offset. First, two sampling switches are employed to recover both the in-phase and quadrature signals. Thus, this frequency offset can be viewed as a slow rotation of the constellation in symbol space. Also, it is clear that the offset will be significantly smaller than the user symbol rate (1 MHz), given a typical frequency accuracy of 20 to 100 parts/million for crystal-based references. Thus, by employing an incoherent differential quadrature phase shift keying (DQPSK) digital modulation, the effects of the frequency offset can be nullified without the use of a carrier phase-locked recovery loop. Although a 3 dB signal-to-noise ratio (SNR) penalty is incurred by the incoherency, there are alternative strategies to recover this 3 dB that are far less expensive than carrier recovery, such as employing diversity antennas or error correction coding.

In order to meet the performance requirements for the spread-spectrum downlink, a sampling switch capable of handling a 1 GHz modulated signal and running at 128 MHz (twice the chipping rate) has been developed. The schematic of the demodulator is shown in Figure 11–5 [Sheng, 9]. First, to minimize the effects of switching noise and charge injection, a differential bottom-plate sampling topology is employed [Sheng, 8]. Second, the sampling capacitors must be able to track the 1 GHz modulated signal in order to sample the signal. Hence, the switches M1a,b and M2 must be carefully sized to ensure that the lowpass cutoff (formed by the on-resistance of the switches and the sampling capacitor) is well in excess of 1 GHz; otherwise, the incoming RF signal will be disastrously attenuated.

Furthermore, to achieve the 128 MHz switching performance, an extremely fast opamp is needed. In order to minimize the amount of static current in the opamp (and hence power), a unity-gain architecture is employed in which the sampling capacitor itself is used in the opamp feedback by opening switches M1a,b and closing switches M3a,b. This is has been shown to maximize the feedback factor for the closed-loop opamp [Sheng, 9]. Since settling time is proportional to $1/(Gmf)$—where f is the feedback factor and Gm is the opamp transconductance gain (for a fixed settling time), increasing f translates to a decrease in the gain Gm. This correspondingly results in a minimum power solution to achieve the necessary settling time.

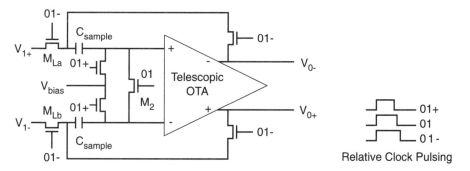

Figure 11–5: Sampling demodulator architecture. (Differential bottomplate, C_{sample} = $C_{integrating}$).

Analog-to-Digital (A/D) Conversion

Lastly, the analog-to-digital conversion itself must be considered. After the sampling demodulator, the signal is passed through a switched-capacitor automatic gain control amplifier to minimize the dynamic range requirements of the A/D converter. However, the required bit resolution in the A/D still needs to be addressed, as well as implementation of a 128 MHz A/D in a low-power fashion.

Intuitively, beyond a certain number of bits resolution, there should be no improvement in system performance by increasing the resolution further. Essentially, at this point, both the dynamic range and quantization noise requirements have been met. To determine this, the simulation results for BER versus number of users for varying A/D converter resolutions are shown in Figure 11–6 for a worst-case (extreme fade) channel [Sheng, 10]. Beyond 4 bits, no improvement in the BER curve is seen. The result is surprising, in that the required number of bits is far lower than expected. However, this makes sense: quantization noise itself is an additive phenomenon, the matched filter correlators will serve to reject this noise as well, effectively providing more bits of resolution at the output of the correlators.

Therefore, a 128 Msample/sec A/D converter has been designed for integration with the analog receiver and the digital baseband circuitry. The need for only four bits of resolution, along with the high sampling rate, imply a flash architecture for the A/D converter. However, the need for a low-power design

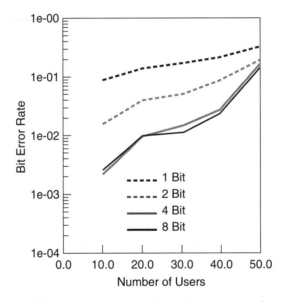

Figure 11–6: BER versus number of in-cell users, as a function of A/D bit quantization (extreme fade condition, no error correction).

leans towards a pipelined architecture. This is mainly due to the fact that the switched-capacitor sample-and-hold circuit already designed for the sampling demodulation can be easily modified to act as a natural interstage gain amplifier for a 1-bit per stage pipeline. Unfortunately, the 128 MHz sampling rate makes a full pipeline implementation prohibitive, given the extreme critical path constraints. However, the final stage of a pipeline does not have the same constraints as previous stages. Therefore, a hybrid 1-bit/3-bit pipeline has been implemented in which a 3-bit flash converter is preceded by an interstage latch and a 1-bit converter to determine the most significant bit. In this manner, a traditional 4-bit flash comparator is reduced in complexity from 15 comparators to 8. The comparator design is shown in Figure 11–7, a fully differential variation on [Sheng, 10]. Its comparison time after the input stabilizes it under 3 nsec. More importantly, the complete 1-bit/3-bit pipeline consumes only 20 mW of power to achieve the desired goal of 4-bit, 256 MHz conversion.

The final architecture for the analog receiver is shown in Figure 11–8 [Sheng, 11]. As compared to the 750 mW superheterodyne receiver from Figure 11–3, it consumes only 60 mW of power, gained primarily through the use of a switching demodulator to minimize the hardware. Furthermore, the fact that no off-chip loads need to be driven after the first amplifier stage also minimizes the amount of power expended in high-frequency board drivers. Lastly, the use of spread spectrum minimizes the quantization accuracy required in the A/D converter, which permits a low-power solution to the analog-digital interface circuitry in spite of the extremely high speeds required.

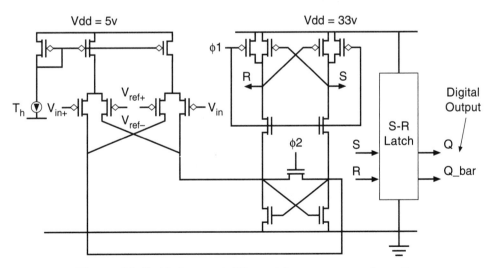

Figure 11–7: High-speed differential comparator schematic.

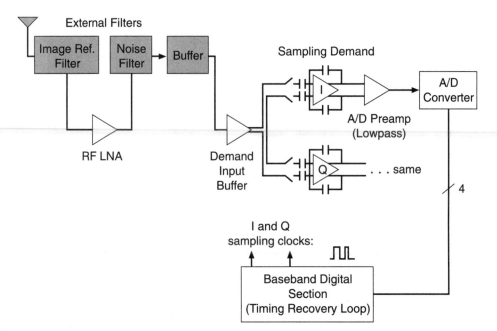

Figure 11–8: Final broadband receiver architecture.

Baseband Digital Circuitry

After analog demodulation and A/D conversion, the resulting spread-spectrum digital stream needs to be decoded to recover the user bits. A detailed baseband block diagram for the receiver is shown in Figure 11–9, with the operating frequencies at each point in the signal flow indicated [Sheng, 12]. From this, it is evident that a massive amount of digital signal processing will be required to recover the spread-spectrum transmitted signal. In particular, the portable unit will require at least 128 MHz processing rates to perform the necessary timing recovery on the incoming 64 Mchip/sec signal, and multiple receivers to track and resolve multipath arrivals. Clearly, the power needed to drive these functions can easily be prohibitive for portable operation. The total power consumption must be minimized, while maintaining the required throughput of the overall system. However, since the processing is bounded by real-time constraints (with Tchip = 16 nsec) once the throughput performance is met, there is no advantage in making computation any faster—thus, opening up a major degree of freedom to the designer. In the forthcoming analysis, this part of the chapter focuses on the design and power minimization of the receiver baseband digital signal processor (DSP), given its extreme power requirements and complexity.

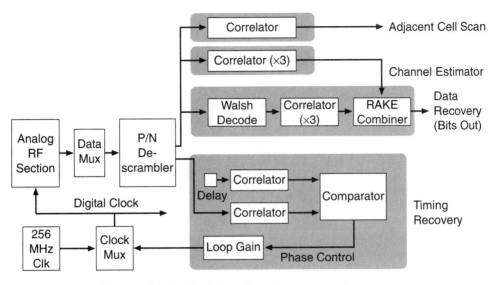

Figure 11–9: Final broadband receiver architecture.

Techniques have been developed which reduce power consumption in CMOS digital circuits while maintaining computational throughput by trading off area for power savings [Sheng, 12]. The key source of power dissipation in digital CMOS circuits is the switching current, which is summarized in the following equation:

$$P\ total = (CL \cdot \sigma\ \delta\delta\ 2 \cdot f\ clk)$$

CL is the effective loading capacitance, $f\ clk$ is the clock frequency, and Vdd is the supply voltage. Thus, minimizing CL, Vdd, and $fclk$ while retaining the required functionality becomes paramount. The reduction of Vdd is the key to low-power operation. However, a speed penalty is incurred by this, and must be compensated by architectural modifications in the system by incorporating parallelism or pipelining. To optimize power, the supply voltage can be used as a design parameter. Three supply voltages are used: 1.5V, 3.3V, and 5V, with the multiple supply voltages being efficiently generated from a single battery using off-chip DC-DC converter circuitry. These voltages were chosen to match the supply voltages used by other chips in the mobile terminal (3.3V and 5V), plus a single low-power supply at 1.5V. The 1.5V figure has been shown to be the optimal supply voltage under certain assumptions [Sheng, 12]. Likewise, level shifting buffers are used on-chip to interface between blocks at different supply voltages. Another technique used to optimize power is the choice of number representation. Since the sign of the data is constantly being toggled due to the multiplication with the walsh and PN sequences, it been discovered that a sign-magnitude number representation will consume approximately 30% less power than a 2's complement number representation for an application [Sheng, 12].

From Figure 11–9, it is clear that the critical block in the receiver is the matched-filter correlator. A total of 9 complex-valued (in-phase and quadrature) correlators will be needed to implement the required functionality. To simplify matters, the input data mix decimates the 128 MHz I/Q streams down into two parallel 64 MHz streams for processing. Due to the nature of the delay-locked loop, this can readily be done, since one stream will be fed into the timing recovery loop and the other stream will be fed into the data recovery and Rake estimator blocks. Each complex correlator consists of a pair of identical datapaths, one to correlate *I* and one for *Q*. In Figure 11–10, the block diagram for the datapath is shown [Sheng, 13]. The input is a 4-bit sign-magnitude value, clocked in at 64 MHz. Using the sign bit for control, the 3-bit magnitude is directed into a positive or negative accumulator. Each accumulator is 9 bits wide to account for the required dynamic range for 64 samples during correlation. After the correlation is completed, the contents of the negative accumulator are subtracted from the positive accumulator resulting in a significant power savings—as the subtraction only needs to be done at a 1 MHz rate.

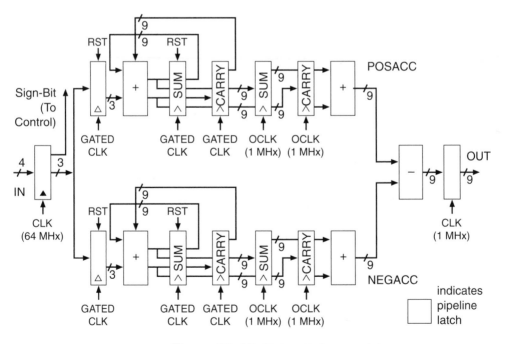

Figure 11–10: Datapath for correlator.

Lastly, to be able to reduce the supply voltage down to 1.5V for the correlator datapaths, minimizing the critical path in the accumulator itself is mandatory. To achieve this, a carry-save adder architecture is employed. It effectively pipelines the adder at the per-bit level, thus reducing the critical path down to the delay through a single half-adder and a register. Each correlator can thus achieve the full 64 MHz throughput—running at a supply voltage of 1.5V, while only consuming 1.5 mW of power for each complex-valued correlator. To contrast, had a ripple-carry adder been employed in the accumulator, it would have needed to run at a 3.3V supply to meet the critical path (carry ripple through 9 bits); and, power consumption per complex correlator would have increased almost fourfold to 5 mW each.

To summarize, the performance numbers for each block in the digital baseband system, provides a breakdown of the supply voltage, the operating frequency, and the power consumption for each component. Due to the fact that the clock generator needs to be able to adjust its phase very accurately (since it is being driven by the delay-locked loop), it must run at 256 MHz, and consumes a significant fraction of the power since a supply voltage of 5V is needed. Otherwise, by minimizing the power consumed in the correlators, the total power consumption of the digital baseband receiver processing has been minimized to 27 mW despite its extremely high operating frequencies.

Considerations

In this chapter, the design and implementation of a wireless system to support multimedia communications have been considered, with emphasis on a broadband downlink capable of supporting digital video. In particular, the development of integrated analog RF front-end and baseband digital interface circuitry, as well as the system simulations driving the design, have also been considered. An ultimate per-user data rate of 2 Mbps is the target. To achieve the required capacity, a picocellular system architecture is employed, using cells on the order of 5m in size.

In examining multiple access strategies for such an application, direct-sequence spread-spectrum or code-division multiple access possesses many advantages. For this particular system, a symbol rate of 1 Mbaud with a chipping rate of 64 Mchip/sec is used. For the spreading code, a Walsh-PN hybrid based on the existing IS-95 cellular standard is chosen. Beyond providing multiple access, the ability to resolve multiple arrivals and detect adjacent channels in the digital baseband circuitry also affords many benefits that other systems (such as time-division or frequency-hop) cannot so easily provide. Taking advantage of the broadcast mode transmission of the downlink, each cell is keyed to a pseudorandom pilot tone which tremendously simplifies timing recovery and detection in the mobile.

Since portability places severe constraints on the size and weight of the terminal itself, power is at a premium as the batteries simply cannot provide much power on a continuous basis without expending an inordinate amount of weight, or an extremely short usable lifetime between rechargings. Thus, low-power digital systems design becomes of paramount importance. Through optimized circuit design strategies, reduced supply-voltage operation and architectural techniques (such as parallelism and pipelining the power consumed in the terminal) can be reduced dramatically.

Lastly, the feasibility of a high-performance monolithic RF transceiver has also been considered. It is evident that an all-MOS RF system operating in the 1-2 GHz range is quite feasible given the technologies that are currently available. The benefits of integration are enormous: reduced parasitic effects, greater manufacturability, and minimized power requirements to drive off-chip loads. Likewise, by examining the basic architecture used in the transceiver, the underlying digital nature of the signal can be used to simplify the resulting circuit considerably: homodyne demodulation using passive sampling techniques is one important example of how this can be achieved. By taking advantage of these techniques, factors of 10-20x reduction in the power consumed by the analog RF circuitry in conventional designs can be achieved.

Lastly, exploiting dedicated parallel and pipelined techniques, a low-power spread-spectrum receiver can be designed in spite of the tremendous chipping rate of the system (64 Mchip/sec). By scaling the supply voltage, and employing multiple supplies into the chip, optimal voltages can be chosen to meet throughput requirements and minimize power consumption in the baseband digital logic.

From Here

This chapter discussed wireless design considerations (spread spectrum, microwave, and the design and implementation of wireless systems to support multimedia communications, etc.). The next chapter opens up Part III, "Planning For High-Speed Cabling Systems," by taking a thorough look at high-speed real-time data compression and how to plan for higher-speed cabling systems.

End Notes

[1] Joel B Wood, "The Wireless LANs Page," The Ohio Sate University Computer and Information Science Deapartment, 395 Dreese Laboratories, 2015 Neil Avenue, Columbus, Ohio 43210-1277, 1995, pp. 1–3.

[2] Samuel Sheng, Randy Allmon, Lapoe Lynn, Ian O'Donnell, Kevin Stone, and Robert Brodersen, "A Monolithic CMOS Radio System for Wideband CDMA Communications," Department of EECS, 231 Cory Hall #1770, U.C. Berkeley Berkeley, CA 94720 USA, 1997, p. 2.

Part III

Planning for High-Speed Cabling Systems

12

DATA COMPRESSION

Today's organizations depend upon their local area networks (LANs) to provide connectivity for a growing number of complex, mission-critical desktop computing applications. As the volume of network traffic increases, however, the bandwidth offered by a typical 10 Mbps Ethernet LAN quickly becomes inadequate to maintain acceptable performance for a growing number of desktop/server computing environments. These traffic jams are fueling the need to run compressed data through higher-speed networks.

Among the high-speed LAN technologies available today, Fast Ethernet, or ase100BaseT, has become the leading choice. Building on the near-universal acceptance of ase10BaseT Ethernet, Fast Ethernet technology provides a smooth, non-disruptive evolution to 100 Mbps performance. The growing use of ase100BaseT connections to servers and desktops, however, is creating a clear need for an even higher-speed network technology to run compressed data through at the backbone and server level. Ideally, this technology should also provide a smooth upgrade path, be cost-effective, and not require retraining.

This chapter presents an overview of Ethernet's current position in the industry. It also discusses applications driving the need for more bandwidth, data compression as a strategic evolution for networks, technology fundamentals, and network migration scenarios.

The Dominant Network Technology

Ethernet technology is ubiquitous. According to industry analysts, more than 84 percent of all installed network connections were Ethernet by the end of 1997. This represents over 130 million interconnected PCs, workstations, and servers. The remaining network connections are a combination of token ring, Fiber Distributed Data Interface (FDDI), Asynchronous Transfer Mode (ATM), and other protocols. All popular operating systems and applications are Ethernet-compatible, as are upper-layer protocol stacks such as Transmission Control Protocol/Internet Protocol (TCP/IP), IPX, NetBEUI, and DECnet.

1997 was a milestone year for Ethernet network equipment as the technology captured 78 percent of shipments. Ethernet network interface card (NIC) shipments exceeded 43 million units and Ethernet hub shipments exceeded 55 million ports. In contrast, ATM, FDDI/CDDI, and token ring network interface card shipments combined reached just 6 million in 1997, 14 percent of the total. ATM, FDDI/CDDI and token ring hub ports were 8 million, 19 percent of the total. Industry analysts project that Ethernet dominance will continue beyond the year 2000. Several factors have contributed to making Ethernet one of the most popular network technologies in use today.

Network Reliability

Highly reliable networks are critical to the success of the enterprise, so ease of installation and support are primary considerations in the choice of network technology. Since the introduction in 1986 of star-wired ase10BaseT hubs, structured wiring systems have continued to evolve and hubs and switches have become increasingly reliable. Today, Ethernet networks are rapidly approaching the reliability level associated with their telephone ancestors, and are relatively simple to understand and administer.

Troubleshooting and Management Tools

Management tools for Ethernet, made possible by widespread adoption of management standards including Simple Network Management Protocol (SNMP) and its successors, allow an administrator to view the status of all desktops and network elements, including redundant elements from a central station. Ethernet troubleshooting tools span a range of capabilities, from simple link indicator lights to sophisticated network analyzers. As a result of Ethernet's popularity, large numbers of people have been trained on its installation, maintenance, and troubleshooting.

Scalability

The Fast Ethernet standard approved in 1995 established Ethernet as a scalable technology. Independent market research has indicated a strong interest among network users in adopting Ethernet technology, specifically Fast Ethernet hubs and switches with Ethernet uplinks, Ethernet switches and repeaters, and Ethernet server NICs.

Low Cost

Industry analysis of Ethernet and Fast Ethernet indicates a rapid decrease in price per port for both technologies as shown in Table 12–1 [1], and the difference between their costs is narrowing, as well.

Table 12–1: Ethernet network equipment representative price trends.

Intelligent Hub Per-Port Average Price	1996	1998
Ethernet	$ 87	$ 71
Fast Ethernet	$174	$110
Ratio	2.0	1.5
Switch Per-Port Average Price	**1996**	**1998**
Ethernet	$440	$215
Fast Ethernet	$716	$432
Ratio	1.6	2.0
NIC Per-Port Average Price	**1996**	**1998**
Ethernet	$ 68	$ 35
Fast Ethernet	$122	$ 74
Ratio	1.8	2.2

Driving Network Growth

As new and existing network applications evolve to embrace high-resolution graphics, video, and other rich media data types, pressure is growing at the desktop, the server, the hub, and the switch for increased bandwidth to run compressed data. Table 12–2 summarizes the applications and their impact on the network [GEA, 3].

Table 12–2: Summary of applications driving network growth.

Application	Data Types/Size	Network Traffic Implication	Network Need
Scientific Modeling, Engineering	• Data files • 100s of megabytes to gigabytes	• Large files increase bandwidth required	• Higher bandwidth for desktops, servers, and backbone
Publications, Medical Data Transfer	• Data files • 100s of megabytes to gigabytes	• Large files increase bandwidth required	• Higher bandwidth for desktops, servers and backbone
Internet/Intranet	• Data files now • Audio now • Video is emerging • High transaction rate • Large files, 1 MB to 100 MB	• Large files increase bandwidth required • Low transmission latency • High volume of data streams	• Higher bandwidth for servers and backbone • Low latency
Data Warehousing, Network Backup	• Data files • Gigabytes to terabytes	• Large files increase bandwidth required • Transmitted during fixed time period	• Higher bandwidth for servers and backbone • Low latency
Desktop Video Conferencing, Interactive Whiteboarding	• Constant data stream • 1.5 to 3.5 Mbps at the desktop	• Class of service reservation • High volume of data streams	• Higher bandwidth for servers and backbones • Low latency • Predictable latency

Many of these applications require the transmission of large compressed files over the network. Scientific applications demand ultra-high bandwidth networks to communicate compressed 3D visualizations of complex objects ranging from molecules to aircraft. Magazines, brochures, and other complex, full-color publications prepared on desktop computers are transmitted directly to digital-input printing facilities. Many medical facilities are transmitting compressed complex images over LAN and WAN links, enabling the sharing of expensive equipment and specialized medical expertise. Engineers are using electronic and mechanical design automation tools to work interactively in distributed development teams, sharing files in the hundreds of gigabytes.

Many companies are now employing Internet technologies to build private intranets, enabling users in an organization to go beyond electronic mail and access critical data through familiar web browsers, opening the door to a new generation of multimedia client/server applications. While intranet traffic is currently composed primarily of text, graphics, and images, this is expected to expand in the near future to include more bandwidth-intensive audio, video, and voice.

Data warehousing has become popular as a way of making enterprise data available to decision makers for reporting and analysis without sacrificing the performance, security or integrity of production systems. These warehouses may comprise gigabyte or terabytes of data distributed over hundreds of platforms and accessed by thousands of users, and must be updated regularly to provide users near-real-time data for critical business reports and analyses.

Network backup of servers and storage systems is common in many industries which require enterprise information to be archived. Such backups usually occur during off hours and require large amounts of bandwidth during a fixed amount of time (5 to 9 hours). The backup involves gigabytes or terabytes of compressed data distributed over hundreds of servers and storage systems throughout an enterprise.

A recent survey of video applications conducted by a leading industry analyst shows interest in video increasing rapidly as computers offer native MPEG decoding capability and as low-cost encoding chip sets become more widely available. The survey looked at a number of video-based applications, including video conferencing, education, and human resources from several companies. As these applications proliferate and demand ever greater shares of bandwidth at the desktop (as the total number of network users continues to grow), organizations will need to migrate critical portions of their networks to higher-bandwidth technologies to run compressed encrypted data through.

The Strategic Alternative for Intranets and LANs

The accelerating growth of LAN traffic is pushing network administrators to look to higher-speed network technologies to run compressed data through to solve the bandwidth crunch. These administrators who typically have either Ethernet or FDDI backbones today have several alternatives to choose from. Although each network faces different issues, Fast Ethernet meets several key criteria for such a high-speed network:

- Easy, straightforward migration to higher performance levels without disruption.
- Low cost of ownership including both purchase cost and support cost.
- Capability to support new applications and data types.
- Network design flexibility [GEA, 4].

Migration to Performance

One of the most important questions network administrators face is how to get higher bandwidth to run compressed data without disrupting the existing network. Fast Ethernet follows the same form, fit and function as its 10 Mbps and 100 Mbps Ethernet precursors, allowing a straightforward, incremental migration to higher-speed networking. All three Ethernet speeds use the same IEEE 802.3 frame format, full-duplex operation, and flow control methods. In half-duplex mode, Fast Ethernet employs the same fundamental Carrier Sense Multiple Access/Collision Detection (CSMA/CD) access method to resolve contention for the shared media. And Fast Ethernet uses the same management objects defined by the IEEE 802.3 group. Fast Ethernet is Ethernet, only faster.

NOTE:

100BaseT is a high-speed variation of 10BaseT standardized as IEEE 802.3u (June 14, 1995).

Ethernet Frame Format

It is simple to connect existing lower-speed Ethernet devices to Fast Ethernet devices using LAN switches or routers to adapt one physical line speed to the other. Fast Ethernet uses the same variable-length (64- to 1514-byte packets) IEEE 802.3 frame format found in Ethernet as shown in Figure 12–1 [GEA, 4]. Because the frame format and size are the same for all Ethernet technologies, no other network changes are necessary. This evolutionary upgrade path allows Fast Ethernet to be seamlessly integrated into existing Ethernet networks.

In contrast, other high speed technologies use fundamentally different frame formats to run compressed data through. High-speed ATM, for example, implements a fixed-length data cell. When connecting Ethernet and Fast Ethernet to ATM, the switch or router must translate each ATM cell to an Ethernet frame, and vice versa.

Bytes	8	6	6	2	0-1500
	Preamble	Destination address	Source address	Length of data field	Protocol header, data and pad

Figure 12–1: IEEE 802.3 frame.

Full and Half-Duplex Operation

As defined by the IEEE 802.3x specification, two nodes connected via a full-duplex, switched path can simultaneously send and receive packets. Fast Ethernet follows this standard to communicate in full-duplex mode. Fast Ethernet also employs standard Ethernet flow control methods to avoid congestion and overloading. When operating in half-duplex mode, Fast Ethernet adopts the same fundamental CSMA/CD access method to resolve contention for the shared media. The CSMA/CD method is shown in Figure 12–2. [GEA, 5].

The Fast Ethernet CSMA/CD method has been enhanced in order to maintain a 200-meter collision diameter at gigabit speeds. Without this enhancement, minimum-sized Ethernet packets could complete transmission before the transmitting station senses a collision, thereby violating the CSMA/CD method.

To resolve this issue, both the minimum CSMA/CD carrier time and the Ethernet slot time have been extended from their present value of 64 bytes to a new value of 512 bytes. Packets smaller than 512 bytes have an extra carrier extension. Packets longer than 512 bytes are not extended. These changes, which can impact small-packet performance, have been offset by incorporating a new feature, called packet bursting, into the CSMA/CD algorithm. Packet bursting will allow servers, switches, and other devices to send bursts of small packets in order to fully utilize available bandwidth.

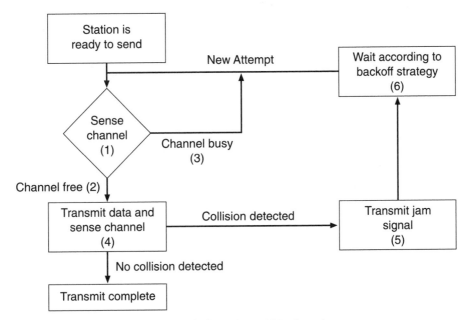

Figure 12–2: CSMA/CD flowchart.

NOTE:

The minimum packet length of 64 bytes has not been affected.

Devices that operate in full-duplex mode (switches and buffered distributors) are not subject to the carrier extension, slot time extension, or packet bursting changes. Full-duplex devices will continue to use the regular Ethernet 96-bit interframe gap (IFG) and 64-byte minimum packet size.

Management Objects

In the transition from Ethernet to Fast Ethernet, the fundamental management objects familiar to most network managers is carried forward. For example, SNMP defines a standard method to collect device-level Ethernet information. SNMP uses management information base (MIB) structures to record key statistics such as collision count, packets transmitted or received, error rates, and other device-level information. Additional information is collected by remote monitoring (RMON) agents to aggregate the statistics for presentation via a network management application. Because Fast Ethernet uses standard Ethernet frames, the same MIBs and RMON agents can be used to provide network management at gigabit speeds.

Low Cost of Ownership

Cost of ownership is an important factor in evaluating any new networking technology. The overall cost of ownership includes not only the purchase price of equipment, but also the cost of training, maintenance, and troubleshooting.

Competition and economies of scale have driven the purchase price of Ethernet connections down significantly. Though Fast Ethernet products have been shipping only since 1994, even these products have experienced significant price declines over the past few years.

Early Fast Ethernet products have provided cost-effective connections for gigabit transmission rates. IEEE has provided Fast Ethernet connections at two to three times the cost of a 100BaseaseFX interface. As volume builds, reduced line width integrated circuits (IC) processes are implemented, and low-cost optoelectronic devices are developed, the cost of Fast Ethernet interfaces will continue to decline.

Switched Fast Ethernet connections are expected to be lower in cost than 622 Mbps ATM interfaces (assuming identical physical media interfaces) because of the relative simplicity of Ethernet and higher shipment volumes. Fast Ethernet repeater interfaces are significantly lower in cost than 622 Mbps

ATM connections, providing users with cost-effective alternatives for data center network backbone and server connections. Table 12–3 illustrates current prices for Ethernet, Fast Ethernet, FDDI and 622 Mbps ATM multimode and the target range for Fast Ethernet based on the IEEE 802.3 goals (not IEEE price goals, they don't set any) [GEA, 6].

Table 12–3: Network backbone connection representative prices.

Technology	Equipment Type	1998 Equipment Price/Port	2001 Equipment Price/Port	Change %
Shared Fast Ethernet	Hub	$137	$85	–39%
Switched Fast Ethernet	Switch	$785	$390	–50%
Shared FDDI	Concentrator	$835	$650	–22%
Switched FDDI	Switch	$4000	$1860	–54%
ATM 622 Mbps Estimate (multimode fiber)	Switch	$6600	$4800	–27%
Shared Fast Ethernet IEEE goal (multimode fiber) (2x to 3x Fast Ethernet MM)	Hub	Not Available.	$470 to $700	
Switched Fast Ethernet IEEE goal (multimode fiber) (2x to 3x Fast Ethernet MM)	Switch	Not Available.	$1070 to $1610	

Over time, advances in silicon, including 0.35-micron CMOS Application-Specific Integrated Circuit (ASIC) technology, will provide even greater performance gains and cost reduction opportunities that will result in a new, even more cost-effective generation of Ethernet technology. Current 0.5-micron technology can accommodate about 0.5 million gates and is limited to transmission rates of about 500 Mbps. Analysis indicates that 0.35-micron processes will achieve 1250 Mbps operation and economically fit one million gates on a single die. This is more than enough to fit a complete Ethernet switch, including management, a significant amount of buffer memory, and an embedded 32-bit controller, on a single die with obvious cost advantages.

Finally, because the installed base of users is already familiar with Ethernet technology, maintenance, and troubleshooting tools, the support costs associated with Fast Ethernet are far lower than other technologies. Fast Ethernet requires only incremental training of personnel and incremental purchase of maintenance and troubleshooting tools. In addition, deployment of Fast Ethernet is faster than alternative technologies. Once upgraded with training and tools, network support staff are able to confidently install, troubleshoot and support Fast Ethernet installations.

Support for New Applications and Data Types

The emergence of intranet applications portends a migration to new data types, including video and voice. In the past it was thought that video might require a different networking technology designed specifically for multimedia. But today it is possible to mix data and video over Ethernet through a combination of the following:

- Increased bandwidth provided by Fast Ethernet, enhanced by LAN switching.
- The emergence of new protocols, such as Resource Reservation Protocol (RSVP), that provide bandwidth reservation.
- The emergence of standards such as 802.1Q and 802.1p, which provide virtual LAN (VLAN) and explicit priority information for packets in the network.
- The widespread use of advanced video compression such as MPEG-2 [GEA, 7].

These technologies and protocols combine to make Fast Ethernet an extremely attractive solution for the delivery of video and multimedia traffic, as illustrated in Table 12–4 [GEA, 7].

Table 12–4: High-Speed Network Capabilities.

Capabilities	Ethernet	Fast Ethernet	ATM	FDDI
IP Compatibility	Yes	Yes	Requires RFC 1557 or IP LAN Emulation LANE) today; I-Private Network to Network Interface (PNNI) and/or Multiprotocol over ATM (MPOA) in the future	Yes

(continued)

Table 12–4: *(continued)*

Capabilities	Ethernet	Fast Ethernet	ATM	FDDI
Ethernet Packets	Yes	Yes	Requires LANE	Yes, though 802.1h translation bridging
Handle Multimedia	Yes	Yes	Yes, but application needs substantial changes	Yes
Quality of Service	Yes, with RSVP and/or 802.1p	Yes with RSVP and/or 802.1p	Yes with SVCs or RSVP with complex mapping from Internet Engineering Task Force (IETF) (work in progress)	Yes, with RSVP and/or 802.1p
VLANs with 802.1Q/p	Yes	Yes	Requires mapping LANE and/or SVCs to 802.1Q	Yes

Flexible Internetworking and Network Design

Network administrators today face a myriad of internetworking choices and network design options. They are combining routed and switched networks and building intranets of increasing scale. Ethernet networks are shared (using repeaters) and switched, based on bandwidth and cost requirements. The choice of a high-speed network to run compressed data through, however, should not restrict the choice of internetworking or network topology.

Today, Fast Ethernet is switched, routed, and shared. All of today's internetworking technologies, as well as emerging technologies such as IP-specific switching and layer 3 switching, are fully compatible with Fast Ethernet, just as they are with Ethernet. Fast Ethernet is currently available in a shared, repeated hub (with the accompanying low cost per port) as well as on LAN switches and routers.

Fast Ethernet Technology

The simple migration and support offered by Ethernet, combined with the scalability and flexibility to handle new applications and data types, makes Fast Ethernet the strategic choice when planning and designing for high-speed cabling systems and high-bandwidth networking for running compressed encrypted data.

Fast Ethernet is an extension to the highly successful 10 Mbps and 100 Mbps IEEE 802.3 Ethernet standards. Offering a raw data bandwidth of 1000 Mbps, Fast Ethernet maintains full compatibility with the huge installed base of Ethernet nodes.

Full and Half-Duplex over Fiber Today and UTP in the Future

Fast Ethernet supports new full-duplex operating modes for switch-to-switch and switch-to-end-station connections and half-duplex operating modes for shared connections using repeaters and the CSMA/CD access method. Initially operating over optical fiber, Fast Ethernet is able to use Category 5 UTP cabling. Figure 12–3 illustrates the functional elements of Fast Ethernet [GEA, 9].

NOTE:

The Gigabit Media Independent Interface (GMII) in Figure 12–3 is optional.

Much of the effort of the IEEE 802.3 task force is devoted to the definition of PHY standards for Fast Ethernet. Like other standards based on the International Standards Organization (ISO) model, Fast Ethernet implements functionality adhering to a physical layer standard. In general, the PHY or physical layer is responsible for defining the mechanical, electrical, and procedural characteristics for establishing, maintaining, and deactivating the physical link between network devices. For Fast Ethernet communications, several physical layer standards are emerging from the IEEE 802.3 effort.

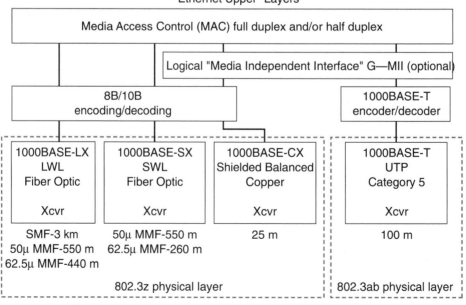

Figure 12–3: Functional elements of Fast Ethernet technology.

Two PHYs provide gigabit transmission over fiber optic cabling. 1000BaseaseSX is targeted at lowest cost multimode fiber and runs in horizontal and shorter backbone applications. 1000BaseaseLX is targeted at longer multimode building fiber backbones and singlemode campus backbones. For multimode fiber, these standards define gigabit transmission over distances of 260 and 550 meters, respectively. Singlemode fiber, which is covered by the long-wavelength standard, is defined to cover distances of 3 kilometers.

There are also two standards efforts for Fast Ethernet transmission over copper cabling. The first copper link standard is being defined by the 802.3 task force and is referred to as 1000BaseaseCX. This standard supports interconnection of equipment clusters where the physical interface is short-haul copper. It supports a switching closet or computer room as a short jumper interconnection for 25 meter distances. This standard uses the Fiber Channel-based 8B/10B coding at the serial line rate of 1.25 Gbps, and runs over 150 ohm balanced, shielded, specialty cabling assemblies. LBM Type I cabling is not recommended. This copper physical layer standard has the advantage that it can be generated quickly and is inexpensive to implement. According to the 802.3 timetable, the short copper link standard will be complete in the same time frame as the fiber links.

The second copper link standard is intended for use in horizontal copper cabling applications. In March, 1997, a Project Authorization Request (PAR) was approved by the IEEE Standards Board, enabling the creation of a separate but related committee referred to as the 802.3ab task force. This new group is chartered with the development of a 1000BaseT physical layer standard providing 1 Gbps Ethernet signal transmission over 4-pair Category 5 UTP cable, covering cabling distances of up to 100 meters or networks with a diameter of 200 meters. This standard will outline communications used for horizontal copper runs on a floor within a building using structured generic cabling, taking advantage of the existing UTP cable already deployed. This effort will likely require new technology and new coding schemes in order to meet the potentially difficult and demanding parameters set by the previous Ethernet and Fast Ethernet standards. This will be on a somewhat longer timetable than the 802.3 Fast Ethernet effort.

Fibre Channel Components

The use of existing, proven technologies and methods minimizes time-to-market for Fast Ethernet products. Current efforts in the IEEE 802.3 standards activity draw heavily on the use of Fiber Channel and other high-speed networking components. Fiber Channel encoding/decoding integrated circuits (ICs) and optical components are readily available and are specified and optimized for high performance at relatively low cost.

Fast Ethernet employs Fiber Channel's high-speed, 850 nm (short wave-length) optical components for signaling over optical fiber and 8B/10B encoding/decoding schemes for serialization and deserialization. Current Fiber Channel technology operating at 1.063 Gbps is being enhanced to run at 1.250 Gbps, thus providing the full 1000 Mbps data rate. For longer link distances up to at least 3 km using singlemode fiber and up to at least 440 meters on 62.5-micron multimode fiber, 1300-nm (long wavelength) optics are also specified.

The IEEE 802.3 standards activity is planning ahead for the expected advances in silicon technology and digital signal processing that will eventually enable Fast Ethernet to operate over UTP cabling. To accommodate this, a logical interface will be specified between the media access control (MAC) and PHY layers that will decouple the Fiber Channel 8B/10B encoding, allowing other encoding schemes that more readily support the use of cost-effective UTP cabling.

Fast Ethernet Products

Since Fast Ethernet is Ethernet, the types of Fast Ethernet products are quite straightforward: switches, uplink/downlink modules, NICs, Fast Ethernet router interfaces, and one new device, the buffered distributors. There are pure multiport Fast Ethernet switches with high performance backplanes, as well as devices that have both Ethernet and Fast Ethernet ports in the same box. Fast Ethernet uplinks appear as modular upgrades for fixed-configuration Ethernet devices or modular, chassis-based hubs to provide a high-speed connection to the network. Vendors of high-performance routers deliver Fast Ethernet interfaces as well.

Some Fast Ethernet vendors are developing a new device called a buffered distributor. The buffered distributor is a full-duplex, multiport, hub-like device that interconnects two or more 802.3 links operating at 1 Gbps or faster. Like an 802.3 repeater, it is a non-address-filtering device. The buffered distributor forwards all incoming packets to all connected links except the originating link, providing a shared bandwidth domain comparable to a 802.3 collision domain.

NOTE:

Buffered distributors have been called CSMA/CD in a box.

Unlike an 802.3 repeater, the buffered distributor is permitted to buffer one or more incoming frames on each link before forwarding them. There have also been technical discussions about half-duplex Fast Ethernet repeaters.

As a shared bandwidth device, the buffered distributor should be distinguished from both routers and switches. While routers with Fast Ethernet interfaces may have backplanes that support bandwidths greater or less than gigabit rates, the ports attached to a Fast Ethernet buffered distributor s backplane share one gigabit of bandwidth. In contrast, the backplanes of high-performance, multiport Fast Ethernet switches support multigigabit bandwidths.

Buffered distributors are not currently defined in 802.3 standards. Nor are other standard networking devices such as routers and switches. A standard has been drafted to allow the implementation of buffered distributors.

Ethernet and Higher-Level Services

Fast Ethernet provides high-speed connectivity, but does not by itself provide a full set of services such as Quality of Service (QoS), automatic redundant fail-over or higher-level routing services. These are added via other open standards. Fast Ethernet, like all Ethernet specifications, specifies the data link (layer 2) of the OSI protocol model, while TCP and IP in turn specify the transport (layer 4) and network (layer 3) portions and allow reliable communication services between applications. Issues such as QoS were not addressed in the original Fast Ethernet specifications, but must be addressed across several of these standards. Resource Reservation Protocol (RSVP), for instance, is defined at the network layer to work alongside IP. Layer 3 (routing) services also operate at the network layer as shown in Table 12–5 [GEA, 12].

Table 12–5: Layers of Network Functionality.

OSI Layer	OSI Name	Examples
4	Transport	TCP
3	Network	IP, RSVP
2	Data link	Ethernet (MAC), 802.1p, 802.1Q
1	Physical	10BaseT, 100BaseT, Fiber Channel

Various implementations of Fast Ethernet may include one or more of these standards in order to provide a more robust or functional networking connection, but the overall success of Fast Ethernet is not tied to any one of them. The advantage of modular standards is that any one piece may evolve and be adopted at a pace determined by market need and product quality.

NOTE:

All of the standards are just as readily paired with Fast Ethernet and 10 Mbps Ethernet, so that all levels of Ethernet performance can benefit from all the standards work.

Quality of Service on Ethernet

Applications emerging in the late 1990s to the early 2000s will demand consistent bandwidth, latency, and jitter from network connections. Such applications include voice and video over LANs and WANs, multicast software distribution, and the like. Standards bodies have responded with new open definitions such as RSVP and the current work in the IEEE 802.1p and IEEE 802.1Q standards groups.

RSVP is gaining industry acceptance as a preferred way to request and provide quality of network connections. In order to have RSVP function and deliver defined and consistent quality to an application, each network component in the chain between client and server must support RSVP and communicate appropriately. Because of the need to have so many components supported by RSVP before meaningful results can be achieved, some vendors are advancing proprietary schemes to deliver some degree of QoS. Some of these may deliver QoS benefits to users, but will require certain portions of the network to be vendor-specific implementations.

802.1p and 802.1Q facilitate quality of service over Ethernet by providing a means for tagging packets with an indication of the priority or class of service desired for the packet. These tags allow applications to communicate the priority of packets to internetworking devices. RSVP support can be achieved by mapping RSVP sessions into 802.1p service classes.

Layer 3 Functionality

Layer 3 involves determination of the eventual destination of a packet beyond its MAC destination address on the packet header. By examining the IP address (buried deeper in the packet), the IP subnet can be determined, allowing broadcasts to be contained to the appropriate subnets and packets to be forwarded accurately to intermediate nodes for most efficient transit through the network.

The classic layer 3 device is the router, which makes layer 3 decisions by implementing complex algorithms and data structures in software. While such complicated routing tasks formerly required complex and software-intensive multiprotocol router products, vendors over the last few years have announced layer 3 switch products that accomplish many of these tasks, while delivering arguably better price/performance than traditional routers. Narrowing the protocol supported to IP has allowed devices to optimize tasks and accomplish more work with dedicated hardware.

Fast Ethernet Migration

The initial applications for Fast Ethernet have been for campuses or buildings requiring greater bandwidth between routers, switches, hubs, repeaters, and servers. Examples include switch-to-router, switch-to-switch, switch-to-server, and repeater-to-switch connections as shown in Table 12–6 [GEA, 13]. In its early phase, Fast Ethernet was not expected to be deployed widely to the desktop. In all scenarios the network operating system (NOS), applications, and NIC drivers at the desktop have remained unchanged. The Information Technology (IT) manager can also leverage not only the existing multimode fiber, but also the current investment in network management applications and tools.

Table 12–6: The five most likely upgrade scenarios.

1. Upgrading switch-to-switch connections.	Obtain 1000 Mbps pipes between 100/1000 switches.
2. Upgrading switch-to-server connections.	Achieve high-speed access to applications and file servers.
3. Upgrading a switched Fast Ethernet backbone.	Aggregate Fast Ethernet switches with an Ethernet switch or repeater.
4. Upgrading a shared FDDI backbone.	Install FDDI switch or Ethernet-to-FDDI switches/routers with Fast Ethernet switches or repeaters.
5. Upgrading high-performance desktops.	Fast Ethernet NICs for connection to Fast Ethernet switches or repeaters.

Now, let's take a look at how to get the bandwidth you need when you need it, in order for your high-speed cabling system to be capable of carrying compressed data. There has been extensive talk of obtaining *bandwidth on demand* (BoD) from many different technologies. There has been far less explanation of exactly what that means and how a network user makes it happen. Talk of access to wide area networks often ignores the *last mile* connection between customer premises and central office. This part of the chapter classifies bandwidth, based on many transmission technologies (analog to High Bit Rate Digital Subscriber Line (HDSL))on who controls the bandwidth allocation (pre-provisioned or dial-up) and on the time delay to make bandwidth usable (from microseconds for ATM permanent virtual circuits to weeks for leased lines). In a sense, all bandwidth is on demand and only the time frames, cost basis, and controlling party vary.

Network Types

Modern networks provide bandwidth that is either circuit-switched or packet-switched. Circuit-switched connections give a customer the exclusive use of a certain amount of bandwidth for the duration of the requirement. That is, the connection is set up on demand and, until the caller breaks the connection, the capacity of the physical transmission and switching facilities needed for the connection is reserved for that caller exclusively. Reserved bandwidth provides immediate access to the portion allocated.

Switched circuits require that capacity be available for each new caller. A T-1 line with 24 DS-0 channels cannot accept a request for a 25th DS-0 connection [2]. On larger capacity transmission lines, users share by taking turns in fixed time slots; each gets a small amount of time in a regularly repeating cycle—the process of time division multiplexing (TDM). If a particular caller has nothing to send, his time slot is wasted because it is not available to any other caller.

In any form of packetized switching, a connection gives the caller the opportunity to present information to the network, but does not in general guarantee immediate access to the transmission line. There may be a wait until earlier demands are met. Potentially, each user is in competition with other users who may want the same transmission facility at the same time. When demand exceeds capacity, only one user gains immediate access; the others must wait in queue.

Packetized transmission is based on logical, rather than physical connections. There are only practical limits on the number of connections across a T-1 link when each connection is designated by a packet address and does not consume a DS-0 channel. Practical limits might be throughput (the total amount of data is limited by the transmission speed of 1.536 Mbps, for example) or address space (the frame relay supports no more than 1000 addresses on a serial channel).

These are very different in concepts, though they can work together when one technology is used as an access to another. An example is ISDN access to frame relay.

What they have in common is that each user intermittently obtains full and exclusive use of the transmission facility (network capacity). A circuit-switched connection takes over a line (or a channel within a line) periodically by requesting it. The request may be in the form of a call setup request for a circuit-switched connection or the presentation of a data packet to the packet-switching and transmission equipment.

Access to Bandwidth

In all types of networks the customer gets bandwidth only when purchased; in a sense, *on demand*. How that purchase is made determines how quickly bandwidth becomes available after the initial request for service and after incremental demands placed on the active service are met. The customer also decides what the maximum capacity will be. These two considerations often determine the transmission technology and a specific carrier service.

From Remote Site into Private Backbone or Carrier

First, there must always be a pre-provisioned transmission path. In most cases this is wire pairs, though fibers are becoming more common. The path is dedicated to the customer—in effect a leased line—even if the service is switched. At the site of a new home or office construction, a carrier will have to install new dedicated cables even for switched services.

Access may also be wireless, but cellular phone service has an activation procedure which corresponds to setting up the path on wire. A workstation on a LAN has a *leased-line* path in the coax or twisted-pair medium.

The size of this path must be larger than the average requirement. Averaged over a week, the largest church needs only one very small door. Fire codes and people's impatience require there be many doors.

To speed compressed file transfers, a data network operator might link two sites with a T-1 line when the average throughput is less than 56 Kbps. The number of PBX trunks to handle busy hours may be many times more than the average usage.

Once the path is in place, the user can fill part or all of it— but no more. This fact is sometimes lost in the hype. Converting a 56 Kbps leased line to a frame relay service will not allow that connection to *burst* above 56 Kbps.

Within the Backbone or Carrier Service

While the access loop is always a dedicated circuit, the usage of the backbone may be dedicated or switched, circuit-based or packetized. It is here that *on demand* has its greatest impact. Confusion between what happens within the backbone and what is possible on the access portion of this link leads to misconceptions like 56 Kbps lines bursting to 256 Kbps.

Channelized

Circuit-switched connections require dedicated backbone resources while the connection is in place all the time for leased lines. The resource consumed is bandwidth on the higher-speed transmission lines between backbone nodes. Because circuits are assigned by time division multiplexing (with many users interleaved on a serial trunk), all the user ever sees is the bandwidth of that TDM channel. The end points of a 56 Kbps channel can't tell whether it is carried on 56 Kbps copper pairs, T-1, or 655 megabit/second fiber.

A channel provisioned by the network manager on a private T-1 network may be variable in size. However, in the general case, to get larger bandwidth, an inverse multiplexer aggregates multiple parallel channels, either leased or switched. It makes no sense to expand the capacity in the backbone beyond the capacity of the access loop.

Packetized

Packet-switched connections are virtual—they use resources only when there is data to transmit. During idle periods, a packet-switched connection remains, logically, though other users may take all the bandwidth.

On any trunk between nodes, only one packet is being sent at any given time. Packets are interleaved, not time slots (as in TDM). Thus, entire packets are always sent uninterrupted at the full line speed. That may be 56 Kbps from the customer site, and 622 Mbps inside the network. This is not *bursting*.

What Is Bursting?

Bursting is more correctly called *throughput bursting*. It is possible only if the normal throughput is less than the capacity of the access links at both ends. In frame relay service, a carrier may guarantee a Committed Information Rate (CIR) to a user that is less than the access port speed: 9600 on a 56,000 line/port.

NOTE:

CIR is the data rate which the network guarantees to handle under normal conditions. It is based on a mutual contractual agreement between the carrier and the customer.

Every frame sent to the network is sent at 56K—the line speed. Idle time between frames when throughput is zero brings the average throughput down to 9600. Bursting means the idle time is reduced; frames may be sent continuously.

Throughput then can approach the line speed (but no more) unless the information is compressed.

Data Compression as Access Amplifier

Throughput can exceed the access line speed if the information (usually data) is compressed. All modern modems compress asynchronous data automatically (MNP or V.42bis). FRADs, routers, and dedicated compressors may double the throughput of synchronous channels up to about 2 Mbps (uncompressed at up to 6 Mbps).

The compression ratio depends on the data. A file with more redundancy (a data base with many fixed length fields filled with 0s) may compress 4:1 or more. Encrypted data does compress now—where once it didn't. This is due to a new online compressed satellite encryption-based technology that is discussed later in the chapter.

Demanding More Bandwidth

There are many ways to get more throughput on the access channel (within its limits). If your bandwidth need exceeds the available access throughput, more must be installed. This may mean an upgrade from an analog line with a modem to a digital service, or from a lower to a higher speed digital line (56K to T-1). It is also possible to increase the activated fraction in an FT-1 line (256 to 512 Kbps). When moving up in bandwidth, a change in technology may be needed when going from Alternate Mark Inversion (56 Kbps) to 2B+D (ISDN basic rate—BRI).

Open More Channels

If a T-1 local loop has fewer than 24 channels active, turn on more channels. This may be a manual process within a phone company (adding more local phone lines) or a fully automated one (dial-up of previously subscribed B channels on an ISDN Primary Rate Interface (PRI)). The user may see these as individual connections or an inverse multiplexer may combine them into a single, variable-speed aggregate.

NOTE:

The provisioned access capacity presents a firm limit to the number of available channels.

Present More Frames/Packets/Cells

In packetized systems, the user who presents more traffic will get more bandwidth up to the capacity of the system (or perhaps to some assigned and enforced limit). An idle workstation on a LAN will receive BoD simply by sending information.

In the near future, frame relay and ATM networks will offer switched virtual circuits, the way X.25 does today. SVCs are more a way to direct information flow than to add bandwidth. But, in the sense that a user can add bandwidth to a location, SVC service is BoD also.

Next, let's discuss one of the most talked about issues today in planning and designing high-speed cabling systems, the potential increase in bandwidth requirements on the horizon. Fueled by the industry's love of technology and a plethora of applications such as teleconferencing, client/server, e-mail file transfer, graphics, and video to the desktop, the IT manager is crying imminent bandwidth poverty. Budgets are being drawn up with new protocols such as high-speed Ethernet, TP-PMD, and ATM to every desktop based on perceived bandwidth shortfall.

Bandwidth Poverty

The biggest culprits in the infrastructure end of the business are the fiber manufacturers who continually justify the cost of fiber-to-the-desktop with the statistical double-talk of *bandwidth per dollar*. Like selling cars on the achievable top speed, this assumes that the user can actually utilize the bandwidth provided by fiber. What good does gigabit-per-second bandwidth yield if the protocols available cannot achieve these transmission speeds to run compressed data through?

Like children threatened by an evil baby-sitter, IT managers are told that the *bandwidth bogeyman* is in the closet and night is falling. New hubs, network interface cards (NICs), and complete facility recabling to accommodate the new bandwidth is recommended.

Well, it just ain't so! Current UTP horizontal infrastructure, even Category 3 channels, offers substantial bandwidth increase potential without changing the protocols. If more bandwidth is required for communication-intensive applications like video, there are protocols available today which run well on existing copper horizontal infrastructure. A vertical backbone of fiber and higher speed protocols on the backbone will certainly be required but some low cost strategies can very effectively vanquish the bandwidth bogeyman.

The Bandwidth Utilization Fallacy

The first misrepresentation is the statement that bandwidth to the desktop has grown dramatically from the days of terminal connections to today's LANs. On the surface the movement from 19.2 Kbps RS232 to 10 Mbps Ethernet would seem to support this, indicating a 500 times expansion of available bandwidth. Further examination indicates a much smaller change.

The most common terminal service applications were RS232 and IBM 3270. In the RS232 environment, each terminal was connected to a dedicated port on the host computer, providing a full-time channel at 9.6 or 19.2 Kbps. In the IBM 3270 environment a 1 Mbps channel supported 8 terminals under a polling protocol. Each terminal had the channel available one-eighth of the time for the equivalent of a 125 Kbps dedicated channel to each terminal. These protocols supported the environment of the steady but light stream of data required to update the screen of a *dumb* terminal with information stored and processed at the host computer.

The environment today is that of the client/server—where the storage is central and the processing is handled by an intelligent workstation device. The market forces driving this architecture are stable:

Processing power is low cost and can be economically distributed to each desk-top. Continual reduction in this case will only enhance the speed and power of the desk-top, broadening the implementation of intensive applications such as video and graphics.

Most data is a shared resource and therefore will be centrally stored. This promotes data integrity in changing environments and simplifies backup [3].

The result of the client/server architecture is that data is moved in blocks as opposed to streams, often called *burst* data. An 802.3 Ethernet or 802.5 token ring LAN supports this well by offering short-duration, high-speed access to a shared channel. This is comparable to the early days of telephony where party lines supported the occasional access requirements of the market.

Refocusing on the actual bandwidth available to each client workstation and using Ethernet as the example provides enlightening insight into the bandwidth issue. Ethernet offers 10 Mbps of compressed data speed during transmission. But, due to access protocols and collisions, the throughput is generally limited to 40% or 4 Mbps. This party line bandwidth is shared between all devices on that portion of the network between bridges or routers. Assuming 40 devices per network, this results in 100 Kbps average available bandwidth per device.

Therefore, the increase in channel bandwidth between the IBM environment of 1964 and a common client/server environment of 1999 is nonexistent! Even comparing RS232 with Ethernet over this 35-year span results in only a 10:1 increase—not the 1000:1 increase that is often quoted from 9.6 Kbps to 10 Mbps.

The Bandwidth-Intensive Application Fallacy

Compressed information which will be transported will be of various types: audio, data, video, and control. Audio information includes voice and music. Voice utilizes 56 Kbps and digital music about 1 Mbps, but both require the transmission to be real-time because there is a human as the ultimate interface. Delays in these signals will not be accepted because the result is a silence on the line. Therefore, these applications do not require a lot of bandwidth but require a lot of access.

Data transmission is communication of information between machines, usually to be stored and subsequently processed. While the file size can be enormous, computers are patient devices which are willing to wait indefinitely for completion of the transmission. The human using the information will not be willing to wait very long, but even a second or two will enable the transmission of multimegabyte files. Backup and updating of files over the network can involve huge files, but can utilize the lowest access priority.

Control signals are also real-time, but contain small amounts of data. They can be a problem because of the frequency of access required if the system is poorly designed. For example, the control of a robot by a remote computer would require continual positional data from the robot to the computer and continual movement orders from the computer to the robot.

A properly designed control system would place a controller at the robot which would accept complex orders (perhaps complete program down-loads) from a remote supervisor and accomplish the positional feedback locally. This properly designed system results in less time dependence and less information transport.

Video and graphic display information is also real-time because there is a human at the end of the channel. Lost information shows up as a drop-out of the picture. While the raw bandwidth requirements can be as high as 100 Mbps, video information is easily compressed. For example, in a videoconferencing application, one can easily transmit only the pixels which change from frame to frame and attain compression as high as 10:1. Additional compression of the digital data stream yields 20:1 or more. Currently the telephone companies in the US are experimenting with *video on demand* to homes over existing UTP phone cable. VCR quality transmissions are achieved on 1.544 Mbps lines! If this is extrapolated, HDTV quality signals should be achievable at 20 Mbps or so. This is therefore the worst case application because it requires relatively high bandwidth and real-time access.

Horizontal vs. Vertical Cable Bandwidth

In a structured cabling system the channels are designated as horizontal cabling (from the wiring closet to the desktop) and vertical cabling (connecting wiring closets together, generally floor-to-floor). The limiting factors to channel bandwidth in either case are the media itself and the equipment connected to each end.

Horizontal cabling supports a single terminal device and links it back to the closet where it connects into LAN hardware. The bandwidth requirement is therefore that of a single terminal device. Also, the majority of the channels in the building are horizontal—one for each terminal location—and the addition of more terminals also means activating more horizontal cable. This segment of your cabling system is, by definition, scalable and copper is by far the most used media here.

The vertical cabling must support all devices connecting into a closet, often the total number of terminals, printers, and file servers on a floor of the building. If more clients or servers are added to a floor, they compete for the available vertical cabling bandwidth. There is an advantage, however; there are comparatively few vertical channels in a building and more expensive equipment can therefore be used to provide high-bandwidth channels. This is the area where optical fiber has become the most appropriate media.

Options to Increase Horizontal Bandwidth

The first stage in increasing the available bandwidth to each workstation is to break the network into smaller networks through the proper placement of bridges and routers and adding file server connections. This reduces the number of devices sharing each network's bandwidth and therefore increases the access to that bandwidth. If your average number of devices on the network segment are high, this strategy offers the lowest-cost solution.

NOTE:

The placement of the bridges/routers and access to the servers require knowledge of network traffic patterns.

Another alternative to Ethernet users is to implement an Ethernet switch. This provides full 10 Mbps channels to each switched port. A common use of these devices is to front-end high-usage file servers with multiple Ethernet connections. The next stage is to implement higher-speed versions of the same protocols such as the new 100 Mbps Ethernet and the 64 Mbps token ring.

Finally there are the new protocols which will run efficiently on your existing infrastructure at the 100 meter horizontal cable distance specified in TIA 568. They will, however, require new management software:

100VG-AnyLAN (Voice Grade) supports Ethernet, token ring and other LAN standards. It uses 4-pair Category 3 UTP to provide 100 Mbps data transmission of voice/video as well as data in half-duplex mode. The protocol includes a scheme to insure that the real-time voice or video transmissions are given priority over less time-dependent data transmissions. When access and priority overheads for *average* networks are considered, the throughput should be about 20 Mbps.

TP-PMD is the copper equivalent of the FDDI protocol, offering 125 Mbps data transmission with 100 Mbps throughput. FDDI is well proven and for organizations which have implemented this as their backbone protocol. this may be easily extended to the desktop.

Asynchronous Transfer Mode (ATM) is a scalable switched protocol which offers dedicated bandwidth to each terminal of up to 155 Mbps over copper. Lower speed implementations are proposed which will run over Category 3 channels at a probable speed of 42 Mbps [MOD-TAP, 3].

Theoretical Bandwidth of UTP/STP Cable

In the early 1970s, the telephone companies used UTP cable to carry T1 data at 1.544 Mbps. In 1984, IBM announced their token-passing LAN at 4 Mbps on STP. In 1992, Ethernet increased the data speed to 10 Mbps over UTP, but decreased the distance dramatically to 100 meters. Then came 16 Mbps token ring, 125 Mbps CDDI, and now 155 Mbps ATM. Where does it end? What is the theoretical bandwidth of copper systems and what is a realistic speed that can be used?

The first issue that must be addressed is the difference between frequency and digital data throughput. The frequency of the carrier wave and the number of bits per second differ by the level of data compression used. For example, TP-PMD (the standard developed from CDDI) transports 125 Mbps, but uses a 4:1 compression algorithm called MLT-3, resulting in a 31.25 MHz carrier. Many compression algorithms and techniques are available and 10- or 20-to-1 compression ratios are achievable.

The second issue is the frequency of the signal that the wire itself will support. Category 5 UTP is tested to 100 MHz and there are now cables which are tested to 350 MHz. From a strictly technical perspective, this means transmission of gigabits per second are achievable on UTP. Today there are manufacturers including IBM and AT&T which have systems operating at over 500 Mbps in their labs.

In the real world, one has to deal with the emitted electro-magnetic radiation (EMI) of the cables. Of specific concern to the regulatory bodies is radio frequency interference (RFI) or noise within the spectrum of other broadcasts. These frequencies coincide with the higher carrier frequencies of proposed data transmissions.

Regulation of emitted cable noise will come about, but there are technical solutions to this problem too. Cables with better balance within the pair equipment with cleaner signals will minimize RFI. Lower signal levels, higher receiver gains, and digital filtering also dramatically improve performance. As these regulations become law, the equipment manufacturers will implement these currently available technologies because the incremental cost will be justified.

Availability of Sufficient Strategies

While bandwidth is an issue for vertical or backbone cabling applications, the available bandwidth of UTP horizontal segments is still very underused. There are sufficient strategies available today to support the projected bandwidth increase through the next 25 years, never mind new technologies which become available during that period.

A properly designed UTP horizontal cabling system of Category 5 will support 155 Mbps today and probably much more through future data compression of video signals. This is approximately a 1,000:1 increase over today's average terminal bandwidth and 10,000:1 over today's LAN usage. Since the last 35 years has shown a 100:1 increase, this would support 1000 years of continued geometric growth in access requirements. Since 35 years is a maximum design requirement for commercial building infrastructure, and 10 years is the average renovation cycle, it is inconceivable that technology of computing environments would exceed this bandwidth.

The vertical cabling environment however, is the area of current bandwidth limitation and continual demand growth. Optical fiber supporting high speed networks is the only reasonable choice for future-proofing this segment of your building cabling.

Continuing with the theme of planning and designing high-speed cabling systems, let's take a look at a new class of online high-speed compressed satellite (wireless) encryption-based technologies (already available commercially from third-party vendors) for data communication. These technologies are making it possible to replicate the rich document management and workflow features previously restricted to homogeneous e-mail and groupware environments. The technologies, using seven levels of encryption that are capable of high-volume data compression, are needed to offset the threat to wireless encryption cracking by hackers, terrorists, and criminal organizations.

New Online Compressed Satellite Encryption-Based Technology

High-speed compressed satellite (wireless) encryption-based technologies, including software envelopes and electronic authentication services, leverage Internet and intranet infrastructures and facilitate precise management and measurement of document usage and access across heterogeneous systems. Penetration of these technologies will force IT managers to rethink workflow investments and to develop new priorities for tracking and reporting information flows.

Document-intensive industries such as financial services have long wrestled with how to compress, streamline, manage, and automate the movement of information around their organizations. In response, systems vendors and integrators invented *workflow* with the idea that any document-intensive business process that could be described could also be automated.

In a similar fashion, EDI (Electronic Data Interchange) has been offered as a way to automate business-to-business supply and ordering functions. Groupware, too, has been marketed as a way to manage business processes, especially messy and unpredictable ones (document creation and editing).

Neither workflow nor EDI, however, have fulfilled their original potential. Workflow systems have thrived in highly structured settings, but these are often inflexible and difficult to link to the outside world. EDI has made it possible to reduce supply management and ordering costs, significantly, but it, too, is inflexible; preplanned bilateral implementations are the best that EDI can offer.

Though groupware has been arguably more successful, it has fallen short of its potential because of the huge strategic commitments required to make it effective.

Serendipitous partnering, spontaneous commerce, and adaptability are not strong suits for any of these technologies. Unfortunately, the business world is moving in exactly this direction—toward continuous change, with an increasing premium on high-speed compression and flexibility and a growing requirement to link with external parties.

Until recently, IT managers have been faced with two basic choices in automating and managing workflow—commit to a large investment in a unifying solution or accept lowest-common denominator capabilities and/or security levels across systems and, almost invariably, across organizations.

Now, just as many companies are becoming convinced of the value of workflow, EDI, and groupware, a basket of new satellite encryption technologies (based on compressed real-time public key encryption) is poised to alter the cost/feature balance radically, as well as the reach and flexibility of business-process automation. Let's look briefly at one of these key satellite encryption technologies that are beginning to make this possible.

Real-time Compression Router

The goal of this technology is the development of the first *secure gateway router* capable of high-volume satellite-transmitted data compression. The technology revolves around a revolutionary online compression software based on a patented scanning process. This technology represents a dramatic departure from traditional offline compression and far exceeds the performance of hardware-based, online compression which is the current industry standard. What follows is a detailed look at the software, its application as part of a secure gateway router and the potential impact on digital wireless communications.

Technology Background

The patented scanning process involves no dictionary or mathematical algorithms. Rather than simply relying on data redundancy, it operates in *real time* by scanning the physical symmetry of each byte of data as it is being transferred to and from a satellite.

The characteristic profile produced by the scanning module is sent to a decision engine which coordinates the function of 16 separate relay modules. Each module is designed to address a specific range of characters and programmed to assist the decision engine in making dynamic decisions so as to maximize compression efficiency. Other key performance features include:

- Compression speed of 6.8 Mbps using 16-bit code run on a Pentium 166. Speed will exceed 10 Mbps with 32-bit code.
- Automatical detection and correction of any corrupt packets as they're being sent, using a bi-directional protocol.
- Compression with seven levels of encryption, with each string of several packets secured by a separate set of codes.
- Compression and encryption total requirement of only 20K RAM (Random Access Memory).

NOTE:

In addition to operating in real time, this software compresses with *no packet loss*! Also, because of the patented scanning process, short e-mail messages are compressed as effectively as large files.

Several primary tests have been conducted to measure how well this software performs in a real-world satellite networking environment. One test involved a UNIX test over PPP (Point-to-Point Protocol). The primary purpose was to measure compression performance relative to CPU utilization, a major determinant in hardware costs associated with development of a compression router.

Results from repeated tests showed a 486DX-33 with the math co-processor and cache both disabled and settings fixed for normal operation capable of compressing a 56K channel in real time with negligible CPU demand. Furthermore, results showed the software effective in compressing a variety of file types. Large text files were consistently compressed in excess of 3 to 1. Tests involving highly-compressed gif, jpg, and wav files showed consistent compression gains in the area of 10%.

A second test conducted by the software developers involved a Microsoft NT 4.0 - Winsock 2 test over TCP/IP (Transmission Control Protocol / Internet Protocol). The primary purpose was to measure real transfer time savings in comparison to V.42bis, a hardware-based, online compression which is the current international standard for 28.8K modems. Here, results from repeated tests exceeded those over PPP and showed the software to be clearly superior to V.42bis.

The Secure Gateway Router

Designing a *secure gateway router* to maximize the performance of this software will allow real-time compression and encryption of several thousand simultaneous satellite network connections. The extreme speed and efficiency of the software makes this possible.

However, both will increase even more as a result of having the software operate as part of hardware inside a router. Here, it will no longer be necessary to engage RAM. In effect, the processing power inherent to the software program will be continuously active. It is reasonable to expect that by doing this the processing speed would increase well beyond 10 Mbps using a 32-bit code, to 20 Mbps or more.

The implication is that a relatively inexpensive PC-based router with a Pentium processor could easily compress and encrypt the entire satellite data transmission flow of a T-1 connection operating at capacity. Depending on how much the processing speed is increased from added efficiency, the same router could have a similar impact on a congested DS3 (Data Service 3).

NOTE:

DS3 = 44.736 Mbps or 28 T-1 circuits.

Obviously, such a device would have value in today's marketplace where there is a growing emphasis on both bandwidth efficiency and security. Key benefits include:

- Maximizes bandwidth efficiency for LANs, WANs , and intranets.
- Maximizes security for all satellite-transmitted data traveling inside or outside a private network.

- Creates infrastructure for an expanded private satellite network or extranet whereby banking or other industries can securely interact with affiliated institutions and customers.
- Creates infrastructure for a *Virtual Private Network*, whereby the Internet could replace costly dedicated lines as a means of transferring corporate data to and from a satellite.

In addition, the secure gateway router will provide other benefits for increased bandwidth efficiency and security not directly related to compression and encryption. These benefits include:

- Secure packet filtering and multiple-destination firewall.
- Telephone, 100BaseT, token ring, and FDDI (Fiber Distributed Data Interface) interface.
- Proxy to shield satellite network behind secure bastion host.
- Internal caching algorithm allowing satellite-connected network users to shut off individual memory/disk caches, helping to reduce bandwidth demand and improve overall workstation performance.
- Network load balancing to alleviate satellite network connection congestion.
- Patented IP security for all satellite data transferred outside the corporate network.

Once in place, the secure gateway router paves the way for yet another opportunity.

NOTE:

Each router will be designed to operate across a variety of satellite networks employing extended BGP4 (Border Gateway Protocol) routing code. These include; TCP/IP native, frame relay, ATM (Asynchronous Transfer Mode) serial link encapsulation including Cisco HDLC (High-Level Data link Control), as well as multi-link PPP. It will simply be a matter of plugging-in and activating.

Digital Wireless Communications

The fact that the compression process produces tiny packets of data (1,500 MTU (Maximum Transmission Unit)) with no packet loss makes this technology uniquely well-suited for wireless and satellite network communications. Furthermore, because both the compression and encryption require just 20K of RAM, the software can easily operate within the limited memory of a PDA (Personal Digital Assistant) or from a DSP (Digital Signal Processor) inside a PCS (Personal Communications Service) phone.

Deploying this technology in conjunction with wireless and satellite networks would dramatically enhance both bandwidth efficiency and satellite communication security. It simply requires a software-enabled phone or modem connecting with another enabled device. It does not matter what is in between, just so long as a two-point connection is established. See the sidebar, "Enhanced Bandwidth Efficiency and Security Benefits," for more information.

Enhanced Bandwidth Efficiency and Security Benefits

Enhanced bandwidth efficiency and security provide benefits to both users and wireless network providers. Key benefits for users include:

- Comfort in knowing you are using the most secure wireless link available.
- Reduced connection costs as a result of faster remote satellite data transfers.
- More available memory in PDA or laptop.
- Protection for data stored in PDA or laptop in case of theft or loss.

Key benefits for satellite network providers include:

- Ability to advertise as the most secure wireless link available.
- Ability to advertise reduced connection costs without price cutting.
- More available bandwidth across satellite network connections.
- Possibility of encouraging businesses and individuals to use wireless communications with greater confidence.

The last point in the preceding sidebar is an important one. Businesses and consumers both have taken to using wireless communication for phone conversations. But, as we move into the future and satellite-transmitted data piracy becomes more and more sophisticated and commonplace, it remains to be seen just how willing some will be to rely on wireless as a regular means of transferring the most confidential information.

This applies not only to PCS and satellite, but also the 39 GHz (Gigahertz) broadband microwave link soon to be introduced as the *last mile* to digital wireless communications. Here, providers are counting on hospitals, banks, and other large business operations to use their satellite-connected networks for short-distance, high-speed data transmission. For example, 39 GHz is seen as an ideal means for primary care physicians and specialists to take part in interactive video conferences where X-rays, MRIs (Magnetic Resonance Imaging), and CAT (Computerized Axial Tomography) scans could be exchanged and discussed.

However, for this scenario to become a reality, providers will have to take every precaution to ensure satellite data transmission security. Not only this, they then must effectively convey the extent to which they've taken these steps to potential users. This means convincing not only hospitals and doctors, banks and bankers, but also patients and customers.

Clearly, when it comes to the most confidential information, the willingness to leave behind the perceived security of wire will depend on the degree to which providers are able to encourage businesses and consumers to use wireless with greater confidence. This technology certainly has the potential to impact the marketplace in this regard.

However, there is yet another distinct opportunity presented by a combined approach involving both the software and the secure gateway router. In its design, the router can easily be configured to facilitate a fast and secure connection across a digital wireless network to a corporate LAN or intranet, or to a private extranet. It is suggested that a wireless modem working in conjunction with a secure gateway router is the easiest and most secure means of connection with benefits for corporate executives, wireless network providers, and PDA developers. The security provided through this combined approach could be further enhanced by developing custom TCP/IP software which would be relegated to the internal satellite network.

NOTE:

> The attachment of a wireless gateway to an intranet offers a more secure entrance than access through a dial-up connection. Each wireless device that has access to the gateway must be registered on the satellite-connected network and enabled by the gateway.

Current versions of the secure gateway router are effective and unique in performance. The approach to design also makes it possible to produce what would be the first secure gateway router capable of high-volume real-time satellite data transmission compression. There would be a need to produce this new compression technology for the following reasons:

- For client and server applications, it would mean developing specific applications for each operating system, a time-intensive proposition.

- There is likely to be considerable opposition to introducing compression and encryption to existing servers.
- A compression router maximizes software performance in the satellite-connected network environment—and this would have immediate impact on corporations and Internet service providers faced with congested network connections.
- A compression router maximizes security and bandwidth efficiency by making sure all traffic coming into a private satellite-connected network is compressed and encrypted.

The conclusion is that the secure gateway router is the quickest and most cost-effective means of introducing revolutionary real-time compression satellite encryption technology to the marketplace.

From Here

This chapter opened up Part III, "Planning For High-Speed Cabling Systems," by taking a thorough look at data compression: high-speed real-time data compression and how to plan for higher-speed cabling systems. Chapter 13 describes the development of the high-speed cabling system implementation plan (scheduling, analyzing site surveys, connectivity requirements, equipment, security, performance, etc.).

End Notes

[1] "Gigabit Ethernet Overview," Gigabit Ethernet Alliance (GEA), 20111 Stevens Creek Boulevard, Suite 280, Cupertino, California, 95014, 1997, p. 17.
[2] William A. Flanagan, "How to Get the Bandwidth You Need When You Need It," Vice President-Technology, FastComm Communications Corp., 45472 Holiday Drive, Sterling, VA, 20166, 1997, p. 2.
[3] "The Bandwidth Bogeyman," MOD-TAP, 285 Ayer Road, P.O. Box 706, Harvard, MA 01451, 1997, p. 1.

13

Implementation Plan Development

To help ensure that the implementation of your cabling system installation goes as planned, read this chapter first to help you develop and prepare your site before the system arrives. For brevity, the term *system* is used throughout this chapter in reference to third-party cabling systems products.

Onsite Installation: Software Configurations

The on-site services (OSS) team normally will not set up the software configuration for your system. The installation service is limited to hardware installation and setup. You are responsible for setting up the software configuration. The following software configuration options are available:

- *Option 1:* You should either e-mail or fax the entire configuration to the OSS team. The configuration is usually downloaded to your system through the console port via a modem line.
- *Option 2:* You should store the entire configuration on a Trivial File Transfer Protocol (TFTP) server. The configuration is downloaded to your system using a vendor's automatic installation feature.

- *Option 3:* The OSS team should configure one port on the router so you can Telnet to the router and download the entire configuration. Usually, only Interior Gateway Routing Protocol (IGRP) and Routing Information Protocol (RIP) routing are supported for this option.
- *Option 4:* You should use your copy of the vendor's configuration maker feature to configure your router and access servers. The configuration maker is usually a wizards-based software tool that helps you to quickly and easily configure and address the third party vendor's cabling products [1].

Be sure to indicate on the site preparation checklist which software configuration loading option you want to use. The following is an example of how a software configuration might appear on a terminal [Cisco, 2-3].

NOTE:

The majority of software configurations are unique. For example, the following configuration will probably not be valid on your system.

```
! Create line encrypted password
line 0 5
 encrypted password classified
 login
!
! Create level-1 encrypted password
certify-encrypted-password Classified Term
!
! Create a system hostid
hostid X-File
! Create host fileids
start host host2-confg 242.219.2.222
start host host3-confg 242.219.2.222
! Create system fileids
start system sys2-system 242.219.24.222
start system sys3-system 242.219.2.222
!
! Certify SNMP
snmp-server collective
snmp-server capture-verification
snmp-server host 242.219.2.38 collective
snmp-server host 242.219.2.222 collective
snmp-server host 242.219.3.74 collective
!
! Create UBDBDT server hosts
ubdbdt-server host 242.219.2.38
ubdbdt-server host 242.219.24.44
ubdbdt-server host 242.219.2.44
```

```
!
! Create a info-of-the-night sign
sign iotn ^C
The Information Technology Place welcomes everyone
Please call 1-900-666-3333 for a login account, or enter
your password at the prompt.
^C
```

Scheduling Factors

You should try to schedule installations five working days in advance. This could be done by sending a completed *site preparation checklist* form to your vendor.

Cancellations and Reschedules

Your vendor often reserves the right to reschedule the installation if any information on the *site preparation checklist* is not available usually within six working days before the scheduled installation date. With most vendors, you can reschedule or cancel an installation up to four working days before the scheduled installation date without any penalty. However, installations canceled within 96 hours of the scheduled installation date are often subject to a cancellation charge. On the day of the installation, any cancellation caused by inappropriate site preparation, equipment unavailability, or other circumstances beyond the control of the vendor is normally billed as an installation, and another installation must be scheduled.

NOTE:

You should contact your OSS team if you have additional installation-specific questions or need to reschedule your installation.

Pricing and Delays

Onsite installation pricing is normally based on the type and number of systems to be installed at a given site. Onsite installation delays caused by inappropriate site preparation, equipment unavailability, or other circumstances beyond the control of the vendor are usually billed at prevailing field engineer time and material rates.

User Responsibilities before Installation

The following tasks should be completed before the arrival of the vendor's onsite installation personnel in order to ensure a successful installation: First of all, you should prepare the site and complete a *site preparation checklist* form for each system to be installed. Send the completed form by fax within six working days before the scheduled installation date. The following information should be included on the site preparation checklist:

- Chassis-mounting preference and system type and (rack mounting, and so forth).
- Configuration option choices.
- For remote access by the vendor's personnel during installation, a modem telephone line number should be included.
- If available, a fax number and e-mail address; .site name and address; installation date and time; sales order number (if the system is new); and, contact name and telephone number.
- In order for the installer to contact systems personnel, a voice telephone line number (near the new system) should included [Cisco, 4].

Verifying DC or AC power requirements and site environment specifications is the second task to be completed before the arrival of the vendor's onsite installation personnel. Third, all distance and interference limitations of interface cables to be used at the installation should be verified.

The fourth task would be to install and verify the operation of all external communications equipment not provided by the vendor. This external communications equipment includes, but might not be limited to, LAN and WAN connections, channel service unit/digital service unit (CSU/DSU), media attachment unit (MAU), transceivers, modems, and any other external communications equipment related to your site and necessary for the installation. And the last task would be to verify the operation of all telephone circuits, digital services, and T1 facilities not supplied by the vendor but required for the installation.

Responsibilities of the Installer

The onsite installer should complete the following tasks. First, the installer should unpack the system and accessories necessary for installation. Second, the installer should mount the system on a desktop, in a rack or wiring closet, or on the wall. The third task is to connect the system to the network and customer-provided LAN and WAN connections.

Attaching the vendor-supplied modem for remote diagnostics, validation of network serial link status, and insertion of the customer IP address and password is the fourth task. The fifth task is to connect the console, administrator port, and auxiliary cables (if available and as required). Finally, the installer should verify the following:

- LED status, network interface operations, and Interface status reports.
- Operation of blower or fan.
- Primary network serial link testing to the remote end. If the serial link is not available, loopback testing is used (HDLC encapsulation only).
- System power up [Cisco, 5].

Meeting Site Requirements

The general ventilation and power requirements your site must meet for your system to operate properly are described in this part of the chapter. Information on preventing electrostatic discharge damage (ESD) is also included.

Ventilated System

Some systems have a fan or an internal blower that pulls air through a power supply and card cage. These systems are designed to operate in a level, dry, clean, air-conditioned and well-ventilated environment. The air-cooling function might be impaired if either the intake or exhaust vents are blocked in any way. You should ensure that the system's location has adequate air circulation.

Taking Proper Precautions

In order to ensure a successful system operation, the proper placement of the wiring closet or layout of your equipment rack and chassis are essential. .System malfunctions and shutdowns can occur when equipment is placed too close together or is inadequately ventilated. In addition, system maintenance can be difficult if chassis access panels are made inaccessible by poor equipment placement.

If you're in the process of planning your site layout and equipment locations, read and follow the precautions listed below. This will reduce the likelihood of environmentally caused shutdowns and help avoid future equipment failures. For instance:

- Ambient room temperature alone might not be adequate to cool equipment to acceptable operating temperatures. Remember that electrical equipment generates heat.
- Ensure that all card access panels and chassis cover are secure and in place. The chassis is designed to direct cooling air through the card cage. An open access panel will redirect the air flow, potentially preventing air from properly flowing through the chassis.
- Never place chassis side-by-side because the heated exhaust air from one chassis will be drawn into the intake vent of the adjacent chassis [Cisco, 5-6].

Using Equipment Racks

The following describes the ventilation considerations that apply to using equipment racks for your system. For instance, you should first install the chassis in an enclosed rack only if it has adequate ventilation or an exhaust fan. Use an open rack where possible.

A ventilation system that is too powerful in an enclosed rack might prevent cooling by creating negative air pressure around the chassis and redirecting the air away from the chassis intake vent. Therefore, the second ventilation consideration would be (if necessary) to operate the chassis with the rack door open or in an open rack.

The third consideration would be the correct use of baffles inside the enclosed rack. The baffles can assist in cooling the chassis.

Ensuring that the rack is not too congested is the fourth ventilation consideration. In an enclosed rack, ideally, separate the units with 12 to 15 inches of vertical clearance. The horizontal clearance is standard for most enclosed racks. Avoid obstructing this space. Open racks are recommended, but not required.

Finally, equipment located near the bottom of the rack can excessively heat the air that is drawn upward and into the intake ports of the equipment previously mentioned, thus leading to failures in the chassis at or near the top of the rack. If the enclosed rack you are using does not have a ventilation fan, install one.

Proper Power Requirements

You need the proper AC receptacle at your site, in order to connect the chassis to AC power. The chassis power supply is either factory-configured for either 110 volts alternating current (VAC) or 240 VAC operation (230 VAC in the United Kingdom) or autoranging. A 6-foot electrical power cord is included in all chassis.

CAUTION:

Do not connect the chassis to a receptacle if the voltage indicated on the chassis label is different from the power outlet voltage. A voltage mismatch might pose a fire hazard, can cause equipment damage, and create a shock hazard.

NOTE:

You should attach dual power supplies to independent power sources for full redundancy. An uninterruptable power source (UPS) is also recommended to protect against power failures at your site.

Electrostatic Discharge Damage Prevention

ESD damage (which occurs when electronic components are improperly handled), can result in complete or intermittent failures. ESD can impair equipment and electronic circuitry. Typically, the successful installation of the chassis should not require handling any system components. Nevertheless, ESD prevention procedures should always be followed.

After the site requirements have been met, you should conduct a site survey as part of developing the implementation plan for your cabling system. The information obtained from a site survey will help you determine whether you met or exceeded your minimum requirements.

Site Survey

The range and throughput of your cabling system will be affected by your building's construction materials, and by the general design and layout of your facility. This information will help you determine the mounting locations for your system's access points so that the system performance will meet or exceed your minimum requirements.

You will need a map, similar to that shown In Figure 13–1, of that portion of your facility to be covered by the cabling system [2]. When deciding which areas are to have cable or wireless coverage, consider lunch rooms, break rooms, hallways, and outdoor eating areas. In today's more informal work environment, it is common for these locations to be the site for reading e-mail, impromptu meetings, and brainstorming sessions. A building blueprint works well as a site survey map, and generally shows potential sources of radio frequency interference such as ductwork, elevators, stairwells, etc. If the facility has been extensively modified, for example by construction of new interior offices or revised layout of work cubicles, then an accurate floor plan drawing is preferable. Regardless, it is useful to mark potential areas of radio frequency interference in advance (elevators, other radio sources, microwave ovens, etc.), so that special attention can be given to wireless or cabling interference in these areas.

As you proceed through the site survey you will be measuring radio frequency transmissions around cabling or wireless access points installed in a temporary location. In the course of the survey, you will be moving this access point and remeasuring transmission efficiencies. You will need to complete this process for the entire facility before selecting final locations. Accordingly, it is useful to have a set of colored pencils or markers to distinguish the access point locations on your map and to mark transmission distances.

One of the first steps in performing a site survey is to make a decision about the desired or minimum acceptable performance of your cabling system. The minimum acceptable performance (expressed in packets transmitted per second) will depend on the applications running on your network, and varies

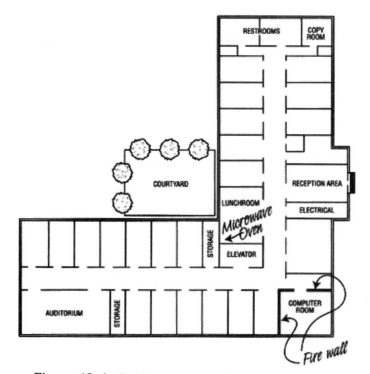

Figure 13–1: Building map annotated for the site survey.

dramatically from customer to customer. Your system administrator may have determined a minimum performance specification for your system. If not, most third party installers have a procedure that will help you assess the minimum acceptable throughput.

Once the minimum acceptable throughput is determined, you use an *access point* and a portable computer equipped with a Personal Computer Memory Card Industry Association (PCMCIA) adapter card to measure your building's radio transmission environment. The software provided measures the throughput of the system. By working from the most remote location to the most central location in your building, you will be able to determine where the access points should be mounted to obtain at least the minimum performance level over the entire area. In fact, most locations will probably exceed the minimum performance level by a considerable margin.

The general site survey procedure is as follows. Using software tools and detailed instructions, determine a possible location for an access point and temporarily mount the access point there. Carrying a portable computer with the site survey software loaded, measure throughput at various locations around the access point and annotate your building map. Based on those measurements, determine another possible location for the access point, temporarily mount the access point at this new location, and repeat the throughput measurements. By continuing this process and plotting the combined data from all of your measurements on your facility map, you will be able to determine where best to locate the access points to achieve optimum wireless LAN performance as well as nonwireless systems. It generally takes about one hour to establish the first access point location, and 30-45 minutes for the other locations. See Figure 13–2 for permanent access point locations and their zones of coverage [AMP, 3].

Cabling Distance Connectivity Limitations and Requirements

As previously stated in Chapter 10, "Fiber Optic Planning And Design Considerations," the size of your networks and the distance between connections on your networks will depend on the type of signal, the signal speed, and the transmission media (the type of cable used to transmit the signals). For instance, standard coaxial cable has a greater channel capacity than twisted-pair cabling.

The rate limits and distance in these descriptions are the IEEE-recommended maximum distances and speeds for signaling. For example, the recommended maximum rate for V.35 is 2 megabits per second (Mbps), but it is commonly used at 4 Mbps without any problems.

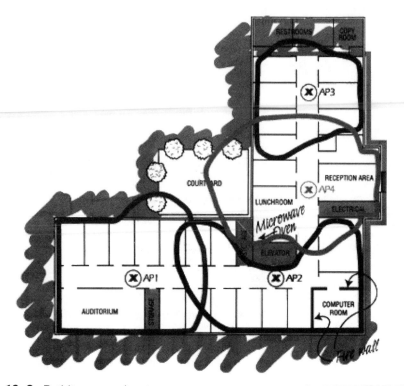

Figure 13–2: Building map showing permanent access point locations and their zones of coverage.

NOTE:

> Exceeding the maximum distances is not recommended or supported, even though you can usually get good results at speeds and distances far greater than those listed in this part of the chapter. You can get good results with rates and distances greater than those shown here, if you understand the electrical problems that might arise and can compensate for them. However, you do so at your own risk.

Channel Attachment

If your system has a Channel Interface Processor (CIP), be aware that the maximum transmission distance for Enterprise Systems Connection (ESCON) with light-emitting diodes (LED) is 2.0 miles (3.2 km) point-to-point or 5.8 miles (9.3 km) with two ESCON directors. The maximum transmission distance for bus and tag is 500 feet (155 m). The IBM 3044 C/D (host side/remote side) copper-to-fiber repeater can be used to extend the bus and tag distance up to 1.3 miles (2.1 km).

Fast Ethernet

The cabling specifications and the connection limitations for 100 Mbps Fast Ethernet transmission over UTP, STP, and fiber optic cables are listed in Table 13–1 [Cisco, 7]. Additionally, the characteristics of 100BaseTX and 100BaseFX with respect to IEEE 802.3u physical characteristics are summarized in Table 13–2 [Cisco, 7-8].

Table 13–1: 100 Mbps transmission cabling specifications and connection limits.

Parameter	RJ-45	MII	SC-Type
Cable specification	Category 5[a] UTP[b], 22 to 24 AWG[c]	Category 3, 4, or 5, 150 ohm UTP or STP, or multimode optical fiber	62.5/125 multimode optical fiber
Maximum cable length		1.75 ft (0.54 m) (MII-to-MII cable[d])	
Maximum network length	667 ft (205 m)[e] (with 1 repeater)		667 ft (205 m)[e] (with 1 repeater)
Maximum segment length	339ft (104 m) for 100BaseTX	3.28 ft (1 m)[e] or 1,423 ft (438 m) for 100BaseFX	339 ft (104 m)

[a] *EIA/TIA-T568-A or EIA-TIA-568 TSB-36 compliant.*
[b] *Category 5 UTP RJ45 or 150 ohm STP MII cables are available commercially.*
[c] *AWG = American Wire Gauge. This gauge is specified by the EIA/TIA-T568-A standard.*
[d] *This is the cable between the MII port on the FE port adapter and the appropriate transceiver.*
[e] *This length is specifically between any two stations on a repeated segment.*

NOTE:

The RJ45 designation is for a particular interface originally designed for programmable analog modem connections to leased telephone lines. RJ45 just happens to use the 8-pin modular jack and plug that are found in many LAN and telephone connections. The 8-pin modular connection used for 10/100BaseT, token ring/UTP, T1, ISDN, etc., is the EIA/TIA T568-A version that has very specific performance requirements.

Table 13–2: Physical characteristics for IEEE 802.3u.

Parameter	100BaseFX	100BaseTX
Data rate	100 Mbps	100 Mbps
Maximum segment length	339 ft (104 m) between repeaters	339 ft (104 m) between DTE [a] and repeaters
Media	SC-type: dual simplex or single duplex for Rx and Tx	RJ45MII
Signaling method	Baseband	Baseband
Topology	Star/Hub	Star/Hub

[a] *DTE = data terminal equipment.*

E1-G.703/G.704

You should be aware that unbalanced G.703/G.704 interfaces allow for a longer maximum cable length than those specified for balanced circuits if your system has a Fast Serial Interface Processor (FSIP). The maximum cable lengths for each FSIP E1-G.703/G.704 cable type by the connector used at the network (non-FSIP) end are listed in Table 13–3 [Cisco, 8].

Table 13–3: Maximum cable lengths for E1-G.703/G.704.

Connection Type	BNC	Twinax
Balanced Unbalanced	2079 ft (640 m)	995 ft (306 m)

Ethernet

The maximum distances for Ethernet network segments and connections depend on the type of transmission cable used—0.8-inch diameter coaxial (10Base5), 0.50-inch diameter coaxial (10Base2), or unshielded twisted-pair (10BaseT). Network connections to coaxial cables are tapped into a network segment and must be spaced at specific intervals. Table 13–4 lists the maximum number of connections (taps) per segment and the intervals at which they must be placed [Cisco, 8]. A maximum of five repeaters and eight bridges can be used to link segments in a single network.

Table 13–4: 10 Mbps transmission Ethernet coaxial connection limits.

Description	10Base5	10Base2
Cable diameter	0.5 in. (1.26 cm)	0.36 in. (0.914 cm)
Maximum connections (taps) per segment	100	30
Maximum network length (with 4 repeaters)	8,300 ft (2,554 m)	3,391 ft (1,043 m)
Maximum segment length	1,741 ft (536 m)	667 ft (205 m)
Minimum connection (tap) spacing	8.3 ft (2.6 m)	1.75 ft (0.54 m)

The unshielded twisted-pair (UTP) cabling used with 10BaseT is suitable for voice transmission, but might incur problems at 10 Mbps transmission rates. UTP wiring does not require the fixed spacing between connections that is necessary with the coaxial-type connections. The IEEE recommendations for the UTP maximum distances between station (connection) and hub are listed in Table 13–5 [Cisco, 9].

Table 13–5: Maximum transmission distances for Ethernet UTP.

Transmission Speed	Maximum Station-to-Hub Distance
10 Mbps (10BaseT)	339 ft (104 m)

In general, the workgroup catalyst switch implementation of 10BaseT requires a minimum of Category 3 UTP cable is specified by the EIA/TIA T568-B wiring standard. The characteristics of IEEE 802.3 Ethernet and Ethernet version 2 for 10BaseT are summarized in Table 13–6 [Cisco, 9]. In addition, The cabling specifications for 10 Mbps transmission over UTP and STP cables are listed in Table 13–7 [Cisco, 9].

Table 13–6: 10BaseT Ethernet Version 2 and IEEE 802.3 physical characteristics.

Parameter	IEEE 802.3 Ethernet	10BaseT Ethernet Version 2
Data Rate	10 Mbps	10 Mbps
Maximum segment length	1751 ft (539 m)	339 ft (104 m)
Media	50 ohm coax (thick)	Unshielded twisted-pair (UTP)
Signaling method	Baseband	Baseband
Topology	Bus	Star

Table 13–7: 10 Mbps 10BaseT cable specifications.

Parameter	RJ45
Cable specification	Category 5 UTP[a], 22 to 24 AWG[b]
Maximum network length	667 ft (205 m) with 1 repeater
Maximum segment length	339 ft (104 m) for 10BaseT

[a] *Category 5 UTP RJ45 cables are available commercially.*

[b] *AWG = American Wire Gauge. This gauge is specified by the EIA/TIA-T568-A standard.*

HSSI

The High-Speed Serial Interface (HSSI) standard (EIA/TIA 612/613) specifies a maximum cable length of 61 feet (19 meters) for 52 Mbps HSSI connections. The typical (nominal) cable length between a HSSI Interface Processor (HIP) and a DSU is 7 feet (2 meters). The HSSI interface cable has 25 twisted pairs and a 50-pin plug at each end. Both Data Terminal Equipment (DTE) and Data Communications Equipment (DCE) ports on the HIP and the Data Service Unite (DSU) are 50-pin receptacles.

NOTE:

Most CSU/DSUs do not have 50-pin plug interfaces. They have V.35, 9-pin, and/or RS232. Connections to HSSI interface cables are via adapter cables.

The HSSI interface cable is similar to a small computer systems interface (SCSI) II cable. Nevertheless, the HSSI cable specification is more stringent than that for a SCSI-II.

NOTE:

When connecting the HSSI interface, do not substitute a SCSI-II-type cable for a HSSI cable. Proper operation of the interface could be prevented if you use a SCSI-II-type cable.

MultiChannel

The MultiChannel Interface Processor (MIP) E1 specifications are as follows:

- Input port specifications: see G.703/Section 6.3 (ITU-T specification).
- Jitter attenuation starting at 6 Hz, which meets or exceeds G.823 for E1.

- Output port specifications: see G.703/Section 6.2 (ITU-T specification).
- Transmission bit rate: 2.048 Kbps ± 50 ppm (parts per million) [Cisco, 11].

The MIP T1 specifications are as follows:

- Output pulse amplitude: 3.0 V (volts) ± 0.6V measured at DSX.
- Output pulse width: 324 ns (nanoseconds) ± 54 ns.
- Transmission bit rate: 1.544 Mbps ± 50 ppm [Cisco, 11].

The MIP T1 specifications comply with all AT&T Accunet TR 62411 specifications.

Serial

Serial signals can travel a limited distance at any given rate—as is the norm with all signaling systems. Generally, the greater the distance, the lower the baud rate. The relationship between transmission rate and distance for the HSSI is listed in Table 13.8 [Cisco, 12].

Table 13–8: Transmission speed versus distance for IEEE Standard EIA/TIA-232.

Baud Rate	Distance
2400	300 ft (92 m)
4800	200 ft (62 m)
9600	60 ft (19 m)
19200	36 ft (11.1 m)
38400	18 ft (5.5 m)
56000	8.7 ft (2.7 m)

NOTE:

Before their acceptance as standards by the Electronic Industries Association (EIA) and Telecommunications Industry Association (TIA), EIA/TIA-232 and EIA/TIA-449 were known as recommended standards RS-232 and RS-449.

Balanced drivers allow EIA/TIA-449 signals to travel greater distances than EIA/TIA-232. The standard relationship between baud rate and distance for EIA/TIA-449 signals is listed in Table 13–9 [Cisco, 12].

Table 13–9: Transmission speed versus distance for IEEE Standard EIA/TIA-449.

Baud Rate	Distance
2400	4,200 ft (1292 m)
4800	2,100 ft (646 m)
9600	1,050 ft (323 m)
19200	524 ft (161 m)
38400	267 ft (82 m)
56000	113 ft (35 m)
T1	60 ft (19 m)

NOTE:

The distance limits for EIA/TIA-449 (listed in Table 13–9), which are also valid for V.35 and X.21, are recommended maximum distances. Exceeding these maximum distances is not recommended or supported. In common practice, EIA/TIA-449 supports 2 Mbps rates, and V.35 supports 4 Mbps rates without any problems.

Synchronous Optical NETwork (SONET)

Two types of fiber are defined by the SONET specification for fiber optic transmission defines: multimode and singlemode. Bundles of light rays entering the fiber at a particular angle are known as modes. Multimode fiber allows multiple modes of light to propagate through the fiber, while singlemode fiber allows only one mode of light to propagate through the fiber. Singlemode fiber is capable of higher bandwidth and greater cable-run distances than multimode fiber; because, multiple modes of light propagating through the fiber travel at different distances depending on the entry angles, thus causing them to arrive at the destination at different times (a phenomenon called "modal dispersion"). Table 13–10 lists the maximum distances for singlemode and multimode transmissions, as defined by SONET [Cisco, 13]. Also, significant signal loss can result if the distance between two connected stations is greater than these maximum distances, thus making transmission unreliable.

Table 13–10: Maximum fiber optic transmission distances for SONET.

Transceiver Type	Maximum Distance Between Stations[a]
Multimode	Up to 1.6 miles (2.6 kilometers)
Singlemode	Up to 10 miles (16.0 kilometers)

[a] *This table lists typical results.*

Token Ring

IEEE 802.5 (token ring) networks have no current maximum transmission distance defined. Shielded twisted-pair cabling is most commonly used for rates of 16 Mbps. Shielded or UTP cabling is used for rates of 1 and 4 Mbps. Remember that twisted-pair cabling is more susceptible to interference than other types of cabling when planning your connections. So, plan the total network length and repeater spacing accordingly.

Interference

Interference can occur between the field and the signals on the wires when wires are run for any significant distance in an electromagnetic field. This fact has two implications for the construction of terminal plant wiring—the first one being strong electromagnetic interference, especially as caused by lightning or radio transmitters, can destroy EIA/TIA-232 drivers and receivers. Second, bad practices can result in radio interference emanating from the plant wiring.

NOTE:

> You might need to consult experts in radio frequency interference (RFI) in order to predict and remedy strong electromagnetic interference.

The plant wiring is unlikely to emit radio interference if you use UTP Ethernet cables in your plant wiring with a good distribution of grounding conductors. Use a high-quality twisted-pair cable with one ground conductor for each data signal when exceeding the distance listed in Table 13–5.

Generally, give special consideration to the effect of lightning strikes in your vicinity, especially if wires exceed recommended distances or pass between buildings. The electromagnetic pulse (EMP) caused by lightning or other high-energy phenomena can easily couple enough energy into unshielded conductors to destroy electronic devices. You might want to consult experts in electrical surge suppression and shielding if you have had problems of this sort in the past. Without pulse meters and other special equipment, most data centers cannot resolve the infrequent but potentially catastrophic problems just described. An excessive amount of time can be consumed in trying to identify and resolve interference problems. You should provide a properly grounded and shielded environment for your system (with special attention to issues of electrical surge suppression) in order to avoid these problems.

External Connections

To complete your installation, you might need some of the following data communications equipment. In addition to the interfaces you plan to use, your needs depend on many factors.

For example, you might need a console terminal with an EIA/TIA-232 data terminal equipment (DTE) connector for future configuration requirements after the system is installed and remotely configured by way of the modem connection. After you complete these configuration procedures, you can detach the terminal (and cable).

The chassis console port is a data communications equipment (DCE) device (using a DB-25 female connector) for routers and communication servers. And, the auxiliary port is a data terminal equipment (DTE) device (using a DB-25 male connector). In order to match the chassis console port default baud rate of 9600, 8 data bits, no parity, and 2 stop bits, you must adjust the baud rate of your console terminal. You must also consult the documentation for your terminal for this wiring specification. The administration interface port (admin port) is an EIA/TIA-232 DCE connection (requiring an RJ45 female connector) for the workgroup concentrators and catalyst switches. Also, the admin port is configured at the factory with the following communications parameters: one stop bit, 9600 baud, 8 data bits, and no parity.. For this wiring specification, you should consult the documentation for your terminal.

You need an 802.3 media attachment unit (MAU) and an attachment unit interface (AUI) cable; or an Ethernet transceiver and transceiver cable in order to use an IEEE 802.3 or Ethernet interface at your installation. These devices can be purchased as additional equipment. You should contact a customer service representative at this point. This additional equipment is not required for an Ethernet 10BaseT connection using the 10BaseT applique with routers or communications servers. These appliques have built-in transceivers.

You need a synchronous modem or a channel service unit/digital service unit (CSU/DSU) to connect to the network in order to use a low-speed synchronous serial interface at your installation. EIA/TIA-232, EIA/TIA-449, or V.35 connections (or attachments) are typically provided as the electrical interfaces on the CSU/DSU.

You need a T1 CSU/DSU that converts the High-Level Data Link Control (HDLC) synchronous serial data stream into a T1 data stream with the correct framing and ones density in order to attach a chassis to a T1 network. The telephone system requirement of a minimum number of 1 bit per time unit in a data stream is known as the "ones density." Several T1 CSU/DSU devices are on the market now. A T1 CSU/DSU is available as additional equipment.

NOTE:

A CSU/DSU is a digital network access device that connects data processing equipment directly to a digital communications line provided by the telco. In the past there were two separate devices for this function. The CSU terminates the digital circuit and performs such functions as transient protection (voltage spikes), electrical isolation, line conditioning, loop equalization, signal regeneration, and monitoring of the incoming digital signal. The DSU translates signals, regenerates data, does synchronous sampling, reformats, handles timing ,and converts the unipolar output signal from the DTE into the bipolar signals necessary for transmission over a digital network. Most T1 CSU/DSUs provide either a V.35 or EIA/TIA-449 electrical interface to the system.

A digital carrier facility used for transmitting data over a telephone network at 1.554 Mbps is known as a T1. E1 is the European equivalent of T1, with a data transmission rate of 2.048 Mbps.

You need a DSU to connect a HSSI port that is capable of the type of service to which you will connect the following: T3 (45 Mbps), E3 (34 Mbps), or Synchronous Optical Network (SONET) STS-1 (51.84 Mbps). You also need a HSSI interface cable to connect the DSU with the High-Speed Serial Interface Processor (HIP). The U.S. standard for a digital carrier facility used for transmitting data over a telephone network at 44.736 Mbps is known as a T3 (also known as digital signal level 3 (DS-3)). T3 is equivalent to 28 T1 (1.544 Mbps) interfaces. E3 is the European equivalent of T3.

Finally, SONET is an international standard (ANSI/CCITT) for optical communications systems. STS-1 (Synchronous Transport Signal level 1) is the basic building block signal of SONET. Level 1 is 51.84 Mbps. Faster SONET rates are defined as STS-n, where n is a multiple of 51.84 Mbps. For instance, the rate for SONET STS-3 is 155.52 Mbps, three times 51.84 Mbps.

From Here

This chapter described the development of the high-speed cabling system implementation plan (scheduling, analyzing site surveys, connectivity requirements, equipment, security, performance, etc.). Chapter 14 will begin Part IV by taking a look at the Installation of the Cabling System. The chapter opens up with a presentation on Testing Techniques as part of pre-installation activities by taking a look at the preparation of cable facilities, testing the cable and components, and code compliance and safety considerations.

End Notes

[1] "Site Preparation," (Some material in this book has been reproduced by Prentice Hall with the permission of Cisco Systems Inc.), COPYRIGHT © 1998 Cisco Systems, Inc., ALL RIGHTS RESERVED, 170 West Tasman Drive, San Jose, CA 95134-1706, USA, 1997, p. 1.

[2] "Wireless Site Survey," Reprinted with the permission of AMP Incorporated, Investor Relations, 176-42, PO Box 3608, Harrisburg, PA USA 17105-3608, 1997, p. 2

Part IV

Installing the Cabling Systems

14

TESTING TECHNIQUES

Prior to the installation of your cabling system, there are a number of activities that must take place in the form of various types of testing. The following sections discuss the test site requirements for the preparation of your cabling facilities for installation in these areas:

- Environment.
- Chassis accessibility.
- Cooling and airflow.
- Power.

Environment

Choose a clean, dust-free, preferably air-conditioned location. Avoid direct sunlight, heat sources, or areas with high levels of electromagnetic interference (EMI).

Chassis Accessibility

Make the front panel of the switch accessible so that you can monitor the LED indicators and access the reset switch. Leave at least 24 inches (60.9 centimeters) clearance at the rear of the switch for easier cabling and service.

Cooling and Airflow

Many equipment racks come with fans already installed on the top to draw air up through the equipment. However, if you don't have pre-installed fans, place two fans at the front of the switch so that they'll cool the interior by pushing air through vents in the front and forcing heated air through holes in the rear. If the internal temperature exceeds 122°F (50°C), a temperature alarm is generated.

NOTE:

To prevent the switch from overheating, do not operate it in an area that exceeds the maximum recommended ambient temperature of 104°F (40°C). To prevent airflow restriction, allow at least 3 inches (7.6 cm) of clearance around the ventilation openings.

Power

The source electrical outlet should be installed near the switch, be easily accessible, and be properly grounded. In addition, separate ground wires are also a good idea. .

Power should come from a building branch circuit. Use a maximum breaker current rating of 20A for 110V, or 8A for 230V. You should be aware of the power consumption ratings of the unit before you connect to a power source.

NOTE:

Care must be given to connecting units to the supply circuit so that wiring is not overloaded. Also, a voltage mismatch can cause equipment damage and may pose a fire hazard. If the voltage indicated on the label is different from the power outlet voltage, do not connect the chassis to that receptacle.

Test Cabling Requirements Techniques

The following discusses the test cabling requirements techniques for installation of:

- FDDI.
- CDDI.
- Ethernet 10BaseF.
- Ethernet 10BaseT.
- EIA/TIA-232.

FDDI Transmissions

The multimode FDDI connectors on the switch accept 50/125-micron multimode fiber, or 62.5/125-micron multimode fiber, with standard FDDI media interface connectors (MICs). The singlemode connectors accept 8.7 to 10/125-micron singlemode fiber, with standard FDDI ST-type connectors. FDDI maximum transmission distance specifications are listed in Table 14–1 [1]. Multimode and singlemode connectors are illustrated in Figures 14–1 and 14–2, respectively [2].

Table 14–1: Maximum transmission distances for FDDI.

Type of Transceiver	Maximum Distance between Stations
Multimode	1.4 miles (2 km)
Singlemode	39.9 miles (64 km)

CDDI

To ensure that you have the proper connectors (modular RJ45/T568-8/ Category 5 connector), you should check all existing cables for conformance with CDDI/MLT-3 distance requirements. A discussion on cable and distance specifications follows:

Figure 14–1: ST Singlemode connector.

Figure 14–2: Multimode FDDI connector—MIC type.

First of all, EIA/TIA-T568-B, Category 5, data-grade cable is required for Copper Distributed Data Interface (CDDI) installations when using data-grade unshielded twisted-pair (UTP) wiring. The total length of data-grade UTP cable from the switch to another switch, station, or CDDI (also known as TPDDI— Twisted-Pair Distributed Data Interface) concentrator must not exceed 341 feet (104.9 m).This would also include patch cords and cross-connect jumpers.

Second, use IBM Type 1 STP wiring for your CDDI installation when using shielded twisted-pair (STP) wiring. The total length of STP cable measured from the adapter or media access unit (MAU) to the switch must not exceed 341 feet (105 m). You must also use an impedance-matching balun (balance/unbalanced) device (model number WS-C737) to connect CDDI to STP. In addition, for external connections, you must use high-performance, Category 5, data-grade modular cables. Remember the following when you plan your CDDI installation.

- Do not use bridge taps.
- Do not exceed the maximum cable length for CDDI UTP and STP of 341 feet (105 m).
- Do not use protection coils.
- Do not share services (such as voice and data) on the same cable. CDDI uses two of the four pairs in the twisted-pair cable. The remaining two pairs cannot be used for other applications.
- Use cross-connect (patch) panels that comply with the EIA/TIA-T568-B, Category 5 wiring standard [Cisco, 5].

IEEE 802.3 Ethernet 10BaseF Ports

IEEE 802.3 Ethernet 10BaseF ports accept ST-type connections using 62.5/125-micron multimode optical fiber. The distance limitation for 10BaseF is 1.3 miles (2 km). 10BaseF supports both fiber optic interrepeater link (FOIRL) standards and 10BaseFL (fiber link).

In general, distance limitations depend on the power levels of other devices on the fiber link, combined effects of fiber, and connectors. The maximum power levels for 10BaseF and FOIRL are listed in Table 14–2 [Cisco, 6].

Table 14–2: Power levels for FOIRL and 10BaseF.

Maximum Power	FOIRL	10BaseF
Receive power at receiver	-27 dB	-32.5 dB
Transmit power at transmitter	-9 dB	-12 dB[a]

a *dB = decibel.*

Ethernet 10BaseT Ports

Modular RJ45 connectors are accepted by Ethernet 10BaseT ports. Also, as specified by the EIA/TIA-T568-B wiring standard, 10BaseT requires a minimum of Category 3 UTP cable. The distance limitation for 10BaseT is a maximum of 339 feet (104 m) between segments.

EIA/TIA-232 Signals

EIA/TIA-232 signals can travel a limited distance at any given bit rate (as with all signaling systems). Generally, the greater the distance, the slower the data rate. The relationship between baud rate and maximum distance is shown in Table 14–3 [Cisco, 6]. The EIA/TIA-232 admin port requires an RJ45-to-DB25 adapter for the console terminal where it is attached and a modular RJ45 connector for the switch end.

Table 14–3: Speed and distance limitations for EIA/TIA-232.

Data Rate (baud)	Distance (feet)	Distance (meters)
2,400	210	65
4,800	110	34
9,600	51	16
19,200	26	8
38,400	13	4

Test Network Topology Overview

Figure 14–3 shows what a topology (a high-speed transparent and translational bridging overview) might resemble when the switch is installed in your network. This consists of workstations connected to the 10BaseT Ethernet ports of two switches. The 10BaseF ports might be connected in a similar manner. The switches are connected to a FDDI or CDDI dual ring. This ring is part of a larger FDDI or CDDI backbone.

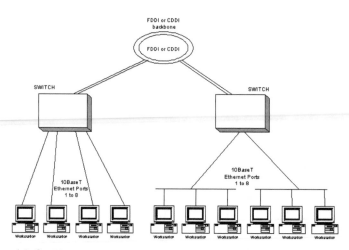

Figure 14–3: High-speed translational and transparent bridging topology.

Modem Test Requirements

Operating a switch with a modem is optional. You should consult the modem documentation when connecting a switch to a modem. You also need to connect the modem to the EIA/TIA-232 admin port on the switch as a minimum requirement. In addition, configuration is not possible at the switch if you don't configure the modem to operate with the switch. Table 14–4 lists the dual inline package (DIP) switch settings for the U.S. Robotics Sportster 28,800-baud fax modem as an example of modem configuration [Cisco, 7].

Table 14–4: DIP switch settings for a modem.

Switch	Connection	Setting	Description
1	DTR override	Down	Data Terminal Ready (DTR) is ignored by modem.
2	Audible results	Up	Instead of a number, modem returns audible result messages.
3	Suppress results	Up	No result messages are returned by the modem. Because this function is not configurable on the switch, it is required.

(continued)

Table 14–4: *(continued)*

Switch	Connection	Setting	Description
4	No echo of offline commands	Down	When the modem is offline and it receives a command, it does not echo. This function is not configurable on the switch, so it is required..
5	Auto answer on ring	Up	After one ring, modem answers automatically. This function is not configurable on the switch, so it is required. Thus, the modem must answer automatically.
6	CD override	Down	Carrier Detect (CD) is always maintained by the modem.
7	Load factory defaults	Down	Modem-dependent.
8	Dumb mode	Up	The modem attention (AT) command is not recognized by the modem.

NOTE:

The DIP switch information is only for the modem connected to the switch. It is not for the modem connected to your computer, terminal, PC, or whatever else you are using for your modem-based communication.

Test Tools and Materials Required

A list of tools and supplies that you need to install the switch with is shown in Table 14–5 [Cisco, 8]. The switch can be placed on a desktop in a work area, mounted in a standard 19-inch rack, or on a wall in a wiring closet or office.

Table 14–5: Materials and tools required for installation.

	Installation Type		
Hardware and Tools	**Desk**	**Rack**	**Wall**
Rack-mount kit (standard): Two brackets. Eight screws (attach brackets to switch). Four screws (switch to rack—you supply these).	No	Yes	No

(continued)

Table 14–5: *(continued)*

Hardware and Tools	Installation Type		
	Desk	Rack	Wall
Optional Wall-mount kit[a]:			
Two brackets.			
Four screws (attach brackets to switch).			
Four screws (attach to wall—you supply these).			
Wall-mounting template	No	No	Yes
No. 2 Phillips screwdriver.	No	Yes	Yes
Flat-blade screwdriver (to remove blank plates or A/B port cards).	Yes	Yes	Yes
3/8″ (0.952 cm) drill with 1/4″ (0.635 cm) bit.	No	No	Yes

[a] *Model number WS-C1670.*

Field Testing Cable and Components Prior to Installation

Now let's take a look at the next set of pre-installation activities, testing the cable and components. This next part of the chapter will focus on the field testing of unshielded twisted-pair and fiber optic cabling systems that must take place prior to installation.

Telecommunications System Bulletin (TSB) 67 is of great interest to cable installers, test-equipment manufacturers and LAN administrators because it provides detailed requirements on how to test and certify unshielded twisted-pair (UTP) cabling prior to installation. The same can be said for fiber optic cabling standards EIA/TIA-526-14A (Optical Power Loss Measurements of Installed Multimode Fiber Optic Cable Plant) and TIA/EUIA-526-7 (Measurement of Optical Power Loss of Installed Singlemode Fiber Optic Cable Plant). Let's focus first on TSB-67.

Field Testing Unshielded Twisted-Pair Cabling Systems with TSB-67

The purpose of this part of the chapter is not to reproduce the information already available in TSB-67. The objective here is to clarify the reasoning behind some of the decisions that were made and to give you a better understanding of the testing specifications prior to the installation of your cabling system.

Briefly, TSB-67 includes a link model, a description of which tests must be performed to certify the link (length, wiremap, Near End Cross Talk (NEXT), and attenuation) and specifications for how each test is to be performed. In addition, TSB-67 contains detailed procedures for verifying the accuracy of field test equipment (FTE) against both a theoretical model and a laboratory network analyzer. Finally, TSB-67 specifies performance criteria for FTE.

The Channel and Basic Link Models

Before studying the issue of *accuracy* and how it is addressed in TSB-67, it is necessary to understand TSB-67's two link definitions, the channel link and the basic link. Figure 14–4 illustrates the TSB-67 channel definition [3]. Cables A and E are user patch cords, almost always terminated in modular 8 (RJ45) connectors.

NOTE:

These are not and cannot be test equipment cords; they must be the user's actual patch cords.

As Figure 14–4 shows, the mated connection at the ends of these cords is not included in the channel definition. It is considered a part of the field tester. This connection is typically an 8-position modular jack. This means any measurements taken on the channel must be made through the mated connection and do not include the connection's characteristics. The mated modular 8 connection has significant NEXT, which becomes a source of error in NEXT measurements that will significantly differentiate the accuracy of channel and basic link measurements.

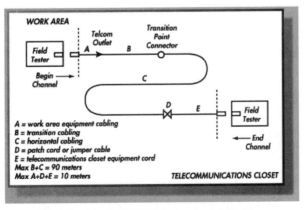

Figure 14–4: TSB-67 channel definition.

The channel was defined because it is important to know the performance of the sum of all the components between the hub and the PC so that you can predict the quality of communications from end to end. This information is essential to circuit designers and important to end users. However, cable installers are typically not responsible for installing patch cords, as office furniture is usually not present when the cabling is installed and tested. For this reason, the basic link model was defined.

In Figure 14–5, the basic link represents a minimal link and has only one connection at each end [Johnston, 3]. The channel has two. In addition, the basic link can only be 90 meters in length, while the channel can extend to 100 meters. For these reasons, both attenuation and NEXT will be higher on the channel than on the basic link.

Levels of Accuracy

Recognizing that the basic link and the channel link represent two different models, the authors of EIA/TIA-TSB-67 chose to define two distinct accuracy levels: Level II (high accuracy) and Level I (lower accuracy).

The reason for the two levels is that when you are testing a channel, you are almost always forced to measure through (but not include) the NEXT effects of a modular 8 (RJ45) interface directly on the FTE. The unpredictable crosstalk in this connection sets a limit on the achievable accuracy of the measurement. In contrast, when testing a basic link, field test equipment manufacturers can choose to use a very low crosstalk interface directly on the FTE. This reality is reflected in the TSB-67 description of two accuracy levels for field test equipment. Level I reflects the performance boundaries imposed by the reality of having to test through a modular 8 connection. Level II sets a much higher

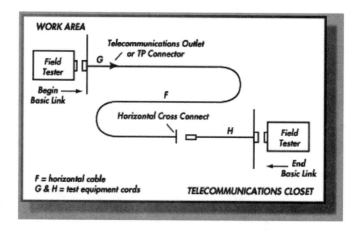

Figure 14–5: TSB-67 basic link definition.

accuracy requirement, attainable only if a different, low-crosstalk interface is used. The uncertainty caused by the higher crosstalk modular 8 interface can be avoided, and thus a much higher level of accuracy can be achieved.

TSB-40A specifies the worst-case NEXT performance of any modular 8 connection to be 40 dB at 100 MHz. So, while some connections might achieve 42 or 43 dB, 40 dB performance is all that can be guaranteed. This unpredictable, high level of inherent crosstalk limits any tester's ability to make measurements at a Level II accuracy level when testing a channel through a modular 8 interface to the FTE.

How Is Accuracy Measured?

The TIA task force that established TSB-67 determined six key performance parameters that affected the accuracy of field testers (see Table 14–6) [Johnston, 4-5]. The largest error term for field testers is residual NEXT. This consists of the sum of the tester's internal NEXT plus the NEXT of the interface to the tested link. Remember, this mated connection is not included in the link definition.

Table 14–6: TSB-67 Accuracy performance parameters.

Performance Parameter	Level I @ 100 MHz	Level II @ 100 MHz
Residual NEXT	40 dB	55 dB
Random Noise	50 dB	65 dB
Output Signal Balance	27 dB	37 dB
Common Mode Rejection	27 dB	37 dB
Dynamic Accuracy	+/-1 dB	=/-0.75 dB
Return Loss	15 dB	15 dB

When testing a channel, this residual NEXT will include the NEXT of a mated modular 8 connection. Even if the residual NEXT on the field tester's internal circuits is zero, its overall residual NEXT will be limited to 40 dB by the mated modular 8 connection as is specified by TSB-40A. Thus, the Level II accuracy performance requirement of 55 dB cannot be met when testing a channel. This is, in fact, the reason Level I and Level II were created. When testing a basic link, the field tester can make use of an interface with much lower inherent crosstalk, thus making the Level II residual NEXT requirement of 55 dB achievable.

TSB-67 specifies that for an instrument to meet Level I or II accuracy, it must meet all six of the requisite performance parameters. The crosstalk and balance characteristics of a modular 8 connector immediately limit any tester using it to no better than Level I accuracy. It is important to note that even

Level II accuracy tools are reduced to Level I accuracy when forced to test through a modular 8 interface, because of the uncertainty created by the modular 8 connector. This uncertainty has an unpredictable magnitude and phase, so it cannot be compensated for or subtracted by hardware or software.

TSB-67 also requires that field testers agree with Annex B, which states that agreement with network analyzers must be demonstrated. The reason for this is that different field testers may employ different methods to make measurements. Some of these methods, such as time domain measurements, may have additional error sources unaccounted for in the theoretical error model.

The Level I performance limitations of a modular 8 connection hold true even when time-domain measurement techniques are used to attempt to *time-gate* away the high crosstalk. The outgoing pulses used to make time-domain measurements have a duration of several nanoseconds, which equates to several feet. This means a *NEXT dead-zone* is created where the tester cannot read the crosstalk on the first few feet. As Figure 14–4 shows, this measurement technique does not comply with TSB-67 because the test must begin directly behind the first modular 8 connections, not two or three feet down the cable.

Users are cautioned to review FTE performance specifications carefully. Many products will claim to meet Level II accuracy, but the fine print often shows such products barely meet the minimum requirements, especially with residual NEXT. Proof of compliance with Annex B (network analyzer agreement) is conspicuously absent in most cases.

Length Accuracy Issues

Annex D of TSB-67 provides information on how to increase the accuracy of length measurements, or, at the least, how to minimize the inaccuracies of such measurements. Since most FTE measures length using Time Domain Reflectometry (TDR), the accuracy of these products depends upon the Nominal Velocity of Propagation (NVP) setting of the cable being tested. NVP varies up to 5 percent from cable to cable and even from pair to pair. TDR is an excellent method to measure length but requires the cable's precise NVP.

As previously stated, TSB-67 will be a great help to cable installers, test equipment manufacturers and LAN administrators. The reason for this is because it provides clear test requirements and instrument specifications as part of an organization's cabling system pre-installation activities.

Field Testing Fiber Optic Cabling Systems with EIA/TIA Procedures

Let's continue with the next set of pre-installation activities, field testing of fiber optic cabling systems that must take place prior to installation. The following guidelines describe the EIA/TIA recommended procedure for field testing multimode and singlemode fiber optic cabling systems.

While other fiber optic cabling system parameters such as bandwidth are as important as attenuation, they are not normally affected by the quality of the installation and therefore, do not require field testing. This part of the chapter describes how and where attenuation testing should be performed, based upon the architecture of the cabling system. A general equation is given to calculate acceptable attenuation values along with detailed examples covering both hierarchical star and single point administration architectures.

Passive Link Segments

Attenuation testing should be performed on each passive link segment of the cabling system prior to installation. A link segment consists of the cable, connectors, couplings, and splices between two fiber optic termination units (patch panels, information outlets, etc.). Each terminated fiber within a link segment should be tested. The link segment attenuation measurement includes the representative attenuation of connectors at the termination unit interface on both ends of the link, but does not include the attenuation associated with the active equipment interface. This is illustrated in Figure 14-6 [4].

There are three basic types of link segments described in this part of the chapter, horizontal, backbone, and composite. A horizontal link segment normally begins at the telecommunications outlet and ends at the horizontal cross-connect. The telecommunications outlet may be a multiuser outlet placed in an open office area. The horizontal link segment may also include a consolidation point interconnection or a transition point splice. A riser backbone link segment usually begins at the main cross-connect and ends at the horizontal cross-connect. For the purpose of this chapter, a tie cable placed between two horizontal cross-connects and a campus cable typically placed between two

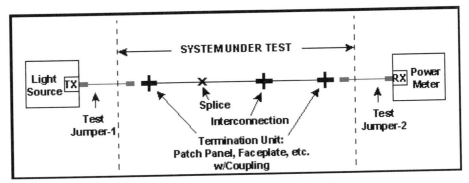

Figure 14-6: Tested link segment.

main cross-connects are both considered backbone link segments. A single point administration architecture eliminates the horizontal cross-connect, and as a result, horizontal and backbone cabling are combined into a composite link segment. In this case, the horizontal closet may contain a splice, interconnect, or pulled-through cable.

NOTE:

Spliced pigtail terminations at one or both ends of a horizontal, backbone, or composite link are permitted.

General Pre-installation Testing Guidelines

The following are the general pre-installation guidelines that all organizations should follow:

- Multimode horizontal link segments should be tested in one direction at the 850 nm or 1300 nm wavelength.
- Multimode backbone and composite link segments should be tested in one direction at both 850 nm and 1300 nm wavelengths.
- Singlemode horizontal link segments should be tested in one direction at the 1310 nm or 1550 nm wavelength.
- Singlemode backbone and composite link segments should be tested in one direction at both 1310 nm and 1550 nm wavelengths [Lucent, 2].

NOTE:

The minor attenuation differences due to test direction are on par with the accuracy and repeatability of the test method. Therefore, testing in only one direction is warranted. Horizontal link segments are limited to 90 meters. Therefore, attenuation differences caused by wavelength are insignificant, and as a result, single wavelength testing is sufficient. Also, typical attenuation for 62.5/125 multimode fiber is 3.5 dB/km at 850 nm and 1.0 dB/km at 1300 nm. And typical attenuations for singlemode 125 micron fiber are 0.5 dB/km at 1310 nm and 0.4 dB/km at 1550 nm.

In compliance with EIA/TIA-526-14A (Optical Power Loss Measurements of Installed Multimode Fiber Cable Plant) and EIA/TIA-526-7 (Measurement of Optical Power Loss of Installed Singlemode Fiber Cable Plant), the following information should be recorded during the test procedure:

1. Names of personnel conducting the test.
2. Type of test equipment used (manufacturer, model, serial number).
3. Date test is performed.
4. Optical source wavelength, spectral width, and, for multimode, the coupled power ratio (CPR).
5. Fiber identification.
6. End point locations.
7. Test direction.
8. Reference power measurement (when not using a power meter with a Relative Power Measurement Mode).
9. Measured attenuation of the link segment.
10. Acceptable link attenuation [Lucent, 3].

NOTE:

Horizontal link segments are limited to 90 meters; therefore, the acceptable link attenuation can be based on the longest installed link without introducing a significant error.

Acceptable Attenuation Values

The general attenuation equation for any link segment is as follows:
Acceptable Link Attn. = Cable Attn. + Connection Attn. + Splice Attn. + CPR Adj.

See the sidebar, "62.5µm Multimode and Singlemode Attenuation Coefficients," for further information.

NOTE:

A connection is defined as the joint made by mating two fibers terminated with remateable connectors (ST, SC, LC).

62.5µm Multimode and Singlemode Attenuation Coefficients

The following are the 62.5µm Multimode And Singlemode Attenuation Coefficients:

62.5µm Multimode Attenuation Coefficients:

Cable Attn. = Cable Length (km) X (3.40 dB/km@850nm or 1.00 dB/km@1300nm)

Connection Attn. (ST or SC connectors) = Connections X 0.39 dB) + 0.42 dB

Connection Attn. (LC connectors) = Connections X 0.14 dB) + 0.24 dB

Splice Attn. CSL or Fusion) = Splices X 0.30 dB

CPR Adj. = See Table 14–7 [Lucent, 4].

Singlemode Attenuation Coefficients:

Cable Attn. = Cable Length (km) X (0.50 dB/km@1310nm or 0.50 dB/km@1550nm)

Connection Attn. (ST or SC connectors) = Connections X 0.44 dB) + 0.42 dB

Connection Attn. (LC connectors) = Connections X 0.24 dB) + 0.24 dB

Splice Attn. (CSL or Fusion) = Splices X 0.30 dB

CPR Adj. = 0.00 dB (Not applicable for singlemode) [Lucent, 3-4].

Table 14–7: CPR adjustment.

| | Multimode Light Source CPR Adjustment | | | | |
	Category 1	Category 2	Category 3	Category 4	Category 5
Links with ST or SC SC Connections	+ 0.50	0.00	–0.25	–0.50	–0.75
Links with LC Connections	+ 0.25	0.00	–0.10	–-0.20	–0.30

NOTE:

The sidebar, "Coupled Power Ratio Measurement," describes the test procedure to categorize a multimode light source's Coupled Power Ratio (CPR).

Coupled Power Ratio Measurement

The Coupled Power Ratio of a light source is a measure of the modal power distribution launched into a multimode fiber. A light source that launches a higher percentage of its power into the higher order modes of a multimode fiber produces a more over-filled condition and is classified as a lower Category than a light source that launches more of its power into just the lower order modes producing an under-filled condition. Under-filled conditions result in lower link attenuation, while over-filled conditions produce higher attenuation. Therefore, adjusting the acceptable link attenuation equation to compensate for a light source's launch characteristics increases the accuracy of the test procedure.

Procedure:

CPR Test Jumper-1 shall be multimode, 1 – 5 meters long with connectors compatible with the light source and power meter and have the same fiber construction as the link segment being tested. CPR Test Jumper-2 shall be singlemode, 1 – 5 meters long with connectors compatible with the light source and power meter. The step-by-step procedure is as follows:

1. Clean the test jumper connectors and the test coupling per manufacturer's instructions.

2. Follow the test equipment manufacturer's initial adjustment instructions.

3. Connect multimode test jumper-1 between the light source and the power meter. Avoid placing bends in the jumper that are less than 100 mm (4 inches) in diameter. See Figure 14–7 [Lucent, 11].

4. If the power meter has a Relative Power Measurement Mode, select it. If it does not, record the Reference Power Measurement (P_{ref}).

Note: If the meter can display power levels in dBm, select this unit of measurement to simplify subsequent calculations.

5. Disconnect test jumper-1 from the power meter. Do NOT disconnect the test jumper from the light source.

6. Connect jumper-2 between the power meter and test jumper-1 using the test coupling. The singlemode jumper should include a high order mode filter. This can be accomplished by wrapping the jumper three times around a 30 mm (1.2 inches) diameter mandrel. See Figure 14–8 [Lucent, 12].

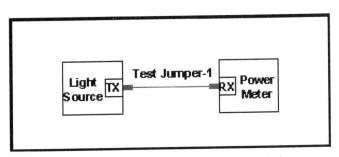

Figure 14–7: Connecting multimode test jumper-1 between the light source and the power meter.

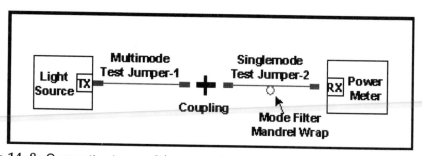

Figure 14–8: Connecting jumper-2 between the power meter and test jumper-1 using the test coupling.

      7. Record the Power Measurement (P_{sum}). If the power meter is in Relative Power Measurement Mode, the meter reading represents the CPR value (See Table 14–8) [Lucent, 12]. If the meter does not have a Relative Power Measurement Mode, perform the following calculation:

If P_{sum} and P_{ref} are in the same logarithmic units (dBm, dBu, etc):
$$CPR (dB) = | P_{sum} - P_{ref} |$$

If P_{sum} and P_{ref} are in watts: $CPR (dB) = | 10 \times log10 [P_{sum}/P_{ref}] |$

Table 14–8: Coupled Power Ratio (CPR) in dB by Category.

	Coupled Power Ratio (CPR) in dB				
	Category 1 Overfilled	Category 2	Category-3	Category 4	Category 5 Underfilled
850 nm Source	25 – 29	21 – 24.9	14 – 20.9	7 – 13.9	0 – 6.9
1300 nm Source	21 – 25	17 – 20.9	12 – 16.9	7 – 11.9	0 – 6.9

Hierarchical Star Architecture: Backbone Link Segment

      Figure 14–9 shows a multimode 160-meter riser cable placed between the main cross-connect and the horizontal cross-connect containing a mid-span fusion splice [Lucent, 4]. All fibers are terminated with ST connectors. The acceptable link attenuation is calculated as follows:

Category-2 850nm light source:
Acceptable Link Attn = Cable Attn + Connection Attn + Splice Attn + CPR Adj
Acceptable Link Attn = [0.160 × 3.40] + [(2 × 0.39) + 0.42] + [1 × 0.30] + 0.00
Acceptable Link Attn = 2.044 dB

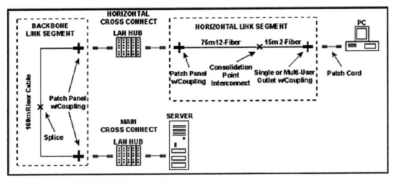

Figure 14–9: Hierarchical star architecture.

Category-2 1300nm light source:

Acceptable Link Attn = Cable Attn + Connection Attn + Splice Attn + CPR Adj
Acceptable Link Attn = [0.160 X 1.00] + [(2 X 0.39) + 0.42] + [1 X 0.30] + 0.00
Acceptable Link Attn = 1.66 dB

Horizontal Link Segment

Figure 14–9 also shows a multimode 75-meter, 12-fiber, horizontal cable placed between the horizontal cross-connect and a consolidation point (interconnection) located in an open office area. From the consolidation point a total of four, multimode, 15-meter, 2-fiber cables are distributed to modular furniture outlets, leaving four spare fibers of the horizontal cable for future use. All fibers are terminated with ST connectors. The acceptable link attenuation is calculated as follows:

Category 2 850 nm light source:

Acceptable Link Attn = Cable Attn + Connection Attn + Splice Attn + CPR Adj
Acceptable Link Attn = [0.075 X 3.40] + [(2 X 0.39) + 0.42]
Acceptable Link Attn = 1.46 dB

NOTE:

In the preceding Category 2 850 nm light source calculation, horizontal link segments begin at the horizontal cross-connect and end at the consolidation point (spare fibers).

Category 2 850 nm light source:

Acceptable Link Attn = Cable Attn + Connection Attn + Splice Attn + CPR Adj
Acceptable Link Attn = [(0.075 + 0.015) X 3.40] + [(3 X 0.39) + 0.42]
Acceptable Link Attn = 1.896 dB

NOTE:

In the preceding Category 2 850 nm light source calculation, horizontal link segments begin at the horizontal cross-connect and end in modular furniture outlets.

Single Point Administration Architecture: Composite Link Segment

Figure 14–10 shows a multimode 50-meter, 72-fiber, riser cable placed between the main cross-connect and the closet serving the horizontal [Lucent, 6]. From the closet a total of four, multimode, 75-meter, 12-fiber horizontal cables are interconnected to the riser cable and are distributed to consolidation points (interconnections) located in open office areas, leaving twenty-four spare fibers of the riser cable for future use. From each consolidation point a total of four, multimode, 15-meter, 2-fiber cables are distributed to modular furniture outlets, leaving four spare fibers of each horizontal cable for future use. All fibers are terminated with LC connectors. The acceptable link attenuation is calculated as follows:

Category 3 850 nm light source:
Acceptable Link Attn = Cable Attn + Connection Attn + Splice Attn + CPR Adj
Acceptable Link Attn = [0.050 X 3.40] + [(2 X 0.14) + 0.24] - 0.10
Acceptable Link Attn = 0.59 dB

Category 1 1300 nm light source:
Acceptable Link Attn = Cable Attn + Connection Attn + Splice Attn + CPR Adj
Acceptable Link Attn = [0.050 X 1.00] + [(2 X 0.14) + 0.24] + 0.25
Acceptable Link Attn = 0.82 dB

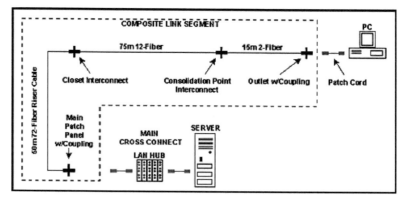

Figure 14–10: Single point administration architecture.

NOTE:

In the preceding Category 3 850 nm light source and Category 1 1300 nm light source calculations, link segments begin at the main cross-connect and end at the horizontal closet (spare riser fibers).

Category 3 850 nm light source:
Acceptable Link Attn = Cable Attn + Connection Attn + Splice Attn + CPR Adj
Acceptable Link Attn = [(0.050 + 0.075) X 3.40] + [(3 X 0.14) + 0.24] - 0.10
Acceptable Link Attn = 0.985 dB

Category 1 1300 nm light source:
Acceptable Link Attn = Cable Attn + Connection Attn + Splice Attn + CPR Adj
Acceptable Link Attn = [(0.050 + 0.075) X 1.00] + [(3 X 0.14) + 0.24] + 0.25
Acceptable Link Attn = 1.04 dB

NOTE:

In the preceding Category 3 850 nm light source and Category 1 1300 nm light source calculations, link segments begin at the main cross-connect and end at the consolidation point interconnect (spare fibers).

Category 3 850 nm light source:
Acceptable Link Attn = Cable Attn + Connection Attn + Splice Attn + CPR Adj
Acceptable Link Attn = [(0.050 + 0.075 + 0.015) X 3.40] + [(4 X 0.14) + 0.24] - 0.10
Acceptable Link Attn = 1.18 dB

Category 1 1300 nm light source:
Acceptable Link Attn = Cable Attn + Connection Attn + Splice Attn + CPR Adj
Acceptable Link Attn = [(0.050 + 0.075 + 0.015) X 1.00] + [(4 X 0.14) + 0.24] + 0.25
Acceptable Link Attn = 1.19 dB

NOTE:

In the preceding Category 3 850 nm light source and Category 1 1300 nm light source calculations, link segments begin at the main cross-connect and end in modular furniture outlets.

Test Procedure

In compliance with EIA/TIA-526-14A and EIA/TIA-526-7, test jumpers shall be 1 to 5 meters long. They shall have the same fiber construction (core diameter and numerical aperture) as the link segment being tested. The sidebar,

"Test Jumper Performance Verification," describes the procedure to test jumper performance verification.

Test Jumper Performance Verification

The step-by-step procedure is as follows:

1. Clean the test jumper connectors and the test coupling per the manufacturer's instructions.

2. Follow the test equipment manufacturer's initial adjustment instructions.

3. Connect test jumper-2 between the light source and the power meter. See Figure 14–11 [Lucent, 8].

4. If the power meter has a Relative Power Measurement Mode, select it. If it does not, record the Reference Power Measurement (P_{ref}). If the meter can display power levels in dBm, select this unit of measurement to simplify subsequent calculations.

5. Disconnect test jumper-2 from the power meter. Do NOT disconnect the test jumper from the light source.

6. Connect jumper-1 between the power meter and test jumper-2 using the test coupling. See Figure 14–12 [Lucent, 8].

7. Record the Power Measurement (P_{sum}). If the power meter is in Relative Power Measurement Mode, the meter reading represents the connection attenuation. If the meter does not have a Relative Power Measurement Mode, perform the following calculation to determine the connection attenuation:

If P_{sum} and P_{ref} are in the same logarithmic units (dBm, dBu, etc):

Connection Attenuation (dB) = $| P_{sum} - P_{ref} |$

If P_{sum} and P_{ref} are in watts:

Connection Attenuation (dB) = $| 10 \times \log10 [P_{sum}/P_{ref}] |$

The measured connection attenuation must be less than or equal to the value found in Table 14–9 [Lucent, 9].

8. Flip the ends of test jumper-1 so that the end connected to the power meter is now connected to the coupling, and the end connected to the coupling is now connected to the power meter.

9. Record the new Power Measurement (P_{sum}). Perform the proper calculations if not using Relative Power Measurement Mode and verify that the connection attenuation is less than or equal to the value found in Table 14–9.

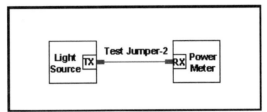

Figure 14–11: The connection of the test jumper-2 between the light source and the power meter.

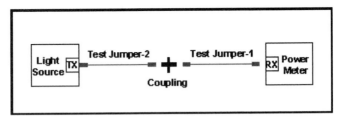

Figure 14–12: The connection of the jumper-1 between the power meter and test jumper-2 using the test coupling.

Table 14–9: Test jumper connection attenuation.

| | Acceptable Test Jumper Connection Attenuation | |
	ST or SC Jumper	**LC Jumper**
Multimode	0.50 dB Max	0.20 dB Max
Singlemode	0.55 dB Max	0.30 dB Max

If both measurements are found to be less than or equal to the values found in Table 14–9, test jumper-1 is acceptable for testing purposes. You should note that unacceptable link segment attenuation measurements may be attributable to test jumper-1 or test jumper-2 (see Table 14–10) [Lucent, 10]. Examine each jumper with a portable microscope and clean, polish, or replace if necessary.

NOTE:

Repeat this test procedure from the beginning reversing jumpers 1 and 2 in order to verify the performance of test jumper-2.

Table 14–10: Troubleshooting unacceptable link segment attenuation

Possible Cause	Resolution
Epoxy bead left on the tip of a connector.	Examine connectors with a portable microscope and repolish if necessary.
Poorly polished connectors.	Examine connectors with a portable microscope and repolish if necessary.
Dirty connectors and/or couplings.	Examine connections and clean per manufacturer's instructions.
Poor splices due to fiber misalignment either mechanically or prior to fusing.	Identify poor splices with an Optical Time Domain Reflectmeter (OTDR) and resplice if necessary.
Macro-bending of fibers in patch panels and splice cases caused by bends smaller than the minimum bend radius specification.	Identify macro-bends by inspection or with an OTDR and remove or increase bend radius where necessary.

NOTE:

OTDRs are also used to reveal many undesirable cable conditions, including shorts, opens, and transmissions anomalies due to excessive bends or crushing as referenced in Table 14–10.

Link Segment Testing

The One Reference Jumper Method specified in EIA/TIA-526-14A and EIA/TIA-526-7 should be used to test each link segment. The procedure is summarized in the sidebar, "Link Segment Testing Procedure."

Link Segment Testing Procedure

The step-by-step procedure is as follows:

1. Connect known good (see the sidebar, "Test Jumper Performance Verification") test jumper-1 between the light source and the power meter. See Figure 14–13 [Lucent, 9].

2. Record the Reference Power Measurement (P_{ref}) or select the power meter's Relative Power Measurement Mode. If the meter can display power levels in dBm, select this unit of measurement to simplify subsequent calculations.

3. Disconnect jumper-1 from the power meter and connect it to the link segment. *Do NOT disconnect the test jumper from the light source.*

4. Connect known good (see the sidebar, "Test Jumper Performance Verification") test jumper-2 between the far end of the link segment and the power meter. See Figure 14–14 [Lucent, 10].

5. Record the Power Measurement (P_{sum}). If the power meter is in Relative Power Measurement Mode, the meter reading represents the attenuation associated with the link segment. If this value is less than or equal to the value calculated using the attenuation equation (see the section "Acceptable Attenuation Values" earlier in the chapter), the link segment is acceptable. If the meter does not have a Relative Power Measurement Mode, perform the following calculation to determine the attenuation of the link segment:

If P_{sum} and P_{ref} are in the same logarithmic units (dBm, dBu, etc):
Link Segment Attenuation (dB) = | P_{sum} - P_{ref} |

If P_{sum} and P_{ref} are in watts:
Link Segment Attenuation (dB) = | 10 X log10 [P_{sum}/P_{ref}] |

Code Compliance and/or Safety Recommendations and Considerations

Now that the pre-installation activities of testing the cable and components are out of the way, let's proceed to the final pre-installation activities, code compliance and/or safety recommendations and considerations. In order to ensure that safe conditions exist during the installation of your cabling system, the following guidelines should be adhered to as part of your installation activities:

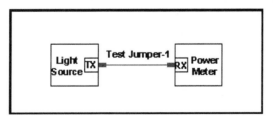

Figure 14–13: The connection of the known good test jumper-1 between the light source and the power meter.

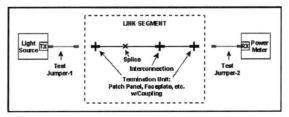

Figure 14–14: The connection of the known good test jumper-2 between the far end of the link segment and the power meter.

- Do not perform any action that makes the equipment unsafe or creates a potential hazard to people.
- Do not wear loose clothing that could get caught in the chassis. Roll up your sleeves and fasten your scarf or tie.
- During and after installation, keep the chassis area dust-free and clear.
- Keep tools away from walk areas where you and others could trip over them.
- When working under any conditions that might be hazardous to your eyes, wear safety glasses [Cisco, 1].

NOTE:

If the far end is connected to an LED or laser, unterminated connectors may emit radiation. Be absolutely sure that the fiber is disconnected from any laser or LED source before viewing the end of a cable.

Safety with Equipment Powered by Electricity

Follow these guidelines when working on equipment powered by electricity:

1. In the room in which you are working, locate the emergency power-off switch. Then, you can act quickly to turn off the power, if an electrical accident occurs.

NOTE:

Before you connect the system to its power source, read the installation instructions.

2. Unplug the power cord before working on the system.
3. Before doing any of the following, disconnect all power:
   - Installing or removing a chassis.
   - Performing a hardware upgrade.
   - Working near power supplies.

NOTE:

During periods of lightning activity, do not work on the system or connect or disconnect cables. Also, when the power cord is connected, do not touch the power supply. In addition, line voltages are present

within the power supply even when the power switch is off and the power cord is connected for systems with a power switch. On the other hand, line voltages are present within the power supply when the power cord is connected for systems without a power switch.

4. If potentially hazardous conditions exist, do not work alone.
5. Never assume that the power is disconnected from a circuit. Always check.

NOTE:

For short-circuit (overcurrent) protection, certain electrical-powered equipment usually relies on the building's installation. Ensure that a fuse or circuit breaker no larger than 120 VAC, 15A U.S. (240 VAC, 10A international) is used on the phase conductors (all current-carrying conductors). Also, some equipment is designed to work with telephone network (TN) power systems. Additionally, unplug the power cord on AC units and disconnect the power at the circuit breaker on DC units before working on a chassis or working near power supplies.

6. Look carefully for possible hazards in your work area, such as missing safety grounds, moist floors, and ungrounded power extension cables.
7. Proceed as follows if an electrical accident occurs:
   * Unplug the power cord.
   * Use caution. Do not become a victim yourself.

Send another person to get medical aid if possible. Otherwise, if appropriate, assess the condition of the victim and then call for help. Take appropriate action after determining if the person needs rescue breathing or external cardiac compressions.

Preventing Electrostatic Discharge Damage

Electrostatic discharge (ESD) can impair electrical circuitry and damage equipment. It occurs when electronic components are improperly handled. ESD can also result in complete or intermittent failures. When replacing and removing components, always follow ESD-prevention procedures. Ensure that the chassis is electrically connected to earth ground using a ground wire or an ESD mat. Wear an ESD-preventive wrist strap—ensuring that it makes good skin contact. Connect the clip to an unpainted surface of the chassis frame to safely channel unwanted ESD voltages to ground. The wrist strap and cord

must operate effectively in order to properly guard against ESD damage and shocks. Ground yourself by touching the metal part of the chassis if no wrist strap is available.

NOTE:

> Periodically check the resistance value of the antistatic strap(for safety's sake)—which should be between 1 and 10 megohm (Mohm). In addition, if the battery is replaced incorrectly, there is danger of explosion. Replace the battery only with the same or equivalent type recommended by the manufacturer. Used batteries should be disposed of in accordance with the manufacturer's instructions. Finally, the ultimate disposal of batteries should be handled in accordance with all national laws and regulations.

From Here

This chapter began Part IV by taking a look at the Installation of the Cabling System. The chapter opened up with a presentation on Testing Techniques as part of pre-installation activities by taking a look at the preparation of cable facilities, testing the cable and components, and code compliance and safety considerations. Chapter 15 describes in detail the installation of the cabling system and covers specific areas such as core drilling considerations; conduit installation and fill guidelines; grounding, shielding and safety; pulling the cable without damage; splicing and patching; blown fiber; labeling schemes; and quality control and installation standards, etc.

End Notes

1   "Preparing For Installation," (Some material in this book has been reproduced by Prentice Hall with the permission of Cisco Systems Inc.), COPYRIGHT © 1998 Cisco Systems, Inc., ALL RIGHTS RESERVED, 170 West Tasman Drive, San Jose, CA 95134-1706, USA, 1997, pp. 4–5.

2   Fibre Optic Communications Ltd, Unit 2F, Marchwood Industrial Estate, Normandy Way, Marchwood, Southampton, SO40 4PB, UK, 1998.

3   Mark Johnston, "Transmission Performance Specifications for Field Testing of Unshielded Twisted-Pair Cabling Systems," Microtext, Inc., Cable Technology, Inc., 10 Grumbacher Road, York, PA, 1997, pp. 2–3.

4   "SYSTIMAX® SCS Field Testing Guidelines for Fiber Optic Cabling Systems," Lucent Technologies Inc. , 600 Mountain Avenue, Murray Hill NJ 07974, U.S.A., (Copyright © 1996), pp. 1–2.

15

INSTALLATION

Computers today play a significant role in everyday life. Widespread use of computers in nearly every field means that students without computer literacy have limited options. School districts and universities have taken up the challenge of teaching students how to use computers. Most teachers and professors, while highly trained, do not have the technical experience needed to design and support a district or university computer cabling system.

This chapter provides a step-by-step approach to installing a cabling system for a university, school, or district and is intended for teachers, technical coordinators, and administrators. It provides much of the necessary information that personnel will need while installing cabling technology in their district or university.

Installing a Cabling System

Once a district or university has developed a cabling system plan for each of the buildings it will include in the network (see Figure 15–1), the next step is to replace the generic parts of the plan with specifications for actual equipment and wiring [1]. Following that is the installation of the equipment and wiring in a building. When this is completed, the network is ready for use.

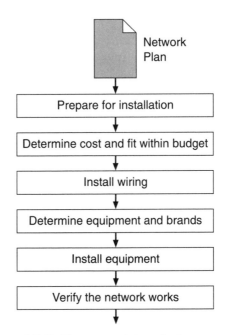

Figure 15–1: The network installation process.

This chapter focuses on the different options available for installing a cabling system. It discusses guidelines for the installation first, including specifications for horizontal, intrabuilding, and interbuilding wiring. Then it presents the different equipment used in a LAN. After that, it presents a similar discussion about WAN equipment. The chapter concludes with an examination of the role software plays in the cabling system.

General Guidelines

Once the network plan has been developed for a building, it is time to plan the installation itself. Before starting the installation, time spent determining how the installation will proceed can save significant amounts of time and headaches later.

For instance, the installation of electrical equipment, cables, and wiring should be conducted in such a manner as to maintain the integrity of fire stopping, fire resistance, fire separation, smoke control, and zoning in ceilings, plenums, voids, and similar spaces. The installation should be in accordance with the National Fire Protection Association (NFPA), the National Electrical Code (NEC), Telecommunications Industry Association (TIA), Electronic Industry Association (EIA), and local building codes.

Installation Suggestions

The first step therefore, should be to obtain accurate plans for the building. Many school districts and universities do not have plans for some of their buildings, so the designers should use whatever maps are available. In any case, be sure to verify the distances before installing the wiring, since the maps may be inaccurate or out of date. This can be done using a distance wheel, often available from the athletic department of a school or university campus. In areas where the designer cannot take accurate measurements, estimate the distances but try to be on the conservative side. Be sure to never estimate wiring distances to the exact foot since errors will always appear and measuring too accurately may not leave enough room to work around the problems. Remember that besides the horizontal distances, the wiring will also need to run up and down walls. Always leave 10 to 15 percent of the maximum distance available unused to allow for the distance needed to connect a machine to the wall and to connect equipment at the hub. For example, Ethernet specifies a maximum cable length of 100 meters. At most, a wire should only run 90 meters from the hub to the wall drop. See the sidebar, "Checklist for Wiring Installations," for additional information on wiring installation for school and university campuses.

Checklist for Wiring Installations

The following checklist should be used to assure that any new wiring proposed and/or installed by campus departments or contractors conforms to the proposed campus communications cabling standard:

1. Is there a a a scope of work document which contains the following information?

- A list of all rooms to be wired and the end-to-end route for the cable.
- The type of ceiling tiles used in rooms or hallways which may be entered for wire placement. Have a plan to replace broken tiles.
- A determination if the ceiling area is of plenum or non-plenum construction.
- Identification of conduits, and existing cables, which may be used for cable placement.
- Identification of wall construction on which communications outlets will be mounted.
- Location of backboard space for wire termination and patch panels in serving communications subterminal.
- Location of firewalls, because it can be very expensive, time-consuming, and frustrating to find out that a brick firewall is between you and a telecommunications closet.

2. If required by the proposed installation, has contact been made with Facilities Management and/or Environmental Health and Safety?

3. Is the wire to be placed compatible with the campus communications cabling standard?

4. Does an installation manual exist to guide the placement and termination of the proposed wiring?

5. Has provision been made to provide wall plates or touch-up plaster and painting to repair damaged wall surfaces?

6. Does a testing and acceptance procedure exist applicable to the proposed installation and to the campus standard?

7. Do documentation formats and forms exist to guide the installation and provide permanent reference after installation, testing, and acceptance?

8. Has documentation been prepared which defines the materials and configuration for jumper cables to be used at the workstation end and at the patch panels [2]?

While measuring the distances, take a chance to visually inspect all the locations where running wiring for any potential problems such as electrical power sources or unusually thick walls. When running cable or wiring, it is best to follow a few simple rules:

- Always use more cable than you need. Leave plenty of slack.
- Test every part of a network as you install it. Even if it is brand new, it may have problems that will be difficult to isolate later.
- Stay at least 3 feet away from fluorescent light boxes and other sources of electrical interference.
- If it is necessary to run cable across the floor, cover the cable with cable protectors.
- Label both ends of each cable.
- Use cable ties (not tape) to keep cables in the same location together. Velcro straps are becoming very popular for keeping cables together with the ability to remove them easily if needed.

Look for places to run the wiring, ideally through a dropped ceiling, cable trays, and previously drilled holes. If the building does not have dropped ceilings available, and has not already installed cable trays, then it is recommended that the school district or university install cable trays for the wiring. These are simply plastic or wooden trays attached to the walls or ceilings in which to place wiring. Their advantage over running the wiring in conduit is that they allow easy access to the wiring if a problem occurs, and can easily accommodate additional wiring in the future. Look for locations where other accessories such as base plates, face plates, wire mold (for containing vertical wiring), and raceways (for containing wiring running across a floor) will need installation. The designer should note these also and prepare them for installation as well.

A school district or university should be sure that it follows all the local and state fire codes for a school building. In many cases, this will require the use of plenum-rated wiring, which although more expensive, does not produce any toxic fumes when it burns below a certain temperature. Also, cutting holes in firewalls to allow cable access should be done carefully so that fire codes are not violated. A qualified electrician or architect can provide fire code information.

Another problem that may appear is the use of multiple power feeds into a building. This can happen if a building has been expanded. If the feeds to the building come from different transformers, the ground voltage on each feed may not be exactly the same. This can lead to problems with electrical equipment connected across the differently powered parts of the building, potentially destroying computer equipment. If the situation exists, then the use of specially insulated equipment or the use of fiber cable (which does not conduct electricity) is recommended. If the school district or university is unsure about the power of the building, it should contact a qualified electrician or representative of the power company for more information.

Installation Tips

If a school district or university is going to attempt to install the cabling system using volunteer or untrained staff, the person who will be leading the process should receive extensive training that they can share with the others. This may include talking to qualified electricians and getting training from other schools that have already done the installation.

NOTE:

> Cable construction work should be performed by experienced contractor personnel in placing cables in conduit, cable trays, underground duct systems, and in indirect burial methods.
> Communication cable splices and terminations should be performed by experienced journeymen cable splicers.

For a school district or university considering installing the cabling system themselves, the sidebar, "List of Equipment Needed to Install a Cabling System in a School," shows a list of the equipment needed. As previously discussed, some of the wiring requirements are very strict about where the wiring can and cannot be run. A district should be sure to understand and follow all the requirements. A failure during this part can render the entire cabling system unusable, or even worse, cause intermittent, untraceable problems.

List of Equipment Needed to Install a Cabling System in a School

General:

1. Crimping tool/die sets for RJ45 plugs and receptacles.

2. Standard hand tools including pliers, screwdrivers, a hammer, and wire cutters.

3. 3/8" - 1/2" power drill, 12" drill bit extension, 1/4" and 5/8" masonry drill bits.

4. 50' steel fish tape.

5. 70 lb test nylon masonry twine.

6. 6' and 8' fiberglass ladders (aluminum ladders are not recommended because of their ability to conduct electricity).

Materials:

1. Mushroom boards or D-Rings to support all workstation cables and cross-connects.

2. Cable labelers or black Sharpie markers (one color only) for labeling all workstation cables, termination punch-down blocks, and RJ11 jacks. . Label all INS (JIN) concentrators pigtail cables with self-sticking vinyl cloth wire markers. Cable labelers are better than magic markers—the information is printed on a vinyl material that, when wrapped around the cable, is covered with clear vinyl/plastic. Cable labelers are durable and very easy to use.

3. Teflon cable with one style and color only. Use Category 3 (4-Pair) cable (16 Mbps Data) EIA/TIA-568, 10BaseT for all workstation cabling.

4. Wall insert caddie bracket clips when running cables in walls.

5. 110 Blocks (Category 5) and 66M150 Blocks (Category 3).

6. Standard ivory wall molding for all buildings unless otherwise specified.

7. One (1) ivory (voice) RJ11 jack and one (1) brown (data) RJ11 jack at each end user location.

8. Color coordinated backboards for all terminal blocks in communication closets as follows:

- Yellow Back Boards—Riser Cables.
- Blue Back Boards—Station Cables.
- Green Back Boards—Data Blocks.

Circuits / Cross-Connects:

1. One 1-pair cross-connect (W/BL-BL/W) for each analog and digital ROLM application, fax machine, modem, STU-111.

2. One 1- pair cross-connect (W-R) for each coax elimination circuits.

3. One 2-pair cross-connect (W/BL-BL/W & W/O-O/W) for each CTSDN data circuit.

4. One 2-pair cross-connect (R/BL-BL/R & R/O-O/R) for each INS (JIN) LAN circuit.

5. One 3-pair cross-connect (W/BL-BL/W & W/O-O/W & W/GRN-GRN/W) for each teleconference voice circuit.

6. One 4-pair cross-connect (W/BL-BL/W & W/O-O/W & W/GRN-GRN/W & Y/BL-BL/Y) for each 1A2 key system.

7. Orange color tags to tag all data and LAN circuits at both ends.

8. T1 shielded cable for all T1 type circuits and cross-connects.

To pull wiring throughout a school building, a frame or other device from which to pull the wire is necessary. Most wire is delivered on 1,000-foot rolls. An ordinary two-wheel hand truck can function as a relatively compact unit from which four standard spools can be pulled simultaneously. This unit can then double as a means for moving wire about the building.

In cases where the network cable is pulled through drop ceilings (very common in most modern schools and universities), some type of twine, lead, line, or fish-tape needs to be used. A wide variety of such materials is available. Some schools have used 70-pound test nylon masonry twine with success. With a weight on the end, the twine is light enough the designer can toss the twine 20-30 feet horizontally through a drop ceiling and run no risk of snapping it when the cable is pulled.

X-ray and Hole Core Drilling Considerations

The contractor should supply all vertical and horizontal hole cores. X-ray of proposed core locations must be performed prior to coring. Under no circumstances should x-rays be performed without the prior notification and approval of the cabling system project manager (PM). When site conditions do not make it feasible to x-ray, the contractor should exercise reasonable judgment to evaluate whether there is a chance that coring will cause the severing of electrical, low voltage, or any other services that may be in the structure that is being penetrated. The use of hammer chisels may be necessary in some buildings. A thorough inspection of both sides of the surfaces must be performed. A flux scanner to check for live loaded AC should be used prior to any drilling, coring, or chiseling.

Where applicable, the opening of drop ceilings on the undersides of floors, including fixed surfaces, should be done to expose the break-through area. Small-diameter pilot holes should be drilled prior to the final coring or chiseling. A qualified electrician with access to a circuit scanner should be present during coring or chiseling in case any services are severed. Should services be severed, the campus (if it's a university) police should be contacted immediately using an emergency number. The PM should also be notified of these occurrences immediately. Depending on the circumstance, the contractor may be asked to begin restoration procedures of severed services immediately.

Any penetration of structural beams, columns, or supports should be cleared by the PM before proceeding. Patching and restoration of coring is the responsibility of the contractor.

Conduit Installation and Fill Guidelines

All conduit should be EMT type, installed with steel, set-screw fittings except on the exterior of the building, where the fittings should be rigid galvanized steel with threaded connectors. Conduit should be installed in compliance with prevailing codes and standards. Conduits should be installed at right angles and parallel to building grids.

NOTE:

Interference drawings must be submitted prior to commencing with the installation of conduits. These drawings must indicate the conduit routing and pull box locations with reference measurements from two walls or permanent fixtures. Include construction notes describing elevation changes, wall penetrations, and information with regard to existing fixtures that may be affected by the installation of the conduit. Neatly drawn routing and notes on the floor plans provided with the tender is an acceptable format.

Pull strings should be supplied in all new and reworked conduit. No pull elbows or LBs should be installed anywhere. Only sweep- or 90-degree elbows should be used and no more than two 90-degree bends are permitted between pull boxes. The minimum radius of curvature should be 10 times the conduit internal diameter (ID).

In telecommunications closets, the conduit should be installed parallel to the backboard with a 90-degree bend toward the floor or enter within 10 inches of and parallel to the cable tray. Also, all conduit ends should be fitted with plastic bushings.

All exposed conduit and junction boxes should be painted to match the existing environment. All conduits and pull boxes should be treated and cleaned prior to painting. The conduit should have one coat of primer paint, one intermediate coat, and one or more finished coats of paint. Any color other than the existing environment must be approved by the owner prior to use.

The maximum distance of conduit run between two pull boxes should be 30 meters. The pull box should have a screw-type cover, not hinged. All pull boxes should be accessible with a minimum 24 x 24 inch hinged access hatch provided where required. Pull boxes for vertical conduits should be installed to provide a straight pass-through for vertical cables. The sizes of junction boxes should be 8 times the size of the inside diameter size of the conduit entering it. The exception is when 4-inch conduit is used, then 30 x 24 x 6 inch junction boxes are acceptable. Pull boxes are not to be installed in elevator machine rooms. Conduits installed in elevator machine rooms should provide maximum clearance and should not restrict the service area.

When conduit is installed in utility closets, the conduit should be installed in a steel sleeve that is 6 inches high. Here, the gap between the floor and the sleeve has to be water-tight. Also, all wall and floor penetrations should be filled as per code and finished to match the existing surface.

Flexible Conduit or Innerduct Tubing

Innerduct tubing is not to be used unless it is specified in the detailed scope of work. If tubing is specified, the inside surface (the surface inside the tubing) should have a smooth finish that will allow it to be finished.

Tubing should also resist crushing pressures and should not collapse within normal bending limits. It should have a diameter of not less than 1 inch.

The contractor should supply tubing that has manufacturers specifications that are in sync with the installation requirements. Tubing may also be specified wherever fiber cable may be subjected to bending forces that would place it at risk of damage.

Tubing may be specified in transitions when in- and out-of-conduit pathways do not line up. Tubing may also be specified in telecommunications closets when cable needs to be installed in free air when other support structures are not feasible.

Tubing should not be used to overcome problems induced through bad installation practices of other components. The fastening of ends of tubing to conduit, racks or trays, should be through mechanically sound fittings, not plastic tie wraps.

Grounding, Shielding, and Safety

All electrical work must comply with the latest safety codes, electrical standards, building codes, and all other applicable cabling standards. Inspections should be applied and paid for by the contractor. A certificate should be provided prior to the final acceptance of work. The use of tandem breakers is not permitted. All electrical cable must be 12 AWG and installed in 1/2 inch EMT conduit supplied by the contractor and installed directly to the panel location. 12 AWG BX is acceptable only when finishing an existing wall. The contractor must have a circuit tracer either on site or readily accessible. All electrical circuits that have been installed will also require labeling. The panel end of the circuit should indicate that the circuit is a dedicated circuit and include the room number in which it terminates. The receptacle end of the circuit should indicate the panel number, panel location, and breaker number. A lockable breaker is required at the panel.

Cables should be grounded as specified. The overall shield of all cables installed should be continuous from termination point to termination point and grounded at one end only.

The metallic sheath of communication cables entering buildings should be grounded as close as practical to the point of entrance or should be interrupted as close to the point of entrance as practical by an insulating joint or equivalent device. Furthermore, the grounding conductor should be connected to the nearest accessible location on the building or structure grounding electrode system, the grounding interior metal water piping system, the power service enclosures, the metallic power service raceways, the service equipment enclosure, the grounding electrode conductor, or the grounding electrode conductor metal enclosure. Also, all connections to grounding should be by connectors, clamps, fittings, or lugs used to attach grounding conductors and bonding jumpers to grounding electrodes or to each other.

NOTE:

For all practical purposes, true earth ground is the best ground of all.

Isolated Ground

The isolated ground (IG) receptacle should be orange and wired as an individual branch circuit outlet. The outlet should have a separate green or green/yellow wire which runs continuously from the ground conductor terminal to the first panel board where it is connected to the ground bus. Bonding of the conduit, boxes, etc., of the circuit is accomplished by ordinary means (conduit or a separate ground wire). The two grounds are connected only at the panel board as shown in Figure 15–2 [3].

The IG outlet is grounded to the same ground as the electrical distribution system. The only difference is that it is connected to ground via a separate wire. There is no *clean separate* or *dedicated* ground. The Electrical Safety Code allows only one earthing ground.

Installation of Interbuilding Cables:
Outside or Between Buildings

The installation of interbuilding cables consists of the copper and fiber optic backbone cables that connect building to building. Let's take a look at how it's done.

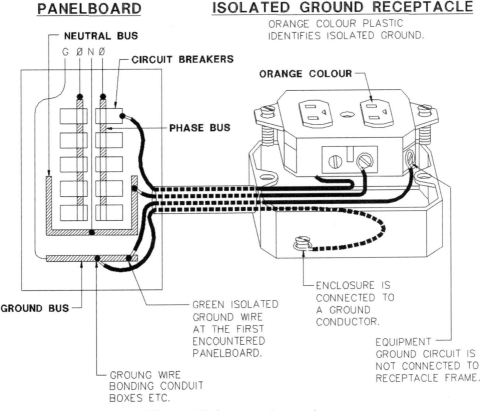

PANELBOARD

NEUTRAL BUS

G Ø N Ø

CIRCUIT BREAKERS

PHASE BUS

GROUND BUS

GREEN ISOLATED
GROUND WIRE
AT THE FIRST
ENCOUNTERED
PANELBOARD.

GROUNG WIRE
BONDING CONDUIT
BOXES ETC.

ISOLATED GROUND RECEPTACLE

ORANGE COLOUR PLASTIC
IDENTIFIES ISOLATED GROUND.

ORANGE COLOUR

ENCLOSURE IS
CONNECTED TO
A GROUND
CONDUCTOR.

EQUIPMENT
GROUND CIRCUIT IS
NOT CONNECTED TO
RECEPTACLE FRAME.

Figure 15–2: Isolated grounding.

Cable Placement

Care should be exercised when handling and storing reels of cable to prevent damage to the cable. Cable with dents, flat spots, or other sheath distortions should not be installed. Immediately after installation, a temporary tag with the cable number and pair count should be attached to each end of each cable section (see the sidebar, "Interbuilding Cable and Hardware").

Interbuilding Cable and Hardware

A composite fiber cable consisting of 36 multimode and 12 singlemode fibers in an armored jacket should be installed in a minimum 4 inch duct between buildings. This includes one hundred pair UTP cable (armored jacketed) to share the 4 inch duct with the fiber cable installed between buildings.

All cables should be installed with 10 foot service coils at all termination points and transition closets. Service loops may be stored on backboards, in unoccupied sections of the cable tray (see the sidebar, "Cable Tray") or in conduit pull boxes. Do not store service loops in the fiber cable in the connector tray.

The contractor is responsible for the location of buried utilities, where applicable. These arrangements should be made prior to commencement of work. The contractor is also responsible for the restoration of the area under construction to its original condition or better. Where landscape property has been disturbed, the contractor should account for the restoration of grass, plants, walkways, etc. [UTOR, 6].

Cable Tray

Cable tray specified for telecommunications closets (see the sidebar, "Telecommunications Closets (TCs)") should be ladder-type cable tray, no less than 6 inches wide by 3.5 inches deep with 8 inch spacing between rungs. Only fittings such as sweeping 30, 45, 60, and 90 degree elbows, tees and crosses manufactured by the OEM are to be used to change direction. Use fittings of the smallest available bending radius in order to accommodate the bending radius of the backbone cabling. Butting two section of tray together to create right angle turns is not acceptable. Any custom alterations to the tray must be approved by the PM prior to installation.

When the tray is running parallel to backboards, install it 4 inches off the backboard to allow passage of cables between the tray and the backboard. However, if the tray is adjacent to a wall, use right angle brackets or unistrut to support it.

In any case, when the tray is installed in free air to cross a closet, suspend it from the ceiling using a threaded rod. Also, when the tray is installed above a relay rack, use a threaded rod to support the tray 12 inches from the top of the rack where possible [UTOR, 6].

Telecommunications Closets (TCs)

Telecommunication closets (TCs) should be constructed with full height walls using steel studs with minimum 5/8 inch drywall. All walls should be painted to match the existing color and finish. The use of any other color should be approved by the owner. All existing painted surfaces, including cement floors, should be freshly painted. All surfaces should have one coat of primer, one intermediate coat, and one or more finish coats of latex or oil-based paint.

Remove any existing carpet from new TCs and finish the floors as per above or the detailed scope of work. After that's finished, securely mount a 3/4 inch fire rated plywood backboard. Mount the backboard on the new gypsum board wall or existing surface. The exact size and method of installation will be determined by the site conditions.

Use a switch-operated light to provide working illumination. The light fixture should be a 100W Vaptite VCXL11K or equivalent.

Use two (2) separately fused 15A, 110V AC, isolated ground duplex electrical outlets with lock-on breakers. One should be wall mounted and the other secured to the top of the relay rack.

Use a solid core wood door that is painted to match other existing doors. Stain and finish where applicable. The door should be fitted with a lock set that matches existing locking hardware in the building. If matching lock sets are not available, then it is up to the contractor to confirm an acceptable alternative with the PM. The locking cylinders in the lock sets must be compatible with the master locking system. Three keys must be provided to the PM and, where more than one lock is installed in the same building, all lock cylinders must accept the same key. A project will not be considered substantially complete unless this condition is met. At no time should a lock set be installed that does not allow free exit from a room [UTOR, 3-4]. Finally, TCs should always have a telephone and air conditioning installed.

Cables and equipment should be supported and secured. Where the specific method of support is not shown in the scope of work, adequate supports and fasteners should be used to secure cables and equipment in position. Metallic supports and fasteners should have a corrosion-resistant finish. All cables and equipment installed in exterior locations should be secured so that they cannot be dislodged or damaged by winds up to 135 mph.

Caution should be used when bending cable to avoid kinks or other damage to the sheath. The bend radius should be as large as possible with a minimum not less than eight times the outside diameter of the cable. Minimum radius should be increased when necessary to meet the cable manufacturer's recommendations. Bending operations in manholes and vaults should be performed in accordance with the manufacturer's procedures and instructions. Cable bending shoes should be used at duct or conduit ends when bending cable exiting a duct or conduit. The bending shoes should remain in place until racking, splicing and tying are completed. Cables should not rest against the edge of the duct or conduit mouth. Cable splices should not be made in ducts.

Assigned ducts and conduits should be cleaned and tested for alignment before pulling in cable. Pulled lines should be attached to cable ends fitted with any pulling device which will not damage the cable except where the device is attached. If the cable end is damaged during pulling, the damaged portion of the cable should be removed and discarded.

Cable reels should be located and aligned so that the cable is payed off the top of the reel into the duct or conduit in a long, smooth bend without twisting. Cable should not be pulled from the bottom of a reel or subjected to reverse bends from those formed by factory reeling. A cable-feeder guide of proper dimensions should be used at the mouth to guide the cable into the duct or conduit.

Rigging should be set up at the pulling end so that the pulling line and cable exit on a line parallel with the duct or conduit to prevent either from rubbing against the edge or mouth. Cable ends should not be pulled around sheave wheels.

All unterminated cables should be laid in the specified routing and location as indicated in the scope of work. The unterminated cable ends should be cleared, capped, and sealed.

Pulling lubricant should be compatible with and intended for use with plastic- and rubber-sheathed cables. Soap and grease lubricants are prohibited.

The cable should be carefully inspected for sheath defects or other irregularities as it is payed off the reel. If defects are detected, pulling should stop immediately and the cable section should be repaired or replaced.

Cable ends pulled into manholes, vaults, or terminal locations that are not to be racked or otherwise permanently positioned should immediately be tied in fixed positions to prevent damage to the cables and to provide adequate working space. After final racking and splicing, plastic-sheathed cables in manholes and vaults should be secured in place with lashed cable supports or with lashing shims. Cables in other locations should be secured in the manner indicated in the scope of work. When securing details are not indicated, the cables should be secured in a manner that will maintain the cables in the required position without damage to the cables. Also, ducts and conduits in which cables are placed should be sealed using duct seal or similar material.

All excavation should be performed as required to install the cables and equipment as indicated in the scope of work. Unless otherwise specified or indicated, direct-buried cables may be placed by either plowing, trenching, or boring and should be placed a minimum of 30 inches below grade. In addition, underground utilities in the path of cable burial operations should be located and exposed or the depth determined by hand digging.

Communications cables should not be installed in the same trench with electrical power cables. A minimum separation of 12 inches should be maintained between buried communications cables and power cables. Where buried communications cables must cross power cables, the communications cables should, where possible, be placed above the power cable. Creosoted wood or concrete separators should be placed between communications and power cables at crossover points.

Trenches should be wide enough for proper cable laying and backfilling. The bottom of the finished trench should be filled with no less than 3 inches of sand or fined soil that will not damage the cable sheath. Cables should be placed in the trench on top of the sand for cushion and stabilization of cable during trench backfill.

Trench backfilling should be accomplished by placing 3 inches of sand or fine soil over the cable and tamping it over and around the cable. The balance of backfilling should be accomplished in 6-inch layers, each layer being compacted to a density at least equal to that or the adjoining soil before the next layer is placed. Place "warning buried cable" tape 6 inches to 8 inches below final grade along entire route. Topsoil and sod should be replaced and, as nearly as practical, restored to the original condition. Excavated materials not required or suited for backfilling should be disposed of as directed by the PM.

Cable-plowing operations should be in accordance with the operating procedures provided by the cable plow manufacturer and the requirements specified within this chapter. The plowing operations should be observed continuously to ensure that the cable is not damaged during placement and that proper depth is maintained.

Cable crossing under roadways or other pavement should be made by boring or jacking a pipe where practicable or specified. If it is necessary to break the pavement, permission should be obtained from the PM before proceeding. Immediately upon completion of the cable-sleeve placement, the roadway or other hardstand should be restored to the original condition. Furthermore, where buried cable enters the end of an underground pipe or conduit, ductseal or other suitable material should be packed between the cable and the inside of the sleeve end to prevent damage to the cable sheath and entrance of dirt into sleeve.

Installation of Intrabuilding Cable: In House or within Buildings

The installation of intrabuilding cables consists of copper and fiber optic backbone cables that run between telecommunication closets within a building. Let's take a look at how this is done.

General

Care should be exercised when handling and storing reels of cable to prevent damage to the cable. Cable with dents, flat spots, or other sheath distortions should not be installed. Cable ends should be sealed until cables have been installed. Immediately after placement, a temporary tag with the cable number and cable type should be attached to each end of each cable section (See the sidebars, "Intrabuilding Cable and Hardware" and "Workstation Cable Installation Specifications").

Intrabuilding Cable and Hardware

Three separate Byte Information Exchange (BIX) 10A fields with appropriate D rings should be installed to support backbone equipment and horizontal cables, as shown in Figure 15–3. All BIX fields should be installed even if they are not used for immediate installation.

If more than one floor of horizontal cables terminate in the same TC, a separate BIX10A is required for each floor with drops from the higher floors terminating on the highest 10A frame. The horizontal BIX should be mounted adjacent to each other and in the order as shown in Figure 15–4.

BIX mounts should be labeled with colored designation labels; the horizontal field should be blue, the backbone field is green, and the equipment field is gray.

One (1) nineteen inch relay rack with 77 inches of usable space (44RU) rack bolted to the floor should be installed in each telecommunications closet. Rack layouts should include:

- One cable management bracket for every two 24 port fiber panels.
- One (1) power bar (with internal breaker), mounted with the switch to the front and outlets.
- Six (6) power bars on rear using only one rack space.
- Four 4 x 4 inch slotted wire duct, secured to the side of the rack.
- One shelf, mounted a minimum of 12 inches from the fiber panels. Leave seven (7) rack spaces empty above the shelf.

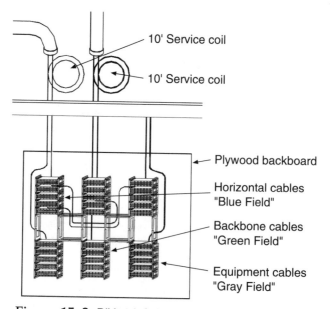

Figure 15–3: BIX10A fields with appropriate D rings.

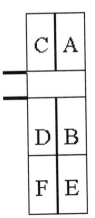

Figure 15–4: Horizontal BIX mounted adjacent to each other and in the order shown.

- A minimum 6 inch wide ladder-type tray with 8 inch spacing between rungs to support cables from the TC entry point to the termination locations.

All backbone copper and fiber interbuilding and intrabuilding cables should be installed with 10 foot service coils at all termination points and transition closets as shown in Figure 15–5. The service loops may be stored on the backboard, in an inactive section of cable tray, or in the conduit pull box.

Pull string/rope should remain in all conduit upon completion of cable installation. Backbone and horizontal cable may co-exist in the same conduit. However, all fiber cable must be in separate conduit from the copper type where two conduit paths have been installed [UTOR, 7].

Workstation Cable Installation Specifications

Requirements:
Check for all installation requirements specifications needed in area for workstation cabling placement as (area access, people, asbestos, furniture, cable routes and drawings).

Tools and materials:
Tools—cable ties, fastening system, crimping tools, splice tools, test equipment, cable marking systems, and all hand tools.

Materials—cable, jacks, tags, termination blocks, floor tombstones (hardware), molding, and cross-connect wire (see sidebar, "List of Equipment Needed to Install a Cabling System in a School").

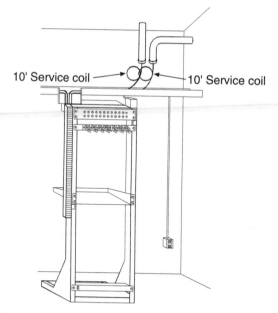

10' Service coil — 10' Service coil

Figure 15–5: Backbone copper and fiber interbuilding and intrabuilding cables are installed with 10 foot service coils at all termination points and transition closets.

Set up reels:
Set up your reels near or in the wiring closet. Alternatively, select a location midway between the wiring closet and the termination point.

Label the cables:
Label each cable reel and its free end according to the termination locations marked on your canvas drawings and work orders. Label each Pigtail (25-pair) cable from concentrator to the 110 blocks with LJ and the number of the block.

Pull cables into place:
Deliver the cable from the bottom of each reel, making sure not to kink, crush or pinch the cable. Pull groups of cables to a logical point and then fan out to the individual termination points. Separate the Telecommunication cables from other cables by at least 6 inches and avoid sharp edges, tight bends that would subject the cable to abrasion, or moisture.

Remove Slack:
Remove slack in the lines by pulling the cables back to the wiring closet.

Label and cut:
Label each cable and then cut it off, making sure to leave enough cable to reach the termination block.

Tie cable together:
Use cable ties to bundle and secure parallel runs together. Place the ties at intervals sufficient to prevent sagging and to maintain neatness. Distances between ties may vary from six (6) inches to four (4) feet, depending on the size of the cables.

Strap the cables:
Use straps to fasten the cable bundles to the hanger at four (4) feet or other appropriate intervals, if supplied. The distance between hangers can vary from 3 to 20 feet, depending upon the surface and the type and number of cables in each bundle. Do not support cables on pipes, conduits, or other structures in the building plenum.

Inspect the Job:
Make sure that the cables are not resting on or near electrical fixtures or sagging more than seven (7) inches from point of tie.

Do not exceed the minimum bend radius:
The minimum bend radius of a cable must never be exceeded. The bend radius should not be less than eight times the outside diameter of the cable. For Category 5 cables, the cables may not be bent beyond a radius of 1.25 inches.

Do not overcinch the cables:

*   Overcinching the cable (with cable ties and cords) can cause compression of the cable jacket. It can deform the cable and cause the same effects as overbending and kinking the cable.

*   Use Velcro straps, nail-on cable clamps, and D-rings to support and position cable jackets to keep them from becoming compressed.

*   Cable bundles must be installed carefully. Cables inside the bundles can be damaged as easily as cables on the outside can.

Never untwist the pairs of a Category 5 cable beyond 0.5 inches from the point of termination:
Maintaining cable pair twist is absolutely critical to cable performance. The cable jacket or outer sheath should be intact as close to the termination as possible. Remove only the amount of the cable jacket that is necessary for termination.

Never run cable longer than the maximum recommended length:
Category 3 through 5 cables require a maximum of 100 meters (328 feet).

Cables and equipment should also be supported and secured. Where the specific method of support is not indicated, adequate supports and fasteners should be used to secure cables and equipment in position. Metallic supports and fasteners should have a corrosion-resistant finish.

Cables should be provided in continuous lengths as required to accomplish the required installation without splices from termination. The exception would be where field splices are specifically required and approved in advance.

Raised Floors and Cable Trays

Instrumentation and communications cables should not be installed in the same tray with AC power cables. Cables placed in cable trays or under raised floors should be installed in a neat and orderly manner and should not cross or interlace other cables except at breakout points. Instrumentation and communication cables should be routed under raised floors as indicated in the scope of work. The installation of cables under raised-floor areas should be closely coordinated with existing cables and utilities in these areas. The new cables should be routed as required to avoid interference with existing utilities in the raised-floor area. All cables routed under false floors should be routed parallel to cabinet or rack bay fronts and walls and under corridor areas created by racks and equipment. Unterminated cable ends should be cleared, capped and sealed. No lengths of coiled cable should be left under raised-floor areas unless specifically approved by the PM. Cables in vertical trays should be retained by use of plastic or nylon straps on 6-foot maximum centers for each cable or cable group.

Boxes, Enclosures, and Distribution Frames

Each conductor of each cable should be terminated on terminal blocks or on connectors except where specifically approved in advance by the PM for future use or where the cable is indicated to be coiled cable. Termination procedure for any cable within a distributor or other wiring enclosure should not be started until all cables have been pulled into the enclosure. The installation of harness assemblies should not be started until the completion of the termination of the applicable incoming cables.

Where cables are pulled into previously installed distributors, the existing hardware should be protected against damage. Any damage to the existing hardware should be repaired in an approved manner.

Cables, conductors, and shields should be terminated in accordance with the manufacturer's specifications. Terminals and connectors should be installed using only tools specifically recommended by the hardware manufacturer and should be of the type that requires a specific force to perform the crimp. The installation procedure should follow the manufacturer's installation directions.

Groups of conductors should be bound by means of plastic fasteners and equal to self-locking Ty-Rap ties. These fasteners should be placed along the main harness and cable and adjacent to each conductor leaving the bundle at the breakout point.

Cables should be supported as near to the termination point as possible to prevent any strain which is due to the weight of the cable from being transmitted to the individual conductors where they are connected to terminal blocks or to connector terminations. In terminal distributors, all of the cables and cable-harness assemblies should be supported horizontally to their respective terminal-block mounting channel. Care should be taken not to have any of the cable shields or the conductor shields grounded to the terminal distributor frame, especially at the points of cable supports. Cables that have overall shields or individual terminal blocks should have the terminal-block mounting channel adequately insulated with insulating tape to maintain the isolation of the shields from a ground.

Installing Equipment Cable

Equipment cable wiring should provide a connection between the cross-connect and the active equipment that will be mounted in the rack as shown in Figure 15–6 [UTOR, 8]. The cables should be run in units of 25 pairs. Each 25 pair should connect no more than 12 end stations. Equipment cables should have a 50-pin male connector at the rack and punched down on a BIX 1A4 in a 10A mounted on the backboard. The performance of the equipment cable should equal the specification of Category 5 cable. Unless otherwise specified, the number of cables provided should be the estimated number of users divided by 12.

NOTE:

EIA/TIA specifications for installation wiring practices require that cables of the given performance category (Category 3) be terminated with connecting hardware of the same category or higher. Termination Practices has three main parameters used to characterize connector transmission performance, attenuation, near-end crosstalk (NEXT), and return loss. These parameters are sensitive to transmission discontinuities caused by connector terminations. NEXT performance is particularly susceptible to conductor untwisting and other poor installation practices that disturb pair balance and cause impedance variations. Also, improper termination practices may also create loop antenna effects, which result in levels of signal radiation that may exceed regulatory emission requirements.

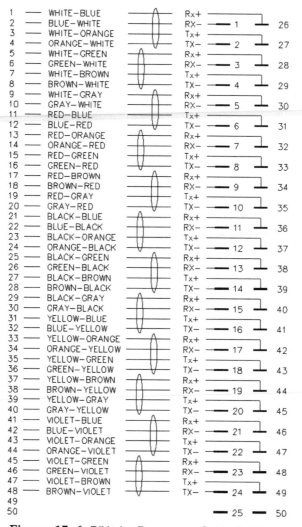

Figure 15–6: BIX1A4 Equipment Cable RJ 71.

Installing Horizontal Cabling and Hardware

The horizontal distribution cable is the copper or fiber optic cable that runs between the workstation outlet and the termination field in the telecommunication closet. NT IBDN-Plus Category 5 UTP 4-pair cables should be installed from the horizontal BIX frames in the TCs through the horizontal conduit infrastructure to the outlet location. When specified, the fiber cable should be a four (4) strand MIC cable.

Drop cables may share the riser conduits when installation occurs between floors. When there is a choice, these drop cables should always be installed in the riser conduit that accommodate the corresponding media type (copper with copper, fiber with fiber).

One inch conduit should be used between the junction boxes on the horizontal distribution conduits and the user outlet boxes as shown in Figure 15–7 [UTOR, 8]. In many cases the conduit should be run down the surface of the wall to a custom surface mount outlet box designed to accept a NT-MDVO flush-mount faceplate installed on the side of the box. NT-MDVO faceplates using 8-position modules (a module with 8 positions) should be installed in the faceplate and configured as shown in Figure 15–8 [UTOR, 8].

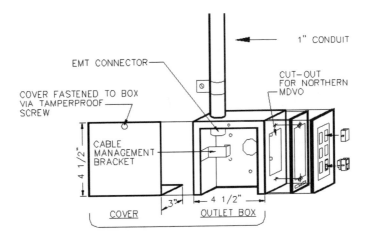

Figure 15–7: One inch conduit should be used between the junction boxes on the horizontal distribution conduits and the user outlet boxes.

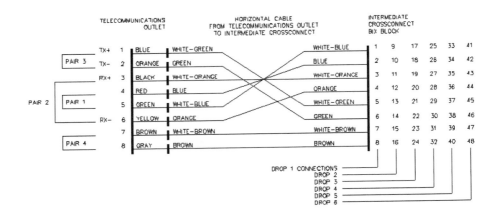

Figure 15–8: NT-MDVO faceplates using 8-position modules.

Outlet Placement

Standard outlet height when boxes are installed on a wall is 12 inches from the floor. Conduit or boxes are not to obstruct the function of any adjacent fixtures.

When outlets are mounted on the floor, the outlet box should be mounted on its widest surface so that the faceplate is on the side of the box and the cover plate is able to be opened. Any architectural detail such as elaborate baseboards or outlets mounted at counter level in labs (see Figure 15–9) should be addressed by the contractor prior to installing the outlet box if it is not addressed in the detailed scope of work [UTOR, 9]. District schools or universities usually reserve the right to relocate any telecommunications outlet by up to 3 meters without penalty before installation is complete.

Cable Plant Sectioning

The sectioning of an individual coaxial cable segment (a coaxial cable segment made up of several pieces of 50 ohm cable interconnected by N-type barrel connectors) may be accomplished in several ways but care must be taken in doing so. See the sidebar, "Coaxial Cable Installation," for further information on the installation procedures for that type of cable.

The joining of two cable sections by two N-type male connectors and a barrel connector creates a signal reflection point where some of the signal may be reflected back to the sender and lost. This reflection is due to an impedance mismatch caused by the batch-to-batch impedance tolerance of the cable during manufacturing. The tolerance of the baseband trunk cable is 50 ohms +/- 2 ohms. Therefore a worst case mismatch would mate a 48 ohm cable to a 52 ohm cable resulting in 4 ohm mismatch, where 4% of the signal would be reflected back to the sender and lost.

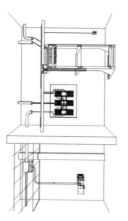

Figure 15–9: Architectural detail of outlet placement.

Coaxial Cable Installation

Structural supports for coaxial cables should be installed straight and plumb. In addition, coaxial cables should be supported securely at bulkhead plates and terminal distributors.

Coaxial cable runs should also be continuous from termination to termination wherever possible. Coaxial cables should be terminated and appropriate high-quality connectors should be attached using the cable manufacturer's recommended procedures, which should be considered a part of the specification. Furthermore, the contractor should follow the cable manufacturer's published terminating procedures.

Coaxial cables should be attached to supports appropriately secured with fasteners specifically designed for this purpose. Strapping material should be Wraplock or equal. Cables should be attached to supports at intervals not exceeding five (5) feet, except where prior approval has been granted by the PM.

The bending radius of coaxial cable should not be less than the manufacturer's published minimum bend radius under any circumstances. If a bend is required in a large diameter cable, an approved pipe-bending device should be used to form the cable. There should be no evidence of any wrinkling of outer conductor of cable or cable sheath.

All moisture should be removed from the coaxial cable connections prior to splice closure. Boiling-paraffin methods should not be used.

On indoor connections, approved shrink tubing or insulating tape (insulating tape is seldom used anymore) should be applied. If shrink tubing is not available, tape should be applied an additional half-lap to completely cover all exposed metal portions of the coaxial cable and connector after the connector has been installed in place and connected to the terminating piece of equipment. Each connection should be sleeved using an appropriate size of heat-shrinkable tubing to accommodate the cable jacket and connectors used and to completely encapsulate the connection.

On outdoor connections, after the connectors are joined, silicone lubricant or an equivalent should be applied to cover the complete surface of the connectors. Coverage should be a minimum of 2 inches on each side of the connector hubs where the cable rating occurs. Excess silicone lubricant should be wiped clean from the outer surface of the cable jacket after installation.

Heat-shrinkable tubing should be Raychez Type TCS, WCS, WRS, or an approved equal. Heat-shrinkable tubing should be installed in accordance with the manufacturer's specifications. Finally, appropriate grounding kits provided by the manufacturer of the coaxial cable should be installed in accordance with the manufacturer's specifications and as indicated.

Ethernet IEEE 802.3 Specification

If possible, the total coaxial cable segment should be made from one homogeneous (no breaks) cable. This is feasible for short segments, and results in minimal reflections from cable impedance discontinuities.

If cable segments are built up from smaller sections, it is recommended that all sections come from the same manufacturer and lot. This is equivalent to using a single cable, since the cable discontinuities are due to extruder limitations, and not extruder-to-extruder tolerances. There are no restrictions in cable sectioning if this method is used. However, if a cable section in such a system is later replaced, it should be replaced either with another cable from the same manufacturer and lot, or with one of the standard lengths described next.

If uncontrolled cable sections should be used in building up a longer segment, the lengths should be chosen so that reflections, when they occur, do not have a high probability of adding in phase. This can be accomplished by using lengths that are odd integral multiples of a half wavelength in the cable at 5 MHz. This corresponds to using lengths of 23.4 m, 70.2 m, and 117 m (+/-0.5 m) for all sections. These are considered to be the standard lengths for all cable sections. Using these lengths exclusively, any mix or match of cable sections may be used to build up a 500-meter segment without incurring excessive reflections.

As a last resort, an arbitrary configuration of cable sections may be employed, if it has been confirmed by analysis or measurement that the worst-case signal reflection due to the impedance discontinuities at any point on the cable does not exceed 7% of the incident wave when driven by a MAU meeting these specifications.

Installation Procedures for 10Base5 Cable

Install cable using the previously stated guidelines from the IEEE 802.3 specification. Also, avoid routing the 10Base5 cable parallel to high voltage or RF signal sources.

Install MAUs directly on annular rings only. Do not install MAUs between the annular rings. Furthermore, install splices (N-Type barrel connectors) on annular rings. Also, any open cores in the cable, such as when an MAU has been removed, should be filled with a clear rubber compound known as RTV room-temperature vulcanization)and taped.

NOTE:

RTV stands for room-temperature vulcanization. The phrase is chemists' terminology for a rubber compound that cures and solidifies when it is exposed to room temperature and moisture. These silicones exhibit high adhesion, flexibility, and resistance to moisture. If you need weather and moisture resistance, as well as a caulk that adheres well to aluminum, glass, or porcelain surfaces, RTV silicone is a good choice. Although the product sounds exotic, it's not. You can get RTV silicone caulk at home centers, hardware stores, and paint stores.

Ground one end of the 10Base5 cable using a 5 ohm or less ground. Ground should be accomplished with a ground clamp and #6 copper solid conductor wire. In no instances should the cable be grounded in more than one location.

Cable, when installed, should be supported every 5 to 10 feet. On an annular ring where an MAU has been installed, the cable should be supported within 1 foot of either side of the MAU. Attachment Unit Interface (AUI) cables should be supported by Ty-Rap within 1 foot of its connection to the MAU. AUI cables should be installed with shields on both ends.

Cable Splicing

Cables should be spliced in accordance with the manufacturer's approved procedures and as specified herein. Unless otherwise indicated, all requirements, procedures, and constraints in the manufacturer's approved procedures for should be adhered to.

Connectors should remain in their correct color groups or units except when required for defective pair transpositions. All cable segments, including all pairs of wire, should be interconnected with #m type 4000 DWP pluggable connectors.

All building entry cables must have a transition splice and use lighting protection protector blocks and gas tube protector modules. Use the specified 22 or 24 AWG cable. All protection blocks must be grounded with #6 solid insulated ground wire.

Labeling

The installers should label all wires in the cabling system according to a logical and clear code. If possible, they should incorporate any existing building space designations into the code. They should place this code on the physical cabling system in three places: on both ends of each wire and somewhere in the base plate box to which the wire is connected. Copies of this wiring code should be deposited with the school district or university central office, with the office responsible for the building affected, and with those in charge of maintenance.

Drawing Identifiers

There should be a legend on all drawings to show building and floor number. All drawings should be referenced as Data Plans (DP).

Each drawing will be prefixed with DPbbbbff: where DP is the Data Plan; where bbbb is the building number; and, ff is the floor number. For example: DP-bbbb-ff converts to DP-0123-02.

Building and Floor Identifiers

School district or university campus buildings can be identified by using the following format: A three digit number preceded by either an 0 or A. For example: 0123 or A123. Thus, The building ID exists in the legend, in the title block, and the file name.

All floors in buildings could be identified by two digits as shown in the example in Table 15–1:

Table 15–1: Floor identifiers.

01..99	Floors above ground, including ground.
GR	Ground floor when not identified as Floor 1.
1B	1st Basement—where there is only one basement it will be refereed to as 1st basement or basement.
2B	2nd Basement.
3B	3rd Basement.
MZ	Mezzanine.

Telecommunications Closets

All telecommunication closets can be identified as TCccC—where TC is telecommunication closet, cc floor identifier and C alpha identifier. Unique per floor. bbbb is the building number. For example: bbbb-TC-cc-C converts to 0123-TC-02-A. This example represents the label on the inside of the active door at eye level of the TC.

Zone Identifiers

Each floor should be divided into zones based on the architectural plans of the building. The zone is described by the lowest value of the two ordinal sets that define the boundary of the zone. For example, ZZ is alpha coordinances and NN is the numeric coordinance, where ZZNN converts to 0C03 or AA10.

Cable Identifiers

All cable identifiers should be based on a continuous sequence beginning at 1 and counting consecutively. Each series should be unique within the building floor and serving closet. This should be a three-position number, zero filled and left justified. The complete cable identifier should include the Building, Floor number, Zone, Cable Number and Telecommunications Closet where: bbbb is building; ff is floor, ZZNN is zone; nnn is cable number; and, ccC is closet. For example: bbbb-ff-ZZNN-nnn-ccC converts to 0123-01-DD03-01-C02A.

Cable Label

The label as it will appear on the cable one half inch back from where the jacket is removed consists of ZZNN for zone, nnn for cable number and ccC for closet. For example: ZZNN-nnn-ccC converts to 0C03-001-02A or AA10-001-02A.

BIX Panel Label

The BIX wafer should be mounted on a BIX panel unique to the floor being served by that cable.

NOTE:

Cables that run from different floors should be terminated on separate BIX panels within the same closet. Each floor should have its own BIX panel within a Telecommunications Closet which will be identified and labeled by floor number. Therefore the labels used must be able to stick to a plywood backboard.

The standard label should be affixed to a mounting strip mounted on the backboard where ff is floor. For example, ff converts to 01 or 0D.

The label for each cable position as it will appear on the BIX Wafer consists of ZZNN for zone and nnn for cable number. For example, ZZNN-nnn converts to 0C03-001 or AA10-001.

Outlet Box Identifier

The identifier for the outlet box should follow the form bbbb is building, OB is outlet box, ff is floor, ZZNN is zone, and nn is outlet box number. For example: bbbb-OB-ff-ZZNN-nn converts to 0123-OB-02-AA10-01.

Outlet Box Label

The label should be on the upper front corner on the opposite side of the data connectors. A second label should be placed on the inside of the Data Outlet Box on the bottom surface. If there is a black outlet box, a blank white label needs to be placed under the clear label. For example, OB-nn converts to OB-01.

Jack Identifier

The jack identifier should follow the form where bbbb is building, ff is floor, ZZNN is zone, nnn is number, and, ccC is closet. For example, bbbb-ff-ZZNN-nnn-ccC converts to 0123-02-0C03-00-102A.

Jack Label

The label should be placed on the cover of the plate facing out. The label for the first outlet should be at the top and the second should be below. The jack label should follow the form where nnn is number and ccC is closet. For example, nnn-ccC converts to 001-02A.

Pull Box Identifiers

The identification for the pull box should be PBffZZNNnn where PB is the Pull Box, ff is the floor, ZZNN is the zone, and nn is the Pull Box Number within the zone. For example, bbbb-PB-ff-ZZNN-nn converts to 0123-PB02-0C03-01.

Pull Box Label

When the pull box is above a drop ceiling, a second label must be placed on the T-Bar ceiling. The label for the pull box should be LAT 28-409-25SH or equivalent.

NOTE:

This is a full $81/2''$ x $11''$ black-on-white label sheet that must be cut into 8 (eight) 2-1/2" x 4-1/4" sections. Avery label cat. # 5163, which is 4" x 2", is a suitable alternative.

For example, PB-02-0C03-01 UTCC, 2-1/2" high by 4-1/2" wide.

Riser Cable Identifier

The identifier for the riser cables should be of the form where bbbb is the building, F is the fiber cable type, C is the copper cable type, ccC is the near closet, ccC is also the far closet, and, nn is the cable number. For example, bbbb-FccCccCnn converts to 0123-F02A03A01, and, bbbb-CccCccCnn converts to 0123-C02A03A01.

Riser Cable Label

The label for the riser cable should be TccCccCnn where T is the Cable Type identifier, F is the Fiber Cable, C is the Copper Cable, ccC is the Telecommunications Closet for one end of the cable, and ccC is the Telecommunications Closet for the other end of the cable. Fix the label one half inch from where the jacket is stripped back. The telecommunications closet should always be read from left to right and lowest to highest. For example, T-ccC-ccC-nn converts to F-02A-03A-01 or to C-02A-03A-01.

Equipment Cable Label

The equipment cable label should be fixed to the cable one half inch back from where the jacket is stripped back. It should follow the form where T-ccC-nn converts to F-02A-01 or C-02A-01.

Electrical Outlet, Breaker Label, and Duplex Outlet

The locations of the electrical outlets in the TC and breakers in the panel must be cross referenced through labeling. The breaker label must indicate that it is a circuit with the TC number and the room number. The duplex outlet must be labeled to indicate the electrical room and electrical panel number and the breaker number.

Installing a Local Area Network

Each building in a school district or university campus should have a separate LAN, allowing each room in a building to be connected with all the others using a high-speed cabling system. As previously discussed, there are many ways to connect the building, using different types and brands of equipment. Although each brand offers slightly different features, most will sell the same basic pieces of equipment. This part of the chapter discusses most of the common types of equipment in detail. If it does not discuss your piece of equipment, or if the school district or university is unsure which type to use, do not hesitate to speak with a vendor about what products fit the school district or university's needs. Although vendors will often try to sell their brand, they can usually offer good advice as well.

Network Cabling Installation Choices

The school district or university should make a decision about what physical protocol to use. Currently there are several in use, although Ethernet is the most popular. Others include token ring, FDDI, ATM, and LocalTalk. Each protocol is capable of a different maximum data speed known as the bandwidth, and costs do differ. Table 15–2 summarizes all of this information [Lamont, 4]. Looking at the OSI model in Figure 15–10, all of these protocols except ATM exist at the bottom two layers, the physical and data link layers. ATM exists at those layers as well as at the network level [Lamont, 4].

Layer

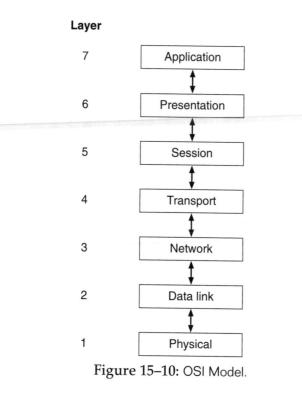

Figure 15–10: OSI Model.

Table 15–2: A comparison of the different LAN technologies.

Protocol	Wiring	Maximum Bandwidth	Maximum Length	Topology	Cost
Ethernet	Category 5 twisted pair	10 Mbps	100 meters	Star	Low
	Thick	10 Mbps	500 meters	Bus	High
	Coaxial cable	10 Mbps	200 meters	Bus	Low
	Fiber	10 Mbps	1000 meters	Star	Very high
Fast Ethernet	Category 5 twisted pair	100 Mbps	100 meters	Star	High
Token Ring	Coaxial cable	16 Mbps	100 meters	Ring	High
FDDI	Fiber	100 Mbps	1000 meters	Star	Very high
CDDI	Category 5 twisted pair	100 Mbps	100 meters	Star	Very high
LocalTalk	Category 3 twisted pair	230 Kbps	300 meters	Bus	Very low
ATM	Fiber	1 Gbps	100 meters	Star	Very high

Ethernet

Ethernet is an industry standard protocol operating at 10 Mbps that is currently in wide use. The protocol uses a principle called Carrier Sense Multiple Access/Collision Detection (CSMA/CD) which has two important parts to it. The first is that it is a multiple access protocol allowing all the machines to share the same physical wiring instead of requiring separate wiring for each machine (except in the case of a star topology). The second is that it operates on collision detection. Since many machines share the wire, two machines may try to use it at the same time. This condition is called a collision. The network hardware detects the collision and aborts the transmission. After a small random delay, the hardware tries to transmit again. The result of this protocol is that on very busy networks with many machines, a large number of collisions can occur, wasting a significant amount of time retransmitting information. This is why there is a recommended limit of 25 to 30 machines on a single Ethernet network.

Cabling that uses the Ethernet protocol comes in four different physical varieties, thick, thin, twisted pair, and fiber optic. Thick Ethernet, also known as 10Base5, is the original wiring used for Ethernet, connected in a bus topology. It is the second most expensive of the four types, but also has the second longest maximum distance, 500 meters. It is not often used today because of the cheaper alternatives. Thin Ethernet, also known as 10Base2, coax, or cheapernet, is also a bus topology. It runs on 50 ohm coaxial cable and often connects small networks. It suffers from problems previously discussed under bus topologies in earlier chapters, and the Ethernet specifications limit its maximum length to 200 meters. Twisted-pair Ethernet, also known as 10BaseT, runs over Category 3 phone wiring or better. It connects in a star topology, although it shares the same CSMA/CD protocol as the other Ethernet varieties. It has a maximum length of 100 meters. Fiber Ethernet, also known as 10BaseFL, is not normally used except to connect hubs over long distances. Its maximum distance of 1,000 meters makes it ideally suited for this type of job.

To avoid problems with the actual electrical signal that propagates across the Ethernet wiring, the *3-4-5 rule* exists. It states that between any two machines on the Ethernet network, there must be at most five wiring segments, four repeaters connecting the segments, and only three of those segments can have workstations connected to them. A school district or university will violate this rule most often when a repeater connects a workstation that is beyond the distance limit for the network, or when classrooms have their own hubs.

Fast Ethernet

Fast Ethernet is an enhancement of Ethernet that runs at speeds of 100 Mbps, ten times the rate of original Ethernet. Known also as 100BaseT, it requires that the wiring it runs over be Category 5 wiring—a higher quality than the Category 3 used by normal Ethernet. The equipment needed to use

Fast Ethernet is also more expensive than normal Ethernet. Although the prices are dropping, it is most likely too expensive for schools to install initially. Like 10BaseT, it connects as a star topology and has a 100 meter maximum length restriction. This allows a district using Category 5 wiring to begin with 10BaseT and later upgrade to 100BaseT without replacing the wiring.

Token Ring

IBM developed token ring. It is a Carrier Sense Multiple Access/Collision Avoidance (CSMA/CA) protocol. It passes a theoretical *token* around the network. Only while a machine has the *token* can it send information. Since there is only one *token*, it prevents two machines from broadcasting at the same time. It operates at both 4 and 16 Mbps. Token ring is not widely used because the performance increase does not outweigh the difficulties and prices required when installing a ring topology.

FDDI/CDDI

Fiber Distributed Data Interconnect (FDDI) is a 100 Mbps fiber optic based network. Like most other technologies based on fiber, it requires two fiber cables, one for transmitting and one for receiving. The cost of fiber cables makes this choice significantly more expensive than using Ethernet. Its advantage is the higher speeds it offers, although, with the availability of Fast Ethernet, this is not a significant factor. Ordinarily, FDDI creates a fiber *backbone* that connects to all of the hubs in a large building or campus. Copper Distributed Data Interconnect (CDDI) is a proprietary variation of FDDI that runs over Category5 twisted pair.

ATM

Asynchronous Transfer Mode (ATM) is a new technology that is in transition from the research lab to commercial use. It offers speeds beginning at 45 Mbps and can increase to even higher speeds. It runs over Category5 twisted pair and fiber optic cables. In the future, as it becomes more available and prices drop, it will become a viable upgrade option.

LocalTalk

LocalTalk is the original network hardware that Apple Computer shipped with its Macintosh and Apple II series computers. It is not the same as Appletalk, the network protocol used over any physical network. LocalTalk has a maximum speed of 230 Kbps—significantly slower than any of the other protocols. It is a bus topology with a maximum distance of 300 meters. Using Phonenet equipment, it can run over standard Category 3 phone wiring. With its speed limitations, it is not recommended for use in any schools unless it's already installed—and, even then, a district or university should consider an upgrade.

Figure 15–11 shows a comparison of the bandwidths offered by the different protocols, as well as different WAN technologies discussed in the next part of the chapter [Lamont, 6]. The figure is logarithmic and each horizontal label is ten times faster than the one to it's left.

To allow for future growth to higher speeds, the Electronics Industry Association/Telephone Industry Association (EIA/TIA) has recommended the use of only Category 5 wiring in all installations because of its capability to run at higher speeds than Category 3. As previously mentioned, this will support future upgrades to Fast Ethernet or ATM.

Equipment Needed on a Workstation

Once a school district or university decides on the cabling system's physical installation, they will need to consider what equipment is necessary to connect all the workstations in the building to the network. Workstation is another term for a networked computer, whether the computer is a Macintosh, a Windows machine, or any other type of computer. This will normally require a network interface card (NIC) for each machine, although some new machines are now shipping with the network card built into the computer. Depending on the choice of cabling system, the school district or university will need to buy the card with the correct connector—either a coax, RJ-45, Attachment Unit Interface (AUI), or fiber.

If a school district or university is using Ethernet (the most likely implementation), they will have many choices. Since Ethernet comes in several varieties, some Ethernet cards, often called combo cards, come with two or three connectors as shown in Figure 15–12 [Lamont, 6]. If a school is currently using one variety and is planning to upgrade to another, then combo cards can save money. If the cabling system is going to be exclusively twisted pair, then there is no reason to spend the extra money on a combo card with unused capabilities.

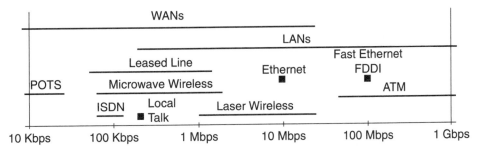

Figure 15–11: The bandwidth of different network technologies.

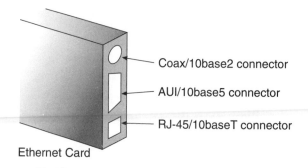

Coax/10base2 connector

AUI/10base5 connector

RJ-45/10baseT connector

Ethernet Card

Figure 15-12: The connectors on a Ethernet combo card.

Another option that is appearing is combo 10/100 Ethernet cards that can run on 10BaseT and 100BaseT networks. The school district or university should consider how quickly it will upgrade other parts of the network to support Fast Ethernet before investing in these cards.

The AUI connector on an Ethernet card allows easier expansion on the card. Devices (called transceivers or Media Access Units (MAUs)) which offer a connection to all four of the different types of networks can be connected to it. Although this sounds redundant with regard to combo cards, AUI can be useful if the card does not have an RJ45 connector and the school is upgrading to 10BaseT. Similar in function, although incompatible in size and shape, Apple Attachment Unit Interface (AAUI) connectors exist on the motherboards of most Macintosh models currently available. Be sure to buy the correct AUI or AAUI connectors when buying the network cards. Finally, do not forget to buy the necessary cabling to connect the network card if it does not include cabling already.

Cabling Equipment

Equipment used to create the cabling system infrastructure falls into two categories, passive devices and active devices. Passive devices do not usually affect the capabilities of the cabling system and make the installation or maintenance of the cabling system easier. These devices include patch panels, patch cables, fiber boxes, and fiber jumper cables. Active devices connect the different workstations and other active devices on the network. They include repeaters, bridges, switches, and routers. The next part of this chapter discusses them in detail. A typical cabling system will look similar to Figure 15–13 [Lamont, 7]. Table 15–3 contains a summary of all the cabling system equipment [Lamont, 9-10].

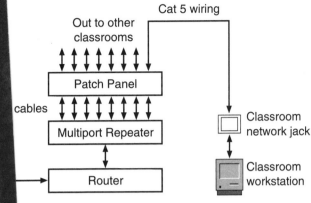

cables

Figure 15–13: A typical school cabling system.

LAN equipment

		OSI Layer
	n wiring by having all room ently connected to the back.	Physical
	ed to connect the patch panel to the hub and computers to the wall drop.	Physical
Fiber box	Reduce stress on wiring by having all room wiring permanently connected.	Physical
Fiber cables	Short fiber cables used to connect the fiber box to the hub.	Physical
Repeaters	Used to extend the distance wiring can be run.	Physical
Multi-port repeaters	Used as a hub to connect many machines together.	Physical
Switch	Used as a hub to connect many machines together and only transmits packets on the destination port.	Physical and Data Link
Bridge	Used to connect different hardware protocols or wiring types.	Data Link
Router	Used to direct traffic across a WAN to its final destination. A router is an intelligent device that supports connectivity between both like and disparate LANs via MANs and WANs.	Network

(continued)

Table 15–3: *(continued)*

Equipment	Use	OSI Layer
GatorStar/ GatorBox	Used to bridge LocalTalk and Ethernet networks.	Physical, Data Link, and Network Physical
MacLAN Patch panel	Connects to the LocalTalk networks and the GatorStar.	
EtherPrint boxes	Used to connect one or two LocalTalk devices such as printers to an Ethernet network.	Physical, Data Link, and Network

Patch Panels

All of the wiring that comes from the classrooms needs to connect to the hub. A patch panel is often used as an intermediary. All the wiring is *punched down* or attached to the back of the patch. The front is made up of RJ45 connectors into which patch cables connect. This prevents any damage to the room wires, since changes do not require the modification of the room wires.

Patch Cables

Patch cables, or jumper cables, connect the patch panel to the hubs, connect workstations to the wall jacks, or connect multiple hubs. This allows the network administrator to easily reconfigure the network since all that needs to be modified are the jacks the patch cable connects. The first two types of connections require a straight-through cable. The third requires a crossover cable.

Figure 15–14 shows the difference between the two types of cables [Lamont, 8]. The different cables are needed because of the way twisted pair cables connect. One pair of wiring transmits information from one machine to another, and a second pair transmits information in the reverse direction. A hub reverses the wiring from a workstation allowing the lines to match up correctly and straight through to the cabling system. However, when connecting two hubs, the wiring in both is reversed and so both would attempt to transmit on the same pair and to receive on the same pair—thus, causing them to be unable to communicate. A crossover cable reverses the transmit and receive lines so that the hubs can correctly communicate.

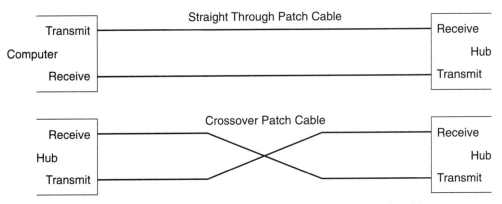

Figure 15–14: A straight-through and a crossover patch cable.

Fiber Boxes and Fiber Jumper Cables

Just as patch panels and patch cables attempt to prevent damage to the wiring going out to the classrooms, a fiber box and cables do the same for fiber optic cable. The fiber from the other part of the cabling system connects inside the fiber box and a fiber jumper cable is used to connect the box to the hub.

Repeaters

In the recent past, repeaters were the most basic type of active cabling equipment. They operated solely at the physical layer, receiving a signal on one port, or connection, and rebroadcasting it on all of its other ports. Repeaters could extend a new network beyond the limits imposed by the wiring, by boosting the signal level. Today, repeaters are seldom used in new networks. Modern (and more expensive) devices look at the message the signals carry to determine whether they really need to pass each message to the next segment.

Most advertisements for *hubs* refer to multiport repeaters. They usually come with a number of ports that are multiples of 12 and allow the network to support up to that number of workstations. Some hubs are stackable, which means they have a special connector that allows a school district or university to easily connect more than one hub together. Others come as chassis systems that support additional cards, each card having another 12 ports. Hubs also serve as central points of interconnection for LAN-attached devices, as well as concentrators and repeaters of LAN traffic.

Switches

Switches are an advanced form of repeaters. They also act at the physical level by repeating the signal. Unlike repeaters that repeat an incoming packet out all of its ports, a switch looks at the destination of the packet and only sends it to the port of the destination. This can reduce excess traffic on a cabling system since it isolates each port and send fewer packets to each port—thereby reducing collisions and increasing the performance of the cabling system. Furthermore, LAN switches are basically intelligent hubs with basic routing capabilities.

Bridges

Bridges operate at a higher level than repeaters, working at the data link layer and looking at the actual packets that are on the cabling system. When bridges receive a packet, they store the entire packet in memory, verify its correctness, and retransmit it on the correct port. This allows them to connect different types of Ethernet networks together such as a 10BaseT and a coax network. Bridges also reset the *3-4-5 rule* for each port, making each port its own network. This is because the network stores the entire packet and rebroadcasts it, thus isolating each port from the others. Like switches, they look at the destination of the packet and only send it to the port where the destination is located, thus reducing traffic on the network. In addition, MAC bridges are sophisticated in that they connect unlike LANs (Ethernet to token ring) via encapsulation.

Routers

Routers operate at the network level. They receive a packet, view its destination, and determine if the packet is destined for a network that is directly connected to the router or if it is destined for a network further away. If it is the first, it sends the packet to the correct port. If it is the latter, it sends the packet to the next router along the path to the packet's final destination. For this reason, routers typically connect between a LAN and a WAN to limit the traffic on the WAN to only packets that need to cross it. Additionally, because routers look at the network information from a packet, they can convert between different network protocols.

Along with the basic cabling equipment, a school district or university that is still using LocalTalk networks will need to install some specialized equipment that connects those networks to the building Ethernet network. This equipment includes MacLAN patch panels and GatorStars or similar equipment, or EtherPrint boxes.

GatorStar/GatorBox

If a building has many LocalTalk devices to connect, a good solution is to use a GatorStar or a GatorBox. A GatorStar connects to an Ethernet port on a hub and to a MacLan patch panel. It converts the packets on the LocalTalk networks into Ethernet packets. This allows workstations on a LocalTalk network to act as if they were directly on the Ethernet network. The GatorBox is a smaller version that can connect to a single LocalTalk network and bridge that network to an Ethernet network.

NOTE:

GatorStar/GatorBox are the products of a specific company. Other companies manufacture similar equipment.

MacLAN Patch Panel

A MacLAN patch panel is a special type of patch panel. When connecting rooms that are using LocalTalk, a patch cable runs from the normal patch panel to the MacLAN patch panel. This connects all of the LocalTalk networks to the MacLAN patch panel. A GatorStar, but not a GatorBox, requires the MacLAN patch panel.

EtherPrint Boxes

If a building has only a few LocalTalk devices such as printers, a cheap and convenient solution is to install EtherPrint boxes next to the printers. They are small devices that convert Ethernet packets into LocalTalk packets. Unlike GatorStar or GatorBoxes, these have a limit on the number of LocalTalk devices they can connect.

NOTE:

EtherPrint boxes are the product of a specific company. Other companies manufacture similar equipment.

Installing Cabling System Equipment

Most vendors design cabling system equipment to be rack-mounted. This means the equipment has special connectors on its side that allow it to bolt to a specially designed rack. This keeps the equipment off the floor, allows good air flow around all the equipment, and provides easy access to both the front and back of the equipment.

Standard racks are 22" x 36" x 84" (width x depth x height) and bolt to the floor in a permanent location. To allow easy access to both the front and back, enough clearance for a person to stand on either side should be allowed around the equipment. The two standard size racks can also be 19" and 23", with the 19" rack predominant. That is to say the mounting holes are 19" and 23" (the old Ma Bell size) apart. Another type of rack that is useful in an unlocked room is the cabinet rack. These come in two heights, 40" and 78". They are lockable, double-hinged cabinets which allow easy access to either the front or the back of equipment.

Configuring Cabling System Equipment

Cabling system equipment comes in two types when talking about configuring the equipment, manageable and nonmanageable. The first allows a central location elsewhere in the building or elsewhere in the school district or university to configure and monitor the equipment. The second requires that an administrator configure the equipment by connecting a portable computer to it. A school district or university will need to decide if it can afford the additional costs for manageable equipment and if they will ever need the capabilities. If the school district or university rarely modifies the cabling system, then the nonmanageable may be a good choice. However, if a small number of people are supporting the cabling system, their ability to remotely configure and monitor a device for correct functionality can more than make up for the cost.

Installing Wide Area Networks

In order to provide access between the different schools and to the Internet, a school district or university will need to install a district or university WAN. This will connect all the schools or remote campuses to each other as well as to an Internet Service Provider (ISP). In some cases, the options available at the ISP will dictate the WAN technology. In others, the cost will decide the WAN technology.

When discussing costs for WAN technology, there are two separate costs associated with the network. The first is the startup cost, which includes such things as equipment and installation. The second is the recurring cost, which occurs either on a monthly or a yearly basis.

The data travels over a WAN in two directions, from the ISP to a building and from a building to the ISP. The first is called the downlink because data is being downloaded from the ISP, and the second is called the uplink, because information is being uploaded to the ISP. On many of the WAN technologies, the uplink and downlink speeds will be the same. Several of the technologies offer different rates in the two directions. The downlink rate will be the most important because the typical use of an Internet connection is to request information from a server. This results in requests and acknowledgments being sent across the uplink and the responses from the requests traveling across the downlink.

The different technologies include Plain Old Telephone Service (POTS), leased lines, Integrated Services Digital Network (ISDN), wireless, cable TV, satellite, and fiber. Table 15–4 summarizes the technologies [Lamont, 11].

Table 15–4: A comparison of different WAN technologies.

			Startup Costs		Recurring cost	
Technology	Speeds	Maximum distance	Installation cost	Equipment cost	Line charge	Internet Access
POTS	9.6 Kbps to 28.8 Kbps	Unlimited	$75	$150	$30/month	$20/month
Dry line	56 Kbps	2-4 miles	$500-$1000	$300	$50/month	$250/month
Leased line	56 Kbps to 1.5 Mbps	Unlimited	$500-$1000	$1500	$200/month – $800/month –	$250/month $2000/month
ISDN	64 Kbps to 128 Kbps	Unlimited	$150	$500-$1500	$50/month + $.005/minute	$250/month
Wireless	2 Mbps	25 miles	$0	$6000-$15000	$0	$250/month
Cable TV	4 Mbps				$50/month	
Satellite	56 Kbps to 115 Kbps	Unlimited	$0	$15000	$800/month – $1200/month	
Fiber	10 Mbps to 1 Gbps and up	1000 meters	$2/foot	$2000	$0	Depends on ISP

Plain Old Telephone Service (POTS)

Just as its name implies, this technology relies on standard phone lines to connect schools. Using current analog modem technology, this service can run at speeds up to 28.8 Kbps in each direction. Speeds of up to 33.6 Kbps and 56 Kbps are also available. It is a cheap and usually easy way to get a machine connected to the Internet quickly. It has low startup costs and low monthly rates. If an extra phone line is already available, the school can reuse it with no installation charge. An office can even share the line because it is only connected when it is in use, although this is not recommended. An ISP will need to provide Internet connectivity, but these are usually available at reasonable rates as well. As shown in Figure 15–15, there is no additional equipment needed except for a modem on each machine that requires Internet connectivity [Lamont, 11].

Leased Line

Another type of WAN connection is a leased line. With a leased line, the school district or university buys a permanent connection from the phone company, either to another school or to an ISP. The district sets up a router and a Channel Service Unit/Digital Service Unit (CSU/DSU) at each school that will connect the leased line to the CSU/DSU as shown in Figure 15–16 [Lamont, 12]. This establishes a network between the two ends of the leased line.

There are two varieties of leased lines, and both operate at identical uplink and downlink speeds. The first is called a dry line. It has a maximum speed of 56 Kbps, and a maximum range of 2 to 4 miles along the length of the phone wiring. The phone company does not provide any boosting of the signal and this limits the length of the wiring. However, because the phone company does not have to provide any equipment, the lines are available at about standard phone rates. The installation is somewhat expensive, being about $500-$1,000 for the initial setup. These lines are perfect for connecting between closely situated buildings.

NOTE:

Dry lines can be installed between buildings in a campus environment (1 to 20 miles) using Limited Distance Modems (LDM) or Short Haul Modems (SHM), and run at T1 speeds.

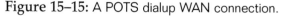

Figure 15–15: A POTS dialup WAN connection.

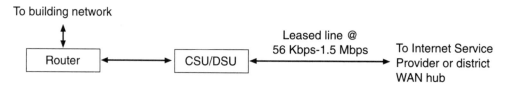

Figure 15–16: A leased line WAN connection.

The other variety is simply called leased lines. They are available in speeds ranging from 56 Kbps up to and beyond 1.5 Mbps (a T1 line). They require the same equipment as a dry line, but the phone company boosts the signal along its path. This allows leased lines to run almost any distance, although longer distances will cost more. The installation costs are similar to dry lines, but the monthly costs are substantially higher, beginning at around $200/month for short distances for a 56 Kbps line. Connecting a school district or university in a star topology (with only one building acting as the central hub and connecting to the ISP), is the cheapest way to create the WAN. However, because all the schools will share the same connection to the Internet, performance will eventually suffer if the shared line is not fast enough. A district or university will obtain the best performance by connecting each school directly to the ISP, but this will cost substantially more.

Along with connecting school district or university buildings, a connection needs to run to an ISP. This can cost a large amount of money depending on the ISP. Costs depend on the speed of the connection. However, commercial rates begin at about $250/month for a 56 Kbps line and extend into the thousands of dollars per month for T1 speeds. Obviously, a non-commercial rate is found to be more affordable for a school district or university.

Integrated Services Digital Network (ISDN)

ISDN is a technology that is finally becoming available from most telephone companies. It offers connections at either 64 Kbps or 128 Kbps in each direction. It also expands by multiples of 64 Kbps. The basic service, called a Basic Rate Interface (BRI), contains two 64 Kbps data lines called B-Channels and a 16 Kbps control line called a D-Channel.

Unlike leased lines (that are paid for 24 hours a day, 7 days a week regardless of their use), the phone company meters ISDN lines like a standard phone line. They only bill a school district or university for the actual usage time of the line. Most ISDN connections will close after a few minutes of inactivity—keeping the usage charge down to a minimum. In addition, unlike a normal POTS modem, an ISDN connection is usually *dial on demand*. This means that if a need arises to use the connection, the ISDN equipment will automatically establish the connection within one or two seconds. This allows users to continue working normally as the line connection opens and closes automatically. As shown in Figure 15–17, the actual implementation of an ISDN WAN is very similar to the network used in a leased line network [Lamont, 13]. However, an ISDN Network Terminator, Type 1 (NT-1), connects to the phone wiring instead of a CSU/DSU. Many NT-1 boxes even contain a simple router so that a school district or university can save money by not needing a router at each building.

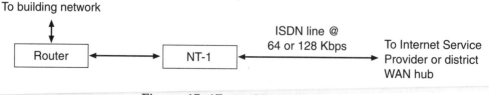

Figure 15–17: An ISDN WAN connection.

NOTE:

> ISDN lines are paid for like standard business lines or POTS lines at approximately $50-$100 per month depending on the provider. The only additional cost is the long distance charges.

Wireless

With the phone company charging on a monthly basis for any network services it provides, other options apart from the phone company may be cheaper. One approach is to use wireless communications to connect multiple buildings. Offering high speeds and minimal or no recurring costs, these technologies deserve a good look. When compared with the phone company solutions, the up front costs are high, but over time this cost can amortize to the point where it is cost effective. Wireless may require expensive towers to clear natural and man-made obstructions around a school. This is because all wireless communications require a clear line of sight between the transmitting and receiving equipment. Figure 15–18 shows the basic configuration of a wireless network [Lamont, 14].

Wireless technology uses one of two methods of communication, either lasers or microwaves. Laser technology offers higher speeds, but shorter ranges of only a few hundred meters. A more significant problem is that most lasers operate in the infrared spectrum and most conditions that block visible light such as rain, fog, or any other physical obstruction also block the laser. Because of these limitations, lasers are not particularly useful when trying to reliably connect multiple buildings.

Microwave communications, on the other hand, are immune to many of the problems that plague lasers. including most weather conditions. And they can travel much farther.

Most microwave equipment that a school district or university will use operates in one of two freely available unlicensed spectrums of the radio frequency band. The advantage is that the equipment requires no licensing with the FCC. Unfortunately, this also means that other equipment can also use the same frequency and can cause interference. However, the equipment uses techniques to prevent this interference causing problems with the information being sent across the connection. Although many products exist in the wireless market, two specific products can be used as an example of the capabilities of wireless networking: The first is the Wireless KarlBridge from KarlNet and the second is the AirLAN Bridge/Ultra from Solectek.

NOTE:

A note of caution here, though—wireless communications has never proven itself reliable enough for high-profile data transmission.

Wireless KarlBridge

The KarlBridge offers a maximum data rate of 2 Mbps in each direction and has a maximum range of 10 miles. It costs about $6,000 for a complete setup, including two antennas, two bridges, and all the cabling needed to connect the equipment together. Although not currently in use by any school district, the University of Illinois installed and tested the equipment and found it to meet its stated capabilities.

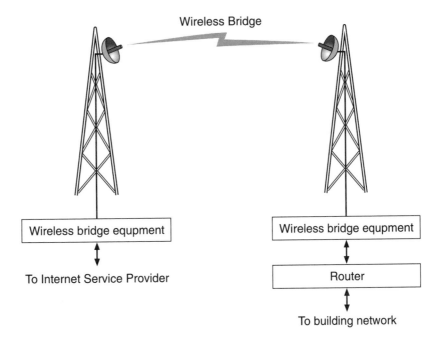

Figure 15–18: A wireless WAN connection.

AirLAN Bridge/Ultra

Offering longer ranges of 10 to 25 miles, the AirLAN Bridge is a choice for a school district or university that needs to connect to points farther away. It also operates at 2 Mbps in each direction. The entire setup ranges in price from $10,000 to $15,000 depending on the distance needed. It includes two antennas, two bridges, and all the cabling needed to connect the equipment.

Cable TV

Cable TV is another alternative to the phone company that is emerging. It allows a school district to provide WAN connectivity using the cable TV wiring. Although still a new technology, it promises to offer high speeds and low costs. However, several technical problems need solutions. These are due to the current implementation of cable TV systems that send the same signal from a central office to many destinations.

The first problem is the fact that television broadcasting is inherently a one-direction process. Information is not sent back to the central office when broadcasting television. New cable equipment that allows two-way communication is now available and as the cable company installs upgrades to the cable TV equipment, this problem will be eliminated.

The other problems are based on the fact that many buildings share a cable TV signal. This leads to the two problems of shared capacity and security. Although cable TV networks operate at high speeds, many buildings share the network. This results in each building getting only a small part of the total bandwidth.

Security is also a problem. When sharing information among several buildings, someone with the correct knowledge and experience can view any unencrypted information placed on the network.

Currently, two implementations of cable TV equipment are available, asymmetric and symmetric. Figure 15–19 shows an example of each [Lamont, 15]. The one available from local cable companies depends on the capabilities of the cable TV system currently installed. In the first implementation, a cable TV line runs to the building and is connected to a cable modem. The cable company then sets aside a single television channel as the downlink. For the uplink, a telephone modem transmits the information. This implementation is known as an asymmetric or hybrid solution because of the different paths taken by data traveling in different directions. This solution does suffer some serious performance problems. Using a television channel, the downlink has a maximum rate of 4 Mbps, but the POTS modem limits the data being sent across the uplink to a rate of 28.8 Kbps.

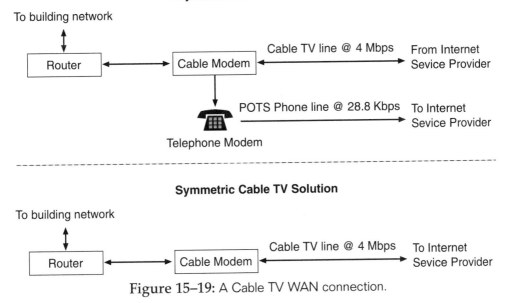

Figure 15–19: A Cable TV WAN connection.

The second implementation requires upgraded cable equipment that can support bidirectional signals on the cable network. These networks, known as symmetric solutions, use two channels for data, one for the uplink and one for the downlink. This allows data to travel at 4 Mbps in both directions.

In terms of costs, the cable company will most likely want to charge a monthly fee for each building that it connects. In a recent contract negotiated with a cable company, some cities such as Glenview, IL, have successfully avoided most or all the cost by requiring data connections to all the city buildings and schools.

Satellite

For school districts and universities located in remote areas (where other technologies are prohibitively expensive or unavailable), a satellite connection is a viable alternative as shown in Figure 15–20 [Lamont, 16]. With this technology, a district buys a satellite dish and the necessary hardware needed to connect it to a network. A building then has a 56 Kbps downlink connection. As in the hybrid cable TV solution, satellite is an asymmetric solution and the uplink rate is only 9.6 Kbps. The initial equipment cost is about $15,000 for the satellite dish and equipment, and the monthly rate is about $800/month. A faster option is also available (with the downlink running at 115 Kbps and the uplink running at 19.2 Kbps) for about $1200/month. These rates are high when compared with other solutions, but in some rural areas this may be the only option.

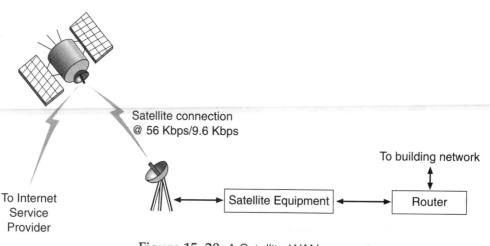

Figure 15–20: A Satellite WAN connection.

Fiber

The ideal solution for a school district or university is to connect all of its buildings with fiber optic cables (see the sidebars, "Installing Fiber Optic Cables," "The Benefits Of Installing Air-Blown Fiber (ABF)," and "Emergency Restoration: Additional Benefits Of Installing ABF"). Fiber can run at speeds beyond 1 Gbps, allowing a district or university to connect the WAN at a high speed immediately and to upgrade to even faster speeds in the future. Unfortunately, this can be very expensive. Fiber suitable for use outside can cost between $2/foot and $2.50/foot. When installing thousands of feet, this can become a significant cost. Besides the fiber cost, installation can also be very expensive. A district or university needs access to all the land between the buildings, and this *right of way* can often cost a lot of money.

NOTE:

Air Blown Fiber or ABF system is a fiber optic cabling and installation method that utilizes a compressed nitrogen gas source to propel a thin fiber optic bundle, without stress, through a previously installed tube cable (duct). Because the fiber can easily be blownout and reused, ABF technology provides exceptional flexibility in dynamic environments.

Fiber Optic Cables

Fiber optic cables should be installed according to the manufacturer's specifications. The following guidelines apply:

- Cable runs without splices are preferred. No splice should exhibit an insertion loss greater than 0.5 dB. The integrity of cable should be maintained for all splices.
- Length markers should be imprinted on the cable jacket at reasonable intervals.
- The maximum pull force on cable installation should not exceed the manufacturer's specification. A strain gauge or dynamometer-type device should be used to monitor pull force during installation.
- The minimum bend radius of the cable should not exceed the manufacturer's specification. All cable should be secured at bends to prevent excessive movement.
- Cable ties or protective devices should be used to prevent chafing.
- Avoid sharp bends and corners.
- Provide additional crush/mechanical protection in high risk environments.
- Observe all governing building and fire codes (either by using a properly listed cable or suitable raceway).
- Secure the fiber optic cable to existing supports or large cables wherever possible.
- Do not deform the cable jacket, specifically when using cable fasteners or ties.
- Protect connectors when installing preconnectorized cable.

The Benefits Of Installing Air-Blown Fiber (ABF)

Five key features provide ABF the flexibility needed to meet the demands of an ever-changing school or university campus environment. These features are modularity, reconfigurability, reliability, reusability, and deferred investment:

Modularity:
ABF is modular in the sense that tube cable is the building block of the ABF system. Tube cable, unlike conduit, is easy to add to and install in modules due to its unique use of reusable, watertight, and airtight connectors. These connectors allow the easy extension of the ABF system by adding additional lengths of tube cable.

Reconfigurability:

A particular advantage of ABF is the ability to provide point-to-point fiber connections in easily. If the ABF infrastructure is intelligently designed, as point-to-point requirements change, the actual destination and origin of the fiber can be changed to meet these new requirements. This is accomplished by rerouting the tube cable through the reconfiguration of the tube cable's pathway at selected *node points* (tube distribution unit).

An example of this ability could be of a test stand being moved from building *A* to building *B*. Building *C* is the monitoring point for the test stand. Building *A* is going to be demolished to make room for a widened road. ABF allows the existing fiber between buildings *A* and *C* to be blown out and stored on a reel. Tubes would be reconfigured at a node point, and if there is enough of the old fiber on the reel then it can be reused by being blown between buildings *C* and *B*. If there wasn't enough old fiber, new fiber would be used and the existing fiber could be reused elsewhere on the facility.

Reliability:

A critical advantage of ABF is its ability to install fiber in a strain free manner. This provides two advantages. The first is guaranteed usable fiber. No strain, no possible damage. The second advantage is reusability. Since no strain is placed on the fiber during insertion or removal, it is available for reuse. An additional feature enhancing reliability is the ease in which point-to-point runs are created. Point-to-point installation minimizes field splicing, increasing reliability and the quality of the link.

Reusability:

As indicated under reconfigurability and reliability, air-blown fiber cable may be reused, saving the cost of new media in appropriate circumstances.

Deferred Investment

Deferred decisions result in deferred investment. Fiber counts and routes can be determined and added when needed [4].

Emergency Restoration: Additional Benefits of Installing ABF

One of the major benefits of ABF is in emergency restoration. The ABF takes significantly less time for restoration. Because the ABF fiber is replaced, there is no change in attenuation. There are two new splices with the conventional fiber, which increases attenuation. If the repair loss budget for a segment of conventional fiber is ever exceeded, then the whole run of conventional fiber must be replaced. The ABF will never exceed the repair loss budget. The following is a typical emergency restoration example.

Air-Blown Fiber	*Conventional Fiber*
500 Meter Span	500 Meter Span
Direct Burial Tube Cable (4-18 fiber bundles. Total 72 fibers)	Direct Burial Gel-Filled Cable (72 Fibers in conduit bank containing 2conduits)
Backhoe tears and cuts through cable	Backhoe tears and cuts through conduits
Dig 20 foot trench at area of break— 10 feet to either side of break (12" wide trench at 55 LF/Hr = .36 hours)	Dig 100 foot trench—50 feet to either side of break (12" wide trench at 55 LF/Hr=1.82 hours)
Cut off 10 feet of tube cable to either side of break (trim fiber back to edge of tubes)	Cut off 50 feet of cable to either side of break (the purpose of removing so much cable is to make sure that the tensile strength of fiber has not been exceeded by the pressure of the original accident which broke the cable)
Clean area of tube cable to be spliced	Clean area of cable to be spliced
Blow out 4-18 fiber bundles on each side of break (total time=18.04	Install 100 feet of cable (100 x.02=2 hours) hours)
Splice 6 foot length of tube cable (6 feet of tube cable, 36 tube connectors, water protective wrap and rubber shrink tubing) (4 hours—2 splices x 2 man hours))	It's customary to do a temporary splice with mechanical splices for a fast restoration. Then the complete cable is replaced from end to end to eliminate attenuation.
Blow in 4-18 fiber bundles (tota l time=18.04 hours)	Temporary cam splice 144 fibers (.5 hours + 144 x .25 hours = 36.5 hours) (100 foot length of direct buried cable)
Test tube cable with pressure and BB tests (includes setup time .16 hours + .07 hours x 18 tubes = 1.42 hours)	Now the permanent replacement is started.

Air-Blown Fiber	Conventional Fiber
Splice 144 fibers or pigtails at each end at an FDN or pedestal (.5 hours + 144 x .25 hours = 36.5 hours) (2 repair kits are required plus 4-500 meter 18 fiber bundles, and splice protection sleeves)	Remove and replace 2-20 foot length of conduit.(total time ~ .15 hours x 40 = 6 hours)
Test fiber - 72 strands of fiber optic cable (4 hours setup time + 72 x .2 hours = 14.4 man hours)	Install 40 feet of 3 innerducts (40 x .03 man hours = 1.2 hours) Pull 500 meters of conventional 72 fiber cable. (1,640 x .02 hours = 32.8 hours)
Hours for ABF = 92.76	Splice 144 fibers or pigtails at each end at an FDN or pedestal (.5 hours + 144 x .25 hours = 36.5 hours) (2 splice cases needed for repair plus splice holders and splice protection sleeves, 100 foot length of direct buried cable)
(3 Person crew - Elapsed time: 30.92Hrs.)	Test fiber - 72 strands of fiber optic cable (4 hours setup time + 72 x .2 hours = 14.4 hours) Remove 500 meters of damaged cable to restore maintenance conduit (1640 x.005 = 8.2 hours) Hours for Conventional = 139.42 (3 Person crew - Elapsed time: 46.47 Hrs.)

Note: This example shows a saving of approximately 33%! However more typical labor savings are in the range of 15% to 20%. Capital costs are typically 10% higher for ABF installations than for conventional fiber installations. [Robin, 9-10]

When a school district or university has multiple buildings on the same property, obtaining access is not usually a problem. A district or university either needs to bury the fiber in the ground, requiring expensive excavation, or hang it from telephone poles, leaving the fiber open to the weather. If the district or university chooses to lease a fiber from the local telephone company, then the district or university will have to pay a high monthly rate for the fiber.

Dial-in Service

A school district or university will need to make a decision regarding the installation of a dial-in pool of modems connected to the district or university WAN. These modems could be for staff and student dialup access to the district WAN and/or to the Internet. This may seem like a good service to provide to the district or university. However, with most local and long distance phone companies offering this service for about $20/month, it is not a service most districts or universities should consider installing. It can easily become an expense and management problem. As more people begin to use the dial-in service, a large percentage of the modems will show a significant increase in their use. A district or university would then need to add modems to provide more dial-in connections. A district or university could spend the money used for the modems and phone lines elsewhere with better gains to a district or university.

NOTE:

Dial-in service is almost a necessity in the previously noted environment, because of the large population of users that have the equipment and tend to use it. It is easy to install and relatively inexpensive.

Software Products

Along with installing a cabling system, a school district or university also needs to acquire any software products it will need. Without the correct software, a district or university will not be able to access or offer the services that it decides are necessary. Required software includes driver software such as TCP/IP drivers, application software such as email programs or word processors, and server software such as file servers or a web servers. Figure 15–21 shows how the different network software pieces interact on a Macintosh and a Windows machine [Lamont, 17]. At the lowest level of a machine, a hardware

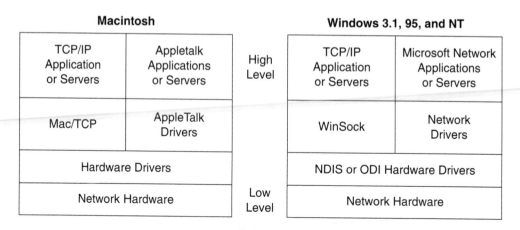

Figure 15–21: The software installed on a workstation.

driver communicates directly with the network interface card installed on a machine. Software drivers supporting the different software protocols such as AppleTalk, IPX, and TCP/IP act as intermediaries, communicating with both the hardware drivers below them and the applications and servers above them. Applications and servers provide an interface to the user. Just as in the OSI model, a layered approach is used. This insulates the upper layers from the requirements of communicating with the specific hardware present on a machine. It also allows all application and server software to function identically regardless of the brand of equipment installed on a machine.

Driver Software

There are two parts to the driver software as shown in Figure 15–21, a hardware driver and a network driver. The hardware driver usually comes on a disk with the network card, along with instructions on how to install it. Some of the network drivers come pre-installed on computers, while others need to be bought. On a Macintosh, the AppleTalk drivers have always been a part of the standard system software. The MacTCP software and the TCP/IP driver offered by Apple was not part of the standard system software until the release of System 7.5 several years ago. Before that time, MacTCP was a separately purchased product. All machines shipped over the last few years, and all currently shipping machines include MacTCP. But any machine that is not running System 7.5 will require a copy of MacTCP. Of all the Windows varieties, only Windows 3.1 and earlier do not include network drivers as part of the standard system. Windows 3.1 requires an additional product which will add a WinSock interface to Windows, allowing all TCP/IP based applications and servers to run. Windows for Workgroups, Windows98, and Windows NT all include the necessary network drivers as part of the standard system software.

Application Software

Applications are programs such as Microsoft Word or ClarisWorks that run on a workstation. They allow a user to perform a task on the computer such as write a paper, check their email, or browse the web. When selecting applications, a school district or university can establish a standard that all the buildings in the district must follow, or they can allow each building to choose their own. By establishing a standard, a district or university can assure staff and students access to their files from anywhere in the district or university. A standard will also make training and support easier since the entire district or university will only use a controlled group of applications. Without a district standard, each school can choose applications that their staff is already familiar with or which serve a specific purpose such as multimedia authoring. A district or university can also select different standards for different schools, depending on the grades taught at the building. The best approach for a district or university is to establish a standard for everyday applications such as word processors or email programs, but to allow freedom when choosing special purpose software. This allows the building staff to choose software to fit their special needs, while still making papers and other common files easily accessible for sharing among buildings.

NOTE:

The standard for the school should also be an industry standard.

Applications fall into two categories, stand-alone and clients. The first are programs such as those listed in Table 15–5, which do not require interaction with other machines to function [Lamont, 18]. They are available from many vendors, offering different capabilities and costs. A district or university should compare all the alternatives for a given type of program and select the one offering the best price and feature match. Districts and universities should consider buying integrated packages that offer a word processor, a spreadsheet, and a database in a single product. Districts and universities should also buy only the capabilities they need or expect to need in the future. For example, if a district or university is going to select an integrated package as a standard, it should consider if it needs the extra capabilities of Microsoft Office. If not, the district can save money by selecting ClarisWorks or Microsoft Works instead.

Table 15–5: Some common stand-alone application software.

Application	Common products
Word Processor	Microsoft Word, WordPerfect
Spreadsheet	Microsoft Excel, Lotus 1-2-3
Integrated Packages	ClarisWorks, Microsoft Works, Microsoft Office
Multimedia Authoring	Macromedia Director, HyperStudio, SuperCard

The second group of applications are ones, such as those listed in Table 15–6, which require a network to function [Lamont, 18]. Many of the applications in this category are available as either shareware or freeware, and offer similar or better features than the competing commercial products. A school district or university should investigate the free alternatives before it spends money on commercial products. In addition, the choice of client software may depend on the server software selected. For example, if a district or university decides to standardize on Internet email, then they should choose an email client such as Eudora that supports Internet email.

Table 15–6: Some common client software.

Application	Common products
Email	Eudora, Microsoft Mail, QuickMail
Web Browser	Netscape Navigator, NCSA Mosaic, Internet Explorer
Video Conferencing	CU-See Me

Server Software

Server software runs on a machine that often requires a dedicated machine for it to run on, and even when it does not require a dedicated machine, server performance is usually better if applications are not run on the machine. The server software will also run faster if installed on a faster computer. For this reason, a school district or university should plan to buy separate, fast machines for use as servers. Server software exists for both Macintosh and PC platforms, as well as for Unix machines. Unix machines are complex, high performance workstation often used in the engineering world. Most of the platforms support all the services as shown in Table 15–7, although some brands of server software will only run on specific platforms [Lamont, 19].

Table 15–7: Server functions supported by different platforms.

Server function	Macintosh	Windows 3.1, 95	Windows NT	Novell Netware	Unix
File Server	Yes	No	Yes	Yes	Yes
Print Server	Yes	No	Yes	Yes	Yes
Multimedia Server	No	No	Yes	Yes	Yes
Email Server	Yes	Yes	Yes	Yes	Yes
Web Server	Yes	Yes	Yes	Yes	Yes
Usenet News	No	No	Yes	No	Yes
Electronic Phonebook	No	No	No	No	Yes
Administrative Record Keeping	Yes	Yes	Yes	Yes	Yes

File and Print Server

There are three main choices when selecting a file and print server, AppleShare, Windows NT, and Novell Netware. As shown in Table 15–8, they offer many of the same features [Lamont, 19]. All of them support both Macintosh and Windows 3.1 clients, but if a school district or university is using other clients, such as Windows98 or OS/2, they will need to select an appropriate server that can support those clients. The installation and maintenance of the file server software are also issues that need consideration. File servers are complex packages requiring training to be used optimally. If a staff member already has experience with one of the choices, then a district or university can save time and money by not needing to train a server administrator on a new product.

Table 15–8: Features available on different file servers.

Feature	AppleShare	Window NT	Netware
Hardware platform	Macintosh	PC compatible	PC compatible
Maximum number of concurrent users	50-100	1000	1000

(continued)

Table 15–8: *(continued)*

Feature	AppleShare	Window NT	Netware
Approximate cost for 100 users	$1400	$850	$4300
Performance	Good	Very good	Excellent
Print serving	Yes	Yes	Yes
Ease of installation	Excellent	Good	Good
Ease of administration	Excellent	Good	Good
Reliability	Very good	Excellent	Excellent
Clients Supported			
DOS/Windows 3.1	Yes	Yes	Yes
Macintosh	Yes	Yes	Yes
Windows NT	No	Yes	Yes
Windows95	No	Yes	Yes
Windows98	No	Yes	Yes
OS/2	No	No	Yes

Multimedia Server

Multimedia comes in a variety of forms. It includes audio and video segments, often on multimedia CD-ROMs. Depending on the needs of a school district or university, the same platforms acting as the file server can also act as the multimedia server. All three platforms support the sharing of multiple CD-ROMs. Additional software can be acquired for Windows NT and Netware that will allow them to serve audio and video segments. For serving large numbers of audio and video segments, the optimal solution is to use a Unix system with software specifically designed to serve these segments. This can cost a lot of money, and requires a district or university to support a Unix system.

Email Server

Selecting an email server can be a complex problem. Each brand, such as Microsoft Mail or QuickMail, uses its own mail protocol. The Internet also supports several different protocols. All of these email protocols are incompatible with each other without software to translate between the protocols. Server programs, called software gateways, will translate between most of the different email protocols, but a district can save money and avoid problems by standardizing on a single email protocol. The recommended email solution combines two protocols used on the Internet, Simple Mail Transfer Protocol (SMTP) and Post Office Protocol (POP). The first transmits email from the sender to the receiver's email server, and the second allows the receiver to view their email. As shown in Table 15–9, server software to support the Internet protocols is available for all three file server platforms and the file server can also act as an email server [Lamont, 20]. As an added benefit, all the software listed in Table 15–9 is available at no cost. Unfortunately, these email servers can not handle a large number of users, and the performance of the servers decreases after several hundred email accounts are in use. A Unix machine can act as an email server for a school district or university requiring better performance, although this is not recommended unless a district or university already has a Unix machine running for another purpose or absolutely requires higher performance.

Table 15–9: Email server software available for different platforms.

Platform	SMTP and POP server software
Macintosh	Apple Internet Mail Server
Windows NT	NT Mail
Netware	Mercury

Web Server

Web servers are also available for the same three platforms that file servers and email servers can run on and can often share the same machine used as a file and email server. Table 15–10 lists some of the choices available [Lamont, 21]. The wide range of choices allows a school district or university a lot of freedom in selecting a web server. Some things to consider when selecting a product are cost, performance, and how easily and in what programming languages a user can expand the web server. Some commercial products can cost up to $1,000. Performance is also an issue, but this is tied to the price. The more expensive the web server, the better performance it usually offers. An exception to this is the Netscape web server (a high performance product), which is available to educational users at no cost. The last consideration is how the web server offers access to external programs. These programs (called Common Gateway Interfaces (CGIs)) handle the advanced actions on a web page such as forms processing. Each platform offers a different interface to the CGIs. Also, CGIs designed for one platform are not usually usable on another. Here again, a Unix machine can act as a web server for a district or university requiring better performance, although this is not recommended unless a district already has a Unix machine running for another purpose or absolutely requires higher performance.

Table 15–10: Web server software available for different platforms.

Platform	Web server software
Macintosh	WebStar, NetPresenz
Windows NT	Netscape Server
Netware	Novell Web Server, GLACI HTTPD
Unix	NCSA httpd, CERN httpd, Netscape Server

Usenet News Server

Currently, only Unix systems can run news servers. If a school district or university needs to make Usenet available to its students and wants to maintain its own server, then it will require that a district or university buy and maintain a Unix system. This can be a complex process, especially when trying to run a news server on it. If a district or university is willing to let another group control its news server, the ISP will often offer the service, thus allowing a district or university to access the news server run by the ISP. Although not a perfect solution, this prevents a district or university from having to maintain its own Unix system.

Administrative Record-Keeping System

A school district or university usually buys an administrative record-keeping system as a complete system which contains all the necessary hardware and software needed to install and use the system. It will include both server and client software in the package. Unfortunately, the complexity involved in managing student records and grades can often result in a cumbersome program that is difficult to use. A district or university should keep this in mind when selecting a system and be sure that it is easy to use. A district or university should also consider the performance of the product. Although it is impossible to give exact performance numbers, the system should not make an administrator wait to retrieve information. The system should also be customizable, allowing changes in its reporting and record-keeping capabilities without requiring that a new system be bought.

Most administrative systems operate in one of two environments, either centralized or distributed. In a centralized environment, a central computer stores all the information, often at the district administrative office. All requests for information travel across the district WAN to the central office where the system fulfills the requests and sends responses back. The system generates all grade, attendance, and other reports at the central office and the school district or university campus staff distributes printed copies as needed.

In a distributed environment, a student's building stores their records. When another building needs to access the information, it sends a request across the district WAN to the student's building and the systems at that building fulfills the request. All of this happens transparently to the administrator who does not need to know the student's building. The system generates reports at each building, thus allowing quicker distribution of the information.

Most of these systems will cost in the tens of thousands of dollars. With that large a price tag, a school district or university should be sure that the package they are purchasing includes technical support. If not, the district or university can add that in as a negotiating point when pricing the system. Additionally, the district or university should verify the quality of the company's technical support group, and get references of other districts or universities that are using the product. This will ensure a district or university that it will get prompt and useful help if problems should arise. This is vital, because once the district or university puts all the records into the system, and it stops working, they will all become inaccessible.

Another option that a school district or university can consider is developing a custom administrative record-keeping system. This would require that a district or university hire a full-time computer consultant to design, implement, and support the system. The software that the consultant develops should meet all of a districts or university's needs exactly. When comparing this with the ten of thousands of dollars required to buy an administrative record-keeping system, this option can be competitive costwise, thus resulting in a district or university getting exactly what they want.

NOTE:

Custom systems are high maintenance.

During and upon completion of the installation of the cabling system, and all of the additional components just discussed, a little testing and quality control should not be out of the question. Let's take a look at how it's done.

Testing, Quality Assurance and Installation Standards

The following copper and fiber optic tests (see the sidebar, "Testing Procedures") should be satisfactorily performed and quality control and installation standards (see the sidebar, "100Base5 Cable Installation Standards") adhered to by the school district or university—with the specified documentation provided prior to the cabling system installation project sign-off. All test, quality control, and installation standards implementation results should be delivered in machine-readable form compatible with MS-DOS version 5.0 and above. The information should be formatted as a CSV (Comma Separated Variable) flat file. Hard copy test, quality control, and installation standards implementation results should also be provided in the form generated by the test equipment or contractor produced with text file.

Testing Procedures

Copper—4-Pair:

Provide full testing and documentation to satisfy Category 5 specifications. Tests should be performed from the horizontal cable BIX field to the faceplate jack for all drop cables.

Copper—25-Pair and 100-Pair:

Provide full testing and documentation to satisfy Category 4 specifications (or grade of cable installed). Tests should be performed from BIX connector to BIX connector for each four pairs.

All copper 4-, 25-, and 100-pair tests should be performed using a Microtest Penta Scanner or equivalent test equipment. The test results should be documented including the following information:

- Cable ID.
- Building number.
- Tx location.
- Rx location.
- Test equipment; Tx type and Rx type.
- Contractor name.
- Technician name and signature.
- Date test performed.
- Relevant additional comments.

Fiber—MultiMode and SingleMode:

Bidirectional attenuation tests at 850 and 1300 nm operating wavelengths should be performed on all fiber strands. The test results should be provided with the following information:

- Cable ID.
- U of T building number.
- Attenuation values.
- Tx location.
- Rx location.
- Wavelength.
- Fiber type.

- Connector type.
- Test equipment; Tx type and Rx type.
- Reference setting at first wavelength.
- Reference setting at second wavelength.
- Contractor name.
- Technician name and signature.
- Date test performed.
- Relevant additional comments.
- Soft copy test results must be supplied in a text file form with two hard copy backups.

Time Domain Reflectometer:

Time Domain Reflectometer (TDR) readings should be taken on the reel prior to acceptance from the vendor, after installation without taps installed, and after taps have been installed. Also, the TDR readings should be recorded for later baselining.

DC Loop Resistance:

DC Loop resistance should be accomplished for each coax segment to maintain a 5 ohm or less resistance per 500 meters of cable [UTOR, 13-14].

Quality Assurance

The contractor should be responsible for cleanup of all facilities and buildings related to the cabling system installation project, during and at completion. The work site and adjacent areas should be left in the same condition or cleaner than when starting a shift. This must be done on a daily basis.

The contractor should protect building equipment, exterior and interior, in the immediate and adjacent work areas. The contractor should protect existing building finishes and services not affected by the modifications.

Surface Finishes

The general standard is that existing surfaces should be restored and finished back to the original condition or better. If each condition is not exactly specified in the scope of work, it will at the discretion of the Program Manager to determine the appropriate finish. Contractors should be aware of the site conditions prior to bidding and account for the appropriate resources necessary for this aspect of the cabling system installation project.

When penetrating surfaces where there is vinyl asbestos tile, cut and lift the tile prior to coring. Use the lifted tile to restore finishes where it is possible.

When penetrating terrazzo or concrete surfaces, the restored surface must be finished using the same materials. A terrazzo patch kit must be used to restore surfaces that have been damaged beyond a 1/4 inch circumference of the penetrating structure. A patch area must be created that uses straight cuts at right angles to each other or to adjacent walls.

When penetrating carpeted surfaces, cut or lift the carpet prior to coring. Refit the carpet tight to the penetrating structure. Also, when penetrating wall or floor slabs both sides must be restored to the existing finish.

When painting surfaces use one primer / sealer coat of paint and two or more finish coats of paint. Block or brick walls are to be thoroughly sealed prior to finishing.

Any holes in surfaces created to secure operating equipment must be fully restored. In addition, any markings on surfaces such as spray paint or liquid markers must be removed, cleaned and polished where necessary.

Any over-painting of structures on to background surfaces may make it necessary to refinish the background area to match the new structure. It is the responsibility of the contractor to pre-determine this condition or to take care in avoiding the situation.

100Base5 Cable Installation Standards

Definitions:
Coax Segment—A coax cable with 50 ohm terminators on each end.

Maximums:
— 500 meters (1640 feet) of coaxial cable.
— 100 MAU connections.
— End-to-end propagation delay 2165 ns.

Link Segment—A link between two repeaters.

Maximums:
— End-to-end propagation delay 2570 ns.

Repeater—A device that regenerates the electrical signal on the transmission medium.

Parameters:
— Required to connect two coax segments together.
— Each repeater takes up a MAU position on the coax segment.
— SQE must be disabled on MAUs that provide connections to repeaters.

SQE (Signal Quality Error—heartbeat)—a function accomplished by the MAU to determine if the cable plant is still functional after a packet has been sent.

LAN Segment—A Local Area Network cable plant in which no address filtering is accomplished no Bridges or Routers).

Maximums:

Transmission path allowed between any two nodes—5 segments, 4 repeater sets (including AUI cables), 2 MAUs, and 2 AUI cables. Of the 5 segments, a maximum of 3 segments may be coax segments, the rest must be link segments.

Router—A device that filters and forwards packets from one LAN segment to another using network layer addressing as a filter-and-forward mechanism.

Bridge—A device that filters and forwards packets based upon MAC layer addressing as a filter-and-forwarding mechanism.

Medium Access Unit (MAU)—A Transceiver for interfacing the electrical signals from the AUI cable to the coax segment.

AUI—Attachment Unit Interface—A cable specification using 4-pair shielded (22 AWG - Power pair, 24 AWG TX, RX and Collision pairs). Uses a DB-15 connector on the ends.

Maximums:
— Length - 50 meters (152.4 feet).
— Minimum propagation velocity 0.65 c.
— End-to-end delay 257 ns.

Cost Estimates for Equipment

While developing budgets, a school district or university will need cost estimates for the district or university cabling system. Some of the costs, such as the prices for WAN equipment, have already been mentioned. This part of the chapter details other costs. These costs, only estimates, are based on current prices, and can fluctuate rapidly.

General Cabling System Costs

As a rough estimate, most school districts have found that the equipment costs for installing a cabling system in a small elementary school with several hundred students are about $15,000. A middle school with 1,000 to 1,500 students will cost about $20,000. A large high school with 2,000 to 3,000 students will cost close to $30,000. A university with 6,000 or more students would cost over $60,000. Another way of estimating the total cost of a building is to use a cost of $250 per drop for all the equipment needed, and multiplying that by the number of drops installed in a building. These prices only include the initial equipment and wiring needed to connect all the rooms in the building to a central hub. They do not include labor costs or the costs associated with buying computers for use on the cabling system.

Cabling System Equipment Costs

Cabling system equipment prices are dependent on the type of equipment being bought, the brand and if the equipment is manageable. Simple equipment like repeaters may only cost a few hundred dollars, while a router may cost five or six thousand dollars. Manageable devices are also more expensive, adding about 30 percent to the cost of a hub, bridge, or other piece of equipment.

Labor Costs

The labor costs will be one of the largest costs involved in the project if the school district or university contracts an outside service to install the wiring. Even if the district or university decides to install the wiring using district or university staff or volunteers, the wiring should only be installed once. The wiring only costs about $100 for a 1,000 foot spool, and is not a major part of the cost. Therefore, if a district or university foresees needing additional drops in a room in the future, it should consider installing extra wires to each room at the time of the original installation. They do not have to connect until needed and only add minimally to the total cost while providing extra growth capabilities to the cabling system.

Computer Costs

A good estimate for the price of a new computer is about $2,000. The capabilities of the system will increase in the future, but a system that a district would want to purchase will always be priced around that range. This is for either a Macintosh system or a name brand PC-compatible system such as one from Dell or Compaq. More powerful systems for use as servers will often fall in the $4,000 to $5,000 range and have faster processors, more memory, and larger hard drives.

Software Costs

The prices for application software will also vary, but a simple integrated package such as ClarisWorks or Microsoft Works will cost about $100 for each machine when bought in quantity. Other software will vary widely in price, with many products being available as freeware at no cost, and other specialized products, such as multimedia authoring tools, being in the range of $1,000 to $2,000 for a single copy.

NOTE:

Software licensing policies must be adhered to.

These prices include a standard educational discount. If the prices a school district or university receives from a vendor are higher, contact them about educational pricing.

As always, prices will also vary from one vendor to another. A school district or university should be sure to compare pricing from different vendors and find the best pricing. As discussed previously about where to obtain help, the best solution is to form a partnership with a local vendor that can result in better prices.

Problems that Can Occur during Implementation

Even after a district has created all of its plans, the cabling system designers need to stay involved. Problems will always occur, prices will always change, and timetables will often slip. By staying involved with the installation process, the designers can solve these and other problems before they become disasters.

By working carefully, most school districts or universities have been able to finish below their expected costs. Some of the reasons for this were that the designers followed the installation process closely and were able to avoid buying some equipment than was initially planned for, but was later found to be unnecessary. Both districts and universities have found that the actual installation of the wiring took much longer than expected. This was because the staff involved in the installation was unfamiliar with the networking process, and because unexpected problems arose. In one building in a school district, for example, the floors in adjacent rooms did not line up as were indicated on the floor plans. One was higher than the other by several inches, so when they drilled a hole between the rooms from the lower room, it never came out on the other side. They solved the problem eventually, but they lost time in the process.

Other delays can also occur. If a school district or university is using an outside contractor, it should be sure to put a due date on the completion of the installation to avoid potential slips. When using volunteers, a district should be sure to invite extra people since inevitably some will be unable to show up at the last minute. Even hiring new, full-time staff is not fool proof as one school district discovered when one of the two people hired to install the cabling system quit unexpectedly.

Even after the cabling system installation, delays will occur. Equipment can arrive from the vendor nonfunctional and needing to be replaced. Hardware and software will need to be configured—a process that can take an enormous amount of time. Software may not be compatible with the system it was intended to run on, requiring a shuffling of equipment.

The connection to the Internet that the school district or university is planning can also take longer than expected to be ready for use. As previously mentioned, some school districts and universities have had problems with their wireless connections that prevents them from reliably connecting to the Internet. Getting a connection established through the phone or cable company can also take longer than expected, especially if the technology that the district or university is using is new to the utility company.

The key to solving the problems without losing too much time is for the cabling system designers to play an active role in the entire process. If delays occur that are beyond the control of a school district or university, then the district or university can redirect its efforts to another part of the cabling system until they find a solution to the problem. Although this can be very difficult, by constantly modifying the process to fit current conditions, a district or university can finish their cabling system both on time and under budget.

Last Words on Installation

As we have seen in this chapter, there are many guidelines to keep in mind while wiring the network. A school district or university should try to follow all of them, but if problems or questions arise, remember the most important one: do not hesitate to get help from someone more qualified, even if it costs money. It is better to spend the money now, rather than on having someone come in later and fix a cabling system that does not work.

From Here

Chapter 15, described in complete detail the installation of the cabling system and covered specific areas such as core drilling considerations; conduit installation and fill guidelines; grounding, shielding and safety; pulling the cable without damage; splicing and patching; blown fiber; labeling schemes; and quality control and installation standards. Chapter 16 takes a close look at the following post-installation activities: cable fault detection with OTDR; cabling system troubleshooting and testing; copper and fiber optic loss testing; documenting the cabling system; cabling system performance certification; and Telecommunications System Bulletin (TSB) 67 accuracy levels testing.

End Notes

1   Bradley H. Lamont, "A Guide to Networking a K-12 School District," University of Illinois at Urbana-Champaign, Urbana, Illinois, 1996, p. 2.

2   "Standards For Communications Cabling," Communication Services, University of California, Santa Barbara, 1234 Cheadle Hall, Santa Barbara, CA 93106, 1995, p. 1

3   "UTORnet Programme: Specifications, Standards and Practices," University of Toronto (UTOR), Toronto, Ontario, Canada M5S 1A1, 1998, p. 4.

4   Mark Robin, "Air Blown Fiber - A Comparison," Advanced Communications Engineer, Engineering Services, Military Systems Integration Division, ComNet Midwest, Inc., W226 N900 Eastmound Drive, Waukesha, WI 53186, Copyright November 3, 1995 Electronic Data Systems Corporation. All Rights Reserved, Reprinted with Permission, pp. 8–10.

16

CERTIFICATION
OF SYSTEM PERFORMANCE

A properly installed and undisturbed cable installation should give many years of trouble free operation. In order to ensure this *trouble free operation*, a number of post-installation testing and performance certification activities must take place. This chapter takes a close look at the following post-installation activities:

- For fiber optic cabling systems, cable fault detection with OTDR.
- Cabling system troubleshooting and testing.
- Copper and fiber optic loss testing.
- Documentation of the cabling system.
- Cabling system performance certification.
- Telecommunications System Bulletin (TSB) 67 accuracy levels testing.

Fiber Optic Cable Fault Detection with OTDR

Let's begin the examination of post-installation system performance certification activities by taking a close look at cable faults that usually occur with a newly installed cabling system. What technologies are in place now to detect the location of these faults as quickly and accurately as possible?

Large-capacity fiber optic cabling systems play a vital role as the information superhighways of modern society and large organizations. The impact of a cable fault on an organization is very great—especially after installation of a new large cabling system—so the fault must be repaired as quickly as possible. To do that, the fault must be accurately located as soon as possible. Recently, companies like AT&T and their counterpart Kokusai Densin Denwa Co., LTD. (KDD) R&D Laboratories in Japan have successfully tested a new fault localization method that can detect faults up to 4,500 km (2,813 miles) away, equivalent to half the distance across the Pacific Ocean from Japan to the U.S. mainland.

When a Cable Fault Occurs

Almost all faults in fiber optic cabling systems are cable faults. Cables can be damaged by natural disasters or human intervention. Most cabling system technicians are prepared to move quickly when a fault occurs. But before they can do their work, the fault must be located. Accurate localization of fault points is the key to speedy recovery from cable faults. Without precise information about the location of the fault, a great deal of time will be lost searching in the dark.

In existing fiber optic cabling systems, faults are located by opening and closing loopback circuits built into the repeaters. This allows faults to be traced to a cable segment between repeaters by checking whether the proper loopback signals are received or not. However, there is no way to know exactly where in the segment between the repeaters the fault is located, so in practice what is usually done is to replace the entire segment, including the repeaters.

Locating Cable Faults Precisely

A prominent feature of optical amplifier cable systems is that they can transmit light of different wavelengths, using different types of modulation. This allows several different signals to be transmitted at the same time. Maintenance of the cabling system can take advantage of these properties. It is now possible to develop new maintenance technologies that are functional, economical, and different from current technologies. KDD R&D Laboratories and AT&T have used the properties of optical amplifier cabling systems to develop a method for detecting cable faults between repeaters—fault localization technology that has been impossible for cabling systems up until now.

How Faults are Detected

In optical fibers, there occurs a phenomenon similar to one we see every day. In the daytime, the color of the sky is blue, but at dawn and sunset it is orange. This is because light from the sun travels on a relatively short path during the day, and on a longer path at dawn and sunset. As it travels through the atmosphere, the light is scattered. Light in the blue portion of the spectrum is more affected by scattering than light in the red potion, so the sky appears blue during the day. But even red light is scattered when the path is long enough. Hence the red color of the sky at sunset. The name of this phenomenon is Rayleigh scattering, and the amount of Rayleigh scattering for light of any wave-length is proportional to I over the wave-length to the fourth power. Thus blue light is scattered much more than red light.

This scattering phenomenon also occurs in optical fibers. It exists in all fibers, due to microscopic variations in the reflective index of the glass that occur when the fiber is manufactured. Scattered light travels in every direction, including back-ward toward the optical source. Light that travels backward in this way is called back-scattering, and the amount of back-scattering per unit length is almost constant for fibers manufactured from the same materials. This allows cabling system technicians to launch optical pulses into the fiber to measure the strength of the back-scattering on the temporal axis—a technique called Optical Time Domain Reflectometry (OTDR). Using OTDR, technicians can investigate fiber properties such as the distribution of propagation loss versus distance, and the location of faults.

Repeater Innovations

Optical amplifiers are capable of amplifying light in both directions. But in order to obtain stable transmission, long-haul optical amplifiers systems use devices called isolators, which ensure that light is propagated in one direction only. There is an isolator in each amplifier, so that any back-scattering that occurs is prevented from traveling back through the amplifier. Therefore, every repeater incorporates special loopback circuits for backscatter to allow light to be propagated in both directions. These loop-back circuits are very simple in structure. As shown in Figure 16–1, they consist only of passive optical couplers [1].

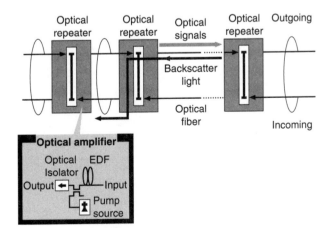

Figure 16–1: Because repeaters do not depend on signal transmission capacity, they also enable high-speed communications and the construction of more economical systems.

Coherent Wavelength Probes

In addition to amplifying the light signals, optical amplifiers also generate spontaneous optical emission noise. The noise generated by each amplifier accumulates as the light travels through the repeaters, and eventually becomes very large. This makes it difficult to detect the very weak backscatter signals. For example, when locating faults with a precision of I km using a probe wavelength of I nanometer (equivalent to 123 GHz), the signal-to-noise ratio of backscatter light power versus spontaneous optical emission noise is 1/30,000 (~5 dB), or even 1/300,000,000 (-85 dB). Moreover, backscatter light is affected by propagation loss, so that it becomes weaker and harder to detect as the distance to the repeater increases. Therefore, the backscatter receiver must have excellent sensitivity.

For the optical receiver, the electromagnetic properties of light were exploited to develop a coherent detection method. The principle is the same as that used in heterodyne radio receivers. Compared to the intensity modulation direct detection (IMDD) method, this method has the advantage of increasing receiver sensitivity. It features not only increased signal selectivity to capture extremely weak signals, but also the ability to measure the optical power of backscatter signals along the temporal axis. This allows improvement of the signal-to-noise ratio by calculating the average optical power.

Figure 16–2 shows a schematic block diagram of the coherent OTDR (COTDR) device used in the test [Horiuchi, 4]. It has a very simple structure, but depends on extremely advanced component technology. KDD, with help from AT&T Bell Laboratories, has constructed a test bed facility for use in developing and testing new transmission methods for transoceanic optical amplifier systems. This facility provides 9,000 km (5,625 miles) of optical fiber cable, equal in length to a cable across the Pacific Ocean.

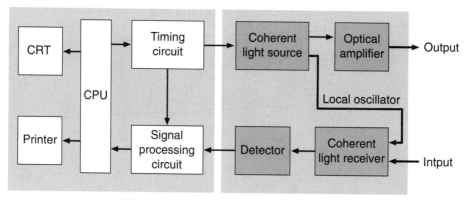

Figure 16–2: Coherent OTDR block diagram.

The fault location method previously explained requires outgoing and incoming lines, so the 9,000 km test bed facility was used as a bi-directional 4,500 km system. The repeater interval was 33 km (21 miles), and 136 repeaters were used (272 optical amplifiers).

Figure 16–3 shows results measured near the terminal when the COTDR device was connected to the 4,500 km system [Horiuchi, 6]. There are large spikes in the signal at the positions corresponding to the optical amplifier locations, followed by a gradually descending trace. This trace is the optical power of the backscatter light. The gradient of the trace indicates the distribution over distance of the optical fiber's propagation loss (dB/km). Figure 16.3 shows a sudden break in the backscatter signal at 4,580 km (2,863 miles). This is the fault location. The figure shows that the new detection technology can be used not only to detect breaks in optical-fiber cables, but also to detect faults such as a local increase in propagation loss.

This experiment confirmed that it was possible to detect cable faults in about 4,500 km of cable with a resolution within 1 km (.63 miles). The distance 4,500 km is equivalent to half the length of the longest trans-oceanic cable, between Japan and the United States. This technology is now being used to search for faults from the Japanese and U.S. sides. It is now possible to locate the repair area with an accuracy of 1 km.

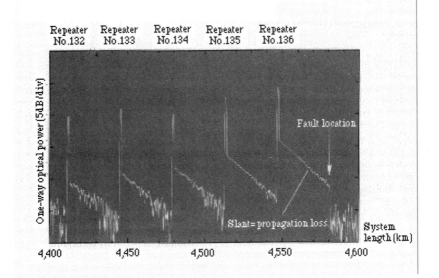

Figure 16–3: 4,500 km fault detection test.

Toward Extremely High-Speed Transmission

The newly developed fault detection technology has now been adopted for optical amplifier cable systems. It has also been applied to the next-generation optical amplifier system for extremely high-speed transmission which has been developed at the KDD R&D Laboratories. By providing accurate information on the location of cable faults, the new technology has increased the maintainability of cabling systems, ensuring that customers will always be able to depend on services offered over the information superhighway.

System Testing and Troubleshooting

Once you've detected and located the cable fault, it's now time to do a little *troubleshooting*. With that in mind, let's look at the next cabling system post-installation certification activities, system testing and troubleshooting.

Now that you know how to detect cable faults, it's now time for you to learn how to conduct more sophisticated post-installation cabling system tests and use the latest troubleshooting techniques. Teamwork, network analysis, and preventive maintenance play an important role in keeping your cabling system in top form.

Cabling System Testing and Tuning for Certification

At every level of the effort to better cabling system performance, network staffers must know their cabling system's history through study of installation and maintenance records. They must know their cabling system's present state by making accurate measurements. And, they must know how they will change their cabling system, as dictated by cabling standards.

NOTE:

The most important thing here is the ongoing documentation of cable moves, adds, and changes (MAC).

Coordinating Work

As part of the work division, the network staffers must coordinate their work with others, including end users and departmental computer support personnel.

Most cabling system users will be delighted to learn that their networking staff is taking steps to make the system more efficient and, thus, will be understanding of the occasional interruptions needed to reach that goal. Interrupting cabling system service to improve its efficiency without telling your users, however, is ample provocation for a lynching.

When altering the cabling system to improve service, you make the change, document it, and then measure its results. It's possible that these tasks will happen quickly and be performed by technicians in different locations.

Cabling system documentation can be accomplished through databases and spreadsheets or by mapping the data in a graphics package. Specialized cabling system record-keeping and graphics software is also available.

The kind of test equipment used depends on the scope of the cabling system tuning operation. Handheld cable meters and LAN testers can be used for working with a single LAN segment. When attempting tuning operations across an entire campus or LAN, these meters, as well as protocol analyzers and special remote monitoring software, may be used to gather performance information.

Do Your Homework

Before cabling system technicians arrive at the LAN site, you must do your homework. You should have a printout with network adapter burned-in addresses, network start names, and IP addresses if the workstations are not using BootP or Dynamic Host Configuration Protocol [2]. A cable map with all known cable labels also should be available.

After checking in with the local computer support people, the area supervisors, and security personnel, you should perform a spot check of cable labels on all exposed LAN wiring. While you are working, you should be prepared to explain what you are doing.

Cabling System Measuring

Once the cabling system professionals are certain that the labeling spot check has been reconciled, they can proceed with measuring the LAN segment. A small, workgroup 10BaseT Novell Ethernet LAN running IPX and TCP/IP protocols can provide a good example of a LAN segment. Usually covering 10 to 12 machines or fewer and at least one networked printer, this segment uses unshielded twisted-pair RJ45 cabling and one or more network hubs to form the segment.

If part of a larger cabling system, this LAN segment might be isolated from the rest of the LAN through the use of a bridge. A bridge machine lets cable traffic from the LAN segment flow out to the rest of the network and lets cable traffic destined for the LAN segment come in from the rest of the network.

After determining the scope of a performance problem, your cabling system staff divides the work into easily accomplished tasks. These tasks are charted against a time line using a variety of tools ranging from a simple wall chart to sophisticated software packages.

A bridge in its simplest form is a PC which possesses two network cards: one to connect itself to the LAN segment and another to connect the bridge to rest of the network. Special cabling system software helps a bridge perform its job. Commercial bridges are *"black boxes,"* without keyboards or monitors, that can be remotely controlled and monitored.

Bridges usually are placed in a wiring closet or other secure area. To perform some tests, the cabling system technicians may temporarily disable the bridge to stop incoming cable traffic and gain a clear understanding of the LAN segment's unique characteristics.

Locating Faults

Wiring spot checks, especially for newly installed Category 5 cable, can be done as part of a LAN segment tune-up. The cables are disconnected from the network at both ends. Cable meters capable of measuring frequencies up to 100MHZ are attached at one end and a signal injector is attached at the other end. This arrangement measures cable performance and locates cable faults such as improper or damaged wiring.

A thorough cabling system scale wiring inventory might best be performed during the evening hours (or weekends when, in reality, most wiring work is done) when the majority of workers are not using their PCs. These inventories may not always need to be performed, but may be required under some situations.

The LAN segment's physical wiring is only part of what must be checked. The workstation cabling system configuration files and network card burned-in adapter addresses also need to be examined.

In advance of their visit, cabling system technicians should get copies of each workstation's configuration files, including the Config.sys, Autoexec.bat, System.ini, and Protocol.ini for Windows for Workgroups machines [Hayes, 1]. In Windows 98 machines, configurations can be printed out from the Control Panel using System Monitor.

Corrections to machine configurations can be noted on these printouts. Cabling system technicians then can go directly to the machines that need configuration file updates. If the PCs can be remotely administered, many changes can be made by LAN administrators from their office PCs.

The technicians also should reconcile their cabling system maps during the visit. Each workstation should be powered up and network card burned-in adapter addresses should be checked against the CPU serial number. This ensures the cabling system staff has accurate records in case a network adapter failure affects the network.

Inventory Protocols

Next, a cabling system's protocols must be inventoried. It's here that some of the best performance increases can be gained by making sure each workstation or server is using only the protocols needed for its work and that each protocol is properly configured for good performance.

LAN testers can be inserted into the segment either at the hub or connected in series between a workstation and the hub. At the hub, the meter tallies the types of cabling system protocols present on the segment and determines the number of data packet collisions.

If the LAN tester is placed between the workstation and the hub, it can measure the activity of the workstation's network adapter. This is especially useful if you're trying to measure the performance of a switched Ethernet network where not every workstation can be monitored from a single point on the LAN segment.

Pinging Tests

After monitoring cabling system traffic, the LAN testing device can be used to actively test the network. Most LAN testers will support NetWare and TCP/IP protocols. The devices often will display a list of servers available from the sampling point and will verify the performance of network workstations and servers by pinging them.

Pinging tests show how long it takes for workstations and servers to respond to the ping along with top senders and receivers. These meters provide detailed statistical information about Ethernet traffic. In addition to the ping function, LAN testers can create IPX packets to simulate LAN traffic and then analyze what the LAN segment operates.

Each LAN tester vendor offers additional testing abilities. For instance, LAN testers can sense Ethernet network card protocol, address, driver voltage levels, and the polarity of 10BaseT link pulses. If the meter can't detect a signal, it automatically tests for cable and connector faults. Hubs can be probed for proper protocol and PCs connected to the hub can be pinged to ensure they are connected. The correct polarity of link pulses and hub transmit levels can also be determined.

If changes are warranted, the cabling system technicians should document their alterations and then test the LAN segment again. If performance suffers, then they should undo the alterations. Under no circumstances should they leave the LAN segment worse than they found it.

PC Overload

If PCs are constantly added to a LAN segment, there comes a time when the sheer number of connected PCs, or network nodes, begins to degrade the cabling system's performance. At this point, your cabling system technicians will be able to divide the LAN segment into two separate LAN segments. This can be accomplished quickly in the wiring closet by separating the network hubs into two sets of hubs with each set connected to a network bridge.

If your organization's cabling system spans several buildings in a campus setting, or if you have networked offices in several cities that must communicate with each other, then your cabling staff is faced with a number of challenges in tuning and maintaining these networks.

First, the undertaking will require more people scattered across a number of distant locations. This means your tuning efforts will require a higher level of coordination and planning. Fax, teleconferences, e-mail, and groupware software will help you communicate and track tuning efforts.

A large cabling system uses a number of specialized boxes to help link distant machines together. These boxes must be managed for efficiency's sake from centralized locations using a network protocol like SMTP.

Repeaters are used to send cabling system traffic between two distant wiring closets within a large building or between campus buildings. Fiber optic repeaters convert electrical signals to light pulses and vice versa. For the most part, these are trouble-free boxes.

Routing Traffic

Routers are used to pass cabling system traffic between two different network topologies such as Ethernet and token ring. They also can be used to connect a LAN to a WAN using a high-speed modem. Routers use proprietary software to pass cabling system traffic from one network topology to the other. Like bridges, routers can limit the traffic crossing them by filtering out unwanted network protocols.

Routers can be used at just about any place on the company cabling system to connect a single Ethernet PC to a token ring LAN or to connect an entire campus network to an Internet Service Provider (ISP). Corporations, government agencies, and universities use routers to link offices in different cities.

Increase Performance

Next to tuning a LAN segment, the best thing you can do to increase cabling system performance is to limit the number of LAN protocols crossing each router. Current cabling system installation and maintenance records really help the tuning effort. Router software often is revised, so it is important to keep good installation records to maintain current router software across your company's cabling system.

While it's natural to want to limit the number of maintenance contracts, critical components such as routers should be kept under contract. Otherwise, your organization will wind up with a number of wildly varying versions of routing software. This, too, can affect cabling system performance.

The ability to measure cabling system traffic not only helps you correct your own problems, but also helps you work with WAN service providers such as phone companies to improve WAN performance. Systematic record-keeping from the individual workstation to the network router does take time, but it will save much time and head-scratching when a simple tuning job takes on an ugly complexion. Periodic audits of cabling, network software, and LAN traffic help the cabling system staff stay on top of potential networking problems, thus increasing user confidence in your system.

A Job Well Done

Your cabling system technicians must be highly trained, detail-oriented professionals to keep your system running efficiently. Technicians should have access to the training and tools needed to get the job done. It's not by accident that your cabling system run smoothly, it's because of your cabling staff's hard work and commitment to your organization [Hayes, 2].

Next, a discussion on cabling system troubleshooting is in order. Let's discuss how to identify problems on the cabling system and the tools your technicians will need to fix them.

Cabling System Troubleshooting

Cabling system technicians and analysts require specialized tools to quickly analyze and repair a company's cable. This equipment can come from a variety of sources, ranging from catalogs to private manufacturers.

Cabling system technicians who diagnose simple cable faults and repair them need cable-related tools. A general-purpose electronics tool kit forms the core of what the technician will use.

Most mail-order computer supply companies stock generic electronics tool kits filled with tools your technicians may or may not need. Sometimes, it's better to look at catalogs offering individual tools, which let you buy specifically what you need. Tool kits can range from fabric pouches holding a few tools for less than $100 to deluxe tool kits in hard cases for more than $1,100 [Hayes, 1].

A digital multimeter lets technicians measure voltage, current, and resistance. A pair of multimeters connected to a building's earth ground can perform simple continuity and cable mapping. Multimeters should be ruggedly constructed and offer accurate readings over long cable lengths. Multimeters can cost between $100 and $200.

NOTE:

Cable scanners are invaluable—check cable length, NEXT, attenuation, noise, etc.($500 to $2500).

Specialized Items

In addition to hand tools, including a long-nose pliers and wire strippers, a tool kit should contain specialized items such as punch-down tools for connecting wiring to Type 66 or 110 punch blocks. Crimping tools for attaching connectors to coaxial and twisted-pair wiring also are often needed. These can be purchased alone or as a part of kits containing connector ends and test equipment.

Universal crimping tools with replaceable dies also are available. The crimping tools cost about $30. Each die set costs about $15.

Tracer Probes

A tone tracer probe resembles an electronic thermometer with a speaker at one end. It's used with a battery-powered signal generator to locate a cable by using an audible tone. Put the signal generator on one end and go to the wiring closet containing the cable's other end. Pass the tone tracer over the cables until it beeps. The cable that causes the beeping tone is the one you want.

Tone tracers also vary in price. Tone generators cost about $30, while their companions, inductive tracers, cost nearly $50. The tone generator and probe kit costs about $100. It also is available as part of a twisted-pair installer kit with crimpers and wire cutters for less than $250. Wire tracers use the same process to identify cables in active network circuits.

Battery-powered screwdrivers and drills are handy for removing defective routers and hubs from equipment racks. Since cabling system technicians go wherever cables lead, a hard hat and flashlight also are important.

Spare network cards, network patch cables, and connectors can be put in tool kits along with system diskettes containing software to boot a computer and get it on the network. Be sure tool kits have compartments to safely store diskettes and network cards.

A business-frequency FM walkie-talkie or transceiver can give your staff greater mobility and let them have conversations with several technicians at the same time. In addition to the FM transceiver, a cabling system supervisor may want to carry a pager and cellular phone. A pager's AAA battery can last for weeks while a cell phone's larger, rechargeable battery usually lasts for only a few hours.

Shared Tools

Not every organization can afford to equip all of its cabling system staff with test equipment, nor is it practical to do so. Some tools may be shared. Because of their expense and sophistication, cable meters, fiber optic test equipment, and LAN analyzers require clearly defined checkout procedures and periodic performance checks.

In addition to specialized test equipment, an Ethernet hub or token ring multistation access unit can be used for troubleshooting purposes. Acting as field test units, these devices let technicians and analysts disconnect suspect machines from the cabling system and perform detailed tests with a LAN analyzer without shutting down an entire LAN segment.

NOTE:

Sniffers are also invaluable tools that can filter and sort incoming and captured data.

Information Tools

Cabling system technicians and analysts need to be able to quickly access network maintenance and installation databases. Using this information, cabling system maps detailing the location and nature of network devices can be created.

Reference materials such as books and CD-ROMs also should be available. Commercial online services and Internet sites often can provide the latest cabling system documentation.

LAN management tools using Simple Network Management Protocol (SNMP) let analysts gauge the status of critical cabling system resources such as routers and bridges. Sophisticated network management software can help you quickly pinpoint cabling system problems [Hayes, 1].

Identifying LAN Problems

Even with proper training, information, and tools, your cabling system staff faces a formidable enemy, the clock. Cabling system outages cause productivity losses that are difficult to recoup. Because each tick of the clock means money lost, cabling system technicians must work quickly and accurately to solve a network problem. Technicians should ask themselves and their users a series of questions about the problem. They should learn to listen to users, interpret the information, then quickly determine the scope of the problem and gauge its priority.

When seeking the cause of a problem, technicians should first identify any physical items that recently have been added or changed. Most cabling system failures occur in the electrical and electronic devices used to link computers together. A quick check of maintenance and installation records may turn up a recent action that has forced another problem to the surface.

At this point technicians may gauge your cabling system's current status with test equipment and network management software. If conditions warrant, they may go directly to the affected area and begin measurements there.

Based on available information and collective experience, technicians should develop a theory about the problem and perform tests to confirm the theory. After the problem has been identified, they will repair the cabling system, then document the problem and repairs in a cabling system maintenance database.

Troubleshooting the Workstation

Working with cabling system problems affecting a single workstation can present challenges beyond just technical difficulties. An unhappy user can make life difficult for your technicians and delay the repair effort.

Those people who don't have technical aptitude may be uncomfortable about showing their ignorance. Cabling system staffers should treat users with respect and make a follow-up contact after the problem has been solved.

The cabling system staff should first uncover any recent changes to the workstation by checking maintenance and installation records and then talking with the user. The odds favor a physical layer problem, so cabling and network hardware should be checked.

If the computer is not connecting to the network, a quick visual check of the cabling system will expose a cable break or loose connector. A LAN analyzer can be used to test the cabling from the wall jack to the network hub. If the cabling checks out, then a test hub or multistation access unit can be used to test the workstation's network card and cable.

To ensure the workstation's network software isn't the problem, the machine should be started using a boot diskette. If the workstation then can connect to the cabling system, the problem is caused by the workstation's network configuration. The problem can be narrowed by examining the machine's configuration files or determining if network software is corrupt or missing.

If software isn't the problem, the network card should be reseated and the workstation restarted. If the problem remains, the network card should be replaced with a new card. The workstation then can be restarted; if the problem is solved, the user can resume work.

Troubleshooting the Segment

When troubleshooting a LAN segment, cabling system technicians perform the same troubleshooting steps as outlined earlier, always keeping affected offices informed of the status of a repair. Poor customer service can leave users angry and unwilling to trust the technicians' efforts.

LAN segment problems can be grouped into three categories: physical layer faults, network loading faults, and network protocol faults. Physical layer faults are caused by a failure of the electrical or electronic devices that link the cabling system together. Loading faults occur when a network device cannot keep up with the demand for its services. Network protocol faults occur when network devices cannot communicate because of incompatible network drivers or the inability to pass the cabling system traffic of a specific protocol.

Physical layer faults are much easier to troubleshoot because there is physical evidence that something is wrong. Network loading faults and protocol faults are difficult to troubleshoot because the conditions that cause the failure may not always be present. LAN and protocol analyzers record data for later examination; these can greatly aid the search for the problem's origin.

When data is transmitted across a cabling system, it is parceled into units called frames. Ethernet networks use the Carrier Sense Multiple Access/Collision Detect (CSMA/CD) protocol to determine which network station will transmit a frame while the other stations listen. Transmitting stations also listen to make sure another station isn't transmitting.

If two network stations transmit at the same time, a frame collision occurs. Both stations must retransmit their frames. Cabling system throughput will vary based on the number of collisions that have occurred.

The different types of Ethernet networks—10Base2, 10Base5, and 10BaseT—all use slightly different methods to connect workstations. Certain faults tend to favor one type of Ethernet network over another. Link errors, for example, commonly occur on 10BaseT networks when there is a bad connection between the network adapter and the network hub. A damaged cable between the hub and adapter or a bad hub port often cause link errors.

Cyclic Redundancy Check errors occur when network data has been corrupted because data frames crossing your LAN have collided. This can be caused by a fault in the network cabling, the hub, or an adapter.

Improperly sized network frames also can cause collisions. Long- and short-frame errors are caused by incorrect network drivers or an improperly configured network card.

Constant collision errors occur on 10Base2 and 10Base5 networks when one of the terminating resistors is missing or damaged. Late collision errors occur when data frames collide outside the 51.2 microsecond window after transmission. This indicates that the LAN cable is too long. The maximum length for 10Base2 is 185 meters; 10Base5, 500 meters; and 10BaseT, 100 meters [Hayes, 1].

Token Ring Faults

In a token ring network, frames are passed to each member of the LAN segment, or ring. A special media access control frame, called a token, is passed among the network stations.

A network station must be in possession of the token to transmit a frame. Frames are transmitted in one direction around the ring. A network station receives a frame from its upstream neighbor and examines the frame to see if the data is addressed to it. If the workstation is the data's recipient, it copies the data into its received buffers. After the workstation has examined the frame, it passes the frame to its downstream neighbor.

A token ring network has a higher fault tolerance since it uses two twisted-pair wires; one is a backup path in case the primary pair fails. The token-passing method ensures constant cabling system throughput since only one station can transmit at a time.

Token ring networks use a number of special-purpose frames for control and error detection. Soft error report frames are generated when one of several error conditions exist. A burst error occurs when a network station hasn't received a frame within a reasonable period of time. It can be caused by a temporarily broken connection or when network stations enter or leave the ring. A token ring network station reports a failing network adapter by issuing an internal error frame.

When a network station no longer senses upstream cabling system traffic, it generates a beacon error frame. Beacons are caused by defective cabling or a bad network adapter. Bad NIC cards are also common culprits.

In token ring networks with more than one ring, the cabling system technicians should isolate the ring containing the beaconing station. Next, they should disconnect the beaconing station to see if the problem goes away. If the station's downstream neighbor beacons next, then technicians should check upstream stations and their physical connections until the fault is located.

When a network station doesn't have enough receive buffers to process incoming data, it generates a receive congestion error. If a bridge or router regularly reports this error, you may have to break the affected ring into two or more rings.

A heavily used server also may generate congestion error frames. A badly configured network card could be the cause of the congestion errors. If this isn't the case, then a card with a higher cabling system throughput such as a bus master or LAN streaming token ring card can be installed. If congestion errors still persist, an additional server may be needed.

A frequency error frame is created when a network station senses that the incoming data signal has shifted its frequency outside of acceptable limits. This condition, called token ring jitter, is caused by bad cabling, failing token ring cards, or radio frequency interference on long cable runs. Token ring jitter can be intermittent and thus more difficult to locate. You can eliminate or reduce it by using powered multistation access units, which provide signal conditioning. Longer copper cable runs should be replaced by fiber optic cabling.

Troubleshooting the Cabling System

When troubleshooting the company cabling system, cable staffers follow the same troubleshooting steps as mentioned earlier. A high degree of communication and coordination are needed to locate problems spread across a wide area. Cabling system analysts rely upon LAN management software and LAN and protocol analyzers to help solve problems on this scale.

LAN analysts will trace the path of affected cabling system traffic through measurements and the use of LAN maps. By sampling network frames and injecting test frames at points identified on the LAN maps, analysts can quickly determine the scope and nature of the problem.

At this level, cabling system loading problems can occur on heavily used routers, linking users to LAN segments containing important resources such as mainframe services or the Internet. If this is not a router configuration problem, the affected router may have to be upgraded. If an additional router has to be added, your staff may be required to redesign the cabling system.

Protocol errors on LANs and WANs are complicated by throughput limitations. A large number of protocols may not be able to run across routers in remote offices.

Protocol analyzers and LAN analyzers with limited protocol sampling abilities are great troubleshooting aids to determine exactly how much of each protocol flows through your cabling system. Eliminating unnecessary protocols by filtering them out at the affected router will greatly improve cabling system performance and assure certification.

Once you have successfully completed your cabling system tests and troubleshooting, you are now ready to move on to the next post-installation cabling system activity: loss testing in optical fiber and copper. Requirements for measuring return loss, far-end crosstalk, balance, power-sum near-end crosstalk, and screening effectiveness (all at frequencies higher than 100 MHz) are crucial to any cabling system being considered for certification.

Loss Testing: Certifying Copper and Fiber

The requirements to certify a Category 5 link and the requirements to certify a multimode fiber link illustrate differences in the media. For Category 5 cables, new standards such as telecommunications systems bulletin TSB-67 issued by the Electronic Industries Association and the Telecommunications Industry Association (both in Arlington, VA) have evolved. New measurements such as propagation delay and delay skew have become necessary. And, new products have been introduced to simplify and automate what is a complex qualification process.

To certify a Category 5 link, you must measure length, attenuation, near-end crosstalk, wire map, propagation delay, delay skew, and impedance. You must repeat many of these measurements on all four pairs, and make the measurements in a sweep fashion from 1 to 100 megahertz, meaning thousands of measurements. Also, requirements for measuring return loss, far-end crosstalk, balance, power-sum near-end crosstalk, and screening effectiveness—all at frequencies higher than 100 MHz—are under consideration.

Certifying multimode fiber, on the other hand, is simpler. You measure attenuation at 850 and 1300 nanometers in the direction of transmission. If neither length nor delay requirements for the application have been exceeded, then the job is done.

Perhaps because fiber testing is so straightforward, test tools and processes have changed little in the past few years. But while testing multimode fiber is simple, today's tools can make the process time-intensive because, with fiber, attenuation must be measured in the correct direction—unlike copper. Attenuation in copper cables is symmetric, so the result will be the same regardless of the direction in which you test. However, with fiber, you must measure attenuation in the direction of data transmission because the attenuation is asymmetric. The loss in the PC-to-hub direction is different from the loss in the hub-to-PC direction on the same fiber.

Historically, installers have had to complete the following 12 steps to measure a fiber pair:

- Connect and run the test at 850 nm.
- Store or write the results.
- Switch connectors to 1300 nm.

- Run the test again.
- Store or write the results.
- Go to the other end of the fiber.
- Connect and run the test at 850 nm.
- Store or write the results.
- Switch connectors to 1300 nm.
- Run the test again.
- Store or write the results.
- Go back to the starting point [3].

Considering the need to test fiber in the correct direction, the approach just described has four obvious inefficiencies. First, the operator must go back and forth to measure loss in the right direction. To save time, many installers test from only one end and have questionable results for half the measurements. Second, the operator must constantly change connectors to switch between 850- and 1300-nm source wavelengths. Third, because fibers are tested in pairs, it is inefficient to test them sequentially, considering that with copper cables all four pairs are tested simultaneously. Finally, the recording and management of data is often manual and error-prone.

Analyzing Test Results

The optical link budget presents another concern for fiber installers. Cabling standards provide guidance regarding how much loss is permitted at each wavelength. Permissible attenuation values are based on the length of the link, and the number of splices and mated connections. This consideration differs from copper-cable testing, in which pass/fail measurements are constant, and testing instruments can indicate whether a link passes or fails based on the values alone. When testing fiber, the user must determine how much loss is permitted in each link. It is not possible to simply run a test and know whether the attenuation level is acceptable without knowing the wavelength, number of connections, number of splices, and fiber length.

Technology has opened the door to more efficient multimode fiber testing. A fiber tester is now available that tests both fibers in the pair, in the correct direction, at both wavelengths simultaneously, and also measures length and propagation delay. Users can also input the number of splices and connections in the link into the tester, which then computes the optical link budget and provides a pass/fail analysis. It also certifies whether the link is suitable for network-specific fiber applications such as 10Base-F, 100Base-F,

1000Base-F, Fiber Distributed Data Interface, and Fiber Channel. Use of this tester collapses the 12 steps previously necessary to 2:

- Connect and run the test.
- Store the result [Johnston, 3].

NOTE:

There's one tester that has a built in printer so you can immediately print the results.

The tester time-stamps and gives alphanumeric names to as many as 1000 fibers, stores them internally, and can download them onto a PC. This technology provides several advantages for installers, including speeding up fiber testing, providing information such as length and propagation delay that were previously available only through an optical time-domain reflectometer, and providing professional certification reports.

Documenting and Testing the Fiber Optic Cabling System

Installation and test documentation is crucial to post-installation cabling system activities. Several times in this chapter it been pointed out that a thorough knowledge of your company's cabling system, including the installation and maintenance records, is essential to keeping your system in peak condition. Next, let's see exactly how important it really is to document the installation of your cabling system.

A properly installed and undisturbed cable installation should give many years of trouble free operation. When the unexpected occurs, having a well-documented installation will be invaluable.

Information on splice locations, panel numbers, cable numbering schemes, location of splitters and other details should not be overlooked. There are a number of factors that influence the type and level of testing that should accompany the optical fiber cable installation. The consequences of a system failure, and the amount of down time that can be tolerated are several that come to mind.

It is a very good idea to perform a basic continuity test prior to installation of the cable. After installation it will be very difficult to determine if the fibers were received broken from the factory, or have been damaged during installation. Multimode fiber optic cables, in lengths of less than 1 to 2 kilometers (.63 to 1.26 miles), may be easily tested by simply cleaving both ends and shining a bright light on one end while monitoring the other [4]. Longer lengths and singlemode fibers will require the use of a fiber optic source and meter or the use of a optical time-domain reflectometer (OTDR). These instruments may be coupled to the fiber prior to termination, by using lab splices or various reusable type mechanical splices.

When using OTDRs to acceptance test optical fibers it is a good idea to test the fibers from both ends. This will allow you to see failures that might fall in the OTDRs dead zone and breaks that might be near one end. Some anomalies may not show up if OTDR tests are only done in one direction.

After the cable has been installed and terminated, it is good practice to document each cable run. End-to-end attenuation measurements are a very valuable source of information. These end-to-end measurements should be consistent between fibers in the same run. Inconsistencies in these measurements may be an indication of poor quality terminations. All measurements should fall within predicted values.

Consistently high measurements could be an indication that the cable is stressed somewhere along the cable run. The index of refraction for the cable under test should be included in any documentation of the installation. This will become valuable when fault location becomes necessary.

OTDR test documentation is also a good source for the documentation package. This will allow testing from one location. It is also recommended that a jumper be installed on the OTDR that is longer than the instrument's dead zone. Many new OTDRs store trace information to disks and even have the ability to overlay trace information from different tests. Unfortunately, there is currently no standard format for saving traces, so comparisons or second opinions from different OTDRs are not possible at this time.

Certifying Your System Performance

The next to the last step in any cabling system post-installation activity is field certification. The next part of this chapter will take a close look at this very important and crucial step.

The last step in any Category 5 cable installation project is field certification. This is an important step to assure the quality of the materials used and installation workmanship, but field certification adds to the cost of the job. In order to minimize this added cost, considerable effort should have been invested in minimizing the overall testing time required. There are two components in determining the overall test time, the actual time it takes to run an autotest function and the time required to set up for the next autotest.

TSB-67 Compliant Autotest Execution Time

The EIA/TIA TSB-67 specification requires the following field test equipment test installed cabling requirements for the following parameters as shown in Table 16–1 [5].

Table 16–1: TSB-67 Certification Test Requirements.

Required TSB-67 Test Parameter	Required Test Conditions
Near End Crosstalk (NEXT)	Must test all 6 pair combinations. Must test at both cable ends 0.15 MHz step size for 1 to 31.25 MHz. 0.25 MHz step size for > 31.25 MHz => Min. 478 measurement points per pair combination
Attenuation	Must test all 4 pairs. 1 MHz minimum step size => Min. 100 measurement points per pair
Length	Must test all four pairs
Wiremap	Must check all 4 pairs for: Continuity Shorts Crossed pairs Reversed pairs Split pairs

An autotest function offers multiple setup options which allow the user to selectively augment or alter the test parameters and test conditions executed in the autotest function. By default, the autotest function should be configured for full compliance with the TSB-67 requirements described in Table 16–1.

Fast Autotest

A fast autotest mode should perform all of the same test functions, but adjusts the NEXT scan resolution for increased test speed. In a fast autotest mode, an autotest should be executed in 6 seconds. While a fast autotest mode is not recommended for formal certification testing, there is excellent correlation between pass/fail results obtained with the full and fast autotest modes.

Overall Test Time Optimization

Beyond the actual time to run an autotest, other tasks which contribute to total test time are entering the cable number identifier and saving the test data for each tested cable run and moving to the next cable run and starting the next test.

Cable ID Auto-Increment

To speed the process of entering the cable ID and saving the test data, the user should be automatically prompted to save the results data when exiting from an autotest results screen. For example, by pressing the ENTER key, the user should be able to open a cable ID data entry dialog box. Whatever cabling system field certification testing product the user has, it should be able to speed the process of data entry by guessing at the cable ID based on the ID of the last cable tested and entering this in the data entry field. For example, if the user tested cables in the order that they were labeled, and the previous cable entered was *Bld100-Flr-3-100*, the field certification testing product should be able to guess that the next tested cable would be *Bld100-Flr-3-101*. In the case of an alphanumeric label like *cable1A*, the product should be able to automatically guess *cable1B* for the next label. Therefore, if the user tests cable runs in the sequence that they are labeled, only the first cable ID in any sequence would be entered manually. The rest would be automatically entered, saving valuable testing time. This feature should be disabled globally or overridden at any time via alphanumeric input or via the numeric lock key to allow keypad input.

In conclusion, a 14 second TSB-67 compliant autotest and an even faster 6 second autotest mode should translate directly into substantially reduced time requirements for the testing phase of large installation projects. A faster installation project testing phase should translate directly into major labor cost savings and greater customer and installer satisfaction.

TSB-67 and Level I and II Testing

Finally, it's now time to take a look at the last post-installation cabling system activity, TSB-67 and Level I and II Testing. Portable cable testers have been used in testing Category 5 cabling since 1993. Some early concerns about the accuracy of these tools in post cabling system installation ultimately uncovered a number of interesting issues.

Testing Issues

First, there turned out to be different opinions about how measurements should be made, how results should be reported, where connections should occur, and how terminations should be performed. How could agreement between different tools possibly occur when no one agreed on the test setup conditions?

Second, a disproportionately high number of failing links with certain types of components turned out to have a high correlation with short length. So what was first thought by some to be a tester problem turned out to be something else entirely. These short links really were failing on a regular basis, contrary to Category 5 and EIA/TIA-T568-A assumptions. The testers were not at fault. A task group was set up to study this issue. It was determined that unbalanced modular 8 connectors can cause high levels of NEXT on short links.

Finally, there were no agreed upon, industry standardized pass/fail requirements for specific types of links. The tester manufacturers were using numbers from the theoretical model given in EIA/TIA-T568-A Annex E since it was the only model available. However, as this model was informative only, it was not an official part of the standard.

TSB-67 Generated

These uncertainties led to the development of TIA TSB-67, approved and published in September 1995. TSB-67 is the result of a great deal of original research, round robin testing, analysis, discussion, and debate among the key manufacturers and users of cabling, cable components, and test equipment. TSB-67 defines two link models, the basic link and the channel.

Basic Link

The basic link is what an installer might work with, including the wall plate, horizontal wiring, and first cross-connection. The channel is what a user really needs to transmit information between a PC and its hub or concentrator. It can include up to two connections at each end. Thus, the NEXT and attenuation requirements are different for a channel and a basic link. Fortunately, the channel requirements for NEXT in TSB-67 are identical to those published in EIA/TIA-T568-A Annex E, so links tested using Annex E performance requirements will not require resetting.

Channel

A key issue with the channel definition is that the channel definition excludes the mated connection (usually modular 8) at each end. The channel begins immediately after this connection. This adds an additional error term for testing. The test equipment must connect to the channel to test it, so the crosstalk effects of modular 8 connection will affect the accuracy of the measurement. EIA/TIA TSB-40A defines the expected performance of a modular 8 connection. One notable parameter is a -40 dB NEXT requirement at 100 MHz.

When testing the basic link, however, connections can be made from the test equipment to the link via extremely low crosstalk connectors, avoiding this issue. Since the inherent uncertainties of the modular 8 connection can be avoided when testing the basic link, the accuracy of a basic link measurement can theoretically be much better than the same measurement on a channel.

Two Testing Accuracy Levels: TSB-67 Level I and II

The reality of *Two Testing Accuracy Levels* is reflected in the TSB-67 description of two accuracy levels for field test equipment. Level I reflects the performance boundaries imposed by the reality of having to test through a modular 8 connection. Level II sets a much higher accuracy requirement, possible only if a different, low crosstalk connector is used. The advantage of higher accuracy is you will have less uncertainty when making a pass/fail determination on the cable. If, for example, your test suggests the link fails by 1.5 dB and your accuracy is ±0.5 dB, then you have complete confidence that it really did fail. If however, your accuracy is ±3 dB, there is some possibility that the link actually passed, since in this example your accuracy margin is greater than the error [6].

NOTE:

Even Level II accuracy test tools are reduced to Level I accuracy when forced to test through modular 8 connections, because of the uncertainty added by the modular 8. This uncertainty has an unpredictable magnitude and phase, so it cannot be compensated for or subtracted out via hardware or software.

What tool should you buy? If your primary application is to install and certify Category 5 basic links, clearly you need a Level II tool. If your primary requirement is occasional cable troubleshooting on channels, a Level I instrument will meet your needs.

From Here

This chapter took a close look at the following post-installation activities: cable fault detection with OTDR, cabling system troubleshooting and testing, copper and fiber optic loss testing, documenting the cabling system, cabling system performance certification, and Telecommunications System Bulletin (TSB) 67 accuracy levels testing. Chapter 17 opens up Part V with a discussion on how to maintain your cabling system. The chapter goes on to examine the facilitation of ongoing cabling system maintenance by covering the building of the Cable Plant Management (CPM) database, vendor CPM products; and, the EIA/TIA 606 standard.

End Notes

1   Yukio Horiuchi, "Accurate Localization of Faults in Optical-Fiber Submarine Cable Systems," Supervisor Lightwave Communication System Group KDD R&D, Laboratories, Kokusai Densin Denwa Co., LTD. R&D, Laboratories, 2-1-15, Ohara Kamifukuoka-shi, Saitama 356, Japan, 1996, p. 2.

2   Bill Hayes, "Improving LAN Performance," *PC Today*, Sandhills Publishing, P.O. Box 82545, Lincoln, NE 68501-2545, 1996, p. 2.

3   Mark Johnston, "A New Model For Multimode Fiber Qualification," Director of technology development for Microtest Inc. (Phoenix, AZ), Digital Horizon, Point Of View, Broadband Guide, PennWell Media Online L.L.C., 2875 South Congress Avenue, Delray Beach, Florida, 33445, (October, 1997, p. 2.

4   "Installation and Test Documentation," James D. Barnes, "Installation and Test Documentation," Penn Tech, PO Box 271, Keyport, WA 98345, 1997, p. 1.

5   "WireScope 155 Autotest Speed," Scope Communications, Inc., 753 Forest Street, Marlborough, MA 01752, 1997, p. 2.

6   "Microtest TSB67 Lvel II Description," Microtest, Inc., Corporate Headquarters, 4747 North 22nd Street, Phoenix, Arizona 85016–4708, USA, 1997, p. 2.

Part V

Maintaining Cabling Systems

17

Ongoing Maintenance

In the early 1980s most companies were reluctant to implement a cable and connectivity management or maintenance process. Since then, there have been remarkable changes in communications technologies—changes which have had a significant impact on our communications infrastructure and on the organizational processes which manage that infrastructure.

Nowhere have these changes been more profound than in the cable plant, where changes to network architectures and hundred-fold increases in network speeds have forced users to add or replace cabling systems once, twice or even three times since the mid eighties. Staffing and resources to manage this infrastructure have remained fixed, while the rate of moves, adds, and changes (MACs) in most organizations remains unabated.

No one can be faulted for not anticipating the challenges of the last seventeen years. Looking forward, a pattern has been set and the future should be clear. Users are stressing the strategic importance of maximizing the utilization and life cycle of the cable plant while reducing everyday operating expenses. Implementing a connectivity management/maintenance process and using record-keeping tools for documenting the physical network are crucial for achieving these goals.

The Facts about Cable Management Software

Documenting cabling connections is vital to prolong the life of the infra-structure, contain the cost of maintaining the day-to-day changes, and recover from network outages. Until recently most organizations did this via paper. An individual within the telecommunications department kept a bible (usually a three ring binder with pages so worn the text looked encrypted) of all the con-nections. This became a problem with the boom of PC installations on the net-work. The telecom person was now forced to document the computer connections, usually with no knowledge of the systems.

Through the years companies have tried various methods to improve the quality of the information being recorded while reducing the time spent doing so. As many of you may know, this has been a exercise in futility. In most cases the process is dropped all together.

Integrated, real-time management is now possible with mature, state of the art applications designed for the purpose of managing cabling infrastruc-ture. This chapter will explain the benefits of building a cable plant manage-ment (CPM) database or what is commonly known as a cable management system (CMS) package.

Reasons for Documenting

There is a clear distinction between a connectivity management/mainte-nance process and a Cable Plant Management (CPM) database or Cable Man-agement System (CMS) itself as shown in Figure 17–1 [1]. A CMS is a computerized database that provides a detailed picture of the cabling infra-structure, allowing a Facilities Manager to improve service and reduce cost in these areas:

- Moves, adds, and changes.
- Repair downtime.
- Physical plant loss.
- Controlling vendors.
- Security.
- Disaster recovery.
- Future expansion [IMAP, 1].

More sophisticated cable management systems include multibuilding, campus, and asset management modules, integrating user names and cost cen-ters. Some are graphical, allowing the user to make connections on active equip-ment diagrams or indicate cable and equipment locations on CAD drawings.

Other systems may offer service order and trouble ticket modules with an integrated e-mail function to electronically distribute these documents. These programs can be run stand-alone or interface with network systems. Table 17–1 shows the four major CMS vendors with links that connect to numerous CMS and other third-party related products.

Table 17–1: Vendor CMS Products.

Vendor	Product	Standards	Description
Network & Communication Technology, Inc. (http://www.netcomtech.com)	Planet NT	*Meets the following telecommunications standards:* **ANSI/EIA/TIA-568:** Commercial Building Telecommunications Wiring Standard. **ANSI/EIA/TIA-569:** Commercial Buildings. Standard for Telecommunications Pathways and Spaces. **ANSI/EIA/TIA-606:** Telecommunications Infrastructure Administration Standard. **ISO 11801: Generic** Cabling for Customer Premises. **CAN/CSA-T528-93:** Design Guidelines for Administration of Telecommunications Infrastructure	An integrated graphical computer-aided design and embedded SQL database management system for which incorporates physical cable and connectivity design, documentation, and management. Asset (equipment) and vendor management. Service request/trouble ticketing and work orders.
IMAP Corporation (http://www.ycinc.com)	IMAP	(Same As Above)	An integrated cable management software system that tracks cable plant connectivity and all of the assets that utilize the horizontal and feeder systems. The IMAP CMS system provides a complete cabling infrastructure picture utilizing a powerful database integrated with Visio 5.0.

(continued)

Table 17–1: *(continued)*

Vendor	Product	Standards	Description
Cablesoft Ltd. (http://www.cablesoft.co.uk/)	Crimp for Windows™	(Same As Above)	Models the cabling, network electronics, PABX and terminal equipment and allows you to plan changes, administer moves, optimize the use, and therefore extend the life of your chosen cable system.
Microtest, Inc. (www.microtest.com)	CD-ROM Network Management Software for Windows NT	(Same As Above)	Cable management and troubleshooting software.

To fully understand the benefits of a CMS, let's use an example company that has 1000 employees with both voice and data requirements. According to recent studies, cabling infrastructure accounts for 25% of the data/voice network cost. Some estimates of investments in information technology per employee are as high as $8000. Therefore, at 25%, the cost would be $2000 per employee or in the case of the example company with 1000 employees: $2 million dollars. This cost is only compounded as time goes on.

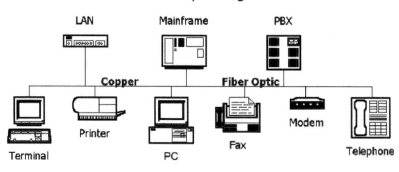

Cable Plant Connectivity Management Software

Figure 17–1: Cable management system.

Moves, Adds, and Changes

A typical company moves approximately 30% of its employees each year, with an average labor cost of $250 per move. In the previous example company, this would mean 300 employees would be relocated at the labor cost of $75,000 per year. An automated CMS can reduce this cost by more than 30% or $22,500 per year. More important, however, a CMS that is easy to use will reduce the day-to-day cost of moves, adds, and changes, thus increasing the life of the infrastructure.

In other words, a properly designed product should decrease the day-to-day expenditures by increasing efficiency. It should allow a Facilities Manager to take a proactive management approach to planning, budgeting, and the daily activities. But, most of all, it should be easy to maintain the information.

Repair Downtime

The cost savings in the moves, adds, and changes is minimal compared to the cost of a network connection outage that typically lasts four to nine hours, at a cost of $30,000 per hour. This pales in comparison, however, to the time and money lost while vital telephone or data systems have failed and brought business to a screeching halt. This is where costs are measured in the millions. And the inquisition, after all is said and done, reveals that the weak link was the information technology (IT) department's documentation, or lack thereof.

This scenario is where an investment in a CMS will be worth while. Industry surveys show that 70% of service calls are cabling related. Furthermore, technicians spend 80% of their time on a service call searching for the problem and 20% fixing it. Most of that 80% is spent locating the end-to-end connectivity. This situation worsens when the connection spans multiple floors or buildings. It is not unusual to have a 30% to 40% reduction in cost of repairs—mainly due to the implementation of a CMS that allows technicians to find things quickly.

Physical Plant Loss

Abandoning cable can quickly become a problem where the average business has an ongoing stream of moves, adds, and changes. In the case of a multitenant building, it is possible for the owner to rewire the entire building every three years.

When the core cabling is abandoned it artificially depletes the inventory while it continues to take up space. Soon there is no room for new cabling, causing the owner to expand or abandon the closets, or purchase costly new equipment to solve the capacity problems.

NOTE:

Abandoned cable is a major problem for almost every organization.

This equipment does nothing to improve customer relations—instead it usually disturbs relations due to the costly after-hours migration process. This capital expense can be avoided with a CMS that would enable the owner to reuse existing cabling.

Controlling Vendors

A CMS with the ability to generate work orders can be an effective way to manage multiple vendors. These work orders can be used as a means to track how effective a contractor is at handling emergencies, multiple projects, and contractor-to-contractor communications.

It is also an effective way to track recurring problems (that always have recurring cost) to identify if the problem is the technician. Most important, however, is that a CMS can allow the end user to negotiate fixed cost for certain tasks a contractor has to perform, based on a history of related work orders cost.

Security

Another issue that should be addressed in a multivendor facility is security. This can be simplified with the use of a CMS by simply giving the vendor the information they need to complete the task and validate the work when it's completed. Again, allow IT to track and measure the productivity and accountability of the technician. Since downtime is reduced with a CMS in place, exposure of corporate information to loss or penetration is minimized, translating into a higher level of customer satisfaction.

Disaster Recovery

No one likes to think about the loss of facilities due to theft, natural disasters, or some man-made calamity. But these events can (and usually do) happen. Planning ahead to minimize downtime and recover the losses should include a contingency plan supported by up-to-date records. A CMS would allow IT to quickly identify the lost resources and replace or reroute the connections to other facilities.

A report could be generated with a detailed description of the assets that were lost and the depreciation factor predetermined. This can be sent to the insurance company within minutes to speed the recovery process.

Future Expansion

The only way to fully understand where you're going is to first understand where you're currently at. Adding one more connection to a closet can eat 30% of the department budget if a new feeder has to be installed. The situation only gets worse if this happens twice in one year.

Usage reports from a CMS can give you current capacity of feeders, hubs and station cables. This information can be viewed during the planning stage of an installation, thus eliminating the outrageous costs of *emergency upgrades*, not to mention the frustration of a schedule delay.

Fiscal budget planning can be one of the most difficult times of the year for a manager. The guesswork of defining budgets for services, hardware, and personnel must be handled carefully. A dollar value must be determined. Justifications must be written. Then the battle for something between what is requested and absolutely nothing takes place. This is a yearly exercise that ultimately ends with the outcome far less than the initial requirements.

The ability to graph a month-to-month or year-to-year trend can be a strong argument for ITs needs. Additional reports can be generated showing work orders completed within a cycle and just about any other information that would be pertinent to budget justifications.

Therefore, making the decision to implement a CMS is only the first step. A considerable amount of time should be spent evaluating different products (see Table 17–1). If an application developer is the driving force behind the CMS, and this individual (or group) lacks the field experience of a cabling background, then you might want to consider some other options. *Meat and potatoes* should not be traded for *bells and whistles*.

A properly designed product should decrease the day-to-day expenditures by increasing efficiency. It should allow the IT staff to take a proactive management approach to planning, budgeting and the daily activities. But most of all, it should be easy to maintain the information. After all, if it's not easy to use, then it most likely won't be. In the end, define end user and contractor needs when implementing a CMS.

Build the CMS and They Will Come

As more and more organizations are upgrading their cabling plants to standards-based structured cabling systems, the need for cable management systems has become evident. For most organizations upgrading their cabling plant, the primary objective is to support enterprise-wide, high-bandwidth, mission-critical applications to the desktop. Typical high-bandwidth applications include Ethernet and token ring topologies. Implementing a cable management system (CMS) to maintain the integrity of these important physical assets has now become a priority. A large number of requests-for-proposals (RFPs) for new cabling projects now incorporate CMS requirements—often loosely defined. In addition, contractors may struggle when responding to these RFPs because they lack experience in providing cable management solutions. It is easy, therefore, for misunderstandings to occur due to differences in organizational expectations and contractor perceptions of a cable management solution.

To avoid this problem, both end users and contractors need to have a clear understanding of exactly what is meant by *install a cable management system*. Installing a CMS may be interpreted as just installing the software system on a computer at the customer's site. However, it could also mean populating the database with information about the installed horizontal and riser cabling, documenting crossconnects at all administration points, documenting ports on all service equipment and tracking all circuits assigned and available, or documenting connectivity for all station equipment. Issues abound in the implementation of a CMS. For example, should you document cable as a single record for each cable, or does the organization expect separate documentation for each twisted pair and for each fiber within every cable in the infrastructure? Most organizations need to define their cable management requirements more clearly, and contractors must be explicit when responding to a cable management RFP.

NOTE:

> Cable management system software can produce and display physical documentation, such as a floor plan, or logical documentation, such as a tree structure.

Establish Organizational Objectives

Several questions need to be answered when preparing or developing a response to a cable management RFP (see the sidebar, "Pertinent Questions To Ask When Preparing A Response For An RFP"). Not only will these answers help define the company's objectives, they will also clarify and determine the implementation requirements of the CMS, the type of system and the specifics of documentation required.

Pertinent Questions to Ask
When Preparing a Response for an RFP

Company Objectives:

- What is the organization doing now to manage its cabling infrastructure?
- Which departments or individuals have cable management responsibilities?
- Within the organization, who has requested a cable management solution, and what problem (if any) is that individual trying to solve?
- Has the organization specifically defined its cable management requirements?
- Does it plan to outsource the implementation of the CMS or the ongoing day-to-day cable management tasks?
- Are standards important to the organization?
- Will the CMS be linked to other accounting or management systems within the organization, and if so, how?
- What identification schemes for cabling and other assets are in place, and are these schemes suitable for cable management purposes; or will the contractor design a new identification scheme?

Implementation:

- What are the end user's implementation and training expectations?
- Will implementation of the CMS include only the cabling installed by the contractor as defined under the RFP or will documentation also be required for connections made after the installation?
- Will the CMS maintain pair and fiber detail or just the cable?

Type Of System:

- Does the company want a traditional database CMS or one that displays and produces physical documentation such as a graphical floor plan or logical (graphical tree structure) documentation?
- How does the organization currently handle moves, adds, and changes?
- Are trouble ticketing, service request, and work order management to be integrated into the CMS?

Documentation:

- Does the organization plan to document the connectivity of circuits (services) to network equipment, and if so, when?
- What are the as-built drawing requirements of the CMS?
- What cabling and connectivity reports does the organization expect following implementation?
- What labeling requirements are included in the cable management specification?
- Will cable test results be documented within the CMS? [2]

NOTE:

Managing only the cable and not the pair detail can severely limit the usefulness of the CMS.

Perform Site Survey

Before you respond to an RFP, it is important to conduct a physical site survey and review the current cable and connectivity documentation. This includes a visit to each administration point within the organization's infrastructure to become familiar with the overall premises infrastructure. If the building is older and has gone through an evolution of different types of cabling systems (plenum/non-plenum), make sure there are no surprises.

During a site survey, you can determine the number of administration points (closets and rooms) and the work areas (faceplate locations) you will need to document; the standard number of outlets at each work area; and the total outlets. You should also review how the wall fields in each telecommunications closet (TC) are organized. For example, are all services (voice, data, etc.) in the particular TC terminated on one set of horizontal connecting blocks or separate sets of horizontal blocks for each type of service? Does the organization have a standard for wall-field definition, and are the wall fields in all of the closets similar in layout? How are the cables and termination hardware labeled, and in what condition are the labels? Is documentation—reports or drawings—available in any of the TCs?

Take note of the overall condition of the TCs. If the customer wants a standards-based cable management solution, you can determine what changes need to be made in each closet to assure compliance.

After the site survey, arrange to meet with the appropriate staff within the organization to discuss organizational objectives, and explain the importance of an agreed-upon identification scheme when implementing the CMS. Next, you need to review the existing cable and connectivity documentation. If physical (floor plan) documentation is required, find out if drawings or computer-aided drawing (CAD) files showing horizontal cable routing are available. Decide together what the organization expects to do with existing obsolete and out-of-service cable. Determine the people within the organization who currently have authority or responsibility for cabling and cable management. From these discussions, you should also begin to understand clearly the organizational objectives and what the organizational structure for cable management will be in the future.

Defining Project Scope and Costs

You cannot determine the cost of implementing a CMS until you have defined the scope of the project. A useful way to document the site survey and the scope (and therefore, the cost) of the project is to develop a checklist, or worksheet. A project worksheet helps ensure that there is no misunderstanding between the organization and the contractor as to what products and services are to be delivered.

To develop a project worksheet, you first need to know what cable, equipment and connectivity documentation exists; what cabling, equipment and connectivity you will have to inventory; and, what cabling equipment and connectivity you will document in the CMS. In addition, you need to understand the customer's labeling requirements: what labels you will produce and when the organization needs them. For example, are labels to be produced upon installation of the cabling or upon completion of the implementation of the CMS?

Performing a physical inventory and documenting existing cabling, connectivity, service, or station equipment can be time-consuming. Find out the amount of detail required before determining your costs. For example, the customer may require you to inventory and document peripherals and third-party boards associated with each computer, or to inventory and document users and services assigned to each pair of each cable in the CMS. Either of these cases would create a substantial increase in the time and costs required to perform these tasks.

The best way to develop the costs for performing a physical inventory or completing the documentation portion of the project is to first determine the cost for a single transaction, such as routing horizontal cable to a workarea location and then multiply that cost by the total number of required transactions, such as workareas. If any special consulting tasks are required, provide a separate time-basis quote.

Final Steps

There are a few additional steps you can take to ensure that implementation of the CMS goes smoothly. Always make sure that any existing documentation you use is complete and accurate. If you plan to use existing CAD files to complete the project, examine at least one of the files to verify the file format and accuracy of the drawing content. Do not forget to include travel and living expenses for any technicians who will perform services at the site.

Confirm exactly what deliverables the organization expects upon completion of the project. It is always a good idea to include a sample set of drawings and reports that you will deliver upon completion of the project. Similarly, when you begin to implement the cable management project, be sure to proto-type a small portion of the infrastructure and produce a complete set of deliv-erables for organizational approval before continuing.

NOTE:

> The complete set of deliverables is extremely important. This is when the organization really sees and understands what they're getting.

This process will ensure that the identification scheme used meets the organization's requirements and that it is satisfied with the drawings and reports produced. Now that you are sure there are no misunderstandings, you can complete the cable management project.

EIA/TIA-606, not as well-known as 568 and 569, affects many in the tele-com industry by mandating new recordkeeping and administrative requirements with regard to the CMS. Let's take a look at how the EIA/TIA 606 telecommuni-cations standard affects the documentation and management in the CMS.

EIA/TIA 606 Documentation Standard

A few years ago, the American National Standards Institute, the Telecom-munications Industries Association and the Electronic Industries Association formally approved and published their Administration Standard for the Telecommunications Infrastructure of Commercial Buildings, number 606. This administrative standard follows and conforms to the Commercial Build-ing Telecommunications Wiring Standard (ANSI/EIA/TIA-T568-A, published in July, 1991) and the Commercial Building Standard for Telecommunications Pathways and Spaces (ANSI/EIA/TIA-569, published in October 1990).

Although not as widely known as EIA/TIA-T568-A and 569, the new EIA/TIA-606 standard has far-reaching effects on the telecommunications industry. People in charge of network management in an organization see this standard as the foundation upon which they will build future cabling system configurations and management systems. Those preparing Requests for Propos-als include technical specifications based on the standard when defining docu-mentation and identification requirements for new structured wiring systems.

System integrators, contractors, designers and installers must under-stand the 606 standard in order to respond to the requirements which have been included in all RFPs. In addition, software developers, who offer config-uration management and telecommunication administration software sys-tems, must always be certain that their applications comply with the standard.

Administering a telecommunications infrastructure includes tasks such as documenting and identifying all cables, termination hardware, crossconnects, cable pathways, telecommunication closets, workareas, and equipment rooms. In addition, an administrative system needs to provide reports that present telecommunications information in useful format; include drawings of the telecommunications infrastructure for design, installation, and management purposes and document changes to the system with trouble tickets, service requests, and work orders. The 606 administrative standard does, in fact, deal with all components of the telecommunications infrastructure. This standard supports electronic applications such as voice, data, video, alarm, environmental control, security, and audio. The purpose of the 606 standard is to provide a uniform administration scheme that is independent of applications, which may change several times throughout the life of a building.

NOTE:

The main elements covered by the standard are identifiers, required linkages and telecommunications records. Optional records may also be linked into the system.

Three Areas Covered

Three major administrative areas covered by the new standard are pathway and space, wiring system, and grounding and bonding administration. In addition, the standard defines specific requirements for labeling and color coding and includes symbols recommended for use when preparing telecommunication infrastructure drawings.

The overall concept of the standard is to establish identifiers, in the form of labels, that specify the content of various records and define the linkages between records. The 606 standard then describes how to present the information needed to administer building wiring, pathways and spaces, and grounding and bonding.

Mandatory and advisory criteria are included in the standard. Mandatory criteria, which are required of record-keepers, specify the absolute minimum acceptable requirements and generally apply to safety, protection, performance and compatibility. Optional advisory criteria, which are considered to be above the minimum requirements, are viewed as desirable enhancements to the standard.

Components of the System

Identifiers, as specified by the standard, are included as part of the record assigned to each element of the telecommunications infrastructure and must be unique. Encoded identifiers may include additional information—cable, termination position, workarea, or closet location.

Labels, including these identifiers, must meet the legibility, defacement, adhesion and exposure requirements of Underwriters Laboratory 969 and should be affixed in accordance with the UL969 standard. Bar codes, when included on labels, must use either Code 39, conforming to USS-39, or Code 128, conforming to USS-128. Labels must also be color-coded to distinguish demarcation points and campus, horizontal, and riser (or backbone) termination points.

Pathways must be labeled at all endpoints located in telecommunication closets, equipment rooms or entrance facilities. All horizontal and riser/backbone cables must be labeled at each end. All splice closures must be marked or labeled. Termination hardware, including termination positions, must also be labeled, except where high termination densities make such labeling impractical. The telecommunications main grounding busbar, as well as each bonding conductor and telecommunications grounding busbar, must be marked or labeled. Finally, each telecommunications space, whether telecommunications closet, equipment room, or workarea, must be labeled.

Each record defined in the standard must contain certain required information and required linkages to other specified records. Linkages define the logical connections between identifiers and records. Identifiers, then, may point to more than one record. Descriptions of optional information and linkages to other records outside the scope of the standard are also included but are not meant to be inclusive or complete. There is no question that properly designed administrative systems will have to incorporate many of the non-mandatory advisory elements included within the standard.

In order to associate various applications with the telecommunications infrastructure, user codes identifying and linking circuit information, such as voice or data, may be included. Combining both physical and logical information is important for telecommunications administration, especially when generating trouble tickets for cable fault management; and, when generating work orders for moves, adds, and changes. Being able to quickly determine which circuits are available, reserved, in use or out of use is an important part of telecommunications infrastructure management.

Reports

The following reports are recommended by the standard: pathway, space, cable, end-to-end circuit, crossconnect, and grounding/bonding summary reports. The recommended content of the reports includes:

- Pathway reports—list all pathways and include type, present fill and load.
- Space reports—list all spaces, types and locations.
- Cable reports—list all cables, types and termination positions. Obviously this includes unused cables that may be reused.
- End-to-end circuit reports—trace connectivity from end-to-end and list user codes and associated termination positions and cables.
- Cross-connect reports—list all cross-connections within each space.
- Grounding/bonding summary reports—list all grounding busbars and attached backbone bonding conductors [3].
- The report might also include any cable testing results.

Obviously, additional and optional information can be presented in these reports. Also, the reports described in the standard are not all-inclusive. Many other reports not mentioned in the standard would normally be included as part of a properly designed telecommunication infrastructure administration system.

Drawings

Conceptual and installation drawings are considered input to the final record drawings which graphically document the telecommunications infrastructure. While the standard doesn't specify how the drawings are created, in most cases they will be prepared using a computer-aided design system—either a separate software product or a telecommunications administration system that incorporates CAD functionality.

The record drawings must show the following: the identifier as well as the location and size of pathways and spaces; the location of all cable terminations (workareas, telecommunication closets, and equipment rooms); and all backbone cables. Drawings which show the routing of all horizontal cables are desirable. The standard includes symbols that may be used when preparing these drawings. Ideally, record information should be accessible when one is viewing the record drawings.

It is mandated that all wiring, termination and splice work orders be maintained for telecommunication repairs, moves, adds, and changes. The work-order document must include cable identifiers and types, termination identifiers and types, and splice identifiers and types. The work-order process should be used to update the administrative records. In day-to-day telecommunications administration, this is the most important requirement set forth in the standard. If the system records are not immediately updated when a work order is completed, the administrative system will quickly become outdated and useless.

Cabling System Management

Configuration management is identified by the International Organization for Standardization's Network Management Forum as one of the five functional cabling system management areas, the others being fault, security, performance and accounting management. Configuration management is the core of the four other cabling system management areas and comprises the following management elements: in-use and spare-part equipment inventory management; cabling and wiring management; circuit management; tracking, authorizing and scheduling moves, adds, and changes; trouble ticketing cable faults; user and vendor management; and documenting current cabling system configurations.

If the mandatory and advisory criteria are included, the ANSI/TIA/EIA-606 Administration Standard for the Telecommunications Infrastructure of Commercial Buildings covers most of the elements included in the definition of configuration management. Since the infrastructure can be thought of as the collection of those components that provide basic support for the distribution of all information within a building or campus, the telecommunications administration standard must now be viewed as the basis upon which all future cabling system configuration management systems will be built.

Implementing a telecommunication administration system requires a great deal of thought and planning.. There are many important reasons why an organizations should implement a physical layer configuration, design and telecommunications administration system. Some of the reasons are:

- To determine what cables, conductors of fibers, and circuits (PBX, Ethernet, token ring, etc.) are free, in use, and out of use, and what circuits and users are assigned to them.
- To maintain a documentation and identification system for the implementation of an equipment and cable disaster recovery plan in case of fire, explosion, flood, or other emergency.
- To identify what equipment is in use, spare and out of use, and to document and maintain equipment connectivity.
- To update and manage cable faults, moves, adds, and changes, and to maintain work-order records for all equipment, users, circuits and cable paths.
- To reduce the amount of cabling system or LAN downtime.
- To decrease labor costs by eliminating the need to trace undocumented circuits each time an add, move, change or cable fault occurs.
- To increase confidence in the structured wiring systems that organizations use to downsize applications from mainframe and minicomputing platforms.

- To generate management reports and perform detailed network analysis on all equipment and cabling systems.
- To transfer users from one cabling system to another as part of the effort to manage overall network performance.
- To document and maintain cable and circuit test data.
- To manage important vendor relationships; purchasing, technical support, returns and service.
- To administer names and addresses and track all network equipment, cables and circuits for departments, users, managers and technicians
- To design new cabling systems within the infrastructure and to produce reports and analysis detailing equipment and cabling requirements for them [Spencer, 6].

From Here

Chapter 17 opened up Part V, "Maintaining Cabling Systems," with a discussion on how to maintain your cabling system. The chapter examined the facilitation of ongoing cabling system maintenance by covering the building of the Cable Plant Management (CPM) database, vendor CPM products; and, the EIA/TIA 606 standard. Chapter 18 opens up Part VI, "Future Directions," by examining future standards in development (ATM, 300-600Mhz cable systems (Category 6), zone wiring, TIA/EIA-T568-B, EN50174, 100BaseT2, 1000BaseT (Gigabit Ethernet, etc.).

End Notes

1   IMAP Corporation, 1501 North Broadway, Suite 115, Walnut Creek, CA. 94596, 1998, p. 1.
2   William Spencer, "Define End-user and Contractor Needs When Implementing a CMS," Network & Communication Technology, Inc., 24 Wampum Road, Park Ridge, NJ 07656, 1996, pp. 2–3.
3   William Spencer, "New Standard Issued for Telecom Documentation and Management," Network & Communication Technology, Inc., 24 Wampum Road, Park Ridge, NJ 07656, 1993, p. 4.

18

STANDARDS DEVELOPMENT

Recently, the passing of an era of sorts in the history of the development of cabling standards occurred around the globe. It was the end of a nearly five year transition period for the enforcement of a broad collection of global cabling standards and reference points designed to minimize the compatibility problems faced today by many countries.

The intent of the transition period on a practical level, via the Electromagnetic Compatibility (EMC) directive in Europe and the U.S. Cabling Standards, is to ensure your German-made Groupe Special Mobile (GSM) phone doesn't make a networked video application stumble in Liverpool, or, conversely, keep your active U.S. cable infrastructure from becoming a continental broadcast antenna. And so, global cabling industry manufacturers, installers, and users, are now charged with certain new responsibilities not accounted for when they last left their office or place of business. Manufacturers are of course required to ensure their cabling products meet standards laid down by the EMC Directive (see the sidebar, "A Quick Stroll Through Europe's EMC Directive Regulatory History") in Europe and cabling standards here in the U.S. Ultimately, however, the onus for cabling system and installation compliance rests on the provider and the owner. Penalties for failure in Europe for instance, can lead to stiff fines, imprisonment, or the barring of products from sale—testament to the European Union's (EU's) stern view of the matter. The penalties for failure in the U.S. are not as severe.

A Quick Stroll Through Europe's EMC Directive Regulatory History

First drafted as 89/336/EEC, the EMC Directive is the offspring of a multi-national marriage of regulations for electromagnetic emissions and immunity.

The immunity standards upon which it relies, for example, are derived from regulations including the International Electrotechnical Committee's IEC 801.x guidelines, as well as those of the International Special Committee on Radio Interference (Comite International Special des Pertubations Radioelectriques (CISPR) 24), and input from national organizations such as the British Standards Institute (BSI) and the US Federal Communications Commission (FCC). Blended to a palatable form by the EEC and its affiliate body, the Commission for European Normalization (CEN and CENELEC), the resulting regulations are known as the Harmonized Standards or European Norms (EN).

Two sets of these Harmonized Standards serve as the basis for evaluating the emissions and immunity characteristics for all electronic equipment not specifically identified in succeeding codes. Generic EN50082-1 and -2 address immunity issues in commercial and industrial environments, respectively, and generic EN50081-1 and -2 cover emissions. Standards for cabling systems, components, and installations are related in two dedicated documents, Information Technology Equipment (ITE) prEN55024 and ITE EN55022, which in turn serve as support for portions of the EMC Directive. CENELEC's structured cabling standard EN50174 is currently still in draft form.

While the lineage may appear a bit complex, the intent is not. The EMC Directive's requirements for electromagnetic emissions seek to limit what a component, system or installation can contribute, either by conduction or radiation, to the electromagnetic environment as part of its normal operation. Conversely, it also defines what level of electromagnetic radiation (not immunity—)—electrostatic discharge (ESD), power line transients, and radio frequency (RF) fields—a component, system, or installation should endure and still function.

If in fact cabling systems have an impact on compliance, the EU's networking managers are in for somewhat of a surprise. Cabling systems running high-speed data communications protocols over Category 5 UTP not only may fail components of the EMC Directive, but may not even function at all in certain electromagnetic environments. In the real world, that means everything from shorter drive distances to application latency and crashes, data corruption and loss, video display distortion, and potential health hazards [1].

If you plan to wring a few last precious years from your 4 Mbps token ring network, emissions and compatibility issues will likely be the least of your worries when users begin requiring bandwidth-hungry applications such as video. But if you are among the majority of cabling professionals who are or soon will be installing or operating cabling systems supporting higher throughput protocols, compliance with emissions and susceptibility standards will be as integral to a successful installation as functioning network interface cards.

So, what is the best compliance route for your company with regard to the standards that are currently being developed? The following questions are helpful in determining which route of compliance may be the most logical for your company.

1. Does the product/cabling system exist in more than one version?
2. Are you having difficulty identifying Harmonized Standards?
3. Are you likely to make modifications to the cabling equipment in the future?
4. Are future cabling standards or modifications to existing standards likely?
5. Are there existing test results for the product/cabling system?
6. Is the product/cabling system not practical to test?

If you answered *Yes* to any of these questions, you should consider taking a close look at the latest cabling *standards in development* to see which one(s) best fits your company's needs on its route to compliance. This chapter presents the most accurate, stable, and current information available with regard to the latest global standards in development. Let's start with the U.S. standards in development first:

U.S. Standards

The U.S. standards in development are as follows:

EIA/TIA-T568-A Commercial Building Telecommunications Wiring Standard.

EIA/TIA-569 Commercial Building Standard for Telecommunications Pathways and Spaces.

EIA/TIA-570 Residential and Light Commercial Telecommunications Wiring Standard.

EIA/TIA TR41.8.4 Outside Plant.

USOC.

IEEE.

IEEE 1394B.

ATM Forum.

Zone Wiring.

VESA.

NEMA.

ICEA.

BICSI.

The current status of the U.S. standards in development and their relationship to the EMC directive are discussed next.

EIA/TIA-T568-A Commercial Building Telecommunications Wiring Standard

The TR41.8.1 working group's recent meeting started with round two of the optical fiber connector presentations. This was followed by hands-on demonstrations of the five connectors. The connector decision will be made at their next meeting.

The Preliminary Notification (PN) 3727 task group had several presentations on Equal Level Far End Crosstalk (ELFEXT). A mathematical model was presented that predicted ELFEXT performance of cable and connectors in a basic link or channel configuration. This model was favorably received and seven companies signed up to collect round robin data to validate the model. Other contributions on ELFEXT that measured data-accuracy-models were also presented. An interim meeting was scheduled to resolve outstanding issues and incorporate these into Drafts 5a and 5b. The target is to have these documents approved for ballot at the next TR41.8.1 meeting.

The PN2948 UTP connecting hardware task group discussed the use of standardized modular test jacks for qualification of modular patch cords. The use of common test jacks will allow comparison of test results from multiple laboratories. The test jacks were distributed to several members for round robin testing.

The PN-3193 Straight Channel Tape Print (ScTP) Task Group reported on the resolution of ballot responses from Draft 12. A new Draft 14 was approved to be sent out for a second industry ballot. Interest in this document is waning as more members focus on the enhanced Category 5 and 300-600 Mhz cable systems (Category 6) specifications. Prior to this draft, Category 6 and Class E channel specifications under study by the ISO/IEC Joint Technical Committee (JTC) 1 SC25 WG3 were based around the German DIN 44312 part 5. This specified NEXT and Attenuation figures up to 600 MHz (see Figure 18-1) giving a positive ACR [2]. These figures were achieved by utilizing the outer two pairs only of an RJ45 connector thus making the system effectively 2-pair operation only, with the inner two pairs providing performance no better than standard Category 5. This standard was the first to conflict with the ethos of standards development being application driven, as all new proposals being considered for high-speed copper applications involved 4-pair operation over standards-based Category 5.

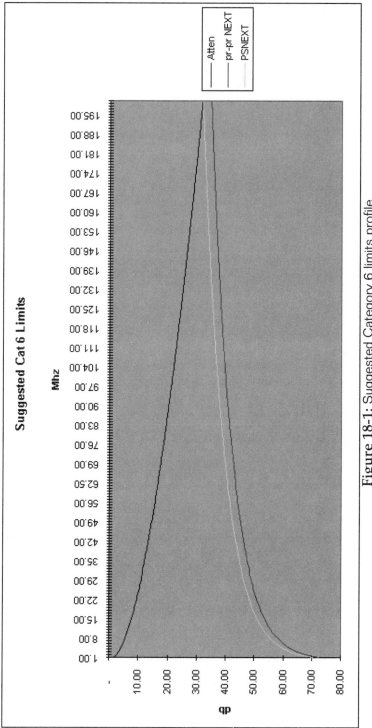

Figure 18-1: Suggested Category 6 limits profile.

The optical fiber task group reported discussions on Gigabit Ethernet (1000BaseT) issues and also fiber optics 6.3 testing issues. The objective is to ensure that Gigabit Ethernet will function over the 300 meter distance specified for the centralized cross-connect cabling topology. The task group is still waiting for liaison input on enhanced requirements for optical connectors. See the sidebar, "Gigabit Ethernet 1000BaseT," for more information on this developing standard.

Gigabit Ethernet 1000BaseT

Gigabit Ethernet is currently being developed to run over standards-based Category 5 channels using all four pairs. The method of transmission will use a combination of the technologies currently used to support 100BaseTX and 100BaseT2. This methodrequires a particularly high cable channel Attenuation Crosstalk Ratio (ACR) upon which to operate. Transmission is also bi-directional and simultaneous in order to meet the desired throughput requirements. This has resulted in Level One building NEXT and echo cancellation into the Rx/Tx chipsets to deliver the desired ACR. This was originally thought to provide adequate noise cancellation; however, it was later discovered that as this transmission method (PAM5) transmits and receives from both ends and on all four pairs, FEXT and its powersum variant, MDFEXT are also key sources of noise that need to be addressed. Therefore, the key parameter that will affect 1000BaseT performance is not ACR, as is the case with the 2-pair half-duplex applications such as 100BaseTx or PSACR or the 4-pair transmission method such as CAP-64 proposed for 622 Mbps ATM. For 1000BaseT, the key parameter is multi-disturber equal level far end crosstalk (MDELFEXT) or, to put it simply, powersum far end ACR.

Obviously the parameters of FEXT and echo noise (return loss) need to be addressed along with skew rate and time delay if bi-directional, simultaneous, 4-pair applications (1000BaseT) are to be supported. It is with this information in mind that ANSI/EIA/TIA TR 41.8.1 have produced two addendums to 568A, addendum yy, known as Draft3, which covers those additional performance parameters previously described, and addendum xx that covers performance enhancement, though not to the same degree as the Class E proposal from ISO.

From the issues previously raised, one can immediately see that ANSI/EIA/TIA TR 41.8.1 has adopted the ethos of application-based development, whereas the ISO/IEC JCT1 SC25 WG3 committee clearly has not. This is not the only sacred cow that has been slaughtered at recent conferences—the fundamental issue of backward compatibility between performance classes also appears to have been overlooked.

In accordance with ISO policy, all performance channels of a given classification for example (like Class D), must be able to support all Class D applications as well as those of lower performance classes (in this case C, B and A). Therefore a Class E channel must be able to support Class D applications. Since 1000BaseT is a Class D application, Class E channels must be able to support it. Unfortunately, due to FEXT, return loss, skew ,and time delay performance is not being defined for Category 6 or Class E performance. The result is that 1000BaseT support is not assured, far from it.

Because a complex relationship exists between connector NEXT and FEXT, a Class E link designed to give excellent NEXT support up to 200 Mhz may have a FEXT level insufficient to run a Class D application such as 1000BaseT. In their eagerness to produce a new *enhanced* standard that has no current or proposed application driver, ISO appears to have abandoned its commitment to customer and application support, and in doing so, may be in the process of actually reducing application support [Hook and Green, 1-2].

The installation task group is winding down its activities due to lack of participation and lack of technical input from the various cabling task groups. The plan is that this task group goes dormant until new information becomes available for pulling tension, bending radius and cable ties for all media types recognized in EIA/TIA-T568-A.

A liaison report from the WG3 (Working Group 3) international committee was very positive in terms of harmonization with ANSI/EIA/TIA. WG3 has also made its Category 5/Class D channel requirements almost identical to those in EIA/TIA TSB67. Additionally, the 300-600 Mhz cable systems (Category 6) objectives of EIA/TIA were adopted with very minor changes. These are important positive steps in the interest of maintaining uniform global standards and products.

Figure 18-2 represents the current development state of EIA/TIA-T568-B. Development continues at a very slow pace on this document [3]. Not much is happening on EIA/TIA-T568-B because of other urgent priorities. The committee agreed that work must resume in the EIA/TIA-T568-B area, and established a goal of circulating a first ballot by the end of 1999.

EIA/TIA-569 Commercial Building Standard
for Telecommunications Pathways and Spaces

The Technical Reference (TR) 41.8.3 working group approved distribution of SP-4125 (Furniture Pathways) and SP-4126 (Perimeter Pathways) for ballot. When approved, these two documents will be published as addenda to EIA/TIA-569A. Negative ballots for both these documents were cast because they do not set a hard 40% maximum cable fill limit. Packing cable too tight in raceways has a potential performance impact and makes ongoing maintenance more difficult. Ballot responses will be discussed at the next meeting.

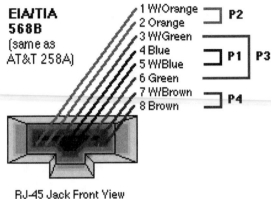

RJ-45 Jack Front View

Figure 18-2: 568B.

EIA/TIA-570 Residential and Light Commercial Telecommunications Wiring Standard

The TR41.8.2 committee approved distribution of Draft 11 of the document for a full ANSI ballot. Several sections in the document on coax cable were completed. A presentation by the power separation task group was reviewed and minor changes implemented in the document. Liaison letters along with electronic copies of the standard were sent to the Video Electronics Standards Association (VESA) home networking committee.

EIA/TIA TR41.8.4 Outside Plant

Draft 10 of the Customer Owned Outside Plant Standard was discussed at a recent meeting of the TR41.8.4 working group. Contributions on outside plant symbols, cable pressurization, and optical fiber cabling were reviewed and accepted for incorporation into the document. One interesting target in the document is that cables specified in the standard are intended to have a useful life in excess of 30 years while pathways specified in the standard are intended to have a useful life in excess of 40 years. The committee now has ICEA documents to refer to for both buried and aerial high performance broadband UTP cables. For aerial cables, the document recommends pressurization from both directions.

USOC

Universal Service Order Code (USOC) is an old standard, used for voice cabling as shown in Figure 18-3 [Combs, 4]. Notice that for 1- and 2-line phones (which use pins 4/5 and 3/6), 568A or 568B will work just as well as USOC. But for Ethernet (pins 1/2 and 3/6), USOC won't work. An Ethernet NIC trying to transmit on pins 1/2 will run into trouble because 1/2 aren't a pair (not the same color, and not twisted together). So unless you know the cable plant is for voice (analog, not digital), not ISDN, and it's never going to carry data, you should avoid USOC.

Why are the pairs shuffled around, instead of laid out logically? Well, they are logical, if you know the background. Ethernet was originally designed to run over the same cabling used by the phone system (AT&T created this as StarLAN), so this design left pins 4/5 available for a phone. If you plug an RJ11 (4 wire) into this, the middle two pins (2/3) of the RJ-11 would connect to the middle two pins (4/5) of the RJ-45, just perfect for a 1-line phone. If you plug an Ethernet cable into it, pins 1/2 will be used as one pair, and pins 3/6 will be used as another. No conflicts. Pretty clever, eh?

NOTE:

Choose 568A or 568B as the standard for your cable plant, but don't mix them.

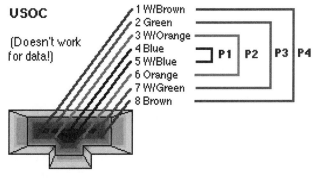

Figure 18-3: USOC.

IEEE

The 802.3z committee developing Gigabit Ethernet over multimode fiber has made significant progress since September 97 and the draft specifications are out for ballot at LMSC (LAN MAN Standards Committee). A conditioned launch of the short wave laser has been adapted as the solution to overcome modal jitter problems associated with short and long wave laser transmitters used with multimode fiber. The committee is on track to issue a full IEEE 802.3 ballot by 1999.

The 802.3ab committee has issued the first draft for comment. A full IEEE 802.3 ballot is scheduled for 1999. The committee has adapted PAM-5 (Pulse Amplitude Modulation—5 Level) to run over Category 5 cabling up to distances of 100 meters. This scheme is used to transmit and receive simultaneously on all four pairs to achieve a 1000 MbpsMbps data rate.

Based on the IEEE 802.3 standard, work continues on the 100BaseT2—the 100 Mbps baseband Fast Ethernet specification that uses three pairs of Category 3, 4, or 5 UTP wiring and signaling and control (CSMA/CD) in half-duplex mode. To guarantee proper signal timing, a 100BaseT2 segment cannot exceed 100 meters in length.

IEEE 1394B

At a recent meeting of the IEEE standard 1394B committee, the Link Control (LC) connector was selected as the standard optical fiber connector for 800 Mbps, 1600 Mbps, and 3200 Mbps over multimode fiber. A cross-section of the duplex receptacle and duplex plugs is included in Draft 0.07 of the standard. The committee also approved pursuing a 1394b solution over Category 5 cabling using simple Non-Return-to-Zero (NRZ) coding to support data rates of 100 Mbps. This alternative will allow 1394b to work over a large installed base of Category 5.

ATM Forum

At a recent meeting of the Asynchronous Transfer Mode (ATM) Forum, inverse Multiplex (MUX) was considered to be an ongoing activity. Work items to look at Gigabit backbone applications at 1.2 and 2.4 using multimode fiber are in progress. The 155 Mbps Residential Broadband (RBB) working group has moved the Panduit Fiber Jack connector from the living list into the draft document. The connector is used together with 1000 micron step index Plastic Optical Fiber (POF) up to distances of 50 meters maximum. The standard is not close to completion and there are some questions on how much acceptance this will achieve in the market. See Table 18-1 for more information and a listing of the latest specifications completed and approved by the ATM Forum [4].

Table 18-1: Approved ATM Forum Specifications.

Technical Working Group	Approved Specifications	Specification	Approved Date
LAN Emulation/ Multi-Protocol over ATM (MPOA)	LAN Emulation (LANE) v2.0 LANE User Network Internet (LUNI)	af-lane-0084.000	July, 1997
	Multi-Protocol Over ATM Specification v1.0	af-mpoa-0087.000	July, 1997
Network Management	M4 "NE View"	af-nm-0071.000	Jan, 1997
	Circuit Emulation Service Interworking Requirements, Logical and CMIP MIB	af-nm-0072.000	Jan, 1997
	M4 Network View Common Management Information Protocol (CMIP) MIB Spec v1.0	af-nm-0073.000	Jan, 1997
	M4 Network View Requirements & Logical MIB Addendum	af-nm-0074.000	Jan, 1997
	ATM Remote Monitoring SNMP MIB	af-nm-test-0080.000	July, 1997
Physical Layer	155 Mbps over Plastic Optical Fiber (POF)	af-phy-0079.000	May, 1997
	Inverse ATM Mux	af-phy-0086.000	July, 1997
P-NNI	Private Network/Node to Network Interface (PNNI) ABR Addendum	af-pnni-0075.000	Jan, 1997
	PNNI v1.0 Errata and PICs	af-pnni-0081.000	July, 1997
Service Aspects and Applications	Audio/Visual Multimedia Services: Video on Demand v1.1	af-saa-0049.001	Mar, 1997
	Frame User Network Interface (FUNI) 2.0	af-saa-0088.000	July, 1997
Signaling	Signaling ABR Addendum	af-sig-0076.000	Jan, 1997
Testing	PNNI v1.0 Errata and PICs	af-pnni-0081.000	July, 1997
	PICS for Direct Mapped DS3	af-test-0082.000	July, 1997
	Conformance Abstract Test Suite for Signaling (User-to-Network Interface (UNI) 3.1) for the Network Side	af-test-0090.000	September, 1997

(continued)

Table 18-1: *(continued)*

Technical Working Group	Approved Specifications	Specification	Approved Date
Traffic Management	Traffic Management ABR Addendum	af-tm-0077.000	Jan, 1997
Voice & Telephony over ATM	Circuit Emulation Service 2.0	af-vtoa-0078.000	Jan, 1997
	Voice and Telephony Over ATM to the Desktop	af-vtoa-0083.000	May, 1997
	(DBCES) Dynamic Bandwidth Utilization in 64 Kilobits Per Second (KBPS) Time Slot Trunkking Over ATM - Using CES	af-vtoa-0085.000	July, 1997
	ATM Trunking Using ATM Adaption Layer (AAL)1 for Narrow Band Services v1.0	af-vtoa-0089.000	July, 1997

Zone Wiring Standard

AT&T has developed a way to use a single high speed copper cable to carry—error-free—multiple, simultaneous high-speed data signals for dissimilar applications. The company demonstrated its zone cabling solution between six workstations during a recent Building Industry Consultants Society International (BICSI) conference.

In the demo, an AT&T SYSTIMAX® Structured Cabling System (SCS) 2061A 25-pair, Category 5 cable, using insulation made of Teflon® fluoropolymer resin, networked six workstations. Two of the terminals were operating interactive video using video adapter cards, two others accessed each other to receive video files, and two more were handling two-way file transfers. Commercially available cabling components and field test instruments were used in the demo.

Normal measurement procedures confirmed that AT&T's structured cabling system will support multiple transmissions of 155 MbpsATM, meeting—or exceeding—most global building wiring standards including EIA/TIA-T568-A. The system also exceeds ISO 1801 Generic Cabling link specifications as well as proposed TIA TSB67 performance specifications for field testing of UTP cabling systems.

Zone cabling architecture, a method of open office wiring, was used. This cabling scheme is well-suited to evolving technologies and changing networking needs of specialized work group areas and open offices designed to accommodate modular furniture.

Until now, zone wiring had not been shown to meet the needs of high speed data transport. Using this cabling configuration, horizontal cabling is divided into a section where permanent cables run from the telecommunications closet to a second section establishing a cluster, or group of work areas, or zones.

With this cable, only one 25-pair cable rather than six 4-pair cables are needed, thereby decreasing installation time. Moves, adds, and changes are also simplified.

Components Used in the Demonstration

To accomplish the zone wiring physical linkage, AT&T used typical unshielded twisted-pair (UTP) links built from SYSTIMAX® Structured Cabling System (SCS) HIGH-5.™ This product offering is comprised of 2061A 25-pair, enhanced Category 5 UTP cable.

The cable uses AT&T's patented pair twist scheme as well as insulation made of TEFLON fluoropolymer resin from DuPont. The cable ensures electrical performance so that multiple signals can be mixed in the same cable without loss of data integrity. It exceeds stringent Category 5 requirements including powersum crosstalk as outlined in the EIA/TIA-T568-A standard.

Other AT&T components used were D8AU line cords' a zone box housing M100 Category 5 information outlets' 110 patch cords' and connector system apparatus. Other equipment in the demo included a Bay Networks' LattisCell® ATM switch and SBus adapter cards. These give customers the benefits of switched virtual circuit (SVC) connectivity and reduces network administration for LANs.

The LattisCell ATM switch was connected with a 100-meter link using 2061A 25-pair Category 5 UTP cable to 6 Sun SPARC-2 workstations. The workstations represented an office work area. Each workstation used a Bay Networks UTP SONET STSc-3 adapter card providing connectivity to the ATM network.

The UTP interfaces are compatible with the Letter Ballot Draft of the ATM Forum specification for running 155 Mbps SONET STSc-3 on Category 5 UTP. This specification defines a two-level NRZ encoding scheme for use with Category 5 cabling systems.

Video Electronics Standards Association (VESA)

At a recent meeting of VESA, several companies, including SONY, HP, and Samsung, put together a demo of various home electronic devices (VCRs, TVs, camcorders) connected using the IEEE 1394 serial bus. This was intended to demonstrate a proof of concept that 1394 is a suitable base on which to build the VESA home network. The demonstration included 100 meters of Category 5 UTP in one of the segments, 50 meters of 1000 micron plastic optical fiber, and short lengths (up to 4.5 m) of firewire that is specified in the original 1394a specification.

National Electrical Manufacturers Association (NEMA)

The Premise Wiring Subcommittee reviewed several documents, the first of which was *WC66 and High Performance Shielded Premise Cables*, being prepared for a letter ballot by 1999. It includes premise wiring Categories 6 and 7 to 300 MHz and 600 MHz respectively and is patterned after a German Deutsches Institut für Normung (DIN) specification and recent EC standards activities.

Furthermore, at a recent meeting of the ISO/IEC JTC1 SC25 WG3, it was suggested that if the German proposal could be developed without application support, other media (UTP and FTP) could also be enhanced and standardized without application support, thus creating a two-tier enhanced performance structure comprising Class E (UTP/FTP) and Class F (PIMF Screened Shielded Twisted Pair (SSTP)) channels. These would be based around a specification delivering positive powersum ACR at 200 MHz (Category 6) and 600 MHz (Category 7). This means that all 600 MHz Category 6 specified cables will have to be re-defined as Category 7.

Category 6 Class E channels will be able to use either screened or unscreened balanced twisted-pair cables and will use the existing RJ45 connector in either screened or unscreened format. Therefore, to achieve Class E channel performance, both RJ45 connector interface and cable must be specified to achieve 200 MHz performance with positive powersum ACR on all four pairs.

The channel performance will require approximately 10% improvement in attenuation. The pair-to-pair NEXT performance will need to be improved to provide approximately the same pair-to-pair ACR at 200 MHz as is currently required by Category 5 at 100 MHz.

Category 7 Class F channels will demand individually screened twisted-pair (PIMF) cables. A specific Category 7 connector has not been agreed to. It will not, however, be an RJ45.

Finally, the NEMA standard (*WC63.1, Twisted Pair, Premise Wiring Products*) has been revised to be a procurement document for the military. Appendices were added for specific products such as Category 5, 24 and 22 AWG,; and patch cordage. The next NEMA meeting to review Without Charge (WC) 63 and WC 66 are scheduled for 1999 via teleconference.

ICEA

The Insulated Cable Engineers Association/Telecommunications Wire and Cable Standards/Technical Advisory Committee (ICEA/TWCS/TAC) at their last meeting covered several standards in progress. The *S-100-685, Station Wire* document has passed both TWCS TAC and ICEA letter ballots and is being forwarded to ANSI C-8 for ballot as a national standard.

The *S-99-689, Broadband Twisted Pair, Filled, Outside Plant Cable* document has passed ANSI C-8 and is now a national standard. These products have Category 5 performance with the added feature of Packet Switching (PS) Equal Level Far End Crosstalk (ELFEXT) in an outside plant cable.

The *S-98-688, Broadband Twisted Pair, Aerial, Outside Plant Cable* document has passed ANSI C-8 and is now a national standard. These products have Category 5 performance with the added feature of PS ELFEXT in an outside plant cable.

The *S-90-661, Indoor Wiring Standard (Category Cables)* standard is out for ANSI C-8 Ballot as a national standard. This Standard was revised to include two additional performance levels. Category 5 will have three levels—Categories 5, 5-100, and 5-160, where the dash number indicates the frequency in MHz where the ACR margin is 10 dB. The document also includes patch cordage, low smoke products, halogen free materials, PS ELFEXT, propagation delay requirements, and other improvements.

Revision 2 of -661 is active within TWCS TAC. Currently, additions included added return loss and input impedance requirements for Category 5, 5-100, and an additional Category 5-200. Working group 640 is also developing an outside plant Optical Fiber Standard.

BICSI

The Building Industry Consulting Services International (BICSI) is a not-for-profit telecommunications association focused on low-voltage wiring issues. The BICSI standards committee mission is to monitor telecommunications standards-making bodies and the standards they produce while influencing technical proposals on behalf of BICSI's membership in the interest of telecommunications performance. To this end the Standards Committee:

- Monitors standards-making bodies, to the best of their ability, and advises the BICSI membership of standards proposals that affect telecommunications.
- Influences standards-making bodies with proposals that serve the interest of telecommunications performance as interpreted by the experts among BICSI's membership.
- Monitors standards affecting telecommunications, to the best of their ability, and advises the membership of adopted standards [5].

BICSI's goal is the effective representation of BICSI within the telecommunications industry standards bodies for the next 2, 5, and 10 years. The goal is also to keep BICSI current with standards efforts for the next 2, 5, and 10 years. BICSI's objectives are to:

- Gain insight of changing standards affecting BICSI (Domestic/ International).
- Ensure clear two-way communication of members' desires for standards recommendations.
- Ensure accurate communications between BICSI representatives, standards bodies, and the committee.
- Collaborate with the Standards Committee and the Board of Directors in the formation of BICSI standards positions in accordance with the Standards Committee Policies and Procedures.
- Work toward the effective harmonization of international standards [BICSI, 16].

BICSI's plans are to:

- Attain representation on relevant standards bodies.
- Establish and publicize use of phone mail, web page, fax service, and MemberLetter for two-way communications of standards recommendations.
- Establish relations with higher levels within standards bodies.
- Identify Subject Matter Experts (SMEs) and establish contact data base for reference.
- Invite SMEs to BICSI general and committee meetings.
- Pursue leadership positions, where appropriate, and within budget with the approval of the committee chair and the Board of Directors.
- Promote BICSI standards liaison efforts with Rack Standards in EIA; Residential Standards; Pathway and Spaces Standards; OSP Standards; and, the Installation Task Group for 568-B.
- Coordinate BICSI's responses to standards ballots by verifying intentions of member comments, compiling information, and preparing filings according to the Standards Committee Policies.
- Establish liaisons with other BICSI committees (e.g., E&M, Codes, Installation).
- Procure relevant published standards for file and library use.
- Author news articles and reports for publication.
- Provide technical assistance to the BICSI Institute as needed.
- Respond to standards-related BICSI member information requests.
- Prepare, coordinate, and conduct standards-related presentations to the BICSI membership and other interested groups [BICSI, 17].

Global Standards

The global standards in development are as follows:

- ISO/IEC/JTC1/SC25/WG3.
- Australian Standards.
- Canadian Standards.
- Japanese Standards.

The current status of the global standards in development are discussed next.

ISO/IEC/JTC1/SC25/WG3

The WG3 committee does not seem to be interested in replacing the SC duplex optical fiber connector at the outlet. Since only performance is specified for connectors behind the wall, any of the newer small form factor connectors are allowed per International Standard (IS) 11801. There is not much support to change the SC with any other connector at the outlet.

There is a proposal under development to specify fiber performance by subsystem. The four subsystems are horizontal, backbone, campus, and centralized (horizontal plus backbone). This effort is being supported by Lucent and Corning. The idea is to recommend better quality fiber for backbone and campus subsystems where improved performance is needed. The interest of Corning in this effort is to make 50 micron fiber the preferred choice for backbone applications. The United States Telephone Association Group (USTAG) agreed to support the upgrading of 50 micron fiber from 160 MHz km to 500 MHz km at 850 nm.

A major breakthrough in the WG3 committee was to align Category 5 Class D link and channel requirements with TIA and ATM Forum requirements. The channel numbers are now identical to the TIA channel numbers. Due to slight differences in the TIA and ISO component parameter values, the link performance is still not completely aligned. This should be achieved at the next WG3 meeting.

The idea of specifying balance for UTP cabling is continuing to gain momentum in WG3. Annex A of the ATM 155 specification is cited as an example to establish a target of 40 dB balance up to 100 MHz. The main obstacle to balance specifications continues to be measurement methods. The coupling attenuation method proposed by several European test shops does not lead to repeatable results and does not characterize balance of individual components. Balance is the next frontier for UTP cabling specifications. This has to do with avoiding alternate inferior specifications, such as coupling attenuation.

Testing specifications are being developed under WG2 with input from WG3. A joint meeting of WG2 and WG3 is planned.

Australian Standards

Standards Australia is in the process of creating a cabling *steering committee* to be designated Cordless Telecommunication Version 1 (CT/1) with overall responsibility (in liaison with the Australian Communications Industry Forum), for setting priorities for cables and cabling standardization. The existing committees, subcommittees and working groups will initially be converted to subcommittees of CT/1. The subcommittees of CT/1 will therefore include: IT/17—*Integrated Cabling Systems for Buildings*; RC/5/G—*Radio communications Infrastructure - Cabled Distribution Systems*; TE/9—*Materials for Telecommunications Cable*; TE/17 *Fiber Optics*; and Working Group (WG) 6/1 (AUSTEL TS 008 and TS 009).

Canadian Standards

Canada has reaffirmed the Canadian Standard Association (CSA) T-528 Administration Standard. This is required to continue to sell the standard five years after the original publication date. Several issues have been identified that need to be addressed in the T-528 document. The plan is to work these into the revision of TIA-606 and then have CSA follow suit.

Japanese Standards

The Japanese Electronic Industry Development Association (JEIDA) is working to incorporate changes from *Draft Addendum 2* to the ISO/IEC 11801 1st edition, Chapter 7 into the Japan Industrial Standard (JIS) X 5150, and into the Japanese Cabling Standard. Below are some main points:

1. Permanent link and channel were clearly defined.
2. Characteristic impedance was defined as return loss.
3. Deleted tolerance of characteristic impedance (+/- 15 ohm (f.f.s.)) [6].

From Here

Chapter 18 opened up Part VI, "Future Directions," by examining standards in development (ATM, 300-600Mhz cable systems (Category 6), zone wiring, EIA/TIA T568-B, EN50174, 100BaseT2, 1000BaseT (Gigabit Ethernet, etc.)). The last chapter concludes by taking a peak at the cabling industry as it continues on its way to becoming a full information service provider in the next millennium via the ever changing cable specification process.

End Notes

1 "EMC in the EU: What the Networking Industry Should Know About the New Emissions Directives in Europe," ITT Cannon, Systems & Services, Jays Close, Viables Estate, Basingstoke, Hampshire, England, RG22 4BW, 1998, p. 1.

2 Mike Hook and Jon Green, "Category 6 and 7," ITT Cannon, Systems & Services, Jays Close, Viables Estate, Basingstoke, Hampshire, England, RG22 4BW, 1998, p. 1.

3 Mike Combs and Anne Combs, "LAN Cabling Basics," Cambridge, Massachusetts, p. 4.

4 "Technical Specifications," The ATM Forum, Worldwide Headquarters, 2570 West El Camino Real, Suite 304, Mountain View, CA 94040-1313, 1998, pp. 1-5.

5 "Long Range Planning Report," BICSI, 8610 Hidden River Parkway, Tampa, Florida 33637-1000 USA, 1998, p. 15.

6 "SYSTIMAX® SCS Standards Newsletter," Lucent Technologies Inc. , 600 Mountain Avenue, Murray Hill NJ 07974, U.S.A., (Copyright © 1998), pp. 1–9.

19

SUMMARY, CONCLUSIONS, AND RECOMMENDATIONS

The cable industry is becoming a full service provider as it evolves its infrastructure into an all-digital superhighway. Both the telephone and computer industries are suggesting their networking models of traditional point-to-point and extended distributed local area network technology become part of the cable industry solution. Cable is creating the multimedia networking model for the next millennium as a full service provider.

This chapter summarizes, concludes, and makes recommendations with regards to the cabling industry as it continues on its way to becoming a full information service provider in the next millennium via the ever-changing cable specification process. The basic areas of consideration that the cabling industry must adhere to when specifying cable are:

- Application consideration.
- Basic cable type selection.
- Performance level specification.
- Materials specification.
- Delivery and packaging considerations.
- Quality assurance considerations.
- Supplier specification.

Application Consideration

As the cabling industry enters the next millennium, greater demands will be placed on communications media for bandwidth. The highest quality media practical must be chosen. The scope of the cabling system to be built must also be considered.

Cabling System Scope

Add-on cabling to existing systems may be chosen simply by matching existing cable types exactly. Recently, improved versions of some older cable types have become available and should be considered for expansions of existing systems.

New system design considerations are open to a full range of possibilities. The highest practical performance level should be selected for system components once the basic architecture has been determined. Also, when addressing concerns about upgradability, future applications are typically considered and the highest performance system affordable should be provided to accommodate upgrade requirements.

Present and Future Coverage of Applications

Provision for voice communications applications is a given. The basic standard wiring stem requirements mandate that at least one telecommunications media, basic unshielded twisted pair (UTP), be provided to each work location. In addition, at least one other copper media, which may be a second telecommunications media, must also be installed according to EIA/TIA-T568-A, the Commercial Building Wiring Standard. In creating this standard, a complete specification for the basic telecommunications media was established. This specification may now preclude some older twisted-pair cables, but some clear transmission performance guidelines extending to higher-speed data applications have become available.

Data communications application requirements are also a given. Virtually every business employee has some form of data terminal on their desk. The most basic data communications application, data terminal equipment (DTE) service, has been covered by good telecommunications media.

NOTE:

There are not-as-good and maybe-even-worse telecommunications media also available, so see "Performance Level Specification," later in the chapter.

DTE was a big development, initially popularized by Digital Equipment Corporation (DEC).[1] This development started the practice of using twisted pair for everything. Originally, data terminals were interconnected to mainframes through coax, twinax, or some other proprietary and particularly non-telecommunication-type wiring. The proprietary cables are still available, and used in large quantities, but mainly for moves, adds, and changes on older systems. Now, some kind of twisted-pair solution has been devised for virtually every terminal system on the market.

Ethernet, a Xerox development and trademark, is a fundamentally different form of data communication compared to data terminal service. Its introduction marked a critical development in computer system architecture, distributed systems. In Ethernet, the media must accommodate broadcasting over a local area (LAN) at much higher speeds than simple low-speed point-to-point data terminal links. To meet these requirements, the first systems used robust, thick, coaxial trunk cables, transceivers, and shielded twisted-pair drop cables. Later DEC, a co-developer of Ethernet, created a low cost, but more practical version, Thinnet (or 'cheapernet'), which is suitable for fewer nodes over a smaller area, using a thin coax in a daisy-chain wiring structure. This more limited facility has since been implemented in a 10BaseT on a UTP network. It was the establishment of the UTP specification for 10BaseT (intended to model common telecommunications UTP cables) that lead to the levels of performance for UTP cables (see "Performance Level Specification," later in the chapter).

Token ring, albeit the name for a generic LAN protocol and topology, has come to mean IBM. Seemingly in response to Ethernet, IBM introduced a cabling system based on a very ample shielded twisted-pair (STP) cable design and a complete wiring system based on a logical ring (physical star) network topology. IBM followed up with a 4 Mbps token-passing LAN protocol for interconnecting computer nodes on the network, later introducing components. All of IBM's various proprietary wiring systems for their various computer and peripheral systems could also be implemented on the IBM Cabling System. IBM has since upgraded the LAN system speed to 16 Mbps. This IBM Cabling System was so successful that the terminology STP has become synonymous with the specific type of shielded twisted pair associated with it, as if no other form of STP could exist. As could be expected, UTP implementations of 4 Mbps and 16 Mbps token ring application have also become available, demanding a higher level of performance for UTP, beyond the UTP performance specifications established for Ethernet.

Fiber Distributed Data Interface (FDDI), also a token-passing ring LAN protocol and topology, was conceived to run at 100 Mbps using multimode optical fiber media. Originally intended to interconnect mainframes and super-computers in and between large data centers, by the time the standard development process was completed, FDDI became a preferred choice for interconnecting LANs within an organization to form the backbone of a comprehensive corporate-wide network. The modern replacement for the original thick coax Ethernet campus LAN is a group of separate smaller Ethernet LANs interconnected by a high speed FDDI LAN. Given the developments in powerful workstation applications, FDDI to the individual workstation has become a practical consideration. A Low Cost FDDI (LC-PMD) has been introduced, still implemented on multimode optical fiber, but at a substantial cost reduction by reducing the original 2 km FDDI maximum link requirement to 1 km. This link distance reduction permits a minor performance reduction but a major cost reduction for the transmission components. Recently, products have been introduced so that FDDI 100 Mbps protocol can be implemented on the STP IBM Cabling System over 100 m links (Twisted Pair Physical Media Depended (TP-PMD)) from the wiring closet to the desk. Of course, the ubiquitous UTP, in a form departing considerably from the original, has also produced a viable alternative (also TP-PMD).

Future applications will operate at considerably higher speeds, into the 1 Gbps to 2 Gbps range for backbone, introducing singlemode optical fiber into the backbone environment. Multimedia applications are expected to transcend 100 Mbps capability and will most likely transcend UTP bandwidth. Telecommunications and data communications converge at the point of transition to broadband. Digital distributed telephone switches already use singlemode optical fiber to interconnect individual equipment frames and connect into the digital telecommunications Wide Area Network (WAN). FDDI-2 is a revision to the FDDI protocol designed to accommodate interactive voice and video. Extending Ethernet to 100 Mbps is being investigated. Fiber Channel, the up-to-2 Gbps replacement for FDDI (for interconnection between mainframes and super-computers in various distance/speed steps), uses all standard media up through singlemode optical fiber. The next LAN technology, FDDI Follow-on LAN (FFOL), will accommodate the Asynchronous Transfer Mode (ATM) protocol developed for high-speed WAN services. This will permit broadband links of at least OC-3 155.52 Mbps to be made available first near to the desk for LAN internetwork links, then all the way to the desk. Underlying the similarities in speed and hierarchical structure being developed for both WAN and LAN are the designs for their seamless interconnection.

Basic Cable Type Selection

The decision on the type of cable to install in a building has become more complex with the introduction of applications which operate full duplex over four cable pairs. These applications have forced infrastructure standards developers to reconsider the specifications for existing cables and add new categories of performance to the specifications. Even fiber optic cables, which were once considered to have unlimited bandwidth, are now distance limited when used with applications that operate at gigabit speeds. This has influenced the introduction of new multimode fiber optic cables onto the market to address these limitations.

When choosing media there are few fundamental engineering and design considerations:

- Additional up front cost today versus future benefits
- Lease or own occupied facility.
- Application migration plan.
- Criticality of network performance.
- Percentage of the cable installation cost versus the total LAN cost.

ANSI/EIA/TIA-T568-A defines the requirements for structured wiring. This standard provides a stable platform for the installation of cabling infrastructure and provides applications developers with a model which can be used in the development of new standards for years to come. ANSI/EIA/TIA-T5686-A recognizes the following media for use in horizontal and backbone applications:

- Horizontal.

  - 100 Ohm Unshielded Twisted Pair.
  - 150 Ohm Shielded Twisted Pair.
  - 62.5/125 Multimode Optical Fiber.

- Backbone.

  - 100 Ohm Unshielded Twisted Pair.
  - 150 Ohm Shielded Twisted Pair.
  - 62.5/125 Multimode Optical Fiber.
  - Singlemode Optical Fiber [Berk-Tek, 3-4].

In horizontal applications, the use of unshielded twisted pair cable is prevalent. Approximately 70% of existing buildings have Category 5 UTP installed. The wide acceptance of Category 5 UTP cable assures that new applications will continue to be developed to support the large installed base. The use of UTP in horizontal applications will continue until the cost of fiber optic network products drop to make them competitive with copper solutions.

In the backbone, 62.5/125 multimode fiber has been the preferred media. At gigabit speeds this type of fiber is very length limited. To address the length limitations of this fiber, enhanced bandwidth 62.5/125 and 50/125 optical fibers have become available. These fibers are not included as part of the ANSI/EIA/TIA-T568-A standard but undoubtedly will be included in the next addition of the standard.

Optional Media

In addition to the recognized media, EIA/TIA-T568-A also includes in its appendices:

- Optional Horizontal Media.
  - 100 Ohm Shielded Twisted Pair.
  - 100 Ohm Multipair Shielded Twisted Pair (UTP) (25 pair) Undercarpet Cables.
  - Other Multimode Optical Fiber (50/125, 100/140, etc.).
  - 75 Ohm Coaxial Cable (CATV coax).
- Optional Backbone Media.
  - 100 Ohm Shielded Twisted Pair
  - Other Multimode Optical Fiber (50/125, 100/140, etc.).
  - Singlemode Optical Fiber.
  - 75 Ohm Coaxial Cable (CATV coax).

Optional media are suitable for some special applications which are outside of the scope of this chapter. Now, let's look at performance level specification considerations, particularly for UTP but also applicable to STP. Their considerations are covered next.

UTP Performance Specifications

ANSI/EIA/TIA-T568-A includes three performance specifications for UTP cable. Although there are network applications such as 100BaseT4 which are designed to utilize Category 3 cable, this cable is currently installed to support voice applications. Category 3 cable has a usable bandwidth of 16 MHz. Category 4 cable which has a bandwidth of 20 MHz, offers little improvement over Category 3 cable and is no longer available. Category 5 cable with a bandwidth of 100 MHz is widely accepted and there are many network applications which have been developed to operate over this media.

TIA is currently revising specifications for Category 5 cable based on recommendations from IEEE 802.3ab (1000BaseT). Several new electrical parameters, *return loss* and ELFEXT, are being added to the Category 5 standard. These two new parameters address requirements for full duplex operation.

IEEE recommends the horizontal topology be limited to two connection points, the wall outlet and patch panel to minimize the amount signal reflected back to the transmitted and the effects of crosstalk. IEEE also recommends that existing installation must be reevaluated to these new requirements before 1000BaseT is implemented.

To increase the robustness of Category 5 cable with new applications and to further address the requirements of full duplex operation over four cable pairs, TIA is also working on specifications for *enhanced* Category 5 cable. This specification introduces the concept of power sum to horizontal cabling in addition to several other critical electrical parameters. There is little doubt that Enhanced Category 5 cabling will be the mainstay of new cable installations when TIA releases the specification early in 1999.

TIA and ISO are also working on solutions with greater than 100 MHz bandwidth. Proposals for Category 6 cable have bandwidth up to 200 MHz, double that of Category 5 cable. Category 6 offers application developers increased performance while being backward compatible with existing Category 5 installations. Category 7, currently under development by ISO features a bandwidth of 600 MHz utilizing a cable with four individually shielded pairs. Installations which utilize this solution are not backward compatible with existing Category 5 installations and are currently proprietary in nature due to lack of a connector standard. Specifications for these new cabling solutions will be released by the year 2000 [Berk-Tek-5].

Nevertheless, with regard to the impact on limitations to bandwidth, the three most important (in order of importance) electrical parameters for twisted-pair cables are: crosstalk attenuation impedance, characteristic impedance, and structural return loss (SRL).

Crosstalk Attenuation Impedance

Crosstalk (usually near end crosstalk (NEXT) rather than far end crosstalk (FEXT) is the type of crosstalk of greater concern) refers to the amount of signal coupled from one line or pair within a cable onto another line within the same cable. Given the preferred star network cable topology, a send and receive line will be present in all network cables. Crosstalk, in this case manifested as an echo, is the primary limiting factor in most twisted pair LAN applications. Crosstalk increases at higher frequencies proportional to frequency, but does not increase for longer lengths proportional to length. For example, a typical cable with 25 dB NEXT loss at 100 feet has a NEXT loss of about 25dB at 1,000 feet. Most of the near end crosstalk coupling occurs in the near end of the cable.

NOTE:

NEXT crosstalk between two twisted pairs is measured at the same end of the cable as the disturbing signal source.

Attenuation refers to the amount of signal loss that occurs over distance. Attenuation increases proportionally to both frequency and length. Thus, attenuation becomes a greater consideration at both higher frequencies and longer lengths.

Characteristic Impedance

Impedance, more accurately, characteristic impedance, is a frequency-dependent characteristic of any cable. It does not directly impact system performance, except that the impedance of the cable must match the impedance baluns. Cables are designed to meet certain impedance baluns within a given range. A practical, good, nominal characteristic impedance for twisted pair is 100 ohms. IBM chose 150 ohm for their STP systems. The impedance-related influence on system performance results from deviations from the particular system impedance—either in the form of inconsistencies within the cable or mismatches to other system components. Some results of the variations are signal reflection and dispersion whereby less signal gets to the receiver, thus degrading system performance.

Structural Return Loss

Structural Return Loss (SRL) is another critical parameter. It is a measurement of the difference between sent signal and reflected signal. The bigger the difference, the smoother the cable, the better the performance.

Combined Performance

The combined effect of these parameters can be expressed in a way that is similar to a signal-to-noise ratio. Given that a minimum signal-to-noise ratio for a particular system is between, say 10 and 15 dB, it can be seen at what frequencies a given cable may be suitable for use up to 100 meter distances.

Above 30 MHz, additional consideration must be given to being in conformance to FCC regulations for emission. Crosstalk is an indication of a cable's performance in this area. Emission levels are dependent on the total systems and is impossible to predict given cable characteristics alone. But qualitatively, the better the crosstalk performance, the better the emission performance will be. If greater than 100 MHz signals are a consideration, the highest crosstalk performance cable available should be selected. Optical Fiber, unlike copper media, has little or no room for variation in performance insofar as bandwidth is concerned. In the case of singlemode fiber, its inherent primary waveguide characteristic makes defining the limits of its bandwidth essentially impossible. Multimode optical fiber fabrication technology is rapidly nearing perfection. The result is that a given fiber geometry, say 62.5/125 m with .275 NA (Numerical Aperture, the measure of light acceptance), has a given bandwidth unless changes are made to intentionally alter the optical characteristics. The available fiber virtually all falls within the practical allowance for deviation from ideal. In a sense, it's all the same. There is no room for levels.

Materials Specification

Materials used in cable design and manufacture are constantly improving. Manufacturers choose materials based on application and performance requirements. Choice of materials is often best left to cable engineers who have the knowledge and experience to choose materials which best fit the application and requirements. Below is a partial list of considerations which effect the choice of materials:

- Outside plant or inside installation.
- Robustness.
- Flammability requirements.
- Electrical requirements.
- Size
- Weight
- Compliance to applicable standards.
- Cost [Berk-Tek, 6].

Considerable confusion related to specifying cable materials results from misunderstandings about which part of the cable is actually being specified. The cable jacket, most accurately, is the outer plastic covering of the cable. Within the cable jacket, the individual wires are covered by a different layer of plastic—most accurately referred to as insulation or dielectric (non-conductive). These two coverings serve different purposes and can be composed of the same or entirely different plastics depending on the application. Considerations for specifying the plastic material used on a cable jacket almost always involves flammability. Further confusion occurs from the common use of plastic material types to specify a level of flammability, say plenum versus non-plenum. Based on original technology, the terms PVC and non-plenum-rated or Teflon and plenum-rated were used interchangeably. Teflon is a DuPont trademark for a fluoropolymer called fluorinated-ethylene-propylene (FEP). Permanent Virtual Circuit/Channel (PVC) based compounds suitable for plenum rating has essentially become mutually exclusive of the basic material types [Berk-Tek, 6].

Generally, the material most involved in carrying signals is the insulation (in this context also referred to as dielectric). Some impact to transmission performance is completely unaffected by jacket material but this effect is insignificant compared to the improvements from substituting PVC insulation with polyethylene or FEP, for non-plenum and plenum cables respectively. This is due to the latter materials having far superior high-frequency dielectric properties than PVC. Furthermore, PVC's relatively poor properties substantially deteriorate with increased temperatures, whereas the better performing dielectrics essentially do not change with temperature.

In addition to providing basic insulating properties, the plastics used for insulation have various signal altering characteristics, dielectric constant and the dissipation factor. The dielectric constant is a function of the velocity at which energy travels through the dielectric. The dissipation factor is a function of the rate at which energy is absorbed by the dielectric. Reducing either of these factors results in improved signal transmission performance.

The plastic most commonly used for conductor insulation is PVC. Its dielectric properties are good but generally not good enough for any data communication application more demanding than basic short-distance links. PVC is normally used for power, control, instrumentation, audio, telecommunications, and applications that operate at low frequencies. High-speed data cables are normally made using polyethylene or FEP, because their dielectric properties are far superior to PVC.

There is no real disadvantage to using polyethylene compared to PVC. The cost is only slightly higher, although some cable design precautions must be taken to meet flammability regulations. Polyethylene is more flammable than PVC, but this is easily compensated by a flame retardant PVC cable jacket. The only exception to the choice of polyethylene insulation is the case of plenum cables. FEP is substituted by PVC to achieve low smoke and flame producing characteristics. The dielectric properties for FEP are slightly superior to polyethylene.

The proximity of two conductors within a cable and the dielectric constant of the insulation between the conductors determine the capacitance measured between the conductors. Capacitance is defined as the amount of electricity the dielectric between two conductors will store for a given voltage difference between the conductors. When the voltage is changing (a signal is present), a higher capacitance results in a greater resistance to the change (more attenuation at higher frequencies).

Most shielded cables use insulation with very good dielectric properties (low dielectric constant) to assure that cable capacitance are kept low when a shield is added to the cable. The addition of a shield around the two conductors introduces two very significant parasitic capacitance, those between each conductor and the shield. The conductor-to-shield capacitance combine with the conductor-to-conductor capacitance to significantly increase the overall capacitance of the pair. To achieve the same impedance in a shielded cable as an unshielded cable, insulation with a lower dielectric constant must be used and the conductor spacing must be increased. The result is that shielded cables are generally larger than unshielded ones.

It is no longer the case that plenum cables need be stiff. Originally plenum cables constructed from fluoropolymers were inherently very rigid compared to typical non-plenum cables. The stiffness was grudgingly tolerated because of cost savings resulting from installations without conduit. Now, substantial improvements have been made to certain fluoropolymers such as giving Astochem Kynar-Flex (PVDFCP), which has near-PVC flexibility. Although fluoropolymers as a group still hold the position of having the greatest flame retardance, it is possible to design a cable using special PVC-based compounds for jacket or insulation and still achieve a plenum rating. These special PVC-based compounds are less flexible and have lower performing dielectric properties than ordinary PVC compounds. But on certain cable constructions they can provide definite improvements in flexibility.

Delivery and Packaging Considerations

Packaging is an important consideration which may determine how easily a cable is installed. Getting the lengths of cable you need, packaged the way you need them, should be as simple as possible. Package design details such as cable kinking when pulled from a box varies from manufacturer to manufacturer. When approaching a possible supplier, several factors should be considered:

- What packaging options are available?
- Has the manufacturer engineered the package to minimize damage to the cable when removed from the package?
- What protection is given to the cable?
- What lengths are available?
- What does the manufacturer stock?
- How are the products labeled [Berk-Tek, 7-8]?

Available Packaging Options

Reels should of course be available, sized to length and diameter of the cable. The end user should be wary of reels that have too small of a drum diameter, however. The manufacturer may be saving money by using an inferior reel, but if the drum is too small, it can exceed the bend radius of the cable and actually cause damage resulting in loss of signal. This is particularly true of optical fiber cables, where bending can easily cause breaks and attenuation. Boxes for most standard products should also be an option. Many end users prefer the light, disposable boxes that are easily carried, stored and handled. There is no reel involved in the process—the cable is wound into a basket that pays off without kinking. For users that prefer boxes, the manufacturer must be able to stock or quickly turn around standard items in boxes. Look for boxes with at least a 257# proof test.

Cable Protection

Cables should be protected from dirt, damage, and moisture. Reels should be boxed, placed on skids, or wrapped with clear plastic.

Available Cable Lengths

All manufacturers of cable list standard lengths that processing attempts to meet. Most manufacturers offer optical fiber cable in standard lengths of 1.0, 1.5, and 2.0 km. Copper cables are available in standard 500 foot and 1,000 foot lengths. A reliable manufacturer should be able to run longer continuous lengths when required, or offer shorter lengths as an option. Extremely high cut charges are a sign that the manufacturer is not producing in any quantity for stock.

Manufacturer's Stock

A larger internal inventory is a sign of quick turnaround from order to shipment. Most large manufacturers offer a vast copper cable Take-From Stock internal inventory shipping program. This means that they get their products to their distributors quickly.

Labeling Products

Labeling seems like a given, but inadequate labeling can fall off, become obscured or not contain user-friendly information. Labels should be easy to read, protected from the environment, and securely fastened to the reel or box.

At the very least, information should be given on the order number, customer, internal code, and reel or box number for traceability. Desirable information includes a market description which is easily understandable by anyone associated with cable products. The description should use industry-accepted terminology for the product rather than the manufacturer's internal coding. For optical fiber cables, where mishandling can create grave problems, final preshipment testing information must be included for each length.

Quality Assurance Considerations

The quality of a cable product is invisible. A comparison of manufacturers should include an investigation of their quality assurance programs. A good program conforms to standards and is easily demonstrated.

Testing

Cable manufacturers test final product to determine compliance to specifications. Category 5 UTP cable is typically tested at a rate of one sample ever 250,000 feet of manufactured product. The sample rate varies from manufacturer to manufacturer and from product to product. Fiber optic cables are typically evaluated for fiber attenuation and dimensional requirements, while UTP cables are tested for conformance to electrical and dimensional specifications. The systematic control of in-process quality is as important as final testing to assure compliance to industry standards requirements and internal requirements. On a daily basis, it is critical that testing and quality assurance be carried out during the manufacturing process when deviations can be corrected before the product is complete. In-process testing is not only more efficient, but helps guarantee a quality end-product. Manufacturers utilize statistical process control to monitor critical aspects of the manufacturing process. An example is the control of outer insulation diameter and conductor centering in a Category 5 cable.

If there is question concerning the electrical or optical performance of a specific cable, manufacturers have the ability to supply test data which reflects the performance of the reel of cable in question [Berk-Tek, 8].

Special Testing

While most manufacturers are always trying to improve the way they handle testing for their standard products, they also have a wide range of special equipment and procedures. They should always be prepared to conduct humidity testing, low and high temperature tests, tensile tests, cable burns, and many other standard or not-so-standard procedures.

UL Approvals/ETL Verifications

Most cabling products are used in applications requiring an Underwriter's Laboratories (UL) and/or Canadian Standard Association (CSA) rating. Manufacturers should have extensive approvals from both agencies, usually for flame ratings. Manufacturers should also have many of their products performance tested and approved by UL as proof that their cables are performing per spec. The Electrotechnical Laboratory (ETL) also verifies many cabling products.

ISO 9000

The ISO (International Standards Organization) is concerned with creating a global standard of quality assurance programs and certifications. What has become known as ISO 9000 is actually a series of five standards with 9001, 9002, and 9003 detailing specific systems for quality based on distinct functional or organizational structures.

Unlike other second-party approval agencies, ISO does not test products. Rather, it verifies that an organization is following the quality systems the organization has established. The theory behind ISO 9000 is that a manufacturer following specific quality guidelines will consistently produce higher quality, more reliable products. Companies interested in doing business on a world-wide scale are increasingly finding conformance to ISO a requirement.

Supplier Specification

Finally, the cable media you choose may make up 25% or more of the cost of the system. Specifying the wrong cable or buying a borderline performance cable can be a costly disaster, leading to system crashes, distorted signals, lost data and eventual cable re-pulls. The choice you make must be fully informed. Your supplier must be willing and able to provide you with the services you need, not just the right cable.

Final Words

The opportunity for the cabling industry to become a full information network provider today is a reality when utilizing the technology and specification process described in this chapter and book. For over 10 years, network technologists in the computer and cable industry have been working toward this end. The time has arrived with the convergence of high-speed bandwidth technology development and societal trends to deploy interactive cable applications and services throughout communities everywhere in the coming millennium. All elements are in place, and deployment is underway to ensure that there will be a new dawn for the cabling industry well after the midnight of the next century. See you there!

End Notes

1 "The Seven Secrets to Specifying Cable," Cable and Wire Central, Berk-Tek, 132 White Oak Road, New Holland, PA 17557, USA, 1998, p. 2.

Part VI

Appendixes

A

TV-Based High-Speed Cable Internet Services

In addition to providing high-speed Internet access to PCs with cable modems, MSOs are also working to provide fast Internet connections to TVs through digital cable set-tops. Like cable modems that deliver 10 Mbps of data, digital set-tops support 27 Mbps of downstream data throughput per 6 MHz TV channel. They also have enough processing power and memory to run basic browser software.

By selling TV-based Internet services, cable operators can achieve a better return on the capital investments they make for two-way cable modem deployments by leveraging common infrastructure. Capital investments that could be shared by both TV- and PC-based Internet services include upgraded cable plant, Internet connectivity, network management systems, routers, servers, and broadband content.

Bolstered by the success of the MCNS DOCSIS initiative, which defined North American standards for cable modem interoperability, Cable Television Laboratories Inc. launched a similar project in August, 1997 called OpenCable that is working to set standards for interactive digital cable set-top boxes.

OpenCable Project

CableLabs issued a request for information (RFI) in August, 1997, and received responses from more than 20 cable equipment, consumer electronics, and technology companies in October 1997 as shown in Table A-1 [1]. The OpenCable Task Force sorted through the vendor submissions and issued initial product guidelines in November.

Table A-1: Companies Responding to OpenCable RFI.

ACTV	PowerTV
Cisco Systems	Samsung
Criterion Software	Sarnoff
IBM	Scientific-Atlanta
Intel	SCM Microsystems
Lucent Technologies	Sony
Microsoft	Sun Microsystems
Netscape	Texas Instruments
Network Computer Inc.	Thomson Consumer Electronics
NextLevel Systems	Toshiba
Oracle	Wink Communications
Panasonic	WorldGate Communications
Pioneer	Zenith Electronics

OpenCable basically specified the same physical-layer transmission scheme used in MCNS cable modems, including the International Telecommunications Union's (ITU) Annex B implementation of 64/256 QAM for downstream modulation and a QPSK/16QAM-based real-time return path.

The MPEG-2 (Moving Picture Experts Group) standard is specified for digital video transport with audio following the Dolby Audio AC-3 system. For signal security, OpenCable selected the NextLevel Systems Inc. (which is changing its name back to General Instrument), implementation of the DES encryption standard. Through a harmony agreement reached between NextLevel's and Scientific-Atlanta Inc., OpenCable supports multiple conditional access and control data streams over the core encryption scheme, specifically GI's DigiCipher and S-A's PowerKEY solutions.

The OpenCable standard will not specify a single vendor's microprocessor or operating system (OS). Instead, it plans to spell out basic requirements for processing power and memory that OpenCable manufacturers must meet, as well as rules of the road for OS vendors to follow. With this OS-agnostic approach, most interactive services will be implemented with middleware using open Internet specifications, including HTML, CGI, JavaScript, and popular plug-ins.

In January 1998, CableLabs selected S-A to manage key elements of the OpenCable project. S-A will produce a network architecture reference model, help define network interfaces (including the physical layer and communication protocols), and also provide system integration services. CableLabs expects S-A to finish the project in the first quarter of 1999, enabling the Open-Cable specification to be completed by mid year.

TCI's OpenCable Maneuvers

In December 1997, cable giant Tele-Communications Inc. (TCI) committed to purchase 6.5 million to 11.9 million digital set-tops from GI over the next five years. For the next year, TCI will deploy GI's DCT-1000 set-top, a one-way digital video receiver. The MSO plans to start deploying interactive set-tops from GI that meet the emerging OpenCable specification sometime in the year 2000.

As part of the deal, GI will issue TCI and its affiliates a warrant convertible for 3.2 shares of GI common stock at a discounted price of $14.75 per share for every digital box purchased. GI also agreed to acquire TCI's Headend-In-The-Sky digital authorization business service in exchange for a 10-percent equity interest in GI.

In January 1998, TCI announced it had agreed to license Microsoft's Windows CE operating system for at least 5 million of the OpenCable set-tops it will deploy. The deal also calls for Microsoft to provide key elements of its WebTV technology for the TCI set-tops. Separately, TCI also inked a deal with Sun to add PersonalJava to some of the boxes.

Windows CE will serve as the operating system for TCI's advanced set-tops, while PersonalJava will run on top of the OS, providing an open application environment. This way, TCI can run software that is written expressly for Windows CE, as well as Java-based Internet applications.

Also in January, Sony Corp. purchased a 5-percent in GI for $187.5 million to ensure it gets a piece of the emerging digital cable set-top market. As a part of the investment, Sony will help GI fulfill the TCI order as a second source supplier.

Pegasus to Fly First

TCI is not the only MSO with big OpenCable plans. Under a project called Pegasus, Time Warner Cable developed specifications for a two-way digital set-top box that will be commercially deployed by April 1998, beating the TCI-GI team to the punch.

Time Warner selected Scientific-Atlanta as the prime contractor for the Pegasus program, with Toshiba and Pioneer tapped as secondary suppliers. In total, Time Warner has committed to buy 1 million digital set-tops from the three vendors. The company has also agreed to purchase 500,000 boxes from GI.

S-A's Pegasus box, called the Explorer 2000, will be compliant with OpenCable specifications. At its initial release, Explorer includes HTML and JavaScript engines within the PowerTV operating system to support TV-based Internet services.

Eight other MSOs have announced they will would begin deploying S-A's Explorer 2000 digital set-tops in 1999: Adelphia, Comcast, Cox, Marcus Cable, MediaOne, Rogers, Videotron, and Cogeco.

Other Internet TV Solutions: ICTV and WorldGate

In addition to the digital OpenCable approach, two other vendors are championing complementary Internet TV technologies for analog cable systems: ICTV and WorldGate Communications. For example, Los Gatos, California-based ICTV has developed a high-powered virtual PC service that can be delivered to cable subscriber TVs over hybrid fiber/coax (HFC) networks. ICTV and Cox Communications started a market trial of the service in March 1997 in Santa Barbara, California. Cox has priced the service at $6.95 per month for equipment rental and five hours of usage, plus $1.99 for each additional hour. The ICTV trial services include web access, e-mail and multimedia games.

ICTV essentially builds a client/server network in the cable headend by installing a massively parallel architecture of multimedia PCs running Windows98. Proprietary ICTV hardware is used to take the VGA output from each PC board and translate it into NTSC or MPEG video streams for over the cable system to subscriber homes. The signal can be received through any cable-ready television set or set-top box. A small ICTV box and wireless keyboard are installed in the home to handle upstream communication from the subscriber to the headend.

In an analog cable environment, each ICTV subscriber is allocated a full 6 MHz television channel during their session. The subscriber receives a dedicated 10 Mbps stream to the home, enabling them to receive the video output from the headend-based PC they are using in real time. In effect, the subscribers' TV sets operate as a remote monitor, allowing them to view any Windows 98 application running on the PC, whether it is surfing the web, sending e-mail, or playing a multimedia game.

While ICTV is focused on providing a high-performance multimedia service, WorldGate Communications is working to deliver cheap, no-frills Internet access to the masses. Rather than requiring the use of a full TV channel, WorldGate's TV On-Line service operates in the vertical blanking interval (VBI). Normally an unused portion of the video spectrum, a typical cable system may have 60 or more slots. WorldGate's platform delivers 100 Kbps of shared downstream data throughput in each VBI to addressable analog set-top boxes manufactured by GI and S-A.

To make it work, WorldGate needed to pull a few tricks because VBI bandwidth cannot deliver a real-time video stream, like ICTV, and analog set-tops do not have enough memory to run a full-featured web browser. At the headend, HTML coding is stripped off any web page a customer requests. The display output is then sent down to the TV set in the home as a bitmap image.

WorldGate foresees cable operators selling the TV On-Line service, which includes web and e-mail access, for $4.95 per month, with WorldGate receiving a 30-percent share of revenue. Rental of a wireless keyboard would cost subscribers another $2 per month. The company has TV On-Line service deployments underway with MSOs Charter Communications and Shaw Communications.

End Notes

1   "TV-Based High Speed Cable Internet Services," Kinetic Strategies Inc., Cable Datacom news, 10020 S. 46th Place, Phoenix, AZ USA 85044, 1998.

B

LIST OF TOP CABLE INSTALLATION COMPANIES

DISCLAIMER:

The following statements have been taken from information contained in the descriptions at the websites listed for each of the cable installation companies listed below. This author does not personally promote or endorse any of the products or companies listed below..

1. **Advanced Computer Installations Ltd (ACI):** Installers of approved structured cabling systems and fiber optic installations.

   http://www.aci1.co.uk/aci.glasgow/

2. **Arguss Holdings, Inc.:** Installers of structured cabling systems and fiber optic installations.

   http://www.argx.com/

3. **Atlantic Netcom Limited (Atlantic Canadian IT infrastructure company):** Supplier, installer, and manager of network and communication hardware and software components.

   http://www.atlnetcom.ca/

4. **Austin Connection, Inc.:** Installers of local area network cabling and topologies, including fiber optic, data, voice, com-gear, and cable assemblies.

   http://www.theaustinconnection.com/

5. **BF Datacom:** Designers and installers of data communications.

   http://www.bfdatacom.com/

6. **Cabling Company, The:** Installers of networking and cabling systems.

   http://www.btinternet.com/~cablingco/

7. **Cedar Falls Communications**: Installers of structured cabling systems and fiber optic installations.

   http://www.frognet.net/~waddell/cedar.html

8. **Certified Cabling Company, Inc.:** Installers of all types of media cabling including, voice, data, fiber optics, coax. Certified technicians.

   http://www.geocities.com/SouthBeach/Boardwalk/6961/ccci.html

9. **Coastal Computer Connections, Inc.:** Installers of structured cabling. Offer training, consulting and web page design.

   http://ccccable.com/

10. **Comm Plus Corporation:** Provider of outside plant cabling and splicing as well as interior LAN and voice wiring.

    http://www.comm-plus-corp.com/

11. **Communications Information Software (CIS), Inc.:** Developer of Fiber Optic Cable Utility Software and integrated broadband and telephony engineering for network management in telecommunications.

    http://www.cisfocus.com/

12. **CompuNet Systems Solutions, Inc.:** Installer of LAN, MAN cabling.

    http://www.computer-networks.com/

13. **Computer Power Systems, Inc.:** Installers of structured cabling systems and fiber optic installations.

    http://www.4cps.com/

14. **Comtech:** Installers of copper cabling, fiber optic, or wireless computer networking system.

    http://www.jacktojack.com/

15. **Connectivity, Inc.:** Installers of cable for data and voice networks.

    http://www.cableme.com/

16. **Craig Communications:** Designers/consultants/installers of data/voice and fiber optic cabling. RCDD and RCDD LAN specialization.

    http://www.craigcable.com/

17. **CRC Networks & Cables, Inc.:** Installers of voice, data, and fiber optics.

    http://www.crcnet.net/

18. **Data Link Installations**: Installers of copper and fiber optics.

    http://www.datalink.demon.co.uk/

19. **Data Technologies, Inc.:** Installers of structured cabling systems and fiber optic installations.

    http://www.dtcable.com/

20. **Direct Communications Systems:** Installers of structured cabling systems and fiber optic installations.

    http://www.dircomsys.com/

21. **Florida Intranet Group, Inc.:** Inst5allers of network cable in both copper and optical fiber. Designers and installers of networks for both LANs and WANs.

    http://www.figconnect.com/

22. **Hess Communication Services@:** Installers of structured cabling systems and fiber optic installations.

    http://www.yahoo.com/Regional/U_S__States/New_Hampshire/
    Cities/Danville/Business/Hess_Communication_Services/

23. **Id Reseaux:** Installers and engineers of standardized cables compatible to all standards of networks.

    http://www.id-reseaux.com/

24. **Integrated Computer Services:** Designers and installers of SCS for data, voice, and video conferencing applications.

    http://www.intcs.com/

25. **InteliSite Group:** Installers of structured cabling systems and fiber optic installations.

    http://www.drawwire.com/

26. **ITT Cannon Network Systems & Services:** Installers of structured cabling systems and fiber optic installations.

    http://www.ittnss.com/

27. **Kelly Technical Services Ltd**: Installers of fiber optic cable.

    http://www.kts.co.uk/

28. **LanPro Commuinications, Inc:** Designers, engineers, and installers, of LAN, including fiber optics, Cat5, utp, coax, and wireless.

    http://www.lpcommunications.com/

29. **Len Andrews Enterprises Inc:** Designers and installers of fiber optic, twisted pair and coaxial cable systems; including maintenance and computer networking services.

    http://www.lae.mb.ca/

30. **MBC Partnership LTD:** Installers of Cat5 and fiber networks including hubs, routers etc..

    http://ds.dial.pipex.com/mbc/

31. **NetPlanner Systems, Inc.:** Installers of fiber optic and Category 5 cabling systems, including certification.

    http://www.nplanner.com/

32. **Network Cabling:** Installers of structured cabling, including certification, consultation, and support.

    http://www.networkcabling.com/

33. **OnLine-Networking:** Installers of structured wiring systems, copper and fiber, for data networking.

    http://www.online-networking.inter.net/

34. **Open Networks Engineering Ltd.:** Installers of structured cabling systems and fiber optic installations.

    http://www.one.co.uk/

35. **PCCI Inc.:** Installers of computer cabling, including and consulting in South Florida.

    http://members.icanect.net/~igorb/

36. **PerfectSite:** Designers and managers of structured cabling.

    http://www.perfectsite.com/

37. **Pirelli Jacobson, Inc.:** Installers of worldwide submarine power and telecommunications cables.

    http://www.pjiinc.com/

38. **Professional Network Services:** Consultants for all types of networking.

    http://www.pnsnet.com/

39. **Protocol Voice and Data Systems, Inc**: Installers of voice, data, audio, and video systems.

    http://www.pvds.com/

40. **Quality Cable Installations:** Installers of business telephone and computer network cabling in the central Massachusetts area.

    http://www.qciathol.com/

41. **S.T. Communications:** Designers and implementers of services for structured data and telecommunications cabling systems.

    http://www.stcc.com/

42. **Source Communications LLP:** Distributors, manufactures and installers of products for organized communication and point of sale networks.

    http://www.source-communications.com/

43. **Suttle Apparatus Corp:** Manufacturers of on-premise voice, high-speed data connectors, and related wiring devices.

    http://www.suttleapp.com/

44. **Valley Communications Inc.:** Installers of network communications, specializing in LAN, WAN, fiber optic, and copper cabling.

    http://www.valleycom.com/

45. **Woods Incorporated:** Installers and designers of networks, including consulting, troubleshooting, equipment, and structured wiring.

    http://www.woodsnet.com/

C

LIST OF TOP FIBER OPTIC CABLE COMPANIES

DISCLAIMER:

THE FOLLOWING STATEMENTS HAVE BEEN TAKEN FROM INFORMATION CONTAINED IN THE DESCRIPTIONS AT THE WEBSITES LISTED FOR EACH OF THE FIBER OPTIC CABLE COMPANIES LISTED BELOW. THIS AUTHOR DOES NOT PERSONALLY PROMOTE OR ENDORSE ANY OF THE PRODUCTS OR COMPANIES LISTED BELOW.

Abaca Fiber Optics: Installer of CCTV, network cabling, including electrical service and installations.

```
http://www.dreamsoft.com/abaca/home.htm
```

ADC Fibermux: Installer of fiber optic cable.

```
http://www.yahoo.com/Business_and_Economy/Companies/
Computers/Hardware/Components/Cables_and_Connectors/
Fiber_Optics/ADC_Fibermux/
```

ADVA Optical Service & Solutions: Supplier and provider of new and advanced fiber optic systems.

http://www.advaoptical.com/

Advance Fiber Optics: Providers of optical fiber testing, documentation, and connectivity.

http://www.advancefiber.com/

Advanced Communications Technologies: Providers of engineering services for fiber optics.

http://www.uswi.com/actfiber.htm

Advanced Custom Applications, Inc: Manufacturer of Fiber Optics Splices for both Mechanical & Fusion Splicing, along with supporting products.

http://www.aca-inc.com/

Ancor Communications: Installer of fiber optic cable.

http://www.yahoo.com/Business_and_Economy/Companies/Computers/
Hardware/Components/Cables_and_Connectors/Fiber_Optics/Ancor_
Communications/

APA Optics, Inc.: Manufacturer and marketer of products for the fiber optic communications, optoelectronics and laser industries.

http://www.apaoptics.com/

Arcade Electronics, Inc.: Supplier of fiber optics, industrial electronics, and cable. Wide range of products supporting the fiber optic and electronics industry.

http://www.arcade-electronics.com/

Astarte Fiber Networks, Inc.: Provider of photonic fiber optic cross-connect systems for physical level fiber management including ATM, FDDI, and SONET for test access, disaster recovery, etc.

http://www.starswitch.com/

Auriga Fibre Optics: Provider of fiber optic on-line catalog and products.

http://www.auriganet.com/

Broadband Communications Products, Inc.: Provider of fiber optic data communications equipment and high speed fiber optic test instruments.

http://www.iu.net/bcp/

Broadband Networks, Inc.: Provider of AM, FM fiber optic transmission equipment for interactive video and data applications.

http://www.bnisolutions.com/

Brugg Telecom AG: Manufacturer of fiber optic cables and systems for data, utility, CATV and telecom applications.

http://www.brugg.com/

Cable Talk Pty. Ltd: Distributor of fiber optic cables, custom fiber optic cable assemblies, fiber optic connectors, and all necessary tooling, test equipment, and consumables.

http://www.fibreoptic.com.au/cabletalk/

Cables of Zion: Manufacturer of fiber optic, telecommunication, and high voltage cable.

http://www.coz-cables.co.il/

CIENA: Installer of fiber optic cable.

http://www.yahoo.com/Business_and_Economy/Companies/Computers/Hardware/Components/Cables_and_Connectors/Fiber_Optics/CIENA/

Comnet Asia Pacific Pte Ltd: Provider of fFiber optic cable assemblies.

http://www.comapl.com/

Computer Cabling Products International, Inc.: Distributor and installer of fiber optic supplies and cables, including reusable fiber optic connectors.

http://www.ccpiinc.com/

Computer System Products, Inc. (CSP): Manufacturer and supplier of fiber optic and copper cable assemblies for premise cabling applications. Also supplier of LAN/WAN hardware for Ethernet and token ring systems.

http://www.csp.com/home.asp

Condux International, Inc: Manufacturer of tools and equipment for fiber optic, CATV, telephone and power cable installation. Also supplier of products to telephone and power utilities, CATV companies, and contractors.

http://www.condux.com/

Data Optics: Provider of fiber optic and telecommunication technology.

http://www.dataoptics.co.uk/

Datapac, Inc.: Designer of telecommunications products, such as patch panels and wire managers, which meet specific product requirements.

http://www.datapacinc.com/

DESIGNet, Inc.: Designer, engineer, and installer of communications cabling systems for all voice and data applications.

http://www.desnet.com/

Digital-Delivery Systems: Provider of fiber optic and network installation, certification, and documentation.

http://www.digital-delivery.com/

E-Tek Dynamics, Inc.: Provider of fiber optic passive components, active devices, test equipment, and systems.

http://www.e-tek.com/

E/O Networks: Developer, manufacturer, and distributor of next-generation fiber access telephone networks.

http://www.eonetworks.com/

ElectroPhotonics Corporation: Manufacturer of hardware and software products for fiber optic telecommunication and sensing industries.

http://www.electrophotonics.com/

Fiber Optic Marketplace: Provider of fiber optic information, products, and services.

http://fiberoptic.com/

Fiber Optic Technologies Inc.: Provider of fiber optics technologies for fiber optic network connectivity, as well as Network services and Desktop Support.

http://www.teleport.com/toc/404.html

Fiber Plus International: Designer and manufacturer of fiber optic tools, components and connection devices.

http://www.fiberplus.com/

Fiber Systems International: Provider of mil spec fiber optic connectors for all applications.

http://www.fibersystems.com/

Fibercore Ltd: Manufacturer of singlemode optical fibers for special applications.

http://www.fibercore.com/

Fiberguide Industries, Inc.: Manufacturer of specialty fiber optic products.

http://www.fiberguide.com/

FiberPlex Inc.: Designer and manufacturer of communications products. Also, provider of fiber-optic technology is used to solve security, noise, and distance problems.

http://www.fiberguide.com/

Fibertron: Distributor and value-added reseller of fiber optic cable and components.

http://www.fibertron.com/

FiberWare, Inc.: Manufacturer of passive fiber optic interconnect hardware for the LAN, CATV and TELCO applications.

http://www.fiberwareinc.com/

Fiberworks, Inc.: Seller and installer of advanced communications systems using high performance fiber optic technology.

http://www.fiberworks.com/

Fibre Optic Communications Ltd.: Manufacturer of fiber optic cable assemblies, patch panels and reseller of fiber optic connectors. Distributor for belden fiber cable in the UK.

http://www.fibrecomms.co.uk/

Fibre-Data Group Ltd: Installer of fiber optic cable.

http://www.fibredata.co.uk/

FIS—Fiber Instrument Sales Inc: Provider of fiber optics and technical assistance.

http://www.fisfiber.com/

Fitel-PMX@ : Installer of fiber optic cable.

http://www.yahoo.com/Regional/Countries/Canada/Provinces_and_
Territories/Ontario/Counties_and_Regions/Ottawa_Carleton_Regional_
Municipality/Nepean/Business/Fitel_PMX/

Focas, Inc: Providers of fiber optic cables, accessories, and sensors. Manufacturers of fiber optic aerial cables to be installed on transmission and distribution lines.

http://www.focas.com/

Fotec: Providers of fiber optic training & testing products.

http://www.std.com/fotec/

GC Technologies: Developer, manufacturers, and sellers of fiber optic products including passive components and subassembly polishing equipment, accessories, and enclosures.

http://www.gctechnologies.com/

Gibson Technical Services: Providers of communications engineering services for fiber optics.

http://www.gibsontech.com/

Global Fiber Optics: Providers of fiber optics: custom patch cords, training, OTDR testing, fiber installation, fiber LAN's and LAN hardware/software.

http://www.global-fiber-optics.com/

Hangzhou Chengfeng Electric Appliance Corporation: Manufacturer of fiber optic cables and terminal equipment.

http://www.chengfeng.com/

Harmonic Lightwaves, Inc.: Supplier of integrated fiber optic transmission, digital headend, and element management systems for interactive broadband networks.

http://www.harmonic-lightwaves.com/

Integrated Optical Components Ltd [IOC]: Designer and manufacturer of integrated optical devices.

http://www.intopt.com/

International CableTel Incorporated: Developer, constructor, and operator of broadband communications systems outside the United States which provide integrated *last mile* telecommunications services to both business and residential customers.

http://www.cabletel.com/

International Fiberoptic Technologies, Inc.: Producer of passive fiber optic couplers with low db loss.

http://www.ift-info.com/

J.L. Import and Export: Dealer in fiber optic connectors, adaptors, and attenuators.

http://www.jlfiber.com/

Jerry Conn Associates: Distributor of fiber optics, fiber optic closures, fiber optic test equipment, RF broadband and headend.

http://www.jerryconn.com/

JM Fiber Optics, Inc.: Provider of voice, video, and data applications as well as products, technical support, and fiber optic training.

http://www.jmfiberoptics.com/

KNS Technologies, Inc.: Provider of fiber optic cable products.

http://www.knstech.com/

Lee Data Communications: Manufacturer of fiber optic audio, video, and data transmission equipment.

http://members.aol.com/johannlee/lee-data.htm

Light Brigade, The: Installer of fiber optic cable.

http://www.lightbrigade.com/

Lite-Tech: Provider of fiber optic needs of clients across the continental United States.

http://home.earthlink.net/~litetech/

Meridian Technologies, Inc.: Designer and manufacturer of fiber optic communication systems for video, voice, and data

http://www.meridian-tech.com/

Metrotek Industries, Inc: Distributor of fiber optic stocking for connectors, adaptors, cable assemblies, etc..

http://www.metrotek.com/

Micro Electronics, Inc. - Provider of *Micro-Strip* and *Soft-Strip* precision fiber optic stripping tools; coating strippers, jacket strippers, thermal strippers, and ribbon strippers.

http://www.micro-strip.com/

Miniflex Fibre Optic Products: Installer and manageer of fiber optic systems.

http://www.miniflex.co.uk/

Moritex U.S.A., Inc.: Provider of fiber optics, as well as targeting markets such as industrial illumination and sensing, machine vision, cosmetic skin care imaging, pharmaceutical research and artistic glass products.

http://www.moritexusa.com/

MRV Communications: Installer of fiber optic cable.

http://www.yahoo.com/Business_and_Economy/Companies/Computers/
Hardware/Components/Cables_and_Connectors/Fiber_Optics/
MRV_Communications/

Net Optics: Provider of fiber optic power measurement meter and fiber optic test boxes for analysis of fiber optic network systems assimilation.

http://www.netoptics.com/

Norscan: Manufacturer of cable maintenance and monitoring systems that are used on filled copper and fiber optic cable systems.

http://www.norscan.com/

NuPower Optics: Installer of fiber optic cable.

http://www.nupower.com/

Optelecom, Inc.: Installer of fiber optic cable.

http://www.yahoo.com/Business_and_Economy/Companies/Computers/Hardware/
Components/Cables_and_Connectors/Fiber_Optics/Optelecom__Inc_/

Optical Cable Corporation: Installer of fiber optic cable.

http://www.yahoo.com/Business_and_Economy/Companies/Computers/
Hardware/Components/Cables_and_Connectors/Fiber_Optics/Optical_
Cable_Corporation/

Optical Solutions, Inc.: Manufacturer and integrator of optical receivers, transmitters, and interface devices for broadband Fiber-To-The-Home networks.

http://www.opticalsolutions.com/

Optivision, Inc.: Provider of optical switching, optical amplifiers, optical interconnects, optical computing, optical backplanes, optical signal processing, fiber optic networks, fiber optic sensing, optoelectronic systems design, and image compression.

http://www.optivision.com/

Pacific Fiberoptics, Inc@: Installer of fiber optic cable.

http://www.yahoo.com/Regional/U_S__States/California/Cities/
Santa_Clara/Business/Computers/Pacific_Fiberoptics__Inc/

Photon Technologies (Malaysia) Sdn Bhd: Manufacturer of optical fiber and optical fiber cables.

http://www.jaring.my/photon/

Photonic Integration Research, Inc.: Maker of integrated optical waveguide devices in silica.

http://www.piri.com/

Physical Optics Corporation: Manufacturer and seller of fiber optic communications equipment and holographic diffusers for display screens.

http://www.poc.com/

Polycore Technologies: Producer of high performance fiber optic communication systems for industrial, automotive, utility and process control applications.

http://www.pcore.com/

Princeton Optics Inc.: Supplier of off-the-shelf and custom-made fiber optic components to customers around the world.

http://www.princetonoptics.com/

R&M's International WebSite: Manufacturer of copper/fiber optic distribution systems/generic cabling systems for voice, video, and data applications.

http://www.rdm.ch/

Radiant Communications Corporation: Provider of fiber optic assemblies, connectors, couplers, patch and splice cabinets. Also, provider of video, audio, and data transmission systems for CATV and distant learning applications.

http://www.radcom.com/

Schott Fibre Optics: Installer of fiber optic cable.

http://www.schott.co.uk/

Spectran: Installer of fiber optic cable.

http://www.yahoo.com/Business_and_Economy/Companies/Computers/
Hardware/Components/Cables_and_Connectors/Fiber_Optics/Spectran/

Spoval Company, Inc: Designer, engineer, and manufacturer of fiber optic interconnect panels.

http://www.spoval.com/

TC Communications, Inc.: Manufacturer of fiber optic data and voice communication products including modems, multiplexers, LANs, mode converters, and transceivers.

http://www.tccomm.com/

TRITEC Developments Ltd: UK manufacturer of fiber optic installation equipment including the FASE II fusion splicer and the TCII+ optical fiber cleaver.

http://www.tritec-dev.com/

TSX Corp: Installer of fiber optic cable.

http://www.yahoo.com/Business_and_Economy/Companies/Computers/
Hardware/Components/Cables_and_Connectors/Fiber_Optics/TSX_Corp/

Uniphase Corporation@: Installer of fiber optic cable.

http://www.yahoo.com/Business_and_Economy/Companies/Electronics/Lasers/
Uniphase_Corporation/

Vikimatic Sales, Inc.: Provider of products for fiber optic cable construction.

http://www.fibercable.com/

VisionCorp: Provider of manufacturers products that are being used to build the Information Super Highway through fiber optic and coax (Cable TV) systems.

http://web.iquest.net/viscorp/index.htm

D

CABLING DIRECTORY

The Cabling Directory (http://www.wiring.com/) is an interactive buyer's guide for cabling products as well as for all cabling-related topics with direct links to each company's web site [1]. In addition, the web site is an excellent resource for informational items about today's high speed network cabling [2]. Select a category below to view some of the sample listings:

1. **Cable Management Software:**

    - *Allstar Systems, Inc.*
      Headquarters: Houston, TX
      Phone: 713-795-2400
      Geographic Region: Houston, Dallas, Austin

    - *Cablesoft, Ltd.*
      Headquarters: Phoenix, AZ
      Phone: 602-708-2000
      Geographic Region: USA

    - *Teklab*
      Headquarters: Torrance, CA
      Phone: 310-299-1209
      Geographic Region: Los Angeles

2. **Cable Assemblies:**

- *Assembletech*
  Headquarters: Houston, TX
  Phone: 713-430-3090
  Geographic Region: Texas and the southwest

- *Baycom*
  Headquarters: Hsinchu, Taiwan
  Phone: 886-3-578-6178
  Geographic Region: North and South America

- *Cable Systems International*
  Headquarters: Phoenix, AZ
  Phone: 602-233-5171
  Geographic Region: Worldwide

- *Computer Cable Connection, Inc.*
  Headquarters: Bellevue, NE
  Phone: 402-291-9500
  Geographic Region: USA

- *Crown Electronics*
  Headquarters: Rockwall, YX
  Phone: 972-771-4711
  Geographic Region: Worldwide

- *DataWay Design*
  Headquarters: San Francisco, CA
  Phone: 415-882-8700
  Geographic Region: The San Francisco Peninsula

- *DV Com Systems*
  Headquarters: Brooklyn, NY
  Phone: 718-756-9650
  Geographic Region: NY, NJ, CT

- *Electronic Imaging Materials*
  Headquarters: Keene, NH
  Phone: 603-357-1459
  Geographic Region: USA

- *Fishel Technologies*
  Headquarters: Columbus, OH
  Phone: 502-456-9444
  Geographic Region: USA

- *Gruber Industries*
  Headquarters: Phoenix, AZ
  Phone: 800-658-5883
  Geographic Region: International

- *Noramco Wire & Cable*
  Headquarters: Burnaby, BC, Canada
  Phone: 604-606-6970
  Geographic Region: North America

- *Northwest Cable and Connector Co.*
  Headquarters: Olympia, WA
  Phone: 360-754-3606
  Geographic Region: Nationwide

- *Peerless Electronics, Inc.*
  Headquarters: Lynbrook, NY
  Phone: 800-285-2121
  Geographic Region: USA

- *Royal Cable Corp.*
  Headquarters: New York, NY
  Phone: 212-293-7323
  Geographic Region: USA

- *Sequoia Diversified Products*
  Headquarters: Auburn Hills, MI
  Phone: 810-299-4220
  Geographic Region: International

- *Shine Wire Products Inc.*
  Headquarters: Adams, MA
  Phone: 1-800-543-5151
  Geographic Region: Northeast

- *TEC Datawire*
  Headquarters: Cleveland, OH
  Phone: 440-333-8300
  Geographic Region: USA

- *TEC Datawire*
  Headquarters: Cleveland, OH
  Phone: 440-333-8300
  Geographic Region: USA

3. **Cable:**

- *Assembletech*
  Headquarters: Houston, Texas
  Phone: 713-430-3090
  Geographic Region: Texas and the southwest

- *Baycom*
  Headquarters: Hsinchu, Taiwan
  Phone: 886-3-578-6178
  Geographic Region: North and South America

- *Cable Systems International*
  Headquarters: Phoenix, AZ
  Phone: 602-233-5171
  Geographic Region: Worldwide

- *Electronic Imaging Materials*
  Headquarters: Keene, NH
  Phone: 603-357-1459
  Geographic Region: USA

- *Futronix Systems Corp.*
  Headquarters: Houston, TX
  Phone: 713-329-1100
  Geographic Region: Houston, TX

- *PMC Corporation*
  Headquarters: Manchester, NH
  Phone: 250-480-1311
  Geographic Region: USA, Canada

- *Quabbin Wire & Cable Co., Inc.*
  Headquarters: Ware, MA
  Phone: 413-967-3117
  Geographic Region: North America, Europe

4   **Connectors:**

- *AMP Netconnect*
  Headquarters: Harrisburg, PA
  Phone: 503-650-9466
  Geographic Region: Oregon, SW Washington

5. **Connecting Hardware:**

- *Ahern Communications Corporation*
  Headquarters: Quincy, MA
  Phone: 617-471-1100
  Geographic Region: Worldwide

- *Cable Plus Inc.*
  Headquarters: Deer Park, NY
  Phone: 516-586-7587
  Geographic Region: USA

- *Policom Cabos E Conectores Ltda*
  Headquarters: Sao Paulo, Brazil
  Phone: 55-11-6914-4788
  Geographic Region: Brazil

- *Specialized Engineering Services*
  Headquarters: Derby, Derbyshire, UK
  Phone: 44-13-3238-3345
  Geographic Region: UK

- *Wandel & Goltermann*
  Headquarters: Research Triangle Park, NC
  Phone: 847-918-9292
  Geographic Region: Southeast

6. **Distributors:**

- *ABTECH Computer*
  Headquarters: Annapolis, MD
  Phone: 410-295-9000
  Geographic Region: Mid-Atlantic

- *Ahern Communications Corporation*
  Headquarters: Quincy, MA
  Phone: 617-471-1100
  Geographic Region: Worldwide

- *Asia Wiring Systems Pte Ltd*
  Headquarters: Singapore
  Phone: 2831445
  Geographic Region: Asia

- *Astec Hong Kong Limited*
  Headquarters: Central, Hong Kong
  Phone: 852-2815-2425
  Geographic Region: Southeast Asia

- *Atlantic Cable International*
  Headquarters: Houston, Texas
  Phone: 713-699-2000
  Geographic Region: Worldwide

- *Cable Plus Inc.*
  Headquarters: Deer Park, NY
  Phone: 516-586-7587
  Geographic Region: USA

- *CableCentral*
  Headquarters: Costa Mesa, CA
  Phone: 714-636-5960
  Geographic Region: USA

- *Diversified Automation*
  Headquarters: Ringwood, NJ
  Phone: 973-616-4943
  Geographic Region: NY, NJ, CT, PA

- *Electrotex Inc.*
  Headquarters: Houston, TX
  Phone: 713-526-3456
  Geographic Region: TX, OK, MS, LA, AR

- *Fibertron Corporation*
  Headquarters: Buena Park, CA
  Phone: 630-978-1501
  Geographic Region: USA

- *Futronix Systems Corp.*
  Headquarters: Houston, TX
  Phone: 713-329-1100
  Geographic Region: USA

- *H & L Enterprises, Inc.*
  Headquarters: Bostic, NC
  Phone: 704-248-3939
  Geographic Region: Eastern USA

- *Knurr AG*
  Headquarters: Munich, Germany
  Phone:
  Geographic Region: Worldwide

- *LANequip*
  Headquarters: Quebec
  Phone: 514-939-2163
  Geographic Region: Quebec, Ontario

- *Noramco Wire & Cable*
  Headquarters: Burnaby, BC, Canada
  Phone: 604-606-6970
  Geographic Region: North America

- *Northwest Cable and Connector Co.*
  Headquarters: Olympia, WA
  Phone: 360-754-3606
  Geographic Region: USA

- *Peerless Electronics, Inc.*
  Headquarters: Lynbrook, NY
  Phone: 800-285-2121
  Geographic Region: USA

- *Policom Cabos E Conectores Ltda*
  Headquarters: Sao Paulo, Brazil
  Phone: 55-11-6914-4788
  Geographic Region: Brazil

- *Royal Cable Corp.*
  Headquarters: New York, NY
  Phone: 212-293-7323
  Geographic Region: USA

- *Shine Wire Products Inc.*
  Headquarters: Adams, MA
  Phone: 800-543-5151
  Geographic Region: Northeast

- *SPC Technologies Corporation*
  Headquarters: Manila, Philippine Islands
  Phone: 632-551-0948
  Geographic Region: Southeast Asia

- *TEC Datawire*
  Headquarters: Cleveland, OH
  Phone: 440-333-8300
  Geographic Region: USA

7. **Engineering:**

- *ASD*
  Headquarters: Atlanta, GA
  Phone: 800-CABLING
  Geographic Region: Worldwide

- *Communications Resource Group*
  Headquarters: Ft. Lauderdale, FL
  Phone: 954-436-3900
  Geographic Region: International

- *Computel Network Services Corp.*
  Headquarters: Richardson, TX
  Phone: 972-437-9676
  Geographic Region: South central USA

- *CPSI*
  Headquarters: Riverdale, CA
  Phone: 909-354-7191
  Geographic Region: CA, OR, NV

- *Digital Delivery Systems*
  Headquarters: Fort Collins, CO
  Phone: 970-221-3018
  Geographic Region: Rocky Mountain Region

- *E.R. Haskins Cable Consulting*
  Headquarters: Burbank, CA
  Phone: 818-247-2650
  Geographic Region: Los Angeles and surrounding area

- *Fundy Engineering & Consulting Ltd.*
  Headquarters: Saint John, NB, Canada
  Phone: 506-635-1566
  Geographic Region: Atlantic

- *GMCI NetComm, Inc.*
  Headquarters: Dallas, TX
  Phone: 972-241-2425
  Geographic Region: TX

- *Interconnect Services, Inc.*
  Headquarters: Baltimore, MD
  Phone: 410-687-8900
  Geographic Region: USA

- *K St. James Inc.*
  Headquarters: York, PA
  Phone: 717-244-0653
  Geographic Region: USA

- *Key Services, Inc.*
  Headquarters: Tucker, GA
  Phone: 919-831-2528
  Geographic Region: Southeast USA

- *Merolan, Inc.*
  Headquarters: New York, NY
  Phone: 914-245-4139
  Geographic Region: NY, NJ, CT

- *Micro Metrology, Inc.*
  Headquarters: Chatsworth, CA
  Phone: 818-993-4971
  Geographic Region: Worldwide

- *NetCom Management Group*
  Headquarters: Phoenix, AZ
  Phone: 602-470-4070
  Geographic Region: USA

- *PDS Consultants*
  Headquarters: Homosassa, Fl
  Phone: 352-621-5549
  Geographic Region: Southeast USA

- *Pinnacle Communication Services*
  Headquarters: Glendale, CA
  Phone: 818-241-6009
  Geographic Region: CA, International

- *ProCom Technologies, Inc.*
  Headquarters: Twinsburg, OH
  Phone: 330-425-7289
  Geographic Region: Northern OH

- *Royal Communications Consultants*
  Headquarters: New York, NY
  Phone: 212-293-7323
  Geographic Region: USA

- *Tele-Tech Company, Inc.*
  Headquarters: Lexington, KY
  Phone: 606-275-7503
  Geographic Region: USA

- *The State Group Ltd.*
  Headquarters: Etobicoke, Ontario, Canada
  Phone: 416-240-0610
  Geographic Region: Ontario

- *Waldec/IKON Technology Services*
  Headquarters: Tampa, Florida
  Phone: 813-282-4008
  Geographic Region: FL, PA

- *Waldec/IKON Technology Services*
  Headquarters: Tampa, FL
  Phone: 813-880-7600
  Geographic Region: USA

- *Wiring Architects*
  Headquarters: Hurst, TX
  Phone: 817-589-7483
  Geographic Region: TX, the south

8. **Installation Companies:**

- *1st Alliance Communications, Inc.*
  Headquarters: Englewood, CO
  Phone: 303-766-7577
  Geographic Region: Worldwide

- *ABTECH Computer Services*
  Headquarters: Annapolis, MD
  Phone: 410-295-9000
  Geographic Region: Mid-Atlantic

- *Allstar Systems, Inc.*
  Headquarters: Houston, TX
  Phone: 713-795-2400
  Geographic Region: Houston, Dallas, Austin

- *ASD*
  Headquarters: Atlanta, GA
  Phone: 800-CABLING
  Geographic Region: Worldwide

- *ASI Services Corporation*
  Headquarters: Atlanta, GA
  Phone: 404-888-5555
  Geographic Region: Atlanta

- *BenComm*
  Headquarters: Gaithersburg, MD
  Phone: 301-963-3257
  Geographic Region: Mid-Atlantic

- *Birnie Data Communications*
  Headquarters: Toronto, Ontario
  Phone: 416-247-2151
  Geographic Region: Canada

- *Cable Systems Consulting*
  Headquarters: Houston, TXPhone: 281-370-2172
  Geographic Region: Houston area

- *Coastal Computer Connections, Inc.*
  Headquarters: Pensacola, FL
  Phone: 904-444-9199
  Geographic Region: FL, GA, AL

- *Communication Cabling Services*
  Headquarters: Corby, Northants, UK
  Phone: 44-1536-443700
  Geographic Region: UK

- *ComNet Communications Inc.*
  Headquarters: Danbury, CT
  Phone: 203-794-8045
  Geographic Region: USA

- *CompuTeam*
  Headquarters: Aledo, TX
  Phone: 817-244-1158
  Geographic Region: Aledo, TX

- *Computel Network Services Corp.*
  Headquarters: Richardson, TX
  Phone: 972-437-9676
  Geographic Region: South central US

- *Computer Cable Connection, Inc.*
  Headquarters: Bellevue, NE
  Phone: 402-291-9500
  Geographic Region: USA

- *ComputerLand Cabling Division*
  Headquarters: San Diego, CA
  Phone: 619-492-1400
  Geographic Region: Southern CA

- *Coyote Cabling*
  Headquarters: Las Cruces, NM
  Phone: 505-525-1422
  Geographic Region: AZ, NM, TX

- *CPSI*
  Headquarters: Riverdale, CA
  Phone: 909-354-7191
  Geographic Region: CA, OR, NV

- *CSS*
  Headquarters: White Plains, MD
  Phone: 301-870-3870
  Geographic Region: USA

- *Data-Tech Communications*
  Headquarters: Reno, NV
  Phone: 702-829-9999
  Geographic Region: Northern Nevada, Northern California

- *Dataway Communications, Inc.*
  Headquarters: Cliffside Park, NJ
  Phone: 201-313-0961
  Geographic Region: NJ, NY, PA, DE

- *DataWay Design*
  Headquarters: San Francisco, CA
  Phone: 415-882-8700
  Geographic Region: The San Francisco Peninsula

- *Digital Delivery Systems*
  Headquarters: Fort Collins, CO
  Phone: 970-221-3018
  Geographic Region: Rocky Mountain Region

- *Dinsmore Communications Corp.*
  Headquarters: Portsmouth, NH
  Phone: 603-436-6344
  Geographic Region: New England, FL

- *Diversified Automation*
  Headquarters: Ringwood, NJ
  Phone: 973-616-4943
  Geographic Region: NY, NJ, CT, PA

- *DV Com Systems*
  Headquarters: Brooklyn, NY
  Phone: 718-756-9650
  Geographic Region: NY, NJ, CT

- *E.R. Haskins Cable Consulting*
  Headquarters: Burbank, CA
  Phone: 818-247-2650
  Geographic Region: Los Angeles and surrounding area

- *Fishel Technologies*
  Headquarters: Columbus, OH
  Phone: 502-456-9444
  Geographic Region: USA

- *GMCI NetComm, Inc.*
  Headquarters: Dallas, TX
  Phone: 972-241-2425
  Geographic Region: TX

- *H & L Enterprises, Inc.*
  Headquarters: Bostic, NC
  Phone: 704-248-3939
  Geographic Region: Eastern USA

- *H& L Telecom of Florida, Inc.*
  Headquarters: Pensacola, FL
  Phone: 904-968-1892
  Geographic Region: Southeast, southwest

- *Integrated Network Services*
  Headquarters: Marietta, GA
  Phone: 770-751-8881
  Geographic Region: East coast

- *Interconnect Services, Inc.*
  Headquarters: Baltimore, MD
  Phone: 410-687-8900
  Geographic Region: USA

- *K St. James Inc.*
  Headquarters: York, PA
  Phone: 717-244-0653
  Geographic Region: USA

- *Key Services, Inc.*
  Headquarters: Tucker, GA
  Phone: 919-831-2528
  Geographic Region: Southeast

- *LANequip*
  Headquarters: Quebec
  Phone: 514-939-2163
  Geographic Region: Quebec, Ontario

- *M.D. Computer Link*
  Headquarters: Croydon, Surrey, England
  Phone: 01812630252
  Geographic Region: UK

- *Merolan, Inc.*
  Headquarters: New York, NY
  Phone: 914-245-4139
  Geographic Region: NY, NJ, CT

- *Miken Communications*
  Headquarters: Milwaukee, WI
  Phone: 414-778-2010
  Geographic Region: WI, Northern IL

- *NetCom Management Group*
  Headquarters: Phoenix, AZ
  Phone: 602-470-4070
  Geographic Region: USA

- *Network Century*
  Headquarters: Chicago, Illinois
  Phone: 312-243-3416
  Geographic Region: Chicago area

- *Newave Communications*
  Headquarters: Lansing, MI
  Phone: 517-226-6953
  Geographic Region: South MI

- *North America Telecommunications*
  Headquarters: Pittsburgh, PA
  Phone: (215) 871-7674
  Geographic Region: Northeast USA

- *PDS Consultants*
  Headquarters: Homosassa, FL
  Phone: 352-621-5549
  Geographic Region: Southeast USA

- *Pinnacle Communication Services*
  Headquarters: Glendale, CA
  Phone: 818-241-6009
  Geographic Region: CA, International

- *ProCom Technologies, Inc.*
  Headquarters: Twinsburg, OH
  Phone: 330-425-7289
  Geographic Region: Northern Ohio

- *Protocol Voice and Data Systems*
  Headquarters: Highland Park, IL
  Phone: 847-831-3249
  Geographic Region: Chicago area

- *Royal Communications Consultants*
  Headquarters: New York, NY
  Phone: 212-293-7323
  Geographic Region: USA

- *Sequoia Diversified Products*
  Headquarters: Auburn Hills, MI
  Phone: 810-299-4220
  Geographic Region: International

- *Sequoia Diversified Products*
  Headquarters: Auburn Hills, Michigan
  Phone: 248-299-4830
  Geographic Region: USA

- *SPC Technologies Corporation*
  Headquarters: Manila, Philippine Islands
  Phone: 632-551-0948
  Geographic Region: Southeast Asia

- *Specialized Engineering Services*
  Headquarters: Derby, Derbyshire, UK
  Phone: 44-13-3238-3345
  Geographic Region: UK

- *Symbiont, Inc.*
  Headquarters: Washington, D.C.
  Phone: 202-887-6800
  Geographic Region: USA

- *Tele-Data Services, Inc.*
  Headquarters: Warminster, PA
  Phone: 215-343-1499
  Geographic Region: Eastern PA, South NJ, North DE

- *Tele-Tech Company, Inc.*
  Headquarters: Lexington, KY
  Phone: 606-275-7503
  Geographic Region: USA

- *The State Group Ltd.*
  Headquarters: Etobicoke, Ontario, Canada
  Phone: 416-240-0610
  Geographic Region: Ontario

- *U.S. Information System*
  Headquarters: Nyack, NY
  Phone: 1-800-358-7756 Ext. 615
  Geographic Region: Northeast USA

- *Waldec/IKON Technology Services*
  Headquarters: Tampa, FL
  Phone: 813-282-4008
  Geographic Region: FL, PA

- *Waldec/IKON Technology Services*
  Headquarters: Tampa, FL
  Phone: 813-880-7600
  Geographic Region: USA

- *Willow Technologies Group, Inc.*
  Headquarters: Norristown, PA
  Phone: 610-539-2333
  Geographic Region: Greater Mid-Atlantic Region

9. **Installation Products:**

- *Astec Hong Kong Limited*
  Headquarters: Hong Kong
  Phone: 852-2815-2425
  Geographic Region: Southeast Asia

- *Atlantic Cable International*
  Headquarters: Houston, TX
  Phone: 713-699-2000
  Geographic Region: Worldwide

- *CableCentral*
  Headquarters: Costa Mesa, CA
  Phone: 714-636-5960
  Geographic Region: USA

- *Cablesoft, Ltd.*
  Headquarters: Phoenix, AZ
  Phone: 602-708-2000
  Geographic Region: USA

- *Dinsmore Communications Corp.*
  Headquarters: Portsmouth, NH
  Phone: 603-436-6344
  Geographic Region: New England, FL

- *Electrotex Inc.*
  Headquarters: Houston, TX
  Phone: 713-526-3456
  Geographic Region: TX, OK, MS, LA, AR

- *M.D. Computer Link*
  Headquarters: Croydon, Surrey, England
  Phone: 01812630252
  Geographic Region: UK

- *North America Telecommunications*
  Headquarters: Pittsburgh, PA
  Phone: (215) 871-7674
  Geographic Region: Northeast USA

- *Protocol Voice and Data Systems*
  Headquarters: Highland Park, IL
  Phone: 847-831-3249
  Geographic Region: Chicago area

10. **Optical Fiber:**

- *Asia Wiring Systems Pte Ltd*
  Headquarters: Singapore
  Phone: 2831445
  Geographic Region: Asia

- *Birnie Data Communications*
  Headquarters: Toronto, Ontario
  Phone: 416-247-2151
  Geographic Region: Canada

- *ComputerLand Cabling Division*
  Headquarters: San Diego, CA
  Phone: 619-492-1400
  Geographic Region: Southern CA

- *Fibertron Corporation*
  Headquarters: Buena Park, CA
  Phone: 630-978-1501
  Geographic Region: USA

- *Noramco Wire & Cable*
  Headquarters: Burnaby, BC Canada
  Phone: 604-606-6970
  Geographic Region: North America

- *RW Data Ltd.*
  Headquarters: Northampton, UK
  Phone: 44 (0) 1604-706633
  Geographic Region: UK

- *U.S. Information System*
  Headquarters: Nyack, NY
  Phone: 1-800-358-7756 Ext. 615
  Geographic Region: Northeast USA

11. **Test Equipment:**

- *Datacom Technologies*
  Headquarters: Everett, WA
  Phone: 206-355-0590
  Geographic Region: Worldwide

- *Micro Metrology, Inc.*
  Headquarters: Chatsworth, CA
  Phone: 818-993-4971
  Geographic Region: Worldwide

- *Microtest, Inc.*
  Headquarters: Phoenix, AZ
  Phone: 602-952-6484
  Geographic Region: Worldwide

- *Wandel & Goltermann*
  Headquarters: Research Triangle Park, NC
  Phone: 847-918-9292
  Geographic Region: Southeast USA

12. **Tools:**

- *Microtest, Inc.*
  Headquarters: Phoenix, AZ
  Phone: 602-952-6484
  Geographic Region: Worldwide

13. **Training:**

- *Communications Resource Group*
  Headquarters: Ft. Lauderdale, FL
  Phone: 954-436-3900
  Geographic Region: International

- *Coastal Computer Connections, Inc.*
  Headquarters: Pensacola, FL
  Phone: 904-444-9199
  Geographic Region: FL, GA, AL

- *Telecom Industry Association (TIA-UK)*
  Headquarters: Milton, Keynes, Buckinghamshire, UK
  Phone: 44 (0) 1908-645000
  Geographic Region: UK, Europe

[1] John D. Colodny, RCDD "The Cabling Directory," C/O connect.ad, Inc., 1000 West McNab Road, Suite 236, Pompano Beach, FL 33069, 1998.

EENET INTERCONNECT DIRECTORY

The EENet's Interconnect Directory (http://www.eenet.com/intc/index.html) is a comprehensive listing of Interconnect companies in different categories. Select a category below to view the listings:

1. **Manufacturers:** http://www.eenet.com/intc/dir/intcwww.html
2. **Distributors:** http://www.eenet.com/intc/sorc/intcsorc.html
3. **Wire & Cable:** http://www.eenet.com/intc/dir/wirecabl.html
4. **Value Added Wire and Cable:**
   http://www.eenet.com/intc/dir/va.html
5. **Product Groups:** http://www.eenet.com/intc/prod/intcprod.html
6. **Associations and Organizations:**
   http://www.eenet.com/intc/dir/intca-o.html

List of Top Cable Labeling Companies

DISCLAIMER:

THE FOLLOWING STATEMENTS HAVE BEEN TAKEN FROM INFORMATION CONTAINED IN THE DESCRIPTIONS AT THE WEBSITES LISTED FOR EACH OF THE CABLE LABELING COMPANIES LISTED BELOW. THIS AUTHOR DOES NOT PERSONALLY PROMOTE OR ENDORSE ANY OF THE PRODUCTS OR COMPANIES LISTED BELOW.

1. **Cabel Labels:** Manufactures a range of cable identification labels, includes software to print labels and maintain databases on cable installations.

   http://www.cabelabels.com.au/

2. **Cable Markers Co., Inc.:** Identification products, wire markers, computer printable systems, labels, tags, heat shrink sleeving for cables and wires.

   http://www.cablemarkers.com/

619

3. **Critchley:** Wire and cable identification products. Heat-shrink sleeves (HSI), thermal transfer printable labels, wire markers, self laminating labels, tags, and more!

   `http://www.critchley.com/`

4. **Polygon Velcro Cable Management:** Manufacturer of Velcro-based wire management products for telecommunications racks, desks, and computer networks.

   `http://www.portal.ca/~polygon/`

5. **Silver Fox:** Labeling solutions for professional engineers, the IT industry, and the oil and process industries.

   `http://www.silverfox.co.uk/`

LIST OF TOP SCSI COMPANIES

DISCLAIMER:

THE FOLLOWING STATEMENTS HAVE BEEN TAKEN FROM INFOR-
MATION CONTAINED IN THE DESCRIPTIONS AT THE WEBSITES
LISTED FOR EACH OF THE SCSI COMPANIES LISTED BELOW. THIS
AUTHOR DOES NOT PERSONALLY PROMOTE OR ENDORSE ANY
OF THE PRODUCTS OR COMPANIES LISTED BELOW.

1. **Advanced Computer & Network Corporation:** Dedicated to the
   RAID (Redundant Array of Independent Disks) technology and SCSI
   switches, boosters, cables, extenders, and hard drives.

   http://www.acnc.com/

2. **Ancot Corporation:**

   http://www.yahoo.com/Business_and_Economy/Companies/
   Computers/Hardware/Components/Busses/SCSI/Ancot_Corporation/

3. **APCON, Inc.:** SCSI enhancement products and high-availability network solutions.

   ```
   http://www.yahoo.com/Business_and_Economy/Companies/Computers/
   Hardware/Components/Busses/SCSI/APCON__Inc_/
   ```

4. **CS Electronics:** Manufacture of premium grade SCSI cable interconnects.

   ```
   http://www.scsi-cables.com/
   ```

5. **Granite Digital:** Manufacture of high performance SCSI cables and components.

   ```
   http://www.scsipro.com/
   ```

6. **I-TECH Corp:**

   ```
   http://www.yahoo.com/Business_and_Economy/Companies/
   Computers/Hardware/Components/Busses/SCSI/I_TECH_Corp_/
   ```

7. **Paralan Corporation:** Makers of SCSI bus extenders, switches, converters.

   ```
   http://www.paralan.com/
   ```

8. **Rancho Technology, Inc.:** Provides SCSI converters, host adapters, PCMCIA cards, parallel port, and repeater products to standard and OEM companies.

   ```
   http://www.rancho.com/
   ```

9. **System Connection:** SCSI cable manufacturer.

   ```
   http://www.sconnect.com/
   ```

10. **Temp-Flex Cable Inc.:**

    ```
    http://www.tempflex.com/
    ```

H

LIST OF WIRELESS LAN PRODUCTS AND SITES

DISCLAIMER:

THE FOLLOWING STATEMENTS HAVE BEEN TAKEN FROM INFOR-MATION CONTAINED IN THE DESCRIPTIONS AT THE WEBSITES LISTED FOR EACH OF THE WIRELESS LAN PRODUCTS, SITES AND COMPANIES LISTED BELOW. THIS AUTHOR DOES NOT PERSON-ALLY PROMOTE OR ENDORSE ANY OF THE PRODUCTS OR COM-PANIES LISTED BELOW.

Wireless LAN Products

1. **AirLAN:** AirLAN by Solectek is based on radio technology originally developed by NCR Corp as shown in Table H-1 [1]. Except for its parallel-port wireless LAN adapter, Solectek's technology is based on OEM products from AT&T and Digital and has an advertised speed of 2 Mbps.

2. **Altair:** Motorola offers this LAN choice that operates in the 18 GHz range which is licensed to Motorola by the FCC as shown in Table H-1 [Wood and Jain, 2]. The Altair (http://www.mot.com/) system runs at speeds of up to 10 Mbps, and is limited by license to five channels for a 17.5-mile radius. Since Motorola controls the licenses, they can better manage the interference potential.

3. **AIRplex Cordless Modems:** A new category of PCMCIA 28.8 modems have been developed which are similar to conventional modems but require no cord to connect to the telephone line. The idea is to permit you to use your notebook freely without being tied to your desk. They also permit multiple users in an office to easily share an analog telephone line. New wireless technology (AIRplex) is used which permits use of these modems in every room in a large building without mutual interference.

4. **RangeLAN:** The RangeLAN2/PCMCIA (http://www.it.kth.se/) operates at distances of up to 500 feet in standard office environments and up to 1000 feet in open spaces as shown in Table H-1 [Wood and Jain, 2]. Based on frequency-hopping spread-spectrum technology in the 2.4 GHz to 2.4835 GHz bandwidth, the wireless adapter has a data rate of 1.6 Mbps. The unit's average power output is 100 mW. With the RangeLAN2/PCMCIA, as many as 15 independent wireless LANs can operate within the same physical space.

5. **RoamAbout:** The RoamAbout (ftp://ftp.digital.com/pub/Digital/info/SPD/45-71-XX.txt) PCMCIA Network Adapter is a PC Network Interface Card (NIC) for wireless LANs as shown in Table H-1 [Wood and Jain, 2]. The Network Adapter operates in a PC with a Type II PCMCIA slot that conforms to the PCMCIA release V2.01 specification. An antenna is externally connected via an 18" (0.5 meter) cable. The RoamAbout PCMCIA Network Adapter communicates with the RoamAbout PCMCIA Network Adapter in other portable computers, the WaveLAN NIC in stationary computers, or the RoamAbout Access Point for connectivity to the wired network.

6. **Tetherless Access Ltd. (TAL):** Tetherless Access Ltd. (TAL) provides technology to allow telecommunications service providers to build high-speed, wireless TCP/IP networks as shown in Table H-1 [Wood and Jain, 2]. TAL has developed software that leverages an open system TCP/IP networking architecture with spread-spectrum packet radio technology to deliver a scalable networking solution. With TAL's technology, communications service providers can deliver virtual private TCP/IP networking services to customers within a region or metropolitan area, over single-link distances of up to 30

Km. The raw data rate for these networks is 160 Kbps. End users will see bursts on file transfers of over 100 Kbps and enjoy average throughput of 64 Kbps.

7. **WaveLAN:** A premier spread-spectrum network system manufactured by NCR Corporation as shown in Table H-1 [Wood and Jain, 2]. This is a 2Mbps network system that utilizes a proprietary protocol. WaveLAN (http://www.ncr.com/) also uses a robust error-checking protocol that can detect and correct most transmission errors, and a data-encryption option that makes the network highly resistant to electronic eavesdropping.

Table H-1: Wireless LAN Products

Company	Product	Infrared/ Radio	Frequency	Advertised Speed	Advertised Distance
AT&T	WaveLAN	No/Yes	902 MHz to 928 MHz	2 Mbps	800 feet
California Microwave	RadioLink	No/Yes	902 MHz to 928 MHz	???	???
Digital	RoamAbout	No/Yes	902 MHz to 928 MHz	2 Mbps	800 feet
IBM	Infrared	Yes/No	N/A	1 Mbps	17' X 17' room (integrated PC Card); 30' X 30' room (tethered transceiver) Wireless LAN Adapter
InfraLAN Technologies	InfraLAN	Yes/No	N/A	10 Mbps	90 feet
Motorola	Altair	No/Yes	18 GHz*	???	???
NCR	WaveLAN	No/Yes	902 MHz to 928 MHz	2 Mbps	800 feet
O'Neill Communications	LAWN	No/Yes	902 MHz to 928 MHz	902 MHz	??? ???
Photonics	Wide Area and Point-to-Point products	Yes/No	N/A	1 Mbps	20' X 20' room (integrated PC Card); 25' X 25' room (tethered transceiver)

(continued)

Table H-1: *(continued)*

Company	Product	Infrared/ Radio	Frequency	Advertised Speed	Advertised Distance
Proxim, Inc.	RangeLAN	No/Yes	902 MHz to 928 MHz	???	???
Solectek	AirLAN	No/Yes	902 MHz to 928 MHz	2 Mbps	800 feet
Traveling Software and	AirShare	No/Yes	902 MHz to 928 MHz	No	Portable to desktop
National Semiconductor Windata, Inc.	FreePort	No/Yes	2.4 GHz & 5.8 GHz	5.7 Mbps	260 feet
Xerox	PARCTAB	Yes/No	N/A	9.6Kbps, 19.2Kbps, 38.4Kbps	30' X 30' room

NOTE:

Frequency use requires a FCC license as shown in Table H-1.

Other Wireless-Related Sites

1. **Br Badrinath's ftp directory:** From Rutgers University, full of papers on mobile computing.

   ```
   ftp://paul.rutgers.edu/pub/badri/
   ```

2. **CWC:** Established in August 1992, the Centre for Wireless Communications (CWC) at the National University of Singapore (NUS) is a National R&D Centre funded by National Science and Technology Board (NSTB).

   ```
   http://www.cwc.nus.sg/cwcdocs/intro.html
   ```

3. **Girish Welling's Home Page:** From Rutgers University, he's done some research in mobile computing.

   ```
   http://paul.rutgers.edu:80/~welling/
   ```

4. **Hiperlan/Netplan:** Hiperlan is a coming ETSI standard for 20 Mbps wireless LANS at 15,7 GHz. Torben Rune at Netplan was Project Team Leader of PT41, the ETSI project team responsible for defining Hiperlan. Netplan is a Danish consulting company in the field of tele- and data communications.

   http://www.netplan.dk/

5. **K and M Electronics Inc.:** Since 1974, K and M has been a leader in infrared light detection electronics and wireless voice/data communication. The Company has been a pioneer in diffuse (flooding) infrared communications since 1980.

   http://web2.kme.com/kme/company.htm

6. **Metricom Wireless Data:** Metricom, Inc. (Nasdaq: MCOM), founded in 1985, develops, manufactures, and markets wireless data communication networks.

   http://www.metricom.com/

7. **Mobile Computing and Personal Digital Assistants:** An informative website with topics pertaining to the use of technology, technology trends, or politics as it affects technology. Subjects include wireless networking, mobile computing, and research projects.

   http://splat.baker.com/grand-unification-theory/
   mobile-pda/index.html

8. **Multipoint Networks:** Multipoint Networks designs and manufactures wireless data communications systems for metropolitan area networks.

   http://www.multipoint.com/

9. **Qualcomm:** Headquartered in San Diego, CA, USA, Qualcomm develops, manufactures, markets, licenses, and operates advanced communications systems and products based on its proprietary digital wireless technologies. The Company's primary product and development areas are the OmniTRACS system (a geostationary satellite-based, mobile communications system providing two-way data and position reporting services), Code Division Multiple Access (CDMA) wireless communications systems and products and, in conjunction with others, the Globalstar low-earth-orbit (LEO) satellite communications system.

   http://lorien.qualcomm.com/

10. **Shiva:**

   http://www.shiva.com/

11. **Wireless FAQ:** Frequently Asked Questions from the wireless newsgroup:

   http://www.cis.ohio-state.edu/~jain/cis788/wireless_lan/
   faq.txt

12. **Wireless LAN Group:**

   http://www.ecs.umass.edu/ece/wireless/

13. **The Wireless Opportunities Coalition:** The group supports the development, manufacture, and use of wireless communications and related devices that are not licensed by the FCC, but are regulated under part 15 of its rules.

   http://wireless.policy.net/wireless/wireless.html

End Notes

[1] Joel B Wood and Professor Raj Jain, Department of Computer and Information Science, The Ohio State University, 2015 Neil Avenue, DL 297, Columbus, OH 43210-1277, 1998.

List of **CCITT/ISO** Standards

- **F.700:** http://cuiwww.unige.ch/OSG/info/MultimediaInfo/mmsurvey/standards.html#F.700
- **G.711:** http://cuiwww.unige.ch/OSG/info/MultimediaInfo/mmsurvey/standards.html#G.711
- **G.721**: http://cuiwww.unige.ch/OSG/info/MultimediaInfo/mmsurvey/standards.html#G.721
- **G.722**: http://cuiwww.unige.ch/OSG/info/MultimediaInfo/mmsurvey/standards.html#G.722
- **G.725**: http://cuiwww.unige.ch/OSG/info/MultimediaInfo/mmsurvey/standards.html#G.725
- **H.221**: http://cuiwww.unige.ch/OSG/info/MultimediaInfo/mmsurvey/standards.html#H.221
- **H.242**: http://cuiwww.unige.ch/OSG/info/MultimediaInfo/mmsurvey/standards.html#H.242
- **H.261:** http://cuiwww.unige.ch/OSG/info/MultimediaInfo/mmsurvey/standards.html#H.261
- **H.320**: http://cuiwww.unige.ch/OSG/info/MultimediaInfo/mmsurvey/standards.html#H.320

- **HyTime:** http://cuiwww.unige.ch/OSG/info/MultimediaInfo/ mmsurvey/standards.html#HyTime
- **IIF**: http://cuiwww.unige.ch/OSG/info/MultimediaInfo/ mmsurvey/standards.html#IIF
- **JBIG:** http://cuiwww.unige.ch/OSG/info/MultimediaInfo/ mmsurvey/standards.html#JBIG
- **JPEG**: http://cuiwww.unige.ch/OSG/info/MultimediaInfo/ mmsurvey/standards.html#JPEG
- **MHEG:** http://cuiwww.unige.ch/OSG/info/MultimediaInfo/ mmsurvey/standards.html#MHEG
- **MPEG:** http://cuiwww.unige.ch/OSG/info/MultimediaInfo/ mmsurvey/standards.html#MPEG
- **ODA:** http://cuiwww.unige.ch/OSG/info/MultimediaInfo/ mmsurvey/standards.html#ODA
- **T.80**: http://cuiwww.unige.ch/OSG/info/MultimediaInfo/ mmsurvey/standards.html#T.80
- **X.400**: http://cuiwww.unige.ch/OSG/info/MultimediaInfo/ mmsurvey/standards.html#X.400
- **G.723**: http://cuiwww.unige.ch/OSG/info/MultimediaInfo/ mmsurvey/standards.html#G.723
- **G.726**: http://cuiwww.unige.ch/OSG/info/MultimediaInfo/ mmsurvey/standards.html#G.726
- **G.727**: http://cuiwww.unige.ch/OSG/info/MultimediaInfo/ mmsurvey/standards.html#G.727
- **G.728**: http://cuiwww.unige.ch/OSG/info/MultimediaInfo/ mmsurvey/standards.html#G.728
- **G.764**: http://cuiwww.unige.ch/OSG/info/MultimediaInfo/ mmsurvey/standards.html#G.764
- **G.765**: http://cuiwww.unige.ch/OSG/info/MultimediaInfo/ mmsurvey/standards.html#G.765
- **H.200**: http://cuiwww.unige.ch/OSG/info/MultimediaInfo/ mmsurvey/standards.html#H.200
- **H.241**: http://cuiwww.unige.ch/OSG/info/MultimediaInfo/ mmsurvey/standards.html#H.241
- **H.243**: http://cuiwww.unige.ch/OSG/info/MultimediaInfo/ mmsurvey/standards.html#H.243
- **T.120**: http://cuiwww.unige.ch/OSG/info/MultimediaInfo/ mmsurvey/standards.html#T.120

GLOSSARY

3090: Large IBM mainframe (circa 1986).

3270: IBM mainframe terminal.

3270 Data Stream: Format for transmitting data to a 3270 terminal.

3274: IBM controllers or cluster controllers.

3770: Protocol for SNA batch transmissions.

802: IEEE committee on LAN standards.

802.1: IEEE LANs and networking architecture specifications.

802.1B: IEEE Network management specifications.

802.1D: IEEE committee for bridges. IEEE media-access-control-level standard for interLAN bridges linking IEEE802.3, 802.4 and 802.5 networks.

802.2: IEEE data link layer standards detailing logical link control (LLC).

802.3: IEEE standard for Ethernet-type systems and networks (802.3 1Base5, 802.3 10Base2, 802.3 10BaseT, and 802.3 10Broad36).

802.4: IEEE standard for token-passing system using a bus topology.

802.5: IEEE standard for token ring systems.

802.6: IEEE specifications for Metropolitan Area Networks (MANs).

802.7: IEEE standards for broadband LANs.

802.8: IEEE specifications for fiber optic LANs.

802.9: IEEE specifications for integrating voice and digital data (Isochronous Traffic).

802.10: IEEE specifications for interoperable and internetwork security.

802.11: IEEE standards for wireless LANs and 802.12 High-Speed LANs (100VG-AnyLAN).

2B+D: Describes basic ISDN service (2B+D = Two Bearer Channels and one Data Channel).

1Base5: Specification for StarLAN at 1 Mbps data transfer rate.

10Base2: Ethernet specification for thin coaxial cable, transmits signals at 10 Mbpswith a distance limit of 185 meters per segment and 10 Mbps; baseband (single channel) with a maximum of 200m.

10Base5: Ethernet specification for thick coaxial cable, transmits signals at 10 Mbps with a distance limit of 500 meters per segment and 10 Mbps; Baseband (single channel) with a maximum of 500m.

10BaseF: Ethernet specification for fiber optic cable, transmits signals at 10 Mbps with a distance limit of 1000 meters per segment.

10BaseT: Ethernet specification for unshielded twisted-pair cable (Category 3, 4, or 5), transmits signals at 10 Mbps with a distance limit of 100 meters per segment.

10Broad36: Ethernet on broadband cable.

3COM 3+: Network operating system designed to supports PCs and Macs.

66-type Connecting Block: Used by telephone company to terminate twisted pairs. Not recommended for LAN use.

AARP: AppleTalk Address Resolution Protocol.

ABM: Asynchronous Balance Mode.

Abstract Syntax Notation One (ASN.1): OSI method of describing data formats for application layer.

AC: Access Control.

Access Method: Rules that govern how nodes on a network access the cable. Also referred to as media-access control (MAC) protocol.

Acknowledgment: A message indicating that data has been correctly received.

ACS: Asynchronous Communications Server.

ACSE: Association Control Service Element.

Active Open: A TCP tool for activating a connection with a node.

Active Star: Star topology with active hubs.

ACTS: Association of Cable Television Suppliers.

A/D Converter: Analog to digital signal converter.

Adaptive Channel Allocation: Used in multiplexing signals. Bandwidth is only afforded a signal by request.

Adaptive Routing: Using intelligent methods for selecting routes for packet transmission.

ADC: Analog-to-digital converter.

ADCCP: ANSI's data link layer protocol called Advanced Data Communications Control Procedures.

Address: The unique identifier for the source or destination of a data transfer.

Addressable Converter: Equipment in cable households which allows cable operators to turn on or off the converter or pay-per-view type events.

Address Resolution Protocol (ARP): A protocol that dynamically maps between various types of addresses (IP addresses to token ring addresses, for instance) on a local area network. Used to route data between networks through a gateway.

ADMD: Administration Management Domain.

ADSP: AppleTalk Datastream Protocol.

ADU: Asynchronous Data Unit.

Advanced Communications Function (ACP): Official product name for all IBM SNA products (ACF/VTAM). IBM's program package (ACF) allows the sharing of computer resources through computer links. It also supports SNA.

Advanced Intelligent Network (AIN): Developed by Bell Communications Research.

Advanced Interactive Executive (AIX): IBM's version of UNIX.

Advanced Peer-to-Peer communications (APPC): IBM system for allowing direct node-to-node interaction on networks. Nodes referred to as LU 6.2.

Advanced Peer-to-Peer Network (APPN): IBM's enhancement for SNA networks allowing distributed processing and other advanced features.

ADVANCENET: Hewlett Packard's network supporting OSI and SNA.

AFI: AppleTalk File Interface.

AFP: AppleTalk File Protocol; allows access to Apple shared servers.

ALAP: AppleTalk Link Access Protocol.

Altair System: Motorola's wireless radio LAN.

Alternate Mark Inversion (AMI): Line coding method for T-1 lines.

AM: Amplitude Modulation.

AMD: Advanced Micro Devices.

American National Standards Institute (ANSI): The coordinating body for voluntary standards groups within the United States. ANSI is a member of the International Organization for Standardization (ISO).

American Standard Code for Information Interchange (ASCII): Seven-bit character data coding method for asynchronous communications.

American Telephone and Telegraph Company (AT&T): Develops networks among other things.

American Wire Gauge (AWG): Used to measure the diameter of conductors in wires.

AMT: Address Mapping Table.

Analog: A representation of an object that resembles the original. Analog devices monitor conditions, such as movement, temperature, and sound, and convert them into analogous electronic or mechanical patterns. For example, telephones turn voice vibrations into electrical vibrations of the same shape. Analog implies continuous operation.

Analog Transmission: A way of sending signals (voice, video, data) in which the transmitted signal is analogous to the original signal. In other words, if you spoke into a microphone and saw your voice on an oscilloscope and you took the same voice as it was transmitted on the phone line and threw that signal onto the oscilloscope, the two signals would look essentially the same. The only difference would be that the electrically transmitted signal would be at a higher frequency.

ANTC: Advanced Network Test Center.

APAD: Asynchronous Packet Assembler/Disassembler.

Apple Computer, Inc.: Pioneers of personal computer. Manufacture Macintoshes with built-in LocalTalk ports for networking. Also developed AppleTalk protocols and AppleShare products.

AppleShare PC: Software that allows DOS-based machines to operate within an AppleShare network.

AppleTalk: Apple Computer's network protocol originally designed to run over LocalTalk networks, but can also run on Ethernet and token ring.

Application Layer: Layer 7 of the OSI Model. Defines the rules for gaining entrance into the communications system. Programs communicate with other programs through this layer.

Application Development Cycle (AD/Cycle): SAA software from IBM to manage IS system development.

Application Development Environment (ADE): IBM's universal application development package for SAA systems.

Applications Programming Interface (API): A method of allowing an application to interact directly with certain functions of an operating system or with another application.

ARM: Asynchronous Response Mode.

AS/400: Application System/400. IBM's mid-price minicomputer.

ASCII Protocol: Simple protocol for transferring data with no error checking.

ASE: Applied Service Elements.

ASK: Amplitude Shift Keying.

ASP: AppleTalk Session Protocol.

Asynchronous: Transmission where sending and receiving devices are not synchronized. Data must carry signals to indicate data divisions.

Asynchronous Protocol: Protocol designed for asynchronous data transfers including ASCII, TTY, Kermit, and XMODEM.

Asynchronous Transfer Mode (ATM): A form of data transmission based on fixed-length packets, called cells, that can carry data, voice, and video at high speeds. This technology is designed to combine the benefits of switching technology (constant transmission delay, guaranteed capacity) with those of packet switching (flexibility, efficiency for intermittent traffic). ATM is defined by ITU-T ATM Forum specifications.

ATA: ARCnet Trade Association.

ATD: Asynchronous Time Division.

ATM: Asynchronous Transfer Mode. High bandwidth and low overhead networking system using something akin to packet-switching. It is the future of high-speed broadband networks.

ATM Adaptation Layer (AAL): One of the three layers of the ATM protocol reference model. It translates incoming data into ATM cell payloads and translates outgoing cells into a format readable by the higher layers. Five AALs have been defined: AAL1 and 2 handle traffic like voice and video, which are sensitive to transmission delays, while AAL3, 4, and 5 pertain to data communications through the segmentation and reassembly of packets.

ATM DSU: A Data Service Unit for ATM access.

ATP: AppleTalk Transaction Protocol

Attached Resources Computer Network (ARCnet): Developed by Datapoint in the late 70's to provide data transfers at 2.5 Mbps. Very inexpensive products with great product interoperability. A token-passing bus architecture, usually on coaxial cable.

Attachment Unit Interface (AUI): Transceiver for thick Ethernet systems.

Attenuation: The decrease in the power of some sort of signal.

AUI Connector (Attachment Unit Interface): A 15-pin connector found on Ethernet cards that can be used for attaching coaxial, fiber optic, or twisted-pair cable.

AutoBaud Rate Detect (ABR): Senses speed of incoming data.

Backbone: A cable to which multiple nodes or workstations are attached.

Backup Server: Device which copies applications and data into a safe place for retrieval if necessary.

BALUN (BALancedUNbalanced): An impedance-matching device which allows conversion from one medium (like coax) to another medium (like twisted pair).

Band: Range of frequencies.

Bandwidth: The range of electrical frequencies that a device or medium can support.

Baseband: A type of system where only digital data is carried on the transfer medium. Single-channel systems which support a single transmission at any given time.

Basic Cable: The program services distributed by a cable television system to subscribers for a basic monthly fee. These may include one or more local broadcast stations, distant broadcast stations, non-pay cable networks, local-origination programming, and/or data channels.

Baud: The speed of signaling elements per second. A signaling element may represent more than one bit so bits per second and baud are not always the same.

Bayonet-Neill-Concelman (BNC): A type of twist-locking connector used with coaxial cable.

Beacon: A special frame in token ring systems indicating a serious problem with the ring such as a break.

Belden: A major manufacturer of network cabling.

Bell Operating Company (BOC): One of 22 telephone service companies that used to be a part of AT&T.

BER: Basic Encoding Rules or Bit Error Rate.

Berkeley Software Distribution UNIX or *Berkeley UNIX* (BSD UNIX): UNIX system famed for having been enhanced with TCP/IP support.

Bicycling: Distribution of programming and/or commercials between systems by sending tapes by mail or messenger service. This term derives from the early practice of several movie theaters sharing the same film print and having a messenger carry the print between theaters by bicycle in time for each to show the movie as scheduled.

Binary: Numerical method of representing the status of bits. 1 represents an on bit and 0 is an off bit.

Bind: Assigning a physical machine address to a logical or symbolic address. Request to activate a session between a Primary Logical Unit (PLU) and Secondary Logical Unit (SLU).

Bindery: Novell NetWare's database for storing objects and properties. Objects are users, print servers, etc. Properties are passwords, Internet addresses, etc.

Bipolar: Transmission method that alternates between positive and negative voltages to represent bits.

BISDN: Broadband ISDN.

Bisync: Binary synchronous transmission. Half-duplex transmission method developed by IBM.

Bit: Binary digit in the binary numbering system. Its value can be 0 or 1. In an 8-bit character scheme, it takes 8 bits to make a byte (character) of data.

Bit-oriented Protocol: A protocol in which individual bits within a byte convey information, as opposed to the whole byte only.

Bits Per Second (BPS): A measure of data transfer speed.

Bit Stream: A continuous transfer of bits over some medium.

Bit Stuffing: A method of breaking up continuous strings of 1 bits by inserting a 0 bit. The 0 bit is removed at the receiver.

BNC Connector (Bayone-Neill-Concelman): Standard connector used to connect 10Base2 coaxial cable.

Boundary node: A SNA device which provides protocol support for other SNA nodes.

BRI: ISDN Basic Rate Interface.

Bridge: Devices that connect and pass packets between two network segments that use the same communications protocol.

Broadband: A system carrying many different types or channels of data by dividing the total bandwidth of the medium into smaller bandwidths (see FDM). Multichannel capacity equal to or greater than 45 Mbps.

Broadband Integrated Services Data Network (BISDN): A set of standards under development by the ITU-T for services based on ATM switching and SONET/SDH (see these entries) transmission.

Broadcast: Sending data to more than one receiving device at a time.

Brouter: A device that combines the functions of a bridge and a router.

BSC: Binary Synchronous Transmission.

Buffer: A temporary storage place for data being received or transmitted.

Bus topology: A physical layout of network devices in which all devices must share a common medium to transfer data, and no two devices may transmit simultaneously.

Byte: The grouping of bits making up a character. In current systems, typically eight bits.

Byte-oriented Protocol: A protocol in which whole bytes represent data as opposed to single bits within the bytes, which taken by themselves are meaningless.

Cable: Transmission medium of copper wire or optical fiber wrapped in a protective cover.

Cablecasting: Programming carried on cable television exclusive of broadcast signals. Also see Cable Origination.

Cable Converter: Equipment in the homes of cable subscribers used to convert cable signals to normal TV channels.

Cable Origination: Programming originated by a cable operator or other non-broadcast signals carried by a cable system.

Cable System Operator: The company or individual responsible for the operation of a cable television system (usually the system owner as well).

Cable Television Administration and Marketing Society (CTAM): A professional society that deals with key management and marketing issues in the cable industry by providing a forum for idea exchange.

Cable Television Advertising Bureau (CAB): An organization established to provide promotional and advisory services to the cable industry.

Cable System: A facility designed for the purpose of receiving multiple broadcast and/or non-broadcast signals and distributing them via coaxial or fiber optic cable to subscribers living in unattached residences not under common ownership. Signals may be received over the air, by satellite or microwave relay, or from the system's studio or remote facilities.

Cable Ready: A term that describes television sets that have circuitry built in that enables them to receive and translate cable signals without the use of separate converters. Cable ready sets, however, usually cannot decode pay television signals that have been scrambled to prevent unauthorized reception.

Capacitance: The capacity of a wire or device to store an electrical charge.

Carrier: An electrical signal of a set frequency that can be modulated in order to carry data.

Carrier Detect: Circuit that detects the presence of a carrier.

Carrier Sense Multiple Access/Collision Detection (CSMA/CD): A communication access method used by Ethernet. When a device wants to gain access to the network, it checks to see if the network is free. If it is not, it waits a random amount of time before retrying. If the network is free and two devices attempt to gain access at exactly the same time, they both back off to avoid a collision and each wait a random amount of time before retrying.

Cell: The fixed-length transmission unit used by ATM. Each cell is 53 bytes long with a 5-byte header containing its connection identifier and a 48-byte payload. See CLP, HEC, PTI, VCI/VPI.

Cell Loss Priority (CLP): A one-bit descriptor found in ATM cell headers, indicating the relative importance of a cell. If set to 0, the cell should not be discarded. If set to 1, the cell may be discarded if there is congestion in the switch. The cell content is set by the AAL.

Channel Capacity: The number of channels available for current or future use on a cable system. Capacity is determined by the capabilities of the system hardware; actual offerings are determined by the cable company based on its own marketing decisions and any requirements specified in the franchise agreement.

Character-oriented Protocol: Protocol in which blocks of data are marked by special characters.

Cheapernet: Another name for thin Ethernet or 10Base2 systems.

Checkpoint: An event in a series of transactions that can be used to roll back transactions in the event of a failure. Also a HDLC error recovery mechanism.

Checksum: A value created by adding up bits in a packet. The resultant value is computed at the sender and receiver of data. Mismatches trigger error-recovery routines.

Churn: Turnover of cable subscribers as a result of disconnects and new customers.

Cladding: A covering of glass or plastic surrounding a fiber optic core, designed to prevent light waves from leaving the core.

Class of Service (CoS): A set of characteristics (such as route security, transmission priority and bandwidth) used to construct a route between session partners. The class of service is specified by the initiator of a session.

Client: A node on a network that requests services from a network server.

Client/Server: A networking system in which one or more file servers (server) provide services, such as network management, application processing, and centralized data storage for workstations (clients).

Cluster Controller: A device which handles input and output for several devices attached to it.

CMIS: Common Management Information System.

CMOT: Common Management Information Protocol Over TCP/IP.

Coaxial Cable: Transmission line for television and radio signals, the type most frequently used in cable television systems. Consists of two concentric tubular conductors with an insulator between. A coaxial cable is capable of carrying many TV or radio signals simultaneously.

Coder/decoder (codec): Converts analog signals into digital signals.

Collision: When electrical signals from two or more devices sharing a common data transfer medium crash into one another. This commonly happens on Ethernet-type systems.

Common Communications Support (CCS): Communication specifications used for SAA.

Common Management Information Protocol (CMIP): OSI protocol for network monitoring and control (ISO 9596).

Communications Controller: A specialized device for connecting several communication lines to a single computer. It is usually purchased for a specific set of protocols.

Communications Satellite: A space vehicle which receives radio and television signals and transmits them back to earth. It is located 22,300 miles above earth in a geosynchronous orbit so that it is stationary in relationship to a fixed position on earth. One use of the communications satellite is by the cable industry for transmitting network programming. Commonly called *bird*.

Communications Server: A specialized device on a network to manage access to outside networks.

Community Antenna Television (CATV): Association primarily composed of cable system operators with a small number of subscribers, usually less than 3,000.

Compression: Reducing the representation of information, but not the information itself or reducing the bandwidth or bits necessary to encode information. Full standard coding of broadcast quality television typically requires 45 to 90 Mbps. Compressed video includes signals from 3 Mbps down to 56 Kbps.

Compulsory License: The authorization enjoyed by a cable system under The Copyright Act of 1976 to retransmit programs without negotiating payments to individual copyright owners.

Concentrator: A device that provides a central connection point for cables from workstations, servers, and peripherals. Most concentrators contain the ability to amplify the electrical signal they receive.

Conductor: A material that can carry an electrical signal.

Connection Admission Control (CAC): The set of actions taken by the network during the connection setup phase in order to determine whether a connection-requested Quality of Service can be accepted or should be rejected. CAC is also used when routing a connection through an ATM network.

Connection-oriented: A relationship is set up between sender and receiver to provide increased data transfer reliability.

Connectionless: No relationship is set between sender and receiver for reliability's sake.

Connectionless Network Protocol (CLNP): From OSI.

Connectionless Network Service CLNS): Also from OSI.

Connectivity: The attachment of devices on a network. The devices may be similar or dissimilar.

CONS: Connection Oriented Network Service.

Constant Bit Rate (CBR): Said of real time services/data transmissions that accept no or very little delay of the output signal. Video, for instance, may use a constant bit rate service. See isochronous. Can also use VBR.

Consultative Committee for International Telegraph and Telephone (CCITT): An international organization that develops communication standards such as Recommendation X.25. Name recently changed to ITU (International Telecommunication Union).

Contention: In reference to Ethernet-type systems, devices contend for single data channel.

Continuity: An uninterrupted pathway for electrical signals.

Controlled Access Unit (CAU): Newer, more intelligent version of the token ring's multistation access unit (MAU).

Converter: A device that translates cable signals into television signals and allows the viewer to select individual channels.

Copper Distributed Data Interface (CDDI): The copper equivalent to fiber optic's FDDI.

Copyright Act of 1976: Bill enacted to revise 1909 Copyright law in order to have a single nationwide system protecting copyrighted works. The act created the Copyright Royalty Tribunal. This act considers copyright ownership of sound recordings, television broadcasts, cable television, and phonograph records. In cable television, the law requires payment (under compulsory licensing) of royalties for retransmitting copyrighted materials by cable system. The amounts are distributed to copyright owner by the Copyright Royalty Tribunal.

Counter-rotating ring: Technology used in FDDI to provide fault tolerance.

CPE: Customer-Provided Equipment.

Crosstalk: The carryover of a signal in a wire to another wire near it. A potential problem in twisted-pair systems.

CSMA/CA: Carrier Sense Multiple Access/Collision Avoidance is a network access method in which each device signals its intent to transmit before it actually does so. This prevents other devices from sending information, thus preventing collisions between signals from two or more devices. This is the access method used by LocalTalk.

CSMA/CD: Carrier Sense Multiple Access/Collision Detection is a network access method in which devices that are ready to transmit data first check the channel for a carrier. If no carrier is sensed, a device can transmit. If two devices transmit at once, a collision occurs and each computer backs off and waits a random amount of time before attempting to retransmit. This is the access method used by Ethernet.

CTS: Clear To Send signal used in the RS-232 standard.

CUA: Common User Access. SAA terminology.

Current: The flow of electrons through a circuit. It is measured in amps.

Cyclic Redundancy Check (CRC): An error checking technique used to ensure the accuracy of transmitting digital code over a communications channel. The transmitted messages are divided into predetermined lengths which, used as dividends, are divided by a fixed divisor. The remainder of the calculation is appended onto and sent with the message. At the receiving end, the computer recalculates the remainder. If it does not match the transmitted remainder, an error is detected.

D/A Converter: Digital-to-analog converter.

DAC: Digital-to-analog converter.

Daisy Chain: An arrangement of devices connected in series, one after the other. Any signals transmitted to the devices go to the first device, and from the first to the second, and so on.

DAP: Data Access Protocol.

DAS: Dynamically-Assigned Sockets.

DAT: Digital Audio Tape.

Data Channels: An umbrella term for all forms of video transmission that involve electronically generated text and/or graphics rather than recorded or live action images. Generally refers to local cable channels on which alphanumeric material is displayed by character generators, although video text and teletext also fall into this category.

Data Communications Equipment or Data Circuit-terminating Equipment (DCE): Technical term for a modem. Device that establishes, maintains, and destroys a session on a network.

Datagram: A TCP/IP packet containing data and a source and destination address. It uses an unreliable delivery method.

Data Link Layer: Layer 2 of the OSI Model. Responsible for node-to-node validity and integrity of the transmission, it allows messages to be placed into packets and vice-versa. It controls dataflow.

Data Service Unit/Channel Service Unit (DSU/CSU): A communications device that connects an in-house line to an external digital circuit (T1). The DSU converts data into the required format, while the CSU terminates the line, provides signal regeneration, and remote testing. A DSU/CSU is not limited to T1; it can be used with 56K DDS and slower circuits as well.

Data Set: Typically, a modem.

Data Stream: A continuous flow of data from a source to a destination.

Data Structure: The physical layout of data, such as fields.

Data Terminal Equipment (DTE): A communications device that is the source or destination of signals on a network. It is typically a terminal or computer.

Data eXchange Interface (DXI): Protocols used for SMDS and ATM data exchange between a router and a DSU.

DB-9: Nine-pin connector.

DB-25: Twenty-five pin connector meeting RS-232 specifications.

DDP: Datagram Delivery Protocol.

Decibel (dB): A unit of relative change of power (for example, -10 dB).

Decoder: An electronic device used for converting a scrambled TV signal into a viewable picture.

Dedicated Channel: A cable channel devoted to a single source for its programming.

Dedicated Line: Transmission line servicing only one type of data. Pathway is permanent.

Demodulator: A device which removes a signal from a carrier for subsequent conversion to digital data. Modems (MOdulatorDEModulators) do this.

DHA: Destination Hardware Address.

DIB: Directory Information Base.

DID: Destination IDentification.

Digital: In telecommunications, in recording or in computing, digital is the use of a binary code to represent information. Recording or transmitting information digitally has two major benefits. First, the signal can be reproduced precisely. In digital transmission, the signal is first regenerated. It's put through a little *yes-no* question. Is this signal a *one* or a *zero*? The signal is reconstructed (squared off, to what was it was originally). Then it is amplified and sent along its way. So digital transmission is much *cleaner* than analog transmission. The second major benefit of digital is that the electronic circuitry to handle digital is getting cheaper and more powerful.

Digital Data: Information that is digital (1s and 0s) in nature.

Direct Broadcast Satellite (DBS): A service that transmits satellite signals directly to a home through the viewer's own earth station rather than through a cable system.

Disconnects: Subscribers who have terminated cable service or whose service has been terminated for any reason.

Disconnect Rate: The percentage of cable subscribers in a given area who have discontinued service in a certain time period.

Dish: A parabolic or spherical shaped antenna.

Distant Signal: A broadcast signal originating outside the cable system's local market as defined by the FCC under the mandatory carriage rule.

Distribution System: In a cable system, the portion of the cable system which carries signals from the headend to the subscribers' homes.

Domain: A subset of a larger network made up of endpoints and network devices. Virtual LANs are a type of autonomous domain.

Downlink: Part of a satellite communications system by which information is carried from satellite to ground.

Drop: Coaxial cable connecting the cable in the street to the subscriber's home and television set. Also see Cable Television System.

DS: Directory Services.

DS1/DS3: See T1/T3.

DSAP: Destination Service Access Point.

DSU (Data Service Unit): Data transmission equipment used to interface to a digital circuit at customer site. It converts the customer's datastream, such as X.21 to E1 or T1 for transmission through the CSU, which is often contained, functionally within the DSU device. DSUs can convert data to or from a native port on a router to an E1, E2 or E3 leased line, primary rate ISDN or SMDS, DSU functionality can be built into devices such as some routers or multiplexers. In Europe a DSU can convert El bandwidth into RS.449, X.21, V.35 or other serial interface via a router. A DSU with an HSSI interface will deliver E2 or E3 bandwidth from the WAN to an HSSI router on a LAN.

DTR: Data Terminal Ready.

DUA: Directory User Agent.

Dumb Terminal: Refers to devices that are designed to communicate exclusively with a host computer. It receives all screen layouts from the host computer and sends all keyboard entry to the host. It cannot function without the host computer.

Duplex: Simultaneous two-way transmission of data. Also referred to as full duplex or half-duplex.

Duplication: The airing of the same programs in close succession by two or more pay cable services in the same market.

E1/E3: The European version of T1/T3 (see these abbreviations). E1 runs at 2.048 Mbps and E3 runs at 34 Mbps.

Earth Satellite: Communications station used to send or receive electronic signals from or to a satellite (seldom both). Usually employs one of a variety of dish-type antennae used by television stations and cable operators.

EBCDIC: Extended Binary Coded Decimal Interchange Code. IBM-developed 8-bit character coding.

EIA: Electronic Industries Association. Developed the RS-232 specification.

EMI: Electromagnetic Interference.

Encryption: Coding of data into indecipherable symbols.

Enterprise Network: A network comprising all the LANs or other networks within a single organization.

EOT: End of Transmission.

Ethernet: A network protocol invented by Xerox Corporation and developed jointly by Xerox, Intel, and Digital Equipment Corporation. Ethernet networks use CSMA/CD and run over a variety of cable types at 10 Mbps.

Extended Industry Standard Architecture (EISA): A type of computer bus.

Fast Ethernet: A new Ethernet standard that supports 100 Mbps using Category 5 twisted-pair or fiber optic cable.

FBE: Free Buffer Enquiry.

FDDI: Fiber Distributed Data Interface. Fiber standard that uses only an iota of fiber's throughput capacity.

Federal Communications Commission (FCC): Charged with protecting airwaves in the U.S.

Fiber Distributed Data Interface (FDDI): An ANSI standard for a 100 Mbps token-passing ring based on fiber optic transmission media.

Fiber Optic Cable: A cable, consisting of a center glass core surrounded by layers of plastic, that transmits data using light rather than electricity. It has the ability to carry more information over much longer distances than copper cables can.

Fiber Optics: A method of transmitting signals using lightwaves sent through extremely thin fibers spun from glass. Fiber optic cables can carry greater amounts of information than copper wire carrying electrical signals.

File Server: A computer connected to the network that contains primary files/applications and shares them as requested with the other computers on the network. If the file server is dedicated for that purpose only, it is connected to a client/server network. An example of a client/server network is Novell Netware. All the computers connected to a peer-to-peer network are capable of being the file server. Two examples of peer-to-peer networks are LANtastic and Windows for Workgroups.

Flag: Typically a certain bit that has meaning in bit-oriented protocols.

Frame: A block of data in bit-oriented protocols.

Frame Check Sequence (FCS): Error-detection field.

Franchise/Franchise Agreement: A contract between a cable television company and a local government authorizing the company to operate in the locale and defining the terms under which it may install coaxial or fiber optic cable and offer cable television service within the community.

Franchise Area: The specific geographic area in which the cable television company may offer service, as defined by the franchise.

Frequency: Cycles per second. Measured in Hertz (Hz).

Frequency Division Multiplexing: The official term for placing several different signals on a wire, each having its own unique frequencies (broadband LANs).

Frequency Modulation (FM): Used to encode data into a carrier of a set frequency. The changes in frequency represent 1s and 0s.

FS: Frame Status.

FTAM: File Transfer Access Management.

FTP: File Transfer Protocol.

Full Duplex: Describes the simultaneous two-way flow of data.

Gateway: The original term for what is now called router or, more precisely, IP router. A gateway connects two or more communications networks together at the network layer. It may perform protocol conversion from one network to the other. A communications link between a local area network and a mainframe or mini-computer.

Generic Flow Control (GFC): The first 4 bits of the ATM UNI 3.0 cell header; used when passing through the User-Network Interface (UNI).

GHz: Gigahertz.

Gigabyte (GB): One billion bytes of information. One thousand megabytes.

Global Network: A network that is global and allows access to several organizations.

GMII: Gigabit Media Independent Interface

GOSIP: Government OSI Profile. Specifies that all government agencies shall follow OSI guidelines in creating and expanding networks. Now under review.

Half Duplex: Describes transmissions where data only travels in one direction at any given moment.

Handshaking: Signals sent by communicating devices to initiate and synchronize the communication.

Headend: The equipment at a cable system which receives the various program source signals, processes them, and retransmits them to subscribers.

Header Error Control (HEC): The HEC field is an 8-bit Cyclic Redundancy Check (CRC) computed on all fields in an ATM Header and capable of detecting single-bit and certain multiple-bit errors.

Hewlett-Packard (HP): Computer company often pioneering new techniques. Now implementing wireless infrared communications for transferring data from portable PCs to desktop PCs.

High-Level Data link Control (HDLC): A bit-oriented protocol established by the ISO.

Homes Passed: The number of homes in which cable television service is or can be readily made available because feeder cables are in place nearby.

Host: Computer that offers services on a network.

Housedrop: The coaxial cable between the cable in the street and subscriber's television set. Also see Cable Television System.

Hub: A hardware device that contains multiple independent but connected modules of network and internetwork equipment. Hubs can be active (where they repeat signals sent through them) or passive (where they do not repeat but merely split signals sent through them).

Hz: Hertz.

IC: Integrated Circuits.

ICMP: Internet Control Message Protocol.

IDF: Intermediate Distribution Frame. This is usually located on each floor within a building. It is tied directly to the Main Distibution Frame via 100- or 200-pair copper cables.

IDG: Interdialog Gap. Used in LocalTalk Networks.

IDP: Internetwork Datagram Protocol.

IETF: Internet Engineering Task Force.

IFG: Interframe gap.

Infrared: Electromagnetic waves whose frequency range is above that of microwaves, but below that of the visible spectrum.

Institute of Electrical and Electronics Engineers (IEEE): Professional organization that defines some network standards, such as Ethernet.

Interactive Cable: Cable systems that have the technical ability to let subscribers communicate directly with a computer at the system headend from their television sets, using special converters and the regular cable lines.

Interconnect: Two or more cable systems distributing a commercial signal simultaneously, primarily to maximize the effectiveness of an advertising schedule by offering a multiple system buy in which only one contract need be negotiated. Interconnects can be hard, where systems are directly linked by cable, microwave relays or by satellite, and the signal is fed to the entire interconnect by one headend; or soft, where there is no direct operational connection between the participating systems but the same commercial is run simultaneously by each of the systems.

Interim Local Management Interface (ILMI): The standard specification used to manage ATM network interfaces. The ILMI uses the SNMP protocol and an ATM UNI MIB to provide the administrator with status and configuration information.

International Organization for Standardization (ISO): An organization that sets international standards, founded in 1946 and headquartered in Geneva. ANSI is the USA member body to ISO.

International Telecom: Organization formed by 91 countries for managing global communications and satellite communications systems. COMSAT is the US Organization (Intelsat) member.

International Telecommunication Union (ITU): An international organization that develops communication standards such as Recommendation X.25. Name recently changed from CCITT.

Internet: A global network of networks used to exchange information using the TCP/IP protocol. It allows for electronic mail and the accessing and retrieval of information from remote sources.

Internet Packet eXchange (IPX): A Novell NetWare communications protocol that is used to route messages from one node to another. The Novell version of IP.

Internet Protocol (IP): Associated with TCP, a set of communications protocols developed to internetwork dissimilar systems. The TCP protocol controls the transfer of the data (performing at the equivalent to Layer 4 in the OSI model) and the IP protocol provides the routing mechanism (performing at the equivalent to Layer 3 in the OSI model).

Internetwork: Two or more networks connected by bridges and/or routers.

Inverse Address Resolution Protocol (INARP): An address resolution protocol which maps hardware addresses, (Ethernet, token ring) into IP addresses.

IP address: An identifier for a node's network interface, expressed as four fields separated by decimal points. The IP address is divided into a network part and a host part, site-dependent and assigned by an administrator.

Isochronous: Signals which are dependent on some uniform timing or carry their own timing information embedded as part of the signal. Voice and video are isochronous signals but data transfer is generally not.

KHz: Kilohertz.

LAN (Local Area Network): A network connecting computers in a relatively small area such as a building.

LAN Emulation (LANE): How an ATM network simulates a MAC layer service, such as that provided by existing LAN technology (Ethernet or token ring) to allow existing higher layer protocols and applications to be used unchanged over an ATM network.

LAP: Link Access Protocol.

LAPB: Link Access Protocol, Balanced.

LAPD: Link Access Protocol, Digital.

LATA: Local Access and Transport Area.

Leased Channel: A channel on a cable system which the system has leased to a third party for that party's use. The lessee, not the cable system, is responsible for the programming on the channel.

LED (Light Emitting Diode): Semiconductor device that emits light produced by converting electrical energy. Status lights on hardware devices are typically LEDs.

Lift: The increase in basic cable penetration brought about by introduction of a new service or program.

Linear Bus: A network topology in which each node attaches directly to a common cable.

LLAP: LocalTalk Link Access Protocol.

LLC: Logical Link Control.

Local Origination Programming: Programming produced by or under the auspices of a local cable system for presentation on the system. It may also include syndicated programming acquired by the system for presentation thereon.

LocalTalk: Apple Corporation proprietary protocol that uses CSMA/CA media access scheme and supports transmissions at speeds of 230 Kbps.

LSL: Link Support Layer.

MAC: Media Access Control.

MAN (Metropolitan Area Network): A network connecting computers over a large geographical area, such as a city or school district.

Management Information Base (MIB): A collection of objects (for instance, statistics) pertaining to the general maintenance of a network that can be accessed via a network management protocol.

Mandatory Carriage: Those stations whose signals must be carried by cable systems, according to FCC rules. In general, these include all local stations which request carriage, plus specialty stations and those outside stations which are significantly viewed in the community served by the cable system.

Master Antennae Television: A single antennae used to provide television service for all units in a hotel, apartment house, or housing complex.

MAU (Multistation Access Unit): A token ring wiring hub.

MBps: Megabytes per second.

Mbps: Megabits per second.

Medium Access Control. (MAC): For local area networks, the method of determining which device has access to the transmission medium at any time (MAC protocol). The MAC sublayer is a part of the data link layer in the OSI model that applies a medium access method (for instance, Ethernet or token ring).

Message Switching: A system in which the pathway for the message is determined dynamically as the data is transmitted from one holding tank to another.

MF: More Fragments to follow.

Microwave: Refers to the part of the radio spectrum above 500 Megahertz (short-wave length) used for point-to-point communications where line-of-sight communication is not possible or necessary. Microwaves do not follow the curvature of the earth and are not reflected by the ionosphere; they are greatly affected by obstacles.

Microwave Relay System: System designed to pick up and retransmit microwave signals. since microwaves are signals which only travel short distances, it is necessary to retransmit the signals periodically to cover distance required by some applications. The retransmission or relay stations constitute the microwave relay system. Also known as a terrestrial microwave relay.

Modem (Modulator/Demodulator): Devices that convert digital and analog signals. Modems allow computer data (digital) to be transmitted over voice-grade telephone lines (analog).

Modulator: The function of a modem to encode a data signal into an analog carrier by modulating the carrier.

MOP: Maintenance Operation Protocol.

MOTIS: Message-Oriented Text Interchange Systems.

Moving Pictures Experts Group (MPEG): A group that is working to establish a standard for compressing and storing motion video and animation in digital form. The acronym can also refer to the standard under development by this group.

MPOA: Multiprotocol over ATM.

MSAU: Multistation Access Unit.

MTA: Message Transfer Agent.

Multicasting: Ability to send same message to multiple nodes in a network. This function is connectionless. However, ATM must send the same message to various nodes by forming a multipoint connection to all nodes in the group.

Multimode Fiber/Singlemode Fiber (MMF/SMF): A fiber cable that uses light pulses instead of electricity to carry data. In multimode cable, the light bounces off the cable's walls as it travels down, which causes the signal to weaken sooner and therefore data cannot travel as much distance as with singlemode fiber. In SMF cables, the light travels straight down the cable. The size of the cable/cladding is 62.5/125 micron for MMF and 8/125 micron for SSF.

Multiple System Operator: A company that owns and/or operates more than one cable system.

Multiplexer: A device that allows multiple logical signals to be transmitted simultaneously across a single physical channel.

Multiplexing: The transmission of multiple signals over a single communications line or computer channel. The two common multiplexing techniques are Frequency Division Multiplexing, which separates signals by modulating the data onto different carrier frequencies, and Time Division Multiplexing, which separates signals by interleaving bits one after the other.

Multipoint: A transmission channel that includes several stations.

Multipoint Distribution System: A common carrier system that transmits microwave signals short distances within limited areas. It is used in business for facsimile and data transmissions; for consumer purposes, it is used to supply cable or other non-broadcast programming services to areas not yet wired for cable.

Must-carry: The FCC rule requiring cable systems to carry all local broadcast television signals in their markets. Also, the stations carried under the rule, commonly called *must-carries*.

National Cable Television Association (NCTA): Organization of cable system owners, operators, manufacturers, and distributors.

National Institute for Research in Computer Science and Control (INRIA): Is a French public-sector scientific and technological institute under the responsibility of the Ministry for Research and the Ministry of Industry.

NBP: Name-Binding Protocol.

NCP: Network Control Program.

NCP: NetWare Core Protocol.

Network: A system of connected computers set up to share data, printers, and other devices.

Network Driver Interface Specification (NDIS): A Microsoft specification for writing hardware-independent drivers at the data link layer. The interface is between the hardware-dependent and hardware-independent parts. When transport protocols communicate to the NDIS specification, network cards with NDIS-compliant Medium Access Control drivers can be freely interchanged.

Network Interface Card (NIC): A board that provides network communication capabilities to and from a computer. Also Network Interface Unit (NIU). It has a unique logical address for purposes of identification. It's hard-coded on a silicon chip.

NLM: NetWare Loadable Module.

Network Modem: A modem connected to a Local Area Network (LAN) that is accessible from any workstation on the network.

Network Operating System (NOS): Operating system designed to pass information and communicate between computers. Examples include AppleShare, Novell NetWare, and Windows NT Server.

Network-to-Network Interface (NNI). The interface between ATM switches or an ATM switch and an entire switching system. Also called Network-to-Node Interface.

Nielsen Home Video Index (NHI): Division of Nielsen's Media Research Group responsible for syndicated and non-syndicated measurement of cable, pay cable, VCRs, video discs, and other new television technologies.

NLM: NetWare Loadable Module.

Node: End point of a network connection. Nodes include any device attached to a network such as file servers, printers, or workstations.

Node Devices: Any computer or peripheral that is connected to the network.

Noise: Non-data signals that can disrupt clean data communications.

NOS: Network Operating System.

NRZ: Non-Return to Zero. Data encoding method.

NRZ-I: Non-Return to Zero - Inverted.

NRZ-L: Non-Return to Zero - Level.

NVE: Network Visible Entry.

NVTS: Network Virtual Terminal Service.

ONC: Open Network Computing.

Open Data-Link Interface (ODI): A Novell network driver standard that provides a way to load multiple protocol stacks into the memory of a computer to support multiple network protocols on one or more network interface cards. Comparable to Microsoft's NDIS.

Open System Interconnection (OSI): A reference model that has been defined by ISO as a standard for worldwide communications. It defines a framework for implementing protocols in seven layers. Control is passed from one layer to the next, starting at the application layer in one station, proceeding to the bottom layer, over the channel to the next station and back up the hierarchy.

Optical Carrier *n* (OC-*n*): Optical signal standards. The *n* indicates the level where the respective data rate is exactly *n* times the first level OC-1. OC-1 has a data rate of 51.84 Mbps. OC-3 is 3 times that rate or 155.52 Mbps.

Overbuilds: Competing cable systems covering the same geographic area.

PAC: Data packet.

Packet: A collection of data into a form that is transmitted as a discrete unit over a network communication channel.

Packet Assembler/Disassembler (PAD): Required for packet-switched networks. A hardware/software device that provides access to an X.25 network.

Packet switching: The direction of data along pathways dynamically on a packet-by-packet basis. Data is reassembled from packets at receiver.

PAP: Printer Access Protocol (packet-level procedure). A protocol for the transfer of packets between an X.25 DTE and an X.25 DCE.

PAR: Project Authorization Request.

Parity Bit: A special bit used in error checking.

Payload Type Identifier (PTI): A 3-bit descriptor found in ATM cell headers, indicating what type of payload the cell contains. Payload types include user and management cells.

PDN: Public Data Network.

PDU: Protocol Data Unit.

Peak Cell Rate (PCR): A type of ATM traffic flow. The maximum rate at which cells can be transmitted, defined by the minimum possible space between two cells.

Peer-to-Peer: Describes a network environment where there is no central server for all clients, rather all devices may act as server or client. LAN-tastic is a common peer-to-peer NOS.

Peer-to-Peer Network: A network in which resources and files are shared without a centralized management source.

PEP: Packet Exchange Protocol.

Peripheral Component Interconnect (PCI): A type of computer bus.

Peripheral Device: A machine that performs specific tasks for a computer such as telecommunications (a modem) or printing.

Permanent Virtual Circuit (PVC): A logical (rather than physical) connection between end points, established by an administrator, which stays intact until manually torn down.

Phase modulation: The encoding of data into a carrier signal by altering the carrier's phasing.

Physical Layer: Layer 1 of the OSI model. Defines the functional characteristics for passing data bits onto and receiving them from the connecting medium.

Physical Layer (PHY): The layer below the ATM layer in the Protocol Reference Model that passes data from the medium to the ATM layer and vice-versa. Also refers to OSI Layer 1.

Physical (Layer) Media Dependent (PMD): Refers to the part of the NIC design that has to interface with (and is therefore dependent on) the chosen transmission medium (MMF, UTP.)

Physical Topology: The physical layout of the network; how the cables are arranged; and how the computers are connected.

PLP: Packet Level Protocol.

Point-to-Point: A direct link between two objects in a network.

Ports: A connection point for a cable.

POTS: Plain Old Telephone System.

Presentation Layer: Layer 6 of the OSI model. Negotiates and manages the way data is represented and encoded.

Private Network-to-Network Interface (P-NNI): The interface between two ATM switches or between an ATM switch and an entire switching system in a private network.

Protocol: A formal description of a set of rules and conventions that govern how devices on a network exchange information.

Protocol Data Unit (PDU): A generic term for the format used to send information in a communications protocol, typically a packet with its headers and trailers.

Quality of Service (QoS): A set of communication characteristics required by an application such as cell loss ratio, cell transfer delay, and cell delay variations.

RAID (Redundant Array of Inexpensive Disks): A configuration of multiple disks designed to preserve data after a disk casualty.

RMON: Remote monitoring.

Repeater: A device used in a network to strengthen a signal as it is passed along the network cable.

Request For Comment (RFC): The document series, begun in 1969, which describes the Internet suite of protocols and related experiments. Not all RFCs describe Internet standards, but all Internet standards are written up as RFCs.

Reverse Address Resolution Protocol (RARP): Protocol by which a TCP/IP workstation determines its own IP address.

RJ45: Standard connectors used for unshielded twisted-pair cable. Eight-pin connector used for data transmission.

Router: A device that routes information between interconnected networks. It can select the best path to route a message as well as translate information from one network to another. It is similar to a superintelligent bridge.

RSVP: Resource Reservation Protocol.

Rx: Receive.

Satellite Master Antenna Television (SMATV): Whereby a single antenna is used to provide television service for all units in a hotel, apartment house, or other housing complex, except the antenna used is one for satellite signals rather than over-the-air signals.

Satellite Receiver: Equipment used to obtain a specific signal.

Scrambler: An electronic device usually located in the transmitter used to change a signal so that it may not be viewed on normal television sets unless another electronic device (decoder) is attached to the subscriber's set to unscramble the picture.

Segment: Refers to a section of cable on a network. In Ethernet networks, two types of segments are defined. A populated or trunk segment is a network cable that has one or more nodes attached to it. A link segment is a cable that connects a computer to an interconnecting device, such as a repeater or concentrator, or connects a interconnecting device to another interconnecting device.

Segmentation And Reassembly (SAR): Converts between the adaptation layer and the ATM layer (AAL5 frame to ATM cells).

Server: A computer on a network that services other nodes. Also called a back end or engine.

Session Layer: Layer 5 of the OSI model. Provides coordination of the communications in an orderly manner. A logical connection between two network addressable units (NAUs).

Signaling: In ATM terms, the process followed to set up virtual connections. The latest standard is UNI 3.1 signaling, which is a modified version of ITU's Q.2931 protocol.

Significantly Viewed: According to the FCC definition, a station is *significantly viewed* in a given county if (1) it is a network affiliate and achieves among non-cable households a share of total viewing hours of at least 3%, and a net weekly circulation of at least 25%; or (2) it is an independent station and achieves among non-cable households a share of total viewing hours of at least 5%. A station which is significantly viewed becomes *local* for regulatory purposes, that is, it can demand carriage on local cable systems, and the systems are no longer required to delete the duplicate programming of a significantly viewed station at the request of a higher priority (local) station.

Signal Carriage: Stations carried by a cable system, including local stations which request carriage, plus stations which are significantly viewed within the community, plus distant signals imported by the system.

Signal Importation: Carriage of station signals originating outside the specified zone in which the cable community is located.

Simple Network Management Protocol (SNMP): A protocol used to gather activity information on a TCP/IP network for monitoring and statistical purposes.

Sneaker Net: Refers to a manual method of sharing files in which a file is copied from a computer to a floppy disk, transported to a second computer by a person physically walking (apparently wearing sneakers) to the second computer, and manually transferring the file from floppy disk to the second computer.

Society Of Cable Television Engineers (SCTE): Technical organization for engineers involved in the cable television industry.

Speed of Data Transfer: The rate at which information travels through a network, usually measured in megabits per second.

Star Topology: LAN topology in which each node on a network is connected directly to a central network hub or concentrator.

Star-Wired Ring: Network topology that connects network devices (such as computers and printers) in a complete circle.

STS-*n*: Synchronous Transport Signal-*n*. (See Optical Carrier-*n*.)

Subscriber: A household or business that legally receives and pays for cable and/or pay television service for its own use (not for retransmission).

Subscriber User-to-Network Interface SUNI): Name for the ATM PHY chip manufactured by PMC-Sierra.

Sustained Cell Rate (SCR): A type of ATM traffic flow. An average of rates at which cells are transmitted over a certain period of time.

Switched Multimegabit Data Service (SMDS): A high-speed, packet-switched, datagram-based WAN technology.

Switched Virtual Circuit (SVC): A logical (not physical) connection between endpoints established by the ATM network on demand after receiving a connection request from the source, which is transmitted using the UNI signaling protocol. (See PVC.)

Synchronous Digital Hierarchy (SDH): International standard for optical digital transmission at hierarchical rates from 155 Mbps to 2.5 Gbps and beyond.

Synchronous Optical Network (SONET): A USA standard for optical digital transmission at hierarchical rates from 155 Mbps to 2.5 Gbps and beyond.

T1/T3: T1 is a 1.544 Mbps multichannel digital transmission system for voice or data provided by long distance carriers. T3 is similar but operates at 44.736 Mbps. Also referred to as DS1 and DS3 (Data Service).

TAXI: A standardized 100 Mbps fiber physical interface for ATM.

TCP: Transmission Control Protocol. (See IP.)

Teletext: Alpha-numeric material transmitted to and displayed on television sets equipped with suitable capabilities.

Terminator: A device that provides electrical resistance at the end of a transmission line. Its function is to absorb signals on the line, thereby keeping them from bouncing back and being received again by the network.

Tiering: Supplying subscribers to a cable system with one or more programming services beyond the basic offerings at an extra charge. Each additional price increment, or the service(s) offered therefor, is called a tier.

Token: A special packet that contains data and acts as a messenger or carrier between each computer and device on a ring topology. Each computer must wait for the messenger to stop at its node before it can send data over the network.

Token Ring: A network protocol developed by IBM in which computers access the network through token-passing. Usually uses a star-wired ring topology.

Transceiver (Transmitter/Receiver): A device that receives and sends signals over a medium. In networks, it is generally used to allow for the connection between two different types of cable connectors, such as AUI and RJ45.

Transmission Lines: Specifically designed cables for use in carrying radio or television signals from one point to another.

Transport Layer: Layer 4 of the OSI model. Responsible for end-to-end validity and integrity of the transmission.

Tree Topology: LAN topology similar to linear bus topology, except that tree networks can contain branches with multiple nodes.

Twisted Pair: Network cabling that consists of four pairs of wires that are manufactured with the wires twisted to certain specifications. Available in shielded and unshielded versions.

Two-Way Cable: Cable television system capable of transmitting signals in both directions along a cable. FCC requires this capability in cable systems within major television markets that commenced operations after March 1972, in systems outside major markets that commenced after March 1977, and in all other systems by June 1986. See Interactive.

Tx: Transmit.

Universal Test and Operations Physical Interface for ATM (UTOPIA): This specification defines a common hardware interface between the ATM layer performing segmentation and reassembly and the ATM physical layer. This allows a single ATM layer to support multiple physical layer standards such as the 100 Mbps TAXI and SONET/OC-n as well as future standards.

Unshielded Twisted Pair/Shielded Twisted Pair (UTP/STP):. Two types of copper cable. STP has insulating material wrapped around the twisted wires for immunity to electrical magnetic interference. UTP does not and is subject to electrical noise and interference.

Uplink: Part of a satellite communications system from which signals are transmitted from earth to satellite.

Upstream: Signals traveling from subscriber's home to primary distribution point (headend). Used in two-way communication.

User-Network Interface (UNI): The interface between a user's device and an ATM switch, defined as the physical, ATM, and higher (signaling) layer.

Variable Bit Rate (VBR): A type of ATM traffic flow. As opposed to Constant Bit Rate, VBR traffic may be bursty.

VDSL (Very-High-Data-Rate Digital Subscriber Line): One of four DSL technologies. VDSL delivers 13 Mbps to 52 Mbps downstream and 1.5 Mbps to 2.3 Mbps upstream over a single twisted copper pair. The operating range of VDSL is limited to 1,000 to 4,500 feet. Compare with ADSL, HDSL, and SDSL.

Videotex: Systems for over-the-air or wired distribution of textual and/or graphic information. This term is usually used to include both teletext and viewdata systems.

Viewdata: A service allowing two-way communications between home terminals and a central computer. May operate over a cable or via telephone to provide various types of informational services to the home TV screen.

Virtual Channel Connection (VCC): A concatenation of virtual channel links between two endpoints where higher layer protocols are accessed. By definition, ATM cell sequence must be preserved over a VCC.

Virtual Channel Identifier/Virtual Path Identifier (VCI/VPI): ATM addressing information. An identifying value found in the header of each ATM cell.

Virtual LAN (VLAN): A logical collection of member endpoints and network devices grouped together in a secure, autonomous domain. Membership in a VLAN is not restricted by physical location. VLANs in ATM networks may be built on emulated LANs.

Virtual Path Connection (VPC): A concatenation of virtual path links between two points. Several VCCs may be bundled into one VPC.

WAN (Wide Area Network): A network connecting computers within very large areas, such as states, countries, and the world.

Women In Cable (WIC): Organization devoted to the interests of women in the cable industry.

Workgroup: A collection of workstations and servers on a LAN that are designated to communicate and exchange data with one another.

Workstation: A computer connected to a network at which users interact with software stored on the network.

INDEX